THE TRIUMPH OF TRADITION

THE TRIUMPH OF TRADITION

The Emergence of Whitman College
1859 – 1924

G. THOMAS EDWARDS

Whitman College
Walla Walla, Washington

ISBN 0-9632955-3-5

Library of Congress Catalog Number 92-61767

Manufactured in the United States of America.

Dedication

In 1913 Whitman President Stephen B.L. Penrose wrote: "I am proud of the great beauty of the College Campus; I am much more proud of the loyalty and fine spirit of the student body; but I am most proud of the men and women of the Faculty, who by their faithfulness, devotion, scholarship, and personality, have made Whitman College what it is today." During the period from 1882 through 1924 numerous professors and their families made tremendous personal and financial sacrifices to build Whitman College. Those listed below in alphabetical order seem to have been the most significant contributors, and to their memory this history is dedicated.

Eli T. Allen
Alexander J. Anderson
Louisa P. Anderson
Louis F. Anderson
Vincent "Nig" Borleske
Walter A. Bratton
Howard S. Brode
Benjamin H. Brown
Elvira C. Cobleigh
James W. Cooper

Walter Crosby Eells
Frank L. Haigh
Otto A. Hauerbach
Archer W. Hendrick
William D. Lyman
Stephen B.L. Penrose
Helen A. Pepoon
Howard E. Pratt
Edward E. Ruby
Gertrude H. Wylie

Note from the President

Critical to the success, vitality, and longevity of an academic community such as Whitman College is the existence of a reigning mythology, a set of governing principles or beliefs—shared by all members of the community—that explain the institution's past, order its present, and suggest its future. In a culture that encourages and fosters debate, disagreement, and healthy argumentation in pursuit of the truth and the discovery of knowledge, it is the application of this set of beliefs as a context for discourse and for action that focuses the disparate energies into a cohesive and vibrant whole.

At Whitman College this mythology is a powerful force in defining and guiding the institution, and Professor Edwards has done a superb job of portraying the genesis and development of those beliefs in the early years of the college. In particular, we gain precious insight into those early myth-tellers, the founders and presidents of Whitman College whose personal visions and ambitions for the college were transformed—more often than not—into a set of communal goals that eventually were realized in Whitman's continual growth as one of the West's premier institutions of higher learning.

It was a mythology initiated by Cushing Eells, shaped by the inspiration and ingenuity of Stephen B.L. Penrose, and renewed and intensified through the contributions of each successive generation of Whitman people. Not since Penrose's *Whitman: An Unfinished Story* was published in 1935 have we had such significant insight into the philosophical—as well as the practical—genesis of the college, and into the roles that various people played in its formation and development. We are indebted to Dr. Edwards for chronicling for us Whitman's formative years, and for providing the perspective necessary to appreciate the college's past and present, its aspirations, adversities, and achievements.

Whitman College takes great pride in publishing *The Triumph of Tradition*, as it does in the faculty, students, staff, alumni, and friends who have been instrumental in the college's evolution, and who have come together in shared belief in Whitman's mission. We look forward to the next chapters.

David E. Maxwell
President, Whitman College
August, 1992

Contents

Foreword

What Professor Edwards has discovered about Whitman's early days will astonish the most curious reader, and the graceful way he tells the story is delightful. Anyone who expects this subject to be provincial will be pleasantly surprised by its inextricable connection with the history of the nation.

The history of Whitman College begins with the biography of Marcus Whitman and the clash of claims and cultures in the Pacific Northwest of the nineteenth century. The founding of the Whitman Seminary was a datum for anthropology as well as for international relations. The survival of the evolving collegiate institution was dependent upon eastern support for the romantic "Whitman myth," which claimed that the nation owed its northwestern territory to the martyred medical missionary.

Eastern private colleges—principally Williams—as well as their midwestern imitators—particularly Knox—were the models for early Whitman presidents Alexander Jay Anderson (1882–1891) and James F. Eaton (1891–1894). Edwards' detailed discussion of Anderson and Eaton is definitive. The reader is reminded that, as the frontier moved westward, higher education witnessed the same reciprocal relation between that which was imported and the local environment as did all other aspects of life.

A dozen years after the arrival of the third president, Stephen B.L. Penrose (1894–1934), the Greater Whitman plan unsuccessfully attempted to turn a college into a university. The Greater Whitman episode, concluded by 1912, was the most important series of events in the years covered by this volume and is treated extensively. Edwards suggests that the Greater Whitman plan was a plausible attempt by the college to join the main currents of higher education after 1900—which included more vocational training and professional schools—rather than to remain dedicated exclusively to undergraduate arts and sciences. Though it was a plausible attempt, it was unsuccessful.

During and after the First World War, the college settled into being what it would remain, the most traditional transplant in the Pacific Northwest of the elite New England college. By the twenty-fifth anniversary of the beginning of Stephen Penrose's presidency in 1919, Whitman was also Penrose's school. Almost every such institution has a Penrose figure: a founder with a long tenure never later equalled; a teacher of many subjects and a moral exemplar; an administrator of all areas of activity (including students *in loco parentis*); and an indefatigable fund raiser. The quality and success of each college's Penrose figure invariably shaped the nature of each school for decades afterwards. For Whitman this meant a blend of academic aspiration and civic virtue, worldly respectability and family loyalty, all expressed in a plain style reflecting Walla Walla, Washington.

The figure of Stephen Penrose that emerges from Edwards' pages is noble, admirable, heroic and, in some ways at least, tragic. The young visionary of the 1890s—he of the ice-water baths in Dayton—becomes the blind, fatigued president of the 1920s, who cannot summon the necessary resources to finance his collegiate goals. Edwards concludes his narrative, on a relatively high plane of achievement, in 1924. Whitman students had been recognized for their academic prowess; the college, and Penrose himself, were acknowledged to be educational leaders. But even on this high plane of the mid-1920s, the reader is reminded of Chester Maxey's contemporary observation. When Maxey returned as a professor in 1925, thirteen years after he had graduated, he thought that the faculty was weaker than a decade earlier, that the physical plant was more decrepit, and that Penrose should have retired.

The worst was yet to come for Penrose in his last decade, which will begin the next volume of Whitman's history, not yet written. During the deprivation of the Great Depression, the very existence of the college was threatened as it had not been since the beginning of Penrose's tenure. One thinks of many low points for the sightless president in the 1930s. One of the worst must have been the inability, or the unwillingness, of his many friends to respond to personal pleas for money in the winter of 1932–1933. Another must have been his failure to persuade his personal choice to succeed him as president. His favorite, Hugh Elmer "Hez" Brown ('04), told Penrose that he could not afford financially to give up his Evanston, Illinois, Congregational pastorate to become Whitman's president, and that the college should seek a wealthy man who did not need a salary.

Perhaps Penrose's most debilitating point followed his retirement in 1934, when his successor appointed an outside "auditor" to analyze Whitman's situation, and the negative report—which held Penrose partly responsible for the poor health of the institution—was not given to Penrose until he heard about it and requested a copy.

From these Depression depths the financial foundations of the college were rebuilt, mainly by alumni who had been Penrose's students. Edwards' history makes it clear that it was due chiefly to Penrose that Whitman was worthy of saving by those who followed him.

Such a capsule overview barely suggests the liveliness of Edwards' narrative. Nor does it indicate the scholarly detail that he provides. Although necessarily of most interest to Whitman alumni, the history is researched meticulously and is a contribution to the history of higher education in the United States as well as to the history of the Pacific Northwest.

Edwards shows persuasively that Penrose was as preoccupied with raising money as has been any of his successors. No other collegiate history has revealed in more detail the way in which early fund raising was done. Edwards' account makes clear, by implication, how relatively insignificant a role was played by the board of trustees in the successes of the college during the early decades (though this was not true later). And, more explicitly, Edwards reveals how minimal was the financial support offered Whitman College by the local community. (Geographical location has been in some respects the biggest drawback and, in others, the most positive attribute of the college.) By focusing upon these areas, which surviving correspondence and other source material have allowed him to do, Professor Edwards is able to integrate the visible and idealistic leader, Stephen

Penrose, into the less visible financial reality which so constrained his aspirations.

In trying to understand why small colleges develop as they do after the early years—which are so extraordinarily influenced by their founding figures (such as Penrose)—financial condition generally is the most formative factor. Professionalization of faculty and administration since the Second World War has been similar in most institutions, but circumstances of financial health have come to vary greatly. Thus, both earlier and mid-twentieth century comparisons of such western and midwestern private liberal arts colleges as Whitman, the College of Idaho (now Albertson), Linfield, Pomona, Beloit, Knox, Carleton, and Grinnell would reveal them to be generically similar institutions in their faculty and student academic and social styles. Yet, by the 1990s, these institutions have become much more differentiated in their campus academic and social attributes. Varying financial conditions, more than any other factor, explain the differing contemporary nature of the schools, whose endowments ranged from virtually nothing to over $300,000,000 as the century entered its last decade.

The Triumph of Tradition explains the establishment and the character of Whitman College up to 1924, and opens up the proper lines of inquiry for the succeeding chapters, which will tell readers about the more recent developments at Whitman and in higher education. Professor Edwards' history does not peer through rose-colored glasses, but directly confronts Whitman's frustations and failures, as well as its dreams and achievements.

Robert Allen Skotheim
President,
    The Huntington Library, Art Collections, and Botanical Gardens
March, 1992

Preface

Although I have long been aware of Whitman College's history, I did not consider writing a book about it until the mid-1980s. As a Willamette University undergraduate, I had heard an Oregon history professor criticize Whitman College for making too much out of missionary Marcus Whitman. I remembered his opinion because of his angry tone. Years later, while teaching at Whitman, I asked colleagues about the validity of his position and received mixed responses. Meanwhile, I heard older professors and alumni assessing former president Stephen B.L. Penrose, the gifted science faculty, Greater Whitman, meager faculty salaries, and other institutional topics from the "old days" at Whitman. These discussions sparked my interest in writing an essay on President Theodore Roosevelt's 1903 campus visit, and in 1982 I joined others in presentations celebrating Whitman's one-hundredth anniversary as a college.

I had always assumed that my colleague Robert L. Whitner, in his retirement, would write the college history. For about twenty years we had talked about the opportunity and the need to produce a modern account. We thought it fortunate that the college had saved so many of its early primary materials, especially the collections of Cushing and Myron Eells, Stephen Penrose, Archer Hendrick, and Howard Brode. Although Bob Whitner was able to write two fine essays on the college, his untimely death in 1982 ended the projected college history. Thereupon President Robert Skotheim asked if I would take it up. I delayed an answer until I could dip into the various sources; about six months later I accepted the invitation and began by reading university and college histories. Many were sketchy, uncritical, and dull, at odds with my experience as a professor. The people I have encountered are not like the bland characters presented in many college histories. I have found colleges and universities to be lively places with colorful, controversial, contentious, and committed groups of trustees, overseers, presidents, professors, staff members, alumni, students, and friends. So I have endeavored to write a history that includes the lively people and events important to institutional life. I also wanted to explain why Whitman professors, students, and alumni continue to be so loyal to the college.

I found it much easier to write about the presidents during the period covered in this book than about any other college group. Their numerous letters and reports are the basic source concerning institutional development. These materials indicate that all of the early presidents had to serve as fund raisers. The first three presidents—Alexander Jay Anderson, James F. Eaton, and Stephen B.L. Penrose —worried constantly about money for the college. I was prepared for this emphasis because I have served under four presidents, each of whom has campaigned for money. Because the financial side of their work was fundamental—and well-documented—I have given it considerable space in these pages. I also learned that each of the first three presidents had strong ideas about goals and how to achieve them. The presidents recruited faculty and students and played a pivotal role in shaping the curriculum, extracurricular activities, and public relations. I have organized the chapters around the various presidents, emphasizing Stephen Penrose. His forty years as president made him the institution's pivotal leader. This impressive educator kept his enormous letter collection, as well as that of Dean Hendrick, because he hoped to have the college history written. At the conclusion of the First World War, Penrose sought missing college documents and made an arrangement with Professor William D. Lyman to write the history in his retirement.

Unfortunately, although Lyman was uniquely qualified—he had lived through the period and had written important regional histories —his death prevented such an undertaking. Penrose did not find time to write his own college history until the mid-1930s, at the time of his retirement. He believed that the story of the building of a liberal arts college was well worth telling. The boxes of materials that he saved illuminated this story, but blindness prevented him from utilizing the sources that he had accumulated. When writing *Whitman: An Unfinished Story* in 1934, he depended upon recollection rather than a scholarly investigation of the sources.

Since Penrose did not claim to have written the definitive history of Whitman, he and others hoped that a more complete one would eventually be published. Dedicated librarians, especially Ruth Reynolds, saved the records for future use. Despite their watchful eyes, boxes of college materials for the period from 1913 through 1920 disappeared. Chester Maxey informed me that custodians had emptied cartons of documents because they needed boxes. They later swept up and dumped what had been scattered.

The enormous amount of material that did survive clearly demonstrates that the early presidents did not build Whitman unaided. Because missionaries Marcus Whitman and Cushing Eells have received considerable historical attention, I have not provided much detail about their backgrounds. But Marcus Whitman as a symbol and Cushing Eells as the originator of the institution are important to the emergence of Whitman College. Penrose often generously acknowledged the assistance of Eells and many other helping hands. Many people shared his desire to honor Marcus Whitman as well as his joy in building an eastern-style liberal arts college in rural Washington. Obviously, the historic eastern concern about western institutional development worked to Whitman College's advantage. Thus eastern groups and persons including Congregational organizations, benefactor Daniel K. Pearsons, writer Oliver W. Nixon, fund raiser Virginia Dox, donor Julia Billings, and the Rockefeller General Education Board played crucial roles. Walla Wallans Dorsey S. Baker, John F. Boyer, William Kirkman, Nelson G. Blalock, Lettice Reynolds, Harry A. Reynolds, Allen H. Reynolds, Levi Ankeny, and the Reverend Raymond C. Brooks also contributed to the institution's development. The Eells family, the Reverend George H. Atkinson, Judge Thomas Burke, George Turner, and Dr. Park Weed Willis were among the many Pacific Northwest residents who were significant supporters.

Penrose insisted that the faculty was as important as any other group in the emergence of the institution. He hired and retained an exceptionally capable and committed group of men and women who fully shared his lofty ideas and goals. The professors received pitiful salaries, but they and their families took immense satisfaction in what they attained. Unfortunately, the faculty did not leave much of a paper trail; indeed, it is harder to write about them than other groups. Presidents retained correspondence, reports, and writings; boards left minutes and financial accounts; students published a newspaper, a yearbook, and a literary magazine; alumni contributed to a magazine, maintained scrapbooks, and granted oral interviews. Compared to these sources, faculty minutes are frustratingly sketchy. Furthermore, few faculty letters or reports have survived. This is most unfortunate because a group that was intimately involved with the emergence of the school did not record it, or, if they did, their materials have been lost. Surely Lyman must have had papers that he had collected for his projected college history, but they have disappeared.

On the other hand, newspapers of the period provided Whitman with much more space than they do now. By reading those published in Walla Walla, Portland, Spokane, and Seattle, it is possible to learn how these various communities responded to the development of a cultural institution.

Whitman College is essentially a New England institution planted in western soil. Its leaders and faculty came from the East and sought to emulate the solid private schools they had attended. Williams College was particularly influential. Presidents James Eaton and Stephen Penrose had graduated from that fine institution, and so had professors William Lyman and Walter Bratton. They knew about Williams' operation and its importance to the Northeast. Whitman leaders also understood the background and accomplishments of other eastern institutions, including Yale, Oberlin, MIT, the University of Chicago, and the emerging state universities. In the West, it seems that Pacific University, Stanford University, the University of Washington, and Colorado College sometimes served as useful examples to Whitman's leaders in such matters as curriculum and student housing. The Whitman faculty occasionally made detailed investigations of the institutional practices of sister schools and used this information in shaping policy.

Whitman College, of course, did not blindly follow the educational paths that had been blazed by others. Penrose, for example, took pride that his was the first school in the region to terminate its secondary academy and the first to establish a system of required comprehensive examinations for seniors. The college did not slavishly follow a national curriculum; it tried—with varying degrees of success—to offer a relevant curriculum to young people from Washington, Oregon, and Idaho. The institution always anticipated that its graduates would help to build the region's civilization. In its attempt to shape these graduates, the college willingly embraced the doctrine *in loco parentis*, which meant that deans and faculty gave a considerable amount of time to disciplining, advising, and guiding students.

The records for Whitman Seminary for the period from 1866 through 1882 are thin. This history emphasizes the college from its start in the fall of 1882 until the fall of 1924. The narrative ends in 1924, as Penrose completes thirty years as president. This year marked the completion of one stage of the college's history. The institution had emerged and received considerable recognition. In the late 1920s and well into the 1930s the school drifted. Alumni in the 1930s and President Chester Maxey in the 1940s set a new course.

I have attempted to provide the cultural, social, and economic aspects of institutional development and to consider the impact of the college upon the region and its people. The enormous amount of primary materials allows me to tell much of the story in detail, but I am aware that there are basic limitations. Sources do not say very much about faculty politics and personal animosities. It would be helpful to know more about the internal politics that led to the resignations of the college's first two presidents, and it would be similarly useful to know more about those faculty members who grumbled that Penrose remained too long in office.

The delay in writing the college history has meant that it was impossible to interview many who lived through the period from 1882 through 1924. Their oral recollections would have supplemented the written record, and gaps might have been closed. There is much about the college's story that cannot be recaptured, and I hope that the oral history project currently directed by Peggy Corley will provide that type of material which was denied to all of us who have written on the early history.

During the six years that I have worked on this manuscript, I have been indebted to many persons and institutions. Former president

Robert Skotheim, who shares my deep interest in Whitman's development and appreciation for its contributions to students, not only instigated the writing of this manuscript, he also provided encouragement as I plowed through boxes of materials. From the start he has discussed my findings and reviewed my chapters. Many people expressed satisfaction with the way that Skotheim used the college's history, especially that of the Penrose years, in a recent and highly successful fund drive. This warm reception demonstrated that many have an interest in the school's past as well as in its future. Clearly, the past and present are linked; this was exactly Penrose's point of view.

Whitman's current president, David Maxwell, has also been generous in his support of this project. Maxwell, like other eastern educators who have come to Whitman, has had to learn about the college and its region. He told me that he soon discovered that alumni appreciate the school's history. By offering financial support for this book's publication, Maxwell has helped bring Whitman's formative years to all who are interested in the effort and sacrifice required to build a New England type of college.

I owe much to Robert Whitner, whose ideas about Whitman College shaped my thinking. Although he would have written a different history, he would have been pleased to see one made available, for he shared Penrose's respect for institution builders. Whitman historians Donald King and David Schmitz and alumna Jeanne Williams analyzed some chapters. Librarian Marilyn Sparks and former treasurer Pete Reid read the entire manuscript. Curator Larry Dodd unfailingly assisted me while I went through the storehouse of Whitman College materials that he carefully tends. Dodd frequently consulted with me about the various collections and patiently located documents for me.

Many alumni have shared their recollections. Chester Maxey, Henrietta Baker Kennedy, and Donald Sherwood recalled their college days to my advantage. The Penrose daughters, Frances and Maysie, spent hours in oral history sessions providing details, illustrations, and recollections of early Whitman's spirit. Penrose's granddaughter, Frances Stickles, furnished considerable family information.

Research has taken me from one coast to the other. Jessica Goldweig and Harold Worthley at the Congregational Library in Boston and librarians at Williams College provided essential details about Whitman's eastern connections. In the West, librarians Barbara Neilon at the Colorado College, Alex Toth at Pacific University, Keith Richards at the University of Oregon, and Kerry Bartels at the University of Washington all helped me to utilize their institutional archives.

Williams College historian Frederick Rudolph, an authority on higher education, led me to sources in his institution's rich archives and shared his essay on Penrose at Williams. He evaluated many of my interpretations of liberal arts colleges in general and of Williams and Whitman in particular.

Many dedicated Whitman students helped me to research this book. Three in particular spent hours poring through primary materials—Tom Burman, Steve Parkinson, and Tia Kolbaba. Each went on to distinguished graduate school careers. Among the many others who provided valuable assistance are Melissa Carey Saalfield, Diane Chun-Ming Salmon, Charles Byler, Mark Hower, John Bogley, Lisa May, Arlene Weible, Matt Hiefield, Kay Barga, Jim Meadows, Jeremy Kazan, Rebecca Buxton, and Donna Gardner.

I was fortunate to have several competent editors—my colleague Margo Scribner, Susan Applegate, and former student Michael Wyatt Smith made many useful recommendations. Smith also spent long hours locating sources and preparing notes and bibliography. My typist, Karen Zollman, good naturedly and carefully prepared the manuscript.

John Laursen of Press-22 has meticulously copyedited the manuscript and custom designed the book. A graduate of Reed College, he has devoted long hours to making certain that the Whitman College story is told clearly and accurately.

Once again my family provided assistance and encouragement. My son Randall, daughter Stephanie, and wife Nannette have assisted me with research, listened to me formulate interpretations, speculated with me about earlier faculty families, and assured me that this book would come to be.

G. Thomas Edwards
Whitman College
August, 1992

THE TRIUMPH OF TRADITION

I

Cushing Eells and Whitman Seminary
1859 – 1882

The Reverend Cushing Eells established Whitman Seminary—the forerunner of Whitman College—and played a leading role in its turbulent history. In 1838, at the age of twenty-eight, he had married Myra Fairbanks and made an arduous overland trip with her to Oregon. The couple came as a part of the mission reinforcement for the American Board of Commissioners for Foreign Missions and became well acquainted with their co-workers, Marcus and Narcissa Whitman. For nearly nine years the Eellses endured hardships and heartaches as they carried out their missionary duties at Tshimikain, a site located about twenty-five miles from modern-day Spokane. But following the Whitman massacre in late 1847, military volunteers escorted the American Board missionaries out of the Spokane country.

This removal forced Eells to change his career; in the Willamette Valley he farmed a donation claim, preached to small congregations, and through correspondence watched over all the abandoned mission sites in the vast area east of the Cascades. He also began teaching in county schools and sometimes boarded students in his home. In 1848–1849 he and his wife were the faculty of the young Oregon Institute, a Methodist institution that was the forerunner of Willamette University. Several times Eells served on the Tualatin Academy faculty, finally establishing a home in Forest Grove in the late 1850s so that his sons, Edwin and Myron, might be better educated. His experience in two church schools in the Willamette Valley helped him create a new one in the Walla Walla Valley.

Eells, unfulfilled as a farmer and a teacher in western Oregon, yearned to serve again as a missionary at an American Board mission site in what had become Washington Territory. In a letter to the board, he stated that he had "become much attached" to eastern Washington and its Indians.[1] The army, however, forbade settlement in the so-called upper country because some tribes still resisted military authority and because Congress had not yet ratified treaties requiring the natives to move from the Walla Walla Valley. In 1858, following a successful campaign against the Spokanes, the army terminated its restrictions against settlement.

In the following year, Eells joined immigrants moving from the Willamette Valley to the Walla Walla Valley. The majority making this eastward trek sought to establish ranches along the valley's streams, but the ex-missionary had a much different purpose. He had come to investigate Waiilatpu (the Whitman Mission grounds) and to reflect upon the 1847 tragedy. An emotional man, he grieved at the Whitmans' gravesite and resolved "to erect a befitting monument to the memory of our martyred missionary colaborers in the form of a school of high moral character."[2] Eells also wished to preach the gospel to the Walla Walla Valley's early settlers, many of whom, he lamented, were gamblers, horse thieves, and Sabbath-breakers.

After completing his reconnaissance, Eells implemented his ambitious plans. He offered the American Board $1,000 for its 640-acre Whitman Mission site but requested to defer payments because he needed time to sell his donation farm and because he lacked cash. (He had been making donations to a Congregational church and to an endowed professorship at Pacific University.) He asked another eastern institution, the American Home Missionary Society, to underwrite the costs of bringing Christian education to Walla Walla Valley settlers.[3] Eells informed its leaders that it would be expensive to move his family to the mission site—$400 for transportation and $1,000 for the first year's living expenses. He explained why he made this financial request. Eells estimated that one thousand pioneers resided in a forty-mile radius of the old mission site and that five hundred travelers on the Oregon Trail would take homes in the region. This was the beginning, he predicted, of a large settlement between the Blue and Cascade mountains, and children of these pioneers would need the kind of education he had given students in the Willamette Valley.

The Reverend Cushing Eells founded and taught at Whitman Seminary, and in the college's first decade he played a critical role as trustee and fund raiser.

Eells also requested Oregon's Congregational leaders to support his plans. He urged the Home Missionary Society to help him bring religion and education to the distant valley. Wanting to evangelize the eastern frontier, these churchmen endorsed his proposal. Congregationalism had already moved from Portland to The Dalles—Eells had helped dedicate its new church in 1859—and the Walla Walla Valley was the next logical eastern move. "Its occupation," Congregational leaders predicted, "will soon prepare the way for our reaching the Colville gold regions . . . north of Waiilatpu."[4] These Oregonians enthusiastically supported his proposal to the Home Missionary Society because the eastern frontier was attracting settlement. They applauded Eells for his willingness "to leave his comfortable home and devote himself to this service" and predicted that his son Edwin would be the first teacher at the proposed Whitman Seminary. (A "seminary" at this time was not necessarily a school emphasizing theology and preparing its students for the ministry; rather, the term seems to have been used here interchangeably with "academy." Cushing Eells was reported to have wanted "a high school of earnest Christian character."[5])

Eells received help from politicians as well as from churchmen. In December 1859, the Washington territorial legislature passed the Whitman Seminary charter. Almost a replica of the Tualatin Academy's charter that the Oregon legislature had passed in 1849, the document established "an institution of learning" that would provide "instruction of persons of both sexes in science and literature."[6] The charter also provided for a nine-member board of trustees (Eells rejected Willamette University's large board of twenty-two—the decision to have a small board would have many ramifications), named the first group of trustees, and outlined their responsibilities. Eells and others writing the basic document understood that Willamette University's charter reflected a Methodist influence in that new trustees would be selected by a church conference. The Congregationalists founding Whitman Seminary, however, chose to follow the example of Tualatin Academy and refrained from mentioning the denomination in the charter; furthermore, they gave the Congregational Association no power to approve trustees. These decisions were, in part, an attempt to prevent charges of denominationalism, an attempt that had failed at Pacific University, and would also fail at Whitman. All of the seminary's first trustees were Congregationalists,[7] and they would elect the new trustees. This perpetuated the denomination's influence, so Whitman came to be called a Congregational school, not a nondenominational one.

Three of the school's original trustees were former missionaries who had been Marcus Whitman's co-workers—Cushing Eells, Elkanah Walker, and Henry Spalding. It is interesting to note that neither Walker nor Spalding remained on the board very long; neither minister worked to establish an institution honoring his former colleague. Walker, like others living in the Willamette Valley, probably found it too difficult to attend trustee meetings in Walla Walla, although he did not resign from the board until 1872. There is no evidence that Walker made a monetary contribution to Whitman Seminary, but he supported private education by land donations to Pacific University and by serving on its board from 1866 until his death in 1893. As for Spalding, Eells may not have expected much from him, for in letters to the American Board he criticized Spalding, charging that he "appears to suffer from mental or moral obliquity."[8] While Walker and Spalding proved indifferent to their old colleague's plans, the Reverend George H. Atkinson, a Congregationalist and a man of enormous energy, brought important experience to the board. He had played a leading role in advocating and advancing Pacific University, an institution that grew out of Tualatin Academy. His part in establishing Whitman Seminary is unknown, but his later work creating Whitman College won praise from his contemporaries and deserves recognition.

In 1860 and 1861 Cushing Eells and his son Edwin journeyed to the Walla Walla Valley, erected a log house, and farmed the former mission site. Profits from the sale of grain to the garrison at Fort Walla Walla paid for much of the $1,000 Eells owed the American Board for the land. In between farming seasons, Cushing returned to the Willamette Valley and promoted the proposed Whitman Seminary; in December 1860 he assembled its trustees in Forest Grove. At this initial, important meeting, Eells announced to the board that he would give them one-half of his mission claim.[9] The trustees elected him president and adopted a constitution and bylaws. The constitution stated that the seminary would be located on the mission claim, that "the Holy Scriptures shall always be a reading book in the institution," and that "English studies both common and scientific, together with ancient and modern languages shall be taught as far as practicable." The trustees were given a variety of responsibilities: to apply "evangelical principles," to select students and textbooks, and to set tuition costs and teachers' salaries. The document also regulated student behavior. Students would attend morning and evening prayers at the school, as well as Sunday church service. They were prohibited from traveling on the Sabbath and they would be dismissed if discovered to be habitually using "tobacco, or ardent spirits, or . . . profanity."

Without a school to operate, the trustees did not reassemble for four years. Meanwhile, in 1862, the Eells family occupied its Walla Walla Valley farm, a move particularly difficult for Myra Eells. She was feeling her fifty-seven years; furthermore, like hundreds of other women, she lacked her husband's enthusiasm for frontier life and much preferred her Forest Grove home, church, and friends. Her son remembered that she "yielded with regret" but accepted her duty to help establish a school honoring the Whitmans.[10]

Historian William D. Lyman, then a young boy, watched the Eells family leave its western Oregon home for its eastern Washington farm.[11] In an emotional scene similar to those in the Midwest when a family headed out for the Oregon Trail, Forest Grove neighbors cried, prayed, and sang as Cushing, Myra, Edwin, and Myron Eells prepared for travel to a remote and perhaps even dangerous land.

The family saved the income from its new farm for the proposed seminary. In 1863 Edwin briefly conducted a school in their home, but this was not the start of Whitman Seminary. The trustees had not sanctioned this school, which was too remote to attract pupils. While the family worked the land and dreamed of an institution to honor Marcus Whitman, the town of Walla Walla emerged about six miles away. In late 1859, Walla Walla County commissioners met to establish and name a county seat. They had heard settlers favor the names Waiilatpu and Walla Walla. Some even wanted Steptoeville, in honor of an army officer defeated by eastern Washington Indians.[12] Interestingly enough, local residents showed little or no sentiment to name the raw village after Marcus Whitman, the valley's most prominent resident. His courage, energy, and compassion had impressed mountainmen and immigrants, but not town builders. For more than a century historians would heatedly debate his deeds, but in 1859 townspeople saw no compelling reason to honor him. Eells, however, sought to change this situation.

The new town began as an agricultural center, but in 1860 prospectors found gold in what became Idaho. This and subsequent strikes in mountains to the east transformed Walla Walla into an outfitting center for miners. Farmers found a ready market for grain, bacon, lard, and butter; businesses profited from the sale of flour, coffee, picks, shovels, and much more. Saloons, boarding houses, and gambling dens lined Main Street, while in this and other dusty streets crowds of miners, wagons, horses, and pack trains created noise and confusion. Miners abandoned their remote camps and wintered in Walla Walla, which earned a reputation as a tough and frequently lawless community. Its vigilante activities in the mid-1860s attracted regional attention.

While townspeople established all kinds of institutions to serve the mining trade, few helped create the Whitman Seminary, which was designed to benefit local children. Eells knew that he must entice some Walla Wallans to serve as trustees. At a Portland meeting held in the fall of 1864, a quorum elected some of them as board members. The most prominent and influential was the Reverend Peasly B. Chamberlain, a Congregational minister who had left his Portland pastorate and in 1864 established Walla Walla's Congregational church. Pleased with Chamberlain's accomplishment, Eells considered him a useful ally in establishing the seminary. But the two Congregationalists disagreed over the school's location. At a trustee meeting Chamberlain, who spoke for the majority, objected to the seminary's constitutional provision requiring that it be located on the old mission site about six miles from the town. Chamberlain asserted that he and his wife had struggled to open Walla Walla's first non-parochial school; they had worked to operate it because the mining community badly needed basic education and because it helped to limit the Catholic influence. Chamberlain must have reminded trustees that Marcus Whitman had also worked against Catholic influence in the valley; a school honoring his memory should follow his example. Chamberlain reminded them that Walla Walla was expanding and that their proposed seminary would attract the sons and daughters of farmers and townspeople.

But Cushing Eells disagreed. He still wanted to establish the school on the missionary grounds. Eells objected to running a seminary in a roaring mining center. With its long row of saloons, Walla Walla was a far cry from bucolic Forest Grove, a village prohibiting ardent spirits. Myron Eells recalled his father's views: "The first plan had been to build the Seminary at the Whitman Mission and have a small, retired, but moral, educated, and religious town grow up around it, leaving the bulk of business and population to go to Walla Walla, six miles distant."[13]

In other words, a new village on the mission site would have about the same relationship to Walla Walla that Forest Grove had to Portland. Eells knew that Pacific University students were sheltered from urban distraction and temptations; he wanted the same for his seminary students. He recalled also that students at Williams College had been far removed from the allurements of eastern cities.[14] Thus Eells, like numerous other Whitman College leaders who followed him, sought to establish an institution patterned after his alma mater.

Possibly Eells emphasized to the trustees that Walla Walla, like other communities that had depended upon the mining trade, had "no assured existence."[15] He reminded them that the trustees had always planned on building a school on the mission grounds because it would be a persistent reminder of Marcus Whitman's character and martyrdom. Every day students could think of the noble missionary as they trod the historic grounds.

Eells also had economic reasons for locating the institution on the mission site: the school owned half of the land and would not have to buy property. Indeed, the institution could sell or rent lots or acreage to homeseekers and use the income for buildings or operating costs. In other words, Whitman Seminary, like Willamette and Pacific universities, would be supported by the sale or rent of land. Despite his reasonable arguments, Eells yielded. He wanted to open the long-delayed school. Trustees soon amended the school's constitution so that it could operate in or near Walla Walla.

After reaching the crucial decision about location, the trustees then sought a clear title to a desirable piece of Walla Walla property. According to Chamberlain, the trustees, "being only beggars forced to secure grounds as a donation," suffered several disappointments.[16] But in the spring of 1866 the town's richest and most prominent citizen, banker Dorsey S. Baker, offered four acres near his home. Located at the town's edge, this donation is part of the present campus. A four-acre site was very small when compared with either the 320 acres that Eells had proposed or with the original sites of such other pioneer institutions as Willamette, Pacific, the University of Washington, and the University of Oregon. Trustees vainly hoped that the sale or rental of mission lands might provide operating funds and money for the acquisition of additional property. Without urban property, Whitman Seminary and later Whitman College often had either to request or purchase town lots. Limited space has often created problems for Whitman that sister schools, such as Pacific and Willamette, avoided.

With title to property acquired, the board rushed to construct a building for a fall opening in 1866. Trustees heard townspeople call the long-delayed seminary "a castle in the air."[17] In a public letter published in the Walla Walla *Statesman*, Chamberlain optimistically predicted that the school would have the facilities of a good academy, that the Eells gift of half the valuable mission claim would provide "income to meet the demands of any of these pressing wants which frequently occur in the history of all such institutions of learning, without some such regular income . . . [and that] the community must be called upon to help it out of difficulty."[18] Chamberlain had summarized the major problem of the seminary and of the college that followed: a money shortage meant that the school's leaders would frequently solicit community donations. His letter did not stress future financial problems, however; he appealed for immediate gifts to launch the school. The trustees, he wrote, "call at once upon all the friends of true education in this vicinity for the means necessary . . . to prepare the grounds and erect a suitable building." A cheerful and liberal response, he assured, would be interpreted as "a command from the people . . . to go forward and build."

Within two weeks trustees believed that they had received the command. Cash gifts ranging from $2.50 to $250, as well as subscriptions, brought in about $1,800.[19] Assuming that there was a "reasonable prospect of considerable additions," the trustees cheerfully voted to erect their schoolhouse.[20] In September its builders, Dexter and Leidy, submitted bills for about $4,000; fund raisers only reported $3,000 in cash and subscriptions.[21] The trustees then voted to borrow $1,000, using their missionary land as security. They offered these 320 acres for $4,500 and then slashed the price to $2,500. Still no buyer appeared. Thus the school opened its doors in debt, a situation that alarmed the Eells family. Other school supporters probably assured them that debt was so common on the frontier, especially for churches and schools, that Whitman Seminary would be in no particular danger.

The trustees assumed that the building's debt could be overcome if the seminary achieved large enrollments, since a successful institution would attract donors. To provide a school principal whom the town respected, the board appointed trustee Chamberlain, giving him the right to hire an assistant and the responsibility to pay all operating expenses. In return for his services, he would pocket all the proceeds from tuition. The term rates were scaled: primary students $10, advanced students $12, instrumental music students $18 (vocal music was free), and French and Latin students $3.

While builders applied the traditional white paint to the seminary building and installed such basic school furniture as uncomfortable wooden benches for primary pupils, Chamberlain advertised that he, preceptress Mary A. Hodgdon, and assistant Emily V. Sylvester would serve as the faculty. The teachers sought "the patronage of all parents who desire to give their children a thorough and finished education."[22]

At the dedication on October 13, a crowd roamed through the building. Located on a barren field, the schoolhouse was a wood frame structure twenty-five feet wide and forty-six feet long. Both floors had classrooms, and the first included a huge wood-burning stove while the second provided a small instructor's room. Some viewers compared the gleaming white building to a New England schoolhouse; some children counted the windows and excitedly reported to parents that there were twenty-one. Speaking for many admirers, an observer reckoned that it was "possibly the most imposing structure east of the mountains."[23] Settlers inspecting this plain building on its barren site responded differently from those who now look at its stark photograph. In 1866 they fully appreciated beginnings—some compared this fine building with the crude log cabin schools they had attended—and felt assured that after the community matured, better structures made of stone would appear and replace wooden ones. The whole West was covered with fresh starts: homes, barns, stores, shops, mills, schools, churches, lodges, roads, bridges, and boats. Settlers were also used to the fact that many schools and churches struggled with debt or burned. In a land of beginnings it was easier to accept the temporary or permanent closure of institutions.

Speaking to sympathetic townspeople packed into the schoolhouse, Chamberlain presented the dedication address.[24] The listen-

Constructed at a cost of about $4,800 in 1866, the Whitman Seminary building was for years the most impressive such structure in eastern Washington. In 1884 it was added to at the front and it became Ladies' Hall.

ers, who feared his well-known verbosity, anticipated most of his solemn themes. Calling Marcus Whitman "the noble patriot, the devoted missionary, and the glorified martyr," the orator insisted that the man being honored combined "the element of true manhood, true patriotism, and true Christianity." Thus it was proper to start a school "of high intellectual and Christian character designed to reproduce these very elements of character in the successive generations of children who grow up . . . around the resting place of his remains." Those listeners who had read the Reverend Henry Spalding's recent newspaper writings were not surprised when the speaker went on to interpret Marcus Whitman's ride to the east coast in 1843. Thus Chamberlain was the first of many seminary and college teachers who would voice what came to be called the Whitman legend or Whitman myth. Chamberlain taught that Whitman arrived in Washington, D.C. "barely in time to prevent by earnest and determined personal effort with President Tyler the trading away of this whole

North West country with all its untold treasure of silver and gold to Great Britain for some comparatively valueless interest about the cod fisheries of Newfoundland." All those living in the Oregon Country, Chamberlain thundered, must always be grateful for Whitman's courage and patriotism. "Other men," he stressed, "may arise who will render great services to this part of our country but no other man can hardly expect another opportunity of actually saving this whole region to the American people as Dr. Whitman so clearly did." Eells agreed with the speaker's interpretation, but the newspaperman covering the dedication ignored Chamberlain's view of Whitman.

After the principal's stirring words about a local martyr, Chamberlain's other topics were commonplace. He reminded the audience that a seminary, like an academy, linked common schools with colleges. The minister stressed the objectives of education, maintaining that the new school would save families from large expense and emotional separations because children could be educated in Walla Walla and not at some distant institution.

Chamberlain congratulated Eells for finally having his hopes "so fully realized." The treasurer of the trustees spoke next, praising Eells "for the spirit of benevolence ... and for his zealous efforts for the ultimate accomplishment of the establishment of a reputable educational institution." Lacking Chamberlain's gushy manner, Eells set

This 1866 broadside, probably the school's first publica-
tion, announces the opening of Whitman Seminary.

down only a terse summary of this important day in Whitman's history: "The services were of a high order and pleasing character. A good attendance."[25]

Two days after the dedication, Chamberlain and his assistants greeted thirty-six students at the precarious frontier institution. Initially, the seminary prospered; its principal soon boasted that the enrollment had increased to more than fifty.[26] The school, however, faced a crisis in March 1867 when Chamberlain, who had led it through two terms, abruptly resigned.[27] The schoolmaster explained his action: he was too busy as a pastor to continue as a principal. Unable to hire a professional teacher, the board asked Eells to be a replacement. The board, which had long depended upon him for money, now needed his teaching skills. Eells had "hoped his teaching days were over,"[28] but he returned to the classroom because it would damage the institution's reputation to close. He would continue to serve as principal until June 1869.

He complained that "all my strength is required in connection with the school."[29] According to his journal he spent long hours in class preparation (apparently mathematics and bookkeeping proved particularly challenging). He and Hodgdon often evaluated students, disciplined students (after being detained, some left permanently), cut and hauled wood from the seminary's land for the ravenous stove, hammered repairs, and planted shade trees. The schoolmaster struggled to find donors or to collect delinquent tuition fees. During the week Eells lived in the tiny schoolhouse room; on weekends he returned home to his wife.

Despite the fact that Myra Eells complained that her husband worked "to the end of strength,"[30] Cushing Eells took on still another task as he became superintendent of Walla Walla County schools. During the two years he served, it was necessary to travel enormous distances because the county was, its residents boasted, larger than Massachusetts. During vacations and on Saturdays, the educator traveled the county, consulting with school directors, investigating conditions, and examining teachers. Occasionally he passed marginal candidates because it was impossible to find capable ones. His travels boosted the seminary: he recruited promising students and helped place its graduates as teachers in common schools. He used his $500 salary from the county to reduce the seminary's debt. Eells had

signed notes requiring stiff interest rates, and he feared that the builders would repossess the schoolhouse if he failed to make payment.
Eells unsuccessfully asked Walla Wallans to contribute funds so that
the debt owed, including one to Dorsey Baker, might be retired.

Eells had been assured by trustees that a successful school would
be able to cover its debts. But the construction and the outfitting of
the seminary had been more expensive than anticipated (and this was
not the only time in Whitman's history that buildings have cost more
than projected and that anticipated donations were not made). So the
Eells family scrimped and worked to cover the school's debts. Cushing peddled chickens, eggs, and cordwood, and engaged in other
money-raising activities. He was, however, not the only member of
his family who labored to save the school. Myra churned four hundred pounds of butter for the local market.[31] All of them, according
to historian William Lyman, "plowed and reaped, cut wood, raised
chickens, made butter, and devoted the proceeds" to the seminary.[32]
"It is hard to conceive," Lyman judged, "of a more pathetic history
than that of Father Eells and his family, slowly, patiently, saving
every scrap secured by their wearisome toil, in order to give it away
for this purely unselfish purpose." By June 1869 the family had
earned enough to cover all of the school's notes; furthermore, Eells
paid the seminary's board $2,500 to buy back the mission land that
he had donated.

Few enrollment and financial figures for the seminary have survived, but the trustee minutes provide some rough figures.[33] In their
first year, 1867–1868, Eells and Hodgdon attracted some sixty students a term; the following year the enrollment declined to about
forty. Unpredictable enrollment figures were typical of frontier
schools and made educational planning difficult. The decrease in
1868–1869 was attributable to several causes, including a smallpox
excitement. So many parents kept their children at home that Eells,
who had received a precautionary vaccination, grumbled that it made
teaching "tedious."[34] Under pressure from a trustee, the principal
reluctantly granted his students a vacation. The ever-changing classroom attendance (Eells described it as "some come and others go")
determined tuition income.[35] Probably Eells and Hodgdon each received about $825 for the first year and considerably less for the
second. Eells' tremendous efforts on behalf of the school led him to

make a rare complaint: "the more effort I make in behalf of the Seminary the less thanks I receive."[36] With the debts covered and the school operating, the founder could honorably resign as principal. He informed his family that he lacked the energy to continue. His able assistant, Mary Hodgdon, also departed, seeking a more congenial teaching career in Portland.

After his resignation in 1869, the founder gave little time to his seminary. Cushing and Myra Eells farmed without their sons' help until 1872, when their home burned. The fire consumed all of their belongings, including some seminary documents. Myra had always yearned to leave the farm for a town. She had once been asked if she would like to return to Forest Grove and replied that she would travel the three hundred miles "on hands and knees."[37] With the destruction of her home, Myra was bedridden with shock and told her husband, "We can leave now; we have nothing to leave."[38] Cushing agreed. In his view they "were sinking under their burdens;" thus the fire was "a signal relief."[39] He sold his farm for $8,000, giving $1,000 in gold coin to the struggling seminary. The Eells endowment paid for the repairs of the building and fences.

Although Eells would never again live in Walla Walla, his contributions to the seminary as donor and teacher meant that Walla Wallans always considered it to be his institution. According to his friend William Lyman, townspeople often commented about the founder's character, stressing "the industry, frugality, self-denial, curious mixture of sternness and gentleness (the first on principle, the second by nature), the preciseness of speech, the extreme rigidity in Sabbath conduct ... the scrupulous honesty of both word and deed, and the kindly and genial humor, of sort of an Old Testament cast, which made the life of this patron saint of Walla Walla a curiosity, and yet an object of profound respect, to the not remarkably pious or scrupulous inhabitants."[40] Walla Wallans joked about his handmade moccasins that made it possible for him to move "noiseless upon idler or evildoer."[41] The principal's dedication to both the memory of Marcus Whitman and his school impressed everyone.

Some residents recalled that Spokane Indians employed in the Walla Walla Valley visited with Eells, asking economic advice and attending his church services. The minister complained that Indians consumed his time by bringing their troubles to him but also boasted that a greater percentage of Indians than white townspeople attended his religious services.[42] In other words, while Eells sought to instruct the children of pioneers, he still had an influence upon Indians he had taught in the 1840s.

Surviving official records demonstrate that the school made little headway because it suffered from financial and leadership problems until 1882. A shortage of money continued to be the seminary's main problem: it could not build a boarding house, attract a permanent principal, compete well with Episcopal schools established in the early 1870s, or provide an expanded curriculum. Peasly Chamberlain, who argued that the shortage of available teachers was "our chief difficulty," reluctantly taught a term in the 1869–1870 school year.[43] For months afterwards the schoolhouse remained locked.

In 1869 Chamberlain wrote Myron Eells, who then attended a New England seminary, that Whitman trustees failed to find a suitable local teacher and that "in our helplessness we now turn to you and dear old New England the land of school teachers, and I feel not like asking or requesting but demanding. We surely have a right to one little man to save us from a generation of ignorance."[44] The trustee explained that the newcomer must depend upon tuition income, not a guaranteed salary. Chamberlain described the type of help he wanted: "If you can find a man and wife or a man and sister especially if the lady can teach music and drawing it would be the most desirable plan, but the principal is most essential." He and Cushing Eells, he confided, wanted "good sound Congregationalists" who were not "mixed up with Secret Societies and Woman's Rights, but as we have not right to [push] these personal notions upon the Board we of course leave these to your own good sense." He agreed to accept Myron's choice. The new teacher should come by transcontinental train and assume his duties in January 1870. It was hoped that a new person would be a permanent principal. Myron quickly responded that he had asked educational leaders for the names of candidates but learned that the seminary's uncertain salary could only attract a person possessing "a missionary spirit."[45] Young, capable male teachers were in demand in New England, where they earned between $1,000 and $2,000 annually.

Apparently Myron's efforts eventually succeeded, for an easterner with a degree from Dartmouth, W.W. Freeman, crossed the continent and served as the seminary principal in 1870–1871. But Freeman, the school's first professional educator, became frustrated by frontier conditions and soon fled to Portland. Chamberlain returned to the classroom.

In 1872 the trustees, who had been unable to open the school that fall, met to vote on an unusual request. An Episcopal leader, the Reverend Lemuel H. Wells, who had recently established St. Paul's Church, asked to operate an Episcopal school for boys in the vacant seminary building. After a debate the trustees approved by a vote of three to two.[46] But they soon terminated this agreement and reopened the seminary. The Episcopal schools for boys and girls in Walla Walla proved to be formidable competitors. In 1873 a Whitman trustee grumbled that they had "gobbled up about all of the Whitman Seminary scholars."[47] St. Paul's School for Girls opened in 1872, boarded students, and developed into an effective Walla Walla institution. Advertising itself as "the only Protestant school East of the Cascades," it received eastern and local money.[48] The Episcopal institution escaped the severe financial problems besetting the Congregational seminary and was able to pay its faculty and provide a stable curriculum. Wells, who remained ten years, was the community's best-respected educator. His reputation attracted students, and at least one Whitman Seminary trustee sent his children to this robust competitor. By 1880, St. Paul's published an annual catalog, increased its faculty to seven and its student enrollment to eighty, and planned on a new building. An Episcopal bishop, taking into account that children outside of the Walla Walla Valley boarded at the school, boasted that "its influence was felt hundreds of miles in every direction."[49] In the 1870s Catholics opened two institutions—St. Patrick's School and St. Vincent's Academy. These schools apparently did not reduce Whitman's enrollment because Catholics had always shunned the Congregational seminary, knowing that Chamberlain and Eells were hostile to Catholicism.

Whitman lagged in competition with these Christian schools. Its trustees did not meet from 1872 until 1880 and simply allowed Walla Walla trustees to hire teachers. Alexander Jay Anderson, Whitman College's first president, neatly summarized the seminary during these eight years: "the trustees, feeling their financial inability to pay good teachers, acted upon the policy of allowing any teacher of good standing to conduct a school on his own risk and responsibility, in the seminary building."[50] Anderson praised the educators as being "above the average teacher of this newly settled country." But another contemporary maintained that the school's inability to pay salaries meant "a constant change from year to year, frequently being open one or two terms at a time, occasionally falling into strange and incompetent hands, and thus being prevented from establishing a firm position at home or a reputation abroad."[51]

Disgusted with both the decision to permit Episcopalians to use the seminary building and with the fact that the school's irregular operation meant that it could not be "safely and consistently patronized," Peasly Chamberlain in July 1873 resigned as a trustee.[52] He angrily informed Eells that because the school "had been basely ... and hopelessly betrayed" he could operate his own school. In the fall of 1873 Chamberlain reminded the public that he and his wife had "labored faithfully" for Whitman Seminary until "such labors are from various causes no longer hopeful, for the present."[53] He proposed to operate his own private school in "a new and commodious building," promised a broad curriculum and hard school work, "having no confidence in that mental discipline which comes from only a succession of festivals, picnics, concerts, exhibitions, and holidays." Chamberlain pledged that his students would not be forced to hear "denominational creeds or stereotyped prayers." Because the trustees did not meet until 1880, his resignation went unacknowledged. Although he would again serve briefly as principal of Whitman Seminary, Chamberlain took little interest in the school.

Cushing Eells, who had sometimes disapproved of Chamberlain's judgment and religious views, must have been terribly upset with this former trustee for running a competing institution. He also rejected Chamberlain's gloomy assessment of the struggling school, telling a fellow trustee that "I shall be thankful if the Whitman seminary building may be appropriately used, and in it a well conducted school should be taught."[54]

Eells assumed important new tasks in eastern Washington. In the winter he lived with his family and preached at the Skokomish agency on the west side. In the summer he crossed the Cascades by horseback and evangelized the Spokane Indians. But the aging missionary spent even more time preaching in the growing white settlements and establishing Congregational churches, including one in Colfax. In 1878 Eells became superintendent of schools for Whitman County, handling responsibilities similar to those he had performed for Walla Walla County about ten years earlier.

His letters and journal entries from the 1870s elaborate on these new interests and rarely mention the seminary. He did, however, maintain that he and his family had made the Whitman monument, as he called the school, their great objective until their home burned. Cushing told his sons in the early 1870s of his new attitude, "I have said nothing in regard to further efforts to erect a Whitman monument" and that he had "made but few inquiries" about the struggling school.[55] He understood that its persistent financial problems meant that "it languished."[56] Eells donated to other Congregational institutions, including the Colfax church, but he did not enlarge his seminary endowment. (Even in 1880 and 1881 when George Atkinson voiced exciting ideas designed to revive his school, Eells remained indifferent.)

In 1875, however, Eells deftly handled one piece of the seminary's business.[57] Dorsey Baker met with him to discuss some legal problems and to propose a solution. The banker read from the deed signed in 1866 in which he gave land to the seminary under certain conditions. At this meeting he probably emphasized the part of the document in which trustees agreed to use the land "for the purposes" of the seminary and the section reading that if the trustees "shall discontinue indefinitely to use the same for school purposes thereafter the said land shall revert" to the donor. Baker must have questioned Eells if the school was living up to its purposes now that it permitted a series of private schools to operate in the building. In other words, it was possible to argue that the seminary's constitution and bylaws were no longer in force. Baker also concluded that the school's inability to operate every term might also violate the agreement. After presenting these complicated legal problems, Baker stated that they would be resolved if the trustees were willing to exchange the four-acre school site for another piece of his property closer to the city. Eells concluded that Baker wanted the Congregational schoolhouse —it was well located and able to accommodate one hundred pupils —for an Episcopal school. Each seminary trustee, fearful of losing the useful building, informed Eells of his opposition to Baker's pro-

Banker Dorsey S. Baker, Walla Walla's most
prominent citizen, donated four acres of land
south of Boyer Avenue for Whitman Seminary.
In time he doubted the seminary's future, but he
became very involved in the establishment of
Whitman College.

posed land exchange. In giving the results to the banker, Eells added
that he personally opposed the switch because he did not want to
reduce the school's "distance to the center of the city."[58] The church-
man still hoped to protect boys and girls from the dreadful saloons
and from unsavory characters.

For years trustees feared Baker's interpretation of the deed and his
appropriation of the building. Eells wrote in 1879 that "I could see no
way of reasonably attempting to do much more for the Seminary in
its present location without a more satisfactory title."[59] Atkinson,
however, had asked Baker if he would support a surprising proposal
to expand the seminary into a college. Baker, who favored improving
the valley's condition through railroads, schools, and other enterprises, heartily approved, offering additional land and endowment
funds if Whitman offered college courses within two years. Atkinson
could not promise such expansion. Thus in 1881 the board acknowledged that the seminary's frequent suspension "had exposed the title
of its valuable site."[60] In 1882 the school's leaders thought it prudent
to ask the banker, who had once sent his children to the seminary, to
join them. Baker declined to become a trustee. He expressed displeasure with the school's lack of management in the 1870s, but continued to sympathize with plans for a collegiate program. The banker
assured trustees that he would support them when they launched a

college, and, as a sign of friendship, he built a sturdy footbridge across Mill Creek for students. With plans for adding collegiate studies in 1882, the trustees no longer feared Baker's taking legal action against them.

Thus Whitman Seminary suffered from lack of leadership. Eells insisted that all his family had made tremendous sacrifices for the school; in 1880 he listed the major donors—Cushing Eells, $4,600; Edwin Eells, $300; Dorsey Baker, $250; Henry P. Isaacs, $250.[61] The school's founder and benefactor had incorrectly assumed that when he left the classroom the Walla Walla trustees would take good care of this institution that benefitted their community.

Historian Stephen B.L. Penrose also placed the blame for the seminary's problems on Walla Wallans and the board of trustees. The mining town was a poor environment because few of its residents had formal education and were thus initially indifferent to the troubled school. Furthermore, trustees "were not greatly interested in an educational experiment which depended for its maintenance solely upon the tuition received from the students."[62] Penrose understated the case: not a single trustee assisted the school despite the terms of agreement they made when joining the board. The trustees did not make financial contributions to the Eells endowment and did not take other measures that would revive the ailing institution. They knew that an endowment was essential to the security of any frontier school, including those in Walla Walla and Forest Grove, and many heard Eells preach that endowment funds were "indispensable to success."[63] Whitman's moribund trustees compared unfavorably with their fellow townspeople serving on the board for the Episcopal schools. Penrose explained this lack of support: "Few college graduates were numbered among the citizens . . . and the standards were low. People were interested in business [another Congregationalist stated that the region suffered from 'money mania'] and pleasure more than in education."[64] He could have added that some Walla Wallans saw no reason to support the seminary because of its strict Congregational orientation, its inability to raise money, its haphazard curriculum, and its ineffective leadership. It seemed to be another failing frontier institution.

Without direction or community support, the seminary drifted. Some trustees permitted applicants to operate a school in the wood-frame building. Each operated the way he wanted; the trustees took scant interest. William Mariner, L.K. Grim, Horace Lyman, and William Lyman were the most important persons attempting to educate valley children.

William Mariner, a New Englander by birth, a graduate of Harvard, and an experienced teacher of mathematics and foreign languages in Kentucky and Illinois, had impressive credentials and conducted the school on two different occasions. He took up his duties in 1874, but, like W.W. Freeman, found it difficult to instruct frontier children. Penrose neatly summarized the situation: Mariner "was a man of books rather than of practical ability or of close human contacts. Probably his scholarship was too fine for the crude community."[65] William Lyman recalled that the serious and kindly Mariner lived in the seminary building, cooking his own meals. "Very badly cooked, too . . . for he fell sick and was taken by Dr. Blalock and his generous wife to their own home, where after a few weeks' nursing he regained his strength."[66]

The next principal, L.K. Grim, a graduate of the University of Pennsylvania and a Civil War officer, possessed teaching skills and impressed students with his athletic abilities. Arriving in 1876, he immediately made friends. Lyman summarized Grim's character: "a man of fine mind and education, though not apparently having continuity of aims, for he went somewhat irregularly from one occupation to another, sometimes practicing law and sometimes farming, as well as teaching. Some said that he was a confirmed woman hater." He disliked the uncertainty of tuition income, and, to the disappointment of many students and townspeople, he resigned and became a farmer, a more lucrative occupation.

In the fall of 1878, the Reverend Horace Lyman's appointment as principal seemed promising. Lyman had lived in the Pacific Northwest since the 1840s, had founded Portland's Congregational church, had taught for years at Pacific University, and had served as its temporary president. He intended to build up Whitman Seminary by proposing a wide range of academic programs, including "a preparation fully sufficient for entering our best colleges."[67]

Lyman got the school year off to a good start, but then succumbed to typhoid; his son, William—later to be a key faculty member at Whitman College—filled in until he had to resume his own studies.

A champion of Congregationalism who worked hard to establish its churches in eastern Washington, the Reverend George H. Atkinson played a critical role in the early 1880s in the creation of Whitman College.

Responding to a plea to complete the spring term, Grim left his plow and returned to the classroom. Thus, the seminary managed to struggle through another trying year.

Mariner, too, returned to the schoolhouse during the 1880–1881 school year, but illness forced his resignation. The seminary seemed to be even sicker than its last principal; pessimists predicted its demise. Significant changes on the board of trustees, however, revived it. The person who made the greatest difference was George Atkinson. He convinced Eells to call and preside over an October 1880 trustee meeting, the first official one since 1872. Atkinson successfully convinced Eells to regain his old enthusiasm for an institution built to honor the martyred missionary.

At the time that Atkinson plunged into the affairs of the seminary he was an agent of the American Home Mission, serving as superintendent of Oregon and Washington. A prominent Congregational minister, he received a salary and a budget of $1,500 from the eastern organization and donations from western Congregationalists. The superintendent had numerous responsibilities, including the establishment and maintenance of academies and churches. Atkinson told the seminary board about his work and successfully sought reelection to the group. Impressed by his energy and vision, the trustees immediately designated him as financial agent, a position he had once held at Tualatin Academy.[68] For the first time in its history, the school attempted systematic fund raising.

At its next meeting in June 1881, trustees approved Atkinson's circular.[69] Designed to promote the seminary, the document provided information on the school's history, its educational accomplishments, and its resources—a schoolhouse and a $1,000 endowment. Atkinson honestly acknowledged, however, that the school "has been often suspended for want or means to secure good teachers, and has thus exposed the title to its valuable site, and has also lost prestige and influence in a growing community." The seminary could be an influential and permanent institution, its promoter believed, "if it can secure a few thousand dollars endowment; it can be the germ of a Christian college for a large section of the upper Columbia Basin in Oregon and Washington." It pleaded for help to become a school of "sound learning and a center of Christian light and power."

After endorsing the circular, trustees now unanimously passed Atkinson's resolutions, which meant that the board would "adopt a full academic [secondary] and full collegiate course of study, and provide teachers for the same at the earliest practicable moment," would employ a principal and lady assistant for the seminary and pay them $1,500 per year, and would seek a charter granting the seminary "collegiate powers."[70] The trustees, who realized the importance of eastern money to the well-being of Pacific University and to Walla Walla's Episcopal schools, praised Atkinson's attempts to get an endowment from the American College and Education Society of Boston for the proposed Whitman College. Worried about the seminary's future, Eells stated that Atkinson's efforts inspired "hope and confidence."

As the first step to rebuild the seminary, the board offered the Reverend Edwin R. Beach and his wife Lucie $1,500 to reopen the school in September 1881. But this, the last year of the old seminary, proved to be as difficult as many of the others. A solid fall enrollment of sixty seemed to support Atkinson's optimism, but the old gloom returned when news spread that half the students had departed. The alarmed trustees consulted with the Beaches about reasons for the disastrous decline in enrollments. Beach thought the loss of enrollment could be attributed to "disaffection." But historian William

Lyman explained that the one-armed Montanan had intimidated his charges with "a voice so powerful that when lifted in words of admonition, the people around for several blocks would run to their doors to discover the cause."[71] One night, Lyman continued, students angry with Beach began smashing his wagon "when suddenly the Professor ... appeared with a Henry rifle, with which he drove the marauders into Mill Creek, which was in a flood at the time, so that they were nearly drowned. He told the students in the morning how burglars had undertaken to rob the seminary during the night."

The board obtained the Reverend Beach's resignation but retained his wife Lucie. The first woman to have control of the seminary, she soon won friends for it. Lucie had attended South Hadly Seminary in Massachusetts and came to Whitman with good teaching experience, especially in classical and modern languages.

While the school could improve its teaching, it could not raise much money, resolve discipline problems, or offer a consistent curriculum. Atkinson reported difficulty in persuading easterners to donate to either endowments for scholarships or professorships. A perennial money shortage meant that the seminary could not pay faculty. For sixteen years the teachers, like those at the University of Washington, assumed the risk that tuition income would earn them a living. This faculty system led to a steady turnover in teachers and to school closures. The seminary students also presented problems. There was no way to determine how many would enroll for a term and whether they would remain long enough to pay tuition bills. Lyman recalled that his male students enrolled in September, "a deal better posted on downtown matters than they had any right to be, and with no more idea of order and school discipline than so many cayuse ponies."[72] Then boys and girls from the ranches began arriving on horseback; Lyman characterized them as "red-cheeked, round-limbed and independent lasses and big, robust, stentorian-voiced boys, no two of them in the same place in their studies, and everyone expecting special classes to be formed for his special benefit." Farm youngsters left in the spring when parents summoned them back to work, cutting spring enrollments.

Discipline problems challenged all Walla Walla Valley teachers, one of whom stated that they had "to tame [wild country children] into a civilized state and keep them from shouting like Indians....

Walla Walla is a place from which many a teacher and professor has departed discouraged almost to broken-heartedness through the unmanageableness of the youths entrusted to their care."[73] Whitman Seminary records lend some support to this generalization, and discipline, like erratic enrollments, upset teachers. Both sexes created mischief; even girls hurled snowballs through windows. Many students and preceptress Mary A. Hodgdon recalled the techniques Cushing Eells employed to punish wayward boys. Perhaps the best of these accounts appeared in William Lyman's essay:

> [One day schoolboys discovered] a large dam had been formed at the mouth of College creek and salmon trout in great numbers were running up the stream nearly to its head just above where Billings Hall [currently Maxey Hall] is now located. The temptation was too great to be resisted, and every boy in school "cut" that afternoon. Father Eells, who was then teaching, saw that corporal punishment was the only suitable and adequate corrective, but the number of culprits was so large that he was not equal to the task. Therefore he selected a proper number of very effective birch switches, and taking the boys two by two, judiciously selected, he made them a very solemn speech and then had each pair of boys apply the birch to each other. This they did with extreme energy and efficiency, and with great economy of time. At the moment when he judged that they had given and received enough, Father Eells interrupted . . . with uplifted hands, and then after a few affectionate and solemn words he knelt with them in prayer that this experience might be blessed to their souls' good.[74]

The curriculum was another perennial dilemma. Students disagreed with faculty over the courses that should be taught. "Most of them," Lyman complained, "wanted to take arithmetic and bookkeeping, having a vague idea that those studies beyond all others offered an open avenue to wealth and business success." In general the problem was—as it has ever been—between liberal and relevant education. In 1872 Franklin Academy, a new Walla Walla competitor, challenged Whitman Seminary's classical curriculum. This academy offered modern languages, music, and penmanship, expecting to enroll those preferring "practical education, rather than fashionable humbugs."[75] Seeking students from the Walla Walla Valley, a Portland business school advertised its practicality.[76] It asked, "Young men, the future welfare of this coast looks to you. Are you prepared to meet its demands?" The school, of course, had the answer in its theoretical and practical courses in both bookkeeping and merchandising. After a few weeks of study, the student would have obtained "the experience of an ordinary lifetime."

When Chamberlain or Eells taught, the curriculum was primarily the one outlined in 1860 in the seminary's constitution. Other principals brought their own programs. Mariner's, for example, offered an ambitious three-part curriculum: an intermediate department with penmanship, bookkeeping, reading, and spelling; a high school department with higher mathematics, advanced bookkeeping, natural philosophy, and physiology; and a collegiate department with Latin, Greek, and other college preparatory offerings.[77] The jumbled curriculum made academic planning impossible. It was a mixture of what teachers considered to be basic or practical courses offered to generate income for struggling instructors. Parents and students could not depend upon the seminary; this slashed enrollments as families took their children out of the seminary and enrolled them in more dependable institutions. But one rule remained in place: Eells and Hodgdon refused admittance to children under ten; all their successors agreed with their decision.[78]

The seminary's furnishings were typical of frontier schools. Penrose described them: "Hard seats, bare board floor, a wood stove, and a pail of spring water."[79] Lyman was even blunter, pointing out its "poverty, unsightliness, narrowness, and irregularity."[80] Despite its lack of amenities and frequent closures, the seminary still made a positive impact upon some students and townspeople who understood that teachers make schools. Many Walla Wallans appreciated Eells, Chamberlain, Hodgdon, Mariner, Grim, and Beach. These educated men and women helped school the community. Their respect for books and learning, as well as their character, added much to the quality of life in the agricultural center. This legacy meant that a few Walla Walla families would support Whitman trustees when they arranged to offer college instruction.

Student recollections are scarce and sometimes dubious, but some generalizations can be based upon them. The alumni respected the seminary teachers for their wisdom, dedication, and discipline. One praised the faculty for its high standards and for not allowing slow students to set the pace of instruction.[81] One male student bluntly informed Cushing Eells that he had trouble with composition: "I made a fool of myself every week for one year, and I must be excused from making those humiliating efforts or stop."[82] However, he did not expect or receive his teacher's sympathy. Students received grades based upon scholarship, conduct, and attendance. Former students recalled Chamberlain's sternness, powerful character, high ideals, and strong opinions; for example, he rejected the belief that Jesus was born on December 25 and, to the dismay of some students, conducted school on that day. Eells was remembered because of his love of books, precise language, Biblical quotations, serene disposition, kindness, honesty, insistence on order, and method of punishment. Some remembered that he ate cold food that Myra Eells sent to last him for a week.

The seminary faculty compared favorably with that employed by the public schools. A Walla Walla editor complained that county school teachers were "very ordinary ... and in many instances it would seem that it is taken for granted that if a man is fit for nothing else he must surely be a good teacher."[83] Whitman Seminary, on the other hand, continued to attract high-quality teachers; unfortunately, they received poor compensation for their dedication. For decades the same could be said of the college faculty.

Writers provided scanty information about the seminary girls' activities; one alumna explained that in the 1870s "the girls had no sports except the privilege of feasting their eyes on the boys while they were at play."[84] Males enjoyed traditional sports: baseball, footraces, shinny, noon swims in Mill Creek, and after-school horse races down Boyer Avenue. Some activities led to trouble; for example, boys perched on the split rail fence and spat tobacco juice into Dorsey Baker's property.[85] There were school picnics and an occasional debate with a town team, and there were, of course, no dances. Indeed, "There were no seriously love sick boys hence there were no girls with broken hearts."[86]

Thus in 1881 the first stage of Whitman's history ended. The crucial figure in this period had been founder Cushing Eells. His leadership, money, and teaching carried the seminary through a difficult start. Depressed with the inability to secure more helpful hands for the establishment of a school honoring his missionary friend, Eells sometimes walked away from the seminary. But he kept returning to it. Called "Father Eells" because of his deep humility and compassion for others, Eells was only the first of many educators who would devote his or her life to the institution's goals.

Despite the efforts of Eells in the 1860s and several others thereafter, it seemed in the spring of 1882 that the sixteen-year-old institution must permanently close. All across the Pacific Northwest private schools had collapsed; Whitman Seminary seemed doomed to be listed in their ranks. When Alexander Jay Anderson and his family arrived that year to revive the floundering institution, many townspeople must have thought that this well-meaning group would operate the school a few terms and then, like their predecessors, would lock its doors. Surely Walla Wallans were skeptical when they heard that the Andersons planned on operating the old seminary and opening the region's first college on the Boyer Avenue property. Anderson's success would surprise doubters; in fact, he and his family would write a remarkable first chapter in the college's history.

2

Alexander Jay Anderson
Lays the Foundation
1882 – 1891

Alexander Jay Anderson's children often boasted of his accomplishments, especially his important work while president of Whitman College. The family insisted that although Anderson made very little money, his success lay in the hundreds of students in Illinois, Oregon, and Washington who were enriched by his teaching. A son eulogized: "His life work is more and more fully revealed in the lives and achievements of his pupils."[1]

Born in 1832 in Lockport, Illinois, Alexander with his four siblings were reared in poverty by his widowed mother. Encouraged by his family and with only $34 in his pocket, the slight, sandy-haired eighteen-year-old enrolled at Knox College located in Galesburg, Illinois, a town that became a center of abolitionism and other antebellum reforms. He completed two years of the required curriculum, and then, like many of his classmates, dropped out and taught common school to support his family. He returned to college, held part-time jobs, and graduated in 1856.[2]

Knox, opened in 1841 by reform-minded evangelical Presbyterians, had a traditional three-part educational organization: collegiate, female collegiate, and academic, which was "calculated to prepare the pupils for college, for teaching school, and for the various pursuits of life." Founders of the college expected many graduates to become western clergymen. In 1856 there were 431 students, a quarter of them enrolled in the three-year college course. All were closely regulated. The catalog explained that "the discipline is designed to be parental, and conducted on gospel principles. Every student will be expected to abstain from all immoralities, and to exhibit a cheerful promptitude in the discharge of every relative and social duty." Anderson not only accepted such rules, he would later establish similar ones in Seattle and Walla Walla.[3]

Although the students grumbled about the two inadequate college buildings, Knox had a good library and well-stocked science cabinets. But the ten-member faculty made the school. The Reverend Jonathan Blanchard was president during Alexander Anderson's years at the college. (Blanchard, a Congregationalist, was later forced to resign from Knox in a controversy with the Presbyterians over control of the college.) He was a most impressive teacher. In championing reform, inspired teaching, solid administration, and successful money-raising activities, he earned the lifelong admiration of Anderson and won many friends for the school. Faculty members soldiered with Blanchard in the reform ranks and encouraged student organizations to advance such causes as abolition and temperance. In later years Anderson told his children that Knox College was the formative influence in his life; he often praised its president, its professors, its stimulating intellectual climate, and its reform fervor. The college, in sum, gave him a solid grounding in the liberal arts, a love of learning, a desire to teach, and a deep sense of social responsibility.

Anderson became a teacher, and in 1857 married a colleague, Louisa Phelps. A daughter of parents committed to woman's education, Louisa had graduated from Ohio's Willoughby Female Seminary, where she had developed an interest in science. While her husband taught a variety of subjects, especially mathematics and pedagogy, and served as principal of academies and private and public high schools, Louisa taught and helped manage the schools. Although her early career was interrupted—in seven years, she bore five sons: Charles, Oliver, Louis, Alexander, Jr., and George—she was preceptress and teacher of natural sciences, French, and art, and she later designed the first curriculum for Whitman College women. As teachers the Andersons set high academic standards and advocated religion, morality, and self-government. In their thirteen years of teaching in Illinois they won considerable praise. Alexander Anderson supported the Republican Party, served as mayor of Newark, Illinois, spoke for temperance, denounced slavery, and advocated reform in school exercises. In 1863, Wheaton College, then under the presidency of Jonathan Blanchard, recognized his productive career and awarded him an M.A.[4]

Anderson rejected opportunities to become a journalist, business-man, or lawyer, and announced in 1869 that he was moving to Forest Grove, to take charge of Tualatin Academy, a preparatory institution operated by Pacific University. Its trustees had offered him $1,000 a year, the interest on a bond, and free tuition for his children. The Illinois *Schoolmaster*, remembering Anderson's enthusiastic support for common schools and teachers' institutes, reported his departure and concluded: "Illinois loses ... one of her best workers in the educational field."[5]

Soon after his arrival in Oregon, Anderson wrote to an Illinois friend that Forest Grove was "far out of the world" but boasted that the academy and the university had a good library and an $80,000 endowment, but he overestimated the size of the endowment and failed to mention that it funded faculty salaries.[6] Tuition income was small; students paid only $33 a year. There were similarities between Pacific and Knox, but Pacific was much smaller (128 students in 1870, only 13 in the collegiate department), its faculty did not push societal reform, and its president, the Reverend Sidney Harper Marsh, was less dynamic, political, and controversial than Blanchard. Pacific had severe problems, especially a lack of operating money—only a $25 book budget in 1872. Marsh, who had labored diligently to build a reputable institution since 1853, explained: there were too many colleges in the state, Oregon's population was small and scattered and suffered from a "general backwardness in scholarship." Still, he had raised endowment money in the East and had put Portland business-men Henry Failing and Henry Corbett on the school's board of trust-ees, where they wisely managed investments and helped improve faculty morale by increasing salaries.[7]

Anderson spent five years in Forest Grove. He reorganized Tualatin Academy so that it became a high school. He attracted students with his effective teaching. A visitor called him "a perfect disciplinarian and the most exact and truly successful teacher I have found in all my travels." Anderson also took time to serve as county school superintendent and work for his old college interests: temperance, the Republican Party, Congregationalism, and common schools. In

Forest Grove the Andersons had a daughter and named her Helen Hood in honor of Mt. St. Helens and Mt. Hood.[8] In summary, during Anderson's five years in Forest Grove he learned about the problems besetting frontier schools and settlers. His experiences would be of great help in his future educational posts.

In 1874 Alexander Anderson submitted his resignation. The trustees tried to dissuade him by offering him $1,500 per year ($200 more than any other faculty member), but he accepted a position with the Portland public schools for a variety of reasons. Although Anderson had received a professorship at Pacific University and taught mathematics and pedagogy, he still complained that the school's leaders favored the university over the academy. He and Louisa also desired to move so their sons—who ranged from nine years of age to sixteen —could eventually find congenial positions in a large city. So for three years Anderson worked in the Portland schools, becoming principal of the region's only public high school, and finding that urban children needed more discipline than those he had instructed in rural Illinois or in Forest Grove.[9]

In 1877 Anderson, who now had a regional reputation, received two job offers: the presidency of the University of Washington and the principalship of Whitman Seminary. Neither school offered the security and salary he currently enjoyed. In fact, both institutions periodically closed from problems worse than Pacific's. Anderson made a quick trip to Walla Walla, which convinced him that Whitman was in a precarious condition and that its future was much bleaker than that of the University of Washington. Although Whitman had been chartered before the university, it had not yet offered college courses. The opportunity to achieve a career goal—the presidency of a college or university—was the major reason Anderson chose Seattle.

Frontier educators knew that many presidential plans had been crushed at the university; one historian concluded that "the east was the great recruiting grounds, for [presidential] candidates familiar with local conditions were loath to apply." The University of Washington struggled with the same problems that beset Oregon's private schools—a shortage of money, a dearth of qualified students, and charges of denominationalism when a minister served as president. But the university had two unique problems: critics still denounced the school's early leaders for disposing of 40,000 acres of land that should have furnished a good endowment, and they complained that the institution provided mostly elementary and high school education rather than a dependable college program. Outsiders grumbled that Seattle children enjoyed a school funded by all territorial taxpayers, while college students had to go at considerable family expense to Oregon or California to receive a high-quality education.[10]

Compared with Pacific or Willamette, the University of Washington was clearly second rate in its financial structure and curriculum; only after some academic juggling did it award its first bachelor's degree (a B.S.) in 1876. At about the same time, the institution's catalog summarized its troubled past: "The Territory is still in its infancy; society is only in its formative state; nothing as yet is really permanent; the unsettled state of things, and the restlessness of the people have an unfavorable influence, adverse to a thorough and systematic course of study; our common school system is in so imperfect a condition, that the district schools do not to any extent become feeders for a College."[11]

Unable to cope with its various problems, the university closed in the spring of 1877. This was not the first time that regents padlocked its doors, but it prompted yet another effort to revive the institution. Governor Elisha Ferry continued to urge development in stages, the regents wanted a school to manage, and the citizens voiced support for effective educational leadership. There was also a fresh incentive to reopen the school: in 1876 a rival, the University of Oregon, began operation. It attracted considerable support from citizens of Eugene, hired a reputable faculty (including the noted geologist Thomas Condon from Pacific University), and enrolled 177 students for its first term. Since the state of Oregon and Washington Territory competed for trade, immigration, and railroads, Washington promoters protested the closing of an old university in Seattle while a new one opened in Eugene.[12]

The Andersons investigated Seattle, which, with a population of about 3,000, was about the size of Walla Walla. Although the school needed repairs and equipment, the three buildings were substantial and seemed adequate to serve the territory's 75,000 inhabitants. More important to the visitors was the enthusiasm that Governor Ferry had for the university. He predicted a sharp increase in enrollments after the legislature appropriated money for scholarships. Ferry knew that Oregon had used such a scholarship scheme to attract students to Eugene; a similar program, he believed, would entice students to Seattle.

Impressed with the possibilities, Anderson signed a one-year contract requiring him to fulfill the duties of president and to teach in an academic department courses appropriate for an academy or high school. In return for his teaching and leadership, he would receive $500, rents from college housing, and all the tuition income from charges ranging from $8 to $12 per term.

The fall term of 1877 seemed promising; more than fifty students registered. Most of them were between the ages of twelve and twenty-one. Alexander and Louisa Anderson put tremendous energy into the enterprise: they classified each student, set and enforced rules, and taught an enormous range of classes, including algebra, geometry, bookkeeping, rhetoric, physiology, history, literature, Greek, Latin, French, chemistry, botany, and astronomy. Louisa boarded girls in the Anderson home, as the Marshes did at Pacific. Living with the president's family gave female students "not only the comforts of a cultivated home," the regents boasted, "but that moral and aesthetic training so valuable in fitting them for the battle of life."[13]

After visiting the campus, legislators appropriated $3,000 for forty-five two-year scholarships. In December Anderson announced that the university would immediately offer college courses primarily to accommodate scholarship students. Believing that the school had a bright future, Anderson signed a five-year contract and set to work in earnest laying the university's foundation upon his extensive experience and reading. First he designed a curriculum that would maximize the school's appeal. According to one authority, the university offered this curriculum "practically unchanged . . . until 1894."[14] Anderson emphasized the collegiate over the preparatory branch and divided the university into four courses of study: classical with a B.A. degree, scientific with a B.S. degree, normal with a diploma, and commercial with a diploma. The educator knew that enrollments in practical courses—education and commerce—would be heavier than in the classical offerings, but he believed that Latin as well as bookkeeping had an important place in a frontier university. His own sons enrolled in both practical and traditional courses, and eventually four of them were employed as instructors (three in vocational classes). All courses of study were open to all students. By comparison, Pacific University, equal in size to the University of Washington, still operated a separate "Ladies' Course" that led to a Mistress of Science degree; it did not offer commercial or normal courses.

After designing a curriculum Anderson established male and female literary societies like the one that had been so important to him at Knox College. He told the participants how their activities, including debates and speeches, could enrich the school's academic life and provide social opportunities. Next, impressed with the way that Sidney Marsh had won friends for Pacific, Anderson sought to win public support. He publicized school exercises and invited prominent men (among them, Governor William Newell and Judge Matthew Deady) to deliver commencement addresses or to lecture on the law, the Constitution, or other scholarly topics. The school became the center of Seattle's cultural life. The president also delivered reports to the regents, provided information for newspaper editors, promoted the university through contacts made in his travels, and personally conducted campus tours. When politicians from eastern Washington demonstrated little sympathy for the school located west of the Cascades, Anderson helped convince a respected Walla Walla lawyer to serve as a regent.

Anderson's varied efforts to make the institution important to its students and the public succeeded. Citizens collected money for the scientific cabinets and gave gifts, such as government documents, to the library, which was strengthened when the city library was moved to campus. Regents, legislators, residents, and visitors praised the president and the university's expanded role. Pleased with the new life on the slope behind the town, Seattleites could boast that in two years the school had grown to eleven teachers and more than 150 students; furthermore, by 1882 all the courses of study had awarded diplomas or degrees. Louis Anderson, who was the third son and the family scholar, earned the school's first B.A. degree. The college catalog began listing those alumni whose accomplishments received newspaper attention.

Many hands applauded Alexander Anderson. Newspapers carried many positive accounts. One editor said simply that he was "the right man in the right place;" another provided a more complete summary: the university had had "a fitful and sickly existence," until Anderson, "with a thorough training and noble enthusiasm in the work, infused a new healthful life into the decaying carcass, and thenceforth its progress has been onward and upward until now it is entitled to rank with the very best institutions of learning upon the upper Pacific Coast."[15] This educational reform was possible because Anderson, according to Judge James McNaught, "was blessed with one of heaven's greatest boons, good common sense."[16] In a memorial, legislators boasted that the "university had attained a high degree of proficiency" and concluded that "its faculty is composed of persons who are able, experienced, and zealous educators."[17]

Although the institution was prospering, its president was not. The legislature did not appropriate enough money for salaries— $1,500 for 1878 and 1879, and only $1,000 for 1880 and 1881. The scholarship program of 1877 was not renewed, which cut into enrollments. Anderson had hired a large and talented faculty, including his wife and sons, and shared the school's meager income with them. At the 1879 commencement he indicated that his salary covered only necessities; two years later he and Louisa together received $1,620 or about $400 less than he had received as a Portland principal.[18]

Anderson knew that in the late 1870s the legislature had spent ten times as much on convicts as it did on its university students. In 1881 he sought broader financial support from citizens and legislators. The president stated that he and the faculty were trying to operate a school "suited to the present wants and worthy of the future" and that faculty members would "continue their arduous efforts ... provided Seattle and the Territory stand by it and provide for it as they can and should." Anderson argued that "the culture afforded and the instruction given are above the average in the colleges of new states and territories." He reasoned that Seattleites should help repair buildings and provide classroom furniture because they got the greatest benefit from the school. Since private and public institutions, including Harvard, Yale, and California, solicited private support, he asked: "Why then should not the new and struggling University of a Territory ask for private aid and receive it, too, with becoming dignity and gratitude?"[19]

Anderson delivered a comprehensive report to the regents, outlining "the true plan" to support the school: a territorial tax "which would hardly be felt." He also urged that legislators appropriate $3,000 for faculty salaries, create a special scholarship program for those interested in the normal department, and purchase necessary equipment, supplies, and furniture. Regents agreed with Anderson and, along with former governor Ferry and other allies, presented a pamphlet to the legislature. It contained a summary of the university's financial history, recommended "an annual tax of three cents on each hundred dollars" for the university, and called Anderson a "public benefactor" who had developed "one of the best and most thorough educational institutions in the new northwest."[20]

Citizens, editors, and Governor Newell supported Anderson and the regents. Newell, however, considered it prudent to ignore the taxation proposal and to generalize that money spent on education "tends only to the promotion of all good, and to the suppression of all evil." But in 1881 legislators rejected Anderson's plea for a tax that would have guaranteed the university an annual income, and they further showed their disdain by refusing to appropriate any money for the university. Once again, the school faced closure. Friends of the university denounced opponents for their "pygmy display of momentary power" and denied that the school was elitist or was a "white elephant."[21]

Anderson had braced for the legislature's negative decision. He had become acquainted with the railroad magnate Henry Villard, who praised him for his educational accomplishments. Villard had made timely gifts to the University of Oregon, and he wrote Anderson "that should the legislature fail to meet your just wishes, you will find me perfectly ready to assist you."[22] The educator now asked the businessman for money. Villard responded with a gift that kept the university operating. He provided $1,000 for immediate expenses and promised more. Territorial lawmakers were, he complained, "shortsighted," but he put the discouraging vote in perspective: the refusal of legislators "is not an uncommon experience in this country; even in some of the older and more flourishing states the interests of high education are sadly neglected."[23]

Villard's assistance notwithstanding, Anderson resigned. He had earlier announced that he would leave if he did not receive financial assistance from the legislature, and he predicted that his departure would force the community to "see the necessity of doing something." Some sources incorrectly claimed that the Andersons left because Louisa's physician recommended that she live in a drier climate, but it seems clear that Anderson's departure was caused by his frustration with the legislature. Not until 1883 did the legislature provide money and reinstate a scholarship program.[24]

Anderson had been offered several positions, including the Willamette presidency. He again received the invitation to head Whitman Seminary. After the disappointments suffered at the hands of tight-fisted legislators, a private institution financially managed by a sympathetic board of trustees and warmly supported by businessmen seemed attractive. Yet Anderson knew the school's troubled history. Not much had changed at Whitman since he had considered the post five years earlier. In fact, in 1882 the seminary again closed its doors.

One of the institution's trustees, the Reverend George Atkinson, was a home missionary for the Congregational church in the Pacific Northwest, and he promoted regional churches and schools. He had worked to make Pacific University the most prominent institution west of the Cascades and hoped that his denomination could establish the first college to serve eastern Washington, eastern Oregon, and Idaho. Atkinson wanted to set up a network of Congregational schools, including academies at Cheney and in the Yakima Valley, to feed eastern Washington's first college. He considered two possible college sites: railroad leader Henry Villard had offered land for a college in the region; the other choice was to build upon the institution founded by Cushing Eells.

Atkinson needed Eells' support for the Walla Walla site, and he argued its merits: the presence of a Congregational seminary, a large population, railroad service, and a mild climate. The promoter also warned Eells about the Episcopalians and Methodists, both of which denominations understood the importance of Walla Walla as an interior educational center and hoped to acquire the Congregational seminary building.

Atkinson reviewed Whitman's financial problems and argued that the only remedy was additional financial support from Walla Wallans. He emphasized that banker Dorsey Baker had promised land and money to build a college. Baker's alma mater, Illinois College, had been aided by the American College and Education Society (ACES), so he knew that eastern funds could help launch Whitman

College. But Eells had grave doubts about finding much local support. Recalling the painful history of the seminary, he saw little reason why a community would aid a college when it had not done much for the Congregational school. Eells also rehashed the old and current problems at Pacific University: the bitterness between the leadership of the academy and the university, the failure of college programs to attract students, and the admission of the former president, Sidney Marsh, in 1875, that the university had been launched ten years too soon. (To solve its problems, some drastic measures had been proposed: Albany College, a Presbyterian institution, should be merged with Pacific, or Pacific should be moved to a larger city.) Eells feared that a proposed Whitman College would face similar difficulties and might fail. Despite his doubts, however, Eells eventually agreed that Atkinson's ambitious educational plans provided the only way to save his school. Obviously there was no local financial support for Whitman Seminary, but a larger and grander enterprise—Whitman College—might very well attract nearby and distant friends. Eells understood that his dream to honor Marcus Whitman could only be realized by operating an institution of higher learning.

Atkinson won the support of Baker, Eells, and others largely because he predicted that the proposed college would receive eastern financial assistance. Early in 1881 he had visited Boston, where he sought funds for Whitman Seminary and urged officials of the ACES to add Whitman to its list of western institutions deserving eastern help. The ACES had long supported private colleges; for example, Pacific had been receiving vital financial aid for twenty-five years. To get on the society's list, the ACES told Atkinson, Whitman must enroll a college class. This was a major problem for the western church leader, for he feared that the seminary might close permanently. If it did, then Baker would get back his land with its schoolhouse. It was possible that he would then make arrangements with Episcopal leaders who sought a building for a boys' school.

Undoubtedly Atkinson emphasized to Alexander Anderson how he had worked in Boston and Walla Walla to gain support for a proposed college.[25] He had assured regional Congregationalists that they would not lose their Walla Walla seminary; he had convinced Whitman's trustees that they need not close their school. With his assurances Atkinson had rejuvenated the trustees: in 1881 they enthusiastically supported all of his educational plans, including the addition of a collegiate program, the establishment of feeder academies, the proposed aid from the ACES, and the appointment of a new school principal to build up a college program to follow the preparatory classes. Atkinson explained that the school had arranged to offer courses in the 1881–1882 school year, but this was only temporary. The superintendent must also have stated that Anderson was his choice to provide badly needed leadership. His work at the University of Washington had won regional acclaim. He was a devout Congregationalist, a successful frontier teacher, and an able administrator.

Anderson appreciated Atkinson's educational vision and his kind words but refused to make a decision until after the fall meeting of the territorial legislature. If that body did not make a university appropriation, then Anderson said he would consider leaving Seattle and establishing a Christian college in Walla Walla.

After Atkinson read in late 1881 that the legislature had voted against the university, he asked its disappointed president if he were now released "legally and morally." In his letter the superintendent predicted that if Anderson wanted the leadership of the Whitman Seminary he could probably have it. In other words, if Anderson stated he wanted the position, Atkinson believed that he could find a favorable majority among the trustees. Although only Atkinson's letters have survived, they demonstrate that Anderson fully understood Whitman's difficulties and negotiated carefully. At the age of fifty he anticipated that Whitman would probably be his last school, and he did not want to repeat the financial mistakes he had made in his contract with the university's regents. He insisted that his negotiations with Atkinson be confidential, gradually listed his conditions, and asked many questions.

For about four months Anderson refused to commit himself; at one point Atkinson complained that he could not determine whether his correspondent would accept. Anderson's terms included assurance that the schoolhouse would be refurbished, that he and his two assistants would receive $3,000 annually for their teaching, that he would receive the title of president, not principal, and that he would have a seat on the board of trustees. Atkinson happily accepted all of these terms and offered enticements: rich Walla Wallans would aid the institution; the seminary building would be repaired and new

In 1882 the Anderson family—Alexander, Louisa, and Louis—came from Seattle to Walla Walla and served as the college's first faculty. Louis would teach at Whitman for sixty years, a record that will probably not be broken.

Alexander Jay Anderson

equipment installed; a college class would be formed within a year; the Cheney Academy was about to open and would feed the new college; and the resourceful and well-educated Reverend Nelson F. Cobleigh and his wife Elvira had recently come from the East to rebuild the membership of the local Congregational church and would eagerly support a college. Gradually Atkinson told Baker and selected trustees about these confidential negotiations. Baker promised $250 per year for four years. He and his partner, John Boyer, predicted that once the school was "put in shape ... it will be supported. It will depend largely upon the President and his assistants." In other words, businessmen would be generous if the college proved to be successful. Atkinson quoted the trustees and the Cobleighs as concluding that "If President Anderson will do, as his reputation assures, the teaching and organizing of the school so that our boys and girls can be educated at home, he shall not lack for buildings or means to do it."[26]

Louisa P. Anderson   *Louis F. Anderson*

On March 29, 1882, the trustees approved all of Anderson's requirements and sent a special committee, including Cushing Eells,
down Main Street looking for pledges of money to make up the difference between any shortage of tuition income and the $3,000 An-
derson required.[27] Within three hours the solicitors had pledges for
the full amount. Eventually forty men signed the subscription list, but
none had to pay even a dollar because the tuition paid the salaries.
The same day the board received these pledges it offered Anderson
the presidency. He accepted because the immediate future of Whitman seemed better than that of the university. (Atkinson's letters do
not mention Louisa Anderson's poor health as a possible reason for a
move to Walla Walla.) To give Anderson greater prestige as well as to
reward his accomplishments, Atkinson arranged with other Pacific
University trustees to award him an honorary PH.D.[28]

Probably no Whitman College president ever faced more demanding tasks than Alexander Anderson did from the fall of 1882

through the fall of 1883. Maintaining that he worked like two men, Anderson told an audience that he was "tired and taxed ... from teaching and planning and correspondence, and anxiety."[29] He did not exaggerate. To get the school operating, Anderson taught several courses, handled daily administration, reported to trustees, applied to the ACES for the promised eastern assistance, helped raise local money for a new building, cooperated with politicians in getting a new school charter through the legislature, and delivered an address to regional Congregationalists convening in Walla Walla.

His initial responsibility was to publish an announcement that would attract students to the two fall terms. This first Whitman College publication defined the institution: it would be Christian but not sectarian, its government would be "paternal and fraternal," and the institution would offer "a broad and thorough scholarship." To achieve these goals the president explained that the seminary building would be refurbished, that prominent Walla Wallans promised continued support so that within three years the number of faculty and buildings would be increased, and that the ACES would help secure eastern endowment funds as soon as the school had a freshman class.

The publication also announced the curriculum to be offered for the next four years; for the first time families could engage in long-range academic planning. The curriculum was divided into two general categories. The first was a preparatory section requiring three years. It offered an English-Latin program and a classical program that prepared both sexes for college work. The second category, the collegiate program, offered a four-year curriculum leading to an A.B. and a three-year scientific course leading to a B.S.

Because of delay in the arrival of the school's furniture, classes did not meet until September 4, Marcus Whitman's birthday. Because the students brought such a wide range of backgrounds, the Andersons first had to place them in grades and then offer numerous classes. The new teachers proved to be competent and popular. News of their ability spread through the valley, and enrollment increased steadily. Sixty students came on opening day; in the second term there were ninety-one, and many were turned away for lack of space. Even so, nineteen students had no seats. In the second term, the new president hired four part-time faculty members and published specific enrollments. The popular subjects included: algebra, 26 students; arithmetic, 72; bookkeeping, 26; Latin grammar and reader, 48; English grammar, 19; geography, 19; penmanship, 30; and general history, 22. Advanced classes, of course, had much smaller enrollments: analytical geometry, 4; Virgil, 4; zoology, 4; and German, 5.

In his December report to trustees Anderson emphasized the successful start but then lamented that a lack of space "holds us in check at every turn." The president predicted that the institution could enroll 300 students within a year and advised that "The true way to secure students is to be prepared for them."

Knowing that his report would be published, Anderson added some information for those who knew little about eastern Washington's prospects. The Northern Pacific Railroad would soon link the region with the nation and thereby stimulate growth. Several boosters had made that claim, but Anderson added a less familiar argument. Whitman College would also help Walla Walla grow. If the school had land, buildings, a "moderate endowment," and solid administration it would increase the size of the community by up to 3,000. This had happened in other college towns, including Galesburg, Illinois. Anderson concluded that the school with the best foundation would become the regional leader. But the educator did more than appeal to the immediate economic reasons for supporting Whitman. While it was true that a college would mean "a rise of value of corner lots," this was less important than the fact that many generations would benefit from a school that served "as an intellectual center of the highest Christian culture."

To provide space Anderson asked trustees to raise $50,000 for two brick buildings: a classroom building and a ladies' hall. He challenged his community: "Can $50,000 be put to a better use in the oldest, largest, and wealthiest city between the Cascade Range and the Rocky Mountains?" Although buildings had priority, the president also wanted $5,000 for a library and scientific equipment. It is interesting to note that he did not ask local contributors for an endowment, which he anticipated could be raised in the East under the auspices of the ACES, as had happened for Pacific University and other western schools.

Aware that pioneers would scoff at raising $50,000, Anderson asked that if wooden buildings must be substituted, they must not be on "a diminished scale" and that a wing should be attached to the seminary building. In other words, he saw these wooden structures as temporary until local donors furnished funds for stone buildings.

Trustees appreciated Alexander Anderson's plans and began studying them. Their special committee concluded that it was impossible to raise $50,000 but that about $15,000 could be collected. So the architect's drawings for a brick building had to be modified in favor of a wooden one. College Hall, a classroom building, would be constructed first because it was badly needed. In an attempt to broaden the school's support, trustees selected three townspeople who were not on their board to serve as a subscription committee. A decision on Ladies' Hall was deferred until 1884 when trustees devised a novel way to fund it.

In July 1883 a contractor agreed to build College Hall, promising to complete his work in the fall. Although trustees and the subscription committee believed that it would be easy to raise funds, such was not the case. It proved to be as difficult to fund College Hall as it had been in 1866 to pay for the seminary building. The total cost was about $16,000. Subscriptions amounted to $11,000, but $5,000 could not be collected. This was not unusual. College leaders from one coast to the other had this disappointing experience, and the trustees once again had to borrow from Dorsey Baker for a classroom building. This $5,000 debt lingered for several years. Like the earlier debt that the Eellses covered, it worried Whitman's supporters. Anderson must have envied the University of Oregon, which received $7,000 in 1881 from Henry Villard to liquidate the building debt and revitalize the school. Such a gift by Villard or anyone else would have had a similar effect at Whitman, where the deficit resulted in low faculty salaries, limited scholarships, and internal bickering. Atkinson, Baker, Boyer, and others had assured Anderson that once he made a success of his college he would receive financial assistance, but such was not the case. During Anderson's nine-year administration he and the school's treasurer, John Boyer, struggled with debt. Whitman's financial condition was much worse than that of Pacific, which paid faculty out of its endowment or from the sale of land.

While attempts were being made to collect building subscriptions, College Hall opened in the fall. Anderson unsuccessfully tried to convince Cushing Eells to allow him to call it Eells Hall. Located slightly to the north of the present Prentiss Hall, it provided a fine view of the

Blue Mountains. The Walla Walla *Watchman*, on December 7, 1883, described the structure:

> It is a capacious building, amply supplying the college for recitation rooms and is an ornament and credit to the city. The building contains an assembly room in the second story 52½ x 35 feet; two school rooms, 28 x 30 feet each; two professors'

Built in 1883, College Hall contained classrooms, the chapel, and the president's office. It later served as the Conservatory of Music, and the chapel was converted into a girls' gymnasium.

rooms, 22 x 28 feet each; and one room 21½ x 30 feet. These
rooms are all furnished with the latest improved patent hard
wood seats and desks. A library 21½ x 22 feet; the President's
room, 16 x 18 feet; apparatus room, 11 x 13 feet; and laboratory, off the science recitation room, 11 x 13 feet.

The school would soon outgrow this space and would build classrooms in the attic.

In July when the contract was signed for College Hall, delegates
from the Congregational Association of Oregon and Washington met
in Walla Walla. It was important for Anderson to win their approval.
He discussed with them some current educational issues and then
recited Whitman's history. Much of what he told these delegates he
later published in his college catalogs. The president asserted, "There
is a general agreement that the State has a right to require a certain
amount of intelligence on the part of all its citizens, and especially on
the part of its voters; and that it may by general tax establish common
schools."[30] If taxpayers supported them, Anderson favored district
high schools and universities. He championed both state and Christian schools and opposed those who insisted that society needed only
state schools. He predicted that the Christian college, "the most
American of all American institutions," would survive. "The greatest
need of the times," he concluded, "is a true Christian morality in
politics, a true Christian morality in training the young, and a true
Christian morality in every department of life." Thus schools like
Whitman had an important mission. The president emphasized that
the institution was not under the control of any synod, association,
conference, bishop, or state. The school, he promised, would "not be
sectarian." Anderson explained that the "Board of Trustees must always continue to have a majority of evangelical Congregationalists in
its membership, so as to represent parties at the East who bestow the
College," but a minority of trustees would represent "cooperating
evangelical denominations" or Walla Walla.

Anderson then moved from this controversial topic to emphasize
the school's future. It had a prime location: "Looking at a correct
map, Walla Walla City, the seat of Whitman College, will be found to
be the geographical, commercial, and population center of the Upper
Columbia River Basin—a region including all of Oregon and Wash-

ington east of the Cascade mountains and the three northern counties of Idaho." He sounded like President Marsh, Superintendent Atkinson, and other boosters when he praised the region. Anderson boasted it was twice as large as New England and that this western area was "capable of sustaining an equal average population to the square mile" as New England. Anderson wrote of the region's grains, fruits, cattle, manufacturing, and invigorating climate. He stressed that Whitman was the only college east of the Cascades based on the New England type and predicted that it and the region it served would prosper.

The delegates discussed Anderson's paper and then adopted resolutions. The first stated that "We endorse fully the main thought in the essay, that the true prosperity of our country, and the production of the highest type of manhood and womanhood in our land, depend upon the maintenance of the Christian college as the only institution fitted to *finish* and *supplement* the secular education supplied by the state, by supplying moral and religious element."[31] The third resolution was more controversial: "We rejoice at last that an institution has come into existence that is not ashamed to call itself *Congregational.* [This was a slap at Pacific University.] We do not mean by this that we regard Whitman College as in any sense of the word sectarian. We simply mean that we understand Whitman College to be set for the propagation of those principles of democratic, republican liberty in church and state which have been advocated by the sons and daughters of the Pilgrims."

In this resolution the Congregational Association ignored Anderson's views. Anderson had not insisted that Whitman was Congregational; it was the ACES that required the majority of the trustees to be evangelical Congregationalists. He believed, as President Marsh of Pacific had stated, that a college had a brighter future if it could appeal to all denominations, not just Congregationalists. He refused to call the school Congregational—as some delegates wanted—in his annual college catalog. Whitman was, he argued, Christian and nondenominational, and he sought the goodwill of other denominations. Therefore, an early commencement speaker was from the local Cumberland Presbyterian church, many college activities were held in various Protestant churches, and Anderson expressed pleasure that one of the first college graduates was a Roman Catholic.

This whole question of Whitman's being a Congregational institution would later cause Anderson considerable grief. But in 1883 his various administrative duties meant that he could not worry about differences with Congregational leaders. Besides, he expected that Atkinson, a powerful Congregational leader and able ally, would protect him from religious acrimony.

In the fall Anderson switched his attention from churchmen to lawyers and politicians. He huddled with them while preparing a revised Whitman charter that would be introduced in the forthcoming meeting of the territorial legislature. They plotted ways to get the document adopted. Trustees had asked Anderson to get the word "collegiate" in the school charter, but he wrote, with the advice of Walla Walla lawyer Benjamin Sharpstein, a much more comprehensive charter, one that would grant Whitman a tax exemption on its property and endowment. Interestingly enough, it did not increase the number of trustees. Thus Whitman, from its seminary charter in 1859 to the present day, has had a small board of nine.

Anderson, who supported private and public higher education, had definite opinions about the state's responsibility. In 1881 he had favored a tax to support the University of Washington; in 1883 he still favored it. A tax "should be cheerfully paid" to support such a school, "but at the same time the State should as cheerfully release from taxation all the property, including buildings, grounds, and endowments used exclusively for school purposes, and belonging to Christian institutions chartered by the legislature."[32] In a sweeping conclusion the president argued that "there should be no tax upon knowledge, and hence no tax upon schools—the foundations of learning, culture, and ennobling principles."

He expressed to a local politician these views and the fact that for years the Massachusetts legislature had aided Williams College. Sympathetic with Whitman College, Walla Wallan Charles Besserer, a territorial legislator, told Anderson that he would try to obtain both an outright appropriation and a tax exemption for the school. During the legislative session Anderson wrote to legislators on behalf of his college, and he carefully followed their proceedings in the press. In October the legislature granted the University of Washington $6,000 for the biennium. (This favorable action might have been influenced by the fact that in 1882 the Oregon legislature passed a tax bill that provided its university with an annual grant of $5,000 and other forms of assistance.) Although the bill passed by about two-to-one margins in both houses, opponents heatedly denounced it. Some eastern Washington lawmakers complained about granting taxes to a distant institution that did not serve the area east of the Cascades. Besserer, a leading critic of the bill, called the university a white elephant, assumed that the appropriation was so generous that professors would "accumulate nice little fortunes out of the institution," and boasted that if the university had been planted in Walla Walla it would be self-sustaining.[33]

Although he could not prevent the university from receiving an appropriation, Besserer introduced a bill that also provided $6,000 for Whitman. According to one listener, it "caused quite a lively time and developed the elocutionary powers of the representatives to a high degree."[34] In supporting his measure, Besserer argued that the institution perpetuated the memory of a martyr, that the college would become a credit to the whole territory, that President Alexander Anderson's college was equal to the University of Michigan, that it was just as much a public institution as the University of Washington because both charged tuition, and that "The only difference in the two institutions is that one receives the fostering care of a generous government while the other must take care of itself or perish." "Well, gentlemen," the Walla Wallan continued, "it has taken care of itself for these many years and we shall not allow it to perish, even should you act the stepmother toward us." Besserer concluded that support from westside legislators would be a sign of fraternal feelings and recognition that tax money should go to institutions on both sides of the Cascades.

A Puget Sound legislator humorously proposed aiding Whitman because when westside students had "their health endangered in moist climate" they could then be sent to the Walla Walla school and would return to Seattle "robust and hearty."[35] A representative from Whitman County argued at length against the bill, stating that the legislature could not give tax money to a private school and warning that if a Walla Walla County institution received money then all the other counties would expect equal treatment. Another opponent said that if the legislature benefitted Congregationalists, Catholics and Methodists would then seek similar assistance.

Both houses of the legislature passed a bill that provided thirty-six free scholarships to the University of Washington. About this time the lower house rejected the appropriation for Whitman by a vote of two to one. But the upper house and then the lower passed the Whitman College charter and tax exemption. (The lower house was less eager to support Whitman: the vote was close—thirteen to ten, with half of the negative votes from eastsiders.) It is impossible to determine why house members passed the Whitman measure. They no doubt wanted to be fair and to foster education on both sides of the territory. But perhaps the fact that Walla Wallans in Olympia pushed to divide Washington Territory along the Cascades and create a new territory east of the mountains also had some impact. Some politicians said that helping an eastside school would be a sign of westside friendship.

Whitman College was for a time the only territorial institution to enjoy a tax exemption. The upper house passed a bill introduced by a Walla Wallan that would provide tax exemptions for all private schools, churches, and hospitals, but the lower house rejected it. The legislature, however, agreed that voters should decide the matter. In 1886 they approved a general tax-exemption law.

Although Whitman badly needed the $6,000 that Besserer tried to get from the legislature, the revised Whitman charter with its tax exemption was far more important. Anderson and the trustees rejoiced over the decision; at the close of the 1883 legislative session Anderson invited the legislators and legislative officers to a campus celebration. But the trustees did not celebrate. They feared that another vote might reverse the tax exemption and even proposed sending Anderson to Washington "to secure from Congress the validity" of its new charter.[36] Most Walla Wallans probably ignored the issue. To their way of thinking, other controversial measures introduced at the same legislative session seemed far more consequential than a tax exemption: they disagreed over a liquor license bill, a herd law, a compulsory school law, the adoption of women's suffrage, and a memorial that would have divided Washington along the Cascades into two territories. Over the years, friends of the college have consistently stressed the importance of the tax exemption, and those who know Whitman's history have praised Alexander Anderson's accomplishment. Both presidents Stephen Penrose and Chester Maxey lauded their predecessor for his political acumen. Historian Frederick

Rudolph put the issue in historical perspective: "hundreds of colleges with tax exemption enjoyed an indirect subsidy of incalculable and uncalculated worth."[37]

Early in his administration Anderson sought financial support from trustees and businessmen, from regional Congregational leaders, from territorial politicians, and from eastern donors through the ACES. Like other presidents, Anderson understood that easterners gave more money to frontier colleges than westerners. For a variety of reasons the older communities were better able to extend a helping hand. He knew from his experience at Pacific that distant donors could supply money and that local businesses could invest it.

He had every reason to believe that the ACES would support Whitman College. In its 1881 report the society stated that "a college without endowment is as useless as a locomotive without steam."[38] According to the report, the ACES and its predecessor had aided twenty-eight western schools since 1844, sending more than $1,353,000 from eastern contributors. These eastern gifts had stimulated western donors. Such schools as Oberlin, Knox, and Wabash had been taken off the ACES list because they had acquired sufficient financial strength, and newer and needier schools took their places. In 1883 the ACES argued that the Christian college, "one of the initial ideas in our New England civilization," had a tremendous positive influence on frontier life, including its impact on the development of the common schools."[39] Anderson had heard such a claim made at Knox thirty years earlier; his experience in Forest Grove had convinced him that the Christian college played a vital western role.

Getting approved by the ACES was slower than anticipated. Atkinson and the ACES had assured Anderson when he considered accepting the presidency that the Boston organization was eager to help. But the ACES delayed because it had questions about the school. When Anderson applied for assistance he admitted that Whitman had only one college student; the ACES replied that such an enrollment was too low to receive help. But it changed its mind when Anderson reported four doing college work. More important, the ACES delayed action until it saw that Whitman had a majority of Congregationalists on its board. The organization wanted to protect Whitman from sectarian squabbles; this could only be done if the Congregationalists had a majority vote. The ACES did not object to other denominations being represented on the board, but it wanted to assure potential donors in Congregational churches that the money they might give would further their denomination's influence in the West. The ACES's application document, which Anderson and the trustees had to complete, required them to agree to certain conditions: that the school's central aim was "Christian learning," that it would always be free from ecclesiastical or state control, that it would maintain a self-perpetuating board, that it would offer a college curriculum, that it possessed an act of incorporation from the legislature, and that it understood that eastern money should not be used for buildings.

In the spring Whitman learned that it had been placed on the ACES list and could raise money for an endowment, equipment, and faculty salaries. A second communication stated that the college was given permission to seek money among Congregational churches in four New England states. Whitman, in turn, agreed that if it were no longer Christian or if it came under ecclesiastical or state control it must return to the ACES all the funds raised with its help.

The society recommended that either Anderson or Atkinson solicit funds in the East by telling the story of Marcus Whitman. Anderson, of course, could not leave his strenuous presidential duties; therefore, trustees decided to divide the eastern work between George Atkinson and Cushing Eells. Eells felt inadequate. He was seventy-three and often ill, he was not a gifted speaker, and he had not been east since 1838. Atkinson, who had successfully raised eastern funds for Pacific University with the cooperation of the ACES, encouraged the old man to represent the young college. Eells would be successful, he predicted, because his long missionary experience would make him unusual. By simply telling of his work among Indians and frontier settlements and his sacrifices and hopes for Whitman College, he would impress easterners. There were dozens of fund raisers in New England, but no one could match the old missionary's career and character. After considerable prayer, and after rejecting the warnings of his sons that the journey would endanger his health, Eells agreed to join Atkinson.

The two canvassers realized they would compete with the agents of other western schools for eastern contributors. Many of these competitors had considerable experience with fund raising and depended upon valuable eastern contacts. At the time of Whitman's acceptance, the ACES was aiding one school in each western state or territory. The institutions enjoying assistance were Carleton College, Minnesota; Colorado College, Colorado; Doane College, Nebraska; Drury College, Missouri; Iowa (Grinnell) College, Iowa; Olivet College, Michigan; Pacific University, Oregon; Ripon College, Wisconsin; and Washburn College, Kansas.

Crossing the continent by railroad, including the recently opened Northern Pacific, Eells in 1883 and 1884 attended various church meetings where his missionary work among Indians received more attention than his educational cause. At a convention in Concord, New Hampshire, delegates honored Eells and railroad executive Frederick Billings. (The meeting of these two diverse individuals was advantageous because the Billings family later contributed to the college.) At one national meeting where Eells summarized his missionary labors, a reporter called it "one of the most thrilling utterances of the gathering." A delegate jumped to his feet and hailed Eells as "the John the Baptist of the Home Missionary Society."[40] At a Brooklyn meeting, church delegates asked to see and hear the venerable missionary. Eells told a writer that "it required some power of condensation to put the work of forty-five years into a ten-minute speech."[41] At Saratoga he gave another short speech, but the audience insisted that he continue and donated nearly $70 to the college.

In the fall Eells began making calls. An ACES official reported that the canvasser was "breaking ground slowly and getting a good many lines out."[42] But Eells was bitterly disappointed to learn that Atkinson, a skilled fund raiser with many eastern connections, could not leave his obligations and assist him. Obviously the critical task of raising an endowment fell entirely upon the old missionary. Once again the school's future depended on its founder.

For months Eells crisscrossed New England, speaking in church services, Sunday school classes, prayer meetings, lecture halls, and private parlors. In his talks he emphasized Marcus Whitman, the school honoring his memory, his own missionary activities, and the fast-growing Pacific Northwest. He assured a congregation in Salem, Massachusetts that the college could increase from 100 to 250 students if it could house them and expressed optimism about the institution because it "had been established by divine inspiration, born and cradled in prayer."[43]

The canvasser's journal and letters provide considerable detail about his efforts to collect money and about his frequent prayers for the college. He acknowledged the vital help of the ACES and persons like William A. Mowry, a professor studying Marcus Whitman's life. But Eells complained that he was unable "to perform more than a small fraction of what needs to be done" and that it was "uphill work to solicit funds for a college."[44] Confusing rail schedules, sleepless nights, rejections by the wealthy, and ailments of old age prompted Eells to complain of "dreadful fatigue." He sometimes showed a lack of familiarity with American business, worrying unnecessarily about the process of getting money safely from Boston to Walla Walla. Eells showed his provincialism by stating that "John Rockefeller is understood to be wealthy."[45]

Eells took time from his solicitation to visit friends and relatives. His brother, Charles, joined him, and the aged men returned to boyhood haunts. It is surprising that the western visitor wrote so little about New England, a region he had not seen in nearly a half century. Instead he praised the region's learned clergy and Boston's urbanity. A highlight of his trip was a visit to Williams College. Eells grumbled about all the smokers but thoroughly enjoyed his return to his alma mater. While on the campus he solicited help for Whitman. A professor volunteered to order foreign-made laboratory apparatus, and a student quartet gave a concert that resulted in "a thank-offering of four dollars ... to Whitman."[46] Impressed with the collegiate environment he enjoyed at Williams, he sought ways to duplicate it at Whitman. Thus he changed his will so that $6,000 which he had earmarked for various Congregational organizations would instead go to Whitman. The first use of this fund would be for the construction of Ladies' Hall.

Even after fourteen months of fund raising in the East, an effort he found even more arduous than missionary labors in the West, Eells worried that he had not done enough for Whitman College. His son Myron summarized his father's experience: "To be a public beggar was very unpleasant; to meet rebuffs from Christians was more so; but unkind treatment from pastors was most severe of all."[47] The ACES praised his fund raising and invited him to remain and address fresh eastern audiences. Eells did continue a bit longer than scheduled, including some time soliciting in Illinois. But in late September

1884 he decided to quit, informing Anderson that to continue would be "suicidal." After returning to eastern Washington he informed the college that it should not celebrate his eastern fund raising. The school's trustees, however, passed a flattering resolution: "We owe an inexpressible debt of gratitude to the Reverend Cushing Eells, who, alone, during his seventy-fifth year, went to New England, and for a year at his own expense labored, worked, and prayed as few men can or will, for the institution ... and with the help of God secured nearly $8,000 for endowment, $1,500 to supplement teachers' salaries, $500 for apparatus, and books worth nearly $1,000."[48] The list of donors, mostly individuals and some Congregational churches, showed that they gave from $1 to $1,500. Thus this first significant fund drive provided the school with badly needed money and with new friends, including the ACES's officers. The first three Whitman presidents would often base their appeals for money upon the devoted service of Cushing Eells, and donors who had heard him, especially in the East, would make contributions.

While Eells visited eastern communities for endowment funds, an executive committee of the Whitman trustees selected a second fund raiser for a different purpose. It accepted Elvira Cobleigh's proposal that she solicit "under direction of the ACES $6,000 or more to enlarge the Seminary building sufficient for a Ladies' Hall."[49] The committee, which knew that the ACES had successfully helped Pacific University raise funds in the East for its own ladies' hall, also recommended to the full board that Elvira be appointed its superintendent if she raised the money. In other words, by finding at least $6,000, Cobleigh could earn herself a position.

A native of New Hampshire and a graduate of Mount Holyoke, Elvira Cobleigh in 1882 had moved with her husband Nelson to Walla Walla. He began to rebuild its Congregational community; she assisted and also established a private school. Cobleigh provided great help to Anderson by enrolling students too young for Whitman. The Cobleighs and the Andersons worked for the college, the church, and the WCTU. From Elvira Cobleigh the Andersons learned about the current boarding plans of women at eastern institutions like Mount Holyoke—a very successful seminary founded in 1837 by Mary Lyon at South Hadley, Massachusetts. The principal and faculty of Mount Holyoke stressed academics, Christianity, and domestic work. Every

student performed domestic chores because this taught the importance of such labor and because it saved the school money. Cobleigh
related that she had baked the seminary's bread. She probably also
explained that the majority of the school's graduates became teachers
and that some had established other seminaries based on the Mount
Holyoke model. Cobleigh wanted to modify her alma mater's
successful dormitory policies for Whitman College.

The decision to send her to New England was as carefully considered by the president and trustees as the selection of Atkinson and
Eells, and they accepted the method that she presented to them. The
Andersons hoped that a women's dormitory would soon be constructed, for college women seeking housing came to their door.
However, they did not board them into their home as they had done
in Seattle.

In mid-May 1884 Cobleigh arrived in Boston and explained her
goal to Cushing Eells, who heartily approved. She enjoyed success
immediately. Eells marveled that in one of her first calls she obtained
$100 and had the prospect of $500 more. But soon both fund raisers
became depressed over rejections, and they prayed for success. Eells'
later gift to Ladies' Hall resulted partly from his respect for his co-
worker's tenacity and ambitious educational plans.

While Cobleigh began her New England travels, Alexander Anderson explained to the ACES the need for Ladies' Hall. "Walla Walla
has not been built up as a college town, where every family has a spare
room in the house on purpose to board one or two students and thus
help on a new college."[50] In other words, Walla Walla was not Galesburg. The president also provided the eastern society with some local
history: the valley had been important to immigrant travelers, later it
had been home to mining enterprises, and now it had become the
"well-to-do center of the best wheat-raising region in the United
States." He concluded, "not half the girls from the farms and distant
places who wish to attend Whitman College, will be able to do so
until the institution can furnish them a comfortable Christian home
while pursuing their studies."

Cobleigh's reports have not survived, but she raised enough money in the summer that Anderson in his August school announcement
gave considerable attention to the ladies' boarding hall. The future
building would "be under the general supervision of a Ladies' Board

and the immediate supervision of a Lady Superintendent, which will use every endeavor to make the Ladies' Hall a safe, comfortable, Christian home for the girls and young women entrusted to it, thus enabling them to receive all benefits of a female seminary and the additional advantage of co-education."[51]

Eells had worried about Cobleigh's ability to carry out a grueling canvass; he once reported that she was ill for two weeks and halted her work. Despite any health problems Cobleigh's efforts won praise. An editor maintained that "her success is proof of the wisdom of her selection." Anderson hailed her efforts, explaining "that her appeal was made by a woman, to women, for women and proved to be successful."[52] The Reverend Increase Tarbox, secretary of the ACES, had been helping college agents for more than thirty years and praised Cobleigh: "She has worked," he told Anderson, "at her business very wisely and efficiently. . . . She surpasses my expectation and meets with very general favor."[53]

In her talks Cobleigh emphasized the same themes as Eells: the sacrifice of missionaries and the struggle to build a school in Walla Walla. But unlike Eells she stressed to eastern women that their western counterparts badly needed educational opportunities. A boarding house based on the Mount Holyoke model would, she promised, help make this education possible.

According to the record published by the ACES, Elvira Cobleigh raised $9,000, much of it came from Boston, Lawrence, Worcester, Farmington, Hartford, New Haven, Brattleboro, Rutland, and Providence. She did proportionately about as well as Eells; after deducting her travel costs, she had collected enough money to remodel the old seminary building into Ladies' Hall, and the books she collected strengthened the small library. In comparison with Eells, Cobleigh tended to get smaller sums, some as low as twenty-five cents, and she received only one $500 contribution. She also collected more from women, some of whom donated bedding and books. Her most famous contributor was Mark Twain, who gave $20 in books.

Eastern contributions for 1884 and 1885 totaled about $20,000. Although the Walla Walla press expected up to $50,000, Whitman leaders assured friends that Eells and Cobleigh had provided the school a promising start. But from 1886 to 1890 eastern donations totaled only $15,000, and the school would not enjoy another good year until 1891. Anderson's reports do not explain the precipitous decline, but there were at least two reasons. First, schools that were no longer on the ACES list continued to raise eastern money in competition with the newer institutions. At the time that Whitman joined the struggle for funds, churchpeople everywhere complained to the ACES that these dozens of appeals wearied them. Second, Whitman did not get an effective fund raiser in the East after Cobleigh returned. Dr. William Barrows, a Massachusetts writer pushing the Whitman-saved-Oregon theme, replaced her. He had met Whitman in 1843, visited the campus in the 1880s, and successfully applied for the position of fund raiser. In his message to New Englanders, he recalled that their young colleges had necessarily employed canvassers and that their graduates had improved the quality of society. He insisted that Whitman College graduates would help conduct the affairs of Washington. This young state depended upon local young men and women, not transplanted easterners, to advance its civilization. However, his attempt to convince churchpeople that Whitman was actually located in their "vast parish," proved ineffective. Barrows only raised a few hundred dollars annually.

Many colleges sent presidents or professors as their canvassers, but there were many complaints that this procedure disrupted both administration and instruction. Nevertheless, in 1887 trustees released Anderson from his duties and sent him to New England. The president was supposed to work the region for a year, but within a month he became ill from his exhausting labors and returned home. In 1888 trustees asked Myron Eells to accept a five-year term as college agent with an annual salary of $1,200 and expenses. Eells, who was also made a trustee, appreciated the importance of this assignment but rejected a move to Hartford because he wanted to continue his missionary work with Indians.

Late in 1889 the ACES made a significant change in its system: the organization, not the individual colleges, would now solicit funds in New England. The ACES recommended that Whitman raise money in the Pacific Northwest and in the region between western New York and the Mississippi River. The Whitman board responded by appointing the Reverend Jonathan Edwards, a trustee from Spokane, as its financial agent. While Edwards solicited funds in Washington and Minnesota, the ACES in 1890 and 1891 sent its field secretary, the

Reverend John L. Maile, into Connecticut and Vermont, where he raised more money for Whitman than any canvasser since Elvira Cobleigh. The ACES's new system of assigning a fund raiser into a limited region for a single institution worked to Whitman's advantage.

Alexander Anderson, however, was surprised that all these eastern efforts produced much smaller sums than he and Atkinson anticipated. Upon becoming president he had told Walla Wallans of plans to raise a $50,000 endowment, but after eight years Whitman's endowment totaled less than $10,000 and produced about $900 income annually. Most of the eastern money could not be added to the endowment because trustees and Anderson had to use it to cover current operating expenses. Unlike other growing schools, Whitman could not endow professorships or many scholarships. It depressed Anderson to read that his school did worse collecting eastern money than Colorado College, Doane, Grinnell, and Yankton. Between 1886 and 1889, Colorado College, for example, gathered about $15,000 annually compared with Whitman's $3,700 annually.

Anderson continually struggled with financial problems. In 1884 he informed the ACES that Whitman had a $5,000 debt; by 1891 it had increased to about $8,700. To reduce its annual operating deficit, the college trustees once transferred $2,500 from the endowment, gave their own money, solicited local funds, asked the regional Congregational Association for support, and searched for ways to increase the endowment. In 1891 the ACES sent $5,000 for the endowment; in return the school promised that a majority of its trustees would be "Orthodox Congregationalists," although there may have been trustees who were not certain what that term meant.

In his college catalogs, Anderson explained why the school was in debt and why debt must be overcome. The president requested money for faculty salaries, scholarships, buildings, books, equipment, furniture, endowment, and even for twenty-five acres as a future campus. At first Anderson hoped for $50,000 in endowment, but by 1886 he reduced his expectation. Even though he knew other western academies had far more in endowment, he pleaded that if Whitman had only $20,000 "it would be fairly lifted on its feet, and be able to walk alone for several years."[54]

The catalog explained that Whitman's debt began in 1883 with the construction of College Hall and that eight years later it was still trying to liquidate the debt. Anderson explained that tuition income did not cover the annual cost of operations; thus in most years the deficit was met by endowment income and by eastern funds. Although the president explained that it cost money to offer respectable preparatory and collegiate programs, he did not write that faculty salaries were very low—he received $1,600, Louis Anderson got $1,100, and other teachers tried to live on much less.

Whitman's appeal for scholarships, library books, and scientific equipment met with some success. The most important effort to increase the very limited scholarship fund came in 1888 when Atkinson got his fellow trustees to approve his Missionary Memorial Professorship Fund. It would be used "to pay the tuition in whole or in part of the worthy, needy students."[55] The faculty would award the money; if it could not find suitable recipients, then the money could help pay faculty salaries. Atkinson attempted to raise $20,000 in what he called the "Upper Columbia Basin," but his death curtailed this promising scholarship program.

Seeking support for the library, Alexander Anderson insisted that it was "an educating force" and that students were learning how to put the collection to better use. In 1882 the library began when Myron Eells gave ten volumes, fifteen pamphlets, and $25 either for the start of a library endowment or for immediate book purchases. After some deliberation the trustees spent the money for badly needed reference works. The ACES helped by collecting the Washburn Library Fund, a $1,000 endowment providing an annual $100 book budget. By purchase and from donations from both coasts, the fledgling school had in 1891 a serviceable library of 3,700 bound volumes and 2,200 pamphlets.

Meanwhile, the faculty sought to improve science classes by improving their cabinets and laboratories. Louisa Anderson organized collection activities at Whitman as she had at the university. Her husband acknowledged her efforts: "The constantly increasing collection of minerals, shells, specimens of flora and fauna, relics, and curiosities has been carefully arranged in the cabinet room.... The new laboratory has proved especially serviceable for practical work on the part of the students in physics, chemistry, and natural history."[56]

Alexander Anderson and his faculty spent considerable time designing and modifying the curriculum. Only about fifteen percent of

In 1886 the college graduated its first class. Dressed in suitable attire are seniors Lizzie Justice, Emma Stine, George Anderson, and Christopher Columbus Gose.

their students enrolled in college classes, and only seventeen of them earned bachelor's degrees between 1886 and 1890, yet Whitman offered three collegiate courses of study—classical, scientific, and literary. The classical was traditional and the most prestigious because it led to the A.B. degree. Those pursuing it spent four years studying such subjects as Greek, Latin, mathematics, science, literature, and social science. Faculty sometimes revised this curriculum adding, for example, more mathematics and physics classes. The scientific (B.S.) and literary degree (B.L.) programs required three years of study. Neither of these degrees required Greek, but both demanded other subjects listed in the classical curriculum. Modern language was not required for the scientific degree, but German would eventually be included in the literary one. Although the catalog did not mention it, the B.L. was designed for women. The course of study for the B.L. excluded advanced mathematics classes and contained fewer physics classes than the other two. Perhaps Whitman should have followed the example of the University of Washington and dropped its B.L. degree, but a few earned it. Some women earned the more challenging A.B. degree.

The school's degree programs were similar to those at Pacific University and the University of Washington. At the University of Oregon, however, there was an English course that led to the B.A. This program excused students from both classical and modern foreign languages in "an attempt to meet the wants of those who think that a higher discipline of mind can be obtained from the study of the English language than from the study of Greek, German, or French."[57] Whitman, however, would not permit its students to skip foreign languages. The Walla Walla *Union*'s editorial entitled "College Reform," championed modern languages over classical and charged that "Our schools, like our churches are conservative institutions and oppose every threatened innovation with the combined dogged forces of habit and prejudice."[58] The faculty would not bend to the editor or to the growing number of students who also wanted to take German or French, not Greek or Latin. Its degree programs were traditional because the faculty defended such study and because the college sought status. Whitman was a freshwater college, but it required courses offered by the old saltwater institutions.

According to a faculty rule, a candidate for admission to the collegiate programs had to take either a series of examinations in relevant subjects or present a diploma indicating completion of a preparatory course. Few Walla Wallans had either the required background for college work or an interest in a college degree. Thus the majority of Whitman students entered the three-year classical preparatory program or the two-year scientific preparatory program. Both stressed English grammar, arithmetic, Latin, science, and social sciences. Graduates of these programs received a diploma.

Anderson listed these preparatory courses in the catalog under the title "Academic Courses." He also placed in this category a normal course and a business course, each requiring three years of arithmetic, English grammar, history, and science. In their third year these normal and business students took a few college courses, probably both to broaden the students and to show some that they had the ability to earn a bachelor's degree. The normal course required pedagogy and school law; the business course required bookkeeping and commercial law. Those preparing for teaching studied "modern elementary methods" (at one point the college operated a model elementary school), engaged in practice teaching, and took advanced subject courses so that the graduates could teach in a high school or an academy. The normal program remained small because the emerging regional normal schools—such as the one at Ellensburg—provided stiff competition, and because there were only a few secondary positions. Such factors led Pacific University to drop its small normal program, but Anderson maintained and tried to expand Whitman's because he enjoyed teaching pedagogy and believed that the region's common schools badly needed the twenty or so Whitman students who had earned diplomas under his guidance. (Ever since his undergraduate days the president had championed public schools.)

According to its faculty, Whitman's business course of study was better than the popular and practical business schools. By taking solid classes in a variety of subjects, including a year of German, Whitman insisted that its graduates would "know something more than a mere knowledge of bookkeeping, penmanship, and commercial mathematics."[59] The business courses attracted a greater enrollment than the normal classes, but business students, some of whom paid their tuition bills by keeping books for Walla Walla businesses, stayed only long enough to complete the relevant classes.

In 1884 Whitman offered courses in art and music; this was about the same time that Pacific and Washington also listed these subjects in their catalogs. Music courses became so popular that in 1886 Anderson arranged to open a conservatory of music, boasting that it was superior to those at other regional colleges. Its teachers offered three-year programs that led to a diploma in either voice or piano. Students took both theoretical and practical courses; the vocal topics included tone formation, muscular action, the scales and intervals, and numerous other classes. Those in the piano program studied such topics as "New England Conservatory Method," Plaidy's technical studies, Turner's scales, reading at sight, and works by Mendelssohn, Bach, and Chopin. Anderson wrote that the conservatory offered opportunities for "those who desire to fit themselves for the profession, either as performers or teachers."[60] Monthly recitals, he continued, enabled music students "to acquire that confidence and ease of manner so necessary to do themselves credit when appearing in public." A Whitman choral society proved to be very popular. In 1889 the conservatory became a music department with about the same offerings.

Plans for a three-year art program failed, and in 1890 Whitman created a new category, art studies, placing in it painting, drawing, typewriting, shorthand, and penmanship.

Physical education received little or no attention. One Walla Walla editor regretted the neglect of "physical development" in all the local schools and urged them to include gymnastics. Many in the early twentieth century would agree with his criticism: "To cram the head with knowledge and neglect all physical development is calculated to shorten the life of the possessor, and leading on to premature decay of highly gifted persons."[61]

Alexander Anderson favored his collegiate department over the other programs. But he understood from his own experience and from his reading that frontier colleges could not be supported only by college enrollments. It was absolutely necessary to offer preparatory programs so as to train students for college classes and to generate income for the college degree programs. Until there were other academies and public high schools, Whitman, like every other Pacific Northwest college and university, had to operate preparatory programs. The University of Oregon operated an elementary English course that prepared students for its sub-freshman department, a two-year course of study designed to prepare students for the degree programs. Its catalog explained that the university had to offer such basic work until Eugene and other towns operated public high schools. Whitman, unlike Oregon, hoped that courses in education, business, music, and art would not only pay for themselves, but would also help fund the college program. At Whitman and elsewhere a broad curriculum kept the doors open; the average student who passed through them contributed financially to a small elite studying in the prestigious collegiate department.

According to historian Stephen Penrose, Anderson assembled a dedicated and competent faculty. Anderson hired women and men with solid training and teaching ability. Anderson apparently hired most faculty by mail. He asked for letters of recommendation but also asked applicants their height, weight, color of eyes, age, and experience. Anderson responded to one applicant that some easterners could not cope with the demands Whitman placed upon them, but eastern job seekers explained that they wanted to teach in the West because of its beauty or because they saw the need for their services in a growing country.

During the 1880s the outstanding faculty members were the three Andersons (in 1885 ill health forced Louisa's resignation), Abbie E.

Cushman, and Harlan J. Cozine. Cushman had graduated from Oberlin and taught English history. Students appreciated her warm personality, solid teaching, and commitment to temperance. Penrose said she "contributed in no small degree to the success of the institution and its reputation for the excellence of its instruction."[62] Cozine, a graduate of Boston's New England Conservatory of Music, had taught and conducted in New England. He successfully established in Walla Walla a conservatory based on the Boston model. He was a major reason why the music department compiled impressive enrollment figures. Recitals, which were designed to give music pupils confidence for public performance, and the Whitman Choral Society both attracted townspeople to the campus.

To achieve the school's ambitious goals, Anderson's faculty members worked long hours, instructed four to six different classes each term, advised students, and attended weekly and specially called faculty meetings. The president dominated these gatherings because he presided and set the agenda. The secretary recorded faculty attendance and tardiness. Faculty members, who by their own resolution had to vote on all issues, classified students for courses and for compulsory chapel. At many meetings teachers discussed students; for example, "Search was made into the work of pupils and some reported for inferior study." The problems of absence, tardiness, and deportment consumed an enormous amount of time. To improve attendance, the faculty once resorted to awarding prizes to the rooms with the best records. The faculty also evaluated student morale. In 1887, for example, it made "a searching inquiry ... into the poor lessons and general looseness of discipline during the past week." On another occasion the faculty considered deportment, especially whispering and noise.[63] Teachers, not a registrar, recorded student work; those receiving at least seventy percent on a final examination had their name and score listed in the faculty minutes book. Professors worked out schedules for classes, examinations, library hours, and vacations. They chose to excuse classes on Friday of the county fair, but in 1891 reversed themselves because of "some evil associations" at the celebration. The faculty decided on numerous subjects, including the setting of school clocks by a downtown jeweler's time.

Whitman students generally worked hard, although they sometimes asked to be excused from requirements. An unusual action was taken in response to a seminary student's wish that he not have to study Homer; a divided faculty resolved the matter by allowing his father to settle the issue.[64] The required courses demanded study in thick and unillustrated textbooks. Each class had considerable homework, and there was little time for procrastination because oral recitations demanded continuous preparation. Term examinations were partly oral. They were open to the public, and scores were announced at chapel. At commencement those completing preparatory or collegiate programs had to deliver an oration, present an essay, or give some other performance. The faculty and townspeople applauded many students for their academic endeavors.

Because there were no student publications during the 1880s, it is necessary to reconstruct students' concerns and condition from faculty minutes. Some students complained about requirements, especially Greek and Latin. One senior's oration advocated the end of the traditional "treadmill of abstract, dead languages" and the adoption of a modern science program. The faculty sometimes permitted the substitution of classes but opposed the elective system. During a trip to the East in 1885, Louis Anderson had a lengthy conversation with Harvard president Charles William Eliot. Seeking to bring "a new spirit of inquiry and scholarship" to his institution, Eliot had favored a broadly elective course of study rather than the traditional requirements.[65] By 1885 Harvard sophomores, juniors, and seniors had freedom of choice. Louis, a professor of classics, warmly opposed Eliot's liberalism. Upon his return to Walla Walla, Louis summarized this conversation to his father and faculty colleagues. All apparently rejected the eastern unorthodoxy. According to faculty minutes, no one moved to abandon or weaken the traditional curriculum. Thus Whitman professors agreed with the vast majority of faculties in considering Harvard "the bad boy of American higher education."[66]

Teachers not only closely regulated the course of study, they also carefully managed student schedules. From 8:15 AM until 3:45 PM students were required to be in chapel, classes, or study. Most students lived in town; the faculty, struggling with the problem of limited school space, adjusted individual schedules and permitted men and women to study at home if they had acceptable grades and obeyed college rules. Residents in Ladies' Hall received permission to study in their rooms.

Elvira F. Cobleigh served as an eastern fund raiser for Ladies' Hall and then implemented the Mount Holyoke College management system to govern the dormitory's residents. Cobleigh and the faculty often disagreed over her stringent management of Whitman women.

The faculty and trustees gave considerable thought to the management of Ladies' Hall. As soon as Elvira Cobleigh reported that she would raise at least $6,000, the school remodeled, under Louisa Anderson's close supervision, the original seminary building so that it became Ladies' Hall. The school's catalogs stressed that its first dormitory offered large student rooms, a dining room, a laundry room, and bathrooms supplying hot and cold water. (But Stephen Penrose later recalled that it initially lacked toilets.) Two women shared a room; when eighteen occupied the hall they had little space because both art and music classes were taught in the building. Determined to keep rates low, Whitman only charged occupants $4 a week for room, board, and fuel. For a few terms in the 1880s boys were lodged in Ladies' Hall. (Coeducational living thus had occurred long before the 1960s.)

The administration took a great interest in this dormitory, which students called "The Wooden Ladies' Hall." For two years Cobleigh operated a modified version of the Mount Holyoke system, but trustees and faculty supervised her regulations. Each resident worked an hour each day under Superintendent Cobleigh's direction; the president explained that the system was "not specifically for lessening the expense, but rather thereby to secure nature's exercise and to enoble labor."[67] The hall's residents would "learn to do and to esteem honorable the common household duties too often wrongly delegated to the mother or servants." The trustees insisted that the dormitory be self-supporting; the free labor helped make it so. Apparently women complained about the compulsory labor provision, however; in 1887 the trustees ended it and appointed a committee to help Cobleigh revise her rules. Occupants thereafter needed to clean only their private rooms; those who worked in the hall would receive a "reasonable" hourly wage. The superintendent's task was to provide "all the necessities, comforts, and care of a true, sensible, Christian home."[68] The faculty, however, complained that Cobleigh failed to enforce its rules. Trustees acknowledged her "heartfelt work" but asked for her resignation. The board then employed a preceptress and a matron, but this traditional arrangement of operating a dormitory increased operating costs. Then Cobleigh, who had once offered to find eastern money to cover any boarding deficit, was reappointed.

The faculty passed more specific rules for Ladies' Hall than for any other part of the school. Wholly committed to *in loco parentis*, professors established rules for the dormitory. Residents had to attend morning prayer at chapel and church on Sunday, be in their rooms during study hours, and retire by ten. Young women were

"not allowed to go walking or riding with gentlemen, nor to leave town at any time, nor to make or receive calls upon the Sabbath."[69] Each week the residents had to write that they had obeyed all the rules. Besides imposing rules on the residents of Ladies' Hall, the faculty responded to their petitions, including an 1888 request for room keys because money had been stolen, and an 1889 plea to improve dormitory food.

In 1888 the school erected Gentlemen's Hall, its third wooden building. Located behind College Hall, it provided space for a science laboratory and a museum; a few male students roomed on its second floor. Although the faculty paid much less attention to the men's dormitory than to Ladies' Hall, it was necessary for them to enforce the school rules. Anderson wanted only a few general rules because he expected students "to act in accordance with a manly sense of right" and to "render a cheerful compliance with regulations and requirements."[70] Students must not smoke (it was "injurious and foolish"), drink intoxicating beverages, enter a saloon "or other place of evil resort," swear, or be disrespectful. The Whitman rules were not unusual. In fact, they were less extensive than those at the University of Oregon, where the faculty forbade profanity, tobacco, liquor, carrying concealed weapons, idling around school doors,

In the mid-1880s College Hall and Ladies' Hall—the latter was the modified Whitman Seminary building—stood on Boyer Avenue as testimonies to President Alexander Jay Anderson's energetic leadership. In 1899 Memorial Hall would be built on the field in the foreground.

making noise in the halls, leaving town without the president's permission, staying out later than "eleven . . . at night at social gatherings composed in whole or in part of University students," and entering a brewery, saloon, skating rink, or public dance.[71]

Anderson boasted that because students had such a positive attitude, only a few received punishment. Faculty minutes seem to support his view as discipline problems seemed minor, ranging from whispering in chapel to ice skating during classtime. Early in 1891, however, the faculty took drastic action by suspending Fred Schrieber "for transgressions of college rules: use of tobacco on college premises, and use of liquor and profanity, for violation of good order, and for his general demoralizing influences."[72] Classmates unsuccessfully petitioned the faculty to reinstate Schrieber. In most instances, however, the faculty reinstated wrongdoers after they promised to obey school rules and apologize for misdeeds before the student body in chapel. Alumni recalled a few instances of confrontation between teachers and large boys with "wild dispositions." For example, Professor John L. Rand physically prevented one such type from leaving his classroom. Rand won respect, but perhaps this incident convinced him that he should put his Dartmouth degree to other uses. He left teaching and eventually became chief justice of the Oregon Supreme Court.

Whitman took a deep interest in the students' lives out of the classroom; it hoped especially to foster Christianity. The faculty minutes of January 13, 1890, state that President Anderson "spoke of the supreme importance of each member of the faculty exercising every possible influence to lead students to become Christians." The college catalog contained a section entitled "Religious Culture," which summarized the institution's views. It stated in 1891: "Believing that everything we do should be done unto God, we begin each day with prayer, devotional singing, and reading of the Holy Scriptures, usually accompanied with comments and remarks suggestive of the higher and nobler life found only in the personality and teachings of Jesus Christ." Each day opened with a short, required chapel; the school expected students to observe the Sabbath and attend church. The college insisted that students benefitted from membership in Sabbath schools, Christian Endeavor, and college chapters of the YMCA or the YWCA, both of which conducted prayer meetings.

Anderson championed literary societies at Whitman, as he had at the University of Washington, showing students how to prepare charters for faculty approval. The Philomathean for men and the Whittier for women formed in 1882 but died out after a few years. Other groups, including the Adelphi for men and the Narcissa Whitman for women, followed; at Whitman, as at other colleges, the societies played a major role. In their constitution the societies stated that they existed for "the improvement of . . . members and the welfare of the college."[73] They accepted students over the age of fifteen for males, fourteen for females. The societies made the faculty honorary members and acknowledged faculty control as well as supervision of public exercises. At their regularly scheduled meetings literary societies gave members a chance to debate, orate, sing, play an instrument, and learn parliamentary procedures. Students read essays on such topics as regional lava beds. A student explained the importance of such an activity. "In the classroom [the student] receives information. In the society he imparts it to others." The society also taught a member "how to make the best use of his talents . . . for his own enjoyment and that of his fellow men."[74] To enhance the college's academic

In 1890 dapper Professor Benjamin S. Winchester (left), a graduate of Williams College who said he was serving a three-year apprenticeship at Whitman, poses with his biology class.

program, the literary societies sometimes brought speakers to campus.

Fortunately the minutes of an early society, the Adelphi, have survived. This group debated contemporary topics. Debates on President Grover Cleveland and government ownership of the railroad were probably less exciting than those dealing with more local issues, such as "that the treatment of the North American Indians had been unjust," "that the Irish are more detrimental to the United States than the Chinese," or "that the study of Greek in College is not beneficial." The Athenaeum debated "that love of country is a stronger passion than love of money;" and women in the Whittier debated "that the schools on the Pacific Coast are an entire failure."[75] The Adelphi occasionally conducted mock sessions of Whitman faculty meetings, and in 1892 the Athenaeum resolved itself into the Populist Party's national convention. Debates provided fun, an opportunity to research relevant and controversial issues, and even the chance to parody professors and politicians.

The societies' closely regulated parties and weekly meetings promoted fellowship. Adelphi members assessed petty fines and passed humorous motions. They sometimes combined work with pleasure. Students joined the faculty in celebrating Arbor Day by cleaning brush from College Creek. Pleased to be excused from Friday classes, a student wrote that "even the president . . . whose frosted locks bespeak the snows of many winters . . . took a hand."[76] After three hours of labor that left the stream "smiling in radiant beauty," Adelphi members called an unscheduled meeting. It featured a mock political convention and with much hilarity elected Susan B. Anthony as its presidential nominee.

Thus at Whitman, as in other schools, these societies played an important academic and social role. Teachers encouraged students to found and to support literary societies because their activities often supplemented instruction. However, in the 1880s they often expired, apparently from student apathy, not faculty hostility.

On the other hand, a Whitman chorus flourished and performed in the community, and the baseball team was even more popular with students. In early 1886 the faculty chartered the Whitman College Athletic Association. Although Anderson mentioned the literary societies in his catalogs, he ignored this association. Its charter had a general statement exactly like that of the societies: the association

In the late 1880s banjoist Marvin Evans and classmates, wearing a wide variety of hats, enjoy an outing in the Blue Mountains.

was to improve members and to promote the college's welfare. Apparently the major reason for the athletic association was the opportunity to form a Whitman baseball team. Both faculty members and students joined baseball teams that played teams from town or the army garrison. The association complied with rigid faculty rules that regulated all practices and decided on the appropriateness of games. But professors gradually relaxed their rules by permitting away games, approving a combined team with the garrison, allowing a former student to be on the squad, and granting more games, even double-headers. In the 1880s the local newspapers probably did not give more space to baseball than they did to literary exercises. But news about Whitman's baseball teams may have helped recruit males into the various preparatory programs.

Students enjoyed fishing, swimming, skating, bicycling, horseback riding, and other sports, along with picnics, singing, and professional entertainments at Small's Opera House. One student probably spoke for many classmates when he asserted that "persistent application to books so fatigues the mind and exhausts the physical forces that even one day of recreation and social enjoyment is hailed with delight by the weary scholar."[77]

While the students were busy with recreation and studies, their president was busy writing. Every Whitman president has communicated with various constituencies. Alexander Anderson had two general audiences. He appealed through the ACES for eastern financial assistance and wrote hundreds of letters, reports, and other documents in an effort to make his school regionally important.

To build eastern and western support, Anderson emphasized the school's progress. From his long administrative experience and from his reading he understood that Americans equated size with quality. Citizens generally assumed that a large or growing institution was superior to one with smaller enrollment, so Anderson cited examples of growth: the grounds expanded from four to seven acres, the well-trained faculty increased from three to twelve, the student body tripled between 1882 and 1890 (now it was larger than the student body at Pacific University or Colorado College), the collegiate programs attracted a growing number of capable students, the school constructed three buildings and needed even more space, the librarian shelved 3,700 books, and science teachers improved cabinets and laboratories.

While lauding Whitman's progress, Anderson, like other western college presidents, boosted the region it served. He particularly pointed out the increase in railroad construction, wheat production, and immigration. The large immigration to eastern Washington in the 1880s led Anderson and others to predict that eventually this section would be as heavily populated as New England.

The president peppered his writings with references to institutional history. He maintained, for example, that the school possessed "a priceless history, including its heroic origin, its distinctive reason for being, and its hard struggle for continued existence and growth."[78] Marcus Whitman and Cushing Eells had dedicated their lives to others; the faculty, he stated, was also providing such service.

Anderson designed his reports to the ACES to impress both its membership and leadership. Like other frontier college presidents, he tried to reach donors by listing improvements, needs, morale, and environment. His appeal to easterners placed a greater emphasis on the college's religious life and the economic and social aspects of the region. He assumed that Congregationalists were curious about teachers and students at "this Christian College in the far-west Inland

Empire."[79] Occasionally Anderson reported that students worked hard in classes, but he more often emphasized their Christian commitment. Chapel exercises, student prayer meetings, the use of the Bible in classes, Christian Endeavor, and Christian conversion all combatted "evil influences." Anderson reported that in 1882 only a single student was a practicing Christian; in 1889 he boasted that "one-third of them are professing Christians." The faculty was religious. Anderson once reported that each had been converted to Christ, that seven out of the twelve were Congregationalists, and that three faculty members preached in schoolhouses. Anderson concluded that Whitman, "planted in a community and region containing a large element of infidelity and immorality, has fought a good fight for Christ and the truth."[80]

There must have been eastern Congregationalists who read about the fact that Whitman served a booming region (all frontier colleges seemed to be beggars in a rich section) and concluded that those served should donate to the college. Sometimes the president explained why westerners did not provide the college with funds: he mentioned that the seventy regional Congregational churches generally depended upon the Home Missionary Society's help, that Walla Walla's businesses were victims of a railroad monopoly or a slump in trade, and that the valley's farmers suffered from extreme heat or cold. President Anderson ignored local parsimony, but biographer Florence Anderson thought that it was a factor. Walla Wallans, she believed, rejected the president's financial appeals because they believed that the ACES was "a fairy godmother" capable of bringing money from rich easterners.[81]

In his last report to easterners, Anderson made it clear that Whitman College was located on the frontier. The community had twenty-five saloons, the Fort Walla Walla garrison lavished its pay in the town's gambling rooms, and soldiers had avenged a comrade's death by forcing a prisoner out of jail and shooting him dead in the courthouse square. The president explained: "Think not we are an uncivilized people, yet we are on the frontier, battling with giant evils, which are fortified by years of wayward pioneer life, and which are not yet overcome by the Bible, the spelling-book, and the college textbook. Whitman College and the dozen churches of Walla Walla have yet much to do in battling with the evils in this grand empire. We need your prayers, and your aid in all practicable ways."[82]

Although Alexander Anderson wrote extensively to New England Congregationalists, he gave far more time to publicizing his school in the growing region of the interior Northwest. Early in his presidency he acknowledged that Whitman College lacked a reputation. He sought to overcome this by writing to churchpeople, donors, teachers, parents, and common school students. In his hundreds of letters, circulars, reports, and essays, Anderson recorded the college's increasing strength. Whitman and the Inland Empire were both expanding. He reminded his readers that prestigious eastern colleges had once undergone about the same difficulties in their formative periods that Whitman now faced. The ACES and Walla Wallans, he reported, were helping the college gather money, books, and equipment. He did not write, of course, that both easterners and westerners were giving much less than he had anticipated.

Anderson assured residents, especially parents and churchpeople, that every year the institution grew stonger and that it taught academics, culture, and character. "Industry and good conduct characterize its students. The moral tone of the Institution is pronounced and healthy, and its Christian influence grows stronger every year."[83] The educator often underscored the point that the school was "distinctively Christian without being sectarian, and patriotic without

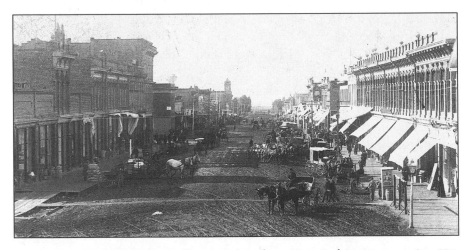

This photograph of Walla Walla was taken from First and Main streets in 1886, when the town claimed 4,500 residents.

partisanship."[84] Apparently Anderson had either lost his enthusiasm for the Republican Party or believed it better to be evenhanded about politics. In a commencement talk, for example, he generalized that the only dispute between the parties was patronage.

The president refused "to resort to the unprofessional practice of personal persuasion to obtain students." One of his circulars, however, provided a very broad invitation. The school's curriculum filled every purpose: "To obtain a college education. To fit for college. To prepare for teaching. To obtain a business education in short time, or to pursue other branches in connection therewith. To take a course of study in vocal or instrumental music or art. To learn typewriting or shorthand. To study German, French, or elocution. To prepare in some way to make the most of one's self and to do the most good."[85]

Anderson commended the learning environment of the college. Each student received individual attention; he explained that the teacher could "get hold upon each scholar."[86] When pious critics charged that Walla Walla was an unsuitable site for a school because intoxicating liquors were sold in the city, Anderson acknowledged that some thought that a college should be in a quiet town. But he then asserted that the students in such a place were no better morally than those who went to a city institution. The leader concluded: "A majority of the best endowed colleges and universities of the land are today in cities, and the idea is fast gaining ground that the city, or its near vicinity, is the better place for institutions of higher learning."[87] Occasionally he voiced a warning to Walla Wallans about the college's site, pointing out that unless they supported Whitman, it might relocate. This threat would be repeated by two later presidents.

Anderson boasted that he employed a competent faculty and summarized its teaching methods: "In all departments and studies great care is taken to lead the pupil to see clearly and grasp firmly the underlying principles, thus enabling him to arrange the great mass of facts into intelligible and useful knowledge. Habits of original investigation and research are fostered."[88] Because of this solid teaching, he concluded, Whitman alums excelled in eastern graduate schools or found rewarding western positions.

Whitman gradually earned a regional reputation and became a vital institution in southeastern Washington, justifying Anderson's optimistic assessment. Historian Stephen Penrose judged that Ander-

*The Whitman faculty in 1890. In the front row are (from left) Mrs. Harlan J.
Cozine (matron), President Alexander Jay Anderson, and Bertha Truesdell
(languages). In the back row are E.H. Thompson (business and education),
Edith L. Parker (music), Benjamin S. Winchester (biology), Harlan J. Cozine (music), Amy B. Richards (math), William D. Lyman (history and English), Ethelyn K. Fenner (art), and Louis F. Anderson (classical languages).*

son, "a great administrator and teacher," had made the school important to the Pacific Northwest.[89] Other writers also have praised
Anderson for laying the foundations of Whitman College.

As the 1880s passed, more and more Walla Wallans supported
Whitman College, appreciating what it had accomplished and what it
would do for the community. Its diverse programs filled a regional
need, but it did much more than provide classes in liberal and practical subjects. It is easier to relate the school's impact on the town than
to enumerate people who moved to Walla Walla for education, but
some did move to the agricultural center because of its educational
opportunities. The college enriched the town's life with the school's
musical performances and special programs such as the one in 1888
that brought Mrs. Elkanah Walker and others to talk about missionary life. Literary exercises, end of term ceremonies, and commencement week soon became very important community events. Eventu-

ally newspapers published and evaluated senior orations, the baccalaureate sermon, and the commencement address. By the late 1880s hundreds of townspeople eagerly looked forward to commencement week; on one occasion 1,000 crammed into Small's Opera House to witness the graduation ceremony.

The college promoted local discussions about education and society. Newspapers carried stories about the need for schools and learning. On August 12, 1882, the Walla Walla *Statesman* requested that a territorial agricultural college be located in the city so it would become both "the great commercial center of the Inland Empire" and the region's educational center. One editor urged students to continue their academic interests, for "He who stops study enters into night."[90] After hearing the orations at a college exercise, a local writer commented upon student optimism: "Youth, yet has a somewhat crude and undefined idea that injustice, wrong, and oppression exist and it cries aloud for a change. . . . It optimistically believes it can to a great extent crush the evils and substitute the good."[91]

The community took pride in the college. In 1883 an editor predicted that it would "become a twin-sister of learning with Eastern institutions, and be the pride and glory of Walla Walla."[92] By the early 1890s some residents enthused that the college was the best one in the Pacific Northwest. Newspapermen asked readers to assist the school; in 1891, for example, the Walla Walla *Union* complained that "one of the things that has held the college back in the past has been its lack of proper campus grounds," and urged a forty-acre donation for its buildings.[93]

Some state Congregational Associations passed flattering resolutions about the work of Anderson and his faculty. The Reverend John Hamilton, secretary of the ACES, having traveled from Boston to a Whitman commencement, reported that the school had a good relationship with his organization, that Anderson provided solid leadership, and that the institution had a promising future. He underscored the fact that Whitman had received meager financial support and concluded, "Nothing but good management and thorough going energy could have accomplished so much with so little."[94]

Most Whitman students appreciated their professors and especially their president. They and townspeople credited Anderson for developing splendid student morale. He was, moreover, a gifted teacher. One of his students recalled that "It was his habit to step into one of the classrooms, interrupt the instructor, and quiz the members of the class on mental arithmetic."[95] While asking questions he paced about, carrying "an old broken-backed knife, flipping a blade back and forth between his fingers." Another remembered that "He had the power of calling out in a student all of his mental strength which he possessed and to arouse a feeling of interest and enthusiasm in subject matter." Students often mentioned that he urged them "to think all around the subject."[96] Alumni remembered that Anderson was a disciplinarian. For instance, George Stone habitually arrived late to morning chapel. The exasperated president asked, "George, why are you late?" The tardy boy replied, "I couldn't find my shirt." Anderson expelled him for a term.[97]

Because Anderson was a successful administrator and teacher, it surprised Walla Wallans in early June 1891 to read about his resignation. He simply explained that he "was almost completely worn out by the labors, cares, anxieties, and even trials" of his position.[98] Privately he wrote: "for the peace and therefore prosperity of Whitman College, and to more readily recover my health, I have resigned."[99] He refused to tell the public that a regional Congregational Association had faulted his administration in a report to Whitman trustees. For three weeks he had pondered his options. His son, Louis Anderson, advised him to continue, but Anderson was hurt and angry and chose to step down, fearing that the trustees might agree with his detractors and ask for his resignation. The local press praised him for building an institution that had served the town and brought it recognition and also published a trustee resolution acclaiming his professional attainments and solid character.

The full story behind Alexander Anderson's resignation cannot be known because not many letters have survived. However, it is possible to patch together the rough outline of this sorry episode. His difficulties resulted in large part from the strain resulting from his heavy administrative responsibilities and his poor health. In late 1887 he had returned from his eastern fund raising in a feeble condition. Louisa, the children, and his physician warned him that he worked too hard and that he should resign. The dedicated leader rejected such advice and continued to teach more than twenty hours a week and to handle diverse and demanding administrative work. Louisa's death in 1889 depressed Anderson, for his wife had been a useful advisor and a sympathetic listener. Friends confided that he became easily irritable without his helpmate.

Increasingly difficult administrative problems arose when illness and death removed some of his other respected helpers. Chairman of the board of trustees Cushing Eells was in precarious health and could do little more than preside at meetings. The deaths of Dorsey Baker, George Atkinson, and Nelson Cobleigh removed a group who would have emphasized Anderson's many accomplishments to all detractors, including those who maintained that Whitman was not closely enough identified with the Congregational church.

Although Stephen Penrose's history erroneously stated that there was harmony as late as commencement 1891, mounting criticism of the president began in 1890 and continued until his departure. There were a variety of detractors: many of the faculty, the school's financial agent, a local Congregational minister, a regional Congregational Association, and some influential townspeople. Perhaps the first important sign of disaffection came from the faculty when William Lyman and Amy Richards disagreed with the president. Lyman accused Anderson of being arbitrary and unwilling to make needed changes. Richards, who had been denied a professorship, grumbled that she would rather have had the salary that went with that position than the honorary M.A. the trustees offered. Both critics resigned. Anderson must have been pleased with Lyman's decision because he believed that the historian was primarily responsible for the lack of "harmony in the faculty."[100] One observer stated that both resignations made Anderson "as pleased as a baby with a new rattler."[101] Lyman's departure upset his students and some college supporters, who argued that he was an innocent victim of the turmoil. The professor, however, spent only a few months teaching at Spokane's new Finney College—a failing institution—and, with trustee approval, returned to Whitman. Lyman assured the trustees that he could serve under Anderson, but he actually resumed efforts to undermine him.

A second problem was Anderson's sharp conflict with the local Congregational minister, the Reverend Eli R. Loomis. The origins of this dispute are unknown, but it is clear that they disliked each other. Loomis was one of those who wanted Anderson to underscore the fact that the college was Congregational. The president, however, thought that such an announcement would reduce financial contributions and enrollments. He also heatedly opposed appointing Loomis to the board of trustees because he lacked a college degree. Loomis, who welcomed complaints about his opponent, helped widen the gap between the local church and the college by repeating the complaints to trustees.

Some prominent Walla Wallans sided with Loomis against Anderson. Others held hard feelings toward the president because they had joined him in a speculative scheme and lost money. In the 1880s and the early 1890s there was a spectacular growth in Puget Sound's population—Seattle had only 3,500 residents in 1880 and soared to 42,800 in 1890; Tacoma jumped from 1,100 to 36,000 in the same time period—and a wave of land speculation swept the entire state. Wealthy Walla Wallans speculated in Puget Sound properties; in fact, there was a Walla Walla addition to Seattle. Some also invested in Spokane, whose population jumped from 350 in 1880 to nearly 20,000 in 1890.

Alexander Anderson responded in two ways to booming Puget Sound: he advertised Whitman in its newspapers and sought to improve his own precarious financial status by joining two of his sons, Charles and Jay, in speculating in land around Lilliwaup Falls. Both attempts failed. Seattleites did not attend Whitman, and the promise of Lilliwaup Falls, located on the west side of Hood Canal, was not realized. Promoters of Lilliwaup Falls, Shelton, Union City, Port Townsend, and other places had boasted that these westside Puget Sound towns would boom; indeed, some might become as large as Seattle or Tacoma. Charles Anderson, a civil and mining engineer in Seattle, knew about rising real estate values all over the Puget Sound country. Thus he and Daniel Troutman, a steamboat captain who owned land near Lilliwaup Falls, convinced Anderson that he should join them in establishing two corporations, the Lilliwaup Land and Improvement Company and the Hood Canal Transportation Company. These men and some others who invested in the new townsite believed that Lilliwaup Falls would enrich them because it was on the proposed Port Townsend Southern Railroad that would link Portland with Port Townsend, because tourists would go through the new town into the Olympics, and because Lilliwaup Falls might become the center for logging, quarrying, and mining copper at Lake

Cushman. In the summer and fall of 1890 the Lilliwaup Land and Improvement Company, which elected Alexander Anderson as its president, widely advertised Lilliwaup Falls as the "Yosemite and Yellowstone of Washington."

The company platted its townsite, naming several streets for prominent Walla Walla families, a few of whom invested in the site, and hired fifty men to build roads, houses, a wharf, a long bridge across the bay, and an improved trail to Lake Cushman. To increase its earnings, the company brought tourists by steamer to Lilliwaup Falls and then transported them by horse to Lake Cushman. While a steady stream of tourists and sightseers came to the emerging town and took rooms in its new three-story hotel, only a few purchased property. After a busy summer and fall, tourism sagged in the winter. Investors rejected the arguments for Lilliwaup Falls and placed money in more promising sites nearer the established cities. But even worse was the fact that the promoters and residents of Lilliwaup Falls learned that they did not have clear title to the site. The company's embattled trustees reincorporated, but President Anderson ended his association with his fellow speculators. The collapse of this promotional scheme ruined Anderson's hopes to improve his financial condition; furthermore, those Walla Wallans—including a Baker and a Boyer—who invested sums in Lilliwaup Falls probably denounced him for their losses. They and some other Walla Wallans grumbled that Anderson should have sought to improve the school's fortune, not his own.

Whitman's financial condition soured in the early 1890s; this led to considerable turmoil—on and off the campus. One trustee made the wild statement that the school was bankrupt, but it was true that it could not raise much money on either coast. To get western help, trustees had chosen the Reverend Jonathan Edwards as a fund raiser at a salary equaling Anderson's. Edwards traveled across the state and to cities in the upper Midwest, but reported that the Old West was unable to assist the New West. The president informed trustees that Edwards raised little money and that Whitman's budget could not tolerate his salary. Aware that Anderson wanted him removed because he was not meeting his agreement with trustees and convinced that the president wanted to dominate his fund-raising activities, Edwards argued that he was not only important as a financial agent but also that he was a mediator between hostile eastern Washington Congregationalists and the college. Edwards became increasingly critical of Anderson, especially for his control over the school's finances and for wielding "an iron hand." He had heard complaints about Anderson and informed fellow trustees that "a change of administration is an absolute necessity and the sooner the better."[102] The president, in turn, wanted Edwards fired. Cushing Eells, an aged and absent chairman of the board of trustees, could not resolve the struggle between the two school leaders, and individual members found it difficult to mend the torn administrative fabric.

College leaders also had to respond to another problem. A story circulated that Presbyterians wanted to buy Whitman College because they had heard that the Congregationalists were about to open new colleges in Olympia and Spokane and dispose of the troubled one in Walla Walla. The ACES in Boston learned about a possible sale and informed Anderson and the trustees that it had invested time and money in Whitman and opposed any deal with Presbyterians. Frightened by the financial troubles at Whitman, the association promised to send more money.

Meanwhile, the Reverend Reuben A. Beard, the well-respected American Home missionary for Washington, lent his voice to the critical chorus. He, like the Reverend Loomis, wanted the college to become more identified with the Congregational church.

Trustees, responding to so many complaints about Anderson, concluded that he should leave. In May 1891 trustee and school treasurer John Boyer traveled to western Washington and conferred with Myron Eells, emphasizing that the trustees wanted the president to resign and that he, Eells, would be a suitable replacement. In a diary entry of May 14, 1891, Eells explained that he had refused because he was not an educator and because he had a weak heart: "The care of a college under my circumstances would likely break me down."

While trustees were reluctantly coming to a decision to replace President Anderson, he often told them that he should keep his position and reminded everyone that he had done much for the school. The action the regional Congregational Association took would soon resolve the issue. In justifying its involvement in the college's affairs, the Association stated that individual Congregational churches had refused to donate to Whitman because there had been reports that

The Reverend Myron Eells was a significant college trustee between 1888 and 1907. He fully understood the problems of founding a frontier college, and he took a special interest in building the college library and museum. He defended the deeds of Marcus Whitman and tried to prevent Congregational ministers from dominating Whitman College.

Anderson was no longer effective in his position, that the school might be sold to Presbyterians, and that the college did not want to identify itself with their denomination. The Association explained that these negative facts had prompted it to select three ministers as an investigative committee.

In the late spring of 1891 the Association committee submitted its findings and recommendations to the Whitman trustees, who were forced to react. They refused to publish the Association report but elected three of their most respected members, Myron Eells, Herbert E. Johnson, and John Boyer to a committee of their own. This group was first to make an immediate, confidential response to the document and then to report to the full board. Eells played the leading role because he was also a Pacific University trustee and had experienced the bitter internal political strife that had weakened it and because he had recently written an essay, "The Relations of the Congregational Colleges to the Congregational Churches."

Trustees chose to approve and publicize the committee report submitted by Eells. Stephen Penrose's history includes this document but not the negative Association report. He judged that the trustee committee's report met the "allegations and suggestions explicitly and with dignity."[103]

But assuming that the committee from the regional church Association acted out of "a spirit of kindness," committeemen Eells, Johnson, and Boyer addressed three general topics: the school's Congregational tie, the need for administrative changes, and Anderson's leadership. The committee believed that Whitman's trustees would be willing to amend the college charter so that its majority would belong to evangelical Congregational churches, but the board feared asking the legislature to revise the charter. Probably they worried about losing the tax exemption. The committee assured them it was unnecessary to amend the charter because the college's agreements with the ACES clearly established legal Congregational control.

The Association report had urged that the Congregational Association of Washington be permitted by authority of the charter to nominate persons to Whitman's board of trustees. (The college had an agreement with the ACES that a majority of the trustees must be Congregationalists.) The charter could not be revised without legislative action, but the trustees promised to amend the school's constitution so that the Association could nominate three persons for a trustee position and that the board would elect one of them at the time of the "first, fourth, and seventh vacancies." The committee also approved other requests: a limited term for trustees, the establishment of a ladies' board, a weekly one-hour Bible study requirement, and a definition of the president's and faculty's duties.

Nearly half of the committee's response concerned Anderson. Before the committee reported, he had resigned. Led by Eells, the committee defended him. It complimented the college's builder: "in our poverty we thank God for sending us so able a Christian and self-denying a man as Dr. Anderson, who has given some of the best years of his life to Whitman at the meager salary of $1,600." In responding to the charge that the president had been arbitrary, the committee reported that Anderson himself admitted that he "may have unconsciously shown arbitrariness." The committee did criticize the Whitman board for giving the president too much power. It handily rejected, however, the charge that Anderson had, by employing his wife and sons, turned the college into "a family affair."

The Association's committee had raised an old issue, one that had been heard in Forest Grove since the 1850s and in Walla Walla in the 1880s: the college president should clearly state that the institution was Congregational. The Reverend Loomis and others charged that Anderson had adopted "the cowardly policy in regard to denomination." The college committee responded that it was actually Anderson who had placed into an agreement with the ACES the clause requiring a majority of the trustees to be Congregationalists. Citing many of Anderson's catalogs and other writings, his defenders pointed out that he had given Congregationalists credit for helping establish the institution. To the major charge that there was a "Want of Christian influence," the committee countered by relating that four of the five most recent college graduates professed Christianity. The response concluded with an appeal for "sympathy, aid, prayers, and general support" from the state's Congregational churches.

The motivation of the Congregational Association is uncertain. Biographer Florence Anderson accuses the Reverend Horace P. James of leading a group that sought to put the college under the control of the Congregational Association. Chester Maxey agrees, arguing that these ministers wanted to take over the college "lock, stock, and barrel."[104] Stephen Penrose, however, explains that the clergymen simply had legitimate concerns and investigated them. Most likely, the Congregational Association wanted to increase its influence, not control the college.

In 1891 the trustees bowed to the Association pressure but did not lose control. The board listened to the ACES plead for harmony between college and church leaders but must have bitterly resented the association's meddling in college affairs by its divisive report. There would not be another attempt by outsiders to shape college management until the federal government became involved in 1918.

After an emotional battle over Anderson, trustees hoped that his faultfinders were right in predicting a brighter college future following administrative change and a revision of the constitution. The board anticipated tranquility on Boyer Avenue, success in fund raising, and an end to stories that Spokane's Finney College would replace Whitman as the region's Congregational college. Some Walla Wallans joined trustees in fearing that Spokane, the largest city in the Inland Empire, would take higher education as well as trade from their city. These friends of the college wanted it stabilized.

In the summer the board faced two tasks. The easier one was to make arrangements for opening the school for the fall term. The other responsibility was to find a suitable president; all would agree with Professor Lyman that "a deadhead would be fatal."[105] Meanwhile, Anderson traveled to the Midwest, visiting his alma mater. Surely the stressful Whitman fight reminded him of the one that occurred soon after his graduation from Knox College. Battles over denominationalism and presidential power had been voiced at Galesburg in the 1850s; the same had happened in Walla Walla in the 1890s. At both Knox and Whitman, trustees, faculty members, clergymen, and townspeople fought over several issues, especially a president's record, and discovered that such an internal political contest created as much stress and excitement as a public political campaign.

Alexander Anderson returned to Whitman hoping to continue building the institution while serving as a professor and as a trustee. (His son Louis Anderson, who was furious with his father's critics, served as temporary president.) To assist the college in recounting its past, Anderson compiled a scrapbook and wrote a brief history. He excluded the reasons for his resignation, however. He denied all of the charges made against him by the Congregational Association's committee and complimented Myron Eells and his committee for "a masterly and true response."[106] Anderson continually accused some regional ministers of taking improper action against him; he charged that these small-minded ministers failed to appreciate the fact that he had developed the only college in the region. He accused Beard and James of pulling strings that created a presidential vacancy so that their Oberlin College classmate, the Reverend James Eaton, might take the position. Anderson even told Eaton, his successor, that he held this position because of these schemers.[107]

It is impossible to substantiate Anderson's accusations. It is true, as Penrose wrote, that some ministers opposed to Anderson had graduated from eastern colleges and did not realize the difficulties of establishing a western one. There is also evidence that Beard worked to have Eaton replace the incumbent, as Anderson charged.

Angry both with continuing criticism voiced by regional ministers and with his successor's accusations that the college was not as academic as eastern colleges, Anderson resigned as professor and trustee in 1892. He removed his daughter from the college and relocated in Seattle; there, because his long years of service gave him no retirement income, he supported himself by tutoring in numerous fields and editing a journal. He maintained, however, a close interest in Whitman—he regarded it as "the special child of his creation"[108]—pushing its fund drive in 1895 and writing an essay on its origins for the Whitman College *Quarterly* in 1899. Anderson informed western friends that he hoped the college could become all that he had dreamed of and wrote an easterner that "I am glad if I shall in any way help the college."[109]

In 1903 the college and community conducted special funeral services for Anderson. The student newspaper reported that the entire student body had marched respectfully from the campus to the cemetery and observed that students "are all profiting now because of his heroic efforts."[110] On March 18, 1903, the Walla Walla *Union* judged that his "nine years were as hard and self-denying work as ever a man performed."

Stephen Penrose's college history carefully analyzed Anderson's achievements, including his ability to win community, regional, and national support, to establish a coherent college curriculum, to build a fine faculty, and to convince students that scholarship and character were worthy goals. The historian concluded: "It is evident that a great administrator and teacher had labored heroically for the little college, and had made an indelible impression upon it. The institution must be ever grateful for his leadership and inspiration."[111]

Unfortunately this did not happen, for Whitman, like the University of Washington, did not honor his memory with a building. But a historian of higher education, Professor Frederick E. Bolton, has emphasized that Alexander, Louisa, and their sons "rendered greater pioneer educational service in the Northwest than any other family group" and that "altogether too little is known of their important and lasting contribution." Novelist Nard Jones agreed, stating that Anderson was an "early day educator [who] had the broadest influence upon the whole Pacific Northwest."[112] Perhaps the final assessment of his educational career belongs to Alexander Jay Anderson himself. He recalled that during forty years of teaching he had held fifteen positions and sighed: "I think I have doubly done my duty."[113]

3

The Troubled Presidency
Of James F. Eaton
1891 – 1894

Whitman's second president, James F. Eaton, came to office in 1891 with more impressive credentials than either his predecessor, Alexander Jay Anderson, or his successor, Stephen Penrose. When Eaton accepted the presidency, delighted trustees, faculty members, and friends spread the word that he was bringing his furniture, an indication that he planned to stay. Details about the process of Eaton's selection have not survived, but trustees chose him partly because they could not appoint Whitman faculty members seeking the position. Both professors Louis Anderson and William Lyman desired the presidency, but each revealed to trustees that he did not want to serve under the other. Trustees asked ACES leaders and former President Anderson to recommend candidates. The reverends Reuben Beard and Horace James had submitted Eaton's name. Impressed with his record, these two former Oberlin classmates knew that he sought a college presidency. In 1891 Beard received an honorary doctorate at Whitman, where he enthusiastically endorsed his friend's candidacy.

Eaton soon furnished trustees biographical information and an impressive set of recommendations. Based on education, experience, and energy, Eaton seemed to be an ideal presidential candidate. Born in New York in 1850, he had been well schooled. After graduating from Delaware Literary Institute, Eaton earned a B.A. from Williams College in 1876. An outstanding scholar, he had won prizes in mathematics and was elected in his junior year to Phi Beta Kappa. Every year his class honored him by electing him its president. Eaton was not a member of a secret society but was active in a literary society. Impressed both with his intellectual abilities and his strong opinions, students nicknamed him "Zeus." Eaton was powerfully built and captained the college crew.[1]

Immediately following graduation he attended Yale Divinity School; after two years he transferred to Oberlin, receiving his B.D. in 1879. Until 1882 he served as a pastor in New York churches; then, like many others, he left preaching for teaching. In fact, all of his life he alternated between the two professions. After brief service as a principal of a Michigan public school, Eaton worked at Ripon College from 1884 to 1889 as principal of its academy and professor of ancient languages. He resigned, moved to Massachusetts, and became principal of Drury Academy, a public high school located in North Adams. Eaton was only a few miles from Williams College, making it possible for him to keep posted on educational affairs at his alma mater. He studied conditions at other prestigious schools such as Smith, Dartmouth, and Yale. By visits, letters, and deeds, Eaton made a reputation among important educators and former classmates, including those in eastern Washington. The ambitious high school principal made plans to become president of a prestigious college; he followed a path that led him through North Adams to distant Walla Walla.

At Drury Academy and at Whitman College, Eaton pushed educational reform and wrote on a variety of educational issues. Although there were many differences between the two educational institutions he led, Eaton championed higher academic standards for each; the educator wanted both schools to place more emphasis upon such divergent requirements as gymnasium work and English literature. In his 1891 principal's report, Eaton explained to Drury Academy patrons his revised school schedule, disciplinary procedures, and curriculum.[2] He also addressed such subjects as the importance of training high school students for either college or business, the need to expel rather than to flog the "idler and the hoodlum" (some parents demanded that teachers "control their boy or girl when they themselves have failed to do it"), the importance of students' developing self-control, the necessity of challenging able students, the importance of accepting a diversity of teaching methods, the duty of the faculty to respect students, and the conclusion that the best way to get "inspiring work" was for friendship to develop between pupils and a teacher. Eaton's writing demonstrated his solid experience, his strong opinions, and his interest in educational thought.

Drury Academy not only gave Eaton an opportunity to enact change and to write on education, it also enriched his career in practical ways. He associated with the primary and grammar school teachers who shared space in his nineteen-room building. He observed the North Adams Training School that prepared Drury high school graduates as local grammar school teachers, and he taught older students in the elementary evening schools for $2 per session.

Eaton's two-year tenure at Drury Academy attracted considerable attention. His superintendent praised him and regretted his resignation. The North Adams *Transcript* also lamented the principal's departure, recounting that the renowned Williams professor, Mark Hopkins, had influenced Eaton and that what "Dr. Hopkins did for Williams, Professor Eaton was beginning to do for our schools: rude boys were becoming ashamed of their rudeness and were yielding to the allurements to higher things that lies in the continual contact with a Christian gentleman."[3]

Other opinion makers also had kind words to say. President Timothy Dwight of Yale stated that Eaton was "a gentleman of high character, of ability as a scholar, and of agreeable manners and disposition."[4] President Franklin Carter of Williams considered him the best man "for any place," and a former colleague at Ripon applauded his scholarship, his ability to discipline young men, and his devotion to duty; in fact, "any institution securing his services may deem itself fortunate." A minister and former Williams classmate concluded that Eaton's "superior cannot be found. He is a man of boundless energy and has the finest physique. He can endure any amount of work and is a man of such broad culture that he could take the place of almost any professor."

A Walla Walla newspaper published these impressive letters of recommendation. Whitman's friends boasted that the newcomer was well suited for the presidency and that he would bring the latest in eastern educational practices to the Walla Walla Valley. Some crowed that Eaton was the most distinguished educator to serve as a college or university president in Oregon or Washington. However, the enthusiasm for the president diminished when he did not arrive until

late November, after the conclusion of the first term. His delay resulted from salary negotiations (he wanted to match the $1,700 he re-
ceived at Drury), from interviews with the presidents of Amherst,
Yale, and Princeton, and from visits with relatives.

While James Eaton, his wife, and three children took nearly three
months to cross the continent, Whitman's senior professor, Louis
Anderson, served as the institution's "temporary executive." Overcoming the campus turmoil of 1890–1891, the faculty closed ranks
and boasted of some physical changes to the campus. Superintendent
Elvira Cobleigh, using her own personal funds, fenced Ladies' Hall
and refurbished its rooms. Trustees agreed to repay her with interest,
but they and Cobleigh would long dispute the amount of her reim-
bursement. Meanwhile, male students raised $300 for a primitive
gymnasium and then erected it.[5]

The executive committee of the board of trustees, not the acting
president, took control. It purchased the school's first typewriter for
teaching purposes; this Yost machine probably created somewhat
similar excitement to that resulting from the school's first computer.[6]
The committee recorded another agreement with the ACES. Apparently because it feared that the trustees might sell the school to Presbyterians, the ACES required a tighter agreement, including the stipulation
that unless the president and the majority of the trustees were Congregationalists, the school must return money received from the ACES.
The committee also established a procedure whereby children of ministers and those preparing for the ministry would pay only half tuition. This prompted the faculty to request successfully that its children pay no tuition in literary subjects and half tuition in all others.

While the term progressed, the faculty and students eagerly
awaited the arrival of the new president. When in late November his
early-morning train pulled into the Walla Walla station, financial
agent Jonathan Edwards and a few male students greeted the Eatons.
The formal reception included brief welcoming comments by students and talks by former President Alexander Anderson, William
Lyman, and Eaton.[7] Anderson sketched the college's history and
heartily welcomed his successor. A writer said that when the two men
shook hands "it seemed as though [it was] completing the tie which
binds a great and good work well done, to a splendid administration
just begun." Lyman recalled his college friendship with Eaton and

promised faculty cooperation. The new president's response assured students that he was "not simply a taskmaster but a sympathizer and helper" and that his recent principalship had helped prepare him for his new tasks.

In late 1891 and through the following summer, the new leader took up various duties, some of which the trustees had set aside until he could assist in their resolution. Immediately he helped write new rules for the executive committee of the board of trustees, he contributed to writing Whitman's new constitution and bylaws, he reformed the school's curriculum and educational practices along eastern models, he toured around town looking at alternative campus locations, and of course he grappled with financial problems.

Eaton and the trustees changed their administrative practices so as to meet the recommendations of the Congregational Association committee report that had faulted Anderson. Under a new system, the executive committee would become more active in managing the college; in fact, it became more important than the full board because the committee met frequently, made major decisions, paid bills, and established a finance committee whose chairman became purchasing agent. The executive committee chose a professor to collect tuitions and appointed a trustee to serve as assistant treasurer. These basic changes meant that Eaton had less financial control and fewer administrative tasks than his predecessor.

In April 1892 trustees unanimously approved a new constitution, one that rested upon the board's experience, the regional Congregational Association report of 1891, and Eaton's ideas. It was a wide-ranging and useful document.[8] In summary, the constitution required the president and the board's majority to be "members of Evangelical Congregational churches." Election or dismissal of a trustee, professor, or president required a two-thirds vote of the trustees; moreover, professorships needed faculty approval. Trustees chose five of their members as an executive committee to meet at least once a term. Its transactions were binding unless the full board reversed them at its next meeting. The officers of the board included a president, a recording secretary, a treasurer, an assistant treasurer, and two auditors. The treasurer paid bills submitted by the assistant and published an annual financial report. The assistant treasurer collected tuitions and helped the president advertise the school, travel for the school, and search for students. The trustees appointed an advisory board; its twelve members enjoyed the same rights, privileges, and duties of trustees except that they could not vote. Three trustees were empowered to invest the permanent endowment but were denied the right to pay current operating expenses out of it.

The college was divided into four departments: collegiate, academic, music, and art. The institution awarded three degrees: A.B., B.S., and B.L., each now requiring four years of study. Master degrees were awarded to those who, three years after their graduation, submitted a thesis or public oration and supplied "evidence of continued pursuit of some line of literary work." A home department supervised by the preceptress—a woman chosen by trustees—made dormitory rules for "the inmates" and received the assistance of an advisory board composed of six women. The faculty and the president controlled the curriculum, the textbook selection, and the discipline of students. A section of the constitution entitled "Religious Element" provided that the "holy scriptures shall be a Textbook ... and instruction shall be given in the Evidence of Christianity, Biblical Literature, and the Relation of Science to Christianity." A separate article permitted the state's Congregational Association to nominate trustees for certain vacancies. This constitution was amended, but it remained in force until 1908. Most articles were closely followed, but the trustees failed to appoint the women to advise the superintendent.

Eaton, who considered himself an authority on educational matters, relished revising the constitution and introducing other changes. The leader placed more responsibility on students by permitting them to study in their rooms or at home. He implemented the religious provisions of the new constitution, scheduled Saturday recitations, and prepared a new catalog that reflected these changes and his educational thought.

Before his first catalog appeared, Eaton wrote a revealing letter to former students at Drury Academy.[9] "When I arrived here," he began, "I found the harness hung up, as it were, as in a fire engine house, ready to drop on me forthwith. The old administration had left matters in sad condition, hence I was met by the need of reorganization, immediate and complete." The writer maintained that the trustees and the faculty supported him and that the students "have responded to my ideas and ideals just about as you did, who so nobly rose to the

*Serving as Whitman College's second
president from 1891 to 1894, James F.
Eaton was an intelligent educator, but his
reforms and his elitism created controversy on the campus and in the community.*

thought of self restraint and self respect. . . . The change here has been
more speedy, more wonderful, and equally gratifying." He stated
that he felt at home and that he appreciated the mild winter, the vast
wheat fields, and the orchards. He complained, however, about the
valley dust that residents called "self-rising."

Evaluating his new western society, Eaton wrote, "The ignorant
and vicious foreign element is not here to any extent. May it so continue." He underscored the fact that he had found quite a few millionaires; moreover, "All the early settlers who have kept clear of gambling dens and saloons are rich." But he complained that the rich
"stick to their wealth as a general thing. If anyone imagines that
western people are more liberal than eastern people I am obliged to
differ with them. Very few there know anything of the joy of giving.
That is yet to be taught them. Good Christians take from twelve to
twenty percent interest and exact the last cent. In line of morality it
seems to me to border close on stage-robbing and cattle stealing." He
praised the Chinese for their productive gardens but tended to favor
the federal exclusion law of 1882. Eaton described blanketed Indians

sitting on Main Street's sidewalks. "A stalwart Indian," he added, "striding along the sidewalk, dressed up in gay colors, not very clean, may be followed by a Chinese dressed in green, baggy pantaloons, yellow jacket, and red trimmings. They are very different, yet present a quite striking resemblance." His children delighted in watching Indians and their Cayuse horses pass their home.

The correspondent also provided a version of the history of his adopted region. He had been told by Cushing Eells that Marcus Whitman had saved the United States by preventing the English from taking the Pacific Northwest:

> If the British had possessed this wonderful country at the time of our civil war there is no question but that they would have taken California, which at that time was weakly attached to the Union. That would have given them without a struggle the Rocky Mountain Basin, including everything west of Colorado, Nebraska, and Dakota. Maximilian with a French Army was at that time in Mexico waiting to see if it would be safe for France to attack us. Had the British had this western country the two governments would have joined the South and destroyed our government.

James Eaton tended to believe this remarkable story, one that would be repeated by those who had even fewer doubts about its truthfulness. The president praised Whitman's "ride to save an empire" and provided an original interpretation: "It was no less thrilling than the ride of Paul Revere ... and is more heroic as it was more prolonged and dangerous."

Eaton's catalogs provided him an opportunity not only to give information about Whitman College but also to express his educational expertise. On one hand, Eaton praised the school's fine faculty, concluding that it was unnecessary to send students to eastern colleges. The president also evaluated new teachers. Anne S. Young, for example, was the "niece of Professor Charles Young, of Princeton College, the foremost living astronomer, and possesses something of his quality of mind." On the other hand, he frankly explained that Whitman was raising its "standard, not up to that of a fully equipped eastern college, which for the present is impossible, but to that of our colleges in the middle west."[10] He also pledged that the school's "methods of instruction" were being harmonized "with the most enlightened views of modern education."

Eaton, who had extended the three college degree programs to four years, maintained that they were of equal difficulty. In this view he obviously had a different idea than his predecessor, Anderson, who had favored three-year programs as being more practical for most westerners but cherished a classical four-year program for those who had the talent and time to complete it. The easterner, however, refused to make distinctions between the length of degree programs, and he expressed another controversial idea. Eaton informed readers that "the tendency now is to consider the A.B. degree as representing, not so much Latin and Greek, but a certain grade of culture." He favored electives but explained that Whitman's poor financial situation meant that it could presently offer only required courses. It must continue "the old method of our colleges," one that well-endowed institutions had dropped. But in time, the educator promised, there would be electives, beginning in the junior year. The Whitman faculty had opposed an elective system but would not fight the president's proposals because they knew the school could not presently afford a liberalized curriculum.

Eaton's catalogs showed a new arrangement of departments. The academy now included college preparatory, business, and normal courses. He continued the music department but dropped the art department because of its low enrollments. Those studying in either the business or normal programs took about the same classes and were excused from ancient languages. Eaton bluntly told readers that courses in literature, history, and science provided information "of which no intelligent business man can afford to be ignorant" and that those desiring to be teachers would learn much from a capable faculty. Whitman's college preparatory classes were better, the president emphasized, than those offered in private academies or public high schools because college professors taught them and because they required the development of study skills. "Unless the student gains scholarly habits," Eaton warned, "the habit of mastering his work and not being mastered by it, at this stage, the chances are against his ever becoming a scholar and thinker."

Two other changes demonstrate Eaton's comprehensive views of education. He added a new sub-preparatory department, which of-

fered the same courses as the public grammar schools and allowed
children as young as ten to enroll in Whitman Academy. Then he
established what he called "the true method for the study of literature." Eaton insisted that students "not spend profitless time ...
studying about literature, but should become actually acquainted
with many productions of the highest order." In Walla Walla, as he
had in North Adams, he arranged required works according to an
increasing level of difficulty. Sub-preparatory students would read
Franklin's *Autobiography*, *Evangeline*, *Ivanhoe*, The Declaration of
Independence, and other appropriate works; preparatory students
would read the addresses of Webster as well as standard literature,
including the works of Hawthorne, Dickens, Scott, Eliot, Shake-
speare, and Chaucer.

Many of Eaton's statements from the 1892 and 1893 catalogs
were sound; others were controversial. He expressed a legitimate fear
that local pride or prejudice might lead to the formation of several
denominational schools, for he had been told by Whitman's financial
agent, Jonathan Edwards, that many churches wanted their own
schools and that many communities favored their own colleges. Although the Adventists had already opened a nearby college, Whitman's leaders believed that a Roman Catholic or a Presbyterian college in the valley threatened Whitman's enrollment. Insisting that
Whitman was nondenominational, he believed that competition between church schools would lead to their mutual destruction. To
Eaton's way of thinking, Whitman and the University of Washington
could meet the state's college needs, but he urged churches to support
badly needed academies. Obviously the president hoped that graduates of such institutions would attend Whitman, which could then
drop much of its non-collegiate work. The easterner warned Washingtonians against expressing too much local pride and becoming
involved in dubious real-estate schemes. Such behavior threatened
"the real hopes of higher Christian education." He assured them that
Whitman was not involved in real-estate speculation and that it desired to earn regional respect.

In his 1892 catalog, Eaton asked residents of Washington, Idaho,
and eastern Oregon to assist the college so "that it may speedily
receive from those to whom a gracious Providence has given abundance, increased facilities for securing and keeping a faculty, and for

the care of worthy students, and for the pursuit of researchers after truth. . . . Only thus can our fair State be preserved from the blight of mere money-getting with no worthy objects as to its expenditure, and from moral and mental darkness." His reading of history led him to argue that "It is enlightened, moral citizens that make a country habitable and life worth living." The Christian colleges graduated desirable citizens; thus residents had "the duty and privilege" to help Whitman carry out this important work.

Some readers must have been startled with the change in tone from Anderson's catalogs to Eaton's. They may have resented a college president lecturing them about the acquisition and expenditure of money and insisting that a college education made superior citizens. Critics could very well have concluded that they were getting a minister's, not an educator's, message. Others considered him an eastern elitist.

In summary, the differences between Alexander Anderson's and James Eaton's educational writings stem from their differing backgrounds. Anderson and many of his classmates had worked their way through Knox, a school championing societal reform. Eaton, on the other hand, had attended a school serving the privileged and supporting the status quo. Anderson aspired to build an institution like his beloved Knox College; Eaton talked in terms of creating a western Williams or Yale. Anderson, a son of the Midwest, hoped that Washington civilization would mature into one approximating Illinois; Eaton wanted Washingtonians to aspire to the culture of Massachusetts, a generous state that championed the Christian college. Neither president expected Whitman to be immediately transformed, but Anderson, who had lived in the Pacific Northwest for more than twenty years, better understood the problems of developing cultural institutions on the frontier. He realized that he could do no more than lay Whitman's foundations; Eaton, however, wanted to do much more. To accomplish his aims he consistently reminded westerners that their civilization, including their schools, lagged behind. The easterner insisted that westerners could be goaded into action.

Eaton's dogmatic statements about eastern superiority would eventually lead to trouble, but in 1892 his high ideals and administrative skills won wide acclaim. He had successfully sought the approval of the Congregational ministers who had faulted the college in 1891.

In the spring of 1892 the regional Congregational Association heard a report delivered by the Reverend Stephen B.L. Penrose, the new Congregational minister of Dayton, Washington, and the chairman of a special education committee appointed by the association.[11] Penrose praised Eaton for opening "a new epoch in the administration," endorsed the reorganization included in the new constitution, approved the educational and religious conditions, and predicted that the school's leaders would raise "Whitman from the level of a school . . . to a first rate college." Penrose's special education committee recommended that the churches assist the college and create "a Whitman Army to rally to its support, each soldier to receive a certificate of membership upon the payment of ten cents." It seemed to the committee members that "If the young people can be interested in higher education and in Whitman College, great good will result to them, to the college, and to the churches."

Impressed by the college's educational and religious orientation, including a series of stimulating addresses given by clergymen in the Cushing Eells lecture series, the Walla Walla Ministerial Union sought aid for Whitman. The churchmen insisted that "no investment will contribute more largely to the upbuilding of this city—both materially and morally—than the aiding of this school." The city's newspapers also championed Eaton; the *Statesman*, for example, boasted that he was "beyond a doubt without a peer in the northwest as an educator."[12] Trustees often congratulated themselves on their choice. John Boyer pledged his "unwavering support" because Eaton was "eminently qualified" and had "no weaknesses or prejudices to gratify"; Myron Eells described the president as "able, wise generally, quiet, efficient, popular, but lacking in goose grease a little."[13] The faculty joined the enthusiastic chorus. Lyman called him "a most excellent and capable man"; Louis Anderson wrote that he "had impressed us as being just the man for the place and is decidedly popular. He believes in the college first and foremost and there has been no hesitation in pursuing the policy outlined by my father."[14] According to Penrose, students were enthusiastic about the president and respected him for urging them to strive for higher standards. The Eaton family mixed socially with students, and the president once closed the school for an impromptu picnic to reward students for their solid work and positive attitude.

Cheered by this widespread and solid support, Eaton found the energy to pursue demanding responsibilities. One problem that ran through his entire administration was the college's location. In his first year Eaton gave considerable thought to its Walla Walla site. Discouraged by the lack of a suitable offer of land for an enlarged campus, Eaton tried to find a site on Puget Sound. During the Anderson administration many complained about the campus's small size, about the need to acquire and sell land so as to finance buildings, and about the possibility of moving to a fast-growing city, such as Seattle, Tacoma, or Spokane. In the early 1890s Whitman's leaders must have looked with envy at the development of Walla Walla College. The Adventists acquired 320 acres a short distance from Walla Walla, subdivided their property into small farms, sold them, and used the profits to build a masonry building. This new college had a permanent structure and a commodious campus before Whitman.

In 1892 the Adventists dedicated their institution while Whitman's president, trustees, faculty, and townspeople debated their college's location. In December 1891 Harry Reynolds, speaking for his mother, Lettice J. Reynolds, and other landholders, had offered land in the Mountain View site situated at the edge of town beyond the cemetery.[15] The major donor, Mrs. Reynolds, proposed to give twenty-eight acres and sell sixty additional acres at $150 each. The donation and two smaller ones would be made only if the school moved to the land she owned and if all money obtained from the sale of the donated land would be used for college buildings and improvements. She also required that a $15,000 building be erected within three years. In evaluating the proposal, trustees understood that the Reynolds family had recently and unsuccessfully offered forty acres to the Adventists as a college site and that they wanted to attract Whitman so as to increase the value of their Mountain View property.

Before responding to Harry Reynolds, trustees passed and published a resolution asking Walla Wallans for gifts of land so that there would be room for large buildings and so that land sales could finance them. The executive committee privately appointed a member "to see various parties and in a quiet way see what can be done in the way of securing more ground, and see whether the offer made by Reynolds can be bettered, anywhere within five miles."[16] Reynolds learned of this attempt to find a better opportunity and angrily withdrew his mother's offer. Because the school could not find suitable acreage on the city's outskirts, the trustees sought to acquire land near the present campus. In asking for terms, landowners learned "that this is the final attempt to retain Whitman College in its present location" and that it needed room for "a well developed college."[17] Whitman trustees also told landholders that the school could only pay "satisfactory rates."

In March 1892 the school considered several offers. Henry P. Isaacs offered land east of the campus at $1,000 per acre and terms of one-fourth down and eight percent annual interest. Executors of the Dorsey Baker estate proposed to sell twenty acres south and east of the campus for $20,000 cash.[18] Professor William Lyman, who favored adding land to the present campus, called this offer "a gratuitous insult" and wrote that Eaton voiced disappointment "over the apparent disinclination of the people here to do anything of free benevolence, but rather to be all the time depending on some real estate string."[19] The professor explained that when Reynolds offered his mother's site it "was not benevolence, but merely a business move of his own to boom Mountain View and street car stock." Even so, Lyman knew that Reynolds was more generous than he seemed and explained that Eaton, unfamiliar with the "bluff way of the wild and woolly west," took Reynolds at his word and feared that the college would be part of a dreaded real-estate scheme. Eaton was chilled by the Reynolds' proposal; convinced that the contiguous land was overpriced, he took the site problem to the public. Perhaps an aroused community would be more generous than a single landholder.

In May 1892 Eaton published in local newspapers a statement to Walla Wallans, explaining the need for a new site.[20] "It is not necessary," he began, "to state that the growth of the school has fallen behind the development of the country about us." This condition, he explained, had led to a thorough discussion about the school's permanent location. The president revealed that the school had received generous offers to move to other parts of the state; although he did not describe them, they probably came from Olympia, Tacoma, and Spokane. Eaton then gave a well-reasoned discussion of the school's location; his arguments would be repeated by other Whitman leaders several years later. He established the case for leaving the city: Walla Walla's "failure to grow, the fact that Walla Walla is in one corner of the State and off the main lines of travel, and that the great College of the State ought to be in the midst of its most densely populated region." He continued, "Over against these we have arguments for its retention in Walla Walla which we deem conclusive." The college should be "in the place made historic by Marcus Whitman," the valley's weather was appealing ("the winters are cold enough to give vigor to our work, yet so mild as not to interfere with it"), the school should be in "a city of homes rather than in a distractive business center," students could board less expensively in Walla Walla than elsewhere, and the railroad service was sufficient for persons who used it infrequently. Eaton then presented his major reason for leaving the college in Walla Walla: the school, "poor and struggling as it is," had many local friends who would assist it.

Without identifying them, Eaton noted that sites on the city's outskirts had been offered and rejected partly because each one would require the construction of expensive dormitories. The school, therefore, had to purchase city property and house students in the old neighborhoods. The best opportunity, the leader argued, was the Bryant tract, which was bordered by Bryant, Park, Division, and Locust streets. (He did not mention that these twenty-eight acres would cost $18,400.) The president glowingly described this property: "It is no exaggeration to say that if this site be provided ... no college in America, unless it be Stanford University, has a more beautiful or suitable location than ours will have." To potential donors he revealed that "We have in mind no small affair, but a great institution like Yale or Oberlin, cosmopolitan and national in scope." Such a school would benefit Walla Walla's economy, and those who gave a building or a professorship would "have their names become household words in the choicest homes all over the country and the world." A generous response, Eaton predicted, would cheer trustees, "who have often almost lost courage from lack of appreciative help." For those who feared that they would be donating to a Congregational school, he carefully explained that the church did not control Whitman and insisted that Yale was "in its organization the most emphatically Congregational college" in the nation but was free from denominationalism. "It is our aim," the president boasted, "to make Whitman a great catholic Christian institution, pervaded by a sweet and reasonable Christianity."

With the support of clergymen, editors, and others, the fund raisers attempted to find subscribers willing to give a total of $18,000 by
November. They failed. Upset by this reversal, Eaton informed Reynolds in December that he favored a move to his mother's Mountain
View site and approved plans for a streetcar line that would link the
business district with the potential campus.[21] In June 1893 Harry
Reynolds, Stephen Penrose, and two others received appointment to
the board of trustees. Reynolds then formally offered about forty-
four acres. Thus for the first time since Dorsey Baker's donation,
Whitman had the opportunity to acquire free local property. Eaton,
however, changed his mind. Historian Penrose wrote that his reasons
could not be "traced."[22] But the old arguments explained why the
"Mountain View Campus" was rejected: the property was too far
from town, the school could not move the old buildings or afford new
ones, the trustees might not legally be able to sell the original site, and
a move might be denounced as a part of a real-estate promotion.
Trustees sided with the president and informed their colleague that
they could not accept his offer.

So Eaton gave up on Walla Walla as the school's site. In 1893 he
reconsidered moving the institution to Puget Sound, and in December
he and a few trustees investigated Tacoma property. After rejecting it
they examined an Olympia site. Myron Eells provided some details
about an unusual offer from this city. John R. Chaplin wanted to
build Olympic University on a Budd Inlet site.[23] He proposed constructing impressive buildings and raising a large endowment. Chaplin insisted that "The name must be Olympic University with Whitman College as a college attached." Agreeing with Eells that the proposed university was "a doubtful experiment," Eaton lost interest.
Fortunately Whitman rejected Chaplin's proposal, for in 1898 he lost
his proposed campus in a sheriff's sale.

In summary, Eaton could not finance an alternative site in Walla
Walla or find one on Puget Sound. This frustrating search for land in
the early 1890s would long be remembered by trustees. Early in the
twentieth century, however, there would be another and greater attempt to move the institution, and arguments raised by Eaton would
be reintroduced. In all these efforts to improve the site there was
considerable complaint about Whitman's small campus; nobody
cared to recall that in the mid 1860s Cushing Eells, in opposing Dor-

sey Baker's offer, had predicted serious problems resulting from a
lack of property.

Whitman was not the only school troubled by its location. In the
early 1890s other private institutions also debated moving from
smaller to larger towns. For years Pacific University had considered a
shift to Portland, but in 1892 its trustees decided to construct Marsh
Hall, an impressive stone building that anchored the school to Forest
Grove. Willamette University, on the other hand, could not reach a
harmonious decision about its location. Believing that Salem had not
been as generous as it could have been and that the university would
become an impressive regional institution in a developing suburb,
some of the Willamette leaders moved to the Oregon metropolis and
launched Portland University.[24] Thus the institution split; the rivals
competed for Methodist support, most of which went to Portland.
Whitman avoided experiencing a similar division because Congregationalists lacked the influence over Whitman that Methodists had on
Willamette and because the majority of Whitman's trustees lived in
Walla Walla and wanted to retain their school.

Throughout his administration Eaton struggled with economics
as well as location. Initially he asked the school's treasurer and financial agent to do what they could about a lack of money. In the spring
of 1892, after working on academic matters and checking various
properties as possible campus sites, the president began grappling
with the deficit. The inability to raise large sums in either the East or
the West meant that money had been taken from the small endowment for operating purposes. Apparently this practice continued even
after the new constitution forbade it. Like Anderson, Eaton tried a
variety of financial strategies, but he left the school in a worse financial condition than when he took charge. In February 1892 Eaton
wrote Myron Eells about his disappointment when he arrived and
learned that the institution possessed only a few acres and buildings.[25] If he had known that the school was so weak, he would "hardly have ventured to take up the work." He revealed that "it never
occurred to me that a college could run nine or ten years, with a name
such as that of Whitman and have accumulated no endowment. I
know nothing like it elsewhere and my acquaintance with colleges in
the west is quite extensive." The educator feared that unless Whitman
stopped living "from hand to mouth" new schools that might open in

Olympia and Spokane would provide too much competition.

John Boyer, president of the Baker-Boyer Bank and treasurer of the college, explained to the president that Whitman was "almost entirely dependent upon the [American] College [and Education] Society for help."[26] Eaton sought to change this situation, for he knew the ACES was also having trouble raising money and that college agents overran New England churches. There was a strong possibility that the ACES would drastically cut its $5,000 annual payment to Whitman, so the school had to raise money and acquire land from local residents. Eaton worked long hours seeking both an improved site and a larger endowment. He and Lyman feared that unless there was a significant increase in local support, the ACES might start assisting another school in the state. At first the president was as optimistic as Anderson had been early in his administration; Eaton, who saw many signs of local wealth, wrote the ACES that he anticipated donations of land and $50,000.[27] He received neither. Financial agent Edwards raised little money and also became pessimistic about the school's future.

Eaton then received unsettling news from the ACES. It could not raise large sums either and could not support seven colleges and eight academies on its approved list. It warned that Whitman might not receive even $5,000 in 1893. Eaton replied that his school must have at least this amount to meet its operating expenses; for example, faculty members could not afford to teach on their current salaries ranging from $800 to $1,100 a year. To raise an endowment for Whitman, especially for faculty salaries, and to assist the ACES with its fund raising, Eaton chose to go to Massachusetts and "plead for money." The ACES accepted this unusual arrangement. In October he visited the World's Fair in Chicago, journeyed to Boston, and began campaigning. Many clergymen and businesspeople gave warm handshakes and gushed over Eaton's dedicated service, but they kept their purses closed. The president reported that this fund raising had taught him "to gently push open doors you find ajar. It is not wise to try to break through any."[28] After subtracting his travel expenses, he probably raised less than $500 for Whitman. He placed this money in his so-called Berkshire Fund in honor of donors residing in western Massachusetts and hoped that eventually it would become a $20,000 endowment for the college.

In a cheerful letter to Whitman students, Eaton described his campaign: "up and down ... the Berkshire Hills, pleading for money to bring west to aid in educating the sons and daughters of far away Washington, that this new country might be helped to attain something of the intelligence and virtue, the Christianity, and prosperity so abounding in the land once trodden by the feet of the pilgrims."[29] Although he succeeded in raising little money, he still praised Massachusetts for its generosity. "No equal portion of the world gives so abundantly and self-denyingly to aid in the salvation and elevation of man beyond its borders."

In the spring of 1893 Eaton wrote to the ACES, listing accomplishments and improvements at Whitman, including the fact that the "trustees are awakening to their duty and are unanimous and hearty in all their actions."[30] Trustee Penrose, for example, even renovated school buildings at his own expense. But the president emphasized that the college could not stand on its own feet and that the ACES must send $5,000 to keep it operating. Obviously the ACES approved of Eaton's work because it increased Whitman's appropriation to $6,000, accompanied by the request that the college match that figure. The president appreciated the extra money and predicted "great things for the college."

Perhaps in normal times the school might have made improvements and matched the ACES gift. Unfortunately, however, eastern Washington, like the nation, suffered from the Panic of 1893. Historian D.W. Meinig summarized conditions in eastern Washington: "wheat prices plummeted, railroads became insolvent, and immigration dwindled."[31] Nature also delivered a blow. Uncharacteristic fall rains sprouted the bagged wheat and turned roads into quagmires. The economic crisis of 1893 to 1895 resulted in low wheat prices, poverty, and pessimism. In 1894 the college fell deeper into debt and could not pay salaries or even buy wood. Trustee Myron Eells hoped that the school would not close and reminded the faculty that the school was "in the position of hundreds of companies, who are unable to pay all their employees and have to discharge some," but Professor Lyman retorted that the trustees could provide something for the pitiful faculty families.[32] He reminded trustees that he had been paid only $495 the past year, that he faced creditors, and that his "wife had almost destroyed her health by hard work and worry."

Beginning in the fall Eaton began alerting the ACES about "hard times," which meant lower enrollments (parents took younger children out of the academy and placed them in public schools), reduction of faculty salaries, and the failure of local fund raisers. Eaton explained, "I have never been in the midst of such wide spread distress. There is evidently no financial foundation to this country yet. . . . If help from the Society now fails us then we can only say 'Lord have mercy upon us!'"[33] Eaton found one benefit in the economic crisis: "several ambitious efforts" to establish other denominational colleges failed; therefore, "Whitman still has the field without any rival."[34] Early in 1894, however, the educator continued to be negative: "This year bears very heavily upon us. For this state is in a most deplorable financial state. Very few have means to pay even the small tuition. . . . Fortunes have vanished and are vanishing on every hand." The worried president called Whitman "a very small affair," but assured the ACES that he would stand by it both for "what it may become and for what it stands for."[35]

Exasperated by Eaton's numerous negative reports about the college's condition, Frank Ferguson, an officer of the ACES, responded in a lengthy, blunt letter.[36] Ferguson told Eaton that he was too pessimistic, that he "discounted the financial ability of the people of Washington," and that he feared "that you having gone from the substantial East to the speculative West have been unduly terrified by the financial bubbles on which you have written so frequently." The pessimistic president should, the writer continued, cheer up, ask Washington Congregationalists for financial help, and try to raise as much of the $6,000 match as possible.

To support his belief that Washington's economy was stronger than Eaton reported, Ferguson pointed out that he knew eastern investors who made steady financial returns from investments in the state and that the state's two academies presently assisted by the ACES did not submit such gloomy news as Whitman. The ACES thus determined that Eaton's 1894 report was too negative and deleted such parts as "would arouse suspicion." The organization also expressed concern about its financial assistance to the school:

> Whitman College has had large and constant assistance from the East, and, notwithstanding the honored names of Whit-

man and Eells, the people of the East will hesitate to continue
their generous support, unless we can persuade them that the
College is appreciated by its own friends, and supported to the
full extent of their ability. There are several sections of the
West much newer and very much poorer than Eastern Washington which have raised a great deal more during the late year
than has been raised by the friends of Whitman.[37]

Ferguson, who scrutinized Whitman's financial situation, added
his own complaint, "I do not see how Washington people can expect
the New England friends of Christian education to build for them a
Christian college in their state." From its experience with many colleges, the ACES had learned that wealthy people "do not always rally
in the support of an institution until it has reached a great crisis." The
eastern organization wanted to hear that Eaton was "stirring up the
Washington people to more generous support of the institution."

Ferguson not only urged Eaton to contact wealthy people in
Washington, he also recommended that he correspond with a Chicago philanthropist who had been aiding colleges that either were on or
had been on the ACES list. The president accepted this advice and
contacted Dr. Daniel "D.K." Pearsons. In late March Pearsons responded, and thus began a long and fruitful relationship between the
millionaire and the impoverished college. D.K. Pearsons lectured
Eaton. "It was time," the blunt philanthropist insisted, "for you to
wake up or for the people of Washington to wake up and act."[38] To
stimulate local donors, Pearsons offered to give $50,000 for an en-
dowment fund if the college raised $150,000 in twenty months. The
Chicagoan insisted that the college should remain east of the Cascades. He concluded by stating that he had donated money to Pacific
University and boasted that every educational institution that had
taken his money enjoyed success.

Excited by Pearsons' offer, Eaton wired his terms to the ACES,
which quickly responded that Pacific had received a more generous
proposal than Whitman. It had only to raise $100,000, not $150,000.
Ferguson urged Eaton to ask Pearsons for the same terms given Pacific and predicted that "New England would respond more generously
to an appeal in behalf of Whitman than to Pacific" because Marcus
Whitman and Cushing Eells were honored names. Eaton unsuccess-

fully sought equal terms and then explained Pearsons' refusal: "His reason for making terms for poorer colleges so hard is to get a sufficient sum to ensure the continuance of the school. He fears to give to a school which has so little that it may not survive."[39] The president added that Pearsons insisted that only the endowment's income could be spent; in fact, this stricture was in accordance with Whitman's new constitution. Eaton thought the endowment earnings should go for faculty salaries because "a good faculty kept is of greater value than a good plant alone." Owing to the local money shortage, he predicted that Whitman would have to take donations of property. (Pearsons agreed that the school should take land, but he wanted to make sure that it was valuable.)

Pearsons' offer meant, Eaton told the ACES, that Washington now had "a chance to wake up and do its part if it ever means to do anything." And the president felt sure that the philanthropist's offer would stimulate other donations. "I feel," he wrote, "that Whitman's day is fast approaching, and that we will succeed in this undertaking. The heroism, wisdom, and patriotism of Whitman and the life long devotion of Dr. Eells are in themselves a rich legacy, but in addition, no young college has a better field or is more needed."

The president then evaluated his own record, boasting that by 1893 he had made the college respectable. "I am," he revealed, "no longer ashamed of Whitman. It now commands general respect. This task has cost me heavily in mental and physical wear, but it has been worth the struggle. . . . We are now ready for advance."

In the hot and economically troubled summer of 1894, the school's leaders sought to make this advance. In June the trustees accepted and announced Pearsons' offer. (In writing him of the board's acceptance, its secretary was so unfamiliar with the donor that he addressed him as "A.T. Pierson.") Meanwhile, trustees appointed five notable Walla Wallans—banker Levi Ankeny, banker Miles C. Moore, merchant William P. Winans, merchant William O'Donnell, and trustee Harry Reynolds—as a local solicitation committee. In July these men published an announcement designed to convince other wealthy Walla Wallans to subscribe money so that the school would receive Pearsons' money.[40] Their statement, of course, stressed economics. Earlier Whitman fund raisers had also insisted that the school would have a noticeable economic impact upon the community, but the reasoning employed in 1894 reflected the community's current economic foundation. The committee stressed the importance of agriculture and deemed it unnecessary to remind citizens that Walla Walla's failure to attract a transcontinental railroad meant that it would not enjoy a significant industrial base. The writers reasoned: "If Walla Walla cannot secure anything else it can secure, and it is more admirably fitted by nature than any other place in the whole Northwest, for . . . a system of schools and colleges which will make it foremost as a city of such substantial prosperity, refinement, and culture as will attract . . . prosperous and educated people, making it essentially a city of finest homes." Walla Walla should become a center for agriculture and education, not transportation or manufacturing, a prediction that was realized. The committee estimated that an expanded college would immediately bring $150,000 into the city's businesses. Its statement made several other points. Whitman College enjoyed "a name which links it to a history that will appeal more strongly to a large class of charitable and patriotic people than any other institution in the Untied States." The school's alumni played important roles in Walla Walla's social and economic life. If the school had an endowment, then "charitable persons" would donate because the college would no longer be "on a precarious basis." In conclusion, trustees assured potential donors that subscriptions would not be binding until the entire sum of $150,000 had been pledged.

After about a week the dispirited solicitation committee met with the executive board, and the two committees jointly decided that because of "the present financial stringency" it would not seek subscriptions until the economy improved. While the solicitation committee delayed its work, however, another new committee had to continue. At the same time that trustees had appointed the solicitation committee, they also created an emergency fund committee, whose task was to raise $3,500 for arrears in faculty salaries. A trustee warned that unless this money was found, the school would not open in September.

The emergency fund committee became very active in August after Eaton wrote to trustees the terms of his resignation, including the payment of his salary. Depressed by Whitman's woeful financial condition, angered by the board's decision to retain Professor William

Lyman, and hurt by the growing opposition to him on and off campus, Eaton had decided to leave. With trustee Reynolds playing a leading role, the emergency fund committee soon raised about $1,700 because it confidentially told donors that their dollars would lead to the president's departure. On September 3, 1894, Eaton resigned.

There was a great contrast between the arrival and the departure of the Eatons. They had crossed the continent seeking a rewarding western adventure: the move was a long step up Eaton's career ladder. They left Walla Walla in a somber mood; in fact, Mrs. Eaton complained several months later that she still suffered from anxiety resulting from her husband's troubled presidency. For years after the Eatons took their eastbound train, townspeople pondered why a brilliant educator who had won diverse initial support failed to retain it. Those providing explanations universally stressed his deep hostility to Professor William Lyman. In 1892 the president had appointed him to be in charge of the college operations while he sought eastern funds. Soon after the leader departed, the teachers began reconsidering the class schedule and voted against the new Saturday morning recitations, a system that Eaton had imposed upon a dubious faculty. They and their students complained about this schedule, arguing that it took time from relaxation, class preparations, and athletics. Lyman also denounced the system because the faculty, suffering from meager salaries, needed Saturday occupations.[41]

Two women faculty members supported the Eaton schedule and immediately informed him about the six-to-two vote against his schedule. He expressed his astonishment that the vote had been taken in his absence. The president also learned that some professors had "raked over and condemned" his administration and complained that students were free from discipline.[42] Diarist Myron Eells wrote that Lyman, aided by Professor Louis Anderson, was guilty of "upsetting Eaton's policy and having but little discipline, so that thirty students left."[43] Trustee John Boyer accused Lyman and Anderson of making "a shameful effort to undermine our esteemed president."[44]

Alarmed by stories of campus difficulties, Eaton hurried from the Berkshire Hills to the Walla Walla Valley, arriving in January 1893. While he sought allies and reasserted his control over what he called deplorable campus conditions, the president received an upsetting telegram from the ACES.[45] Its leaders had heard complaints about

Eaton's administration from a confidential correspondent; the organization would immediately stop making its vital monthly financial payments until he supplied "evidence of harmony." Some regional clergymen and trustees wrote in his defense, stressing his leadership and character. Convinced that Eaton enjoyed broad support, the ACES quickly reinstituted payments.

But Eaton would not drop the matter. He sought to discover the author of the derogatory letters to the ACES. His prolonged search included bitter accusations that would eventually cause him much trouble. At first, he seemed successful. To his great pleasure Louis Anderson, who vigorously denied authorship, resigned. According to the Anderson family historian, he felt "himself hampered in his work by arbitrary surveillance and was disheartened by the growing discontent among his colleagues and the unjust treatment of Lyman."[46]

The extent of student involvement in the Eaton controversy is uncertain; both the president and his faculty foes sought to win student allies. Some students took sides, especially after Lyman was asked to leave and after Anderson actually resigned. A student publication deplored classicist Anderson's decision: "During his professorship . . . there has not been a more thorough teacher . . . and by his tireless energy and persistent labors he has even made the dead languages to live and has maintained an excellence of classic work which is at par with the best."[47] Most students, however, pursued their own interests, not those of the two factions. In 1893 the literary societies, recognizing that the college paper "has become an indispensable factor in college life," launched the *Whitman Collegian*.[48] This first student newspaper reported monthly campus news during the first half of 1893. It informed readers that blue and gold were selected as the school's colors; that male students suffered from "football fever" resulting from the college's first victory—a sixteen-to-zero triumph over the city eleven—and from anticipation of the first full season; that many enjoyed literary societies, musical recitals, and the YWCA and YMCA; and that school athletes competed during spring field day. Female participants appeared "in full dress uniform of blue and gold" and complained about "a fiendish element" that a reporter identified: "Not drug fiends, but Kodak fiends."[49] The *Collegian* described campus conditions during the term's end: "socials, parties, society meetings, lectures, and baseball games took time from study."

The editor complained that his classmates lacked sleep, yawned in class, crammed, procrastinated, and expressed fear of low grades. Nearly a hundred succeeding editors could write about similar conditions during May.

While some students were asked to become involved in the administrative struggle, some townspeople also took sides. Louis Anderson continued his verbal warfare upon the president; for instance, he asked potential donors to reject Eaton's pleas because "the rule of hypocrisy, falsehood, and tryranny still prevail."[50] His influential wife, Mabel, also pitched into the battle. A daughter of Dorsey Baker, she had attended Whitman, and then in 1890 married her former teacher. She pointed out that trustees customarily thanked a resigning professor for his service, but her husband received no such letter in 1893 because Eaton thought him unfaithful. Undoubtedly she spread her bitterness throughout the community, and, in a heated letter to a trustee, she reminded him that her husband had served "faithfully and lovingly" for eleven years and had delayed advanced academic training "until he is past his prime."[51] She confided: "the greatest sorrow that has darkened our path and caused the deepest heartaches has been Whitman."

The resignation of Louis Anderson temporarily ended the Anderson family's long and important connection with the college. In 1892 former President Alexander Anderson had resigned from the board of trustees and removed his daughter Helen from Whitman, enrolling her in the new normal school at Ellensburg. Louis departed the following year. All of Alexander's sons denounced the college. The Andersons had been turned from loyal friends to bitter critics.

In Eaton's mind, however, William Lyman was the chief troublemaker. (President Anderson had made the same charge four years earlier.) Believing that Lyman had undercut his administration and schemed for his position, the president accused him of "plots and politics."[52] He hoped that the professor might transfer to the state college in Pullman. Denying the president's accusations that he could not serve faithfully, and determined to help build Whitman, Lyman remained and asked trustees and others to speak on his behalf to Eaton. Rejecting all explanations about Lyman's actions, the president pressured the faculty and the trustees to support him in his struggle to remove an untrustworthy individual. The president "endeavored to convince the teachers of Lyman's guilt and to even coerce them into admitting that they had grounds for suspicion." A young professor, Edwin Bishop, clashed with the president because he did not agree that Lyman sought to "deliberately and maliciously cripple" his administration.[53] In early 1894 it seemed that Eaton would be victorious. Three westside trustees, including Myron Eells, allied with him. Concluding that they could not pay Lyman's salary, trustees asked for his resignation.[54] The executive committee agreed, voting to terminate his professorship at the end of the spring term and to cut his pay in half immediately by dividing his classes with another teacher. At the same time the committee reduced all faculty salaries by twenty percent.

Probably these trustees believed that Eaton was more important to the school than Lyman, whom they knew had pulled strings to remove Anderson. Eaton often charged that Lyman was uncooperative. But the president soon suffered a blow when alumni, townspeople, and students petitioned the board at its June 1894 meeting, requesting that Lyman be retained. Although the petitions have not survived, each stressed his effective teaching. Affable, intelligent, and dedicated, he was the school's most popular teacher and had won community support through his public lectures and his enthusiasm for the city. Townspeople looked upon him as a westerner with a solid eastern education. The professor understood those he taught and the society they represented better than the president. Both educators had a fine Williams education, but, of course, this in itself did not prepare them for the demands placed upon western teachers.

Impressed with the important names on the petitions and the sincerity of those townspeople who brought them to the meeting, the board questioned both Lyman and Eaton. The advisory board, including those Congregational ministers supporting Eaton, now met regularly with the board of trustees and participated fully in the controversy. After a five-hour session that concluded at an early morning hour, the fourteen-member board summoned Eaton and Lyman, who joined in a deliberation of their relationship. The two then "shook hands, agreeing to work together harmoniously in the interest of the college."[55] Chairman of the board Eells summarized this exhausting meeting. He faulted Lyman's critical letters about the president and complained that Eaton "was morbidly suspicious."[56]

Eells also switched his support from the president to the professor. He predicted that unless Eaton became more reasonable he would fail as a leader. The chairman had discovered that most Walla Wallans, including Congregationalists, opposed the president. Wearied by the long struggle, Eells complained, "O dear they are frittering away valuable strength in petty quarrels."

Trustee Penrose, who helped resolve the dispute, also interpreted it. In his history he explained that Eaton's departure was "inevitable."[57] The Lyman conflict and the economic downturn of the 1890s contributed to his departure, but the major difficulty, he stressed, was Eaton's character. Penrose recalled that the president's "opinions were delivered *ex cathedra* with the assumption that they would be received with the same finality with which they were delivered," that he lacked a sense of humor, and that he was "antagonized by any one who differed from him ... and ... showed a suspiciousness and jealousy which made it impossible for him to treat those who differed from him as though they were his friends and not his enemies." According to Penrose, a majority accepted "the judgments of this wise man of the East who had come from the realms of light into the twilight dawn of the far West." But this acceptance wore thin by 1894. Some students disliked Eaton's arrogance. Harry Painter remembered that the president "believed that New England was the center of all culture, true learning, and piety. He never tried to disguise his contempt for the West, for Western customs, and manners of life. He told us in chapel one time you have no culture or refinement in the West, you must acquire it from those whom the East sends out to you."[58] After quarreling with Eaton, trustee Jonathan Edwards, who had enthusiastically supported him in 1891, resigned as financial agent and sarcastically called him "the wise man from the East." Another trustee tired of the president's complaining that he showed us "all his sores and bruises."[59]

Some people must also have criticized his inconsistency. He wrote in his catalogs, for example, that it was unnecessary for students to go east for a college education, yet he encouraged at least one student, Pearl Gunn, to transfer. In a letter to the Whitman students, Eaton quoted her as saying: "I am very happy here. I delight in Smith. Now I know what you meant when you were trying to make us understand last year what a college is. This is a college."[60]

James Eaton developed many opponents. He denounced Elvira Cobleigh's management of Ladies' Hall and replaced her. Trustee Harry Reynolds disagreed with the president's management, including his opinions about the Mountain View campus and the conditions in the local Congregational church. Eaton wrote that Lyman and Reynolds "were full of malignant hypocrisy."[61] Although he had promised to reconcile his differences with Lyman, Eaton called him a liar and resented the fact that when Eaton announced a trip to California the trustees replaced him with Lyman.

There were several additional reasons for Eaton's growing unpopularity. Townspeople turned against him because they resented his assertion that they did not deserve a college that they had not supported, because they disapproved of his attempts to move the institution to Puget Sound, and because they disliked his telling selected students that their school would not open in the fall. The beleagured leader told Myron Eells and others that he did not care if Whitman "never again shall open in Walla Walla." Alarmed by such words, Eells visited the campus in September and, like other critics, charged that Eaton had "found the institution in successful order and now it is almost a wreck."[62]

Like Anderson, Eaton had created important opponents who now urged trustees to remove him. Anderson's departure came late in his career, but Eaton was only forty-four when he resigned. His manner, not his intelligence, accounted for his failure; and this probably also explains why he failed to attain the presidency of a prestigious college. After Whitman he took a school in Hull, Iowa, where he grumbled to the ACES about how the unreasonable westerners had mistreated him in Walla Walla. He moved on to other midwestern principalships and pastorates before retiring in his beloved New England. There were Walla Wallans who credited him with bringing higher academic standards to Whitman; the majority, however, probably agreed with Lyman's assessment. The historian, who had the last word in his struggle with Eaton, judged that after Anderson's resignation in 1891 "there was a period of loss and uncertainty which was happily ended in 1894."[63]

In the late summer of 1894, trustees and faculty determined to salvage the institution. According to Penrose, trustee Reynolds played the critical role; indeed, "If it had not been for him it may be safely said that the College would have closed its doors perhaps forever."[64] Reynolds provided leadership, courage, time, and money, including $10,000 to help meet the Pearsons offer. Trustees told the public that the school would be delayed until after the fall harvest and that a familiar figure, the Reverend Stephen Penrose, was being offered the presidency and that the popular Lyman was temporarily in charge. Lyman's relationship with Whitman had changed dramatically. In June he had been told that he would be terminated, but in September he headed the institution. Meanwhile, the executive committee "voted to secure students, who could give produce for tuition, but not to advertise for them through the papers."[65] They also worked out financial arrangements with individual professors, handing each a few dollars and a short-term note.

The faculty, too, played a critical role. Although their salaries had been reduced in the 1890s and they all had back pay due them, the teachers wanted the emergency fund, which had been raised for them, to be transferred to Eaton. They would rather be rid of him than to be paid in full. To their way of thinking Whitman would overcome its serious problems, but only under new leadership.

The faculty understood the bitter experience of the school's administrators. Each, in turn, had been frustrated. Peasly Chamberlain, complaining of fatigue, had resigned during the school year; Cushing Eells had paid the school's debt and departed because he received so little community support; Alexander Anderson had worked to the point of exhaustion but had been forced out when clergymen, faculty, trustees, and townspeople combined against him; and James Eaton, who had initially won approval for his ideas and energy, squandered his support and resigned. Each man had taken the leadership with plans and dreams; each had wanted to honor Marcus Whitman by educating the young who lived east of the Cascades. Each had been disillusioned, especially by financial problems. Only Anderson lasted long enough to fulfill many aspirations. Stephen Penrose, who had been offered the presidency, was fully aware of this dismal administrative history, but he was also optimistic about the school's possibility. Penrose had left the East to serve westerners; the Whitman position provided an opportunity. Fortunately for everybody he seized it.

4

The Early Career
Of Stephen B.L. Penrose
1864 – 1894

Early one September morning in 1890 a weary traveler stepped out of a railroad car, stretched his long legs, and studied his new hometown, Dayton, Washington, a farm hamlet that was truly at the end of the tracks. He had enjoyed his travel across the continent, especially the last thirty miles when his train passed through rolling wheat fields. The newcomer made his way to the hotel on dusty Main Street, noting the wood-frame buildings, the farmers who had come to trade, and the Blue Mountains in the background. He acquired a local newspaper and must have laughed at the editor's account of the changing seasons:

> The melancholy days have come, the saddest of the year,
> It's a little too hot for whisky, and a little too cold for beer.[1]

Tall, bespectacled, dignified, and well-mannered, the young man introduced himself as the Reverend Stephen Penrose. His full name was Stephen Beasley Linnard Penrose; his name as well as his degree list were longer than those of anyone else in town. Many new faces had appeared in Dayton during the past several summers as immigration swept across southeastern Washington into the Palouse Country, but Penrose was a unique newcomer. Residents had heard that this new Congregational minister had studied at fancy eastern schools and that he was one of six men—the "Yale band"—that were coming to preach in Washington's small towns. Although each man served in the American Home Mission Society and thus had a

$1,000 salary guaranteed by easterners, most Daytonians probably doubted that the ministers would remain, for others had unsuccessfully attempted to build up small local churches. Surely these well-intentioned urban Congregationalists would also become disenchanted with quiet life in a farm community and would return to their eastern origins.

Penrose recalled that several hundred people jammed the pews to hear his first sermon, but he was disappointed to discover that they had attended because of "the novelty of a young eastern minister ... not a desire to hear the particular kind of gospel which I had to preach."[2] Attendance on following Sundays ranged only between twenty and forty.

While he sought ways to attract a congregation, Penrose necessarily altered his personal life. To his surprise he discovered that there was not a bathtub in town; so every day he bucketed well water into his tub. Some parishioners chuckled over the easterner's admission that he had to learn how to do the church's janitorial work because he had never swept, dusted, or cut firewood. The pastor also had to learn to saddle a horse, though soon after acquiring this skill, the greenhorn was thrown and injured. Penrose laughed at his failings and boasted that he would learn and succeed in his mission.

Penrose was one of the best-educated professional men in southeastern Washington, and rarely was an urbane easterner more at home with simple western people, including Mr. and Mrs. Oliver B. Davis, who boarded him. He was anything but a snob. Interested in the well-being of others, the minister won acceptance because of his affability and optimism. Although he did not expect to stay for more than a couple of years, he remained nearly four. Penrose preached and made calls all over Columbia County, becoming a familiar figure in a cart pulled either by Maud S. or Selim, his reliable horses. The missionary soon became devoted to the inhabitants and the various agricultural landscapes, the "corpulent hay-ricks, crowded barns, and herds of fat cattle and sleek horses." Penrose listened to the merchants who boasted of their lively trade and hoped that Dayton could avoid a country village image by ending "the primitive custom of pasturing cows in the streets" and by attracting new businesses.[3]

To his surprise Penrose discovered that the farm town had an intellectual life, especially in the Blue Mountain Chautauqua Literary

Circle. For nearly four years the young minister attended its weekly meetings. Meanwhile Penrose taught Greek and Hebrew to a bright country editor, lectured to local audiences on topics ranging from astronomy to Whittier, played on a local baseball team, participated in public school programs, served as a city library director, and engaged in popular outdoor sports. In 1891 the "Yale band" went on a fishing and hunting expedition to remote Wallowa Lake. Penrose's friends expressed relief upon learning that an experienced Indian guide led these greenhorns. Such involvement in western amusements and cultural affairs made the young minister popular. Some of these rural folk would help Penrose when he followed a different career in Walla Walla.

Gradually Penrose's congregation learned his biography. He was born in 1864 to Clement and Mary Penrose, a couple that reared two sons and six daughters.[4] Clement was a member of the sixth generation of a Pennsylvania family of English origins, a family noted for its wealth, culture, and politics. Enjoying financial benefits from an inheritance and investments, the family lived well and worked for the well-being of others. Clement Penrose took the classical course at the University of Pennsylvania, read law with his father, and began his law practice in 1853. Twenty-five years later he left his solid law practice to serve as the efficient judge of the Orphans' Court of Philadelphia County. A scholar of the law, an adviser of lawyers and judges, and a well-respected judge, Penrose attracted support from both political parties and easily won several re-elections. He belonged to a number of learned organizations, including the Law Academy of Philadelphia, the state historical society, an archeological association, and the American Academy of Political and Social Science. A member of the Republican Party, which dominated city politics, Clement influenced his family's political thought. (Stephen recalled that he was about twenty-one years old before he discovered that a man could be at the same time a Democrat and honorable.[5])

Mary Penrose handled duties given to women of the upper middle class. She spent her days rearing eight children, directing domestics, being a dutiful daughter to her parents, and assisting her popular and influential Presbyterian church. She took a special interest in the church's foreign missions. Mary and Clement presided over a happy and cultured family that often enjoyed the friendship of numerous aunts, uncles, and cousins. Many of these relatives visited the Penrose home in Germantown, a suburb northwest of Philadelphia. It was hard to find privacy, because twelve occupants lived in the fine house. Three female Irish servants freed the Penroses, including a grandmother, from domestic chores. As Stephen later remembered it, he did not even have to pick up his own dirty clothes. Parents, sisters, and other relatives doted on the lively boy. When he behaved they called him "Little Sunbeam"; when he misbehaved they complained that he had "blackie on his back."[6] The children received musical training; Stephen learned to play the violin, organ, and piano, but he preferred singing.

In later years in the West, Stephen often mentioned his eastern background. His knowledge of the industrial East would assist him when he went there seeking financial assistance for his rural college. He compared the Philadelphia of his youth with Walla Walla, which was the hometown of all his children. He stressed that Philadelphia was very unlike Walla Walla, that he greatly preferred the western community, and that he was one of the few Penroses to leave his hometown. At the time of his boyhood, Philadelphia was America's second largest city and second busiest port. Iron and steel, railroads, and coal were, according to an urban historian, the city's "basic trinity."[7] Philadelphia was a major producer of finished products, ranging from steam engines to carpets. It had an army of skilled or semi-skilled workers, a relatively small percentage of foreign-born inhabitants, and a continuing domination by English, Irish, and German families. Because the city had room, most families lived in small row houses, not multifamily tenements. Complaining of crime, congestion, dirt, and noise, the rich moved to the emerging western suburbs and commuted by the city's extensive horse-car lines. As a boy Stephen gaped at the great railroad terminals, fancy hotels, vast department stores, new skyscrapers, and busy wharves. When he was twelve he enjoyed the Centennial Exposition, the nation's first successful world's fair. Enormous crowds of Americans and Europeans crammed into the city and the exhibition; the year 1876 was an exciting experience that he and other Philadelphians never forgot. The Penrose boys also enjoyed rowing, bicycling, baseball, and tennis. With their family they dined in fancy restaurants, cheered at huge Fourth of July celebrations, heard outdoor music concerts, and drove to the University of Pennsylvania for a variety of cultural offerings.

Stephen Penrose, who was often reminded that he was a member of a significant family, received a stiff code of dress and manners. As he matured he must have learned—as an urban historian summarized—that the goals of middle-class Victorians were "domestic bliss and material comfort." In this smug and uniform society, the professions of law, medicine, and engineering carried more prestige than business careers. The Penrose family pressured Stephen and Charles to choose one of these distinguished professions. Some of Stephen's first cousins, who graduated from Harvard in the 1880s, followed this family advice and became powerful leaders. Boise Penrose went from law and state politics to the United States Senate; Spencer Penrose moved west and made a fortune in Colorado's Cripple Creek mines, becoming a major donor to Colorado College. Stephen Penrose watched these careers and would, one day, turn to each influential cousin on behalf of Whitman College.

No branch of the Penrose family sent its children to public schools, which tended to be overcrowded, rundown, and unsanitary. Clement Penrose placed his intelligent sons in prestigious and demanding private schools, including Philadelphia's William Penn Charter School, which prepared Stephen for college. Under the skilled leadership of Headmaster Richard M. Jones, this school attracted "conservative and cautious parents" from all cultures and suburbs. A large faculty taught a classical curriculum to about a hundred boys crowded into an attractive stone schoolhouse. Jones took pride in the fact that he issued no written rules, for the students had, he boasted, "a healthy sentiment." Penrose enjoyed his studies and remembered that college "had no terrors for me, and I could have a thoroughly good time—which I did."[8]

Clement Penrose then sent both of his sons to Williams College because he greatly admired the aged Professor Mark Hopkins, who still taught a famous course in moral and intellectual philosophy. It is also possible that the father, having himself attended an urban university, agreed with a contemporary who maintained that "Williams College, like the colleges of England, is fortunate in her situation, away from the busy tide, ambitions, and temptations of city life, nestled in the quiet and picturesque hills of Berkshire County, under the guardianship of a conservative faculty, whose Nestor, Dr. Mark

Hopkins, the eminent meta-physician and theologian, has for more than forty years guided and restrained the tide of modern innovations and so-called reforms."[9]

In September 1881 Stephen and Charles traveled by rail to Williamstown, Massachusetts, transferring to the village coach that conveyed them to the college dormitory. Charles, who was a junior at Williams, pointed out to his brother various landmarks, including "Consumption Hill," the high ground that was sometimes contested by struggling freshmen and sophomores.[10] Stephen and eighty-six other men, most of whom came from New York or Massachusetts, made up the freshman class. The Congregational college's new president, Franklin Carter, greeted the 253 students. Carter, a Williams graduate himself, was a brilliant linguist who had taught German at Yale. Historian Frederick Rudolph emphasized that Carter, who was launching his presidency the same year that freshman Stephen Penrose arrived, was the college's "first scholar president." During his long tenure, Carter shaped the institution by hiring brilliant scholars, by introducing limited electives, by delegating authority (he gave the college treasurer more responsibility for internal management), by raising money, by constructing new buildings, by stressing scholarship to students, by delivering fatherly advice to freshmen, and by preaching morality and ethics in chapel sermons. As a college president Penrose would adopt some of Carter's policies and techniques.

But as a student Stephen Penrose was much more interested in classes and activities than in the influential and imaginative Carter administration. Very early in his freshman year, Penrose suggested a cheer which his classmates easily adopted as a bold challenge to sophomores: "Rah, rah, rah, ne-ni-keka," a slogan that translates from the Greek as "We have conquered."[11] Members of the 1885 class, even as old men attending class reunions, still triumphantly shouted their freshman cheer.

Because of his excellent preparation and his ability to learn, Penrose could write that his college work was easy: "After three years of delightful and careless ease, studying enough to keep the good opinion of the faculty ... I had acquired the reputation among my intimate friends of being 'the laziest man in college.'"[12] But Penrose actually studied more than he remembered, since Williams College required students to pass an array of difficult classical classes. It was

William D. Lyman   James F. Eaton

The Williams College connection. Dressed for their senior photographs, William Lyman, James Eaton, Stephen Penrose, and Walter Bratton were distinguished Williams College graduates who

fashionable in his undergraduate years for men to maintain that they had not studied, for as one Williams student stated, "the reputation of a 'grub' is hardly a desirable one."[13] At the end of the first term more than half of the freshmen were academically delinquent, but Penrose received excellent grades and would later become one of four juniors elected to Phi Beta Kappa.

His senior year was the most rewarding, for he finally entered Mark Hopkins' class. Hopkins, then in his eighties, was still a remarkable philosophy professor. Penrose's class, like many predecessors, would select Hopkins as the school's most influential faculty member and would reminisce about his Socratic method. Twenty years after his graduation Penrose described his work with this famous teacher:

> They say we did not learn any philosophy under Dr. Hopkins, and in the technical sense we did not, but we got something better, the strong influence of a noble man, simple as a child in

Stephen B.L. Penrose   Walter A. Bratton

worked to bring the high standards of their alma mater to Whitman College. All but Eaton would spend their careers at Whitman, and all but Lyman would serve as its president.

his intellectual processes, yet weighty, keen, suggestive, and always winning every man in the class to honor righteousness, truth, and reverence.... To the Williams man of that old day he was the college, and while I recall the memories of other teachers, I think of him as the very incarnation of wisdom, unshaken as the eternal hills in his abiding reasonableness, and illustrating best of any man I have ever known the simplicity of greatness.[14]

There were other exciting opportunities in Stephen's senior year, including the selection of some classes. President Carter had established an elective system that was an addition to instead of a replacement for classical courses. Penrose chose biology, which became a favorite class, and Greek. Several honors came to Penrose in his final term: he shared a prize with another senior for having won the most prizes during his collegiate career—in Greek, Latin, German, mathematics, natural science, and rhetoric. He ranked fourth in a graduating class of sixty-two, entitling him to deliver a commencement oration for which he chose the subject of "Personality and Law."

Every semester Penrose became more deeply involved in various extracurricular activities; historian Frederick Rudolph explained that it was possible for him and his classmates to lead strenuous lives because they knew how to organize them. After boarding with his brother in a dormitory for two years, he was "trotted" (this was the term that fraternities used when they entertained prospective members).[15] He joined Delta Kappa Epsilon, the largest of the school's eight fraternities, and enjoyed his Greek experience. Half of his class joined these fraternal organizations, which at Williams, and later at Whitman, would weaken the literary societies. Penrose was a member and debater of the Philologian Society. He was on the editorial staff of a student magazine, was a member of the chess club, and served as president of the college's YMCA. He attended fancy class banquets, including those held at Saratoga, and spoke at one of them. The great majority of Williams men came from wealthy families and could afford these social affairs and other hefty college expenses. In fact, Penrose met only a few students who, like Alexander Jay Anderson, struggled to pay college bills.

Like most of his classmates, Penrose was a member of the college's athletic association. He was active in the bicycle club, played infield on his class baseball team, and qualified for a position on his fraternity's tennis squad. Against class competitors he ran the 220-yard race in twenty-seven seconds and kicked a football 140 feet. As president of the college's baseball association, Penrose scheduled games against Harvard, Dartmouth, Amherst, and others, including professional teams. His position was significant because baseball was the school's most important collegiate game, but he acknowledged that football was rising in popularity and prompting heated disagreement. Faculty, students, alumni, and fans argued over football. Some called it brutal and dangerous; others, including the Williams team, retorted that it was an exhilarating fall game. In 1884 a Williams editor reviewed various arguments over the sport, including the generalization that "the game tends to develop slugging and cheating . . . rather than manly honesty and self-control."[16] The writer predicted that college authorities would prohibit football unless the players themselves insisted upon better rules, improved refereeing, and less emphasis upon college rivalry. This debate over football in New England was similar to the one twenty years later in the Northwest.

Like his classmates, Penrose enjoyed the rhythm of the seasons. In the warm months students organized games, field days, rope pulls, and mountain climbs. During the long cold winter, some of them went tobogganing, but howling winds and treacherous sidewalks meant that most of the students worked out in a primitive gymnasium or remained in their rooms playing whist or chess. Throughout the college calendar the men enjoyed class singing, receptions, or social events in faculty homes.

When seniors gave information for a class magazine,[17] Penrose (called Steve by fellow students) listed his favorites: disputation as a hobby, philosophy as a field of study, William Thackeray as a writer, and Lewis Carroll as a poet. Penrose identified himself as a Presbyterian, a Mugwump in politics, and an advocate of free trade. For social enjoyments he maintained that in summer he liked tennis and flirtation; in winter he preferred sleeping and loafing. According to the information he provided, he was one of the largest men in his class, standing nearly six feet, weighing 173 pounds, and having a big chest and arms.

Stephen Penrose's delightful experience at Williams made him a loyal alumnus, influenced his decision to become an educator, and helped shape his administrative policies when he was a college president. Undoubtedly he would have agreed with a fellow senior who summarized the history of the class of 1885: "we are the largest and strongest class that ever entered this institution; we came in under a new regime; we were the class with which that new regime had to experiment; we were obliged to be the pioneers in many new [policies;] . . . and we proved very unwilling and self-willed subjects, especially when we felt that things were tending back to the 'mother-apron-string' idea."[18] The writer's sentiment about his alma mater was exactly what Penrose would later hope to read from Whitman seniors. "Never will we forget that [Williams] has done very much for us. She has given us her very best: she has broadened and cultivated our minds, she has strengthened and rebuilt our bodies, she has made us largely what we are."

During his senior year, Penrose chose to become a minister. Clement Penrose wanted both his sons to be lawyers, and Charles eventually followed in his father's footsteps, but Stephen refused. Professor Hopkins proposed a compromise, advising Stephen Penrose "on account of his youth, to teach for a few years."[19] The father and son agreed. Thus the young man taught for a year in the Hill School for Boys in Pottstown, Pennsylvania, located about thirty miles from his family home. This first teaching position was valuable, for Penrose served under a remarkable headmaster, John Meigs. A well-educated man, Meigs in 1876 had taken charge of the Hill School and gradually lifted it out of its meager condition by adding students, teachers, buildings, and equipment. Meigs, who respected ordinary as well as gifted boys, taught full-time and handled all administrative matters, including correspondence and discipline. Penrose always praised Meigs and considered himself fortunate to have taught under a master. At the Hill School the young instructor could continue some college interests by playing third base and tennis for its teams and by singing bass in its choir.

Although Penrose enjoyed teaching Greek and Latin to boys, he resigned and accepted a teaching position at his alma mater in 1886 when Carter invited him to return to Williams and instruct lower classmen in Greek and elocution. The inexperienced college teacher probably adopted the teaching methods summarized in the school catalog: "the instruction ... is given by the help of text-books, but these are supplemented by lectures, and the student is made to feel in a more immediate way the influence of the instructor. The examinations on all points presented by lectures are as full and critical as upon those learned from the text-book."[20]

As a faculty member, Penrose found some changes at Williams, including the new gymnasium. Physical training was not compulsory, but students were periodically measured and encouraged to use dumbbells, bars, rings, and other equipment that would develop "special muscles."[21] On the other hand, many things at Williams had not changed. The curriculum for the freshmen and sophomores he instructed was similar to the one he had completed. College problems also remained the same, and now Penrose paid more attention to the college's administration than he had as a student. He watched his colleagues struggle to resolve the perennial problem of student absences by adopting "a system of permitted absences."[22] President Carter explained: "After much deliberation it was finally determined by the faculty to allow a certain number of absences [fifteen] from prayers and recitations without ... penalty."

The faculty also worried about athletics; for example, it sought to establish an appropriate baseball league with colleges, not universities, and to overcome "the evils" connected with its games. The president reported: "The temptation for excitable, untrained minds to profanity and betting and even to worse excess has been repeatedly noted.... Whether the advantages secured to our college by these games outweigh injuries sure to be inflicted on morals, unless some tendencies are checked, is a serious question. The question relates not to the nine, but to the large body to whom the game brings no discipline, only amusement, excitement, temptation, and sometimes demoralization." Penrose, who had experience with the baseball team and thus did not share most of Carter's concerns, would years later join other eastern Washington educators in efforts to resolve the difficulties resulting from intercollegiate athletics.

Late in the spring term the Williams community mourned the death of Professor Mark Hopkins; Penrose was among those who regretted that upcoming senior classes would miss his powerful influence. But the burial of this aged teacher was less painful for Stephen Penrose than the premature death of his brother Charles, who had contracted tuberculosis, unsuccessfully sought recuperation in the West, and died in 1887 at the age of twenty-four.

Penrose's year at Williams was rewarding, and he considered pursuing a professorial career at the college. But he resigned to study for the ministry. President Carter praised him: "He had taught with success ... and leaves us to our great regret."[23] In the fall of 1888 Penrose enrolled at Princeton Theological Seminary. His father agreed to his schooling; perhaps his mother, still enthusiastic about religious missionaries, had successfully pled her son's case. While at Princeton Penrose surprised his parents by announcing that he was transferring in the fall of 1889 to Yale Divinity School. He explained that he was changing schools because he disliked the conservative Presbyterian theology taught at Princeton. Penrose preferred the liberal theology espoused by Mark Hopkins and some others at Williams. His daughter recalled that he simply announced that the "Presbyterian school opened his eyes," and he began a two-year program at Yale.[24]

He studied Congregational theology and in his second year changed his church membership from Presbyterian to Congregationalist. At Yale he became a close friend of a classmate, Frank Shipman, and went to his home for a school vacation. There, in Hartford, Penrose met Mary Shipman. They liked and respected each other and began corresponding. During his 1889 summer vacation he went as an American Home missionary to Colorado and organized a church at Green Mountain Falls. He so enjoyed his western missionary experience that he rejected a call to take the Congregational church at Lenox, Massachusetts, where he had preached as a theology student.

In the spring of 1890 Penrose humorously wrote classmates that he was "as yet uncremated" and that he anticipated moving to a western state. "If missing there," he continued, "search some city's back alleys, and perhaps you will meet me. I am impecunious, immatrimonial, and—well, it is immaterial."[25] Actually Penrose's next move was not as indefinite as he indicated. He later wrote that he and five Yale classmates conceived the idea of organizing a "band" for Home missionary work in order to try out a new plan of cooperative effort. The American Home Missionary Society offered them a wide choice of fields; they decided that the new state of Washington "was the most promising region and that their work would count most for the Kingdom of God."[26]

Penrose arrived in Dayton, Washington, just in time to represent his church at a state Congregational Association meeting in Walla Walla. At this 1890 gathering, Penrose met the church's leadership and received advice on how to rebuild Dayton's congregation. This Congregational church had struggled for thirteen years to find and retain a pastor. Penrose recalled that when he arrived "the church was dead and almost ready for burial. It had six resident members, three of them confirmed invalids and all of them over sixty."[27] The new minister put his enormous energy into building up his church: he preached, taught Sunday school and Christian Endeavor, sang in the choir, did janitorial work, and preached in district schoolhouses. It was exhausting work, and Penrose wrote that "he would lie down on the church floor to rest."[28] From time to time the "Yale band" assembled, shared ministerial techniques, evangelized, and encouraged each other. Penrose regretted that the "Yale band" was breaking up —the members moved to more congenial posts—and that it did not receive young replacements. He was encouraged, however, by the results of his Bible study classes, in which he appealed to the intelligence of listeners. "Ministers heretofore have tried to cram their opinions down people's throats, with the result that many have been disgusted and alienated. To catch trout requires some cunning, and I have learned that it does not do to stand on the bank and shout. The people, like trout, require carefully prepared bait and not noise. I haven't got my creel full yet, but the fish are biting."[29]

While Penrose revived his church he became well acquainted with regional Congregational ministers and with Whitman College. In 1892 the school's trustees elected him to its board, and he was made secretary and a member of the executive committee. This gave him an opportunity to help resolve the school's problems, to become well acquainted with faculty, and to meet students who appreciated his talks and sermons. He told them about seeing Cushing Eells at Williams College. In his history, Penrose explained that Eells was speaking to alumni at commencement. Then a junior, Penrose "happened to be passing by the chapel and was drawn by curiosity to enter and see who was speaking so earnestly.... He did not listen to what the stranger was saying and did not find out until many years after who the speaker was."[30]

Besides serving as an influential Whitman trustee, Penrose played an increasingly important role in the state Congregational Association. At the yearly meetings he delivered sermons and addresses, served on committees, and was chosen as an alternate delegate to a national church meeting in Hartford. This provided him with an opportunity to spend long hours with Mary Shipman. He enthusiastically described to her the physical beauty of rural eastern Washington and compared it favorably to the urban East. Perhaps Penrose also explained how he had discouraged Dayton mothers from attempting to introduce their daughters to him.[31] He had placed a picture of a young woman—it was not Mary—on his dresser, showed it to his landlady, and confided that he was not yet engaged to her. Mrs. Davis, as he anticipated, quickly spread the word to mothers that the young minister had an eastern girl friend and that they were practically engaged. Stephen Penrose informed Mary that he had no interest in or time for squiring local women. Stephen and Mary parted as very good friends, not as an engaged couple. Dozens of their letters to each other would cross the continent; in fact, some of them would cross the Pacific Ocean.

In 1894 the Dayton church was strong enough to support itself, and Penrose felt free to accept an invitation to preach in the Central Union Church in Honolulu. He served much of the summer, enjoyed his environment, but declined an invitation to be the church's permanent pastor. Penrose explained that he found the heat debilitating and warned others only to vacation in Hawaii, not to work there. In mid-September he sailed for San Francisco, where he received a telegram offering him the Whitman College presidency. Penrose replied, "If Whitman can be made a success, a living and growing institution of worth, I shall be willing to put all the energy I have into the work; if this is impossible and it is fated to die, I do not wish to be involved in its funeral. As soon as I conclude definitely as to the likelihood of the one or the other of these alternatives, I will give you official notification of my decision."[32] The former trustee would visit Walla Walla and consult with board members, most of whom he already knew from the time he served with them.

Prior to traveling north from San Francisco, Penrose went south to Stanford University to consult with its president, David Starr Jordan. At that time the university was only three years old. Unlike Whitman College, Stanford had not opened until it had a faculty, buildings, a library, and a solid endowment based upon a valuable land grant. Jordan and his guest strolled the attractive quadrangles; the president pointed out the handsome buildings whose architecture reflected the mission influence. Penrose inquired about the financial contribution of Leland Stanford and his widow and sought advice about college administration. The Stanford president emphasized the need for a competent faculty, praised the late Mark Hopkins, and pointed out that many of the Stanford faculty, like himself, had been educated at Cornell. According to Jordan, a university professor must do original research, but even more important, professors should have character that would "show that virtue and piety really exist."[33] During this memorable day, the two men conversed about such issues as scholarships, tuition (Stanford had not yet imposed it), the need to provide jobs for needy students, and graduation requirements (Stanford with its major and minors practiced an unusual system). At the end of their day, Jordan announced, "Young man, I have only one piece of advice to give you: ... never hold a faculty meeting!"[34] Such meetings, he sighed, only created friction and discord.

Filled with thoughts about Stanford's beautiful campus, impressive faculty, and bright future, Stephen Penrose departed the Santa Clara Valley for the Walla Walla Valley. There an older, mortgaged, unlandscaped school, served by an underpaid faculty teaching in wood-frame buildings awaited his verdict on the offer of its presidency. During his long journey, the traveler must have wondered if this sorry college would ever have even a portion of Stanford's strength and promise. If it were to be so, he must begin his enormous task.

5

Stephen Penrose
And the Establishment of Whitman College
1894 – 1900

Cheering Whitman students greeted Stephen Penrose at the depot, rendered college yells, and begged him to be their president. Faculty members were more subdued but also requested that the young man lead them. College men unhitched the horses, slipped into their traces, and pulled the carriage bearing the visitor up Main Street. Other students, joined by beaming townspeople, waved college banners and rendered cheer after cheer. Penrose assured the celebrants that he would soon decide whether he would accept the presidency. From his previous service as a trustee, he understood the college's wretched condition. He had come to Walla Walla not to evaluate difficulties but to investigate attitudes. Would trustees, professors, students, townspeople, and the state Congregational Association join with him in a determined effort to save Whitman College?

He learned about both general attitudes and specific problems. Wheat had sold at only twenty cents a bushel, thereby restricting local financial contributions to the struggling school. Enrollment was dangerously low, as only forty students in September 1894 had either the tuition money or the confidence in the college to register. The faculty and other employees complained that their meager salaries had not been paid in months. A special committee regretted that it found few donors willing to contribute to the $3,000 owed the faculty. The college treasurer informed Penrose about the $12,000 mortgage and confessed that he had no workable plan to reduce it. Then trustees related yet another problem. A local editor publicly condemned college leaders for violating the school's constitution by taking money from the endowment to cover current expenses. Although the trustees had realized this action would prompt criticism, they argued that they had expended funds from the Eells endowment to keep the school doors open. Somebody had disclosed the use of endowment funds to the Congregational Education Society in Boston (the ACES had become the CES). This group had made timely payments to the school but had not paid the full $4,000 it had recently awarded. Now the CES complained to Whitman trustees that Walla Wallans and Washingtonians had not exhibited the anticipated "spirit of giving."[1] The CES also criticized the decision to dip into the endowment, considered sending a representative to investigate the school's troubled administration, and even threatened to terminate its financial assistance. The CES insisted that it would provide no additional money until the college had accumulated western funds. And Penrose heard still another piece of discouraging news: the committee that failed to match Dr. D.K. Pearsons' money in the spring feared that it could not acquire the money by his December 1895 deadline.

Despite all these discouraging conditions, Penrose informed the board's executive committee on October 5 that he accepted its offer. He would try to do for Whitman College what he had done for Dayton's Congregational church. At the same time he insisted that his presidential salary be cut by $500 to $1,500 and that he would pay his own travel costs as well as the school's printing and postage fees.[2]

Penrose took the position, he explained, because "he was well pleased with the general feelings toward the college," especially the determination and optimism of students and faculty.[3] With promises of assistance from every group, including the state Congregational Association, the new president plunged into his work, assuring faculty members that he "would devote every energy" to build the college and asking them to consider ways to improve their classes.[4] Penrose's decision won considerable local support. An editor, for instance, ruled that the new administrator had the appropriate personality and enthused that "Walla Walla in particular and the whole state are to be congratulated in anchoring Mr. Penrose here for he gave promise of becoming a shining light in educational circles in the Northwest."[5] Some called the thirty-year-old Penrose the youngest college president in the nation; surely he was one of the most optimistic. He predicted that the institution would soon escape poverty, promised Pearsons that a committee could find local money to match his generous offer, and pledged to launch a fund-raising scheme that would provide the college with a solid endowment.

The First Step: Fund Raising

Penrose and college friends argued that the only way to save the college was to raise $150,000 to match the $50,000 offered by D.K. Pearsons. An endowment of $200,000 would give the college a good financial base and would create public confidence. Penrose first sought local funds, explaining that if the college were to remain in Walla Walla then it must immediately collect $50,000. The president, however, did not launch a public drive for money to match Pearsons' offer until he was assured of its success. Like college leaders at Whitman and elsewhere during the twentieth century, Penrose did not announce a public campaign until significant financial pledges had been secured. Penrose, trustees, and friends took nearly two months cultivating donors prior to announcing the endowment campaign.

Although the financial crisis consumed most of his schedule, Penrose taught classes and became better acquainted with faculty and students. The administrator made it clear that he would not have much time to be an educational leader; he must first be a fund raiser. The college was going to have to operate without a president. Once the ship had been anchored, the captain would chart a new course.

Penrose had written philanthropist Pearsons asking whether he retained an interest in Whitman. Pearsons responded that he had an even greater commitment than when he made his initial financial offer. In a series of letters in 1894 Pearsons offered Penrose all kinds of advice. The Chicagoan instructed the president to threaten Walla Wallans that now was their last chance to keep the institution. "Hold the whip over the Walla Walla people," he urged, "strike hard until they shell out. They must endow that college this time or lose it."[6] In another letter he ruled that Whitman needed a $200,000 endowment, and a student body of 400.[7] Such increases, he predicted, would drive up Walla Walla's property values by ten percent. Pearsons advised trustees to seek cash and to accept only productive property, for "Wild lands will not make an endowment." The philanthropist denounced the practice of taking money out of the endowment for current expenses and assumed that once Walla Wallans had determined that they did not want Whitman "to live on and on in a dying condition" then Penrose would find donors. These 1894 letters began a steady stream of correspondence. For about fifteen years the Chicagoan frequently lectured the Walla Wallan on college management. Penrose accepted Pearsons' strictures, in large part, because the college depended upon his money. Pearsons was the closest thing that Whitman then had to a Leland Stanford. (Fortunately, he was not as possessive as the widow Stanford who thought she owned Stanford University and thereby created campus discord.[8] Pearsons was too far away and too busy giving away his money to dictate all policy.)

Before Penrose thought it prudent to announce a local endowment campaign, Pearsons proposed a fresh plan: a national campaign for a $75,000 building that would be a suitable monument to the "brave" Marcus Whitman.[9] Pearsons predicted that such an appeal would receive a "hearty response" and advised: "call together your Congressmen and Governor and your wise patriotic men from all parts of the state and let them have a chance to honor the man who saved Washington and Oregon for our country." Accepting the story that Whitman had indeed saved Oregon, Pearsons assumed that others would also embrace it and would gladly donate to a memorial building honoring a national hero.

Penrose and allies hailed Pearsons' proposal to launch a national campaign for the school's first stone building, but they had to raise $50,000 of the endowment locally. This was a challenge for if the institution could not raise local money, how could it ask for national funds? Penrose optimistically assured Walla Wallans that despite the recent inability to raise money to match Pearsons' offer, it could be collected by Christmas. Thus in early December a committee of prominent citizens led by bankers Levi Ankeny and Miles Moore urged local families to help raise $50,000. The committee's public appeal highlighted Pearsons' attractive three-to-one matching offer, emphasized the need for keeping the college in Walla Walla, explained that the endowment could not be spent, and warned that the community's reputation was at stake, for failure would be an embarrassment. The committeemen said that the school would accept property as well as cash that could be paid in five yearly installments.

Furthermore, donors could make their gifts contingent upon the college securing the full $200,000 in endowment. The committee stressed that Pearsons wanted to build "a $100,000 memorial building to Marcus Whitman as soon as the endowment is secured."[10]

During the winter the college's financial situation improved. Impressed with Penrose's spirit and policies, the CES dispatched money for faculty salaries. But even more important, in January the college received $50,000 in local subscriptions; this was the greatest amount donated since 1866. Although a list of subscribers has not survived, Penrose wrote that Levi Ankeny, Mrs. Dorsey Baker, and Harry Reynolds were major contributors. With this local support as a base, Penrose decided to wage the campaign for the additional $100,000, not in the state, but in the East. The president felt sure that he would have the funds in hand by December. Leaving Professor William Lyman in charge, he departed in January 1895 for Chicago and an eastern appeal. Penrose understood that the future of the college depended on those who had never seen it.

Penrose, like previous Whitman leaders, had concluded that fund raising must center in the Midwest and the East, not the Pacific Northwest. Like Cushing Eells, Alexander Anderson, and James Eaton, he left the campus for eastern campaigning. From his involvement with the state Congregational Association, he realized that it would be impossible to raise $100,000 in Seattle, Tacoma, Portland, and Spokane. This regional church group had enjoyed little success in gathering even modest funds for Whitman; furthermore, the continuing depression discouraged everyone. But the president was also aware that scores of fund raisers from eastern and western schools competed in the East, where there was money and a strong philanthropic tradition. The CES warned him that the New England "field had been trodden by the feet of college solicitors till its whole territory is like one hard-beaten path."[11] To be successful, Penrose needed a compelling message, one that would make his cause stand apart from those of competing colleges. Obviously the best way, if not the only way, was to base his appeal on Marcus Whitman, especially on the assertion that the missionary had saved Old Oregon for the United States. Thus, late in 1894, Penrose prepared both a short pamphlet entitled *The Romance of a College* and an address based upon its major points. Penrose's pamphlet contains a message that he voiced throughout the 1890s. Historian Robert Whitner correctly concluded that this and similar appeals based on Whitman's patriotism brought money "without which Whitman would surely have perished.... That many believed that Marcus Whitman saved Oregon made an enormous difference to Whitman College."[12] Marcus Whitman, in other words, may not actually have saved Oregon, but the Whitman myth saved the college.

Penrose began his pamphlet by recounting the 1830s journey of the Whitmans and the Spaldings to Oregon, a region that the United States and Great Britain owned jointly.[13] Great Britain, however, had actual possession and wanted outright control. Marcus Whitman had learned that the United States was about to surrender its claim, so in the winter of 1842–1843 he made an epic journey through terrible weather to Washington, D.C. and explained to Secretary of State Daniel Webster the "future greatness" of the disputed region. According to Penrose's version of the story, the "indomitable Whitman" arrived just as the Oregon Territory "was about to be traded to Great Britain for a cod-fishery." Although Webster expressed little interest, President John Tyler applauded the missionary's sincerity and his winter ride, promising "that if the accessibility of Whitman's remote region could be demonstrated, it should not be ceded to Great Britain without a question." In 1843, to show that immigrants could reach the Pacific Northwest, Whitman led 1,000 travelers to this promising and productive land. Then Whitman continued "Christianizing the Cayuse" and preparing the way for a future civilization. In 1847 the Cayuse blamed him for a measles epidemic, "surrounded the mission house, slew Whitman and his wife, mutilating their bodies beyond recognition. A few escaped to tell the tale." About twenty years later Cushing Eells founded a school in Whitman's memory. A college grew out of the seminary and stood as a memorial to both Marcus Whitman and Cushing Eells. These two missionaries were, Penrose claimed, "the incarnation of that spirit of Christian fortitude and of enlightened zeal which has animated the missions of the world." Whitman College, serving a region as large as New England and New Jersey combined, was the state's best school. It had many needs, especially an endowment. Penrose hoped that "all intelligent men and women who believe in education as the true basis of citizenship and civilization will desire that Whitman College shall prosper" and would immediately help match Pearsons' offer. The president concluded: "It rests with the people of Washington and of the United States at large to say whether Whitman College, the true monument of a national hero, shall be allowed to perish from the earth."

Penrose's glowing interpretation of the missionary was by no means unique. In early 1895 Republican congressman John L. Wilson, successfully campaigning in Washington for the Senate, advocated that Whitman, "the most heroic figure in the nation's history ... who saved the Pacific Northwest," should be honored by having his statue placed in the capitol's statuary hall. Congregationalists also asserted that Whitman had snatched a rich prize from the grasp of the British lion. Just before Penrose prepared his pamphlet, the state Congregational Association passed a resolution calling Whitman the "martyred benefactor" whose patriotic rides in 1842 and 1843 secured the "entire northwest."[14] Even more important was the publication of Myron Eells' *Father Eells*, a biography of his father. In this as well as his earlier writings, Eells rebutted detractors by maintaining that Whitman saved Oregon. He cited similar interpretations, including Horace E. Scudder's popular textbook, *History of the United States of America*.

Long before Stephen Penrose entered the dispute, there had been a debate over Whitman's actions, especially his travels of 1842 and 1843. The former missionaries, especially Henry Spalding, had argued that Whitman saved Oregon. In the 1880s the Portland *Oregonian*, which complained of a flood of letters on the subject, provided a platform for those who agreed or disagreed with the Whitman-saved-Oregon story. Both sides quoted pioneers. Jesse Applegate, for example, had ridden in 1843 with Whitman and recalled that the missionary had often told him that he had gone East "to prevent his mission board from discontinuing his mission and to furnish more means, that he might be enabled to overcome the influence of the Catholic priests. He never claimed any other purpose."[15] Applegate and another influential pioneer, James Nesmith, insisted that Whitman had not led the 1843 immigration; in fact, they had not met him until he caught up with the wagons along the Platte River. These two and other pioneers insisted that they had never heard a single immigrant state that he had moved to Oregon because of Whitman's influence. Applegate called Whitman a bigot and argued that Thomas Hart

Benton, not the missionary, had inspired Oregon's settlement. In 1886 historian Frances Fuller Victor, writing in Bancroft's *History of Oregon*, rejected the Whitman-saved-Oregon interpretation. Thus many faulted the controversial story.

Penrose had probably heard much of the criticism prior to reading the Eells biography, a book that acknowledged detractors. The president knew that he, too, would be accused of perpetuating a myth. Nevertheless, he argued the Whitman-saved-Oregon story because he admired Marcus Whitman and because its repetition provided an opportunity to secure eastern money and thereby save the college. There was still another reason why he emphasized the missionary. Such eastern supporters as D.K. Pearsons and Chicago editor Oliver W. Nixon repeatedly urged him to instruct citizens about the nation's indebtedness to the heroic Whitman.

The president understood that only a few westerners disputed the Whitman myth and that America was awash in legends perpetuated by such poets as Henry Wadsworth Longfellow and by scores of historical writers who mythologized such figures as Columbus, Revere, Washington, Jackson, Lee, Lincoln, and Custer. Americans wanted to believe in heroism and patriotism, and they generally dismissed the scholarship that demolished popular myths. As a perceptive easterner, Penrose knew that the Whitman-saved-Oregon episode would arouse admiration and pride among the class of citizens he had known in Philadelphia, Williamstown, and Hartford. The missionary's "amazing history" was "a basis of appeal to patriotic people."[16] By the end of 1895 many Americans had come to believe that a Protestant and patriotic easterner had saved a western empire and had died a martyr's death.

Early in the twentieth century some eastern scholars denounced the Whitman legend, thereby arousing skepticism among some thoughtful citizens, and a few expressed doubts to Penrose. By then it was no longer necessary to stress a mythical Marcus Whitman; college leaders could shift to other themes, such as the accomplishments and value of the institution. But Penrose had repeated the story about Whitman so many times that he had become captured by it. He never changed his basic story.

As his Great Northern train steamed eastward through communities suffering from both the cold weather and the depression of the

1890s, Penrose considered his situation. In his later history he admitted that "He had made no study of the history or science of education, had had neither experience nor training in the art of raising money.... He had the advantage of youth, of unflagging courage, of a strong religious faith, and of a sound though brief teaching experience. He had been well educated as education went in those days, and had learned while a Home missionary pastor to speak effectively in public and to rely upon himself while taking counsel with other people."[17]

In 1895 Penrose saved the institution by raising money, publicizing the college, making friends, placating the CES, and employing two skilled canvassers. His first stop in this 1895 campaign was the Chicago *Tribune* building, for calls upon philanthropist Pearsons and journalist Nixon. Penrose often recounted his initial meeting with D.K. Pearsons, "a tall, handsome, and bright eyed old man."[18] The seventy-five-year-old Chicagoan immediately dominated the conversation by delivering "a tirade upon the financial ignorance of colleges, upon college football which he detested, and upon the inadequacies of college presidents whom he had known." Suddenly Pearsons instructed the young man to return to his office tomorrow and bolted to the train station. At the second meeting Pearsons resumed his lecture, but suddenly he relaxed and asked questions. A mutual respect and friendship grew out of this conversation, which would have enormous ramifications for Whitman College.

Enthusiastic about the school and pleased with Penrose's dedication, Pearsons talked about the eastern campaign, especially the opportunity to solicit funds in numerous Congregational churches in Chicago. (With more than fifty Congregational churches—a greater number than there were even in Boston—Chicago in the 1890s was a national center of Congregationalism.) Pearsons took control of the crucial Chicago effort by introducing Penrose to wealthy men, arranging for him to give talks, and urging the Congregational Ministers Union of Chicago to organize an effort to preach on Marcus Whitman as a patriot and missionary. The ministers established Sunday, March 10, as "Whitman Day." In one of Chicago's largest Congregational churches an authority talked about the missionary and used a stereopticon to illustrate his points. Although the speaker made some horrendous historical errors, especially the assertion that the Nez Perce Indians had killed the Whitmans, his use of illustrations

Dr. D.K. Pearsons of Chicago donated large (and timely) sums of money for Whitman's endowment and buildings. The philanthropist consistently provided President Penrose with both advice and emotional support.

proved effective. The crowd even applauded an illustration of Whitman College.[19] Many churches far from Chicago also participated and collected money to honor Marcus Whitman.

A few days later, Dr. Frank W. Gunsaulus addressed the Chicago Congregational Club on the subject "The Place of Whitman in History." The speaker argued that Marcus Whitman was more important to the Pacific Northwest than John Harvard had been to the Northeast. The minister even ranked Whitman with Washington and Lincoln. The Chicago press, including the *Tribune, Post, News, Inter-Ocean,* and *Advance,* all endorsed struggling Whitman College. The *Times-Herald,* for example, printed parts of Penrose's pamphlet, and also enthused that the college's football team had removed sagebrush from the mass grave of Waiilatpu and planted grass and wild flowers. According to one interpretation, "In Whitman's life and death, self-sacrifice, and martyrdom, are all the materials for an epic; they await the coming of another Homer."

Excited by this extensive publicity, Penrose said that "Chicago has never been as much interested in any cause outside of its own borders as it is now in the movement to make Whitman College the worthy memorial of a national hero."[20] The president wrote to Walla Wallans that Chicago leaders appreciated the fact that they had made a $50,000 contribution to the college during "the hardest time which ever befell the country."

The Congregational ministers aided Penrose, and D.K. Pearsons was his most important ally, but Oliver Nixon, editor of the Chicago *Inter-Ocean*, also lent significant assistance. Nixon was cheerful and sympathetic; his calm demeanor contrasted sharply with Pearsons'. He fully shared the philanthropist's enthusiasm for Marcus Whitman and the college. In 1850 Nixon had traveled to the Pacific Northwest; during his short stay he had learned about the missionary. After he became a Chicago journalist, Nixon wrote a story praising the Whitmans every November 29, the anniversary of the massacre. Nixon aided Penrose by writing newspaper stories designed to promote his fund raising, by introducing him to editors, and by providing warm encouragement. The editor promised financial assistance through the sale of his book, *How Marcus Whitman Saved Oregon*. In his preface Nixon emphasized "the heroism and Christian patriotism of the man who rendered great and distinguished service to his country, which has never been fully appreciated or recognized."[21] Nixon admitted that he depended upon his memory, not scholarly research, and that the book had no claims to "high literary excellence." The manuscript had been rushed into print. The rambling narrative contained many stories and themes as well as material Penrose had brought East, including photographs. The author solicited donations: "If Whitman College is to be the Yale and Harvard and Chicago University of the Far West, it must meet with a generous response from liberal givers."[22] Penrose was correct that the Whitman story would attract attention, and he insisted that this campaign book "did more than anything else to develop public interest."[23] Nixon's hasty book went through several editions; according to biographer Clifford M. Drury it was the "most popular book on Whitman of that generation."[24]

This Chicago campaign was the highlight of Penrose's 1895 fund raising, but he did not linger in Chicago. In late January he traveled to Germantown and asked friends and relatives to give money to Whitman; even his grandmother promised $500. Then he dashed north to Boston for important conversations with the Congregational Educa-

Chicago editor Oliver W. Nixon enthusiastically supported missionary Marcus Whitman and the college honoring his memory. Nixon's biography, How Marcus Whitman Saved Oregon, *helped publicize the college and prompted historical debate from one coast to the other.*

tion Society. Whitman badly needed the continuing help of this institution. The secretary of the CES, John A. Hamilton, had been critical of the college's administration in 1894 but wrote to Penrose early in 1895 that the CES directors applauded his energetic leadership. They concluded that the college was "coming out of darkness into light, and out of chaos into order."[25] Penrose received particular praise for "beginning at Jerusalem," in other words finding local money before seeking eastern help.

Although Hamilton praised Penrose's work, he disapproved of Pearsons' Chicago campaign for Whitman because it threatened his society's annual solicitation. Hamilton sympathized with the "Whitman movement" and congratulated Penrose for arousing Pearsons' enthusiasm, but he warned that the CES would be "in a desperate plight if all monies in the wake of that movement are swept in for Whitman's endowment."[26] Hamilton had recently urged his Chicago representative, who feared that Penrose might "camp" in his field, to stand firm and "not to quail before the coming Whitman storm."[27] Hamilton gently reminded Pearsons in a letter that the society had to collect Chicago money for the beleaguered Yankton College.

In his Boston meeting with Penrose, Hamilton related these concerns, talked about the society's efforts in Chicago—he called it "a polygot good and wicked city"—and cautioned that the CES must not offend Pearsons.[28] Penrose agreed with the secretary that the CES should conduct a campaign in Chicago before "Whitman Day," and Hamilton promised that his society would pay its annual $4,000 allotment because Whitman had raised $50,000 in Walla Walla. He insisted, however, that the school's trustees pledge never again to use endowment money for current expenses. Penrose promised that he would secure such a pledge and that the college would pay back the money taken from the endowment. The president did not know the exact sum that had been expended but later discovered that expenses had consumed about half of the $7,000 endowment. Penrose asked about campaigning in New England; Hamilton told him that the CES would not permit a college it aided to seek funds in this region without permission. The two men agreed that Penrose would do some campaigning in this section but that an experienced CES field secretary, John Maile, would be the college's New England solicitor, concentrating on Connecticut. This appointment meant that Penrose would have more time to seek help in Pennsylvania, New York, Ohio, and Illinois. However, Penrose did make one New England stop that did not require the consent of the CES. In February he went to Hartford, where he and Mary Shipman announced their engagement.

In March and April Penrose canvassed the middle Atlantic states and then returned to the Midwest, speaking in such places as Cleveland, Peoria, Beloit College, and Knox College. He sought professional advice from college presidents, especially University of Chicago president William Rainey Harper, a former Yale classmate of Penrose. The noted Chicago educator discussed the responsibilities he faced as his institution's first president. Penrose probably recognized that few problems of a prestigious, urban school were exactly like those of little-known and remote Whitman.

In churches, homes, halls, and editorial offices of the Midwest, Penrose told the story of the missionary and the college. He distributed his pamphlet, illustrations, and books by Myron Eells and Oliver Nixon. Penrose consistently made a favorable impression. He looked like a college president: his hair was turning a premature gray, he wore a neatly trimmed mustache, he peered through pince-nez, and he had grown portly. His energy, dedication, intelligence, voice, and concern for others had made him popular in Williamstown and Dayton and now made an impression on those who heard his appeals for

Whitman College. Rarely did he seem discouraged; in mid-April he estimated that he had raised $50,000 and predicted that he would have $100,000 in hand by September 1895.[29]

While Penrose pursued funds in the Midwest, he learned that Professor Lyman had written to the CES that he and his colleagues suffered from lack of pay and begged the society to make an additional appropriation. Secretary Hamilton asked Penrose to aid "these poor needy friends" by seeking a donation for current operating expenses.[30] The president replied that he would borrow $12,500 for the college to cover all debts, including back salaries. At a May meeting, Penrose nervously told D.K. Pearsons that the college had to meet its debts and that he hoped that a friend would lend him $12,500 at a rate lower than the eight percent the school was paying. Pearsons roared, "Nonsense.... It's not a business proposition. Nobody would lend you the money." The philanthropist lectured the chastened Penrose "upon the heinousness of all debts in general and of this debt in particular."[31] Then to the young man's surprise, Pearsons shouted that he would lend the money. Penrose gave his personal note for $12,500 at six percent. Opposed to such loans, the financier made an exception because he concluded that Penrose "was designed by a good Providence for this Whitman work."[32]

Prior to leaving for Whitman's commencement, the president and the benefactor decided that the school not only needed John Maile as its New England representative, it also required another experienced solicitor to work the Midwest. Pearsons and Nixon highly recommended Virginia Dox, who eagerly accepted the appointment because she admired Marcus and Narcissa Whitman. Thus the college employed two able fund raisers; both would play important roles in the late 1890s.

Meanwhile, Nixon publicized the college by leading a party of eastern newspapermen to the Walla Walla Valley. Arriving in a private railroad coach the journalists visited the mission, the college, and the town. In late May Nixon spoke in Spokane and Walla Walla, stressing the Whitman-saved-Oregon theme. He predicted great things for the college, lauded its president, and advised students: "talk Whitman, preach Whitman, and sing Whitman songs. Show to the world the grand character of the man that pettifogging historians have endeavored to hide."[33]

Penrose returned home in early June and summarized his eastern campaign: "My chief work was in getting the story of Marcus Whitman before the people and presenting the need of this great country for a first-rate college. . . . I knew that ninety-nine out of every hundred in the United States never had heard of Marcus Whitman, nor knew that he was a great national hero, and so I decided that it was necessary . . . to conduct an educational campaign and teach a new chapter in American history, the founding of the Northwest."[34] He boasted that every eastern editor he contacted had published a story.

Back at home the local newspapers praised Penrose's work and his character. A local editor correctly emphasized that Penrose cherished the missionary "with the profoundest respect and reverence."[35] Walla Wallans praised the president for publicizing the city and rebuilding the college with the energy of a football captain. An editor called him a "hustler"; others praised his skill and devotion.

Exhausted by his travel, the president found little rest during commencement week. He helped organize the ceremonies that honored five seniors, preached the baccalaureate sermon, delivered his inaugural address, prepared his first presidential report to the trustees, and attended long trustee meetings. In his inaugural address he praised the missionary: "The nation will never forget, when the stars and stripes are waving before its eyes, that three of the stars of that flag are due to Marcus Whitman, and the red of that flag may well stand for the outpoured blood with which he baptized this country, in the name of God and of the United States."[36] The president then elaborated on goals for the college and the community. The large crowd seated in the city's opera house applauded his inspiring words.

While Penrose's inaugural address considered the future, his report to the trustees stressed the immediate past. Rarely would a Whitman president accomplish so much in nine months. His financial report was most important: he had led an effort that raised $50,000 in local money, convinced the CES to give $4,000, obtained an unspecified but significant amount of money in his eastern campaign, and borrowed $12,500 at six percent from Pearsons. He stressed that Pearsons was an eager friend, that Nixon had publicized the college, and that his own efforts had gotten the Whitman story "in almost all the leading newspapers of the country. From the seed thus sown an abundant harvest ought to be reaped."[37] The school's financial situation had improved tremendously, he boasted, from what it had been in the gloomy fall of 1894. The president reminded trustees that they must be responsible for the school's financial management, including the establishment of a committee to invest the endowment that would total $200,000. He urged them to employ Thompson Coit Elliott as a full-time treasurer. In Penrose's first year, school finances had been managed by its part-time treasurer who shared the responsibility with an overworked faculty member. That system failed. Following Franklin Carter's lead at Williams and the advice he received from other presidents, Penrose sought to shift the financial management from himself to a full-time treasurer; this would provide more time for fund raising and other presidential responsibilities.

His report praised the loyal faculty for its teaching and listed the fall staff, including Louis Anderson, who would be rehired as professor of Greek. Penrose asked that Nixon receive an honorary doctorate "for his eminent services in the cause of history and education."

Impressed by all that the young president had accomplished, the trustees took the actions he recommended. They balked at only one part of his report, a proposal to move the college to a new site at Fort Walla Walla. Penrose had visited the War Department and had learned unofficially that it wanted to abandon the post and move the garrison to Spokane. Penrose told trustees that he wished to help push a bill through Congress that would "transfer the property to the College in recognition of the services of Marcus Whitman to the United States."[38] He thought Congress would agree and that the college could build "a superb campus, equal to that of any institution." The buildings at the fort could serve until the school built permanent ones. In other words, he proposed a way to acquire an attractive and free campus site! Walla Wallans, however, were jealous of Spokane's rise to regional economic domination and loudly protested the fort's closing. The garrison generated income; Walla Wallans, including Whitman's trustees, wanted both the established fort and the emerging college. Penrose understood but rejected the view of residents. He was not yet willing to abandon his promising plan, and he quietly waited for the army to close the site.

Penrose later listed four problems encountered in his early administration: "First, that of securing the Pearsons endowment, indispensable to the life of the institution. Second, the making of a college faculty, which would lift the institution to a higher academic level. Third, the securing of additional campus and adequate buildings for the college when it should begin to grow ... and, fourth, the invigoration of the life of the college with a new spirit and new ideals."[39] By early 1900 the president had met these problems; the school's foundation was in place.

Penrose considered the raising of the endowment money to be his most important responsibility, for such a fund would build confidence and provide for current expenses, scholarships, and faculty salaries. Although he had predicted that the $150,000 in endowment to match Pearsons' offer would be in hand by September 1, 1895, the campaign dragged into early 1898. The continuing depression, the competition with other college fund raisers, and the inability to collect local subscriptions hampered solicitors. To raise money Penrose spent much of 1895 and 1896 in the East; in the following year he concentrated on the Pacific Northwest, searching for funds as well as for students and friends. The long struggle sometimes frustrated him. His extensive travel wearied him, kept him from home, and prevented him from addressing other college problems, especially the construction of permanent stone buildings.

Always optimistic, D.K. Pearsons was anxious to help Penrose complete his endowment canvass, and he again played a crucial role. Chicago was the center of the school's eastern effort, so the philanthropist pressured its Congregational ministers and Congregational club. On June 30, 1895, many Congregational churches in or near Chicago celebrated "Whitman Day," sending donations for the martyr's school. One Congregational minister favorably compared the missionary with more famous men and groups. Paul Revere rode only one night and Whitman rode for a year; the Pilgrims had each other's courage, but Whitman "was alone, sharing his secret purpose with none lest his effort might be betrayed too soon," and the minutemen at Concord and Lexington fought "for their firesides and their sacred honor," but Whitman struggled for others. This speaker's history was unconventional, and so was his geography when he described the 1843 wagons as rolling "down the western slopes of the Blue Mountains into the beautiful valley of the Willamette."[40]

One Congregationalist acknowledged that the college had been assisted by the large churches, but he thought it was more remarkable that "there have been small remittances from Bohemian, Welsh, and German as well as English churches—and Whitman was preached in all these languages."[41] Some Christian Endeavor groups also donated a few dollars.

The Chicago Congregational Club hosted 450 guests for a Thanksgiving banquet, where Penrose, the president of Pomona College, and others lauded Marcus Whitman. The club collected $1,000. Meanwhile, Pearsons continually pushed the CES to lead in the drive for Whitman's endowment. Telling its officials that Marcus Whitman was "the greatest man of the century," he argued that the CES should stress the missionary in all its funding efforts in order to place the organization "in the patriotic fold."[42] As an experienced businessman Pearsons concluded that the Whitman story was actually the CES's "great opportunity of the century." The philanthropist told the CES that when ministers asked him for money he turned them down unless they had preached on Whitman, that his future relationship with their organization depended upon its assistance to Penrose, and that he worked harder for Whitman than for any other college. One CES administrator complained that Pearsons was "so full of Whitman that he is rather blind to the other lines of work."[43] The CES refused to give the college more than $4,000 for annual 1889 operating expenses, but it paid the salary of fund-raiser Maile and guaranteed a $25,000 payment from his efforts.

Pearsons assisted in still other ways. He favored Whitman over other schools trying to meet operating costs. Pacific University, for example, in its unsuccessful request to the philanthropist reported that its investment property returned only a small income and that its faculty needed a year's back pay. One visitor to Pearsons' offices found it crowded with "hungry presidents," some of whom had $300,000 endowments.[44] A few desperate college leaders even informed the philanthropist that he should aid them and abandon such weak schools as Whitman. But Pearsons rejected them "in great sorrow" and feared that he was growing "ugly."[45]

Although Whitman had not raised the entire $150,000 by the December 1895 deadline, Pearsons gave $25,000 because Penrose had accumulated more than half of the matching money and because he wanted the college to have an endowment to earn funds for operating expenses. About two years later Pearsons gave the remaining

$25,000; he delayed because he wanted to force Walla Wallans into paying their subscriptions.

In 1896, looking for additional ways to assist Penrose, Pearsons returned the $750 interest on Whitman's $12,500 note and then gave Mary Shipman the note signed by Penrose, explaining, "I give the Note to you as a wedding present, and also as a sample of the faith and courage of your future Husband."[46] Pearsons advised Penrose to raise $20,000 in his bride's hometown, take a short three-day honeymoon, and then solicit endowment funds with his wife.

As Penrose traveled long distances seeking endowment funds, he received the assistance of Nixon, Maile, and Dox. Nixon wrote letters to the Baker family and to Levi Ankeny, requesting them to help Whitman financially. In a letter to Mary Penrose, he recommended that she ask western women for donations. He advised Penrose to help defeat Democratic presidential candidate William Jennings Bryan. If the apostle of free silver won the 1896 election, Pearsons and Nixon warned, it would delay the nation's economic recovery and thereby frustrate Whitman's fund raisers.

For two years John Maile served as Whitman's principal canvasser in New England and New York. A Civil War veteran, a graduate of Oberlin Theological Seminary, and an American Home missionary, Maile also admired Marcus Whitman. Maile, who would later write a stirring account of his experience in Andersonville Military Prison, believed that he and the missionary had both served and sacrificed for church and country. By early 1897 he curtailed calls in the smaller communities and established himself in New York City. The CES paid him and received his reports; however, Maile wrote directly to Penrose about his strategy and success. The fund raiser designed an interesting letterhead that identified him as field secretary for Whitman's memorial fund and that carried quotations by prominent Protestants, including Josiah Strong, the noted author of *Our Country*. Strong maintained that "Whitman saved Oregon to the United States; the East may help to save it to Christian civilization by giving a worthy endowment to the college which bears the hero's name."[47] To avoid charges of denominationalism Maile did not identify Strong as a Congregationalist, but other supporters quoted on the letterhead were identified as Baptist and Presbyterian. Maile was unwilling to use the word Congregational because "to put the denominational idea first and foremost is to create hindrance and invite failure."[48] He would discuss Congregationalism only if a potential donor asked about the school's church affiliation. Penrose heartily approved, informing Maile that to get wider support he had encouraged the establishment of an "Episcopal Scholars" fund at Whitman.[49]

Maile carefully prepared for his calls on wealthy men, including John D. Rockefeller and J.P. Morgan. Penrose instructed Maile to show Rockefeller the college catalog because it was "evidence of thorough, honest work." This evidence made little impact, however. Unable to find the full $25,000 anywhere in the Northeast, Maile complained about the "continued business depression" and resigned in May 1897. He left his difficult labors and became the American Home Missionary Society superintendent of North Dakota.[50] Penrose applauded Maile for "the noble campaign" in difficult times and invited him to visit Whitman, "which you have helped build up."[51]

Maile's resignation came during a dispute between Penrose and the CES leadership, especially with field secretary Frank Ferguson. In 1895 the CES had pledged $25,000 for Whitman if it agreed to keep its fund raisers out of New England. After Maile's failure to secure $25,000 in 1896, the society promised to continue its effort and to pay six percent interest on this unpaid balance. Beset by money problems in the prolonged depression (in 1897 Pearsons declared that the CES was broke) the society tried to provide funds for all the colleges and academies on its approved list. Ferguson and other CES leaders concluded that Penrose failed to understand the society's financial difficulties. They voiced other complaints: Virginia Dox unfairly sought money through letters to New Englanders; Whitman did not properly credit the society with all the funds it collected; and the college should base its appeal on the desperate need for operating expenses, not the endowment.

Then Penrose expressed his grievances with the CES. He argued that Ferguson, who had once faulted President James Eaton's gloomy reports, was indifferent to Whitman's future, that the society had not helped Maile wage an energetic Whitman campaign in New England, and that the CES had not given the full $4,000 awarded for the 1895–1896 school year, thereby increasing the college's debt. Whatever the merits of the disagreements, which were expressed in numerous letters, Penrose in September 1897 removed his college from the society's list, complaining that its proposed financial agreement "would effectually cripple the college in its future growth."[52] Penrose knew that this separation was significant because the CES had supported Whitman College for about fifteen years. But he concluded that the school had outgrown this relationship and accused the CES leaders of lacking enthusiasm for Whitman.

During the controversy both sides curried Pearsons' favor. He attempted to mediate. The philanthropist urged Penrose not to fret over the issue and to learn about the business world from his clash with Ferguson, but he also pressured the CES to help conclude Whitman's endowment campaign. In 1895 Ferguson resigned to become president of Pomona College; Pearsons joked that he wished "to make Southern California into the Athens of America."[53] Penrose now competed with President Ferguson for Pearsons' financial assistance. The philanthropist provided critical assistance to both presidents but was more generous with Penrose. (It probably came as no surprise to Penrose that Ferguson's brief, stormy administration led Pomona trustees to request his resignation in 1901.) In the meantime, Penrose continued his disagreement with the CES over the promised money. In 1909, exasperated by the quarreling, Pearsons finally presented Whitman with $9,100, a figure that he declared was what the society still owed.

The break with CES meant that Virginia Dox, who shared Penrose's zeal for the college, would replace the society in seeking a harvest in the New England field. While Maile and Penrose conducted typical fund-raising campaigns that featured calls upon prominent people and appearances before wealthy congregations, Dox waged a much different one. To find endowment money, she enthusiastically praised Whitman to ordinary citizens in their midwestern homes, stores, and churches. Penrose later recalled: "She begged for gifts, large or small, and by her thrilling oratory as well as by personal persistence she completed the raising of the fund within the given time."[54] Because of her success in the Midwest, Penrose wanted Dox, and not the lethargic CES, to canvass New England.[55] In 1897 she moved into that region and reported her tactics. (Virginia Dox's work is discussed in Appendix B.)

Mary Penrose: Stephen's Major Supporter

Penrose not only sought money, he also taught classes and administered the college. In 1897, in the middle of his hectic schedule, he went to Hartford for his marriage. Mary Deming Shipman Penrose, like many presidential wives at Whitman and other colleges, would be a tremendous asset. She shared Stephen's dreams, joys, and frustrations. Their union turned out to be as successful as both anticipated.

In many ways Mary's background was similar to her husband's; perhaps that explains their attraction. Her parents, like his, enjoyed wealth and status; valued education, church, and missionary activity; and rendered public service. Both fathers were well educated, staunch Republicans, and respected judges; the capable mothers were equally concerned with social reform.

Judge Nathaniel Shipman, Mary's father, was the seventh generation of his family to live in New England. A brilliant student, he graduated Phi Beta Kappa from Yale in 1848, and later his alma mater awarded him an honorary doctorate. He studied law, helped establish the Republican Party in Connecticut, served a term in the state legislature, and early in the Civil War became the governor's executive secretary. In 1873 President Ulysses S. Grant appointed him judge of a United States district court; in 1892 he was elevated to a United States circuit court of appeals. Shipman was a director of several insurance companies and served as an officer in organizations concerned with the insane, deaf, and juveniles. In 1859 he had married Mary Caroline Robinson, who came from another distinguished Hartford family. She was a founder and diligent worker in the Union for Home Work in Hartford, an organization that provided working mothers with day-care nurseries. The Shipmans had five children; three sons and Mary reached maturity. She was born in 1868 and was reared in a loving, caring family. As Mary assessed her family, her mother "was the most perfect lady ever. Not strong in health, but strong in spirit, always thinking of others ... delicate, humorous, wise." Nathaniel Shipman was "wise, just, sane, and clement" and taught her to "look always at the side of the other person." She learned much about the law from her father's discussion of cases. Her brothers gave her "the masculine viewpoint and training."

Mary Shipman received a solid education that would serve her well as a president's wife. She attended a public grammar school that enrolled the children of the wealthy and of the slums. Because she contracted lice—not bad ideas—from her poor schoolmates, her mother moved her to a prestigious private school, Hartford Female Seminary, where she developed a lifelong interest in Latin.[56] After four years in this school her parents—who probably responded to their democratic sentiments—placed Mary in a public high school. At this coeducational institution, she met a variety of young men and women. A friendship with classmate Harriet Cheney would later be rewarding to both in eastern Washington. The high school provided a solid faculty; Mary concluded that "my three years there were probably the most profitable in study of any of my rather checkered school life." But she was transferred again, for her mother insisted that she spend her last year at an institution that had influenced her—Miss Porter's School at Farmington, Connecticut. In her famous school for girls, Miss Sarah Porter stressed character as well as scholarship. Mary summarized the experience: "the biggest thing [I] learned was that all opportunity—wealth, learning, gifts of any sort—are a trust to be used in the service of others." Mary had heard her parents and fiancé express similar sentiments.

After completing her formal schooling, she continued to study modern languages. Mary Shipman participated in a women's club that enjoyed various teachers, including Mark Twain.

Her diary for 1886 and her summary of an 1888 outing in the Adirondacks provide insights to her character. She was devoted, lively, dependable, honest, intelligent, fun-loving, conversational, and concerned about her tendency to gain weight. Mary respected the devoted, lively Irish domestics who helped rear her. Like other young women in her economic class, she was excused from kitchen duties and never acquired cooking skills.

Her two older brothers attended their father's university and took her to New Haven for special school dances. They brought classmates, including Stephen Penrose, to their home. One visitor wrote, "the Shipmans are a delightful family; they take life so as to get the most out of it."[57] For Mary, visits to New Haven and visitors to her home provided insights into college life. Her schooling and that of family members prepared her for a life in higher education.

She traveled with her father to New York City, shopping in fashionable stores and dining in famous restaurants. In 1893 Mary and her older brother, Frank, thoroughly enjoyed a six-month tour of Europe. Unfortunately, Mary destroyed her love letters to Stephen Penrose, letters which detailed their lives and aspirations, including the building of a useful western educational institution.

On June 18, 1896, they married in the bride's home.[58] Frank Shipman, who had introduced the couple while he attended Yale Divinity School, performed the ceremony. Other members of both families participated in the wedding. The Reverend Edward L. Smith, a former member of the "Yale band" and Walla Walla's Congregational minister and a Whitman booster, served as best man.

Following a brief honeymoon in Maine they traveled the East Coast as Penrose resumed his fund raising. It must have been difficult for the Shipmans to bid farewell to their daughter as she and her husband departed for Walla Walla. But they took solace in the fact that Mary was helping him establish a Congregational college and that the couple promised to return home every summer. The newlyweds stopped in Chicago, where Stephen introduced his wife to Dr. and Mrs. Pearsons and Oliver Nixon. Mary impressed all three. D.K. Pearsons took a great interest in this sprightly, intelligent twenty-eight-year-old woman, praising her for going into western missionary work. He compared her with Narcissa Whitman; undoubtedly his continuing support of Whitman College resulted in part from his admiration for Mary Penrose.

The Penroses arrived in Walla Walla on September 9. Two days later they were guests at a reception, where a cavalry orchestra played while 500 Walla Wallans welcomed and congratulated them.[59] The new bride enjoyed this western hospitality. When asked about her thoughts of Walla Walla, she explained that while traveling across the dreary sections of the West her husband had reassured her that Walla Walla was beautiful, green, and well-watered.

A few days after the reception, Mary rushed to College Hall, where Stephen skillfully directed a bucket brigade that fought a roof fire.[60] Everyone praised his cool action and the fire department's new chemical engine for saving the building, the library, and nearby wooden buildings. Soon afterwards, the Penroses traveled to Tacoma where they attended a meeting of the Congregational Association.

The newlyweds closely followed the hotly contested state election of
1896 and voiced their displeasure over Republican defeats. Thus
Mary's early introduction to the West included exposure to western
culture and politics.

Publicizing the College

At this Tacoma Congregational Association meeting and many others subsequently held in the state, Penrose sought to win support and
attract publicity. Mary assisted by serving as a church delegate and
committee member. To help further publicize the college, Penrose
launched the Whitman College *Quarterly* and pushed the celebration
of the fiftieth anniversary of the Whitman massacre. Penrose only had
time and energy to write and edit the *Quarterly* for three years. It
carried school news, requests for assistance to Whitman College, and
missionary history, including essays on Marcus Whitman, Cushing
Eells, and Henry Spalding. Penrose boasted that his publication was
"the only historical magazine published in the Northwest."[61] The
Quarterly—paid for by a fund to cover the endowment campaign—
was distributed to friends and potential donors. Pearsons warned
that Whitman was too weak to provide "a free lunch"; the president
eventually agreed and charged a token $1 annual subscription fee.

In the first issue, editor Penrose provided a biography of Whitman
longer than *The Romance of the College*. Again he lauded the heroic
Whitman and now maintained that the Indians scalped him and his
wife. (The writer quickly acknowledged his error; others, however,
continued to make it. In 1938 Richard L. Neuberger, for example,
provided a sensational account: "Narcissa's blond scalp . . . dangled
against the greasy thigh of a Cayuse warrior.")[62] Penrose also explained in the *Quarterly* that the college's "primal purpose is to promote that Christian education which shall unite the resolute purpose
which characterized Marcus Whitman with the lofty consecration of
Cushing Eells. . . . Its aim is to give the most thorough education
which it is possible for a student of the Northwest to receive, and to
permeate that education with the finer spirit of Christ."[63] Penrose
promised that "The College will not undertake more than it can accomplish. It has no University aspirations."[64] He also assured donors
that a finance committee "composed of the most experienced and the

most conservative men in the community," carefully invested endowment money.[65] In 1897 the *Quarterly* requested more mining stocks (these shares "may mean little or they may mean a great deal"[66]), library books, contributions for the Spencer F. Baird Professorship of Natural Science, and the establishment of a department of economics and social science. With the addition of this new department the school could offer "economic education" that was needed because of "the political unrest and uncertainty of the present."[67] Penrose was actually appealing to wealthy Republicans to establish a department that would rebut the free-silver argument that Bryan and Democrats had successfully advocated in carrying the state in 1896. In other issues of the *Quarterly* Penrose listed more conventional needs, including buildings, scholarships, and scientific equipment.

In 1897 Penrose became very involved with a project to honor the missionaries and to publicize the college. For years, some residents in the Pacific Northwest had supported the idea of building a Whitman monument; in the spring of 1897 a committee led by prominent Pacific Northwest citizens decided to raise money for both a mausoleum encased with a marble top and a shaft to be placed on high ground near the gravesite. Dedication ceremonies would be held on November 29 and 30, the fiftieth anniversary of the massacre. Special trains brought visitors from Portland and Pendleton, including Congregationalists coming to a state meeting in Walla Walla. On Monday evening, November 29, the Whitman College board of trustees presented a program in the opera house to "an eager mass of humanity."[68] City dignitaries, college trustees and faculty, and nine survivors of the Whitman massacre had prominent platform places. The program featured the Whitman Memorial Chorus of sixty voices and an oration by the Reverend Leavitt H. Hallock of Mills College. Hallock was given this honor because he was an effective speaker, had helped Penrose as an eastern fund raiser, and had been a Whitman College trustee. In his lengthy and impassioned address to a sober audience, he covered such topics as missionary and diplomatic history. In his controversial explanation for the Whitman massacre he stated that in 1847 British settlers realized that they had lost Oregon, but "Tools for vengeance or redemption were near. The red men were susceptible, the Jesuit capable."[69] As proof of such treachery, the orator recalled that George Washington in 1794 blamed the British for promoting Indian hostilities on the frontier. The Cayuse, too, had been aroused by Englishmen. The speaker praised Cushing Eells, D.K. Pearsons, and the college. Hallock concluded: "Monuments chiselled in stone are worth building, but Christian colleges that carve crude souls along fine lines of clean and Christlike character as they pass in ceaseless procession, and send them out to bless the world, are unspeakably more excellent."

On Tuesday morning a procession including the city's band, survivors of the Whitman massacre, Indian War veterans, the Grand Army of the Republic, the Whitman faculty and students, and townspeople marched through the streets to the railroad depot. Businesspeople closed their stores so that they and their employees might be among the crowd that took the special trains to Waiilatpu.[70] Perhaps as many as 3,000 visited the old missionary ground, heard music, bowed in prayer, watched the survivors move slowly by the new mausoleum, and listened to survivor Catherine Sager Pringle's short speech. The shaft had not arrived, and because of mud and poor weather the crowd returned to the opera house. Here the Fort Walla Walla band and the Reverend James Wilson, a Portland teacher, were featured attractions. Wilson delivered another long history of missionary activity, but he was much more restrained than Hallock.[71] Unsure of all the reasons for Whitman's ride, he thought it was obvious that the missionary had gone east to get the government to protect the Oregon Trail and to encourage immigration. He concluded, "We may, confidently expect that the final verdict of history will be, that to Whitman more than to any other man we owe it that the valley of the Columbia was saved to the United States." In this version, Whitman may not have saved what became Oregon, Washington, and Idaho, but at the least he had secured an important valley.

These various activities were reported in regional newspapers, including the Walla Walla *Union*, which ran a special edition, and the *Oregonian*, which published a long front-page story with illustrations of the monument, mausoleum, and survivors. Even distant newspapers provided brief accounts. Penrose reported that the opera house exercises helped widen the fame of Whitman College, the martyr's memorial.[72]

The college had scheduled a football game to attract many visitors and provide diversion from the solemn anniversary celebration. An editor noted that this game with Washington Agricultural College—then called Pullman for short—was "morally" clean, that those who had come "to see some one pounded to a jelly or knocked out" left disappointed, that Penrose jumped up and down in a mud puddle to encourage cheering and shouted to trustee Levi Ankeny to yell.[73] "The sedate Levi forgot he was lame, and was soon as demonstrative as any of the crowd." Despite the encouragement of a thousand voices, Whitman lost twelve to four; there would have been a rematch, but "the Pullman boys were compelled to return on account of their dormitory having been burned."

While the two-day celebration and the football game had been hosted by those honoring Protestant missionaries, a critic also drew a large crowd into Walla Walla's St. Patrick's church. Father Michael Flohr announced that he would give a Sunday evening lecture entitled "The Other Side; or Oregon Saved Without Whitman."[74] The college community and townspeople crammed into the church to hear Flohr state that he spoke as a citizen, not as a priest. He immediately charged that Whitman had not saved Oregon, that the missionary's sole reason for going east was to save his mission, and that Oregon would have been saved even if Whitman had never been born. The critic denounced Henry Spalding, not Marcus Whitman, for fabricating anti-Catholic stories, including a malicious one that Catholics had perpetrated the Whitman massacre. Flohr generalized that Protestants (such as Spalding and Hallock) whacked the pope because "it works on their hearers in the same manner as when you give oats to a horse—it makes them feel good." Maintaining that Spalding "was not sane," he concluded on a humorous note. Spalding blamed Jesuits for murdering Whitman, thus "We will leave him with the Jesuits. He will be in good company, and they will take care of him."

Mary Penrose reported on this lecture to her mother. She stated that Flohr spoke "as an offset to the celebration," that he said nothing new, and "that he was not—contrary to our expectation—in the least unpleasant or abusive toward Whitman, Eells, Steve, or the college, but contented himself with trying to discredit Spalding." However, she did not report that without mentioning names Flohr had criticized Penrose for mixing politics and religion in an attempt to get the million-dollar Fort Walla Walla "as an endowment for a sectarian institution." This charge would be revived a few years later.

Penrose did not publicly object to the address; in fact, he assured friends that the summaries of Flohr's speech given in the regional press provided publicity for the college. He assumed that the opponents to the Whitman-saved-Oregon story would be proved wrong. Flohr's account obviously fueled the Whitman controversy. He repeated his version of the Whitman story at the Chicago Historical Society. Oliver Nixon's book published in 1895 had also aroused critics and defenders. Frances Fuller Victor denounced Nixon in the San Francisco *Call*; Nixon replied in the same press. Newspapers in the Pacific Northwest reprinted the lively disagreement. Editors took sides: the Walla Walla *Union*, the Spokane *Spokesman-Review*, and the Seattle *Post-Intelligencer* endorsed Nixon; the Portland *Oregonian* rejected him and disliked Hallock's anti-Catholicism. Historian George Himes denounced Methodist Harvey K. Hines' criticism of the missionary.

In late 1897 Whitman College received national publicity. In November the *Ladies Home Journal* carried a well-illustrated article entitled "When Dr. Whitman Added Three Stars to Our Flag."[75] In an essay that stressed the travel of Narcissa Whitman and Eliza Spalding across the continent and Whitman's ride, Professor George Weed, who had met Marcus Whitman in 1843, praised the college. "It is a reality worthy of the confidence and aid of all American citizens in remembrance of the hero and heroine the patriot martyrs of Oregon—Marcus and Narcissa Whitman." The writer concluded that Bunker Hill Monument on one coast and Whitman College on the other are "suggestive of patriotism equally pure, and blood equally precious. 'Long may the first beams of the morning gild the one, and the last rays of evening linger and play upon the other.'"

In December Penrose learned of two other events that publicized Whitman. In the nation's capital a Congregational church observed the anniversary of the Whitman massacre. Prominent men praised the missionary: Supreme Court Justice David J. Brewer, a popular orator, supported missions, observing that the current Alaska gold rush brought William H. Seward just recognition for his Alaska purchase and that Marcus Whitman, who had saved a vast, valuable region, was also receiving approval.[76] Civil War general O.O. Howard recounted Whitman's career and even blamed his death upon the Hudson's Bay Company because of its sale of liquor and guns to

Indians. The general charged that "After the Hudson's Bay people saw the awful work they had instigated, they tried to shift the blame to the shoulders of missionaries of the other sects, but without avail."

On the opposite coast a Seattleite recommended in a public letter that Mount Rainier be renamed as Mount Whitman.[77] He favored the change because "Admiral Peter Rainier was obscure even to Englishmen and had rendered no service to mankind." The *Post-Intelligencer*, however, opposed the proposal because Whitman's accomplishments had been overrated and because "the name Rainier is strong and permanently identified with Seattle."

Penrose, who had spent countless hours preparing for the fiftieth anniversary celebration, congratulated participants for helping erect "the Pacific Northwest's first historic monument."[78] A shaft overlooking Waiilatpu was significant, but he had a much greater objective in mind: "we want the people of the United States to feel that [Whitman College] can be made into a national monument to a national hero."[79] This 1897 celebration had publicized Marcus Whitman and the college that honored him, but Penrose understood that work and money, more than popular sentiment, were required to build a school that would be a living monument to the missionary's "inestimable services."

The First Masonry Buildings

With the college enjoying considerable publicity and with the endowment campaign nearly completed, Penrose in early 1898 sought funds for stone buildings, especially a recitation hall and a men's dormitory. The first question was their location. Penrose had watched Eaton unsuccessfully seek an alternative site within the city, and he agreed with his predecessor that the present location of about six acres south of Boyer Avenue was too restrictive. He wanted either the military post or a large donated site, and had told an eastern friend that the school "will not spend one dollar for a site, it must be provided by the people of this place."[80] In his 1896 report, Penrose had argued again that the fort property "was ideally adapted for the growth of a great institution."[81] The president assumed that if the college obtained this choice site, then donors would provide buildings and that the government's donation would acknowledge the heroic missionary "and would give to the college a national standing." But the problem, he complained, was not the distant politicians who could donate federal property; it was the "conservatism of businessmen of Walla Walla." They did not want to take any action that might prompt the garrison's transfer. Penrose had been advised by both Oliver Nixon and D.K. Pearsons to accept defeat and purchase land adjoining the campus. He now asked the prices of property across the avenue from the campus. Penrose suffered a reversal by having to buy land. Like his predecessor he could not find free property. In summary, it proved too difficult to get either large cash donations or major properties from tight-fisted Walla Wallans. Yet even while the school purchased six nearby acres, Penrose and a few others still complained that the school should be situated on a larger suburban tract.

While seeking a larger campus, Penrose explained to the trustees, the faculty, Chicago friends, and many others the need for permanent buildings. He wrote that the college "is rapidly growing out of its old clothes. Its sleeves are too short and its clothes are so old that they cannot be lengthened out. What it needs is a new suit throughout. We must have new buildings within two years or we shall be a case of arrested development."[82] The educator claimed that "we have actually the poorest buildings of any college in the country." The wooden halls were crowded and run down. "Our buildings," Penrose lamented, "are heated by wood-stoves in each room and lighted dimly by oil lamps. We suffer greatly by comparison with the state institutions."[83] Walla Walla supporters agreed and pointed out that the nearby Adventist school operated in a much better facility than did Whitman.

Insisting that the college was "crippled by wretched and inadequate accommodations,"[84] Penrose knew that substantial halls, well-outfitted laboratories, and dormitories appealed to potential students, faculty members, and donors. He used Pomona as an example in arguing that better buildings would help raise the endowment, "for people would rather give to a successful cause than to an unsuccessful one, and while they will give very small sums to a very poor institution out of compassion, they will give larger sums to an institution which they feel is on a sure foundation and bound to succeed."[85]

From every possible angle Penrose argued for new buildings. Influenced by his undergraduate experience at Williams, the president predicted that dormitories would create fellowship, leadership, and school spirit. Moreover, a dormitory would keep young men out of boarding houses and place them on campus, where they would be away from the city's "demoralizing influences."[86] A recitation hall was also badly needed. Cramped laboratories and a lack of classrooms frustrated professors. In fact, Penrose had to surrender his own office so that a class might use it.

The president frequently urged construction of buildings, but he actually had little confidence in a fund-raising campaign to pay for them. He hoped that friends of the college would give the badly needed buildings, but he had been chastened and fatigued by the long endowment campaign and had doubted his fund-raising ability: "I have failed to make people give to the college by appearing to them to be too sure of success. Yet the plaintive strain is not much in my make up, and I do not like to beg. In fact, I never have been a successful solicitor for the college."[87] He told a friend that he would rather be killed than to beg but assured him that he would do the necessary fund raising.[88] Penrose urged Virginia Dox to remind D.K. Pearsons that the financier had promised "that I should never have to solicit again."[89] To the president's way of thinking he could "do a great deal more for the college by staying here and developing it internally than by going around the country with my hat in my hand with a look of poverty upon my face."

Penrose wrote Pearsons that an unsuccessful canvass would embarrass him and his school. Pearsons disagreed. The philanthropist, as usual, provided all kinds of advice, urging the educator to regain his optimism. After all, "a faint heart never won Mrs. Penrose."[90] Pearsons encouraged him to hire an architect and workers, who should start digging foundations. He assured Penrose that donors would then complete the buildings. Nixon wrote that to start construction without money was risky, but he predicted that if Penrose "would hustle," the buildings would be placed in fresh excavations.[91]

Pearsons predicted that there would be no trouble finding dollars for the two proposed buildings. The optimist wrote that Penrose's efforts since 1895 had "sown seed enough to bring the money," that trustees could help find funds, that the local community could be taught that a stronger college would boost the local economy, that letters to fifty or more persons would bring financial results, that

Pomona had so successfully raised money that Pearsons gave a $25,000 science building, and that either Penrose or Dox would be able to "touch the hearts" of wealthy eastern men and women. Pearsons expected that dozens of potential donors only awaited a call. The millionaire maintained that he was currently unable to give Whitman additional financial assistance and made no mention of his old offer to finance a building. He tantalizingly stated, however, that at some unspecified date he would deliver another check; meanwhile, he advised that the proposed recitation hall should have a good sewage system and should be modeled after Pacific University's Marsh Hall, which was the appropriate size.[92]

Nixon often wrote to Penrose about Pearsons' opinions; for example, Pearsons insisted that Whitman had a great future but concluded that he would not provide it with additional financial assistance until Walla Wallans and Washingtonians treated it more generously. Penrose disagreed and asked Dox to impress upon Pearsons that Walla Wallans, who had suffered economically since 1894, had been generous and that a new local request "would be disastrous to the college."[93] Perhaps this argument changed the financier's mind. In March 1898 Pearsons informed Nixon, who then rushed the news to Penrose, of a proposal to give $50,000 for a recitation building if local residents raised $25,000 for a dormitory. This was an even better match than the $1 for $3 he had given for the endowment.

After Nixon related this tentative proposal, the president immediately engaged a competent Walla Walla architect, George W. Babcock. He designed a handsome recitation building in the Richardsonian Romanesque style and simultaneously sought funds for it through the Whitman *Quarterly*. In June, Penrose showed Babcock's dormitory plans to potential local donors.

Penrose informed Pearsons about some pledges he had received and sent plans for the recitation hall as well as ideas about a dormitory designed for seventy men. Pleased with this correspondence, the benefactor in mid-July offered Whitman the generous match he had mentioned to Nixon. The only condition was that the $50,000 building must be called Whitman Memorial Hall.[94]

Announcing that this splendid offer had lifted a cloud from over the school, Penrose and the trustees immediately solicited $25,000 for the proposed dormitory. In the late summer of 1898, Penrose escorted his wife and infant daughter to Hartford. Following Pearsons' advice, he sought eastern money for the dormitory, but failed as he had anticipated.

The increased fall enrollment forced all new students to board in town. The president prayed and begged for buildings to house and instruct the growing student body, but he refused to launch a public campaign. Discouraged, the educator informed his benefactor that the college could not accept his generous match. Disgusted with this pessimism, the Chicagoan poured out a torrent of advice. He insisted that Penrose shift all the fund raising to the trustees, reasoning that these businessmen would find money that seemed to elude the president. Having lost confidence in Penrose's ability as a solicitor, he urged him to "stand back a little and keep as calm as 3 summer mornings" and stick to teaching because it "is your work and you want to put your personality into the pupils."⁹⁵ He continued, "It is better for you to get a reputation as an able teacher than a beggar." Pearsons also concluded that the proposed Whitman Memorial Hall should be cut from 172 to 150 feet because the extra length made it look like a barn, because the college did not need space for more than 300 students, and because the savings from construction could be applied to the cost of furnishings. The financier also suggested that underpaid faculty could be accommodated in the new dormitory at $1.50 a week. Penrose refused to reduce the building's dimensions but agreed to offer bachelor teachers space in the hall.

Penrose asked Pearsons if Dox might seek dormitory money in the East. The Chicagoan heatedly rejected the idea and insisted that Walla Wallans raise its full amount. But Pearsons enthusiastically proposed a new plan: Dox should be brought from Massachusetts and be made a Whitman faculty member. She would teach several months and then seek western students and money; furthermore, she could reduce Penrose's workload by representing him at various meetings. The president could do nothing but accept this unusual proposition, one that he came to like.

In February 1899 Penrose suffered a setback. He had frequently urged banker Levi Ankeny to give all or most of the required $25,000. The wealthy trustee finally refused, and Penrose expressed bitter disappointment. Nixon cautioned him not to be critical of Ankeny, for "we are beggars not critics." But Nixon also reminded him that Pearsons absolutely insisted that local money must be raised before he would give any portion of his $50,000 match. The journalist, who did not "want to put up the shutters and sound lights out,"[96] urged a vigorous search for building funds.

Pearsons, on the other hand, drew lessons from Ankeny's refusal. "It is not," the Chicagoan lectured, "manly or wise to let small matters fret you or discourage you. It is well for you to meet reverses and disappointments. You will meet many before you get to be seventy-nine-years old. Take everything in a manly spirit and never say die."[97] A few days later Pearsons softened his response by permitting Dox to raise part of the $25,000 in New England, although this delayed her faculty appointment. Penrose hoped that her assistance would mean that the two buildings might be completed late in 1899.

College trustees also tried to find funds for the dormitory by offering anybody who gave $10,000 the privilege of naming the hall. They also established a special committee, including the mayor, to raise the approximately $15,000 still required. Penrose remembered that the community had already given about $70,000 in five years, which would make it difficult to find donors for the dormitory. Meanwhile, the special nine-man committee spearheaded the fund raising and pledged contributions. Journalists, clergymen, and others lent assistance. The Walla Walla *Statesman*, for example, reminded the community that it was fortunate to have the Whitman story and the college, for both set the city apart from other aspiring towns. Editor Frank J. Parker growled that it would be "criminal" not to collect the matching money,[98] and attempted to win support from the "practical businessmen and men of affairs" who saw nothing "practical about college men."[99] He grumbled that "A certain class of people seem to think that financial sharpness and accumulation of money constitute the whole sum of practicality." Such persons needed to learn that "Money is a means to an end, not an end in itself." In his discussion of practicality, he asserted that "The play of Hamlet is just as practical as a sausage cutter or cross-cut saw." Boys reared in business, Parker acknowledged, had more technical proficiency than college graduates, but he maintained that all businessmen admitted "that a college man has a ready and general intelligence and a far-seeking grasp of the principles of business which more than compensate." Once the two buildings were operating, the editor predicted, the practical advantages of a college education would become obvious to the "most sensible and hard headed of practical business men."

Meanwhile the college's admirers had already joined the newly launched campaign. In early April 1899 the Whitman faculty was asked to help raise the $3,000 still required. Although professors received small salaries and had previously donated to the building fund, they now pledged another $1,075. Professor Benjamin Brown probably made the greatest sacrifice. Receiving only a $1,100 salary, he supported a wife, child, mother, and grandmother; furthermore, he was putting his sister through Whitman. The professor borrowed $100, donated it to the fund, and explained that these proposed halls were "essential to the life of the college."[100]

The faculty decided that the students, too, should be asked to contribute. After chapel a teacher challenged: "Do you want these new buildings?" "Yes! Yes! came with thundering zeal from boys and girls alike."[101] With sophomore Ross Brattain presiding at a special meeting, several classmates delivered stirring speeches, insisting that they, not their parents, should donate. Enthusiastic voices soon pledged about $1,000, which would be earned by mowing lawns, working harvest, mending, or selling refreshments. Some promised dollars they had planned to use for other purposes: a young man pledged $10 that he was going to use for summer clothes and revealed that he would get the girls to mend his old ones; another gave $50 he was going to spend for a new camera. Catching the spirit, a Chinese cook in Ladies' Hall donated $2.

During the evening, students chaperoned by the college matron and several faculty members spread their spirit around the campus. They visited the Penrose home and gave several cheers, such as:

> Here's to Whitman College
> Here's to the thousand dollars,
>   Drink it down, drink it down;
> Here's to the thousand dollars
>   Drink it down, drink it down;
> Here's to the thousand dollars
> That was raised by Whitman scholars
>   Drink it down, drink it down,
>   Drink it down, down, down![102]

The excited students marched to other faculty homes, rendering college yells and songs. The evening concluded with professors and students dining on the ground where the new halls would stand. Pleased and surprised by this student support, Penrose said that "those who had forfeited certain rights and privileges had been fully restored, because of their manifest loyalty to the college." The *Statesman* congratulated the students and faculty for generously giving $2,000 from their meager incomes. For many years afterward, April 4 would be remembered as a red-letter day. Students and faculty members boasted that their effort influenced others, including alumni, to contribute and that their effort convinced trustees to begin construction.

With more than $15,000 pledged, with confidence that Dox in New England could raise a significant amount, and with Penrose saying he would borrow $10,000 "on my personal security," trustees, in April 1899, asked regional building contractors to submit bids. Apparently the decision to use two contractors came from Pearsons, who had advised that "two men . . . will have a little rivalry and finish them much quicker and better."[103] In mid-May the trustees accepted bids from Walla Walla contractors: Bailey and Cox would build Memorial Hall for $43,792 and E.R. Parkes would erect the dormitory for $23,211.[104] Pressed bricks would be used because they were cheaper than stones. Other contractors would provide heat, light, and water. Trustees appointed Penrose as head of a committee to provide the necessary furnishings. He also had to raise $10,000 to furnish the dormitory, so he urged Dox to help find a major donor.

In an expansive mood, the trustees borrowed from the endowment to purchase the necessary land from Henry Isaacs, Mrs. Dorsey Baker, and others. College leaders had hoped that Isaacs might give the land because in 1896 he had donated six acres near the campus for the Odd Fellows' home. These purchases increased the size of the campus to twenty-three acres; Penrose had added seventeen of them.

The college's growth in buildings and grounds fit neatly into the city's expansion. The three banks enjoyed large deposits that funded the construction of new business buildings and homes. In the late 1890s Walla Walla visitors commented upon its prosperity, which one believed resulted from "its soil and the good crops and good prices."[105] Enjoying good wheat prices (about fifty cents a bushel in 1899) and an abundance of farm loan money, local farmers flocked into town. Their purchases stimulated retail sales. In this healthy economy, owners tore down small wooden buildings and replaced them with brick ones. It surprised one traveler that he could not find an elevator in these new structures. He joked that "every man must be his own yeast cake."[106]

Proud of the building boom, residents drove their buggies around town, observing new neighborhood homes, Mayor Jacob Betz's four-story brewery, and the two attractive brick and stone structures that were emerging among the orchard and shade trees on the expanded campus. Both the city and the college were expanding after a period of stagnation.

Penrose spent a frantic summer rushing the construction of the two halls, for he wanted to use them in late 1899. Virginia Dox wrote that she and D.K. Pearsons worried that he would work too hard and would become "a nervous, fidgety, and broken-down President." She reminded him that it was "easy to find good teachers and solicitors, but an exceedingly difficult matter to find good ... college presidents."[104] Too busy to make the annual trek to Hartford, Penrose sent his pregnant wife and his young daughter. Pearsons called her a brave woman for taking the trip alone.

Although an expert actually oversaw construction, Penrose spent long hours with the architect, the contractors, the furnishings committee, and the trustees. He often summoned the trustees' executive committee, which made decisions about the buildings and about the purchase of additional acreage. The president worried about the contractors' progress, for they once halted work because they ran out of building materials. Foundation stones, not concrete, were used in the 1890s, and the sandstone had to be shipped across the Cascades from a Tenino quarry. Soon after emplacement of the foundation stones, the building sites again grew silent because of the city's so-called "brick-famines." An Oregon supplier soon delivered the necessary cream-colored bricks. Then Penrose became exasperated to learn that there were not enough building stones on hand; finally an additional supply and a skilled stone mason arrived, and the arches were built. In mid-October workmen installed furnishings. Penrose's committee on furnishings had asked individuals to outfit a room with bed, mattress, shelves, table, chairs, and toilet set, for $40. In recognition, a tablet with the donor's name would be placed in the dormitory room. Because William H. Cowles, publisher of the Spokane *Spokes-man-Review*, and his wife, Harriet Cheney Cowles, were friends of the Penroses, the newspaper donated $300 for tables, table linen, silverware, crockery, sideboards, and other items needed in the dormitory's dining room.

In mid-July Penrose received a splendid letter from Dox. It began, "Something grand is on its way to you! I received a check for $5,000 this morning from Mrs. Billings."[108] Widow Julia Billings had earlier declined to contribute to the dormitory but had introduced Dox to wealthy people. Apparently Billings changed her mind because of Dox's efforts and because her husband, Frederick Billings, had contributed to Whitman years earlier when he heard Cushing Eells' eloquent plea for money. At first Mrs. Billings insisted on anonymity, fearing that other colleges would beg for similar amounts. When she was told that she could name the building because her gifts of more than $6,000 were the major donation, she rejected the name Cushing Eells Hall—it "would not be euphonious"—and called the dormitory Billings Hall in memory of her two sons, Parmly and Ehrick. Thus two easterners—Pearsons and Billings—gave the largest amounts to a recitation hall and a dormitory and chose the names. As Penrose had often predicted, these new buildings would open "a new era in the life of the College."[109] Always looking to the future, he asked friends to visit the construction site and contribute to a girls' dormitory that would be equal in size to Billings Hall.

Penrose could not spend his days with contractors. In mid-1899 he traveled nine days in Oregon, lecturing, preaching, and recruiting students and friends. The heavy schedule and the heat wearied him; he called his effort "a severe tax."[110] He could not ignore eastern fund raising either; therefore, he wrote many letters, reporting the college's progress and predicting a bright future. In a typical letter he explained, "If the people of the East appreciated the immensity of our field they would understand better that the future of the college is certain to be brilliant. We are the only institution doing distinctly college work in a region larger than the New England States and New York and Pennsylvania, and we draw students from beyond that great area."

In the October 1899 *Quarterly* Penrose described the new buildings. He boasted that there was a splendid view from the Billings tower. One could see the "Blue Mountains to the southeast and the whole of the lovely Walla Walla Valley. The town embordered in trees lies southwest and west." The building contained forty-eight bedrooms, a parlor, a dining room, and a kitchen. The furnace and kitchen were in the basement. There were bathrooms and toilet rooms on each floor and an elevator. The president praised Whitman Memorial Hall for its "dignity, grace, and beauty." He described other features: "In both front and rear is an arched entrance of massive stone work, which on the front rises into a tower over a hundred feet high, built of brick above the second story to give more of grace and lightness. The same effect is produced by the dormer windows in the third story which redeem the roof from an appearance of too great weight and solidity." He maintained that both buildings "in beauty of form and excellence of workmanship compare favorably with those of any college East or West." Penrose, however, complained that "The unsightly holes in the [Memorial] tower mar the appearance . . . and the need of a clock is much felt in the running of the College."[111]

In December the first of eighty men began moving into Billings Hall and reported comfortable accommodations. They were "all happy as clams at high tide."[112] The four professors housed with noisy teenagers on the second floor were less ecstatic about living conditions. Early the next month carpenters completed Memorial Hall's interior. Classes then moved across Boyer Avenue from College Hall, which now housed the conservatory of music. Everyone rejoiced over the new hall's spaciousness: it housed fourteen recitation rooms, laboratories, a library and reading room, a chapel seating 400 persons, and executive offices. Unlike Billings Hall it was lighted with gas, not electricity, and, like the new downtown buildings, it lacked an elevator.

The dedication of Billings Hall and Whitman Memorial Hall was a major occasion. Penrose had hoped that D.K. Pearsons, who had dedicated his gifts in person at other college commencements, would do the same in Walla Walla. But Oliver Nixon substituted for him at the 1900 commencement. In his dedication oration, this devoted friend of the college praised a variety of people and groups, including the Whitmans, the Eellses, Pearsons ("the saviour of the college"), Penrose ("the right man in the right place . . . an inspiration and an untiring worker"), Dox ("heroic and successful"), women ("they love heroic acts and they easily see the great part acted by a woman in the life of Marcus Whitman"), and the donors, including the faculty, students, and Mrs. Billings ("she sympathized with homeless young men").[113] Still embroiled in the battle with detractors over the deeds of Marcus Whitman, the orator defended him, pointing out that Washington, Lincoln, and Grant had also been denounced by "pretended historians." He hoped that the college's graduates would "with justice and enthusiasm ... fight the [religious and patriotic] battles of the heroes resting in the great grave [at Waiilatpu]." Nixon recited highlights of the college's history and predicted a glorious future for it and the region it served. "Now if Portland, and Seattle, and Tacoma, would aspire to be a Liverpool, or a New York, or a Boston, and build great warehouses; Walla Walla will be equally wise to aspire to be a New Haven, or a Cambridge, or Ann Arbor, and build a great college. . . . There is no reason why Whitman College may not stand proudly in the front rank of institutions of learning." But he cautioned the college not to enroll more than 800 students, pointing out that those with 2,000 did not "do the good work of a smaller college"; furthermore, when professors did not know "even the names of half the students," college life lost much of its charm. "Great buildings," he predicted, "are yet to be erected, and such endowment as will make college doors open to the rich and poor alike." The speaker charged: "May Whitman College in memory of a great name and a noble purpose, send out undiminished and ever-increasing blessings to the generations to follow."

The second speaker, former governor Miles Moore, responded to Nixon. He praised the orator for his writing, which "has aroused a wide-spread interest in the life and services of the martyred missionary" and for his devotion to the college.[114] "Whitman College," Moore went on to conclude, "seems now firmly established on a solid foundation and suitably housed. The dream of Father Eells at last is realized."

A Whitman professor concluded the program by reading Pearsons' letter. The donor insisted that Whitman's ride saved Oregon and "No college in the country has such a history, or rests on more honorable foundations."[115] He then explained that he supported the institution because it "has a strategic position and is likely to grow . . .

it has the missionary spirit, the spirit of true Christian patriotism and self-obliteration behind it. It is to emphasize and perpetuate this spirit that [my] money has been given for the Administration Building and for endowment." He judged that others had also donated because "They believe that this spirit will live in its students, that it will prove to be the most intelligent, the most American, the most prophetic, the noblest, the most manly, and the most Christian to be met with among any body of students in our country."

The large audience appreciated the speakers and congratulated Penrose for having done so much to improve his college. While the official emphasis had been on the successful endowment drive and the construction of two handsome buildings, Penrose had also been recruiting a larger and better faculty and student body.

Building the Faculty

To build a strong institution, Penrose knew it was critically important to strengthen the faculty. In his first year he added well-trained women and men. Despite the depression and the school's deficit, by 1900 he had doubled the faculty from seven to fourteen. William Lyman in history and political science and Helen Pepoon in Latin were influential carryovers, and Louis Anderson returned as professor of Greek. In 1895, while fund raising in the East, Penrose sought "a few young men of ability and faith who would be willing to join in the adventure of trying to build Whitman College into a first-class institution."[116] Fortunately he hired Benjamin H. Brown, professor of natural sciences; Walter A. Bratton, professor of mathematics; and Otto A. Hauerbach, professor of oratory and elocution. There were other consequential additions, especially in 1899 when Howard S. Brode was appointed professor of natural sciences. Brode's arrival meant that Brown shifted to physics and chemistry.

By 1900 this diverse and talented faculty had earned a regional reputation and was attracting and retaining young people, one of whom judged that their professors came from eastern "boasted" schools and "combined the culture and the learning of the East, with the acquired whole-heartedness and enthusiasm of the West."[117] The writer added that his classmates were "spared the humiliation of a faculty at war with each other and students at war with them."

The community knew something about each professor's background. Walter Bratton was born in Vermont, and at Williams College distinguished himself in mathematics. He was a debater, member of Phi Beta Kappa, and speaker at his 1895 commencement. That year, at the age of twenty-one, he began his long and influential career at Whitman. Quickly demonstrating administrative skills, he received various responsibilities, including supervision of Whitman athletics. Active in the state's Democratic Party, Bratton irritated many Walla Wallans by supporting Democratic presidential candidate William Jennings Bryan's monetary ideas. Although most of the Whitman community favored the Republican Party, Bratton and Lyman provided a limited degree of political balance by espousing the Democratic Party. But faculty favoring free silver had little influence; Penrose rejoiced in the fact that in 1897 Whitman students opposed the proposal by a vote of ninety-eight to four.

Benjamin Brown had a different kind of background than Bratton. He was born in 1866 in Wisconsin and was twenty-one before he could leave the family farm. He entered the preparatory department of Ripon; in 1884, after seven years of study, he received a B.S. A

The Whitman faculty in 1897. Seated are (from left) Jean Reynaud (modern languages), Helen Pepoon (Latin), Stephen Penrose, (philosophy), Louise Loomis (Latin and English), and William Lyman (political science and history). Standing are Otto Hauerbach (oratory and elocution), Bert Thomas (science and mathematics), Benjamin Brown (natural sciences), Louis Anderson (Greek), and Walter Bratton (mathematics).

mature student, he established a fine record. After a year of public school teaching, he came to Whitman, where, Penrose humorously recalled, "he occupied a settee rather than a chair, for the poverty of the college required that he should teach three natural sciences . . . in all of which he was . . . equally interested and at home."[118] In 1897 he married Maud Merrell, the daughter of Ripon College's president. Because of his farming background, his enthusiasm for science, and his affable disposition, Brown had a strong influence on Whitman students and the community.

Helen Pepoon had been hired by President James Eaton. A native of Ohio and an 1878 graduate of Oberlin, she had taught in a women's academy in Wisconsin and had been a principal of a seminary in Honolulu. Following a year of graduate study at her alma mater, she moved to Whitman as lady principal and professor of Latin. A gracious woman, Pepoon gave enormous amounts of time to students. She was an effective, popular, and precise language teacher who appreciated the fact that Penrose increased her salary to about the same level as her male colleagues.

Otto Hauerbach was born in Salt Lake City in 1873, where he received his preparatory training. He graduated in 1895 from Knox College; after some advanced work he received an M.A. from his alma mater. Hauerbach impressed Walla Wallans with his public readings. He helped many students overcome nervousness and prepare for required orations. Pearsons hailed Hauerbach because he had started as a "lonely shepherd boy" in Utah and had become a professor and effective Mormon critic.

Howard Brode was born in Illinois, graduated from its state normal school in 1888, worked for four years as assistant in zoology at the University of Illinois, served as a member of a federal fish commission that visited Yellowstone Park, taught in a marine biology laboratory in Massachusetts, and in 1896 completed a PH.D. in zoology at the University of Chicago, where his major professor stated that "he was the best man in Biology he had ever known."[119] After three years teaching in the academy at Beloit College, he came to Whitman in 1899. Brode was the school's best-educated faculty member, and, as befitted his training, he was appointed Spencer F. Baird Professor of Natural Sciences. Proud of his colleague, Penrose wrote that Brode was "a scientist in the true sense of the word" and an excellent teacher.

Born in 1900 to Catherine and Howard Brode, Wallace, Robert, and Malcolm attracted considerable attention from Whitman faculty, students, and visitors. The triplets all graduated from Whitman, went on to earn doctorate degrees, and enjoyed distinguished careers.

S. Harrison Lovewell was born in Massachusetts; after seven years of study he graduated from the New England Conservatory of Music. He specialized on the pipe organ and was church organist, private teacher, and college instructor prior to becoming the director of the Whitman Conservatory of Music in 1898.

A talented teacher, Penrose taught freshmen and sophomores in his Bible classes and upperclass members in his philosophy courses. Students enjoyed these required classes but some grumbled about their teacher's frequent absences and his rigorous grading. All praised him for his knowledge, enthusiasm, wit, and dedication.

From his experiences at Williams College and from his discussions with President Jordan at Stanford, Penrose knew the importance of these effective teachers. In his inaugural address he had insisted, "It is the faculty who make a college great." In 1899 he boasted that "We have a first-rate faculty who make up largely for poor buildings."[120] Not only could Penrose identify talented professors, he also had the ability to retain them for their entire careers. Lyman, Pepoon, Anderson, Brown, Bratton, and Brode served for decades, providing a solid nucleus. According to Penrose they liked Walla Walla, accepting the fact that it could not provide the art, music, and lectures of eastern urban centers. More important, they all shared their leader's dream of making a first-rate liberal arts college in rural Washington.

The faculty appreciated Penrose's leadership and would have endorsed his generalization: "None of the faculty are made to walk in a line not of their drawing, but rather are left as free as possible to develop their best powers."[121] Many of the professors had overcome obstacles to educate themselves; they appreciated the fact that most of those sitting in their classes were making a similar effort. In summary, these young people typically demonstrated an "earnestness of purpose."

In private and in public the president praised his staff. He told trustees that the "brave teachers ... had stood nobly by Whitman through the dark hours of its uncertainty." In 1898 Penrose emphasized that they

> have labored incessantly and zealously on salaries not at all commensurate with their abilities or experience, and have given their best strength without reserve to the college. I hope that you will always bear in mind that the work in which these men and women are engaged is truly a missionary labor. That they could go elsewhere and obtain much larger salaries but that they stay here because they love the college, and because they want to do what they can in building up an institution whose future we all feel, will be glorious.[122]

He often boasted that the faculty was "strong and vigorous" and that there was "perfect harmony among the members of the faculty, who all seem inspired to join in making the college second to none in the northwest."[123] The president delighted to tell the story of a student who had transferred to Stanford, found that its faculty was not better than Whitman's, and returned to Walla Walla.

Penrose consistently worried about the faculty's inadequate compensation, warning trustees that some would resign unless they received salary increases. In the 1890s the faculty often received notes, not cash. These dedicated women and men knew about this bleak situation when they chose their profession, and faculty families struggled to pay bills. The large Lyman and Brode families particularly suffered from inadequate compensation. The president's appeals for additional salary for needy colleagues rarely succeeded. At Whitman, as at most colleges, the sacrifices of professors made it possible to operate. The fine professors that Stephen Penrose hired in 1895 received only $1,000 each; after five years of service each had received only a $100 annual increase. Experienced faculty members got little more than newcomers; for example, Lyman was paid only $1,200. Low salaries were by no means unique to Whitman; Penrose learned that salary reductions at Pomona College meant that its faculty made slightly less than Whitman's. Pearsons was disgusted that Penrose would take only a paltry $1,500, noting that Pomona paid its president $250 more.

Despite these low salaries, their total was greater than tuition income. The endowment was too small to cover both this difference and the other college expenditures, including the fact that Billings Hall had cost several thousand dollars more than budgeted. Thus Whitman struggled with deficits. Angry with this financial situation, Pearsons told Penrose to slash his operating costs, emphasizing that the faculty was too large for the small student body. But Penrose argued that he must have at least seven professors and four instructors, predicting that his teachers would build the college's reputation.

The faculty's first obligation, of course, was to teach a basic set of courses. Probably there was general agreement as to what needed to be covered. In early 1900 the president extolled his school's curriculum: "Whitman College is conspicuous in the northwest as much for what it does not undertake to do as for what it does. It does not call itself a university or aspire to give technical or professional training. It does not try to catch the eye of the public by appeals for cheap notoriety nor by professing to offer courses which it does not give; but in the line which it has marked out it offers opportunity for a thorough, deep, and broad education equal to the best colleges of the east."[124]

The school continued to offer three college degree programs—classical, literary, and scientific—which, according to the catalog, required equal work. Other west coast Congregational schools, Pacific and Pomona, also offered the same three degree programs. Pacific, however, designed its literature course "for women who do not wish to pursue the study of Greek, higher mathematics, or advanced science."[125] Because of distinguished teachers and student interest, the scientific program became the most popular at Whitman. Each program required many demanding courses; students wholeheartedly agreed with the president who warned that there were no "snap courses for weak students." Penrose eschewed the elective system of Williams, for Whitman's faculty was too small to offer anything but the traditional classes in the humanities and sciences. Students, however, might sometimes substitute a class; for example, a modern language might replace Latin.

Interested in music and appealing to parents who wanted their children to sing or play an instrument, the president immediately took steps to strengthen the Whitman Conservatory of Music. Its director maintained that it was better for teachers to be in the conservatory's atmosphere than to be in a private home, "contending with parental criticisms, ill-adapted rooms, or badly kept instruments."[126] For several years the conservatory operated off campus in a downtown site in order to accommodate families, and it offered a choice of two programs: the regular course for those who wanted to teach or perform and a course for amateurs "who aim at personal improvement and musical enjoyment."

The Whitman Academy still enrolled those interested in going on to college or in seeking a basic education. Like the college, the academy also offered classical, scientific, and literary programs. There were no electives; history, classical and modern languages, science, mathematics, and English were the basis of a demanding curriculum. It was necessary to operate the academy because very few of the region's secondary schools offered a solid preparatory program. Whitman leaders emphasized the superiority of their institution over the public high schools and academies in eastern Washington, eastern Oregon, and Idaho. College professors, they stressed, did the actual teaching in the Whitman Academy and were much superior to typical secondary staffs.

Whitman College's curriculum quickly evolved under the new president. In his first year Penrose announced that the business and normal courses would be dropped, making "the curriculum ... less complicated and [of] a higher standard."[127] Because of his own preferences, the leader immediately emphasized music, religion, philosophy, biology, and modern languages. These curricular changes found support, but a department of art which he instituted was not successful. It was designed "to give thorough instruction, and to teach true standards in Art, thus developing a taste for the beautiful and artistic in home, gallery, and nature."[128] The college catalog also insisted that "The education of no man or woman is complete without training in these subjects." Penrose hired a talented and experienced art teacher, whose salary was paid for by friends of the college. But after fewer than two years, the president terminated the department because of small enrollments.

Teaching Conditions

Faculty struggled under heavy teaching loads: they had to teach out of their specialties, and they instructed in both the college and the academy. Penrose reported that "at present our professors have to spread themselves over more than their chair."[129] No doubt Penrose promised that eventually professors could enjoy specialization, but in the 1890s tremendous burdens were placed upon them. In 1899, for example, Brown taught two courses in chemistry, two in physics, and a course in scientific literature (Darwin, Spencer, and Huxley) for the college. In addition he taught physics, physical geography, physiology, botany, and geography in the academy. Hauerbach taught expression, rhetoric, literary criticism, English literature, and Old English at the college level. Assisted by an instructor, he taught grammar, masterpieces, and rhetoric, and oversaw rhetoricals in the academy. For a time he even gave violin lessons in the conservatory. The president conducted a full load of classes in addition to his administrative duties. At the college level he taught logic, psychology, philosophy, and religion; in the academy he gave a required course in Bible study. Penrose explained his objective: "I should be sorry to turn out students from the college who were not well versed in the Bible."[130]

The college catalogs provided only the basic information about the material covered in classes, but the description of Lyman's history class was an exception. Pointing out to students that they lived in the region's formative period, he sought "to train the class in methods of original research and independent judgment, and at the same time impress them with a sense of the duties, the responsibilities, and the opportunities of the American citizen."[131]

Penrose had participated in a highly structured faculty committee system at Williams College and brought a similar one to his own school. In the 1898 college catalog he published a list of standing committees, including discipline and general regulations; library, chapel, and study hours; scholarships and degrees; and athletics. These and ad hoc committees reported findings at faculty meetings and called for action. Faculty members advised student groups and conducted public and chapel programs. They even staffed the college's administrative positions. The librarian, registrar, and excusing officer were also professors. The excusing officer had the onerous task of evaluating student excuses for missing class and chapel.

At the frequent, required, and often lengthy faculty meetings, professors considered a variety of topics, including committee reports, scheduling of classes, examinations, commencement, student organizations, library procedures, and the disciplining of students. Teachers gave considerable time to scheduling; in 1899 they finally shelved the term system for the semester system. But the placement of students— who came from a variety of private and public schools—into the appropriate college and academy classes proved to be the faculty's most fatiguing responsibility.

The faculty also had the task of building the library. Located miles from the nearest major collection, Whitman teachers depended upon the 9,200 items, including 3,000 government publications, housed on campus. A faculty member served as librarian and tried to assist students, most of whom had never used a library. Professors grumbled that too many volumes were of marginal use; for example, many retired ministers gave useless items. The campus community hoped for an enlarged, well-selected collection. Thus in 1898 the school's treasurer stated that there was greater need of a library endowment than of an increased scholarship endowment.

Besides their multitude of teaching duties, these overworked persons were expected to become involved in their community. Most of the faculty members spoke in churches, supported cultural societies, worked in political parties, attended county teachers' association meetings, and responded to other calls upon their time, including traveling to recruit students. Although there were no publishing demands, professors read in their disciplines. It was difficult, however, to keep informed; for example, Penrose asked a university professor for suggestions about "the progress of philosophy." The members of the Whitman faculty, he explained, "are somewhat out of the world here, and I have no one to keep me touched up on recent philosophical works."[132]

It is hard to see how a married teacher had time for family matters; obviously it was necessary to keep a strict schedule. Faculty members frequently visited and dined together and helped each other in times of emergency or childhood sickness. Their children became close friends, growing up together on the campus.[133]

The faculty was expected to have a parental relationship with students. Although the term *in loco parentis* was not used in official sources, the faculty, the administrators, and the matrons practiced it. To be a professor was to be interested in the students' character development, admonishing those who were lazy, untruthful, insubordinate, crude, or immoral. A dean assured parents that Whitman would provide "an excellent intellectual training" and a "good environment." He told a mother, "We desire to give a course of study . . . with the notion of making a young man fitted on any walk of life with a character somewhat formed, and with principles and influences which are directed towards right living and high thinking."[134] In some of Penrose's correspondence he sounded more like a minister than a professor. On one occasion he encouraged a Dayton woman to give complete control of her headstrong daughter to the school's matron. If this were done, the president predicted, "she will make a noble woman in time." He reminded the mother "that we are interested in her welfare, and shall do all that we can for her growth in true womanliness."[135] Penrose's moralizing and expounding on the meaning of life are exemplified in an 1898 letter to Henrietta Moritz, who had left for Seattle. "As to your going on the stage, I should be very sorry indeed to hear that you had done that. You would be thrown with unfavorable associates and would find nothing helpful or uplifting in the life. It seems to me that what you need, as does every Christian, is to find some work in which you can do more than selfishly make money."[136]

Although the school kept an eagle eye on its charges, apparently some parents thought it was nearly blind. In 1898 a Starbuck mother, for example, bitterly complained that her son, who had been a fine violin student and faithful Sunday school scholar, had at Whitman "soon drifted out into the channel of disobedience."[137] Her son Ray, she complained, stopped taking violin lessons; instead he fished and rode "a wheel." He got into mischief by bringing a cow into the dormitory and by polishing himself and other students with shoe blackening. Upset by these deeds, the mother said it made her sick to think that his teachers did not keep track of Ray and that the negligent school had the nerve to charge a tuition.

Student Life

Another of Penrose's initial goals was to increase the size, diversity, and quality of the student body. In his early years, Whitman's enrollment increased notably: from 60 in 1894 to 293 in 1900. The school's two modern buildings, energetic president, skilled teachers, and loyal students were all reasons for growing numbers. Penrose hoped to add another hundred students within a few semesters. A larger enrollment would increase tuition income and would bring more publicity. But it proved easier to find talented eastern professors than capable western students. Whitman, like Willamette University, Colorado College, and others, developed a system of so-called feeder schools. Perhaps Willamette was the best regional model. Since the 1880s the Methodist institution had worked with "correlated academies"; in the 1890s such institutions in The Dalles and Pendleton sent graduates to Salem. Working through the state Congregational Association, Whitman hoped that Puget Sound Academy in Snohomish, Ahtanum Academy (later changed to Woodcock Academy) near Yakima, and Cushing Eells Academy in Colville would each develop a curriculum that prepared its graduates for Whitman. Penrose sometimes advised these academies and Weiser Academy in Idaho about fund raising, staffing, and course offerings. Some tailored their curricula after Whitman Academy, but few of their graduates continued their education in Walla Walla. As late as 1900, nearly all Whitman students came from southeastern Washington.

The college could not be supplied adequately by feeders; thus it would be necessary to attract more freshmen from the growing numbers of public high schools and from the various denominational academies. Whitman leaders also hoped that their own academy might prepare even more students for the college's freshman class. Penrose explained to a New Englander that Whitman was "obligated to maintain a preparatory school because of the lack of secondary education."[138] But it was clear that this academy would not provide many students: in the 1890s it graduated only about ten students every spring, and some rejected further study.

Obviously Whitman, like other western schools, would have to build its enrollment from the graduates of public high schools, but

The well-dressed and mature-looking 1896 graduates of Whitman Academy proudly hold their diplomas.

Penrose complained that very few of them prepared young people for the college and noted that "The public school system . . . is decidedly non-Christian." Thus it would be up to his institution to provide both secular and Christian education. Fully aware of the problems and potential of the high schools, the Whitman faculty in the late 1890s considered ways to get on closer terms with them so as "to secure desirable students in greater numbers."[139] Thus faculty recruiters began to travel to high schools and attend county teachers' association meetings hoping to improve public education. At these gatherings, one of which was held on the college campus, the faculty joined public and private school teachers in discussing educational problems and asked teachers to send promising graduates to Whitman. In the summer of 1900, the college operated its first summer school, offering courses (only three students were needed to make a class) to about fifty teachers and a special course designed to prepare those wanting to take the state teachers' examination. Meanwhile, Penrose worked to publicize the college in newspapers. Because of his friendship with the publisher of the Spokane *Spokesman-Review*, the college got considerable publicity but few Spokane students.

To be admitted to the college, an applicant must either pass an examination administered at the college or present a certificate from an accredited institution, such as a Congregational or other denominational academy, or a public high school. Applicants must have had work in geography, history, English, science, and classical and modern languages. In 1898 Penrose boasted that "our standard of admission is the same as to Dartmouth, Williams, Amherst, and Yale."[140] Whitman applicants had to submit a letter of recommendation and provide information about previous study, current academic interest, and intended place of residence in Walla Walla. Admission to the academy was also by certificate or by examination.

In 1900 college costs, including room, board, heat, light, laundry, textbooks, and library fee ranged from $178 to $394. To help pay these charges needy students could work for fifteen cents an hour under the supervision of the janitor on either the buildings or the grounds. Special jobs were created to help students pay all or part of the tuition, including clerical work for the president or for the director of the conservatory.

The school also offered a few scholarships, which required "a high standard of faithfulness and conduct."[141] Academy scholarships provided less money than those for the college. One interesting scholarship program offered a year's tuition in either the college or the academy to the "graduate of highest standing in each of the High Schools and Academies of Idaho, Oregon, and Washington."[142] Scholarship holders might "be required by the Faculty to do a limited amount of literary or clerical work."[143] Donors establishing scholarships often presented notes, not cash. A gift of $200 a year for a five-year term provided a $1,000 scholarship.

From a typical $1,000 scholarship the recipient received only its earnings, or about $80 per year.[144] This was less than half of a student's yearly school expense. Trying to help as many persons as possible, the school would not provide any additional money to scholarship students, but they might work on campus up to two hours a day. No student could work longer because the faculty feared it would detract from class work. To earn money for college, men were encouraged to labor in summer harvest, and during the school year men and women often worked for room and board in local homes. Most students put themselves through Whitman. Occasionally Penrose and faculty members gave a few dollars out of their own pockets so that the needy might continue. The president and faculty regretted that the institution, with its limited scholarship program, had to reject needy applicants, especially during the depression years of 1894 through 1897.

For a month after the school's fall opening, students—as had been their custom since the institution's founding—drifted into the classrooms from their family farms. Penrose compared those whom he taught at Whitman with his Williams classmates. At Williams he associated with young men of sophistication and means—few worked their way through school. Many had traveled extensively and had familiarity with eastern cultural institutions. By contrast, in Walla Walla he instructed poor and parochial students; they typically depended upon scholarships and jobs and admitted that they had never visited a large city or seen the Pacific Ocean. Nevertheless, the new students quickly learned about their professors' expectations and about the college's mission. They learned that professors set high standards, that the college was in its formative stage, and that it would become a vital regional institution. By their accomplishments as students and then as alumni, these young men and women would help, they were told, build a western college. Penrose frequently described students as being "hard working, industrious, and faithful. I think that in a general way the character of the students and their earnestness will compare favorably with those in any college of the country."[145] The president told his classes and everybody else that Whitman offered work comparable with eastern colleges and that its standards exceeded those of the University of Washington. To his way of thinking, scholarship, student support, and public esteem steadily increased. Many students, like their professors, voiced a lofty institutional vision. A student writer summarized: "There is a feeling of fellowship between the faculty and students without which success would be impossible."[146]

Students, of course, grumbled about academic demands, especially those imposed in the spring. One writer, speaking for Whitman students past and future, found it difficult to meet academic requirements in the spring "when all nature is rejoicing and tempting him forth."[147] Another complained that there was no time for outside reading, writing papers, or physical exercise. To prove the assertion the grumbler presented a statement of time expended during an average week:[148]

Recitation periods, per week	18½ hours
Time spent in study, per week	49 hours
In going to and from school, per week	5 hours
Time spent in work, per week	18 hours
Time spent in chapel, per week	1½ hours
Worship on Sunday	5 hours
Time spent at meals, per week	11 hours
Time spent in sleep, per week	56 hours
Time left for exercise, per week	4 hours
Total number of hours per week	168 hours

The students' religious life was another vital concern of the college. At 8:45 AM they attended chapel, consisting of scripture reading, prayer, music, and an occasional sermon or lecture. The YMCA and the YWCA conducted weekly prayer service for the faculty and students; furthermore, the school "strongly urged" students to attend a church of their choice on Sunday. Penrose had unsuccessfully asked trustees to make church attendance a school requirement.

All groups at Whitman wanted schooling to be enjoyable and broad. To provide breadth of learning, the college brought in speakers, including Civil War general O.O. Howard and poet Joaquin Miller. Raising money for the gymnasium, Whitman's athletic association sponsored a visiting Shakespearean reader. A variety of activities promoted social skills, fun, fellowship, leadership, and loyalty. A student wrote that "the friendships begun while in school ... will prove more lasting than any others." Speaking for many, a college editor concluded that "There are three channels in College open as outlets for the reservoirs of intellectual force. They are: the classroom, which is the chief outlet; the College publication; and the student organizations."[149] Although the students did not govern the classroom, they had considerable influence on the other outlets. There were numerous extracurricular activities, including a mandolin and guitar club, glee clubs, an oratorical association, debate, library societies, and athletic associations for both sexes, as well as a lively college newspaper.

The *Collegian*, Whitman's first newspaper, ran for a few months in 1893 and then fell victim to the regional economic collapse. In 1896 the *Pioneer* appeared. Penrose, who had enjoyed journalism at Williams, played a leading role in establishing this new student newspaper. "Its name," he explained, "was suggested by Oliver Nixon of the Chicago *Inter-Ocean* to suggest the spirit which he hoped the paper and the institution would always embody."[150] The president anticipated that it would provide good training for editors, play a major role in shaping student opinion, and arouse school spirit. The editorial staff wrote editorials, news stories, and specialty columns on a wide range of subjects, including poetry and alumni news. Students controlled their monthly newspaper; according to one of them, it was the "index of their minds and methods of thought;" furthermore, the publication reflected "something of the spirit of the institution."[151] The newspaper set itself above popular journalism because students wanted "meritorious articles [and] did not demand sensational and sentimental matter that lowers the standard of many ... able journals." Proud of the *Pioneer*, Penrose recommended it to supporters for details about "the inner life of the college."[152]

Literary societies for men and women were important social and educational organizations on college campuses from one coast to the other, but at Whitman they lacked vitality until the 1899–1900 school year. In 1897 women in the Alcott Society withdrew their memberships; in 1900 the Libethrean Society replaced it. Both had about the same object: "the development ... of literary study and criticism, oratory, debate, extemporaneous speaking, and dramatic interpretation."[153] Most Whitman women were eligible for membership, but an application had to receive a favorable vote—the Libethrean, for example, required a three-quarters vote. Rarely was a woman denied admission. Membership in the Alcott averaged around twenty, and the Libethrean started with even fewer numbers, so everybody held office, served on committees, or actively participated in weekly programs. In answering the roll call, women sometimes recited famous or original poetry. Attendance was mandatory; those attending voted on the validity of excuses. Small membership fees and fines were imposed. The emphasis of each meeting was literary: recitations, readings, essays, musical performances, and speeches. Sometimes the program was a topic such as "an evening with great composers," including talks and musical performances. Members sometimes debated current political topics ("That foreign immigration should be prohibited"), social questions ("That marriage is not a failure" or "That college theatricals are correct"), or informal topics ("That the horse is more useful than the cow"). Rarely did the secretary comment on the quality of the performance, but the minutes sometimes praised speeches, including "a spicy address on women in politics," a heated debate, or an excellent recitation. Some meetings were public; a few young men were elected as honorary members. There was a close relationship between the societies and the classroom; members might discuss such a question as "Which is better, to study one author thoroughly or gain a general idea of many?" The societies, which met in campus rooms, had fun and developed loyalty. The college community praised the societies for their programs, decorum, and socials.

The objectives, membership requirements, structure, and fees for the men's groups were similar to those for women. There was similarity in the literary exercises, but the men emphasized extemporaneous speaking and debate. These topics, which were generally given in advance, covered a wide range—football, prizefighting, Cuba, direct election of senators, women's suffrage, tariffs, and trusts. There were a few more original subjects, including "That our country is not what our forefathers intended it should be," "That Brutus was justified in killing Caesar," "That the liberty of the press should be curtailed," and "That the republic is in more danger of centralization than disintegration." Debaters sometimes enjoyed a humorous topic, such as a proposal to remove the state capital to raw Pasco, or whether women guests at the literary society's social needed refreshments in addition to "an intellectual feast." To improve the debates, Professor Hauerbach was appointed as a critic; he warned that eloquence and enthusiasm could not make up for a lack of preparation. The male societies sometime debated each other; at these occasions the men waved colors and delivered yells. The societies played an important role in training men for the school's oratorical and debate contests.

The Athenaeum and the Phrenokosomian, literary societies for men, sometimes wasted time correcting unruly members. The minutes of the Athenaeum contain complaints about noise, irrelevant discussions, and tobacco spitting, which led to a resolution prohibiting chewing and spitting at the group's social. The college newspaper said that students and faculty concluded that the organization was a "howling failure."[154] The societies sometime expelled delinquent members. As part of an initiation, members threw men on a canvas or dunked them in the campus stream. Despite their occasionally unruly behavior, members received social and academic benefits from the societies. The faculty regulated and supported the groups, considering them an integral part of college life. Attempts to make the literary societies coeducational drew considerable student support but little from teachers.

Sponsored by the men's literary societies, debate and oratory became important activities. Townspeople and students had often attended campus debates. But in the late 1890s intercollegiate debate created a much greater interest. In 1897 Whitman, the University of Idaho (UI), and Washington Agricultural College (WAC) established an association that adopted rules for intercollegiate oratory and debate. The *Pioneer* and Walla Walla newspapers traced the history of intercollegiate debate since 1892 and explained how important it was to participants. The intercollegiate debate held on March 29, 1898, between Whitman and the University of Idaho was perhaps the first ever held in the Pacific Northwest.[155] The teams considered this question: "Resolved, That it shall be the policy of the United States to

The Athenaeum Society had been founded in 1891; it took great pride in its debating skills and its fellowship. This photograph was taken in 1905.

encourage further territorial expansion." The Walla Walla *Union* promoted the contest, reminding residents of the college town that they should support Whitman's athletic teams and glee clubs, but they should particularly attend debates. The editor insisted that the scheduled topic was important and that the debate would be lively, publicity which helped crowd the opera house. Both sides demonstrated skill, but Whitman, which had the negative side, lost by a split decision. Although the crowd expressed disappointment, it shouted "Long live Idaho."[156]

Whitman was determined to get even. In preparing for a rematch, the Athenaeum researched in the library, the faculty critiqued the speakers, and a local minister served as coach. Wearing the blue and gold of Whitman, a team went to Moscow, where local students greeted the train with the Whitman yell.[157] Names of the visiting team members were posted on bills. The faculty, students, and friends of the university hosted their guests at a reception. At the city hall the colors of both colleges were hung, music was performed, and the question announced, "Resolved, That the late Hispano-American War has been a general benefit to the United States." The visitors won, but the disappointed crowd rendered a Whitman yell.

By 1900 the college not only enjoyed regular debates with its eastern rivals, it also sent an orator to Seattle to compete for cash prizes against the universities of Oregon and Washington in a contest sponsored by the King County Bar Association. Victory celebrations for these forensic contests rivaled those for athletics. For example, a Whitman orator on one occasion defeated those from UI and WAC. Word came to campus; at midnight celebrants pealed the college bell and ignited a bonfire. The fire department rushed to the scene, laid about 500 feet of hose before learning the nature of the fire, and was "not in the best of humor" when departing.[158]

The faculty not only stressed scholarship and supported literary societies and debate, it also urged students to participate in athletics or exercise in the gymnasium. Professors sometimes referred unhealthy men to the president, who, in turn, recommended that they take instruction in the gymnasium.

Athletics followed the same general developmental pattern as forensics: first an effort was made to overcome apathy and expand the program. Obviously Penrose stressed sports. He had thoroughly enjoyed them ever since his undergraduate days and was fully aware that an organized, successful program would provide exercise, build student spirit, and publicize the institution. But, as late as January 1897, students remained rather indifferent to his urgings; a student writer spoke of the need to "awaken an interest in athletics."[159] To accomplish his goal, Penrose, with backing from trustees, the faculty, and students, established prizes for male athletes, assisted a professor in outfitting the gymnasium, encouraged women's sports, established a league with the University of Idaho and Washington Agricultural College, and endorsed athletic competition with the University of Washington (UW).

The school encouraged but controlled women's athletics. In the late 1890s women complained that although they had become interested in athletics, they were denied fair use of the gymnasium and met campus resistance when they attempted to expand their basketball program. According to the *Pioneer*, Walla Wallans saw their first basketball game when a women's team from the college played one from the academy. A condescending student writer stated that "The players showed no roughness nor rudeness." The game proved, he added, that women could run and play silently, which "proved the fallacy ... of man's judgments against women, namely, that when several of them meet together in one room, peace and silence fly out the window."[160]

The Young Women's Athletic Association formed and fought against the male athletic monopoly. But the women found it difficult to secure outdoor playing space or to schedule the gymnasium for basketball.[161] The women organized two school teams, the Bloomers and the Skirts; their intramural games helped raise funds for gymnasium equipment. However, the women's basketball team failed to obtain permission for contests with nearby or distant opponents. According to the Walla Walla *Union* of December 11, 1902, Penrose provided a reason for not permitting women to engage in athletic contests outside of Walla Walla. "We believe," the president explained, "that the girls are under enough strain and expend enough nervous energy in the contests at the school without engaging in intercollegiate games." Whitman women expressed displeasure with this paternalism. In 1903, the women's literary societies, defying rules and tradition, played a baseball game near a city slaughterhouse and

*Student manager and senior Cecil Roy Wade (in bowler hat)
poses with the baseball team in 1902.*

denied admission to all males. Whitman's faculty considered men's
athletics far more important and told women to be content with intramural basketball, gymnastics, and tennis.

Men's basketball gained support slowly because some thought
that the game was feminine, and others did not understand or appreciate it. To advance the sport, the *Pioneer* in 1900 explained the
fundamentals, concluding that "basketball, like baseball and football, calls for a high class of team play; the grandstand player is worse
than useless.... It is a fascinating game, free from injurious qualities."[162] Although college classes competed, there were no intercollegiate basketball contests prior to 1900. Track was also slow to develop, but in 1900 Whitman battled the UW squad and lost every event
except a bicycle race.

Football and baseball were the major college sports. The community supported the Whitman nine, and the faculty often granted them
permission to play out of town. However, far more campus attention
was given to football, a controversial game from one coast to the
other. The *Pioneer*, which gave considerable space to football in the
late 1890s, complained in 1897 about Whitman's lack of interest in
the sport. After pointing out that the athletic association had im-

proved the gymnasium and the field, an editor concluded, "Under these auspicious circumstances, let an endeavor be made to put football in its rightful position—the first rank in college athletics."[163] Apparently the newspaper, Penrose, and other boosters succeeded, for in 1897 the college scheduled its longest football season, which resulted in victories over the Whitman Academy, Waitsburg Academy, and Walla Walla High School, and a defeat at the hands of WAC. Students enthusiastically embraced the game: at the gridiron they wore and waved the school colors, blew horns, and rendered yells in support of teams defending "Whitman's glory and honor." Whitman women honored the players with a reception which "took away the sting of . . . defeat."[164]

Every year the *Pioneer* continued to advocate football, insisting that the game was rough, not brutal, that it required brains as well as muscles. In fact, "It makes the blood course faster through every vein; it makes the heart beat faster; it makes one tingle with excitement; and it thrills one with the joy of living."[165] An editorial entitled "Ethics of Football" complained about professional, semi-professional, and brutal players. The author concluded that the honorable player "holds himself proudly above every unfair and cowardly advantage . . . [and] fights a hard fight and fights it fairly."[166] Another writer noted the national debate over football, emphasizing that "faculties, for tolerating such brutalities, are denominated book idiots, devoid of common sense."[167] To attract more players, a Whitman football captain assured his readers that the game "was not incompatible with good scholarship nor with Christian manhood."[168] In fostering football at Whitman, Penrose no doubt introduced arguments he and his classmates at Williams had used.

Football received attention across the Pacific Northwest and, as Penrose had hoped, developed school spirit. The *Pioneer* emphasized the sport, providing extensive accounts of football games and much less coverage of other sports. Football often sparked intercollegiate rivalry. For example, WAC students, upset by refereeing, castigated Whitman, whereupon the *Pioneer* heatedly responded by referring to Pullman students as "the exterminators of potato-bugs and sifters of hay seed."[169]

Whitman football enjoyed a banner season in 1899 with victories over UI and WAC, and, in a game played in the Seattle mud, the blue

and gold lost to uw by a close score of six to five. This contest provided some players with their first glimpse of the ocean. The faculty
prohibited all Whitman athletic teams from traveling on Sundays.

To improve the football squad the trustees in 1900 unsuccessfully
tried to hire Charles W. "Warhorse" Allen, a former University of
Chicago player, as its coach. Obviously Whitman, like many other
institutions, was struck by football fever, and reliance on amateur
faculty and students as coaches was unacceptable. Victory required
skilled coaches, and even debt-ridden Whitman was willing to pay
the price.

In 1900 Professor Walter Bratton wrote a summary of Whitman
athletics for a Spokane newspaper. He called the school the "amateur
champions of Eastern Washington and Idaho," explaining that this
title rested upon training, sportsmanship, and a good athletic field.[170]
The professor stressed "that athletics is not the entire occupation of a
few students . . . for the diversion of the many who themselves get no
exercise." Because the school had so many teams, including three in
football and three in baseball, at least ninety percent of the men were
in one or more sports, which, he boasted, helped maintain "the good
health of the boys and are also conducive to the development of some
of the strongest types of courage, honesty, and manliness."

Sports were not the only test of the school's unity and spirit. The
Spanish-American War of 1898, many believed, had an impact on the
small college and tested its patriotism. Several Whitman students
soon volunteered. Penrose boasted that Whitman had a greater representation in the First Washington Regiment than any other institution. A former United States senator in a chapel address acknowledged that young men wanted to serve, but he suggested that they not
enlist. A *Pioneer* editorial agreed: "At present our country is less in
need of student volunteers than the West has need of educated men to
take the responsibilities of the government of this great common-
wealth in the not far distant future."[171] Students wildly celebrated
Dewey's victory, male students participated in a twice-weekly compulsory military drill led by a Fort Walla Walla lieutenant, and nearly
everybody, including the debate team, took a great interest in the war
and its ramifications. One student urged a current events club to keep
pace with a rapidly changing world. A former Whitmanite in the
Philippines drew the attention of classmates: Albert Knudson rose

from private to chaplain in the Washington regiment, and the *Pioneer* published his war letters. In November 1899 he and five other former students returned with their unit to Walla Walla. Whitman closed in honor of the occasion and unsuccessfully attempted to get the veterans back into classrooms. The six veterans brought a small bell bearing the names of twenty-five Whitman men who had soldiered in the regiment and presented it to "The Young Men's Dormitory."[172] The men claimed to have taken this old bell as a token of war from a fortified place in the Philippines.

The honoring of the college with a bell was an example of the school spirit that Stephen Penrose sought to instill. In 1896 a *Pioneer* editor had defined the importance of college spirit: "a patriotic feeling for one's college determines the success of the school. It is as truly a virtue as is the love for one's country, and as truly exists."[173] Other editors also wrote on the subject, including this sentiment: "May we not have more of the true college spirit which imparts dignity to those who possess it and will make others coming in contact with it feel that it is a privilege and a great honor to be numbered among the students of Whitman?"[174] Students asserted that Penrose's optimism and cheerfulness, faculty and student friendships, and forensics and athletic contests all made for a college spirit. There was continued talk about increasing school loyalty. By 1900 the president hailed the emerging college spirit and predicted that it would help to build a greater institution.

Although the school emphasized this spirit, there were disciplinary problems. The catalog carried a general statement on discipline: "Good manners and proper deportment are required of all students, and those whose character is not satisfactory to the Faculty will not be allowed to attend."[175] If students accumulated more than seven unexcused absences from classes or chapel, they were put on probation and were liable to expulsion. But there were more difficult problems that required faculty action: cheating in class, lying, vandalism, theft of school property, and insubordination. Those charged with such misbehavior were called before the president, the discipline committee, or even the entire faculty. Violators were censured or placed on probation. Parents generally requested reinstatement of expelled sons and daughters. Teenage boys in the academy committed most of the offenses, especially just before school concluded in

May. Disgusted with boys who broke into college buildings and destroyed property, trustees advised the faculty to "hand over to the civil authorities . . . all cases of misdemeanors affecting both the college and the public."[176] Professors rejected this harsh proposal but temporarily employed a special policeman.

In 1897 a long, troubling, and divisive case came before the faculty; it also attracted newspaper attention. Several academy sophomores barricaded Professor Jean Reynaud in his room. A graduate of the University of Paris, and a soldier who taught French at Fort Walla Walla prior to coming to Whitman as a teacher of modern language and gymnastics, Reynaud had outfitted the gymnasium. Although many appreciated the ex-soldier's diverse contributions, several students bristled at his rigidity and arrogance. Reynaud accused a critic, Ben Stone, of blocking his door; an argument ensued and both complained to the faculty that the other had shouted profanity. The faculty decided that Stone, in locking up Reynaud, had "acted in a malicious and ungentlemanly manner," concluding that he had been profane.[177] At a special faculty meeting, Stone and his witnesses testified, whereupon the faculty temporarily suspended all the boys on the grounds of "general delinquence." Several students then sided with their classmates; parents insisted on a full investigation. Concerned about the number of students aligned against its action, the faculty agreed to investigate. Eventually it voted to readmit the suspended males and place them on probation. At this, Reynaud resigned, growling that his colleagues were too soft.

Despite this incident, most observers who understood the school's condition undoubtedly agreed with a trustee who concluded that under Penrose "internal affairs in the college have moved smoothly."[178] Oliver Nixon recalled that during his 1896 visit only a handful of townspeople thought the institution would survive, but when he returned in 1900 the community embraced the school. There were campus squabbles, of course, but evidence about them is sketchy. Faculty members sometimes criticized Penrose's actions; Lyman, for example, complained that their leader did not do enough to improve woeful salaries. Older professors compared Penrose with other college presidents and his two Whitman predecessors. Instructors in the conservatory denounced director S. Harrison Lovewell's autocratic methods, and this criticism eventually led to his resignation. Trustee Myron Eells related that Penrose's move in 1896 to replace treasurer John Boyer with Thompson Coit Elliott ignited a fiery board meeting. Harry Reynolds angrily resigned from the board, but Eells calmed him down.

Although most of Whitman's internal problems were probably typical, there was one serious difficulty that had long-range ramifications. In the summer of 1900 treasurer Elliott was forced to resign and Allen H. Reynolds replaced him. There were probably several reasons for this administrative change. A New Englander, an 1885 Amherst graduate, and a Walla Walla banker since 1886, Elliott was sympathetic with a liberal arts college but argued that it should be managed like a business. He accused President Penrose of ignoring financial details and running up annual deficits. Elliott unsuccessfully attempted to control the president by finding allies in Walla Walla and the East. In a choice between the treasurer and the president, the trustees, who did not share Elliott's alarm about the school's debt, championed Penrose because of his many accomplishments. Elliott fared no better in his appeals to easterners, including Dox. She told Penrose about a letter from Elliott but refused to provide details. Oliver Nixon wrote Elliott that he was too exacting with Penrose and that cooperation and fellowship among the school's leaders and supporters would overcome problems. "Benevolent work," Nixon wrote, "is like a sensitive plant, touch it roughly and the leaves wither and droop."[179] Although Pearsons shared some of Elliott's concerns about Penrose's lack of business sense, he judged that the president was absolutely essential to the school's success. Pearsons heard both sides of the dispute and recommended that Elliott be dismissed.

Elliott and Penrose also heatedly disagreed over the role of Marcus Whitman. Elliott was a well-read local historian and thought the president made too much of the Whitman-saved-Oregon story. Both men were strong-willed, which worsened their relationship. Soon after the treasurer resigned, Penrose received the first of several nasty, unsigned letters which he presumed were written by Elliott, who vigorously denied it. In 1911 Penrose turned the spiteful letters over to the postal authorities. By that time the two Walla Wallans had clashed over other issues.

A Summary of Penrose's First Years

Penrose could look back with satisfaction over his first six years at Whitman. He was content in his personal life. Mary had easily adjusted to western life; she shared his dreams, joys, and frustrations. The Penroses had become parents; their first child was born in 1898. Friends recommended that she be named Narcissa Whitman, but the Penroses preferred Mary, a family name. A sister, Frances, arrived on Whitman Founder's Day, 1900. Penrose called his daughters "creditable western products."[180] In his letters to the Penroses, Pearsons often inquired about their health, provided advice about rearing them, and referred to the first daughter as "Jim Dandy." To escape the heat of a Walla Walla summer and to provide a place for family vacations, the Penroses bought land at Delano Beach in 1900. For years they took summer outings at this Puget Sound site, which is now Penrose Point State Park and offers the public recreational opportunities similar to those the Penrose family enjoyed.

The president's professional career was equally satisfying. During a national depression he had lifted a frontier institution out of a

Mary Penrose quickly adapted to conditions at the young college. In this 1896 photograph she posed (in chair) with the first girl's glee club. Seated directly behind her is Arminda Fix, who graduated from Whitman in 1899 and from then until 1916 served as the college's first librarian.

quagmire and placed it on a firm foundation. He had attracted capable allies who had helped him raise an endowment. He had begun a meaningful scholarship program, increased the size of the campus, erected two impressive and useful buildings, hired a talented faculty, increased the size and quality of the student body, kindled student spirit, and made the school essential to both the local and the state Congregational churches. Penrose had also streamlined the school's administration. He often called meetings of the executive committee of the trustees, which accepted a more active administrative role. At its spring meeting the full board generally approved the actions of the executive committee. Myron Eells found it difficult to get from his Hood Canal home to Walla Walla trustee meetings. Penrose obtained his resignation so that a local man could be president of the board, always at hand to discuss policy.[181] A prominent Walla Wallan, Dr. Nelson G. Blalock, soon filled the position and proved to be an able ally. The board applauded Penrose's vigorous leadership, and on at least one occasion it learned that opposition to his policy would prompt his resignation.

Stephen Penrose must have considered that he had revived the Dayton Congregational church in four years and Whitman College in six. He received supportive letters from many residents of the region; some stated that they no longer worried about the college's future. Penrose's eastern friends expected him to leave the West and become president of a prestigious school. In their view, he had proved himself at a weak institution and now deserved something much better. But Penrose explained why he rejected several such professional opportunities: "It is more fun to make a college than to take one already made."[182]

In 1900 a different opportunity arose. Republicans asked Penrose to run for the state senate. Oliver Nixon advised him against politics: "You are now in your proper place. The trickery necessary in these days for the successful politician is not in you. . . . The time may come . . . when some grand place in public life may be given you, which will not only be an honor but remunerative."[183]

Penrose knew, at the turn of the century, that it was time for the next stage in his building up of the college. To become a regional, not just a local institution, Whitman had to draw students from beyond the Walla Walla Valley. Penrose knew that there were other private schools on the West Coast that aspired to reach beyond their local communities; those that failed often closed. Schools that he most admired—Williams, Amherst, Dartmouth, Yale, Oberlin—and used as a measuring rod for his young institution's growth, had the ability to draw students from major urban centers as well as small towns. By comparison, Whitman, as late as the 1900–1901 school year, had not attracted a single student from Seattle or Portland, and only a couple had come down from Spokane. Penrose had visited these urban centers. He had told Seattle High School's principal that he wanted its graduates. But news stories, advertisements, and these visits had been unproductive. To recruit regional students the college employed a field agent in the summer of 1900.

Penrose thought that a reduction of railroad fares would increase enrollment; therefore, he urged the Northern Pacific and other lines to sell a special student ticket. In 1898 he explained that "Whitman College would draw a number of students who are now deterred from coming by the high rate of railroad fares."[184] To his way of thinking the railroads would benefit from increased travel to Walla Walla. He explained the practices of eastern companies, which charged students the same fees as those who traveled to "political and mercantile gatherings." In Illinois, for example, all the railroads gave special school rates. When the railroad companies refused, Penrose concluded in disgust, "Perhaps the western roads do not as much appreciate the value of educational institutions to a country as the roads of the East."

Another problem was the annual budget deficit. At the end of the 1896, 1897, and 1898 school years, it ran between $2,000 and $2,500, an imbalance resulting primarily from the cost of professors' salaries and from the purchase of additional land. Penrose was not overly concerned about this debt, explaining that "almost every college in the country runs behind each year on its current expenses and makes up the deficiency by appealing to the alumni as does Yale."[185] Apparently Walla Wallans, alumni, or Penrose himself covered these annual debts. The president thought that a little western college would have deficits and gave a general explanation for them: "A college is not like a grocery store which can cut down its stock and curtail its expenses at any time, but a college advertises to do certain work and must do it. It makes a contract with the public to that effect." He also empha-

sized that the school operated on a stringent budget: "certainly salaries here are as low as anywhere, and I think that the only distinction
among college presidents that I enjoy, is that of having the smallest
salary."

In 1900 the deficit increased to about $5,000 because of unantici-
pated costs associated with the construction of Billings Hall. This was
no surprise. From the construction of College Hall in 1888 and for the
next hundred years, campus construction often exceeded predictions.
Billings Hall, for example, was supposed to have cost $25,000, but
furnishings and a heating plant increased the amount by about
$4,000. Much of this debt was met, but then there were new bills for a
new sewer and water system. To cover these needs, the trustees borrowed about $4,500 at a stiff eight percent. Obviously feeling less
alarm than Chicago supporters did, western businessmen were more
accustomed to paper debts. Nixon, however, warned the college "of
the nightmare of a floating debt" that would discourage potential
contributors. "No one," he lectured, "likes to buy an interest in a
dead horse, no matter how good he may have been in life."[186] Pearsons also was angry that the debt had jumped to $5,000 and notified
Penrose not to expect new gifts from him until he balanced the books.

Fund raising dogged the president. The library, scholarship program, laboratories, endowment, grounds, and even a clock to fill the
gaps in Memorial Hall's tower required various sums. Penrose also
wanted to add a gymnasium and a science hall, but the primary need
was a women's dormitory. He had proposed such a building at the
time that he planned for a men's dormitory. The leader chose to build
the one for men first, because of his desire to have men safely housed
on campus and away from urban distractions. The fear that boys and
young men would become ensnared in the city's allurements resulted
from his experience as a teacher in both the East and the West.

Envious of the commodious men's dormitory, women students
complained to the president that Ladies' Hall remained jammed and
that they found it difficult to make college friends when they were
"pastured" in city homes. Protestors wanted accommodations similar to those that male classmates enjoyed at Billings Hall. Penrose
assured the complainers that a local person would see the need for
improved housing and would give $25,000 for a women's dormitory,
which should be called Narcissa Whitman Hall. In 1899 he had rea-

soned that the construction of two handsome stone buildings "would mean a new status for the college in the minds of the community and other buildings will follow fast."[187] Unfortunately, a local donor had not appeared by 1900, and Penrose searched in vain in the East for another Julia Billings.

The need for additional construction reintroduced the controversy over local support. Penrose had praised Walla Wallans for their financial help; for example, he told Virginia Dox to inform easterners that from 1894 through 1899 the college had received a "very creditable" $70,000 from local donors.[188]

Actually the president had no other choice. To have stated that there was little community assistance would have discouraged eastern supporters, especially the CES and Pearsons, who demanded evidence of local help. Both the CES and Pearsons protested that the school had received much less local financial assistance than it merited; the financier maintained that both Colorado College and Pomona College had attracted more help from their communities. Penrose must have privately expressed disappointment over the fact that some of Walla Walla's leading families—Baker, Boyer, Isaacs, Ankeny, and Stubblefield—had not been more generous. Easterners, especially the CES, Pearsons, Billings, and Dox, had provided most of the money that established the institution because they shared Penrose's vision of a small eastern-style college. Penrose had clearly chosen his model. In 1900 he proclaimed that Whitman must always stand "for those ideals of education which have made the New England colleges the best servants of the nation."[189] To provide such a high quality of education, the president understood that he must soon raise more dollars as well as recruit more students in the region Whitman served. Trustees, professors, students, and friends also realized that money and students were the college's basic needs as it entered a new century.

6

Building the Liberal Arts College

1900 — 1907

In his first years as president, the mere survival of the college had been Stephen Penrose's chief concern. But as the college grew stronger, his worries grew more complex. Between 1900 and 1907 he simultaneously considered finances, buildings, faculty, students, curriculum, alumni, boards, and public relations. With a bright memory of his Williams experience and a dogged determination to build a college similar to this eastern model, Penrose plunged into his demanding responsibilities. For those who knew the role of Oberlin in the Midwest and Williams and Yale in New England, he asserted the hope that Whitman might become similarly important to the growing Pacific Northwest. To uninformed westerners, Penrose patiently explained that private colleges offering demanding academic courses and religious instruction provided the best training for the rising generation. In 1906 he summarized his thoughts on education:

> It is the purpose of education, in my judgment, to help to live nobly. Training, technical training, helps to make a living. The State, according to our American system, cannot provide a complete education because at present time it omits the religious element. I think we shall have in the education system of the future, both the endowed college and the state university. The present trend is strongly towards the former, though the latter still holds its own. The endowed college must be managed by men of high integrity and fine sense of honor.[1]

To a minister Penrose expressed his preference for education over evangelism. "I think that a certain amount of evangelism is necessary ... but as Martin Luther said, 'You can't teach old dogs new tricks' and the evangelism of adults undertakes to do that very thing. My suggestion is merely to recognize that the time for teaching dogs is when they are puppies."[2]

For this reason Penrose had to give attention to the academy and the conservatory. The educator wanted the academy to provide a solid foundation for college-bound boys and girls and for boys pursuing business careers. The conservatory should offer solid musical instruction and appreciation. The academy had to be continued until public high schools attained higher standards; the conservatory should be improved so that it would receive at least western recognition. It was the college, however, that was the most important component to him. Penrose wanted it to be the best regional institution, deserving a national reputation. Until 1907 he kept the eastern private college as his standard, but he did not slavishly imitate any one esteemed institution. He hailed the rigorous academics and collegiate spirit of Williams, but he modeled his music program after Oberlin's. Penrose also pushed for curricular changes to meet particular regional needs. For example, using Yale, Colorado College, and others as models, he thought that a traditional college could offer engineering without losing its liberal arts emphasis. Penrose knew that the small colleges must adapt to a changing American society; he was willing to modify the curriculum to meet contemporary needs.

Thus the educational leader established goals and by 1907 had accomplished several. But a variety of setbacks, primarily financial, slowed institutional growth. In the early twentieth century he attracted fewer financial supporters than anticipated. He had incorrectly assumed that a growing institution offering solid courses would appeal to both eastern and western supporters. Penrose's record demonstrates that money was a crucial missing ingredient. If he had received a few million dollars, most of his goals would have been realized. If money had been added to his vision and energy, Whitman might have been an outstanding national college prior to the First World War. Money problems hounded him, and when he was discouraged he talked about abandoning his career as educational builder for a calmer life as a theology professor.

President Penrose was not alone in his dilemma, of course. Many other college builders consistently hammered on the importance of their schools and regions. For instance, in 1904, Bowdoin president William DeWitt Hyde, whom Penrose admired, insisted that a college education could not be measured in money. Like Penrose, Hyde praised his environment: "The Maine air and the Maine climate are good; and the Maine stock is better." Both educational leaders continually pleaded for endowment; Hyde predicted that without it the college "will be crushed out of existence between the rapidly improving high school below and the expanding universities above."[3]

Fund Raising: The Persistent Problem

The president was sure that he was frugal and that the annual debt resulted from two factors: the decision to expand the college and the small endowment. He calculated that the institution had only half the money it needed; the school would have a deficit until it acquired a $500,000 endowment. But Whitman's growth could not wait for a larger endowment, he argued. To build a first-rate college, Penrose and the trustees bought land, erected buildings, and acquired equipment. He sought money for specific building projects—including a women's dormitory, a gymnasium, and a science hall—and for the endowment, the debt, and operating costs. Reporting in 1904, he itemized the debt that created "a heavy load of anxiety":[4] the purchase of land, buildings, equipment, and maintenance resulted in a $59,000 deficit. He explained that any growing college would be in debt and that "the trustees have felt that it would be unwise to check this rapid growth by too rigid economy, and have preferred to incur debt rather than to retard the steady development of the college."[5] The president consistently sought money to reduce the debt and the "heavy burden" of its annual interest, but he also sought to increase faculty salaries, which he said lagged behind those of other northwest schools.[6] He warned that the loss of able faculty would slow development because effective professors attracted and retained students. These objectives seemed more important in the early 1900s than an increase in the scholarship budget.

Records of gifts received in the early twentieth century are sketchy, but donors gave modest amounts of money, land, books, equip-

ment, and other items. A few who had pledged money to Virginia
Dox continued to contribute their $2 to $5 a year; a Marcus Whitman Society in a Columbus, Ohio, Congregational church sent a
small sum, and the ladies of the Eliot Church in Lowell, Massachusetts, shipped sheets and pillowslips for a dormitory room. Such well-
meaning gifts were acknowledged, but of course they did not meet
basic needs.

Penrose tried various, unsuccessful strategies to raise money, but
by 1907 he was so frustrated with his reversals that he told both his
wife and D.K. Pearsons that he might resign. For a time in 1902
matters had looked promising because Pearsons gave a $50,000 en-
dowment to match $25,000 to be raised by the college for a women's
dormitory. Pearsons, who was by far the most generous contributor,
then stopped donating and informed Penrose that he would not give
additional money until he had helped struggling southern schools.
The Chicago benefactor often told Oliver Nixon that Whitman was
doing well and only needed proper fiscal management. Nevertheless,
Penrose hoped that Pearsons would again contribute and often asked
Nixon how to convince him to do so.

Pearsons' attitude meant that Penrose had to seek other contributors. In 1901 he employed a minister as field agent to find donors like
Julia Billings and to recruit students. Penrose was particularly concerned about the $4,500 debt on Billings Hall, realizing that Pearsons
would not give additional funds until it was retired. Because of low
wheat prices Walla Wallans could not be asked for the $4,500; there-
fore, the school's agent set out to solicit Congregational ministers and
businesspeople west of the Cascades.

While this western effort proved unrewarding, Pearsons sent discouraging news about the East. An agent employing Dox's tactics, he
feared, would have scant success in New England. Scores of college
agents and presidents harried potential donors. The school must seek
help in its own locality where there was enough wealth to support the
town's valuable asset.

Stephen Penrose knew from experience that an eastern campaign
would be difficult. He had recently failed to collect money on a swing
through New England, but he convinced himself and the trustees that
a more determined effort would succeed. They all knew that outside
money had been far more important than local funds in building and

operating the college. Whitman still depended a great deal upon eastern assistance.

In 1902 Penrose convinced his board that another field agent
might accomplish two objectives: raising funds from easterners, especially from those who had given to Virginia Dox, and upon his return
recruiting students in the Pacific Northwest. To accomplish these important goals the college selected the Reverend Frank Whitham, a
Congregational minister at Ritzville, and paid him $300 more than
Penrose's salary. The president told Whitham that his position was
one of "honor and great usefulness" and that he would enjoy "the
satisfaction of helping to build up ... one of the great institutions of
the Northwest."[7] After learning the college's history and experiencing its spirit by visiting the campus, the eager agent headed east in
1903. Whitham enthused that "I take up this work in the conviction
that God is leading me."[8] In Chicago, Congregationalists offered
praise of the young college, not cash or pledges. In Hartford, Connecticut, his efforts proved equally fruitless. Penrose urged the agent
on. The college needed money for current expenses and a women's
dormitory; trustees feared closing the school year with "a disastrous
debt."[9] Pressured by Penrose and rejected by potential donors, Whitham wrote that his inability to raise money made it impossible for
him to eat or sleep. He suffered from bronchitis. He complained that
some people whom Penrose identified as donors had refused to meet
him. Others would not give to Whitman because they knew that
Pearsons had generously aided the college, which was now on "its
feet and ought to quit this house to house begging."[10] Even Nathaniel
Shipman, Penrose's father-in-law, advised Whitham to discontinue
Dox's tactic of visiting homes, offices, and churches. Frustrated by
continuing failure, Whitham predicted he could be more successful in
Washington state's Congregational churches than in the homes and
offices of wealthy easterners.

After four months Whitham had raised only $135 and begged
Penrose to send him railroad fare so he could return home. Penrose
refused, saying there "is no reason why you should not make a brilliant success of your work in the East."[11] He insisted that money and
friends were to be found, especially if Whitham followed Dox's example and canvassed small towns. The president told Whitham to
explain that Pearsons had indeed supported Whitman but that the

gifts had actually increased operating costs. In other words, Whitham must join Penrose in explaining to potential donors that a larger institution had greater expenses. However, this approach often failed, because Whitman's handsome buildings, growing student body, and expanding endowment seemed proof of solid financial footing.

By late April Penrose agreed with Whitham, Pearsons, and Shipman, calling his agent's task "discouraging and disheartening."[12] It was clearly impossible to reintroduce Dox's techniques; she simply had greater fund-raising abilities than her successors. There were other realities: eastern perceptions of the college's financial needs had changed, and competition for eastern money had intensified as many schools sought to expand. In the progressive age, colleges like Whitman still turned to the Northeast and to Chicago in search of funds required for buildings, equipment, endowments, scholarships, faculty salaries, and balanced budgets. The pleas for dollars were deafening but largely unanswered.

Whitham's luckless effort was probably not the only school campaign that failed to raise enough money to cover even travel costs. Although he wanted to be rehired and to try again with an improved pitch for Whitman, the trustees refused. Instead of conducting a drive based on the Dox model, they and Penrose decided to concentrate on regional donors and eastern financiers and foundations.

In 1904 the president sought money in two different ways. Emphasizing the need for dollars to cover current expenses, he asked college friends to contribute to a $5,000 annual maintenance fund. Emphasizing that such a sum would reduce anxiety and expand the college, Penrose asked a hundred persons to give $50 each for five years. He assumed that this modest appeal would be successful. At the same time he challenged trustees: "Either we must retrench and do our work with a smaller faculty or we must increase our income."[13] This fund-raising strategy failed, but Penrose repeated it in 1906. He wrote many letters to college friends and to the county's chief taxpayers. Some contributed, but in 1907 the local economy soured and donations declined.

A second 1904 tactic was more ambitious. Following the example of other college and university leaders, Penrose sought funds from famous and wealthy eastern financiers. In 1901 he had unsuccessfully appealed to J.P. Morgan for $35,000. Little is known about this request, but Nixon had encouraged it because he thought that it would elevate Whitman to university status. Pearsons explained that Morgan had forgotten about the letter. Penrose doubted that the financier would give money, but in 1904 it seemed much more likely that another wealthy figure, Andrew Carnegie, would make a sizeable donation because he had provided library buildings at Beloit, Pacific, and Pomona. Penrose did not consider a library among his school's basic needs; the endowment and a gymnasium ranked higher. The president did not anticipate that Carnegie would provide dollars for either of these needs; therefore, he asked the industrialist for a $50,000 science hall. The building would cost $30,000 and the remaining funds would be used to equip and maintain it. Like other college leaders, he mobilized support for his appeal to Carnegie. He turned to two politicians, Levi Ankeny, a Whitman trustee who had been elected to the United States Senate in 1902, and his own cousin, Senator Boise Penrose (who represented Carnegie's home state), urging them to inform the philanthropist about the college's merits. Penrose reminded these senators that a Carnegie gift would encourage other wealthy individuals to make sizeable contributions. Meanwhile, Mary Penrose, who knew both Connecticut senators, convinced them to write supportive letters to Carnegie.

Stephen Penrose also won the assistance of D.K. Pearsons, who promised, "I will do all I can for you with Carnegie but you will have to go slow and watch for the right time to approach him. He is pestered to death with the great crowd. We all know that Whitman is a trump and you are a very good boy."[14] Pearsons expressed a willingness to promote Whitman with Carnegie in New York. He assured Penrose that, "We shall win in the end."[15] Pearsons did not visit Carnegie but wrote him and sent a published speech about the school. In the late summer of 1904 Pearsons wrote, "I have given Carnegie your character and convictions, and it is a case that will appeal to him I think. I feel quite certain that he will look with favor on Whitman. I am delighted with your prospects."[16]

Penrose shared this optimism. In a letter to an alumnus, he confided, "I am expecting to hear from Carnegie offering us $50,000 for a Science Hall but the matter has not yet reached the stage for public notice. He has had the merits of the college brought to his attention in a very forcible way, and I hope it will prove effective."[17]

But the appeal failed. Incomplete college records for 1905 indicate only that in September Penrose submitted a grand proposal to Carnegie. In a letter to James Bertram, Carnegie's secretary, he explained, "We want to establish in the Northwest a scientific school equal in rank to that at Lowell or the Massachusetts Institute of Technology, and I believe that we are unequalled in need and opportunity."[18] If Carnegie gave $500,000 then the school would raise $250,000 as a match. This would be a promising start in an effort to raise the $5,000,000 that would be required in order to realize the educator's long-range goals.

The ambitious and controversial plan to transform Whitman into a western MIT was not publicized. In private letters Penrose explained this so-called new departure. He wrote, "I feel that the establishment of a department of electrical engineering of the highest grade will be the first and most important step towards establishing here in the northwest a great school of science, which in time will be for the Pacific Coast what the Massachusetts Institute of Technology and Cornell are doing for the east."[19] Apparently Penrose, the faculty, and other leaders came to the conclusion that the best way to build the institution was to broaden its curriculum. In other words, a liberal arts college based on a New England model had only a limited appeal. Whitman recruiters learned from potential students, especially in Spokane, Portland, Tacoma, and Seattle, and from business leaders in these cities, that Whitman would be of great service to young men and the growing region if it offered engineering, especially electrical. Those trained in such a program would develop the region's great water-power potential. Penrose explained that Whitman "ought to get hold of the bright, energetic young men who are turning in such large numbers towards electrical engineering. I believe that we could meet a long felt want, and bring to Whitman some of the best young men in the Northwest."[20] Eventually the school would add civil and mechanical engineering; students in these technical programs would, the president assured listeners, receive a thorough grounding in the liberal arts. Penrose called this the Whitman stamp. Although the University of Washington offered electrical and other types of engineering, Penrose reasoned that students would receive a better total education in a small college offering engineering than in a public university.

To make his case Penrose emphasized that Colorado College had in 1903 established a school of engineering, including mining and electrical programs. The addition of applied science classes had strengthened that school; the same, he assumed, could happen at Whitman. In 1905 Penrose visited Colorado College's science hall; two years later he wrote away for its blueprints.

Favoring "the old fashioned college,"[21] Pearsons, who had largely funded Colorado College's hall of science, opposed adding engineering to the Whitman curriculum. This must have frustrated Penrose, who had hoped that the Chicagoan would provide the same kind of aid for Whitman's expanding science program as he had for Colorado's. Pearsons, however, was less important to Penrose than Andrew Carnegie, who might fund a science hall. But Carnegie's secretary, James Bertram, complained that Penrose's request for $500,000 was two times the size of the school's endowment. He bluntly advised, "Now if you will pardon me, Mr. Penrose, the first thing to do is get down from the air onto solid ground."[22] He would not forward Penrose's inflated request to Carnegie but promised to submit to the financier "The one most vital proponent need of the college as it exists."

Stephen Penrose refused to reduce his request and defended it. The president agreed that "Slow growth is ordinarily preferable, but it is not necessary, as witness Cornell and Chicago University. The judgment of some of the best educational experts in the United States is that Whitman College will be the Yale or Harvard of the Pacific Northwest."[23] By calling attention to Cornell, Penrose believed that he would make an impression because Carnegie served as one of its trustees. The applicant also insisted that after twenty-three years as a college Whitman was stronger than Yale after its first hundred years. Explaining that he had considered asking for funds for a library building, a dormitory, or a conservatory of music, Penrose concluded, "The one thing needed now is the establishment in this part of the country of a great school of science where the engineers who shall develop the amazing natural resources of this country can be prepared by a training as rigorous, under influences as inspiring, as those to be found in the best institutions of the East." After establishing a technical school, various departments would be added. If Carnegie gave $500,000, such a great institution would be built within a few years. The president hoped that the philanthropist would also see the need for a Carnegie Institute or an MIT in the Pacific Northwest, that he would learn that Whitman was a solid institution known for "its work and for its high ideals of life and character," and that he would acknowledge that it was at the geographic and strategic center for the young states of Oregon, Washington, and Idaho. In summary, Carnegie could help train skilled engineers and useful citizens in a promising region.

Secretary Bertram remained blind to Penrose's grand vision. He refused to meet Penrose, who had traveled to New York for this purpose, or to introduce him to Carnegie. The secretary curtly explained that his employer did not want to start schools but would assist those that had specific requests "in modest proportion to what exists already."[24] Bertram terminated his exchange with Penrose by noting Whitman's unimpressive financial standing and low enrollment of 107 students and concluded, "I am sorry that I have already given so much time to such an unreasonable application, which of course Mr. Carnegie cannot pay any attention to."

This 1906 failure to secure money from Carnegie did not divert Penrose from his plan to add an engineering department. Perhaps his persistence resulted from Pearsons' admonition: "You lack the power of persuasion, try and acquire it."[25] To an eastern friend Penrose wrote that Carnegie and Rockefeller had rejected his proposals, "but like a proper college president I live in hope, and never know what tomorrow may bring forth."[26] The president got the college's executive board to support another appeal to Carnegie for as much as $500,000; the full board of trustees, however, considered it hopeless.

Early in 1907 Penrose modified his approach, asking Carnegie and the General Education Board, which awarded John D. Rockefeller's money, for $100,000 each. To each potential donor he explained, "We want to have an MIT or a Cornell here in the Northwest ... and we think that electrical engineers will necessarily have a large part to play in the development of this section. We want these men to have a kind of education which Whitman College gives, first class as respects intellectual culture, and according to Christian ideals."[27] The educator repeated other arguments: "I am quite sure that no private college in the west is situated at so strategic a point, has so admirable a history, or is doing work of so high a grade as Whitman

College." Penrose complained that many western schools did not seek to achieve his high standards.[28]

The president explained to the General Education Board why Whitman could not raise $300,000 to match $100,000 that it might give for the endowment. Whitman had only 150 alumni, and the males—most of whom had paid for their own education—had not become wealthy. Penrose explained that the school was coeducational, which reduced "the opportunity for rich men to be developed."[29] He also educated easterners about the Pacific Northwest: its natural resources "are being developed with great rapidity, but with a consequent great strain upon the means of the promoters. All money is necessarily turned back at once into new channels, and the era of philanthropy has naturally therefore not yet come."[30]

Penrose strengthened his application to Carnegie by supportive letters from influential men in Seattle, Spokane, and Portland to whom he grumbled privately that Carnegie's secretary "regards our request as out of proportion to the development of this section of the country and of the college, apparently thinking that we should be content with a third or fourth rate equipment."[31] To overcome this objection, the president asked these leaders, including judges Cornelius H. Hanford and Thomas Burke of Seattle, banker William M. Ladd of Portland, and attorney and former senator George Turner of Spokane, to answer questions about the college and region. Two questions should be emphasized: "Do you consider that the northwest needs today opportunities for scientific instruction of the highest grade?" "Would $100,000 for a completely equipped building for electrical engineering seem . . . out of proportion to the present development of the college and the needs of the northwest?"[32] Penrose forwarded their favorable answers to Carnegie and Rockefeller.

These letters, however, made no impact. The General Education Board had never taken much interest in Whitman. Early in 1907 it replied that Penrose's request was too large, that about 400 schools competed for its limited funds, and that his appeal would be considered when it investigated educational conditions in Washington State. In April 1907 Penrose wrote a dispirited letter to D.K. Pearsons, who continued to be his sounding board.[33] The president reported his inability to convince either eastern source to help Whitman and his pressing need for a larger endowment. Penrose failed to mention the nagging deficit because he knew that Pearsons would lecture him about it. Clearly trying to keep his spirits up, Penrose added that Whitman had "the brightest future of any college that I had known" and that he enjoyed developing it, but he was discouraged: "the building up of Whitman has been so much slower than I ever antici- pated that I think that if I had known how many years it would take before it should have reached this present state, I would have hesitat- ed long before undertaking the task. Even now I often think seriously of giving up the presidency, because I dislike administrative work and feel that I am far more useful as a teacher than as a businessman." The weary leader insisted that the college required a good fund raiser, one who could convince wealthy men to make substantial contributions. "This is not my forte," Penrose judged, "I can develop the college internally, but heaven never designed me for a beggar. If you will give your consent I shall be glad to resign the presidency at any time in favor of a business man."

Pearsons immediately consoled Penrose: "You have had great success."[34] He advised him to remain at his post and make Walla Walla the family home. One of the Penrose boys "must take your place in twenty-five years, or the husband of one of your girls. Keep the college in the family. No better place in the world."[35] Apparently this encouragement had the desired effect. Penrose responded with an optimistic letter, emphasizing that "There is more fun in taking things while they are young and moulding them, than in running an institution which is already moulded. I feel that I am in some degree identified with Whitman College, and I certainly feel responsible for it. I shall not be willing to leave the college until it is absolutely clear from debt."[36] He said that a college should not be judged by the size of its enrollment but predicted that Whitman could double in size if it had the resources. "The trouble is," the writer concluded, "We have to hold in on every side, and cannot for instance offer the scientific training which the young men of the northwest particularly want, just because we have not the means at present."

Despite the money shortage Penrose wrote to Purdue and other schools seeking an assistant professor of engineering to teach me- chanical drawing and elementary mathematics. The president as- sured candidates that he was offering "a great educational opportu- nity," although he acknowledged that a $1,000 starting salary was

very low.[37] A Cornell administrator agreed and refused even to recommend a candidate.

While the school took steps to establish engineering, Penrose and
the trustees carried on important talks with Archer W. Hendrick.
Hendrick, who had been hired in 1902 as an assistant professor of
English and principal of the academy, had the promoter's instinct and
style, and by the spring of 1907 he had risen to the position of dean at
the college. Dean Hendrick formulated plans for a program grander
than just electrical engineering and explained it to the board's executive committee. Enthused by his scheme to enlarge the school, the
committee increased Hendrick's salary to $1,800 and budgeted his
expenses.[38] His educational plans would be announced in December
1907. Penrose thought that Hendrick would become a great fund
raiser, the man he had long sought. Such an individual would give
Penrose a chance to teach and lead.

Buildings and Grounds: Signs of Success

Huddled under umbrellas and sloshing in the mud around a freshly
dug excavation site, a well-dressed crowd enthusiastically applauded
ceremonies associated with the building of a new dormitory. Everybody in this rain-drenched audience knew that the women's dormitory represented another proud moment for Stephen and Mary
Penrose. Masonic Lodge members, a local band, and Whitman students had marched to the construction site on this last day of May
1902; the fraternal order ceremoniously placed the Reynolds Hall
cornerstone. The featured speaker, historian William Mowry, acknowledged their accomplishments in an address entitled "The Education of Women." A New Englander on a Pacific Northwest lecture
tour promoted by Penrose, Mowry sketched and stressed the history
of women's education. The visitor predicted a large increase in the
number of American women holding college degrees. Mowry reported that local residents had asked him, "Where shall we find house-
keepers if so many girls go to college?"[39] He retorted that American
society needed as many educated women as educated men.

The dormitory being erected owed as much to D.K. Pearsons as
did the two other masonry buildings located on the opposite side of
the quadrangle. Once again Pearsons' generosity had initiated action.

In 1901 he had offered $50,000 for the college's endowment if its leaders raised $25,000 for a dormitory to house sixty women. The benefactor required the college, like all the others he helped, to pay an annuity of two percent of his gift, which, in this case, went to the needy Oliver Nixon. (The long-time Whitman supporter had been dismissed by his newspaper.)

In a series of letters Pearsons took a vital interest in the building, even submitting his plans. Thus the new dormitory would be similar to Chapin Hall, a women's residence he had financed at Northwestern University. In advisory letters Pearsons commented on room size, beds, the halls (they were eighteen inches too wide), and the need for a vegetable cellar. His most important recommendation was that wealthy Walla Walla women should raise the building funds and that the dormitory should be named for a local woman, rather than be called Chapin Hall in honor of Pearsons' sister-in-law.[40] In May Pearsons reiterated his hope that "all the money will be given by Walla Walla women; how nice it would be, and I think your people would be much pleased with the result."[41]

The fund raising for this building followed the all-too-familiar pattern. Penrose found it difficult to find donors. Again he expressed his frustration to Pearsons. Again Pearsons bolstered Penrose's spirits. He encouraged him to be patient and "play with the wife and girls a little more. You have a nice family; I hope you know it. Go slow, young man, laugh and grow fat."[42] Again Pearsons provided more than jovial advice. He agreed to provide money even before the school raised $25,000 for the dormitory. From his long experience with college philanthropy, Pearsons assumed that local residents would not allow an uncompleted building to stand on the campus and would donate the remaining costs. This tactic worked; contributions nearly completed the structure. The major gifts were $5,000 each from U.S. Senator Levi Ankeny, a trustee, and from the Reverend and Mrs. Edward L. Smith, close friends of Penrose. The minister had been a member of the "Yale band," and his wife was a daughter of Dorsey Baker. The Smith gift was contingent upon naming the dormitory for Mrs. Lettice Reynolds, who in 1843 as a girl had traveled the Oregon Trail with Marcus Whitman. Her sons, especially Allen, were major college supporters. These two large donations prompted Pearsons to send the $50,000 endowment with the advice

A student's room in Reynolds Hall in 1903 includes among its amenities fish netting, a chafing dish, and a tea set.

that it be wisely invested. The philanthropist also told the president to recognize his own ability as a fund raiser. He added that, "there is no spot in the country where the money will do as much good" as at Whitman,[43] and predicted, "You are to have the leading college of the North West, and it will make Walla Walla a fine point to live."[44]

In the summer of 1902 Penrose did not join his family for the annual trek to visit relatives; he remained in town, consulting with the contractor and seeking funds for the new dormitory. In a few weeks construction gangs had erected the three-story brick building. The reception room, parlors, dining hall, kitchen, and laundry room were on the first floor; single and double rooms were on the other levels.

While the dean of women and the matron supervised, sixty young women moved into Reynolds Hall in the fall of 1902. Bringing their towels, linen, blankets, rugs, and other personal items, the newcomers delighted in furnishing and decorating their rooms. A cameraman recorded these attractive rooms, and his photographs became part of the school's publicity campaign. The new dormitory immediately became the center of the school's social life; men enjoyed dining with its residents. But Reynolds Hall was also an educational center. The

*Another 1903 photograph of Reynolds Hall. The furnishings in
the parlor helped create a pleasant, homelike environment.*

dean and Mrs. Penrose consulted with its occupants and often instructed them in etiquette. In 1906 the first floor served as a laboratory for a domestic science course. Throughout much of the twentieth
century, this functional building would have a tremendous impact
upon students. Years after graduation women came back to see the
rooms that had been so important in their formative years.

While the school's friends rejoiced over the completion of another
substantial building, Stephen Penrose anxiously thought about his
future construction program. His top priority was a gymnasium, but
he also described the need for a science hall, a library, an academy
building (to provide space for the preparatory department so that it
could be separated from the college), and a conservatory of music.
Penrose wrote a friend about the need for buildings: "It is hard to
keep your trousers fitting when you are growing very fast, and we are
rather short in the trouser legs and in the sleeves."[45]

Penrose recommended that buildings be named for those who had
led the college, including Cushing Eells and Alexander Anderson, and
for leading Walla Walla families such as the Kirkmans, Bakers, Boy-
ers, Ankenys, and Yenneys. He reasoned, "The custom heretofore

has been to erect a useless monument or mausoleum in the cemetery. How much better to erect a monument for the living which will preserve the memory as long as one stone stands upon another!"[46]

Penrose repeatedly asked wealthy townspeople to fund a modern gymnasium; from 1900 into 1905 rumors periodically swept the campus that a philanthropist would provide the required $25,000. In 1904 the president emphasized that the state agricultural college at Pullman and the University of Idaho competed for students with Whitman and that both either had or soon would have modern gymnasiums. By contrast, Whitman students and faculty used a small wooden building dating from the 1890s. To meet the competition and to provide "systematic bodily development of the young men and young women," Penrose begged for a new facility.[47] Others emphasized that with basketball becoming a more popular game, the college simply had to have an adequate court. Penrose explained the building's importance: "It will do more for the strengthening of the college through increase of students and improved conditions of living than any other thing."[48]

The biggest problem in constructing such a structure was that the college must, for the first time, fund a stone building without the financial help of Pearsons, who detested collegiate sports, especially football, and angrily rejected all solicitations for gymnasiums. A second difficulty was the fact that Reynolds, like every other hall, had been more expensive than estimated. Penrose had to find funds for this overrun; fortunately, Lettice Reynolds covered most of the outstanding bills for the hall honoring her.

A most unusual faculty member, Archer Hendrick, not President Penrose, discovered a way to erect the badly needed gymnasium. Convinced that no donor would soon provide the gymnasium, Hendrick determined that it must be financed by popular subscription. Early in 1904, faculty members—some of whom must have been dubious because of the failure to attract local money in other fundraising campaigns—agreed with Hendrick and pledged about $1,500 from what a student described as "meager salaries."[49] Immediately after a chapel exercise in February, Hendrick, "the father of the gymnasium scheme," outlined his proposal.[50] He explained that after getting $2,500 in pledges from faculty and students, the college would then solicit from Walla Wallans, alumni, and others. To help

Campus leader Hugh Elmer "Hez" Brown (right) is shown with William Gaius "Sad Eye" Greenslade (left) and Edward D. "Ned" Baldwin; together they composed the successful debating team of 1904. As alumni, Brown and Baldwin maintained a steady interest in the college.

collect local money, potential donors would be told that a gift of $50 or more gave them the right to designate non-Whitman students for gymnasium privileges. Hendrick's plans provided for the construction of a $15,000 building after $12,000 had been raised. The professor stressed the need for the facility, noting that Whitman athletes blamed their recent defeats upon a lack of training facilities.[51]

After Hendrick finished his plea, the faculty filed from the chapel. Then excited students immediately elected a popular leader, Hugh Elmer "Hez" Brown, as chairman. He called upon classmates, especially dynamic speakers, to support Hendrick's plans. Young women and men from various classes presented emotional arguments, including the assertion that "Never again will we have such an opportunity to do so much for our alma mater."[52] Subscription lists were hastily prepared and circulated down the chapel rows. Within fifteen minutes students pledged $1,500 and shouted that the campaign should be waged in the city. When the total subscription was announced, a *Pioneer* reporter wrote, "The whole mass of happy students vented their joy in one terrific yell. Books, hats, pencils, and tablets were thrown in the air as students jumped up on benches to cheer. It was several minutes before even the college yell could be given, and then it was repeated nearly a dozen times before the students could subside enough to give three cheers for the new Gymnasium." The enthusiasm carried over into the evening. Gathered around a bonfire students sang and yelled in what one observer called "the greatest day in the history of the college."[53] Penrose called it the "Second Red Letter Day."

The *Pioneer* editor congratulated classmates for demonstrating through financial contributions their love of Whitman College and encouraged them to canvass for additional sums. Students served on a campaign committee that sought subscriptions from townspeople and alumni. The college newspaper often reported on the campaign's progress and advised readers to remind businesspeople that student expenditures bolstered the local economy. The city's newspapers also presented various arguments for the badly needed gymnasium.

By mid-April about $7,000 had been collected, but many students expressed disappointment over the sluggish campaign and about the building's distant future. Some regretted that they would graduate without having the opportunity to play or swim in it. The *Pioneer* sought to rally readers by reminding them that Whitman teams "always make the bravest stand on our five-yard line," that Marcus Whitman was "no quitter," that Penrose in his presidency "refused to give up the ship," and that "Professor Hendrick labored like a Trojan."[54] In summary the editor urged, "Let us canvass, circulate, agitate, and never say die." Solicitors thought it helpful to denounce their small and poorly equipped gymnasium. One humorously wrote, "A mat, the very same mat that Methusaleh used in his dog kennel, rests its venerable form on the . . . floor—a fit dwelling place for long whiskered mice."[55]

Penrose unsuccessfully offered wealthy men the opportunity to name the gymnasium if they would equip it. He showed architectural plans that he and Hendrick had adapted from those provided by the U.S. Military Academy at West Point. Finally in the fall semester of 1904 excited students watched bricklayers begin to work, and the *Pioneer* predicted that "with a first class gymnasium and a regular athletic instructor Whitman will turn out pennant winning athletic teams"; furthermore, "everyone will exercise and develop his muscle whether he wants to or not."[56]

In January 1905 sophomores secretly and unofficially dedicated the incomplete building. Accompanied by a faculty chaperone and carrying artificial light, they crashed a bottle of ginger ale against a wall. The celebrants boasted about outwitting other classes and played games on the uncompleted floor.

At the end of the 1905 spring term, workmen finished the interior, including the swim tank. Pleased with the result, students congratulated themselves for a building resulting from their "spirit and self-sacrifice." They proclaimed that the gymnasium was the best in the Pacific Northwest and wanted it named Hendrick Gymnasium because of the professor's "energy, persistence, and executive genius."[67] Unfortunately trustees did not comply with the students' wish to honor Hendrick for the splendid facility built along muddy Isaacs Avenue. The gymnasium remained unnamed until its destruction in 1970. The 1905 catalog described the building:

> The Gymnasium is a large and substantial three-story building of brick, 114 feet long by 62 feet deep. On the first floor are separate bathrooms and dressing-rooms for men and for women, a bowling alley and cage for baseball practice, and a fine swimming tank, 52 feet long by 26 feet wide, and ranging in depth from 3 feet 6 inches to 8 feet. On the second floor are the Director's room, trophy and reception rooms, and the main hall for exercise 90 feet long and 60 feet wide. The third story is given up to the gallery. The building will be heated by steam and lighted by electricity.

Early in the new century this gymnasium and Reynolds Hall were the major campus additions, but students also boasted about an improved athletic field. Trustee Levi Ankeny provided money for an athletic field between Billings and Reynolds halls; in 1904 it was called Ankeny Field. With a quarter-mile track, a baseball diamond, and a gridiron, it was "probably the best field in the Pacific Northwest."[68] Only men could use Ankeny Field; women had to exercise and play games on the original playing field behind the conservatory.

In 1904 the college acquired the Baker home and about three acres of land contiguous to the campus, paying $3,000 in cash and giving a note for $11,000 that took years to pay. This property became the Penrose home, and its importance to the social life of the campus more than compensated for the nagging debt. Money was also spent on landscaping the campus. In 1902 a Washington Agricultural College professor presented plans to beautify the campus; donors provided trees, shrubs, lawns, sidewalks, and grading projects. In 1903 the *Pioneer*, speaking for many, praised the improved appearance of the campus: "The smooth lawns ... the handsome walks and driveways, the new trees, ... and last of all our buildings, make a picture most delightful. We can begin to realize what an added incentive these will be for future seekers after knowledge, to come here for their training, and we envy them this greater abundance of adornments."[69]

In late 1906 John C. Olmsted, a famous landscape architect, examined the college and submitted a report.[60] He recommended that the academy should be separated from the college by locating it south of Boyer Avenue. He proposed that a conservatory of music should be built in the same general area but near the streetcar line for the convenience of those coming from town to campus for music lessons, a proposal the school would eventually adopt. Olmsted suggested locations for future buildings and objected to Ankeny Field's location among the buildings, urging the purchase of twenty nearby acres for playing fields. Penrose endorsed this idea and believed that $5,000 would cover the cost of the additional acreage, but he failed to convince the college community. A modern architectural historian has concluded that "Not all of Olmsted's recommendations were carried out to the letter, but they were followed in the general concept, which called for maintaining a large central open space surrounded by an enclosure of buildings."[61]

Meanwhile, everyone applauded several changes made in Memorial Hall. Most obvious was the installation of a tower clock whose illuminated dials and hourly bells soon became familiar. Anonymous donors gave the clock in honor of Penrose's grandmother, Mrs. Stephen B. Linnard. Relatives of Mary Penrose gave an expensive pipe organ memorializing her mother, Mrs. Nathaniel Shipman. Located in the chapel, the instrument allowed the school to create a department of pipe organ: "The growing popularity of the organ and the increased demand for concert and church organizations make this department highly important."[62] Responding to pleas from science professors and from Penrose, donors provided equipment for Memorial Hall's science laboratories. Most gifts were small, but in 1906 the Miles Moore family outfitted a complete electrical laboratory.

While the physical changes impressed campus visitors who hailed the institution's growth, Penrose sought still more. He continued to believe that additional buildings would stimulate interest in the institution, but he could not fund them. His inability to obtain money from Carnegie and Rockefeller meant that the school would not soon enjoy a modern science hall. In 1907 he stressed the need for a heating plant. He also sought local donors who might provide an academy building or a conservatory. Erecting an academy building would provide space for 250 students, including expanded laboratories and a manual training department. Moving younger pupils out of Memorial Hall would provide more room for the college students. Penrose claimed that the "separation would permit a more careful supervision of Academy students and a greater freedom of College students." In urging the construction of a new conservatory, he pointed out the inconveniences of a wooden building constructed in 1883. Penrose envisioned that: "If a modern conservatory was erected with a large concert hall, equipped with pipe organ and grand piano, and with an adequate number of practice rooms, a local need would be met and the people of Walla Walla would have a convenient and attractive place for concerts and entertainments of many kinds."[63] At this time Penrose thought that a library and another men's dormitory were less important than the three other buildings he advocated.

Recruiting and Managing a Faculty

While President Penrose carried on a building program, he also built the faculty. With his broad vision of the kind of school he wanted to build, he understood that the right teachers had to be added just as the proper buildings had to be constructed. Penrose wrote dozens of letters seeking capable additions or replacements. To attract candidates to his remote institution required optimistic letters. Thus the leader predicted a glowing future for Whitman, boasted that the faculty was harmonious, praised Walla Walla's mild climate (he said it compared with Washington, D.C.), and insisted that the cost of living in this agricultural center was considerably less than that of urban centers. He often stressed that the low salaries of Whitman would actually match larger salaries elsewhere because Walla Walla's "scale of living is simple so that personal expenses are reduced almost to a minimum."[64] He thought that $1,200 in Walla Walla equalled $2,400 in an eastern city. Penrose maintained his college town was next only to Colorado Springs as a desirable place to live. He admitted only three shortcomings to life in Walla Walla: the lack of a good hotel, a need for a golf course, and unremitting August heat and dust that drove residents to their mountain camps.

Penrose's correspondence demonstrates that he sought a certain type of professor. In 1907 the president revealed that "In the selection of men for positions on the college faculty, Christian faith and character are an influential factor."[65] Of references for one candidate he asked, "Is he a member of the church? What is his influence upon his scholars outside of school hours?"[66] In building his faculty Penrose did not seek those with doctorates—none of his letters mentions the PH.D.—but he favored graduates of strong character and solid training from prestigious eastern schools. In building its faculty the University of Washington was adding research professors from the best eastern graduate schools. Penrose sought teachers from the same schools but emphasized the need for "Christian character, manliness, and personality"; furthermore, the candidate must "have the tact and mental balance which will fit him for teaching as well as the scholastic training."[67] Undoubtedly Penrose had read William DeWitt Hyde's *The College Man and the College Woman*. Hyde, a successful and noted president of Bowdoin College, argued that in hiring faculty it was important to stress personality over knowledge and reputation. Working along the same guidelines as Hyde, Penrose sought to avoid egotistical, insincere, mean, selfish, and unfair professors.

Interestingly enough, those making recommendations to Penrose gave frank assessments about individuals; for example, a letter from MIT stated that a candidate possessed the requisite knowledge but because he was from Alabama he was "without a vast amount of hustle."[68] Discouraging responses came to Penrose from Yale, the University of Pennsylvania, and MIT because young men objected to being assigned German classes in the academy, considered the $1,000 salary offer to be inadequate, or insisted upon the opportunity to carry on their research. One educator frankly told Penrose that he must be sympathetic with researchers but at the same time he must try to convince them to subordinate their professional work and do "the necessary administrative and teaching work" required in a college.[69]

As he searched for professors, Penrose spent considerable time hiring and retaining an athletic director and coach. In 1901 he wrote a series of letters to Charles Allen of Alma College. He explained that Levi Ankeny had agreed to pay the salary of an athletic director for a year. When Coach Allen wanted more money than Penrose offered, the president explained the salary structure: "Nominally the salaries

Coach Charles Allen stands behind the 1902 basketball team that won the college's intramural championship. The faculty would not allow women athletes to compete on an intercollegiate basis.

of our Professors are $1,400, that is to say the Trustees have set that figure to be approximated as soon as possible, but practically most of them are getting $1,100 and two of the oldest $1,200 a year."[70] Allen came at a salary of $1,200 and the assurance that because there was no city YMCA, people would be willing to pay him for instruction in athletics and gymnastics. Penrose added that "There is more interest in athletics here than ever before, and we have excellent material for foot-ball, base-ball, and track teams."[71]

In 1904 Allen resigned; Penrose now sought to save money by hiring Captain Charles E. Stodter of Fort Walla Walla as professor of military affairs and tactics. This officer would take charge of Whitman's athletic program and also teach. He would receive his military pay and $500 from Whitman. In making application to military authorities, Penrose stated: "The great importance which is being given by the War Department to the military instruction and training of young men of the country justifies the selection and detail of the officers most fit for such duty."[72] To get Captain Stodter, Penrose asked six United States senators—including Boise Penrose—to write Secretary of War William Howard Taft on behalf of Whitman's request. Ensnarled in military red tape, Penrose doggedly pushed the matter with the secretary, even making the point that Mary Penrose's brother had been at Yale with Taft.

But these efforts were unsuccessful, and disgusted by his inability to employ the captain, Penrose now turned his attention to the Ivy League schools for a coach. He wrote to Coach Walter Camp of Yale, the father of modern day football. Penrose explained the need for a coach and gymnasium instructor. "We want a man," he continued, "of sterling Christian character with tact and adaptability who can adapt himself to the conditions of a small western college."[73] Penrose also desired an athlete who brought the prestige of having played on a Yale baseball or football team.

In letters to less prominent individuals, Penrose stated that he looked for someone who could bring the latest in "eastern college life and training methods" and promised that this coach "could develop great influence and accomplish much good work, not only for Whitman College but for the whole Northwest."[74] Penrose spelled out other duties for the coach—he must give gymnastic classes to young women, and it was better for the new person to teach as well as coach. The college hired an athletic director, but Penrose in 1907 again sought a coach. He ranked candidates on the attributes of Christian character, academic standing, and ability to coach. He summarized, "We are anxious to secure a first class man whose character and personal influence will be helpful to the college life, and who will also be able to give the vigorous impetus to clean and hearty athletics which a college today needs."[75]

In 1902 the search began for the first dean of women, whose initial salary was provided by Professor Louis Anderson and his wife Mabel. Penrose insisted upon meeting applicants who might have charge of the school's women. He wanted a person who was "not too young and not too old, with the most attractive Christian Character and Culture able to influence our girls for the best and highest things." Penrose added that the position, which paid $1,000 yearly and room and board, was very attractive, especially "for some lady obliged to support herself, who has the combined qualities of motherliness and business ability."[76]

Another search became necessary in 1903; it proved to be short, for an unusual candidate soon emerged. Gertrude H. Wylie, an 1886 graduate of Smith, wrote that she came from a family of distinguished educators, had taught classical languages and the Bible, had organized a women's department of Moody's Bible Institute, was a graduate student in Bible studies at the University of Chicago, and was a widow and mother of a twelve-year-old daughter. In her application Wylie emphasized, "I love the girls, and they are always devoted to me. I know of no work more beautiful than that of helping to develop their noblest womanhood."[77] During the search Penrose spelled out his concern to one of her references: was the applicant strong enough for the work and did she have the "leadership, which would fit her for inspiring and guiding western girls?"[78] The applicant supplied important letters of recommendation, including one from Whitman benefactor Julia Billings, who agreed to pay Wylie's salary. This generosity terminated the search. Wylie eagerly accepted the position, indicating that she would remain about ten years and concluded, "It is assuredly the Father's plan. There is now no place on earth where I so desire to be next fall as in Walla Walla."[79]

Penrose assured Wylie that her daughter could live in Reynolds Hall although she was too young for the academy program. The president added that he was a friend of Dwight Lyman Moody, founder of Moody's Bible Institute, and appreciated "his rare judgment of men and women."[80]

Wylie informed the president that she could carry a heavy teaching load, preferably in Bible studies, and also manage Reynolds Hall. She asked about its operating procedures; Penrose explained that Sam, a long-time employee, and other "Chinamen" did the cooking and that the residents waited on tables and cleaned the hall.

By 1907 Penrose had built a solid faculty and worked to retain it and keep it harmonious. He often praised his professors and thanked them for their solid contribution. He also sympathized with their financial difficulties. Their salaries lagged behind those at public universities; in 1903 Penrose had to explain to them that they could not receive a deserved increase because of the school's debt.[81]

Their low salaries were not the professors' only financial concern. Although the Whitman faculty was young, it worried about the fact that the institution, unlike some wealthy eastern schools, had no money for a retirement system. Surely Whitman professors read and commented about a 1904 short story in the *Atlantic* dealing with the poverty of aged professors. One writer charged that an unfeeling university was "more barbarous than the Indians whose teepees used to stand where the campus is now."[82]

The teachers weekly spent from eighteen to twenty hours in their classrooms. Penrose admitted that such heavy schedules permitted little time for research but maintained that other college faculties worked even longer hours. Men and women not only struggled with heavy teaching loads, they also taught long hours and in subject areas where they had little training or interest. Upon being told that he must teach mathematics as well as his specialty, a new professor wrote: "I shall be willing . . . to take my medicine along with the rest in this matter of accommodation."[83]

There was one notable exception to the faculty worries about time and money. Because he had married into money, classics professor Louis Anderson reduced his teaching. Complaining of illness and "mental unrest," he received a leave and with his wife spent the spring of 1905 in southern California.[84] In the 1906–1907 school year he took a sabbatical, touring Egypt, Greece, Germany, and England. Upon his return he taught a half load and told Penrose, "I don't want much committee work and *no* chairmanships." His comfortable lifestyle and the commodious home he built near the campus (it is now the Baker Faculty Center) was a far cry from the life that other professors eked out from salaries averaging less than $1,000. Surely the financial discrepancies between the rest of the faculty and Anderson led to all kinds of comment, including talk about the wisdom of marrying the banker's daughter.

Despite low pay and long hours, many professors found time for important service to the college. To publicize the institution, they gave readings, lectures, and musical performances in town and nearby communities. A few professors, like William Lyman, traveled extensively in the summer seeking students. Lyman somehow found time to carry on his important historical research and writing. Science professor Howard Brode combined a vacation with his professional work at the marine station at Friday Harbor. In 1903 Professor Walter Bratton went to Berlin, where he gathered information on the German school system and attended university lectures, carried on laboratory work, and priced instruments for Whitman's science program. Like many other Whitman professors over a long period of time, he rejoiced in the opportunity of using a large library and consulting with like-minded scholars: "One of the greatest advantages I have found ... has been the ability to get whatever book I wanted ... and to find out from the book or the professor what work has been done along a given line."[85]

Lacking a dean, Penrose managed all faculty affairs. He spent time listening to their complaints about salaries, teaching assignments, uninspiring students, colleagues, the library, and other matters. There were resignations primarily because professors wanted to pursue graduate work. Penrose expressed regret upon accepting the resignation of Otto A. Hauerbach, an English professor who had, Penrose explained, "a very rare power of teaching";[86] and that of professor of Greek and oratory Edith B. Merrill, a cooperative, intelligent, and skilled faculty member, who had, Penrose said, inherited her teaching ability from her college president father.[87]

Probably the faculty in the conservatory took more of the president's time than did that in the college. A piano instructor, Harold Loring, was talented and personable, but immature. When he left town, creditors came to Memorial Hall, asking for a forwarding address. In early 1906, perhaps for the first time in his career, Penrose asked a faculty member to resign or he would be fired. S. Harrison Lovewell, a graduate of the New England Conservatory of Music, had initially impressed students, the faculty, and Walla Wallans. Penrose had called him "a most inspiring teacher." Although he had been denied a pay raise he cheerfully responded that he had "the interest of Whitman Conservatory far more at heart than the increase of salary."[88] But he complained that his wife and children had to make sacrifices and that heavy teaching responsibilities, including forty-nine piano pupils, fatigued him. Apparently the strain of work and his inability to support his family, together with what he called "petty jealousies and bickerings" with colleagues, led him to criticize Penrose in his classes.[89] He apologized, and friends asked the president to give him another year, but Lovewell preferred to leave. Penrose, who understood the musician's personal problems, wrote him a solid letter of recommendation.

Another difficulty in the conservatory was not resolved so harmoniously. Violin instructor Edgar Simpson Fischer resigned because the trustees had ruled against him in a dispute over a student registration. His action meant that the school temporarily lacked a violinist. Even worse, Fischer and his wife, a pianist, opened the Fischer School of Music and strenuously competed with the Whitman conservatory.

Seeking stability and excellence in the conservatory, Penrose attempted to hire an experienced musician at a salary of $2,000. The president explained the unusual offer: "We want the conservatory to be a place where the highest musical standards and spirit are maintained"; and he hoped it would attain a national reputation.[90]

Penrose thought that a conservatory was important, and he theorized about how to build such an institution. The major requirement was to employ talented musicians, who provided high-quality vocal and instrumental lessons. He also advised that fees for music lessons should make the conservatory profitable and that a "musical atmosphere be engendered by frequent concerts by both home talent and visiting artists, the maintenance of an orchestra, choral society, etc."[91]

It is not clear what the faculty thought about Penrose's ambitious plans for the conservatory and his concern for harmony between the two parts of the institution. Professor Lyman expressed a negative view of the conservatory because its faculty "generally speaking, do little for the moral or social uplift of the students."[92]

Designing a Curriculum

Penrose had always been interested in the curriculum. In the new century he and the faculty led the institution in some unusual directions. They gave the conservatory only general instructions, but the academy received their constant scrutiny. The 1902 catalog stated that the academy sought two objectives: to prepare its graduates for Whitman or any other college and "to furnish a well-rounded secondary education to those who are unable to take the College course." In 1904 the catalog dropped the second goal. Academy graduates had received solid training in such basic subjects as ancient and foreign languages, literature, science, mathematics, and history. The faculty clearly wanted academy graduates to pursue a college education, preferably at Whitman, where traditional courses of study—classical, scientific, and literary—would challenge them.

Competing with other academies and with many new high schools, Whitman advertised the advantages of its academy and added a business course to its program. Prospective students and their parents learned that an experienced college faculty taught in the academy and took a personal interest in students; moreover, they would be "constantly surrounded by Christian influences."[93] But there were other appeals: academy students could join the college's literary societies, musical groups, and athletic organizations, and they could use the college library and gymnasium. In summary, "What is particularly attractive to the pupil is the fact that in Whitman Academy he is really in the atmosphere of the College, he receives its inspiration and breathes its spirit, and is encouraged to strive for something higher."[94] To attract more academy students, including those who did not want to go beyond the twelfth grade, the faculty in 1903 created a four-year business course. The catalog stated that the new curriculum was "not a short cut to a business career, but prepared adequately and conscientiously for ordinary forms of business life."[95] Those in the business course could delete only the Latin requirement and substitute such classes as commercial arithmetic, bookkeeping, stenography, typewriting, and commercial law.

The president acknowledged that the faculty "felt considerable hesitancy about inaugurating this departure."[96] Even some students feared that Whitman had lowered its standards. Denouncing such classes in a high school or a business college as "a professed short cut to an education ... and a sham and a trap for the ignorant," the *Pioneer* was pleased with the fact that those enrolled in the Whitman business program still had to meet rigorous academy requirements.[97] The appointment of the business teacher at the rank of instructor, not as an assistant professor, indicated that he was less respected than other faculty members. Penrose unsuccessfully argued through his correspondence the advantages of combining traditional and practical courses. Others, however, could not tolerate the intrusion of such classes as bookkeeping and typing in a traditional curriculum. The college quietly discarded the business program in 1906 because it had been less popular and more controversial than anticipated.

Meanwhile, academy enrollments also declined from 175 in 1904 to 146 in 1907. Penrose attributed this problem to competition with the local high school and to Whitman's recruiting emphasis on high school seniors rather than eighth graders. The college debated the academy's future; faculty members appreciated the solid foundation given to secondary school pupils but preferred to concentrate their energy on college students. The second problem was academy boys, boarding in the dormitory, who created more academic and social problems than the older students. In 1906, during a long discussion over the secondary program, Whitman changed the academy's name to Pearsons Academy, after D.K. Pearsons. Unfortunately this major figure was not honored with a major building—other colleges more wisely named such a structure for him. Pearsons deserved lasting recognition at Whitman, for it is hard to see how the institution could have realized many of Penrose's dreams without his practical advice and timely donations. Today only a few appreciate his crucial role.

The most important curricular change since the founding of the college in 1882 was the adoption in 1904 of the elective system, including majors and minors in subject fields. The Whitman faculty's decision to change the curriculum so drastically was part of a national movement. In the late nineteenth century and into the twentieth century, administrators and faculties had waged an extended battle over the elective system. Historian Frederick Rudolph says the battle "was intense, bitter, and prolonged, and it was essentially an eastern affair."[98] Harvard president Charles William Eliot, who served from 1869 to 1909, gradually replaced the traditional prescribed classical curriculum with a broadly elective one. A leader in this educational reform, he marshalled a variety of arguments for this change, insisting that higher education must take individual differences into account. He and allies argued that this reform increased institutional vitality, improved faculty morale, and motivated students. President James McCosh of Princeton spoke for opponents wanting "an essentially prescribed curriculum . . . and limited specialization."[99] Proponents of the old system argued that students would indulge themselves if they were not guided through their undergraduate years and that they would ignore religious studies. At the turn of the century, Harvard, Cornell, and Stanford stood as the leading proponents of the elective system while Yale, Williams, and Columbia still imposed numerous requirements. For a variety of reasons academic reformers in the Progressive Age triumphed. Rudolph summarized: "Electives were unavoidable except in colleges with suicidal tendencies. . . . The classical course was dead."[100] From that time and from one coast to the other, there has been unresolved dispute over the curriculum.

It is not clear how much controversy there was among Whitman faculty members as they debated curricular reform, especially in the fall of 1903. Unfortunately, faculty minutes are very sketchy; furthermore, Penrose's history fails to mention this significant revision. It is clear that classicist Louis Anderson opposed the liberalized curriculum and that mathematician Walter Bratton supported him. On leave in Berlin, Bratton did not participate in the faculty vote. He wrote Penrose about the "malevolence of the faculty" and trusted that it would not make "serious inroads on the curriculum." He acknowledged that there was need for curricular improvement but feared "a greatly changed course."

Penrose played a significant role in this move to reform the curriculum. He understood that both students and teachers wanted more relevant classes; like other administrators throughout the country, he saw the close relationship between admission and curriculum. A greater variety of choice, he knew, would please students and parents. Faculty members supporting a more liberal curriculum argued that electives would mean faculty additions and more specialization.

In 1904, following the precedent of many other institutions, Whitman took a moderate position. The elective principle was adopted; within a few years students could select about sixty percent of their classes. Penrose championed this change, maintaining that it brought the college "into line with the more advanced requirements and methods of the best institutions."[101] According to the 1904 catalog, students must now complete 128 hours (this system of hours had to be carefully explained), declare a major and a minor, and choose electives. Under the title "Prescribed Work," the catalog stated that those seeking a bachelor's degree must take 14 hours of English, 8 hours of American history, 14 hours of philosophy, 4 hours of Biblical literature, 8 hours of a laboratory science, and 12 hours of foreign language. The faculty urged the completion of these requirements in the first two years so that students would use their final semesters for major, minor, and elective courses. The head of the student's major department would aid with the choice of a minor and would also serve as academic counselor. The school continued to offer four degrees: bachelor of arts, bachelor of letters, bachelor of science, and bachelor of music. The students could initially choose majors from these departments: philosophy, history and economics, classics,

Greek, Latin, modern languages, English, mathematics and astronomy, physics, chemistry, biology and geology, and music.

At many meetings faculty debated questions about required classes and major programs. The president and the professors continually
sought an improved curriculum. Penrose had a major voice in the
curricular changes, but the faculty was a loud and generally harmonious chorus. In 1906, for example, they agreed to separate economics
from the department of history and to offer the position to the Reverend William Worthington. Penrose wrote the new teacher that he
hoped that the economics department would become as strong as
those in Latin or mathematics. The faculty wanted Worthington to
take postgraduate classes at the University of Washington and agreed
with Penrose that "We feel that although you are not now technically
equipped as some men who had been specializing in Economics, you
have the character, experience, and mental and teaching ability to fill
the place admirably, and with increasing effectiveness."[102]

The addition of economics was not the only change. The faculty
reduced the English and history requirements, and in 1907 it altered
the prescribed list of courses by including two years of physical training for men and three for women.

Whitman's faculty assured students that the major curricular revision did not alter its high academic standards. In one of his letters,
for example, Penrose wrote: "I think our curriculum will now compare very favorably with that of the best institutions in the East."[103]
Professors often insisted that the accomplishments of their students
proved that Whitman equalled or excelled regional rivals.

To offer its expanded curriculum, the faculty spread class hours
between 8:00 AM and 6:00 PM; the hours from 3:00 PM to 5:00 PM,
however, were reserved for college athletics. Although there was considerable student protest, teachers held some recitations on Saturday
mornings. The faculty modified the academy's offerings to work with
the new college curriculum and retained several degree programs. To
receive the coveted A.B., however, a candidate must have completed
at least a year of Greek.[104]

Another major educational change was the growing importance
of science and mathematics. Enrollments in the courses increased
because of the solid teaching of Benjamin Brown, Howard Brode,
and Walter Bratton; the addition of laboratory equipment; and the

emphasis in society and on campus for science. Penrose praised his science faculty: "They have each shown a genius for getting great results out of a meagre equipment and bringing their students face to face with facts."[105]

At this time Penrose sought more money for laboratories than for the library. In 1904 the *Pioneer* caught the mood: "The College is preparing to lay greater stress upon the sciences than ever before. The laboratories are being fitted up with apparatus adequate for extensive study in these lines."[106] Rural Walla Walla well knew that industrial America wanted scientists and engineers; students in many such farm towns were eager to prepare for these promising professions. In 1907 many Whitman men became excited about the prospect of adding engineering courses.

Engineering interested the men; domestic science attracted the women. From 1907 into 1910 the school offered a new form of practical education. This program was an expansion of a non-credit domestic science program that had been offered to residents of Reynolds Hall. Women faculty members and Mary Penrose had taught residents such subjects as household management and etiquette, and probably they joined many coeds in requesting college credit for this training. Thus in the "Household Economics" section of the catalog, the school explained that these revised courses "include pure and applied science and practice, and are designed for young women who intend to teach cooking or other household arts, or who wish to prepare themselves for a more thoughtful and effective administration of a home."[107] Students might take three courses, covering such topics as "sanitation, including cleaning and laundry work, preserving and fancy cooking, sewing, dietaries cooking, serving and entertaining," and "lectures on the care of children."

Meanwhile, the physical training department expanded because the faculty, "recognizing that physical culture is both hygienic and educative, desire to encourage every reasonable effort in the direction of physical development consistent with strong manhood and womanhood." The major courses were gymnastics, athletics, and hygiene. Men might participate in football, basketball, track, baseball, and tennis and while "assigned to work on the various teams" would be excused from gymnastics. Women might engage in "milder forms of outdoor exercise, such as tennis and field hockey."

Recruiting Students

Penrose wrote an unusually large number of recruitment letters between 1900 and 1904. It was more necessary to solicit students in these early years. In the 1920s when improved instruction, increased scholarships, a new building program, and more comprehensive extracurricular activities had all helped bolster Whitman's reputation, the school attracted larger numbers of applications. So the president wrote letters to prospective students and sought solid recommendations from alumni and current students. Penrose caused his vision of the college to be shared by his students, and many of them became useful recruiters.

The president wanted Whitman to be like Williams in attracting a large percentage of the student body from urban centers. Williams drew students west from the eastern seaboard; Whitman would attract students east from the western seaboard. It was Penrose's and the faculty's belief that students should be educated in the country college, free from urban distractions. A faculty recruiter believed that it would help get western applicants if the school could attract "two or three good students from influential families in Seattle and Tacoma."[108] The pattern of Whitman's early recruitment effort indicated, however, that the emphasis was placed within the Great Columbia Plain, not west of the Cascades, probably because it was much easier to enroll students from the interior than from the coast.

The 250-mile rail journey to Walla Walla seemed to discourage potential students from the coast. Thus the first efforts of Penrose and faculty recruiters were in eastern Oregon, eastern Washington, and southern Idaho. Early in the new century the president expressed pleasure that students came from Cheyenne, Salt Lake City, Tacoma, Seattle, and Portland; the recruiting emphasis, however, had been upon Boise, Spokane, and the numerous farm communities. In 1901, for example, a Whitman recruiter sought students in the Big Bend Country and in small towns within a fifty-mile radius of Spokane. In 1904 Penrose wrote William Cowles, a trustee and newspaper publisher, that Spokanites needed to know and appreciate Whitman. "When they do," he insisted, "many who are now sending their children to Stanford and Berkeley will send them here."[109] Whitman leaders understood that establishing family traditions of sending children from Boise, Spokane, Lewiston, Pendleton, and other places to Walla Walla would bolster Whitman's enrollment. Penrose and his eastern-educated faculty had observed this tradition operating at their alma maters.

Like other schools in progressive America, Whitman sought not only more applicants but larger enrollments. In 1903 Penrose wanted 600 students—half of them in the college program—within ten years. In 1904 Penrose made a great effort to recruit students but provided no public explanation for this decision. The educator, however, did publicize the fact that in 1900 the total enrollment was 238 and in 1908 it reached 370.

Penrose received names of young women and men who might matriculate. Some had been submitted by faculty or student recruiters; others came from students, ministers, alumni, and supporters. The president wrote to potential students and their parents. Sometimes he tried to convince parents of the need for a college education; for example, he reasoned that "In these days the best that a father can give his son is a training for the highest kinds of work, a good education is better than a fortune, and the 20th century demands much more in the way of education than the 19th century did."[110]

Other times the president tried to convince potential students and their parents that Whitman was their best choice because it was "head and shoulders above any other institution in the Northwest."[111] In these early days, as in modern times, Whitman competed with the state colleges and with private eastern schools. In 1904 Professor William Lyman reported that public universities in Oregon and Washington provided stiff competition. In the following year a student recruiter, making personal calls at Goldendale, Washington, stated that several prospects had elected Washington State College. He complained that "Half the people don't know of Whitman's existence. What it needs here is to get a small foothold."[112] A few western parents told Penrose that they sent daughters to Smith, Mount Holyoke, and similar institutions. Penrose responded to the competition. He admitted he could understand such a decision but added, "I believe that you will find here special advantages."[113] Penrose was particularly solicitous about potential female students, assuring parents that their daughters would be associated with "a very desirable class of girls" and would be supervised by caring administrators. He anticipated that some would be homesick, but they "would be looked after with loving care and would soon become accustomed to their new surroundings."[114]

To other students Penrose presented Whitman's advantages in terms of economy and health. He told an Adams, Oregon, boy that he would not save any money by going to the University of Oregon and that if he went to Whitman, "you will have the advantage of being nearer home and with many warm friends."[115] To another student considering higher education in western Oregon, Penrose wrote, "One great advantage which we have here over the Willamette Valley, apart from our better equipment and grade of work, is the climate, which here is clear and dry, far more healthful and invigorating than the damp air of the Valley. This may not seem of much importance to you now, but you will find it much easier to work in this air than there."[116] Penrose advised an Iowa applicant that Walla Walla had a desirable climate; in fact, students from "distant localities are much improved in health."[117]

In recruiting women students, Stephen Penrose and the faculty emphasized that the literary societies offered beneficial intellectual and social opportunities. The Philolithian Society, photographed in 1908, had been formed in 1902. Mrs. Mary Penrose, who is seated in the front row (third from left), served as its advisor.

For years Whitman leaders generally reiterated Penrose's view on where to be educated:

> If you expect to settle down and live in the West, you will do better to take your college courses out here, and go back East for your post graduate work, if you go into a profession. This advice is based on the opinion of many college men with whom I have talked. They all agree that a course in an Eastern college for a young man under twenty-five is apt to have an unsettling effect, and to leave him dissatisfied with western life. On the other hand, if he stays in the West until twenty-five or so he can then go back East for a post graduate course, and withstand its attractions, his standards of life having been formed.[118]

Some of Penrose's appeals stressed the strength of the academy or conservatory. The leader often praised the talented music faculty; in 1904 he boasted that the conservatory was, "I think, without doubt ... the best on the Pacific Coast."[119] To his way of thinking, Whitman's college faculty, which he said came from excellent eastern schools, were offering solid academy classes and the students gained much from boarding in a dormitory. "Our academy boys are expected to live in the young men's dormitory, Billings Hall, where they are under the supervision of the Dean, Professor Hendrick, and other instructors. They are expected to conform to regular ways of study, recreation, etc., and are encouraged as much as possible along the lines of sound moral and mental development."[120]

Most letters stressed the college degree programs. In some Penrose stated that, "Our requirements for admission are fully equal to those at Harvard or Yale, and we are doing the same kind of work as the best New England colleges."[121] To one potential student Penrose was unusually effusive: "President Hadley of Yale said not long ago, I am told, that Whitman was the Yale of the Northwest. I would not claim so high an honor at the present time, but in aims and spirit we have that for our ambition."[122]

The president repeatedly praised the Whitman students for their spirit, energy, and loyalty. He told a parent that "Knowing the type of school that Whitman is, you will realize that these students are of a particularly admirable type. Indeed they are the only class of students

who are attracted by an institution like Whitman."[123] Penrose informed a Canadian: "We are happy to say that we draw from the very
best families in the country boys who are sturdy and good-mannered,
and of rather superior character."[124] The few surviving recruiting
letters composed by faculty members carried about the same message
as those by their leader; Walter Bratton, for example, emphasized the
"spirit of old Whitman," the "many lovely people" in the town, and
the successful alumni.[125]

The president explained to many applicants the value of taking a
liberal arts education prior to specialized education. To a man interested in becoming a physician, Penrose wrote: "If you expect to be a
doctor you ought to get a full college course before going to medical
school."[126] Similar letters went to those interested in theology or law.

Perhaps a typical recruitment letter read: "We now have not only
the best equipment, probably, in the Northwest, but also a vigorous
faculty, and a large enthusiastic body of students. You will find, here,
unsurpassed opportunities for instruction of the highest grade. If you
want the best, you will do well to come here."[127]

The school also sought particular types of students. In 1902 an
anonymous writer recruited football players: "From your appearance," the letter read, "I would imagine that you would take kindly to
athletics. A picture of our football team, I understand, appears this
year in *Spaulding's Guide Book*, we having been scored against only
once during the whole of last season. Don't you want to come down
and help us put it there again?"[128] The recruitment of athletes was
unusual, however. Archer Hendrick, the principal of the academy,
bluntly informed two prospective students seeking financial help in
return for playing college baseball that scholarships were awarded
only on the basis of academics. The educator denounced young men
who "were willing to sell themselves to a college" and warned that
the financial aid awarded by schools to athletes resulted in their personal failure after graduation.[129]

Penrose wanted the brightest young men and women he could
find. Such persons would help build the institution as students and as
alumni. To get promising prospects Whitman trustees provided a full
one-year scholarship to the "graduate of highest standing from each
high school and academy in Oregon, Washington, and Idaho." (To
retain the scholarship in the second Whitman semester it was neces-

sary to earn a grade of at least eighty percent in the first one.) This scholarship program attracted considerable attention. For example, the principal of Salem High School informed the president that Whitman was "held in high esteem in Oregon."[130] Penrose himself felt strongly that his school was "head and shoulders above any other institution in the Northwest."[131] He also pointed out that Whitman's admission standards were the same as those of Yale and Harvard and that students who transferred to prestigious schools held their own. While other regional presidents would challenge Penrose's assertion, there is no doubt that Whitman's high admissions standards, tuition, and challenging curriculum discouraged many weak and unmotivated applicants.

From its establishment in 1882, the college had always depended upon private academies, especially religious ones east of the Cascades, to send their graduates. In the new century these feeder institutions were closing because of the public high school movement. Seeking money and faculty, several troubled academy leaders turned to Penrose for advice. He sought to assist Eells Academy in Colville; Weiser Academy in Idaho; Pendleton Academy in Oregon; and Puget Sound Academy in Snohomish.

Although Eells Academy had not yet put a graduate into Whitman, Penrose appreciated the quality of its instruction and assumed that it would become a helpful feeder.[132] The Congregational Education Society of Boston asked Penrose blunt questions about this Congregational school, for it feared "putting money into a hole."[133] Wanting to keep this church academy from becoming a public school, Penrose unsuccessfully sought eastern and western supporters for it. He got even more involved with Weiser Academy, especially after he visited there. Calling it "the best academy" in Idaho, the president lauded it for sending him able freshmen.[134] He sympathized with the school's fund raising ("trying to raise funds in the East is trying to one's body and soul"), reassured the CES when it complained about the school's being in "the slough in which it has wallowed for so long," recommended faculty, and even served on its board of trustees.[135] Weiser appreciated the college's assistance and standards, and it urged its graduates to attend Whitman. Penrose supported the Idaho school even as it suffered from internal turmoil, lost able faculty members, and sought to pay a crushing mortgage. The president also lent a hand to a closer school, Pendleton Academy, which sent graduates to Whitman. His letters and personal appearance could not, however, revive a dying institution.

Penrose worked to build a meaningful relationship with Puget Sound Academy. This Snohomish institution considered itself to be Whitman's "best fitting school" west of the mountains. The academy's principal urged Penrose, "a man of energy," to help convince D.K. Pearsons to provide matching endowment money. He should be told that Puget Sound Academy, which tried to reflect the New England model, would help Whitman.[136] Penrose agreed to make the appeal and praised the principal for building an endowment. A young Whitman alumnus teaching in the beleaguered school reported the need of an endowment because the academy "is even poorer, if possible, than a student at Whitman."[137] In 1906 the last principal of Puget Sound Academy wrote that after a long struggle the school was settling up its affairs because of "growing doubt in the minds of its chief supporters as to the utility of the institution."[138]

The collapse of this school diminished Whitman's opportunity to attract students west of the Cascades, but it had one positive result. Several Seattleites responded favorably to Penrose's appeal that they give money to his college now that the Congregational academy had shut its doors. He promised that "there is no possibility" of Whitman's failure, and that it was the state's only surviving Congregational institution. Among those who switched allegiance was Seattle's pioneer Denny family.[139]

Penrose generally had more confidence in an academy teacher than in a public high school teacher because the private school instructors were often better educated and sought to inculcate Christianity. Teaching was the critical component, and Penrose kept an eye on many secondary instructors. The principal of Klickitat Academy in Goldendale related that his private school had just been converted into a public high school. He asked Penrose if Whitman would keep it on the accredited list and was assured that if he stayed on as principal, then the college would not change Klickitat's standing.[140]

Penrose also sought to find positions for the competent, idealistic men and women who had led and taught in the closing academies. The failure of the schools that Penrose hoped to develop as feeders made his institution even more dependent upon public high schools.

The failure of these academies had several other implications for Whitman. How much longer could its own academy compete? The academies could not raise local money. If wealthy westerners would allow these private secondary schools to fail in competition with public high schools, would they also fail to support private schools like Whitman in their struggle against the growing state universities? An academy principal stated that there is "a quite general feeling that the day of academies is past" and that clergymen did not promote them because they failed to realize their worth.[141] But Penrose, who had graduated from a private academy and college, believed that such institutions would benefit a maturing society. How could he convince westerners who had not shared his educational experience that they must donate time and money so that regional children would enjoy the benefits of the academic and Christian education that was offered by both Pearsons Academy and Whitman College?

Whitman's recruiting practices shifted in response to the death of private academies and secondary schools and also to the need to recruit west of the Cascades. The college closely studied its own enrollment patterns and pondered the implications of the private secondary schools' demise. Whitman had established a solid reputation in the rural regions but needed to do the same in the urban centers west of the Cascades. Beginning in the fall of 1907 the college would make curriculum decisions based upon the need to attract coastal students and upon the fact that graduates of the public high school, not the private academy, would dominate the freshman class.

In Loco Parentis

In the early progressive period, as in other times, Whitman College sought to play the role of a parent. Although the term *in loco parentis* was not used, the institution would broadly educate, carefully protect, and firmly discipline its students. Whitman acted as an extended family. The wise and experienced administration, faculty, and older students would provide a supportive environment for students as young as thirteen. An alumnus later recalled Penrose's parental role in the early fall semester: "you are answering letters to fond parents about their offspring besides inspiring the Freshmen with awe and at the same time keeping the preps under a parental eye."[142]

Whitman publications stressed that the college stood for character and culture. Professors advocated Christian character in classes, chapel, advising, and activities. In 1903 Penrose publicly explained that he wanted young women and men "to be strong of will, so developed in character that they will all be brave, clean, earnest, and helpful. They will not yield easily to temptation. They will be above the cheap and easy vices which beset young people." At the same time the college punished those lacking character. The discipline code stated that "The name of any student expelled from the institution will be starred in the next College catalogue."[143]

Penrose assured parents that to help students avoid vices, "We look carefully after the lives of our students, aiming to guard them from harm and strengthen their interests in the best things."[144] "Our girls are . . . well cared for . . . under the supervision of a Matron and Lady Principal. I think that a boy or girl can be as safely entrusted to our care as at any school in the country. Whitman tries as best it can to maintain a simple, healthful, inspiring life."[145] In a 1906 letter to a Boise physician Penrose explained:

> The college has made its reputation by insisting upon a high standard of character, and by endeavoring to surround its students with all those influences which make for the best manhood. We believe in looking after the lives of our students, and in lessening as much as possible the temptations which will inevitably beset them. We do not try to save a student from responsibility for his own character and development, but both in our dormitories and in the general life of the college we try to have such standards of thought and living which will help a student to the development of his own best self.[146]

The institution not only set high academic standards, it required chapel attendance, gymnastics or exercise, regular hours, clean dorm rooms, orderly conduct, and good table manners under the supervision of the dormitory deans. Diners in Reynolds Hall had to furnish their own napkin rings.

Acting like concerned parents, the faculty drew up rules. Some general ones applied to the library, to college property, to unexcused class absences, and to the prohibition of tobacco on campus. Each residence hall had a dean, who, with a discipline committee, enforced

Residents of Reynolds Hall were responsible for cleaning the building. This is a "clean-up day" in 1905.

the rules. A basic one read: "The conduct of students in the dormitories should be that of a well-ordered Christian home. Boisterous conduct of any kind; the use of tobacco in any form; disorder or dirt in the rooms; or other reprehensible habits, or any conduct (such as shouting, singing, whistling, or romping in the corridors) which is not in accordance with the object of a students' dormitory, shall be regarded as cause for expulsion from the dormitory."

Students had to make their beds and to have their rooms in order by 10:00 AM. At various times the dean inspected the rooms. Residents were not allowed to take friends to their rooms without the dean's permission, and a student had to receive approval to spend a night out of his or her room. At 10:30 PM the dormitory was locked and lights turned out, but the dean could lend a key. There was even a stricture on soiled clothing: "No person participating in athletic sports, or other forms of recreation which make the clothing too dirty for a sitting room or study will be allowed to enter the corridors of the building. The objectionable clothing must be deposited in rooms provided for that purpose."

The school's leaders hoped to solve problems by enforcing rules and to shape behavior by advising.[147] Students helped regulate their classmates. In 1901, for example, class officers came to a faculty meeting and told of their efforts to control cigarette smoking.

In 1906 the college made a major change in the governance of Billings Hall. Responsibility was transferred from the dean to a committee of five residents, who were elected by their peers and by the faculty. Some insisted that this committee was effective; others disagreed, even complaining about increased noise and "rough housing." In 1907 the *Pioneer* endorsed the system: "Honest hilarity has not been interfered with, but the boys have been allowed to enjoy any fun kept within the bounds of decency. The life at Billings . . . this year has been ideal."[148] The girls' dormitories took less of the faculty's time because there were fewer reports of undesirable behavior.

Relatives sometimes explicitly asked the school's leaders to look after a student. One parent wrote the president about his son: "I want you to keep a special eye on him."[149] Another informed Hendrick, "Be good to the boy for it is the first time he was ever away from home, and he will need your friendship."[150]

The college, however, did not always wait for a parent to show concern. Penrose explained to a mother that her son needed encouragement and that he would "try and put heart into the boy. . . . The worst thing that could happen to him would be if he became a case of undeveloped manhood."[151] Students were encouraged to live on campus and not in private homes; for example, Penrose assured a mother that in a dormitory her daughter would "be under constant care and supervision such as she could not get at any home."[152]

Principal Hendrick confidentially wrote a father that the college concluded that his daughter was working too hard in and out of class and worried that "it would ultimately overcome her physical strength."[153] Hendrick consulted with local doctors, then explained to a mother that her boy's severe headaches resulted from "overwork and lack of exercise as well as from study." The principal advised that the young man should continue his schooling because he would grow out of his difficulty.[154]

Concern about another student prompted an interesting exchange with University of Washington President Thomas Kane. An unhappy Whitman male wrote to the university about transferring; Kane soon alerted Penrose, who talked to the dissatisfied writer.

Penrose wrote Kane that he favored a transfer for the student because "he is one of the kind who always want change and variety." He discovered that the young man had ignored his assignments and concluded, "I hope that if he comes to you severe pressure will be brought to bear on him to make him develop into something of a scholar. He is now ravelling out at the ends through lack of definite and earnest purpose."[155]

The institution also tried to help students with their financial difficulties. The president assured parents: "We do all that we can to find employment for our boys." He described the type of work available for both sexes. Some of our "nicest and brightest girls are working at Reynolds Hall . . . doing housework and waiting on the table, without lowering their standing in the slightest degree." Some women tutored, worked in the college library, or did stenography and typing for business houses.[156] Men working on campus earned about $2 a week, which covered nearly half of their expenses. Some men labored as school or town janitors. Others arose early and fired home furnaces for $20 a month; those who delivered newspapers received $15 a month. However, Penrose emphasized to parents and prospective students that there was greater opportunity in the wheat harvest, where a seasonal field hand earned up to $100.[157] Penrose believed that anyone who brought with them about $100 and worked a few hours each week should not incur a college debt.

Penrose sometimes wrote to the students' former principals about student achievements; instructors sent personal notes to members of their classes about low grades. The president once mailed a girl her grades before her parents received them and added: "This letter is between you and me, and I trust that you will consider it not only confidential but also an expression of the interest which I am taking in your welfare."[158]

Penrose wrote hundreds of letters to parents about student problems. In some letters he expressed frank concern about a student's behavior. The president informed a mother that her son was doing poorly in classes owing not to "a lack of brains, but to a lack of purpose and energy. . . . It seems to me that what he needs most of all is some kind of a spur which will drive him out of his laziness."[159] Penrose judged that another student failed classes because he tried "to bluff his way."[160] The president told a father that his son should move into the dormitory: "Last term he lived in a private house where he was not under our strict supervision and got with bad companions and into bad ways."[161] Penrose notified a parent that Willie had "both neglected his work, violated the regulations of the college, and was untrue to his mother and me; so that you see there was very little ground for my having a great deal of admiration for him."[162] An Oregon father was told that Tom, whose low grades worried everyone, had been moved to the dormitory where he had to keep regular study hours and that he was "not allowed to be on the street unnecessarily." The educator assured parents that, "He is a nice boy and we all like him, although he has not yet developed that earnest love of study which may yet come."[163]

In other letters Penrose contacted parents about delinquent college bills. He explained the college's situation to one family: "We are heavily in debt, owing nearly $50,000 on which we are obliged to pay interest at the bank. Every dollar which a student owes us is a dollar on which we are obliged to pay interest, and we cannot longer go on the policy of allowing students to run up an indebtedness of several hundred dollars."[164]

In still other letters Penrose found it necessary to defend dormitory food when protestors wanted to leave Reynolds Hall. He became involved when students mistreated each other. A lawyer wrote him that his child suffered "brutal and barbarous treatment" at the hands of classmates.[165] Some complained to the president about a professor's arbitrary methods; others denounced required classes, including those in religion. In a few instances Penrose could not mollify those who were upset with the school's discipline, and they withdrew their children.[166]

The personal care and concern shown by college officials prompted favorable letters. One student wrote Penrose his thanks "for your constant kindness. . . . It was an education in itself to be under you." The writer added, "old Whitman: Long may she wave and never waver."[167] A recent graduate wrote that "the students are justly proud of the unselfish devotion of their president."[168]

The faculty spent considerable time discussing and enforcing rules about dancing, smoking, and entertainment. The faculty divided over the propriety of dancing, but an event in 1904 established a policy. A conservatory student and an academy student were punished by Dean Eliza Cobb, a New Englander opposed to dancing. The two girls had attended a Walla Walla dancing class. Angered because the students did not quickly return to campus after she summoned them by telephone, the dean and the discipline committee restricted one of the girls to campus for thirty days (classmates said this was "a month's jail sentence"). The other dancer was suspended partly because of this incident and partly because she had not paid her college bills. The city newspaper account also revealed that the suspended student had once jumped into Lakum Duckum (the campus pond) with a football player.[169]

A new dean sought a more liberalized rule about dancing; the faculty responded by stating that "all girls attending dances shall be required to obtain a written excuse from their parents for each dance."[170] This reform led students to pressure for more campus dances. In 1906 the faculty permitted students "to hold or attend each semester one and only one outside entertainment with dancing." Underage men and women had to have parental permission to attend dances controlled by the committee on student affairs.[171]

After many attempts to prohibit smoking, the faculty realized that it could not be stopped. Bowing to student pressure, it sanctioned smoking in Billings Hall. However, the professors required the building's student committee to "safeguard the comfort of those who do not use tobacco and to discourage the spread of the habit."[172]

While the faculty liberalized the rules on dancing and tobacco, it refused to modify its tough stand against improper amusement. It opposed students attending "Sunday theater or like amusement" and threatened those who violated the rule. At chapel Penrose announced this rule and added: "we do not consider a student, who attends saloons or other questionable resorts, eligible to membership in the institution. We think that a student with tastes for this kind of amusement will not have a taste for those things for which the college stands."[173] According to a city newspaper some upperclass students upheld the rule because they did not want to diminish the school's reputation. An event of December 1907 brought negative publicity as far away as Portland. Penrose had reported to the Walla Walla City Council that saloonkeepers had sold liquor to academy boys as young as sixteen. "The Council was taken by surprise" and promised to prosecute the saloonkeepers.[174]

Students generally abided by the rules and regulations. But a campus rumor that the faculty had ruled that "no young lady should accept the attention of the same young gentleman as escort for three consecutive times," aroused them to protest. Perhaps the faculty had considered such a stricture but wisely did not enact it.[175]

Student scraps and college pranks provided campus excitement and attracted newspaper coverage. Battles between the freshman and sophomore classes were another tradition brought to the West. In the early new century these fall "scraps" at Whitman involved the stealing of the rivals' class colors—they were carried on a flagpole like regimental colors—and fighting to tear down colors that were raised on buildings or flagpoles. The rivals also kidnaped members of the other class and dumped them on upper Mill Creek Road or threw them into Lakum Duckum. Student groups consistently sought to steal each others' party refreshments.

In 1903 five freshmen hoisted their flag over Memorial Hall, taunting sophomores by shouting that they had blankets and food to keep the flag flying for the required twenty-four hours. If it remained in place this long then the freshman class were the victors. Sophomores, therefore, tried to get up the building, but other freshmen contested their effort. An observer reported that, "A window was smashed, water pipes broken, and one face of the clock cracked."[176] Penrose stopped the struggle. Freshmen girls, however, got into the rivalry by placing a flag on top of Reynolds Hall and keeping guard under a blistering sun. The following year there was another battle as freshmen hoisted their banner, a very large green cloth with "1908" in grey figures. In the early morning hours sophomores tried to scale the dormitory and rip down the hated flag. Frustrated in their attempts, they bombarded their opponents with rocks, bruising one. Some sophomores opposed throwing missiles, fearing that the class might have to pay for property damages. Acting president Lyman ended the affair by warning that if property were destroyed he would call the police. The sullen attackers gave up the struggle but threatened revenge. The triumphant class, who flew their flag the required time, shouted their supremacy.[177]

In 1905 the freshmen raised their flag on the college flagpole. The resourceful sophomores surprised the flag's guardians, sent a man up the flagpole, and burned the detested "rag." The freshmen then took several of their rivals three miles into the country and dumped them. They admitted defeat, however, and honored the victors with a banquet at a local hotel.

Penrose as a student had enjoyed such activities; as president he feared injury to participants and school property. The faculty took no "official" action against the rival classes, but considered ways to control this student behavior. Undoubtedly the teachers expressed more concern about student pranks—partly because they were sometimes the victims—than about class fights. Pranks took various forms. Responding to a false fire alarm, fire fighters on one occasion slogged across muddy Ankeny Field. Penrose apologized and urged authorities to find and fine the guilty. A professor sleeping in Billings Hall suffered from the hands of pranksters. Using a log as a battering ram, students broke into his room and threw firecrackers. Less serious pranks included an attempt to steal a banquet's ice cream; failing in their attempt, the boys salted the dessert.[178] The faculty enjoyed a few of the stunts and made no attempt to punish the perpetrators. On Halloween 1903, for example, the Reynolds Hall women locked three dormitory authorities in their rooms. Then "they danced, played the piano, sang, feasted on cider, pickles, and other halloween dainties." Some of the girls had borrowed clothing and dressed as boys. The girls boasted that their great frolic continued unmolested until 3:00 AM.[179]

An unknown number of students were expelled, but not for pranks. Those dismissed had generally failed to meet the school's scholarship rules. After the faculty took action against a student, Penrose or Hendrick wrote to parents. The letters always explained the decision and often provided advice. Hendrick reported that an able but careless boy would be sent home on the train and advised that Carlyle should "stay out . . . for one semester" because it would "probably open his eyes to the necessity of improving his opportunities when they are afforded him."[180] Penrose wrote a mother that her son had been expelled because he would not study and advised that she find a position where "he would be obliged to work."[181] In a similar example, Penrose recommended that one lad who was interested in a good time, not his books, should be sent to a ranch where a year's hard work "would make him appreciate the value of an education."[182] A minister learned that his son was dropped because he lacked "sufficient backbone or will power to keep steadily to one fixed purpose." Penrose informed parents that Orville had made many promises and resolutions "but that his courage seems to ooze out and soon he is as bad as he was before."[183] In an unusual case a male was sent home for being "insulting, vulgar, and profane."[184]

Perhaps the best example of *in loco parentis* occurred in the spring of 1907. A native of Finland, John Eckman, mined in Idaho and Alaska and converted to Christianity. After a few months of study in Seattle he had completed an eighth-grade education and in 1906 he arrived at Whitman without money or extra clothing. An unusual ninth-grader, he paid for his academy expenses by washing windows. Penrose applauded his "remarkable grit" in starting his education with severe handicaps; the college community agreed and provided him with clothing and textbooks. Eckman soon became ill with consumption, and a local physician advised him to hurry to Southern California. Again the college community responded by furnishing a railroad ticket, clothing, and food. Penrose covered Eckman's debts and wrote a friend to care for the invalid. But it was to no avail. Eckman died within a month, and his distraught Whitman admirers paid his $65 burial expense.

Developing Alumni and Board Support

From his experience at Williams, Penrose knew that alumni could help him improve the college. He did not anticipate, however, much immediate assistance because the alumni were "so few and poor." In 1907 he estimated that there were 150 college alumni, but he made no attempt to total the graduates of the conservatory, the academy, and the old seminary, whose records had been lost. The educator reported that not one of the college graduates was worth as much as $200,000, so they had little to give their alma mater.[185] Considering any persons who had attended the institution to be alumni, Penrose generally asked them to express "the Whitman spirit and to help the college at any time."[186] Often he was more specific: he wrote to a few alumni asking them to recruit for the freshman class.[187]

Several alumni informed Penrose that they wanted to help build their alma mater. One of the most useful was the Reverend William H. Proctor of Ritzville, who recommended that the alumni raise endowment money on a matching basis with benefactor D.K. Pearsons. The president preferred an alumnus to serve as a college agent who would promote the college among alumni and other groups. This person must know the faculty, recognize the problems of the trustees, and appreciate the school's history. Penrose sought "a big man, big hearted, whole-souled fellow, who believes in the institution, who is a lover of education, and who is a good mixer. He is not to be found or picked up on any street corner."[188] Unfortunately, he did not find the right man. In 1907 Proctor and other alumni failed to get money from Pearsons or to find a college agent.

To maintain contact with former students, Whitman professors and Penrose sometimes greeted and organized alumni while traveling. Other alumni formed themselves into groups without any college assistance. Perhaps the best example was the Whitman Atlantic Coast Club, which honored "the little western college."[189] Whitman leaders sent personal letters, the *Pioneer*, the *Quarterly*, and other publications to such eastern supporters.

Alumni sometimes held meetings with faculty members; in 1904 an alumna attended such a gathering. She criticized the alumni president for being inefficient but reported one accomplishment: "It was decided to change the college colors to maize and national blue."[190]

Students also appealed to alumni for support, for example, the class of 1906 tried to sell annuals to them by using a humorous message: "Though you are an alumnus, we regard you as not dead but gone before. . . . Perhaps when we are as old as you are, we will follow your example, but we can't think so far ahead just now."[191]

Alumni often asked the faculty and Penrose for recommendations. In response to this growing number of requests, professors established a committee on graduate appointments, which sought "to find suitable positions and to push applications" for alumni.[192] While faculty letters of recommendation have not survived, Penrose's files include several written by the president. According to University of Oregon president Prince Lucien Campbell, Penrose wrote frank and fair evaluations. Penrose did "not wish to recommend a Whitman man who might not prove all that was desired."[193] The president's comprehensive, supportive letters for candidates to eastern graduate schools sometimes included information supplied by faculty members.

Regional schools often wrote to the college seeking Whitman alumni for teachers. One letter from the state normal school in Bellingham asked for "a clean, sane, sensible, active Christian man." The writer explained why he needed such a mature person: "We have three hundred young ladies in our school and while a young man might make no trouble, unless he has good sense and is discreet, some of the girls may make fools of themselves."[194]

Many alumni developed friendships with Penrose and deep loyalty to their alma mater. Alumni sought their president's advice; for instance, he told a young minister to seek a small parish, "where you can have the quiet for deep study which the successful minister must have at the beginning of his ministry, and which he never gets later."[195] Other alumni thanked Whitman for providing a solid education or compared their alma mater with graduate school. One complained that the University of California's science faculty tried to "bluff" him, yet he favored the privacy of a large school "after the publicity of being a senior in a small college." But he concluded, "I feel like I belong to Whitman and not the U. of C."[196] These loyal alumni brought favorable attention to their alma mater. A Walla Walla writer boasted that the college "has turned into the arteries of public life in the Northwest an ever-increasing supply of strong and wholesome blood. Young men and young women have been trained for public service, both as citizens and scholars ... by an institution never ashamed of its Christian ideals."[197]

The institution recorded facts about its alumni. Between 1886 and 1907, 121 women and men graduated. Most remained in Washington, including thirty-six percent in Walla Walla, five percent in Seattle, and five percent in Spokane. The top five professions for male graduates were business, law, teaching, ministry, and medicine. Only fifty-six percent of the females listed a profession, and almost all of them taught.

The board of trustees, like the alumni, helped Penrose with his educational plans. It held annual meetings at commencement, though generally only a bare majority of the nine men attended. Because it met only once a year and delegated considerable responsibility to its executive committee, one of the board's requirements was to approve what had been done by the smaller group. The board handled a variety of other responsibilities—paying bills, supervising the investment of college money, hiring and compensating the faculty, awarding earned and honorary degrees, and passing appropriate resolutions.

In 1907, knowing that the charter restricted the board of trustees to nine, Penrose created an additional advisory board of sixteen so as "to have the advice and support of a large number of business-men."[198] The larger board had all the rights of the smaller one except that its members could not vote on legal matters. The president planned to ask the legislature to enlarge the board of trustees to twenty-one; then the second board would be disbanded. In 1907 four of the trustees, including Professor Louis Anderson, resided in Walla Walla and formed the executive committee. All of the trustees were Washingtonians; the 1907 advisory board counted only two members who lived out of the state, and only three Walla Wallans. One of the more vocal trustees, Seattle physician Park Weed Willis, teased Penrose about his power over the board, referring to him as "Comanche Steve."[199] The president's letters to the board covered various topics, including the school's financial situation, requests to attend meetings, agendas for meetings, and relevant college news.

The trustees' exact role in these early years is hard to discern. Unfortunately these men did not raise much money. Despite the fact that the endowment was of such importance, neither Penrose nor the board could find many contributors to that fund. The president unsuccessfully pleaded that until the endowment increased there was no possibility of eliminating the nagging debt. Penrose spent far more time with the productive finance committee than he did with the two trustee boards. Under the leadership of Walla Walla lawyer Allen Reynolds and other local men, this group huddled several times a year, investing the college's endowment in property mortgages. Wheat growers in Walla Walla, Whitman, and Umatilla counties borrowed from the college. Whitman also lent to some who were developing irrigated tracts in nearby Benton County. Lacking funds, Whitman turned down many potential borrowers, so Penrose appealed to eastern friends for money the college could loan to westerners, assuring them that the school would not make a bad investment because the experienced and conservative finance committee required a unanimous vote on any loan. In 1907 the president reported that "We invest mainly in farm mortgages of a gilt-edged character. The income on the endowment last year was about seven percent net."[200]

Whitman and the Community

Stephen Penrose, the faculty, and faculty spouses played significant roles in Walla Walla's religious, cultural, and political life. All faculty members except one were active in a church; five sometimes preached, and three served as Sunday school superintendents. Faculty families often endorsed Christian missionary activities and various local clubs. Joining with the Penroses they supported the establishment and management of the YMCA and the YWCA. Professors gave lectures or recitals to local audiences. Most were Republicans, favoring trustee Levi Ankeny's successful bid to become a United States senator and endorsing President Theodore Roosevelt's Square Deal. To the disgust of saloonkeepers and other wets, professors supported restrictions on the sale of alcoholic beverages; most probably also joined Penrose in rejecting women's suffrage. Faculty members and their leader wrote about their societal concerns to politicians, especially the governor. Caught up in the progressive movement, these educators encouraged students to follow their example and become concerned about religious, cultural, and political issues, and to continue their activities after they graduated.

Whitman then as now did much for the city's cultural and intellectual life. The school brought musicians, politicians, artists, and lecturers for both cultural and publicity reasons. Penrose realized that by sponsoring a variety of activities he enlightened his neighbors, who, in turn, became more appreciative of his school. The president sought to bring distinguished citizens to Walla Walla; in 1905, for example, he offered Booker T. Washington an opportunity to deliver the commencement address. Impressed with Washington's leadership of southern blacks, Penrose offered to arrange speaking appointments for him. The black educator agreed but then had to cancel his travel plans. Penrose was more successful in bringing other notables, including progressive Republican senator Robert LaFollette Sr., who spoke on corrupt politics, and newspaperman Jacob Riis, who lectured on urban slums.

In 1906–1907 Penrose became frustrated while organizing a series of five cultural programs. One exhausted performer failed to keep her date, and the audience bitterly complained to Penrose. Another entertainer arrived late because of an impossible train schedule. A lecturer unexpectedly switched his topic from Henry Ward Beecher to Oliver Cromwell. The manager of the Keylor Grand Theater—the best site in the city—charged stiff rates, even during the 1907 recession. Penrose had to cover costs of the program out of his own pocket, and thus he lost his enthusiasm for promoting this form of culture in the rural community.

The educator knew that he had to advertise the college in order to build. A traditional technique was to publish brochures and pamphlets showing pictures of faculty and buildings and describing the academy, conservatory, and college. Newspaper advertising was also used. Whitman even provided a picture of Memorial Hall for an advertisement for Nodusto (a household product no longer available). Penrose endorsed the product: "It saves time and labor in sweeping, prevents dust from rising, and gives the floors a rich dark color."[201] An agreement was reached with a few newspapers, including those in Tacoma and Joseph, Oregon, which allowed editors to offer a $50 Whitman scholarship in lieu of being paid to run an advertisement for the college. Eastern publications asked Whitman to advertise in their pages but Penrose responded to *Colliers* that trustees concluded that such advertising would not "pay for itself."[202]

The president publicized Whitman in many ways. He sent information about it to newspapers in Seattle, Portland, and Spokane. Conservatory teachers and students toured eastern Washington, and it must have annoyed the busy college president that he sometimes had to arrange these publicity tour schedules. In 1906 Penrose wrote for membership lists of the university clubs in Tacoma, Seattle, Spokane, and Portland. He explained that he wanted regional college men to learn about his school, "which, I think, deserves their respect and interest."[203] Whitman faculty, and Penrose, publicized the school and offered regional service by delivering high school commencement addresses, participating at teachers' conventions, judging school debates, and delivering speeches. These frequent calls tired faculty participants; Penrose once complained that every week during the school year he delivered at least one address.[204]

In 1902 the college sponsored a month's visit by historian William Mowry, who came to the region to do historical research. Whitman paid him to deliver ten American history lectures, which Penrose praised "as a feast of fat things."[205] Penrose arranged for Mowry, who accepted the Whitman-saved-Oregon story, to visit other schools.

Far more important to publicizing the institution was President Theodore Roosevelt's May 1903 address given from Memorial Hall's porch. The president was on a national tour (which included some campus visits) seeking the 1904 Republican nomination; he came to Walla Walla primarily because it was the home of Senator Levi Ankeny. Penrose worked diligently to get Roosevelt to give his major address from the campus, explaining that it "will be a good advertisement of the college to the people of the United States."[206] On May 25, an estimated 10,000 visitors came to the city to see and hear the popular leader. Prior to his address, Whitman students, standing together near the speaker's platform, rendered Harvard and Whitman yells. Roosevelt praised Marcus Whitman and the college; local and traveling correspondents wrote flattering reports that included the young school.[207] (Pomona College was also visited by Roosevelt on this 1903 tour, which had similar effects on the two small schools: considerable publicity, and a long-remembered glow of pride.)

Penrose continued to boost Marcus Whitman's memory, which brought attention to the missionary and to the college. He worked with historians to get the state legislature to make the old missionary grounds into a park and appealed to the governor to save the monument from vandals. His efforts resulted in a rail fence built by penitentiary inmates. Penrose also played a major role in paying the old monument debt. In 1907 the college duly celebrated the sixtieth anniversary of the Whitman massacre. This grand occasion included the Washington governor, politicians from Idaho and Oregon, troops from Fort Walla Walla, Whitman faculty members and students, and many townspeople.

To recognize accomplishment and probably to attract publicity, the institution awarded a few honorary doctorates. At most commencements none were given, but in 1904 six were awarded. A wide variety of men received the doctorates, including Seattle minister Edward Lincoln Smith, Spokane judge George Turner, and historian William Mowry.

The institution sought publicity at two historical celebrations. In 1905 it displayed publications, photographs, and historical objects at Portland's Lewis and Clark Exposition. The following year it fur-

The most important and dignified structure on the college campus, Whitman Memorial Hall was completed in 1900. Architect George W. Babcock, who enjoyed a reputable Walla Walla practice, designed the building in Richardsonian Romanesque style. The structure contained classrooms, a chapel, a library, offices, and laboratories. This 1903 photograph shows the building outfitted with flags and bunting in honor of President Theodore Roosevelt, who would speak from its front steps. Townspeople and farmers are crowding for a position near the speaker.

nished a campus photograph and college publications to the distant Jamestown Exposition in Virginia.

In 1907 Penrose believed that Whitman deserved a Phi Beta Kappa chapter; he desired national recognition of the regional school's high academic standards. On February 28, 1907, he wrote to five chapters to support Whitman's request to the national organization. Chapters at Beloit, Stanford, Amherst, California, and Williams were informed that the "Whitman standard of scholarship is, we believe, a high one; the entrance requirements are good, and our college students are admitted to other colleges on favorable terms. For example, two years ago a student left us at the end of his junior year; was considered an average student here; entered Amherst without examination and with full credit, and graduated in one year with Phi Beta Kappa standing."[208]

Although it would be a dozen years before the college received a coveted Phi Beta Kappa chapter, Whitman's reputation had spread throughout the region. This was obvious in 1907 when the school requested new support from business leaders, many of whom acknowledged Penrose's successful efforts to build a reputable liberal arts college in rural Washington.

Penrose's Frustrations and Moods

In his dark moods Stephen Penrose suffered from what he saw as a series of setbacks. As indicated, he failed to raise the amounts of money he needed to erect additional buildings, eliminate the debt, increase faculty salaries, and do other things that would help realize his educational dreams. Money problems consistently nagged him. In 1906, for example, the president complained that the school had "to curtail expenses at every possible point, including the implementation of a new accounting system."[209] Probably it was money that prompted the faculty to insist that the students purchase their own examination bluebooks.

A different type of setback came in 1907 with the death of trustee Myron Eells. A firm supporter of the institution, he had written a biography of Marcus Whitman, which Penrose sought to have published. In letters to editors he called Eells "the foremost authority" on Pacific Northwest history, maintained that there was considerable interest in the Whitman story, described the manuscript as both popular and scholarly, and even offered to proof it and cover publication costs. Several firms simply rejected the biography, but one editor criticized it fairly and urged a thorough revision, saying "I think you can put more snap and go into it than it has."[210] It was frustrating to receive numerous rejections, for Penrose wanted easterners to read this book as a counter to Yale historian Edward G. Bourne's "destructive criticism" of Marcus Whitman.[211]

Another of Penrose's disappointments was his inability to limit the growth of the Washington Agricultural College in Pullman. This institution offered courses that competed with Whitman's and duplicated some taught at the University of Washington. Penrose informed a friend at the Spokane *Spokesman-Review* that the state needed an agricultural college but that he hoped "that the excellent institution at Pullman will keep its legitimate place." He protested that the school's leaders used the term "state college" in an "insidious" attempt to prepare the public for its "usurpation."[212]

Penrose tried to make an ally out of President Thomas Kane of the University of Washington. The Seattle educator sympathized, judging that the agricultural college's courses in music and art were "carried primarily as a club to hammer at ... Whitman." Kane did not fear academic competition from Pullman but complained that the college's president, Enoch A. Bryan, received more than his fair share of the legislature's appropriation. Kane ruled that his school was a more suitable place to offer engineering than a school "in a small town like Pullman, where there is so little to illustrate the practical work that [engineering] departments represent."[213]

Various persons and groups agreed with Penrose and Kane, maintaining that Bryan and his supporters were too ambitious. A group calling itself "The Taxpayers of Eastern Washington" circulated a statement entitled *Is it a Scheme and a Graft?* They pointed out the "enormous expense of two state universities duplicating courses ... and calling for great outlays for building and teaching forces."[214] The state legislature rejected such fears and changed the name of the institution to the State College of Washington.

Penrose, however, continued to fight. In an attempt to limit the state college's curriculum, he prepared a bill creating an educational commission and sent it to the governor. In his covering letter the president predicted that such a law would resolve the rivalries between schools in Seattle and Pullman. Penrose warned: "At the present time we have no educational policy and each institution tries to get all that it can and to develop itself to the fullest extent regardless of what every other institution is doing. In consequence there is considerable duplication of work, and an unnecessary burden on the tax payers of the State." The president urged action or there would be "an ever-increasing jealousy and bitterness."[215] Penrose cautioned

Oregon leaders that he hoped there would be no attempt by its agricultural college in Corvallis to make an absurd attempt, like the one
being made in Pullman, where boosters planned to create "a second
State University."[216]

Increasing his burden, Penrose's difficulties with Walla Wallan
Thompson Coit Elliott continued through 1907 and would grow
much more bitter. Penrose and the school's treasurer, Allen Reynolds, concluded that Elliott, who had once served as Whitman's treasurer, was an avowed enemy of the institution and of Marcus Whitman.[217] In 1905 the college transferred its account from Baker-Boyer
Bank (where Elliott was vice president) to the First National Bank
(where Reynolds was vice president). Miles Moore, the president of
Baker-Boyer, protested the closing of a thirty-five-year-old account.
The banker wrote: "I know nothing of the merits of the controversy
between your board and Mr. Elliott, but no matter how flagrant his
offenses, I submit you had no right to attempt to saddle the responsibility upon the bank. . . . So far as I know he has not used his official
title in his warfare on the college." Moore reminded Penrose that the
bank's stockholders had been friends and patrons of the school and
concluded: "The action of your board in this matter seems . . . ill
advised, it lacks breadth, it lacks charity, it betrayed lack of consideration for old time friends who were still anxious to show good will."
He warned Penrose that his own family donations to Whitman would
soon cease.[218]

Treasurer Reynolds responded that he and the board had not
made the decision. Reynolds stated that he had asked Baker-Boyer to
ask Elliott to "cease his efforts to injure the college" or remove Elliott
as vice president. The school official continued: "As Vice President of
the Bank he certainly, to some extent, represents it, and it seems to me
that it is due to a depositor of thirty-five years standing, that the
management of the Bank would be sufficiently interested to, at least,
urge one of its officers not to be saying and doing things for the
evident purpose of injuring that depositor." He bluntly told Moore
that the bank would be better off without Elliott.[219]

Perhaps there was other correspondence between the two men
about Elliott. Surely Moore must have made much of the fact that
Reynolds was vice president of the rival First National Bank, which
was led by Whitman trustee Levi Ankeny. Fortunately, Whitman's

Allen H. Reynolds graduated from Whitman and took legal training at Boston University. He served as Whitman's treasurer and as a trustee. His family had strong Whitman connections: Reynolds Hall was named for his mother, Lettice, a frequent donor to the college; Allen's brother Harry also supported Whitman and served as a trustee; and Allen's daughter Ruth graduated from Whitman and became the school's librarian.

leaders mollified Moore, who continued to support the institution. Surviving records do not indicate exactly what Elliott had done in his battle with Penrose and Reynolds. The president concluded that Elliott had anonymously sent hostile mail to Whitman's friends in the East and West. He even hired a detective to prove authorship. In 1906 an anonymous publication, *Why Whitman College should pay for the Whitman Monument*, faulted the school's leadership. The writer asserted that the college could have paid this debt. Penrose suspected that Elliott had written this criticism, adding "I think the man is insane or in danger of becoming so."[220]

Penrose discussed the Elliott problem with D.K. Pearsons but probably did not tell the benefactor about a more serious difficulty—his own inability to make wise investments. Penrose's daughters later remembered that each had failed. In 1903 he put his own funds into the sandy lands near Two Rivers, a hamlet in western Walla Walla County. Like many other speculators, he hoped that this arid region could be turned into productive orchards by the miracle of irrigation. The skimpy records indicate that Penrose planned to increase the school's endowment through this investment. After four years his 500 acres still had not been watered. Investments in Spokane business property and Idaho silver mines consumed time and brought worry, and neither he nor the college benefitted from them.

In 1907 Penrose's mood fluctuated. In the spring he had confided to Pearsons that he might resign. He wrote to other friends about leaving the college for a professorship in a theological seminary. In 1902 when he felt frustrated with the inability to raise money for Reynolds Hall, he talked about leaving to his old friend, the Reverend Edward Smith. Smith frankly responded: "I do not for one moment think that we could fill your place were you to go. But I do not take any stock whatever in your threat to resign unless this $25,000 is raised. You wouldn't do it, you know you wouldn't."[221]

In 1906 Penrose sighed that his school had a better reputation in the East than in the West and that he lacked support. He wrote a friend that there wasn't much chance of his leaving, but he was considering a position at a theological seminary "otherwise I presume I shall be here for the rest of my natural life."[222] He told a favorite alumnus that teaching at Yale Divinity School seemed attractive. He added, "But after all I guess that I cannot leave the west yet awhile. Certainly not until Whitman has gotten into a more dependable condition than it is at present, with larger endowment and freedom from debt." He considered himself a teacher, not a scholar: "I have long since abandoned the ambition to be a scholar in the fine sense of the term."[223] Depressed by his inability to raise money, he warned, "Help must come from some source, or else there must be a change of administration."[224] In April 1907 Penrose even considered applying for the principalship of an academy at Pocatello that harbored the hope of becoming a college.[225]

Strolling the campus, or in conversation with friends, Penrose was assured of his accomplishments. In 1907 Whitman was indeed a high-quality liberal arts college of regional stature. In the early twentieth century, as in later times, trustees, faculty, alumni, educators, businesspeople, ministers, and many others congratulated him. Trustees passed resolutions praising his talents and emphasized that he had opportunities for other presidencies with a tremendous increase in salary.[226] Educators especially appreciated all that had been done at Whitman. One wrote, "We recognize the fact that you are doing a great work and are adding to the future of our beloved state."[227] An Idaho educator reported that for years in traveling his state or eastern Oregon he met parents and prospective students who praised Whitman. William Mowry, an eastern professor, applauded the quality of the college community: "The students were fully equal to those of similar colleges in New England, and they were ... more in earnest and more devoted to their work."[228] A classmate from Williams participated at a Whitman commencement and observed: "I see the Williams spirit in this college, the broadening of thought and friendship between faculty and students." He and others compared Penrose with Theodore Roosevelt, for both were strenuous presidents.[229] Some praised Penrose's executive ability, concluding that he was building an important regional institution similar to leading eastern schools. Although the publicity of the college stated that Whitman modeled itself after Yale, it is most likely that Penrose more often used Williams as his example because he knew it better and because it was a more realistic comparison. Yale was probably used in publicity because westerners knew it better than Williams.

In 1902 Ripon College awarded Penrose a doctor of divinity degree. Far more important was the fact that Williams College, which had offered him its presidency in 1905, acknowledged his efforts to build a western college with an honorary doctorate.

Penrose's optimistic spirit returned in 1907. A rewarding summer vacation on Puget Sound and a successful fall semester were the reasons; a solid enrollment, good campus morale, a successful football season that united the community and college, and a successful public observation of the sixtieth anniversary of the Whitman massacre that brought regional support to the college sustained the leader. Penrose also expressed pleasure over the fact that the ten-year-old debt on the Whitman Monument had been paid. All of this good news had a local reaction. Penrose told Pearsons: "Now everybody in this region is a friend of Whitman College. The people of the town talk its praises, and are ready to back it financially. The old period of distrust and suspicion, and even hostility has melted away, and our sun has clearly risen above the horizon."[230]

There was another reason for Penrose's improved outlook. In the fall of 1907 he, Archer Hendrick, local trustees, and other supporters again planned the addition of a major engineering program. Insiders applauded the idea. There was campus talk about following this and other new educational paths; Penrose eagerly set out to explore them.

Whitman College in the Fall of its Twenty-Fifth Year

As the summer heat of 1907 subsided, Whitman College stirred to life. Early September advertisements in Walla Walla newspapers for all the city's schools signified the beginning of another academic year. Penrose placed advertisements for the conservatory, the academy, and the college, which called itself "The Yale of the West." The college offered "complete courses in literature, arts, and sciences," and background work in engineering, medicine, law, and teaching.[231] Penrose eagerly anticipated the school's twenty-fifth year, a year he thought to be extremely significant.

Another signal that school soon would start was the arrival of the Penroses, the faculty, and the students. The president returned from an extended outing at Delano Beach on Puget Sound, where two Whitman coeds had helped manage the Penrose children and prepare summer meals, and a male student had operated the family launch. Dean Archer Hendrick arrived at about the same time from Spokane where he had been recruiting academy and college students up to the last few days prior to the fall opening. Students returning by train were met at the city's various depots by classmates and happily escorted to campus. They took assigned rooms in the three dormitories —Reynolds and Prentiss halls for women and Billings Hall for men. The school required women students to live on campus, with relatives, or in approved homes. Men had more options because the college dormitories lacked space. Residents of Billings Hall soon voted on a cooperative method of running the dining room so as to cut board bills.

The students' traditional fall ritual began with an exchange of cheerful greetings, detailed accounts about work and fun during summer vacation, excited talk about upcoming classes and activities, and a close inspection of the campus. Older students probably commented about the fact that the growth of trees and shrubs and the improvement of pathways made the grounds more attractive. Although there were no new buildings to explore, there were new works of art to admire in Memorial Hall: Professor and Mrs. Anderson had recently donated pictures of Grecian ruins and a friend of the college had given three rubbings of ancient Nestoria tablets. At registration the students encountered a few townspeople who had come to enroll in special courses taught by notable faculty. The college was serving the community through this extension program.

At fall convocation, the faculty, trustees, and alumni appeared in caps and gowns and participated in a program featuring college musicians and an address by alumnus Harry Tash. His lecture, "Experiences in the Philippines," related his work in that country's new public schools. Students attended a Penrose-directed morning chapel and learned that daily chapel was required; later they watched football coach Arthur Baird lead a team practice. Meanwhile needy women and men arranged in the president's office for jobs in Walla Walla's homes, gardens, and offices.

The administration, faculty, and students aimed to make everyone feel a part of the college community. In opening week male students attended a mixer where they listened to a new economics professor, to the returning football coach, to representatives of the literary societies, to the *Pioneer* editor, and to others promoting campus activities. This social activity concluded with the singing of "old favorite college songs." Across campus in Reynolds Hall there was a YWCA reception for women. Mary Penrose explained the relationship

Mrs. Mary Penrose and her children in 1909. Clockwise from lower left, they are Clement (Clem), Mary (Maysie), Nathaniel (Nat), Frances, and Virginia. Mary is holding Stephen Beasley Linnard, Jr. (Binks).

of this organization to the college. Participants enjoyed games, refreshments, and the singing of college songs. Surely celebrants must
have talked about current newspaper reports that the University of
Washington's faculty had expelled (students said "canned") twenty-
nine students because they sought pleasure, not knowledge.

Academy boys and college men heard Penrose deliver his annual
warning against hazing: "The malicious infliction of personal indig-
nity in any form will not be tolerated."[232] He also cautioned his audience not to mar campus property, especially by painting class numerals on buildings. Any class committing the vandalism would have
to pay for repairs and a fine. Penrose also announced that he would
soon go east and that Professor William Lyman would be in charge.

At the first student body meeting there were numerous speeches
on student activities, including the men's glee club, the *Pioneer*, and
athletics. A coed reported that "there were five activities open to girls
on the same basis as to the boys, namely, basketball, debate, oratory,
glee club, and tennis."[233] Another important event was a reception
sponsored by the YMCA and the YWCA. This was the first large social
event of the college year, and most students and faculty attended.
Two lines formed and each person went down them, shaking hands
and learning names. Conversation and group singing of college and
football songs also contributed "to the pleasure of the evening."[234]

During the semester compulsory chapel sometimes covered contemporary topics; for example, the Reverend Joseph E. Walker, a son
of Elkanah Walker and a missionary in China for twenty-five years,
complained, "We have been accustomed to regard the Chinaman as a
joke, but he is fast becoming a very serious joke."[235] He warned that
"A martial spirit is pervading the empire." At another chapel an authority on modern Greece discussed "The Greeks of Today." Other
speakers also tried to arouse student interest in national and international conditions.

In 1907, as in later years, students participated in more activities
on than off campus. Many, however, became involved in local
churches, applauded plays at the Keylor Grand Theater (the plays
ranged from the traditional *Uncle Tom's Cabin* to the contemporary
The College Widow), and enjoyed activities in the new YMCA building. The YMCA sponsored a famous and controversial orator, "Pitch-
fork" Ben Tillman.[236] This famous southerner responded to a de-

mand from his large audience for his popular lecture, "The Race Problem." The senator considered it was his duty to lecture northern audiences about the "niggers." Citing difficulties with Hindus and other Asians in Washington State, he compared them with long-standing black problems in southern states. In emotional tones he argued that whites would not be dominated by Negroes and bluntly asked, "How would you like to be governed by the Hindu, Jap, Chinese, or Indian, and how would you like to have the law proclaim the Hindu as good as yourselves?" Surely Tillman's racist address stimulated considerable campus talk long after his departure.

In November there was another chance to hear a politician and other orators. To observe the sixtieth anniversary of the Whitman massacre, students and faculty joined a long procession at the missionary site. The state's governor and other dignitaries from nearby states praised the Whitmans. The sensational Seattle preacher Mark A. Matthews gave the evening oration. Penrose's desire to honor the "martyr" and to keep the students mindful of the school's namesake had been accomplished.

But in the fall of 1907 talk about the football team's prospects dominated. The student football manager predicted both a winning team and a profitable season. Because it cost $1,800 to bring teams to Walla Walla, he stressed the need to sell tickets. The college's trainer, Donald Mitchell, urged men to turn out for the team. He encouraged them to become familiar with the game "so that those who expected to be high school teachers in the northwest would be able to act as football coaches and thus add to the prestige of Whitman."

By 1907 Whitman athletic teams were called Missionaries. Earlier squads had simply been called Whitmanites or even the "Sons of Marcus." At Whitman, as at so many other schools, football was the major extracurricular activity. On the campus and in the town many evaluated the team's prospects and its best players. Four members of the team received considerable publicity. Captain Ralph Dimick, an all-Northwest tackle, and George Philbrook, another talented tackle, were mainstays. A transfer from Carleton College, Walter Brubaker, brother of Whitman professor Howard Brubaker, "was a crack man" at quarterback. Vincent Borleske, considered to be one of the region's best halfbacks, was on his way to becoming a regional football legend. Much was made of the fact that the Missionaries were considered to be very large, averaging about 175 pounds per man.

Before the first game a terrible rumor swept through the dormitories and down Main Street. Captain Dimick had seriously injured himself in practice and might not play a single game. Everyone considered him irreplaceable. He was not missed in the first game, however, as his team rolled over the much smaller Walla Walla High School squad by a score of seventeen to zero. A second high school opponent, Spokane, was more experienced. Although Dimick remained on the sidelines, Whitman won easily, twenty-nine to zero. After these two successes over inferior opponents, some fans anticipated Whitman's winning the northwest championship. To keep fans abreast of the records of all regional teams, the football manager posted a "Football Dope Sheet" by Memorial Hall.

Whitman's third game was with the Multnomah Athletic Club. This was an unusual game because this Portland team was playing its first road game in four years and because Whitman's coach was entitled to play in this non-collegiate contest. During a team practice Penrose returned from the East and hurried to Ankeny Field. "As soon as he appeared, practice was suspended ... while the entire squad joined in giving three rousing 'rahs' for their ... president."[237] Dimick returned to the team and played a major role as the Missionaries "played like demons" and won fourteen to five. This victory brought the team considerable publicity, especially in Portland newspapers. The *Oregonian*, for example, applauded the Whitman team: "The line is heavy, the backs are fast, and every advantage is taken of the new rules."[238] Whitman lived up to its reputation by smashing Whitworth College, which was playing its first intercollegiate game. The powerful Missionaries gained 616 yards to Whitworth's 112.

After four straight victories, the campus and the town hailed the Whitman eleven, especially Vincent Borleske and Bill Martin. Their next opponent was the University of Washington; fans across the Pacific Northwest awaited the outcome of this meaningful regional contest. Washington had been tied by Seattle High School but had then won four straight victories. In its sixth game, however, the university had been outscored by a squad from the battleship *Nebraska*.

Whitman had only defeated the Seattle team once since 1894. At a well-attended chapel rally everyone predicted victory in what was called "Whitman's first big championship game."[239] At the noisy gathering businesspeople promised that nearly every store would close for the Friday afternoon contest so that employees might attend. As enthused about the game as students, teachers had altered the class schedule to provide more daylight for team practices. Professor Gena Branscombe, who was called a brilliant American composer, prepared a song for the rally, including the stanza:

> At Whitman
> At Whitman
> There's where we all acquire knowledge
> Major in English or major in Greek,
> We have more courses than days in the week.

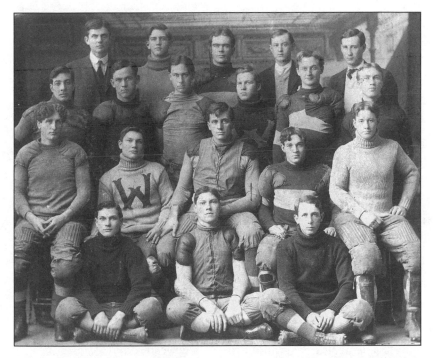

The 1907 football squad had a successful season under Coach J. Arthur Baird (top row, left), a practicing attorney. The team beat the University of Washington by a score of twelve to eight. In the second row are two famous players who went on to coach Whitman teams: halfback Raymond Vincent "Nig" Borleske (second from left) and Charles William "Bill" Martin (fourth from left), an academy student. He later transferred to Notre Dame, where his times as a sprinter led him to be called "the world's fastest human."

Professor Hendrick told the cheering crowd that the eleven deserved support: "We have a purely college team, many of whom are here at considerable sacrifice."

Businessmen later trooped to Billings Hall to meet the players, promising them total support. Enthusiasm for Missionary football had prompted Walla Wallans who had graduated from other colleges to practice Whitman and other school yells that would be delivered during the contest. With a crowd estimated to be well over 2,000— the largest ever to attend a game on Ankeny Field—the local team, "playing like fiends," outscored the University of Washington twelve to eight.[240] Local fans cheered the winner and grumbled that the sore losers refused to return a cheer rendered by the elated victors.

This great triumph prompted students and fans to engage a special train for the University of Idaho game. Meanwhile those with football fever read that Whitman and the Oregon Agricultural College seemed the region's best teams and that they might clash in a championship game. This possibility made the remaining Missionary games with Idaho and Washington State even more important. The varsity went to Idaho a day before the game; the special train, decorated in Whitman's maize and blue colors and with streaming banners, carried the team's substitutes and about 200 enthusiastic fans. Idaho outplayed Whitman and won eleven to zero. But the downcast Whitman rooters were praised as being good sports when they wound their way through the Moscow streets chanting they would win next year's contest. Adversity dogged the travelers on their return: their locomotive broke down. At 4:00 AM the weary rooters finally arrived on campus to be greeted by Reynolds Hall women who had decorated the parlor, burned a fireplace fire, and served refreshments. Many explained that this was the true Whitman spirit. One participant stated, "As long as Whitman exhibits such a spirit in defeat, she need have no fear of her standing"; but, he observed, "There was a general sleepy air about the college yesterday."[241]

During the football season students read that President Penrose sought to form a new and more equitable intercollegiate athletic league. It must have been hard to sustain interest in his effort, for the college always seemed to be involved in negotiations with Oregon and Washington schools in an attempt to improve intercollegiate football. By contrast, a headline in the Walla Walla *Bulletin* sparked considerable interest: "College Players Doped for Games," was a shocking story about a Washington State player who "was doped with strychnine or cocaine" so that he could play. Even more relevant to local readers was the admission by a Whitworth trainer that prior to the Whitman game he had administered cocaine to an injured quarterback.[242]

In the season's final game, played in Walla Walla on Thanksgiving Day, the Washington State team defeated the Missionaries sixteen to eight. What had started out as a memorable season with boasts about a regional championship ended in frustration. The Walla Walla business community, however, expressed pleasure with the enthusiastic crowds on the streets and with the publicity for the town. They praised the student manager for being the first to make a profit from Missionary football. Local businesspeople offered to "secure a first-class coach" from Yale (its use of the forward pass had made a big impact on the Pacific Northwest football writers and rooters) or from some other eastern institution. They would pay the new coach $1,000 for the football season or $1,500 if he would also manage the college baseball team. Students had already indicated to townspeople that they did not believe that they could even raise $400 for a coach's salary. Baird had received only $600 for the 1907 season, and he must have been unhappy with plans for replacing him with an expensive Ivy Leaguer.

A local newspaperman supported the town's offer to the student body: "By its consistent and enthusiastic support of athletics at Whitman College, Walla Walla has gained a wide reputation as being one of the best college towns in the country." It is possible that the remarkable 1907 football season inspired some college friends to pledge support at a December meeting when the college leaders introduced an educational plan that would expand Whitman far beyond what it had been.

7

Greater Whitman:
The Grand Proposal for Regional Service
1907 – 1912

Just before noon on December 14, 1907, about forty well-dressed men assembled in the home of John Langdon, a Whitman trustee and real-estate executive. Identified as "the best people of the town," the diners had been invited to a memorable college gathering.[1]

A local newspaper on the previous day carried the bold headline "To make Whitman the Yale of the Northwest," but it only furnished general information about the luncheon meeting's agenda. A few guests also had only a vague understanding of what would be discussed. Archer Hendrick, who had recently been appointed dean, had written to them that "we are undertaking a plan for enlarging the funds and the education field of Whitman College. The plan contemplates something very much larger than has ever been undertaken, and in the carrying of it out we have the advice and experience of all the friends of the institution."[2] Trustees, however, came to the Langdon home (now the Beta Theta Pi house) well-informed, for at a morning meeting the dean and the president emphasized the major points to be raised at the luncheon. The trustees brought notes about the college's condition, and the dean carried a bold proposal that would dramatically improve it. To help him sell the plan, the dean brought along Seattle financier James A. Moore, whose prestige in the state's business community and whose commitment to the dean's proposal made him invaluable.

Hendrick was the prime mover of the Greater Whitman scheme. The precise date of his original proposal is unknown, but in 1906 he

284

conversed with Stephen Penrose about it when the president recommended the addition of an engineering program. With the instincts of a promoter, Hendrick refined his ideas. In June 1907 he enthusiastically presented plans for Greater Whitman to trustees. Although the board minutes are extremely sketchy, the members obviously caught Hendrick's spirit, endorsed the concept of Greater Whitman, and urged him to take charge of a financial campaign to realize it.

That summer the dean made a pilgrimage to Chicago to explain his ambitious plans to the school's benefactor, Dr. D.K. Pearsons. The old man was initially dubious, for he had heard dozens of impractical educational schemes. Penrose soon visited, however, and changed the philanthropist's mind. Meanwhile, Hendrick and then Penrose talked to mine operators in Wallace, Idaho; business owners in Spokane, Portland, Seattle, and Tacoma; and ministers in Yakima, Ritzville, and elsewhere. Repeatedly those who heard the plan promised to support it. In between scattered railroad trips, Hendrick and sometimes Penrose pushed Greater Whitman to selected Walla Wallans. In summary, the dean could boast that he had won "the very best representative citizens" to his cause.[3]

Hendrick had begged some friends to attend the Walla Walla luncheon, assured that their presence would help him carry his sweeping proposal. The meeting had been delayed because of the 1907 economic downturn—men warned him against talking money at such a time—and because of conflicts in personal schedules.

The diners were trustees (including Edwin Eells, replacing his brother Myron, who had died in January 1907), advisory trustees, businessmen, lawyers, and ministers from Walla Walla and the region. Apparently there was no official record of the meeting, but the correspondence of Hendrick and Penrose and local newspaper stories provide the basic details. The agenda included a thorough assessment of the institution's past, present, and future. Hendrick and trustees, especially Edwin Eells, hailed Penrose for taking a sickly institution in 1894 and transforming it into one of regional acclaim. The dean boasted that the school "enjoys a well-established reputation for high scholarship as well as giving a college life and atmosphere of high Christian ideals and healthy humanity."[4] As evidence of success, the school's friends pointed to its endowment, masonry buildings, impressive academic standards, Christian emphasis, spirited and com-

Archer W. Hendrick came to Whitman in 1902 as a teacher and principal at the academy, and in 1907 rose to the position of dean at the college. Intelligent, energetic, and controversial, he left his mark on the institution, especially as the driving force behind the ambitious proposal for Greater Whitman.

mitted students, dedicated professors, devoted alumni, and numerous friends in Oregon, Washington, and Idaho. At some point speakers stressed the harmony between the campus and town; in part this was owing to the successful football season. Hendrick maintained that the whole community supported the team's victory over the University of Washington and recalled that "the rooting of the town's businessmen was the feature of the game."[5]

Penrose spoke on the subject, "What We Hope to Make of Whitman College," emphasizing that there were several options. Whitman could remain small and hope to reach "an enrollment of 400 like Williams" or it could try to match Yale's 1,400. It might follow Oberlin's example and have a large conservatory of music, or it could have a school of technology like MIT. The president assured his audience that an expanded, practical curriculum would not mean a break "from the legitimate work of a college as distinguished from a university."[6]

Hendrick considered it necessary to reiterate the importance of private education. He anticipated that some would wonder why Whitman would offer programs that competed with the state universities. The dean put forward his position:

I think the history of educated men of the day proves the fact that the college days must be carefully guarded upon the character side, and that an institution which fails in this particular has not any claims upon the wealth of the private individual. If there be anything which is distinctive in the aims and work of Whitman College, it is the fact that they are endeavoring to give their students higher notions and ideals of life, and are paying more attention to the environment and character than are other institutions of the west. This is possible with us because of being a small college wherein the students can come in contact with Christian men who have devoted themselves, in many instances with meager pay, to the carrying forth of the work for which Whitman College stands. It is because of our belief that Whitman College can perform this function and give a better education than is possible in the state institutions of the Pacific Northwest; therefore we make claim for the aid of men of wealth in our territory.[7]

A trustee then related the dismal financial side of the young college. Anticipating that each businessman present understood the crippling effect of long-standing debt, he provided a detailed summary of the one hampering Whitman. For the past ten years the school had struggled with its deficit. Drastic measures—the denial of a faculty pay raise and an inadequate maintenance budget—failed to halt the growing debt, which was about $90,000 in 1907. During the past five years the small endowment had been only minimally increased despite the fact that Penrose and others had urged wealthy persons to enlarge it. The guests were bluntly told that if the endowment could not be significantly increased and if the deficit continued to mount then Whitman would eventually have to suspend its splendid contributions to regional education. It is very possible that some speakers likened Whitman's financial difficulties to those that had defeated many private academies.

Hendrick also emphasized that the enrollment, despite great recruiting efforts, was still too small. He and Penrose must have explained that the elective program, business courses, and domestic science offerings had been enacted, in part, to attract more young people. But even if students came in large numbers from far away,

Whitman lacked the ability to employ more teachers, to build more dormitories, or to add equipment. Student tuition could not cover the school's operating costs; furthermore, the academy was a financial drain. In summary, the educators painted a bleak financial picture for their guests.

All the diners knew, however, that Penrose, Hendrick, trustees, and friends had long contemplated solutions to these old problems. Hendrick told them that expansion was the answer. The dean argued that Whitman must enlarge its curriculum, increase its endowment, construct new buildings, and add equipment and faculty members. There was an historical argument for his proposal. In 1882 George Atkinson, in selling the idea of adding a college, had predicted the seminary's failure because it lacked students and money. By expanding its educational mission at that time, Whitman had weathered the storm. In 1907 enlarging a promising liberal arts college to offer specialized technical training could very well solve current problems. In other words, another ambitious goal, like that of 1882, could again save the institution.

Hendrick now took up a major curricular change that would attract both money and students and make the college more important to the region. The speaker asserted that what "is needed most in this Northwest country is a healthy liberal arts education associated with courses in engineering."[8] Penrose had been attempting to introduce engineering. The dean now also urged such instruction because it would meet regional needs for electric power, irrigation, reforestation, and sanitation.[9] Like other boosters, Hendrick provided figures showing the population growth and predicted that the Pacific Northwest would become one of the nation's most heavily populated regions. In brief, a greater region needed a greater college.

Hendrick predicted that his proposal could lead the school to become the Yale of the West. At other times he used MIT and Cornell for his comparisons, stating that all reputable engineering schools had a $1,000,000 endowment. He did not advocate that Whitman should follow only one example, and stressed the fact that it must develop excellent programs and build a regional reputation comparable to these fine eastern institutions. Hendrick assumed that an expanded Whitman would actually revitalize other regional private schools. He was sure none would threaten Whitman's prominence because of their sectarianism, inadequate resources, and lack of a central location to serve three deserving states.

A discussion of higher education in the Pacific Northwest led to the dean's evaluation of its culture. He judged that it is currently "distinguished for its lack of some of the things which mature civilizations possess. We have no beautiful art or art galleries; or institutions of original research in the professions. We seem satisfied to engraft the help ... of our distinguished brethren whom we import from the East."[10] The dean proposed to remedy this shortage of culture by enhancing Whitman's music conservatory, and by planning a school of art. The cultural side of Greater Whitman, however, was much less important than the scientific one. Hendrick's voluminous correspondence stressed the advancement of technical, rather than artistic, education.

After portraying what Whitman could become, the planner explained the necessary financial steps to realize it. The debt must be eliminated. Joining with Penrose, Hendrick reminded diners that potential donors in the East and West were more likely to be generous if the college paid its deficit. He wanted Walla Walla money to cover the debt: to raise $200,000 in Walla Walla County, the dean and his listeners appointed a committee to solicit funds that would cover the debt, pay for the campaign's cost, and add to the endowment. Hendrick won acceptance for a proposal to raise $1,200,000 for the endowment and another $600,000 for two science buildings, three dormitories, a library, a chapel, a conservatory of music, a separate building for Pearsons Academy, and a central heating plant.

To realize its ambitious goal of $2,000,000, a Pacific Northwest campaign was carefully planned. Leaders appointed one committee of Walla Wallans to find local money and another of twenty-five men from the region to seek funds in the Pacific Northwest, especially in Spokane and Seattle. After these fund raisers accumulated significant donations, there would be an eastern appeal. Donors everywhere would be told the reasons for Greater Whitman that had been presented at the luncheon. However, there would be differences between regional appeals. Westerners would be informed that their sons should receive good positions in the development of regional resources; they would be reminded that better-educated easterners currently got rewarding western positions because deserving local young men lacked the proper training. Whitman hoped to prepare regional sons for rewarding careers.

There was another and more delicate point to be raised in the region. In Oregon, Washington, and Idaho, businesspeople must be reminded that they had too long been involved in the "spirit of commercialism" and should now take up the needs of an emerging civilization, especially private education.[11] Westerners needed to be told that a comprehensive Whitman College would mean that children no longer would have to travel great distances for a superior education. In selling Greater Whitman there should be appeals to regional pride; the Pacific Northwest was the only area of the country without a distinguished private college. That problem could now be resolved.

The appeal for eastern money would follow a different approach. Penrose predicted that Pearsons would probably open his purse again, and he would help open others. Penrose told the assembly about his appeals to foundations established by Andrew Carnegie and John D. Rockefeller and that after meeting with a General Education Board administrator he was optimistic. Penrose, however, explained that he had recently written to the foundation, asking them to delay an investigation of the college until after it launched the campaign. He told the administrator that Whitman would soon make a different type of request.[12]

Hendrick proposed a way to raise eastern money that westerners applauded. He began by stressing that "the Rockefellers, Guggenheims, Harrimans and Hills, the Weyerhaeusers and Goulds, are together with a multitude of other Eastern millionaires interested in the Northwest, namely the railroads, the electrical traction lines, the forest and lumber, and minerals." These wealthy people should be emphatically reminded that they were making money from the resources of Oregon, Washington, and Idaho, but that they were not donating to emerging western institutions. The dean then put his appeal in different words. He explained that the Chinese came to America, made money, and returned home; this was a pattern resented by residents of the Pacific Northwest. The educator then argued that eastern "moneyed capitalists" made money in the West, and, similarly, did not spend it here. Hendrick maintained that the Northwest had contributed to the "intellectual growth of the great eastern part of this country and should receive back from them a tithe of that wealth in order" that western children would receive "as notable and distinctive an education as can be had in any district of the world."[13]

After explaining how the school would seek money on both coasts, Hendrick reminded listeners that gifts to Whitman would add to Walla Walla's reputation and wealth. The town would be looked upon as a regional educational center, and an enlarged school would stimulate the local economy. This was a familiar argument, and so was another one voiced by the promoter. Hendrick insisted that townspeople were more likely to support a major educational enterprise than a small college. They had done so starting in 1882 when Whitman's trustees added a college program in addition to the one offered by the seminary. The dean operated on the obvious premise that Americans appreciated size, so he and others pushing the new educational scheme announced that the school planned an enrollment of one thousand students in 1910. Such a figure would make the city a leading educational center.

The meeting concluded with the participants promising to support Greater Whitman as they congratulated Hendrick for his candor and boldness. The dean's enthusiasm proved infectious far beyond Isaacs Avenue. Walla Walla newspapers cheered the proposal; the *Union*, for example, reminded readers that the college was a "most valuable moral and educational" asset and that it would become even more important economically. "The larger it becomes the greater will be its influence for good and the greater will be its importance as a business institution adding to the trade of our merchants and to the value of . . . real estate." The editor concluded that "Nothing is too good for Whitman College, and it is certain that the city will be behind any movement to make the college bigger and better." The rival *Statesman* also acknowledged the college's significant economic impact and predicted that its plans would contribute to "the city's honor and glory." The editor insisted that "With the immense wealth in this section . . . it would be folly to say we cannot afford it."[14]

Stephen Penrose shared this enthusiasm. The educator said that the various speeches of that day clearly revealed the college's status; Walla Wallans had now gained a solid understanding of the institution. The president boasted, "We feel that for the first time the town is solidly back of the college, and that the businessmen are determined to help its development in every way."[15] He ecstatically predicted that "There is no reason why Whitman College should not rapidly grow and become indeed and in truth the Yale of the Northwest." At some point Whitman would approach Yale in both endowment and equipment.

Penrose also thought it necessary to explain what he called a "new departure." He stated: "Our intention is to make it a representative institution for the three northwestern states, planning to develop it into a true Yale, non-sectarian, but thoroughly Christian, and yet aiming only at doing college work of the highest grade." He explained that the school would gradually adopt technical subjects. A respectable engineering school would be developed by offering basic courses and by adding various types of engineering. Penrose presumed that within two years there should be a change in the school's appearance. "We are not aiming," he assured friends, "at an unreachable ideal, but merely the enlarging of the present college on the lines of greater efficiency without a lowering of standards."[16]

The president put the change into context. The plans for expansion should not have "excited surprise because the college has always intended to develop on some such lines." Penrose concluded, "The difference between us and some institutions is that we have preferred to make our reputation for doing thorough work of the highest grade before beginning to enlarge."[17]

His enthusiasm temporarily waned when he read a letter from Hendrick, written only two days after the luncheon. The dean, who was out of town promoting his proposal, asked to be allowed to resign as leader of Greater Whitman and to return to his teaching duties. Hendrick provided a number of reasons for this startling request: the work required too much nervous energy; he doubted his ability to succeed; he wanted to spend his time studying the law; his personal expenses connected with the campaign would use up his small savings; and somebody else could better "bear the expense and solve the problems." The dean summarized: "the intellect of man refuses to work when his heart strings are pulled because of neglect of home and loved ones."[18] Penrose, who had once told Hendrick that he was vital to the campaign, replied that "I never did think much of the play *Hamlet* with the Dane left out," immediately met with the executive trustee committee.[19] Concluding that only Hendrick could realize the ambitious proposal, the board increased his salary and provided an adequate expense account. It is very possible that some trustees, as Penrose believed, also confided to Hendrick that they preferred Hendrick as college president. Satisfied with the new financial arrangements and with words of encouragement, the energetic dean now entered into an exhaustive battle for Greater Whitman. The community and the campus awaited the verdict.

Early Ramifications

In promoting Greater Whitman, Penrose, Hendrick, and allies moved in carefully planned stages. Between the mid-December meeting and the 1908 commencement, school leaders followed several paths, including the general promotion of Greater Whitman through publications, personal visitations, and group meetings; the solicitation of pledges for $200,000 in Walla Walla; and the assembling of information from various schools about the role of private education.

Benefactor Pearsons had to be kept informed of the proposal. Penrose stressed to him the fact that Whitman would no longer serve a local area but would become "the representative college of the whole northwest." The president reassured his ally that businesspeople hailed Hendrick's proposal and that regional educators congratulated Whitman for electing to remain a college and not to become a university. "We wish to do only first class work on the lines which are open to us," he explained, "and we do not mean to hang out more clothes on the line than we can wash."[20]

While the president acquainted the benefactor with the plan, the dean privately wrote that the school "intended to adopt the three great principles which will make it ultimately the greatest institution west of the Rockies, namely non-sectarian, Christian, and adapting its education to the needs and requirements for the development of the region's resources."[21] Hendrick also informed the public of the new direction through a pamphlet entitled "The New Whitman College and the Old." This brief, widely circulated publication summarized the points that the dean had made in various meetings, including a brief college history, the origins of "The New Whitman," and a survey of its educational programs. He asserted that the institution, which "stands for the highest in scholarship and in character," was located at the geographical center of the Pacific Northwest. Within a

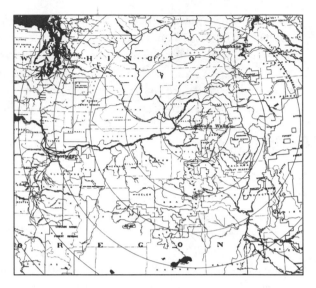

This map, which was designed for the Greater Whitman campaign of 1909, was meant to demonstrate that Walla Walla was the heart of the Pacific Northwest and thus the logical place for the region's major private college.

radius of 250 miles of Walla Walla some 1.5 million people currently resided in a rich area "blest with extraordinary natural resources" that would eventually support a population up to 50 million. The school sought to be of even greater service to this promising region: "What Harvard and Yale are to New England, Whitman hopes to be to the Northwest." To meet regional needs the school would establish a school of technology that would train engineers. Then a school of forestry and irrigation would train experts who would either conserve timber or reclaim land. A school of commerce and banking would help resolve regional economic and financial problems, and a school of art would help enrich Pacific Northwest civilization through instruction in painting, sculpture, and architecture. Whitman Conservatory would become a full-fledged school of music. Whitman would only offer bachelor's degrees and would emphasize quality, not quantity. The pamphlet concluded with a plea for money to cover the cost of buildings and to provide an endowment to meet the expense of maintaining the science departments, the library fund, and an endowment fund that would pay the salaries of twenty additional professors.

In visits to Spokane, Seattle, Tacoma, Portland, Yakima, and Boise, Hendrick huddled with small groups of prominent men and solicited support for Greater Whitman. The dean selected his listeners on the basis of their contribution to the development of the Pacific Northwest; he reasoned that the men who had developed the region economically should be willing to develop it educationally.[22] Hendrick assured them that he sought help only from reputable businesspeople: "I would like to steer clear of any person whose reputation or whose business methods are any way questionable" because the growing institution must be based upon "the finest principles of justice, truth, and character."[23] He boasted that everywhere prominent persons agreed to support his proposal; for example, the dean assured Portland banker William M. Ladd that he had won support from "almost every estimable citizen in the three states whose name is known for integrity and good character."[24] According to the ambitious educator, prominent persons supported his scheme because they agreed that the region needed an impressive private college, one that would rival public institutions and that would increase regional pride. Hendrick not only sought endorsements, he also asked some leaders if they would be willing to serve on a proposed board of overseers. Many agreed to serve.

While the dean acquired backers throughout the three states, he joined his local committee in seeking $200,000 in Walla Walla pledges. Spurred on by Hendrick these local workers called upon fellow townspeople and farmers; meanwhile, the dean held local meetings in which he and committee members explained the proposal and the need for local money. In the spring Hendrick reported that the campaign was "prospering beautifully" and that the goal would soon be attained.[25] But, like so many earlier Whitman campaigns for buildings, this one also faltered. Hendrick grew impatient with delays. In the summer he angrily told a supporter, farm equipment manufacturer Ben C. Holt, that there was no excuse for it. The fund raiser charged that if a new manufacturing enterprise were offered the city, then $200,000 would easily be contributed. The college, however, had no such success, Hendrick grumbled, despite the fact that it was better than a manufacturing plant because it would not bring "an army of wage earners of the varying nationalities."[26] Holt reminded the impatient dean that farmers were busy in the summer and that they would contribute after harvest. Hendrick listed his complaints to another friend: his gift was less than expected; other college leaders had placed all fund-raising responsibilities on him; and if the

campaign collapsed it would ruin the college. The administrator
threatened to resign and blame Walla Wallans for the embarrassing
failure. Apparently Hendrick's fulminations succeeded; in early August he wrote that not only had the city pledged more than $200,000,
but the "subscriptions came very easily."[27]

Promoting his scheme in the region and collecting local pledges
consumed the dean's energy, but he took time to write letters about
two relevant subjects to colleges offering engineering programs. First,
he sought information about launching a program, especially the
costs of a building and classroom equipment; second, he wanted estimates about the minimum endowment that would cover the costs of
an engineering curriculum. Hendrick received plenty of advice and a
variety of estimates; for example, a University of California mining
professor reported—as the dean suspected—that donors preferred
to give to buildings and equipment rather than to the endowment.

Hendrick also requested letters from institutions about the advantages of private schools and of small towns as college sites. Some
distinguished college presidents, including Charles Eliot of Harvard
and Woodrow Wilson of Princeton, provided only sketchy replies,
but others, including David Starr Jordan of Stanford and William
DeWitt Hyde of Bowdoin were informative. Acknowledging that in
the Pacific Northwest public colleges and universities enjoyed considerable favor, Hendrick desired information that would help him win
similar support for private education. His correspondent from Grinnell complained that public universities seeking large enrollments
lowered their academic standards. Carleton's dean informed Hendrick that private schools sought to improve character. Many re-
spondents praised both private and public institutions; President
Thomas Kane of the University of Washington preferred public
schools, and President Prince Lucien Campbell of the University of
Oregon liked "friendly rivalry."[28]

Hendrick asked many educators if small towns, such as Walla
Walla, were the best sites for schools of higher education. Respond-
ents located in such places, of course, answered positively; for example, Carleton's dean affirmed that a small city "is not full of distraction but is conducive to study and good social life" but warned that
places with a population less than 10,000 gave a local school very few
students and little money. The universities of Idaho and Washington

both judged that colleges should be located in small towns and universities in cities.

The summaries of this investigation appeared in some of Hendrick's correspondence, and undoubtedly he used it in selling Greater Whitman. The Whitman faculty supported the dean's defense of private schooling and of the advantage of small towns as college sites.

While the dean gained information from letters, Whitman students received news about Greater Whitman from the *Pioneer*. They must have agreed with Hendrick's explanation that the school's enrollment was low because its standards were high. The dean maintained that Whitman could enlarge its student body through a broader scholarship program and could help attract immigrants into the Pacific Northwest through the dissemination of maps and pamphlets. In a chapel address in late May, Penrose explained Greater Whitman. Responding to a campus rumor about the eventual size of the student body, Penrose promised that the school would never enroll 2,000. He restated the traditional argument—quality was more important than quantity—and that those of upright character were "worth more than three times that number of students of mediocre ability." The leader urged the student body to study the proposed plans for the campus and to become "apostles of Greater Whitman." A *Pioneer* writer enthusiastically agreed, urging each reader to bring another student back in the fall so that "he also may enjoy the glorious privileges and advantages offered by our Alma Mater."[29]

The ramifications of Greater Whitman were obvious during the June 1908 trustee meeting. Prior to its December 1907 meeting, the college had sought to be released from the Congregational Education Society's requirement that the majority of Whitman's board of trustees be "members of evangelical Congregational churches." In the spring Penrose reported to trustees that the school was now—like Williams, Oberlin, and Beloit—free from denominational ties and was "entitled to rank with the undenominational but thoroughly Christian colleges" of the nation.[30] One reason for the break was that the college, in seeking greater regional support, wanted to be known as nonsectarian, not as Congregational. There was another reason for independence: in 1906 the Carnegie Foundation for the Advancement of Teaching listed colleges and universities that would receive benefits, especially "retirement allowances." Penrose immediately sought to participate so that Professor Helen Pepoon, who was feeble and supporting an invalid sister, might receive retirement payments. The foundation rejected the initial request because of Whitman's tie with the CES. Although Penrose would successfully cut ties with the Congregationalists, the Carnegie Foundation continually denied his financial proposals.

In summary, an appeal for broader regional support, the entice- ment of the Carnegie retirement program, and the possibility of im- pressive financial assistance from that foundation led to a break with Congregationalism. Historian Frederick Rudolph wrote that Carne- gie's offers led such schools as Bowdoin, Coe, Hanover, and Occiden- tal to cut their denominational ties; Whitman simply fell into line. Whitman explained the break in the 1909 catalog. Some people, how- ever, still considered the school to be Congregational; Penrose ac- knowledged that it had been founded and nurtured by this denomina- tion.[31] Probably the trustee decision to break the church connection angered some supporters, and Whitworth College, a Presbyterian institution in Tacoma, chided Whitman for its decision and now called itself the leading denominational college.

In 1908 reports to trustees, Penrose and Hendrick stressed Great- er Whitman. The president wrote that the dean's "wise and vigorous- ly executed plans" had resulted in a major change—prominent men in the three Pacific Northwest states now endorsed the college and worked to help it become "the one great, central, endowed, Christian institution."[32] Again Penrose reported an annual deficit, blaming it on an inadequate endowment, but predicted that Hendrick's plan would lead to a "speedy increase of the endowment," whose first earnings should go to experienced faculty. Hoping that the five most senior faculty members might receive $1,600 per annum, the presi- dent asserted that "the increasing cost of living makes it difficult, if not impossible, for a man to support a wife and family on the present meager salaries."

Hendrick's report centered on the new college constitution, which had been introduced in the spring and declared that Whitman was a nonsectarian but Christian school. The dean advocated the creation of a board of overseers. Hendrick acknowledged that the new constitution required that the college president and the majority of the board of trustees must be members of Christian churches, but he preferred that no such requirement should be applied to overseers. He knew that many of them had not affiliated with a church, but he assured trustees that potential overseers possessed "personal character and reputation" and had contributed to the region's "financial and progressive side."

The trustees, influenced in part by Hendrick's forceful opinions, completed the constitution and ratified it at a November meeting. It was a significant document, especially for creating a unique two-board system. In his college history Penrose explained that the trustees accepted the second board because the powerless advisory board had failed and because Harvard president Charles Eliot's writings on a two-board system seemed convincing. Serving four-year terms, the nine-member board of trustees would manage the institution and its properties. The sixty-four members of the board of overseers, serving five-year terms, were given "the power to establish departments of study, to provide means for the maintenance therefor, to direct the financial and educational policy of the institution, and to take such measures as they shall deem necessary for the development of the institution along the lines of its history, traditions, and specific purpose." Both boards elected officers, including an influential seven-member overseer executive committee. The college president's powers remained about the same, but he would assign duties to a dean after consultation. The overseers selected a school treasurer, whose wide authority included the collection of tuition and fees. The treasurer would also serve on a finance committee, which must not dip into the endowment for operating costs and must unanimously approve college investments. All board members, faculty, and administrators must sign a declaration that they would fulfill assigned duties and would support "faithfully the constitution, by-laws, and regulations of Whitman College, in accordance with the Christian principles and spirit of its foundation." A concluding portion stated that trustees could adopt bylaws and amendments by a two-thirds vote.

Trustees chose more than forty men that Hendrick had asked to serve as overseers. These noted men came from all three states and included John C. Ainsworth, Portland banker; G. Scott Anderson, Wallace mine operator; James E. Babb, Lewiston lawyer; Thomas Burke, Seattle lawyer; William Cotton, Portland lawyer; Wayne Darlington, Boise mining officer; Oscar A. Fechter, Yakima banker;

Bishop James B. Funstein, Boise; Governor Frank R. Gooding, Boise; Judge Cornelius H. Hanford, Seattle; Bishop Frederick Keator, Olympia; William M. Ladd, Portland banker; the Reverend Mark A. Matthews, Seattle; Robert McCormick, Tacoma lumberman; James A. Moore, Seattle financier; Miles C. Moore, Walla Walla banker; George S. Long, Tacoma lumberman; Samuel G. Reed, Portland banker; the Reverend William W. Scudder, Seattle; George Turner, Spokane lawyer; and Theodore B. Wilcox, Portland businessman.

The trustees thanked Hendrick for compiling such a distinguished list—no other school in the region had a comparable group—and for his "zeal and efficiency in planning and carrying forward this great movement for the higher development of Whitman College." They also praised Walla Wallans for raising a special fund of $2,500 a year for two years to underwrite the costs of the $2,000,000 campaign.

Supporters acknowledged that the college had raised its sights. Prior to 1908 it had concentrated its efforts east of the Cascades. Now Whitman's new constitution gave the greatest power to overseers who came from just those urban centers the college planned to serve. The June trustee meeting was extremely significant; Hendrick's remaining task was to find the money to attain the ambitious goals.

As if to demonstrate the school's new vitality, the trustees now held monthly meetings. In August 1908 they approved a major proposal. Complaining that he had too much work, Hendrick requested Penrose to leave the presidency for a year and join him in raising funds. The canvasser knew that most potential donors would want to converse with the president, not a dean. Penrose approved of his ally's request provided that competent replacements assumed his responsibilities as president and professor. Professor Louis Anderson agreed to be acting president but only on conditions—the position of vice president must be created and he must be appointed to the office. He also demanded a $2,000 salary, which he donated to the campaign. Anderson might very well have wanted to be vice president so as to rank above Hendrick, who suspected Anderson wanted such an office "because of the social prestige that goes with it."[33]

November 17 and 18, 1908, were memorable days in the era of Greater Whitman. The school hosted an unusual educational congress, convened the board of overseers for its first sessions, and welcomed benefactor D.K. Pearsons to the campus. For months Whitman leaders had been arranging an educational congress designed to provide distinguished eastern educators and resourceful western speakers with an opportunity to address invited guests and Walla Wallans. Stephen Penrose and Archer Hendrick wanted overseers to learn about higher education so that they could intelligently plan the college's future.

Organizing the educational congress consumed vast amounts of time and energy. The first task was to get Pearsons to agree to a Walla Walla visit. Then it was necessary to find speakers and an audience composed of board members, businesspeople, educators, ministers, editors, and townspeople. Arranging for special trains from the coast, housing in Walla Walla (many guests would be hosted in private homes), and a banquet catered by a Seattle firm were some of the major tasks handled by Penrose, Hendrick, and local committees.

In September Walla Wallans learned about the scheduled November meetings, which would feature prominent speakers and would attract as many as 1,000 out-of-town visitors. It would be an opportunity for the community to honor Pearsons, who would deliver a banquet address.

Penrose and Hendrick also wanted distinguished men to speak on private and technical education. To convince reluctant speakers to cross the continent, both men wrote appealing letters, and Penrose made personal calls in the East, including one to Princeton president Woodrow Wilson. In encouraging one person Hendrick wrote: "I feel sure that Yale University would like to share in the formative stages of the developing educational policy of this Pacific Northwest. Whitman College has for years been called by [its] citizens 'The Yale of the West,' and it seems to me it would be a rather fatal mistake if, when a movement as large as this has been started, Yale should fail to make its influence felt in the policy which will be carried out by our overseers at its organization meeting."[34]

Hard work resulted in success. Hendrick boasted that "We have some of the strongest speakers . . . for the exact work which we are trying to lay before the people."[35] University of Minnesota president Cyrus Northrup, whom Hendrick called the "most eloquent college president in America"; the Reverend Anson P. Stokes, secretary of the corporation of Yale University; and Alfred E. Burton, dean of the Massachusetts Institute of Technology, were solid choices. Both E.T.

Allen of the Forest Service and D.C. Henney of the Reclamation Service were Pacific Northwest authorities. In sum, the college offered an unusually attractive array of speakers.

Hendrick bluntly told them what he expected; for example, he explained to President Northrup that "We want to convince these wealthy people of the Northwest that the enterprise in which we are engaged is not in any sense one in opposition to the institutions of the state."[36] He informed Allen that he would like him to speak "upon the economic value to the Pacific Northwest of a first class school of forestry located in this region."[37]

Whitman received considerable encouragement for its curricular proposals and its educational congress. Chief Forester Gifford Pinchot, whom overseers wanted as a speaker, endorsed the idea of a professional school of forestry in a new engineering department. "It ought," he assured Penrose, "to have a field of surpassing usefulness throughout the West." He judged that the Pacific Northwest had the largest stands of timber in the world; therefore, there was a great need for foresters. Pinchot congratulated Whitman for making preparations to train them.[38] Northrup called the plans to expand Whitman "glorious" and thought that a private college would not harm regional universities. President Kane of the University of Washington wished success for Greater Whitman. President Campbell of the University of Oregon sent a similar message about the "great movement" and predicted that it would promote higher education in the region. President Lewis Benbow of the College of Puget Sound thought that Whitman's effort helped all private schools. Editor Albert Shaw of the *American Monthly* concluded that Penrose was "building wisely because he was trying to meet the actual needs" of a growing region.

The president and the dean not only sought outside speakers and supporters, they also labored to attract an audience of 1,000 men and women to the congress. All overseers received special invitations to attend and to participate in their board's initial meeting. Newspaper editors were sent programs and encouraged to cover the talks. Just days before the congress met, Penrose visited with regional overseers, editors, businesspeople, and ministers and urged them all to come to Walla Walla for a major educational meeting.

The Educational Congress

The educational congress was a landmark in Whitman's first half-century. Penrose and Hendrick hoped it would stimulate a regional interest in Greater Whitman, honor Pearsons and win his support for an enlarged college, and provide both the new board of overseers and the board of trustees with vital information about higher education. Between the public sessions of the educational congress, the overseers met privately, conducting business and listening to college leaders report information to be used in shaping educational policy.

The educational congress achieved what its organizers desired. Before its first session the eighty-eight-year-old D.K. Pearsons became the Penroses' house guest. The benefactor told reporters that he appreciated the fact that Walla Wallans had contributed $200,000 to Greater Whitman and predicted additional generosity. The local press acknowledged that the Chicagoan had given the school $160,000 and assumed that he would make another generous gift. Introduced as Whitman's greatest donor, Pearsons appeared at chapel to address Whitman students. He praised those students who worked their way through the college but thought that he had made a greater effort toward this end than any listener. He claimed to have "baked my own johnnycakes, cooked my own potatoes, fried my own meat."[39] The old man argued that anyone who had character could work his way through college unaided. He urged men to put less energy into athletics and more into gardening. You can get, Pearsons lectured, "better and more helpful exercise digging in the garden than playing ... football." At the conclusion of Pearsons' rambling remarks, Penrose provided biographical information about the visitor, emphasizing that he was both a shrewd businessman and an outstanding philanthropist.

While final arrangements were made, including the erection of a temporary chapel gallery, about four hundred guests began to arrive at the depots. Many had ridden in a special train from Puget Sound or in special cars from Portland and from Spokane. The congress began with a brief chapel service and a welcoming talk by Judge Thomas Burke of Seattle, who had just been elected temporary president of the board of overseers. Burke predicted that the congress would stimulate an increased interest in Whitman, which would become "the great private school in the Northwest."[40]

The president, using a stereopticon, showed pictures of the college's history. He stressed the heroism of Marcus Whitman, the self-denial of Cushing Eells, the generosity of D.K. Pearsons, the devotion of students and faculty, and the school's imposing academic standards. Penrose insisted that Whitman's high standards had received recognition in New England and were finally being appreciated in the Pacific Northwest. Because the trustees and overseers had just that morning enacted a new constitution that ended Whitman's ties with the Congregational church, Penrose explained the school's religious affiliation. He recalled that the Reverend Eells, in establishing a school, had wanted it to be nondenominational, but the struggling young college had to be assisted by a Congregational organization, the American College and Education Society. This had made it a denominational institution. Penrose also applauded the contemporary Whitman spirit exemplified by faculty and students. He defined it as "loyalty to high ideals, earnestness of purpose, simplicity of thought and life, and a democracy of the western kind which knows no distinction between rich and poor, strong or weak, but which emphasizes the common brotherhood of all."[41]

When Dean Hendrick spoke, he repeated themes he had employed in selling Greater Whitman: the college served a region that needed both to develop and to conserve its vast natural resources, and the region needed both private and public higher education. He also reviewed the college's new constitution.

In the afternoon, Dean Alfred E. Burton of MIT, who was introduced as an authority in engineering education, summarized the history of technical education, noting that many older schools were currently interested in adding such practical courses. Burton listed the problems of technical education, especially its high cost, which should be covered by the endowment, not by high tuition. Burton thought that Whitman, which served an enormous and promising region, could become as important to the Northwest as MIT was to the Northeast. The dean predicted that Whitman's proposed engineering classes would compete with those at public institutions, and that if Whitman maintained rigorous standards it would succeed. To the pleasure of many Whitman men, he predicted that graduates of a demanding engineering program would find many job opportunities.

In the evening session Judge Burke introduced Cyrus Northrup, who had for about twenty years been a professor at Yale and for about as many years had served as president of the University of Minnesota. Northrup spoke generally on higher education and specifically on Greater Whitman. He asserted that "The safety of the state depends upon education and religion" and stressed the role of colleges: "Higher education means better legislation and a higher type of citizenship."[42] Northrup recalled that denominational schools, including Yale and Harvard, had "thrown off denominational hindrance."[43] Thus he defended what Whitman's leaders had done that very day. Northrup conceded that smaller colleges had traditionally played an important role, but he observed that "the trend of the young is not towards the small college but towards the great universities and colleges." Therefore, he advised that a larger school be built upon the Whitman foundation. He insisted that when a single benefactor could not be found to build Whitman or some other small school, then many men should unite to bring about its growth. Northrup reminded his listeners that strong schools brought benefits to their communities and asserted his opinion that there was not "an enterprise" more noteworthy of time and money than Greater Whitman. To those who assumed that state colleges would oppose the creation of a larger Whitman and wondered if there was even a need for private education, Northrup, who had served both types of institutions, asserted that public schools had "no feeling of jealousy, envy, ... or hostility toward the Christian college" and that because there were so many students who needed schooling, there was a need for both private and public education.

Following Northrup's address, there was a progressive reception in three homes near the campus. An estimated 2,000 guests followed a special route: "Hundreds of small electric lights were strung on wires along the paths leading from one reception place to another."[44]

The following day's program included another eastern college administrator. Introduced as a wealthy person who had given his life "to the betterment of his fellowmen," the Reverend Anson Stokes, secretary of Yale University, emphasized three characteristics of a private school: high scholarship, broad culture, and Christian character. These desirable goals were more likely to be realized at Whitman than at a large school because "there is more contact between students and faculty" and because its faculty were "men of high ideals." Stokes provided considerable advice about the school's policy; for example, it should not become a university. To his way of thinking "a college is just as dignified ... as a university."[45] He exhorted leaders to maintain high standards and to emphasize character development. Stokes saw Whitman as properly sited "away from the corrupting life of the great commercial centers." The speaker called attention to the school's noble history: "I know of no institution which has such an inheritance as has been handed down to you by Whitman, Eells, and the other consecrated men who have made Whitman what she is." Penrose and Hendrick must have beamed during this and the previous two addresses. Each visitor had advanced ideas that they had often stressed.

Two speakers discussed technical education. E.T. Allen, a regional Forest Service official, accused the nation of wasting its wood and water. Graduates of forestry schools, he explained, could help find ways to conserve these vital resources. Allen named the nation's six existing forestry schools, including the University of Washington, and opposed the proliferation of such programs. However, he thought that Whitman might cope with the stiff competition provided by the University of Washington if it offered an outstanding program. Allen advised Whitman to offer course work in forestry even if it could not establish an extensive program.

D.C. Henney, a United States Reclamation Service engineer, summarized the history of western irrigation and recounted the enormous regional benefits resulting from irrigation projects. Henney judged that Whitman was well located to serve the arid districts by offering courses in irrigation engineering and agriculture. In summary, Henney and Allen both stated the problems of technical education and both favored Whitman's offering it, but only if the school offered superior courses.

Portland architect Ellis T. Lawrence then delivered an illustrated demonstration of what Greater Whitman would look like. Using stereopticon pictures, he showed the arrangement of about twenty additional buildings of handsome Georgian classical design. They would be made of red brick with contrasting finish and would be built in groups, such as engineering buildings or dormitories. To make room for these matched buildings, Billings Hall, Reynolds Hall, and the gymnasium must be destroyed. The architect admitted that the new buildings and their furnishings would be expensive—he once estimated that they would cost $3,000,000—but he predicted that they would make Walla Wallans proud and would bring national attention. Local newspapers published pictures of Lawrence's drawings, which won favorable comment.

The educational congress concluded with a seven-course banquet in the gymnasium. The highlight of the evening for the 500 diners was a paper read for D.K. Pearsons, who was too frail to deliver it. The honored guest recounted his own donations to colleges and emphasized how George Peabody, Cecil Rhodes, Andrew Carnegie, and John D. Rockefeller had aided education. Pearsons then recounted his relationship with Whitman College and Penrose and predicted that Greater Whitman would graduate excellent citizens. He exhorted the school to emphasize oratory, for men with strong voices would influence huge crowds. The benefactor favored the development of the "power of speech" rather than the legs of athletes. Pearsons concluded that the Pacific Northwest had a great future and hoped that Whitman would be a major part of it. The college would make its mark by stressing "sincerity, honesty, industry, common sense, . . . and patriotism."[46]

Pearsons won enthusiastic applause, for everyone acquainted with Whitman College's history understood that he was the major benefactor. His generosity had given Penrose an opportunity to realize his ambitious educational plans. Because Pearsons was frail, the audience knew that it would never again have an opportunity to thank him for donating Chicago money to Walla Walla's benefit.

A highlight of the educational congress was the drawing shown on the following pages, which was submitted by architect Ellis Lawrence. In this proposal, Whitman Memorial Hall would have faced a chapel, the two towers separated by Boyer Avenue. Some thought it appropriate that the dormitories for women would be separated by many blocks from those for men, and that the men's dormitories would be in the same quadrangle as the chapel. Many in the Whitman community have pondered what the college might have become had some or all of these grand structures been built.

Women's Dormitories   Refecto

Library and Auditorium and Museum   Biology and Forestry

Civil and Mechanical   Mining   Electrical   Physics   Chemis

Shops and Heating and Power Plant   Administration

ecitation   Men's Gymnasium

Chapel   Men's Dormitories

The Two-Board System

On the morning of November 17, forty-three overseers assembled for
their first meeting. The distinguished, carefully selected group first
elected Judge Thomas Burke as temporary chairman. Then members
signed the required declaration: "In signing this roll I accept the position written in against my name, to which I have been elected by the
constituted authorities of Whitman College. I hereby declare my intention of fulfilling the duties thereof, and of supporting faithfully the
Constitution, By-Laws, and Regulations of Whitman College, in accordance with the Christian principles and spirit of its foundation."[47]

Sandwiching their meetings around the educational congress, the
overseers learned in general about higher education, especially liberal
and practical curricula, and in particular about Whitman. Penrose
and Hendrick had carefully devised the agenda for the two-day gathering. They anticipated that the overseers would help them provide a
relevant curriculum, publicize the college across the region, and,
above all, assist in fund raising. The overseers understood that they
were to be an integral part of the college, an institution that aimed
to play a major cultural role in Oregon, Washington, and Idaho.
Penrose made the point to these men and to the community that "For
the first time in American history three states had united in the plan to
upbuild a great central private college which should be Christian, but
non-sectarian."[48]

The first item on the overseers' agenda was the school's financial
condition, which treasurer Allen Reynolds carefully explained. Apparently he stressed that in 1908 a deficit of $14,000 was accrued—
the largest one reported in the past ten years—and that the endowment had increased by only $3,000 in the past six years. Reynolds
explained that the college kept two sets of books—one for current
expenses and the other for the endowment. He also reported the fact
that the school owned 3,000 acres of profitable farmland. Apparently
overseers gave little time to discussing this important treasurer's report because the school's leaders had candidly discussed its contents
on other occasions.

The overseers divided the three Pacific Northwest states into sev-
en districts, including Portland, Idaho, Seattle, and Spokane, and

then assigned themselves to staggered terms for each. Other administrative business was rapidly concluded.

Then the faculty requested the overseers to shape policy. Professor Walter Bratton spoke to the board on "The Relations of the Sexes in Co-educational Colleges," a topic that he and fellow faculty members thought important to Whitman's future. Bratton acknowledged that both young women and men benefitted from coeducation, but the professor spoke to a problem that resulted when too many women came into such liberal arts departments as foreign languages, English, history, or biology. Discouraged by this influx of women, men then selected another major or even transferred, either to a school offering engineering or to an all-male school. But there was an even graver problem: "a large number" of college women took little interest in scholarship and put their time and effort into "social diversion." This distracted the young men and changed "the ambitions of the student body from intellectual attainment to social prestige and social desirability." Bratton offered two solutions: separate colleges or a limitation on the number of women. The Whitman faculty, he related, opposed the first remedy and endorsed the second. The mathematician explained that he had written to about fifty schools asking about their sex ratio and the way they limited women. State schools reported that they did not limit women, but the president of the University of California recommended that women should not exceed one-third of the student body. The president of Syracuse disagreed: "No limitation: the higher education of women is more important than that of men, for women control men." Carleton, Grinnell, Knox, Pomona, and several other private institutions responded that they worried about admitting too many women. An effective way to limit them was to insist that they live on campus or in approved housing. Although Bratton made it clear that his colleagues worried about increasing female enrollment, currently a bit more than half of the student body, the overseers expressed little concern.

Far more important to the board was the proposal to establish an engineering program. Professor Bratton again initiated the discussion and noted that the addition of engineering would be a significant curricular departure. He said, however, that Whitman wanted to offer it because it would meet "the need of this new country for trained technical experts"; furthermore, "ambitious young men" demanded this type of education. He reported that the faculty did not want the new engineering program to be separate from the traditional curriculum, whose "cultural impulse" had inspired students to "excellent living." The faculty recommended that a competent engineering professor be hired to help launch the program, which required a suitable building, adequate equipment, and an endowment. Bratton listed faculty questions about the type and number of engineering courses to be offered and the number of years required of students to complete the program.

To provide answers to his colleagues' concerns, Bratton had written to sixty institutions offering technical training. The responses indicated that civil engineering was easiest to incorporate into a liberal arts college; furthermore, civil, mechanical, and electrical engineering attracted the largest enrollments. The professor learned that schools generally required a four-year engineering program but that most preferred a required fifth year so that students would take a significant amount of "cultural and technical work." The Whitman faculty supported this view, acknowledging regional need for engineers who knew how to manage people as well as industry. Bratton and his colleagues urged that engineering students take a serious number of liberal arts classes and recommended both a six-year and a four-year program. He reported that the faculty opposed a proliferation of engineering courses but recommended that the school start with three types and add others when possible.

In the wide-ranging discussion Bratton complained that western colleges often hurt their reputation by lowering requirements. Whitman alumnus Dr. Park Weed Willis drew from his profession: "We have plenty of doctors, but comparatively few really good ones." He advocated that Whitman offer a program equal to MIT's. Trustee Miles Moore observed that the only reason for Whitman's existence was the high quality of its work and that it should "make good citizens as well as good engineers."

Hendrick insisted that the overseers must resolve the problems raised by the faculty. Because of their practical experience, overseers knew the types of engineering the Northwest's economy required. The professor added that students preferred a four-year program to a six-year one, but insisted that Whitman must offer a program superior to any currently available in the three states.

Dean Burton of MIT spoke about the proposed engineering program, which he said should be only four years in duration. He favored both civil engineering, as it could prepare men for careers in irrigation and forestry, and mechanical engineering, as it could train men for electrical engineering. A Walla Walla farm equipment manufacturer, Gilbert Hunt, saw the need for mechanical engineers. He knew that such men could help promote regional manufacturing, but he denounced the worthless engineers he had hired from the state institution and would "rather have a Chinaman."

Another overseer, G. Scott Anderson, stated that he had been a mining engineer for twenty-five years and from that experience had judged that "a good engineer is born and not made." Thus he saw little reason for a student to specialize in engineering and thought that a good technical education and common sense were the only requirements. Anderson argued that college course work was of little use to practicing engineers; therefore, a four-year program was important only if the student acquired a lifelong interest in study. One overseer complained that engineering graduates were too young; therefore, Whitman's requirements should result in graduates as old as those who went into law or medicine.

The overseers finally decided that a chair of engineering would be established, that the course would be four years long, and that there would not be a special engineering degree. Specialization might come at a later time.

The overseers then shifted their attention to dormitory designs. Before providing them a choice of building types, Dean Hendrick reminded them that Whitman had always advocated dormitory living. The board was not being asked to endorse this practice; it was being asked to choose between traditional dormitories housing up to 150 students or the so-called cottage design that could accommodate about a third that number. The dean stated that Whitman, in building Billings Hall and Reynolds Hall, had constructed traditional dormitories with long, noisy corridors. He described a cottage dormitory as one without a corridor, with sections, and with a homelike atmosphere. (Lyman Hall would be built in this cottage style in 1923.) The school's architect submitted plans for both types of housing. After studying the drawings and learning that students would dine in a central hall, the overseers selected the cottage plan.

Board members expressed stronger opinions about a scholarship policy than about housing design. Overseers were asked to consider a so-called poor-boy scholarship scheme: a million-dollar endowment that would provide scholarships for one young man from each of the eighty-nine counties in Oregon, Washington, and Idaho. The overseers criticized the proposal. A Portlander feared that "a boy with a good memory . . . who won't last long would receive . . . a free living." He concluded that "Left behind is the somewhat slow, thickheaded boy with slow but strong development." The critic proclaimed that scholarship winners "simply had the ability to memorize the accomplishments of others"; furthermore, "ninety percent of them never amount to anything." He favored helping the "fellow whose head is a little too thick to memorize, but whose head will be hard enough to stand hard knocks in the world."

Judge Burke opposed giving students gifts, for the college did not want those who would accept charity. The Seattleite preferred to lend money, stating that "the work of the world is done by borrowers," and he proposed that worthy boys should receive interest-free loans payable in ten years. Dr. Nelson G. Blalock of Walla Walla countered Burke: "It is rather a dangerous policy to loan money freely to young men, to encourage them to incur indebtedness." It was his opinion that the school should find jobs for needy young men. He compared college students who worked only eight hours a day with farmers who labored for fourteen. Concluding that students could work up to four hours daily at paying jobs, the physician favored establishing a nearby experimental farm, where Whitmanites could earn enough to cover tuition and incidental costs. In the summer these young men would work in harvests—as many currently did—earning as much as $5 per day. The self-made physician preferred those who worked their way through college over those who did not.

Defending the poor-boy scholarship proposal, Archer Hendrick explained that currently male applicants without money feared entering a college unless assured that they could find assistance. Most also lacked courage to ask wealthy persons for college loans. The dean also reported that some Whitman students had to spend so much energy supporting themselves that they could not enjoy their college life. In his defense of the scholarship proposal, the educator insisted that those who received financial help would not live lavish-

ly; in fact, they must work to meet their financial obligations. This
argument failed to convince dubious listeners, who made no vote on
the proposal and turned it over to a large committee for study.

At the next session Hendrick introduced the most important matter of business—the financial campaign. He thought it necessary to
explain again how the school wished to become larger. Taking into
account such factors as the region's "vast richness" and the large
sums that outsiders made from regional investments, it seemed to
Whitman's leaders that there were many rich persons who could provide the means for a Greater Whitman. An expanded Whitman
would help conserve and develop the region's natural resources. Hendrick proposed that a million dollars be raised in Oregon, Washington, and Idaho and that a like amount be raised from those "living
beyond our borders" who had an interest "in our natural wealth."
Probably every overseer had already heard or read these sentiments.
In any event these ideas prompted no debate. Hendrick asked overseers to pledge that they would put him into contact with persons
"you know to be interested in, and to be profiting by the great productive power of this territory." The dean concluded with reading a
subscription statement to be used in raising Pacific Northwest money. Trustee Willis then stressed that the new overseers must "take
upon their shoulders the running of Whitman" and assured them that
the trustees would be of assistance.

The overseers accepted the fund-raising responsibility. James
Moore praised Walla Walla for subscribing $200,000 and predicted
that the region would contribute the required million dollars. The
financier reported that in Seattle he had raised $7,000,000 for various
causes. He pointed out that across the nation wealthy businesspeople
were giving to higher education and assumed that railroad leaders
James J. Hill and Edward H. Harriman, who had helped develop the
region and had profited from investments within it, would consider it
a privilege to give $500,000 each to Greater Whitman. The overseers
endorsed a resolution stating their support of a larger institution and
that citizens should "provide the funds necessary to place Whitman
College in the position of eminence as an institution of learning." The
board also promised to help find donors.

The overseers thanked those who had addressed the educational
congress, elected George Turner as their president, and read a note

from D.K. Pearsons who recommended that the proposed college buildings should be named for Portland, Seattle, Tacoma, Spokane, Idaho, and trustee Nelson Blalock. The benefactor urged the board to make "the new college a strong and beautiful Christian college to meet [regional] educational wants."

Penrose, Hendrick, faculty members, students, board members, and many townspeople considered the educational congress and the first meeting of the overseers to be an enormous success. For many days people recalled the speeches, the banquet, Pearsons, and the report that the overseers had committed themselves to making Greater Whitman a reality. A few overseers confessed that they had arrived as skeptics and were now converts to the proposal. The community had supported the congress by attending the lectures and banquet, where Walla Wallans often told visitors that they embraced the college because it was a great addition to their community. Many women, including the wives of faculty members, had provided hospitality. Classes had been cancelled so that students could attend sessions, sing, cheer, and serve the banquet.

The local press gave the two-day event considerable attention. The Walla Walla *Union* provided extensive coverage—especially of the educational speeches—and editorialized that the educational congress should stir "civic pride" and should be considered one of the city's memorable events.[49] The *Pioneer* devoted its entire November 23 issue to the congress and paid particular attention to D.K. Pearsons. A student editor asserted: "Dr. Pearsons is great. . . . He is great because he has been able to see beauty and read the poetry of humanity in the lives of the humble." The newspaper stated that during Pearsons' second chapel visit he had urged Whitman students to work even harder and prompted laughter by adding: "This advice is . . . not for you, Penrose." In its next issue the *Pioneer* praised Archer Hendrick and the overseers, calling them "the keenest minds of the Northwest."[50] The college editor thanked the board for taking time from busy schedules to be in Walla Walla working to develop a western school equal to the best in the East. Penrose, through the *Pioneer*, urged students to become familiar with "the overseers, in whose hands the destiny of Whitman College now rests."

The *Oregonian* called the congress "the greatest gathering of educational men ever held in the Pacific Northwest" and gave generous space to the speakers and to Greater Whitman.[51] Other metropolitan newspapers provided similar coverage; in fact, an increase in admissions resulted in part from the extensive publicity given to Whitman's "new epoch."

The Early Campaign

To achieve Whitman's "new epoch," Penrose and Hendrick plunged into a fund-raising campaign in early January 1909. They needed to achieve their goal because individual subscription pledges need not be paid until the college had raised the entire million dollars. The two school leaders wrote for donations from corporations and persons who lived outside the Pacific Northwest and had profitable investments within it, but the primary effort was directed at the wealthy living within the region's major cities. At small dinner parties or in individual meetings, Hendrick and Penrose repeated themes they had presented at the educational congress. The two solicitors especially stressed that Whitman wanted to become a "first class college, not a university," and that the institution would combine traditional liberal arts with those types of engineering "which are necessary for the development of the region's natural resources."[52]

For several weeks the president and dean campaigned for $200,000 in Spokane. They believed that if they collected such an impressive amount it would help them achieve their goal of $300,000 each in Seattle and Portland. They tailored their appeal carefully to fit each city. In Portland they based their appeal to Oregonians on "patriotic citizenship" and on the economic fact that Washington communities, especially Walla Walla with its trade in wheat and other commodities, had long contributed to Portland's prosperity.

Hendrick maintained that the way to obtain subscriptions was through personal conversation, not through a public appeal. The dean provided only minimal information about the campaign to newspapers. "We certainly will not answer their criticisms nor contribute to their news columns, anything except what we please."[53]

While the school's leaders worked urban centers, the Reverend Joseph D. Neilan solicited Walla Wallans for money to help cover both campaign costs and the college's current operations. Neilan reported only limited success.

Many supporting Whitman's search for funds had been sure that Edward Harriman, Frederick Weyerhaeuser, and other outside investors in the Pacific Northwest would make major contributions. In his rejection of the college's appeal, Harriman explained that he contributed to New York institutions and not to those located in states his railroads served. Weyerhaeuser also refused to contribute in part because the family preferred to support St. Paul institutions rather than a college in Washington.[54] At this time Hendrick and Penrose were attaining their campaign goals from other sources and seemed unworried by negative replies from Harriman and Weyerhaeuser.

In June Hendrick reported the campaign's progress to the board of trustees and the board of overseers. He boasted that nearly $600,000 had been raised in the Pacific Northwest and that he had not met a single detractor. The dean underscored two major gifts: Stephen H. Matthews of Spokane had given $50,000 for a scholarship loan fund and Margaret L. Denny of Seattle had provided $50,000 for a professorship honoring her mother, Mary A. Denny. Hendrick sought twenty additional professorships honoring the memory of important persons.

To acquire information about educational policy, Hendrick explained that he and Penrose made stops at state universities, including Minnesota, and at private schools, including the University of Chicago and Yale. During this April journey they called upon the Carnegie and Rockefeller foundations and received warm receptions.

Although the campaign's progress was surely the major concern of both of Whitman's boards, they took up other significant matters. In fact, the second overseers' meeting was as significant as the first. At this June 1909 meeting the overseers received unusually long reports from Penrose and Hendrick, both requesting policy decisions. The first overseers meeting in late 1908 had necessarily been a general discussion of educational issues; the second dealt with specifics.

Penrose began his report with issues of general administration; obviously his recommendations were partly based upon educational practices explained to him by eastern school leaders. The president discussed teaching loads, stating that a Whitman faculty member spent twenty hours a week in the classroom. Penrose requested that loads be reduced to no more than sixteen hours and eventually to twelve. He reviewed each academic department and its particular needs for staff, space, and equipment. The most pressing request for change came from physics professor Benjamin Brown, who complained that he needed a new location because by working in a damp corner of Memorial Hall he suffered from "attacks of inflammatory rheumatism."[55] Penrose also recommended the adoption of a regular promotion and salary policy. The faculty should be divided into three ranks according to length of service—instructors, assistant professors, and professors—and they should be paid according to rank. Full professors should receive between $1,800 and $2,500, and department heads should get more. Before a faculty member received an annual increment, a committee on teaching, consisting of the president, the dean, and an overseer, must evaluate his or her teaching. This committee would recommend promotions; those being considered as full professors must have demonstrated "teaching ability, personal character and influence, and value to the institution."[56]

Penrose asked board members to hire a few additional teachers because of increased enrollments and to make modest increases in faculty salaries to "a minimum of decency."[57] He reminded them that for years the faithful faculty had anticipated improved salaries.

Penrose expressed his continuing concern about the academy. To create space in Memorial Hall, he requested that the academy be moved across Boyer Avenue to the old College Hall. He also pointed out that the academy ran at a deficit, thereby draining the college program, which made it necessary to increase tuition. The president wanted the conservatory to be operated separately from the college and pointed out that, unlike the academy, it was making money.

Hendrick's wide-ranging report introduced several important and sometimes interrelated topics. He urged the overseers to decide on the curriculum for an engineering program and to hire a person to teach it. The dean explained that the newspaper publicity resulting from Greater Whitman had increased the student body's size. This presented a variety of problems, including housing, teaching staff, and operating costs. The college housing shortage presented a difficult choice: the school could either limit enrollment, "especially of young ladies," by enforcing a dormitory rule, or it could remove the restriction and allow students to live in homes.[58] Increased enrollments and a small endowment, Hendrick explained, had meant a $20,000 debt in the 1908–1909 school year. The dean offered solutions: a separate budget for the academy and the conservatory, a revised Whitman constitution that would make the overseers more involved in the school's financial affairs, and the addition of a bursar to assist the treasurer. Although the administrator urged retrenchment, he agreed with Penrose that the faculty deserved pay raises. He understood that businessmen on the board would find it difficult to give department heads a $200 raise, but he emphasized that these faculty members had been at Whitman for ten years and were making only $1,400, a salary so low that they could not live "with any decency." The dean stated that every teacher had received offers from other schools that would double his or her salary. Loyalty and belief in Whitman's future, however, prompted each to remain. Hendrick concluded, "I believe it is because of this devotion that the institution has taken such a firm place in the hearts and minds of the citizenship of this Northwest."

In the summer of 1909 two men made diverse contributions to the college's development. D.K. Pearsons gave $50,000, his last gift, which would be used to build the new conservatory. It is regrettable that the benefactor's name was not given to this handsome structure, for a Pearsons Hall would have reminded the community of his critical financial contributions.

A second person helped shape the school that summer. Dr. Henry S. Pritchett, president of the Carnegie Foundation for the Advancement of Teaching, made a study of the college. While in the East, Penrose had met Pritchett, who expressed a willingness to investigate Whitman. Penrose jumped at the chance because he had applied to the foundation for help and because Pritchett was a recognized authority on higher education.

Pritchett enjoyed his visit to Walla Walla, where he interviewed the administrators, faculty, and board members, and read the school records. He was the first outsider to provide a systematic study of the institution. Other eastern educators had offered opinions on educational policy; Pritchett's lengthy report helped identify and resolve some fundamental administrative difficulties. His study noted that all of the Pacific Northwest's small colleges enrolled college, secondary, and special students. This diverse student body mingled in dormitories, classrooms, and other places, and college students often disliked such close association with the younger people.

Pritchett urged Whitman's leaders to resolve two fundamental questions. First, should the institution continue admitting secondary, music, and collegiate students in an attempt to meet the local community's needs, or should it restrict itself to a college program and thereby serve a regional need? The visitor thought that students would not travel a great distance to Walla Walla and attend an institution lacking "the life and the atmosphere of a real college."[59] He warned, "If you are to have a Greater Whitman... you must choose between... a true college and an amalgamation of college, secondary school, and music school." Second, the visitor asked about the type of school Whitman wanted to become. Pritchett listed alternatives, including the traditional classical college emphasizing the liberal arts; second, a more relevant institution that offered courses in the humanities, sciences, and mathematics as background work for those seeking careers in engineering, medicine, and other professions; third, a college offering a school of liberal arts and a school of technology. He warned that teaching too many subjects on a limited income would lead to superficiality. Pritchett delivered another useful piece of advice by pointing out that the overseers were not educational authorities, "and for a right educational policy they must depend entirely on the officers and the faculty of the college."

This report would help Whitman administrators and board members establish educational policy, especially in managing the academy and the conservatory. Penrose praised Pritchett, for he had "intelligently analyzed the situation," particularly in supporting the overseers' decision to separate the academy and conservatory from the college. Over the decades many other authorities would visit Whitman and prepare reports, but few would prove to be as precise and useful as Pritchett's.

The Campaign is Waged in Congress

In the fall of 1909 Penrose resumed presidential and professorial duties. According to historian Chester Maxey he had to give up fund raising and manage the school: "With its president and dean away... the college [had] lapsed into demoralization."[60] Most of the college community assumed that while Penrose administered the school Hendrick and Neilan were harvesting the rest of the million dollars that would complete the campaign's important first stage. Hendrick's travels around the Pacific Northwest and his work in Washington, D.C. seemed to indicate that he was compiling numerous subscribers. He was not. The dean was actually seeking to accomplish a task he considered more important than fund raising. With Penrose's blessing Hendrick was attempting to get legislation through Congress that would permit the college to acquire the Fort Walla Walla property and its buildings from the federal government.

For years Penrose had cast an appreciative eye on this property. When the government had earlier indicated that it would close the fort, the educator had informed some Walla Wallans that the college would like to acquire the beautiful site. But these business leaders, who derived economic and social advantage from the garrison, disagreed and sought to convince the government that it should maintain the post. Senator Levi Ankeny of Walla Walla spearheaded this effort; once again trustee Ankeny disappointed Penrose.

Ankeny's failure to win re-election in 1908 changed the situation because a major force for retaining the post had been lost. According to Hendrick, the War Department in late 1908 informed the college that the post would be closed and asked it to make an application for a donation of the 600 acres. Overseer William Jones of Tacoma provided a fuller explanation: the chief of staff of the army explained to

Located on a beautiful rise near the city, Fort Walla Walla's barracks and grounds seemed to Stephen Penrose and others to be ideally suited for a college campus. For many months the college and various business elements of the city engaged in a bitter contest over the ownership of the 611-acre site.

him that the army was going to concentrate garrisons at larger posts and that Fort Walla Walla could be turned over to "some nonsectarian college ... that was free from graft."[61] In the spring of 1909 Penrose, Hendrick, and a few overseers went to Washington hoping to get Congress to pass a bill prior to June 1 that would transfer the property to the college.[62] Hendrick convinced selected listeners that the acquisition of the property was a splendid way to realize the Greater Whitman proposal, explaining that, even before acquiring a title, the school already had an offer if it wished to sell some of its acreage. Penrose, Hendrick, and a few others planned that the money from such a sale would build and equip a complement of buildings on the attractive military site with its splendid view of the Blue Mountains. Pearsons Academy would remain on the old campus; the separation of the college would strengthen both institutions. Excited by the possibilities of accomplishing his goal, the dean prompted a few influential overseers to write to legislators and urge them to turn over the fort property to Whitman "for college purposes."[63]

At first it seemed impossible to get a bill before Congress. Then the War Department and congressmen suggested that Whitman would more likely get the land if it agreed to educate regional Indians. A reference to such a proposal appeared in a motion adopted by overseers, which authorized Hendrick to make final arrangements "in the matter of the petition to the ... government for the gift of the tract of land to the institution, conditional upon their agreeing to educate the Indians of the Northwest."[64]

In the late fall of 1909 Hendrick intensified his effort to get a bill passed. He urged overseers and alumni to write senators and congressmen about it and alerted those with political connections to prepare for lobbying activity in Washington. The administrator even asked a supporter's wife to attend one function because he relied "upon her diplomacy to win over some of the old cranks of Congress, whom I know no one but a diplomatic woman" could influence.[65] Banker Drew W. Standrod of Pocatello, who responded to Hendrick's plea, was among those who provided reasons why the government should give the post to the college. The addition of the land, he and other board members wrote, would contribute to Greater Whitman, the solid regional college that Pacific Northwest citizens wanted so their children could be educated nearer home and not have to go "so far . . . from us during this critical time in their development."[66] Whitman could become such an impressive institution that students would prefer to be educated there rather than at prestigious eastern schools. Like so many other Whitman supporters, the banker linked the school with the development of the region's natural resources. During their college days men would develop "a strong brotherhood"; these attachments would prove useful when they became businessmen and worked to utilize the region's diverse resources. Standrod concluded by insisting that Marcus Whitman's memory would be properly acknowledged by the government's assisting a school honoring the great patriot. A Spokane overseer put the case for the college in blunter terms: "a high class educational institution at Walla Walla, would have a tendency to take the sting out of the expression 'the wild and woolly West,' and would help to make men and women in keeping with this magnificent country."[67]

Hendrick and Penrose journeyed to Washington to mobilize support, hoping that Congress might pass a favorable fort bill by Christmas. The dean boasted that all the representatives from Oregon, Washington, and Idaho had endorsed it. Some of these politicians convinced him that it would help the cause if fifty leading Walla Wallans would write that they favored the transfer of the fort to the college. Thus businessman Oscar Drumheller wrote to a former congressman, enclosing a copy of *Old Oregon and Whitman College* that explained the Greater Whitman proposal. Drumheller called Hendrick's plan a practical one, pointed out that the region had no major benefactor, and predicted that the fort property would make an ideal college campus. He admitted that "The abandonment of Fort Walla Walla by the War Department is only a matter of time and would have been done before this had not our representatives in Congress used untiring effort to keep the fort alive."[68]

Hendrick obtained support for his bill from such influential easterners as Anson Stokes of Yale and Philip Saltonstall of Boston. Friendly politicians helped him draft a bill and introduced him to influential congressional committee chairmen.

Penrose praised Hendrick for his endeavors: "In the seven years which you have been [at Whitman] you have put new life into it, have opened new horizons for it, and have transformed it with your energy and ability. We shall always be grateful to you."[69] The president, who

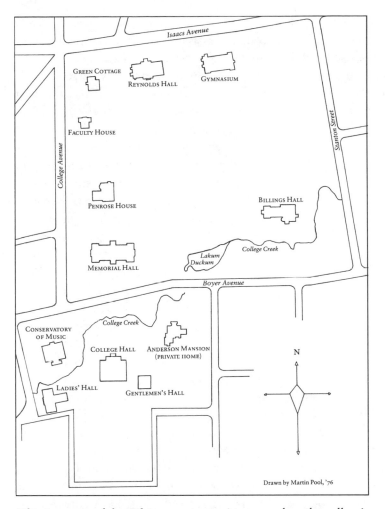

Isaacs Avenue

GREEN COTTAGE

REYNOLDS HALL

GYMNASIUM

Stanton Street

FACULTY HOUSE

College Avenue

PENROSE HOUSE

BILLINGS HALL

College Creek

Lakum
Duckum

MEMORIAL HALL

Boyer Avenue

CONSERVATORY
OF MUSIC

College Creek

COLLEGE HALL

ANDERSON MANSION
(PRIVATE HOME)

N

LADIES' HALL

GENTLEMEN'S HALL

Drawn by Martin Pool, '76

This is a map of the Whitman campus in 1910, when the college's leaders sought to acquire the Fort Walla Walla site. If the effort was successful, the college would be removed to the new property, and the academy and the conservatory would operate in the buildings at the Boyer Avenue location.

also had been seeking regional allies, plunged into lobbying activity. But his cousin, Senator Boise Penrose (who was still an important political connection for the college despite having gained a reputation as a corrupt politician), told him that Congress would not take up his bill until the end of its last session in March 1911.[70]

Just as Congress was to convene for its December session, Walla Walla newspapers gave front-page space to the fact that the fort would be closed and that college officials were in Washington seeking the site. College leaders assured local editors that they had not made an attempt to secure the land until they had learned that the War Department was going to move its garrison. The *Bulletin* of December 6 called the acquisition of the fort "one of the biggest things that has ever occurred in connection with the Greater Whitman Movement." Disgusted by the fact that the fort story had been leaked, Hendrick quickly released a letter giving a history of the college's negotiation for the property. He admitted that a bill had been introduced that would give the college the site, part of which would be sold and used for the endowment, and that Whitman would agree "to educate for all time the Indians who are Government wards in these three states."[71] An alumnus complained that the college should not break with its tradition and educate Indians. He thought the college should "educate a dominant race rather than a decadent one."[72]

In late December Penrose and trustee Blalock returned from Washington and predicted success. Blalock rejoiced that committees had already approved "the Whitman-Fort Walla Walla proposition," that Speaker of the House "Uncle Joe" Cannon (who claimed to know about Marcus Whitman and the college honoring him) favored its passage, and that he had heard no congressional opposition.[73] Penrose also expressed optimism but cautioned that Congress would only transfer the property if the War Department agreed.

Hendrick, who had always feared some type of local opposition, received encouraging letters, assuring him that only a few people questioned the fort bill. Bursar Dorsey Hill stressed that "everyone here feels confident that there can be no opposition"; a physician judged that "the prominent Catholics of Walla Walla endorse the Greater Whitman movement" and that he should make this fact known to a congressman who still recalled the earlier religious controversy over the charge of Catholic involvement in the Whitman massacre.[74] Penrose wrote Hendrick that Walla Wallan Robert Johnson had attempted to protest the transfer but failed to find allies among the directors of the commercial club (an early version of the chamber of commerce). Penrose assumed that the town generally supported the college in the fort matter.[75]

Greater Whitman Becomes Political

In the spring semester of 1910, the campus and community awaited reports of congressional action. Everyone understood that distant politicians would decide Whitman's future location. The acquisition of the fort site would mean a more spacious and beautiful campus; furthermore, the military land had now become an integral part of the Greater Whitman proposal. Penrose sighed that every day he answered 500 questions about the progress of the so-called fort bill. He daily attempted to influence Congress by mobilizing friends on both coasts. Meanwhile, Dean Hendrick and allies in Washington lobbied for the measure. A man of enormous energy and little patience, Hendrick grumbled about congressional inaction, his mounting living expenses, and his rowdy hotel. Frustration and recollections of his recent relationship with the college drained his energy. In November 1909 he had accepted a position offered by overseer James Moore and began working for Western Steel Corporation at the splendid salary of $15,000, with a promise that he might make $50,000 in commissions. According to Hendrick, some Whitman overseers heard of his new position and threatened to resign if he did not resume the school's financial campaign. So Hendrick left Moore's employment and returned full time to his college work. As he waited in his hotel room or a corridor of the Capitol, he must have reflected upon the fact that he had lost considerable personal income. Hendrick related this financial situation to friends, assuring them that he preferred to work for Whitman at a meager salary and to be associated with supportive Walla Wallans.[76]

In early December 1909 Senator Wesley Jones of Washington submitted a bill (S. 3196) that would grant the college the fort property. It was introduced in the Senate, rather than the House, because the school's major supporter in the House, Congressman Miles Poindexter, was a controversial insurgent. Hendrick explained to an overseer that "we preferred to introduce it into the Senate and let it go into the House as a Senate bill."[77] The dean would later regret this crucial political decision.

In January Hendrick appeared before a subcommittee of the Senate Committee on Military Affairs. The chairman explained to him that the members could not favorably report the Senate bill (often called the Jones Bill) because George Washington University had also asked for federal assistance. There was a danger, he warned, that by aiding both applicants Congress could be establishing the precedent of granting federal support to private institutions. But Hendrick had come forewarned. He briefly argued against the committee's decision by listing examples of federal aid to private institutions. Then he introduced a substitute proposal that would make the college a preferred purchaser of the property at $100 per acre; in turn, the Indian education requirement would be deleted. The subcommittee approved, stating that it would rather sell than give the land to the school.

Hendrick immediately informed Penrose and some overseers about this new bill and sought appraisals from knowledgeable Walla Wallans about the post's value. Penrose was delighted with the removal of all conditions in the revised proposal. Probably neither leader liked the idea of offering education to Pacific Northwest Indians "who might be fitted for entrance to Whitman College."

While Hendrick awaited Senate action, the House Committee on Military Affairs considered the original version of Senate Bill 3196. Senator Jones, the first of several speakers supporting the measure, reminded congressmen that the War Department had long been anxious to dispose of the antiquated fort but that the community had successfully blocked such action. Jones mentioned "a slight appropriation for a [fort] building" that had been made four years earlier.

At last Hendrick had his chance to tell a congressional committee why the school desired the property. His wide-ranging testimony stressed Whitman's history, present condition, and promising future. Essentially his presentation continued many of the same themes as his earlier proposals to potential regional allies about Greater Whitman. The dean also championed Marcus Whitman, though claiming less for the missionary than did President Penrose: "Whether or not he was a statesman or a patriot, or had any service in the founding of the Pacific Northwest, his life, nevertheless, for its patriotic devotion to duty and for the lessons which it teaches of fortitude, is a good backdrop upon which to establish the traditions of a great college."

He brought the Whitman controversy to the committee room by citing a recent anonymous letter denying the missionary's historical importance and opposing the college's attempt to acquire the fort site. Hendrick explained: "We are not making an appeal to Congress entirely upon the Whitman story or the reward of Whitman's work in the Pacific Northwest," but he admitted that "We are believers in the Whitman story." So once again the missionary's legacy became a part of efforts to build the institution.

The dean, however, preferred to emphasize the recent accomplishments of the college's overseers rather than those of the controversial missionary. He provided biographical details about these board members, including the fact that ninety percent graduated from good colleges and that these supporters sacrificed time and money to further private education. The lobbyist stated that overseers, like other observers, concluded that the present twenty-acre campus site was inadequate and that the fort property would be an ideal site for Greater Whitman. Hendrick described the 611-acre military installation, stating that there were two useful barracks and that the value of the buildings and grounds was less than $100,000. In his response to questions, the dean assured congressmen that the college had no interest in becoming a university, that it would not offer a broad curriculum in competition with state institutions, that it would offer appropriate engineering courses (including such military subjects as fortifications), and that the college's present site would be used as a preparatory school.

George Turner, who had served a term as senator from Washington, joined Hendrick in lobbying. A savvy politician and a dedicated Whitman overseer, Turner pushed the Senate bill by reminding congressmen about Marcus Whitman's historical importance. The missionary was a "philanthropist and a patriot who had done so much to preserve the northwestern country to the United States." Turner also praised Whitman College leaders for building a solid institution, which had sponsored an impressive educational congress. He considered Whitman to be the geographical center of the three-state region and ideally suited to educate its students. Turner praised Hendrick for raising $600,000 for Greater Whitman. It seemed to the former senator that the fort site, when added to Whitman's other advantages, would make it an outstanding regional institution.

Turner thought the government might sell the abandoned post for $60,000 and judged that such a sum "is a mere bagatelle in comparison with the very great benefit that it would be to the people of the

Pacific Northwest to have it devoted to the purposes of Whitman College."[78] The politician concluded by explaining that one purpose of the federal government was to aid education, especially through the donation of land, and it should now help Whitman, a worthy school with an impressive history and tradition.

John McGraw of Seattle and William Jones of Tacoma also spoke for the bill. They repeated the arguments of the previous speakers, but Jones was particularly direct. He recalled that Walla Wallans had always found the political support to keep the local fort operating and frankly concluded: "It has been practically demonstrated that the post, unless coupled with a proposition to turn it over to a college, is going to remain there, and it is a burden to the Government of the United States." In other words, a gift would actually save federal money. Jones also emphasized that at their first overseers meeting, "hard-headed businessmen [became] wildly enthusiastic over a college." Jones concluded that such a reaction was "the most beautiful sight I ever saw." He predicted that Whitman would become a great school with or without the fort property.

Lewis Pratt of Tacoma, who was not connected with Whitman, testified for the school. He championed the cause of private higher education in general and Whitman in particular. Pratt reminded congressmen of the importance of private colleges in national history and then praised Penrose, his former classmate at Williams, for building a New England type of institution.

Hendrick quickly informed his allies in the Pacific Northwest that the committee hearing had been a great success. He was sure that the House would soon pass the revised Senate bill and that in February he would be in Walla Walla for the overseers meeting. A Walla Walla newspaper reported that if the bill passed, "one of the biggest demonstrations in the history of the college will be given ... and Greater Whitman plans will be given a new impetus."[79]

But there was no immediate congressional action or college celebration. Homesick and frustrated by the Senate's continuing delay, Hendrick confronted Missouri senator William Warner and heatedly reminded him that for two months he had promised the bill's friends that he would call a meeting of his military committee. Hendrick, who had once described Warner as "an old fossil, decrepit, knock-kneed, and incapable of maintaining a chew of tobacco in his mouth without letting most of it go on his vest,"[80] accused the committee chairman of talking "damn nonsense." Hendrick recounted the confrontation to a friend: Warner understood "the roughness with which I attacked him, and I imagine if he looked closely at me he might have realized that I would have enforced it physically."[81]

The angry dean also chastened the college's supporters, especially the overseers, for not applying enough political pressure, warning that if there were no Senate action within a week, "I am going to start west and leave the bill to the fates."[82] Overseers and trustees quickly responded and sent telegrams and letters to congressmen. Seattle physician and alumnus Park Weed Willis was particularly active. In a letter to a friend in New Orleans, for example, the trustee called Fort Walla Walla "a white elephant on the hands of Uncle Sam" and reminded him that Seattle had generously given the land for Fort Lawton. It seemed only fair to him that the government should turn over an abandoned military installation to a nonsectarian college.[83] Overseer Thomas Burke understood Hendrick's frustration: "if you fail to get any bill through, the Board understands the obstacles that have to be overcome and will not be surprised."[84] Penrose often sympathized with Hendrick; he wrote in one letter, "It must be very exasperating to find how many committees of the Senate and House can postpone things ... but the longest road has its turning."[85] Despite such encouragement the weary lobbyist charged that many of the college's friends did not care whether he was successful or not. Hendrick bitterly complained: "But with me it is different, if I fail in this I presume it will injure my reputation and that is what I am working against."[86]

On March 30 Senator Warner presented a revised bill and a committee report, which included the War Department's approval of disposing of the fort site. The new measure would grant the college 611 acres for $150 per acre, a figure established by the subcommittee. Senator Nathan Scott of West Virginia explained that Senator Jones "is anxious about the bill, or I should object to its being taken up at this time."[87] The West Virginian complained about the fact that the college offered $90,000 for the buildings and grounds that the army had evaluated as being worth $162,000, including new brick barracks that in 1907 had cost the government $121,000. Senator Jones countered that the chief of staff wanted to sell the post because it was too small, poorly located, and in bad repair. One senator grumbled

that either Congress or the War Department had blundered by erecting brick buildings and three years later abandoning the reservation.
The Washington senator replied that former senator Levi Ankeny
had responded to local interests by getting the War Department to
erect the barracks. Jones said that he had statements—the ones solicited by Hendrick—that the property was not worth more than $100
per acre because "This land is practically all gravel. There is no water
for irrigation, and the possibilities of getting water for irrigation are
very uncertain." Scott, however, ignored the land's value and stressed
the value of the buildings that could be used as dormitories. He
growled, "Do not let us say that we are selling the land when we
know that we are giving it away."

A week later the bill again came to the Senate floor. Scott immediately reiterated that the fort site was being sold for much less than its
value. The college's political friends, especially Senator William
Borah of Idaho, had prepared for such an accusation. Borah pointed
out that if the government had previously misappropriated money
for post buildings it had nothing to do with the present bill. The
Idahoan argued that the buildings had little use except for military
purposes and that the government should donate the site to show its
appreciation for Marcus Whitman. Senator Samuel Piles of Washington also praised the missionary and added: "A number of distinguished men in Washington, Oregon, and Idaho have subscribed
about a million dollars to construct new and larger buildings on more
capacious grounds, and to make the institution ... worthy of the
memory of that old pioneer, Marcus Whitman."

Senator Joseph Bristow of Kansas denounced an administrative
system that would spend $120,000 on modern barracks at a site that
the War Department now wanted to abandon. The money, he lamented, had simply been "frittered away," an opinion that received
some support in and out of the Senate. To prevent the waste of additional money on the fort, Senator Borah recommended turning it into
a school "so that," he joked, "Congress can not reach it by appropriation." After an exchange with opponents, Borah asserted: "I would
be glad to vote for nine-tenths of the forts of the country being turned
into educational institutions."

Senator Francis Newlands of Nevada denounced the political
spoils system but supported the bill because he judged that the college

was offering a fair sum. Alabama senator Joseph Johnston heatedly disagreed: "The proper way to entitle this bill would be 'A bill to make a donation of $100,000 to Whitman College.'" Johnston suspected a conspiracy: Walla Walla got $135,000 in fort buildings and then proposed that the government abandon the post. Newlands responded that Archer Hendrick had assured him that the barracks were of little use.

There was an extended debate over the $150-per-acre price. A New England senator, who had been lobbied by the college, stated that the federal government ought not to drive a sharp bargain with an educational institution and endorsed Borah's idea of turning army posts into schools. Senator Scott explained that he had raised the price from $100 to $150 per acre because a former resident of West Virginia, A.T. Taylor, had written him from Freewater, Oregon, that he would be willing to pay the higher figure. Scott again emphasized that even at this price Whitman would get a bargain because the modern army barracks could be converted into college dormitories.

Connecticut senator Morgan Bulkeley, who knew about Whitman College from association with Penrose and his Hartford in-laws, brought the debate back to the missionary. He pointed out that Congress had often appropriated sums to honor distinguished citizens. The New Englander concluded: "I do not believe we could do a wiser or a more proper thing than to give this property without any cost to this educational institution, which is largely a memorial to the man to whom the country is indebted for saving to the United States in a large degree this great Northwest Territory." No other senator responded to this controversial interpretation of Whitman's historical role; in fact, the debate wound down, and the bill passed by voice vote.

Delighted with this result, Hendrick now lobbied House members. Penrose informed him that his cousin, Senator Penrose, volunteered to help him find House votes and that he had asked Secretary of the Interior Richard Ballinger, a Williams classmate, to seek President William Howard Taft's support. On May 3 the House Committee on Military Affairs conducted another hearing at which former senator Turner, Hendrick, and others testified. The committee unanimously recommended passage of the Senate bill, stating that the Whitman offer of $150 per acre was more than the government could get for the post property in a sale to a private group. It also concluded

On April 13, 1910, a Walla Walla paper presents the sensational news that the U.S. Senate has agreed to sell the fort property to Whitman College.

that those who had offered to pay more than the college made an offer in "good faith" but had made it "only for the purpose of preventing Whitman College from getting the land."[88] To Hendrick's satisfaction, the committee called Whitman "one of the leading educational institutions of the great Northwest" and indicated that it preferred that the land be used for educational purposes. Among the documents incorporated into the committee report was a lengthy summary of the college's history, its present condition, and its goals.

The Speaker of the House agreed to call up the bill on May 16, but he cautioned Hendrick that this procedure required a two-thirds favorable vote. Realizing that this was probably his only chance to get a vote in this session and that it would be difficult to obtain so many yes votes, Hendrick again turned to his allies for supportive letters to combat the Walla Wallans who opposed the fort bill. In letters to House members, some foes had offered to pay much more than $150 per acre. For example, John Ankeny, the son of banker and former senator Levi Ankeny, and others proposed to pay twice as much as Whitman was offering. Although the House committee had rejected this and other offers as well as some accusations that the college was sectarian, Hendrick understood that land values and religion would be brought up in the House debate.

The bill came before a poorly attended session of the House, but many opponents sat at their desks. The criticism began early when Democrat Oscar Underwood of Alabama reported that he had received letters maintaining that the land was worth much more than $150 per acre and accused the college of planning to divide the post into lucrative town lots. William Kahn of Indiana, who had served on the military committee, countered that many of Walla Walla's leading citizens, including Levi Ankeny and Miles Moore, wrote that $150 was a fair sum. William Cox of Indiana asked why the school wanted the property; Kahn replied that Whitman would build several structures, including an agricultural experiment station. Cox then asked if the college were sectarian as some had charged; Kahn denied the allegation and explained that the committee "felt that that institution of learning should be encouraged; therefore, we decided that they should have the preference in the matter, and so reported this bill."[89] An opponent favored a public auction rather than making Whitman the preferred purchaser and warned: "If we are to enter upon a policy of donation to private colleges of one sort and another, we are opening the door very wide to a dangerous practice."

The debate centered on the land's value, its future use, and past government expenditures on a post building. Texan James Slayden explained that at the committee hearings he had initially criticized the bill but had been convinced that the Whitman offer was fair and that the school was not involved in "a town-lot" speculative scheme. A suspicious congressman, however, favored putting the fort site up for sale; if nobody offered more than the college had, then Whitman would receive the abandoned post for $91,000. New Yorker John Fitzgerald, a determined foe who often faulted the bill, distrusted those Walla Wallans who wrote that the land was worth no more than $150 per acre and requested that the government should get the land appraised "unless Congress is initiating a system of endowment of private institutions." He extended his criticism: "There is something peculiar about land in Washington. When the Government wants to buy it it is the most valuable land to be found in the United States. When it is proposed that the Government sell land it is the poorest land that has ever been located in any State." Fitzgerald's attack aroused Miles Poindexter, a liberal Republican representing eastern Washington, who had promised to support the college. The congressman denied that there was "a speculative motive," defended the $150 price, and insisted that "the great mass of the substantial citizens of all denominations are in favor of it." To his way of thinking Whitman was "the only standard college in that great area" composed of Washington, Oregon, and Idaho. Poindexter wanted Whitman to get the land because it was suited geographically to render significant public service. Congressman William R. Ellis, who lived in nearby Pendleton, rose to defend the school's offer. He said that he knew the property well and joked that even Carnegie would not pay $150 per acre. Henry Clayton of Alabama remained unconvinced: "we ought not to give away 611 acres of land with a building on it worth $100,000 under the pretense that we are selling it for the pitiful sum of $150 an acre."

Washington congressman William McCredie tried to counter Clayton's argument with the claim that the fort site would be more suited for farms than for city residents. Clayton disagreed. He provided details about Walla Walla's growth and concluded that the property could very well be divided into town lots. The Alabaman insisted: "The cry is now back to the farms from the cities."

Fitzgerald persuasively argued that the land should be appraised by "disinterested persons." He then accused Walla Wallans of extorting $100,000 from the government for buildings and now fighting to close the military reservation and paying only a paltry $150 per acre. Perhaps his accusation of a land fraud influenced his colleagues who terminated their debate and voted. To the great disappointment of Hendrick, Penrose, and hundreds of other college supporters, the House voted forty-five to forty against the suspension of the rules. Frustrated by this result, Hendrick soon boarded a train for the long trip to Walla Walla, rehashing the lopsided positive votes in the Senate and in the House Military Affairs Committee and the large negative one in the House. What had gone wrong? What could be done to win passage of the Jones bill in the next session of the Congress?

Mobilizing for the Fort Fight

When he returned to campus, Archer Hendrick immediately joined Stephen Penrose and allies in studying the reasons for the House defeat and in considering ways to overcome each one. For many months those leading the effort to acquire the fort property had looked for signs of opposition and rehashed arguments to rebut them. Everyone anticipated that Walla Wallans profiting from the fort's trade would continue the battle to keep a garrison. To prevent opponents from uniting and waging a fight in Congress through letters and appearances before its committees, Whitman's leaders had kept their plans quiet. But after the newspaper stories of December 1909 Penrose, Dorsey Hill, and friends searched for negative reactions. They asked businessmen about any criticism they heard on sidewalks or at meetings. From such sources Penrose, in January 1910, compiled fairly accurate information for Hendrick. The president's report stated that saloonkeepers feared that they would lose their business if the four companies of cavalry left town. One saloonman grumbled "that a single saloon was worth more to the town than Whitman College."[90] Penrose had also learned that Richard Johnson and some others who supplied horse feed to the cavalrymen attempted to lead the saloonkeepers in a fight against the college bill; furthermore, there was a rumor that some schemed to bring "the Catholic influence" into opposition. The school's long-time foe, Thompson Elliott, was reportedly courting possible allies to fight the school's move to the military site.

In mid-January 1910 Hendrick assured Penrose that he should not worry about this opposition "because there could be no concerted movement which would receive recognition in the face of the petition which we have presented." The dean had reached this conclusion because the community's most distinguished persons supported the college through their persuasive communications to congressmen.[91] In May his confidence waned as the Senate bill came before the House. By then the types of opposition that Penrose had identified had become significant. In the spring and summer of 1910 the president, dean, board members, and others worked to counter them.

To meet the frequent charge that the school would not be paying a fair price for the post property, Penrose and others got leading bankers, realtors, and other informed persons to state that $150 per acre was equitable. The school also discredited the motives of those who raised the value issue. In other words, when opponents offered to give more than $150 the institution challenged their sincerity, arguing that they simply wanted to block the Senate bill so as to keep the fort

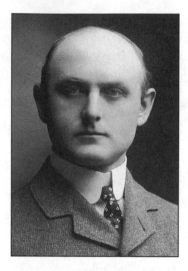

Thompson Coit Elliott graduated from Amherst in 1885 and served as Whitman College treasurer from 1895 to 1900. After his removal from this office he denounced President Stephen Penrose's interpretation of Marcus Whitman as well as Dean Archer Hendrick's attempt to acquire the Fort Walla Walla property for a new campus site. But Elliott supported Whitman through cash donations, and his daughter, Barbara, earned a degree from the institution. Today his fine Pacific Northwest book collection is housed in the Penrose Library.

operating. Richard Johnson, for example, had offered to purchase the fort property for more than the college offered. To counter him, the college submitted quartermaster records demonstrating that in 1908–1909 Johnson had contracts to supply the post with more than $24,000 worth of oats, bran, and hay. Whitman's leadership also gathered documentation to show that John Ankeny's offer for the post property was not genuine, and the House committee soon agreed. However, this decision did not end the dispute. On May 8, 1910, Johnson and Ankeny struck back with an open letter published in the Walla Walla *Union*. Arguing that Hendrick had misled the community and Congress, these writers insisted that Congress would actually enlarge and improve the fort if the Jones bill failed. They reminded readers that the fort annually put about $250,000 into the local economy and that Walla Wallans, including themselves, had always supported the college. Its ambitious leaders, they charged, selfishly pushed the college's interests over the city's.

Elliott was even more persistent than either Johnson or Ankeny. In January Hendrick had received two newspaper clippings from the New York *Tribune* and the New York *Sun*. These two hostile letters to the editor were, Hendrick thought, most likely the underhanded work of Elliott. One letter decried the Whitman myth, accused the college of seeking federal funds for the endowment, and stated that the overseers were "sixty gratuitously selected ... prominent citizens." The letter in the *Sun* charged that the bill was a "plan to endow at the expense of the Government a small sectarian college which continues to live in the glamour of [the Whitman] myth."[92]

On April 9 Elliott sent a letter to Senator Nathan Scott of West Virginia, a fort bill critic, providing reasons for rejecting the measure: Congress should not aid private schools; "the naming of Whitman College as a beneficiary of the National Government raises a historical question involved in doubt and sectarian controversy"; and $450, not $150, per acre was a fair figure. Overseer Miles Moore, who was in Washington assisting Hendrick, attempted to rebut Elliott with his own letter to Scott. Moore stated that he served as president of the bank and that Elliott was a director, not an officer, and thus he should not have used the Baker-Boyer Bank letterhead. Moore rejected the evaluation figure of $450 per acre as "purely arbitrary." He concluded that Elliott's "attitude may be explained by the fact that he was at one time treasurer of the college, and I am informed failed of re-election.... Since that time Elliott has been the relentless enemy of the college."[93]

As Elliott continued to stir up hostility, Hendrick complained that although some citizens enjoyed "knocking" the college, the long-time critic actually favored "the killing of Whitman."[94] Penrose was probably not surprised when Elliott appeared before a House committee and continued his attack. According to the Walla Walla *Bulletin* of June 20, 1910, Elliott told committee members that he would be willing to join others and buy the land at $400 per acre. One congressman alerted the college that this sizeable offer increased opposition to the Jones bill. Despite this growing opposition and his concern about Elliott's congressional appearance, Hendrick still predicted House passage of the Senate bill in next session of Congress. In a private letter to a congressman, Hendrick countered Elliott by charging that he was "avowedly antagonistic not only to this institution but to the interests of the city" and that he fought the college "to satisfy his own personal revenge."[95] The dean then confided that Elliott had married into the wealthy Baker family, whose members detested his methods.

As late as mid-April Hendrick thought that the testimony of Whitman's leaders and the extensive letter writing of its friends had successfully overcome detractors. Congressmen commented on the number of communications: for example, Senator Jones had received two hundred letters for his bill and only two against it. The dean believed that this support showed all groups that Walla Wallans wanted Greater Whitman and that some of its friends had concluded that the institution was in "a life and death struggle."[96]

Unfortunately, in late April Hendrick's battle took a turn for the worse when a Walla Walla priest, Father Harry J. Van de Ven, telegraphed a congressman that "Democrats in Congress on principle should oppose the Jones Senate bill ... for a paltry $150 per acre." The priest urged these politicians to investigate land values. Apparently this was the first time in this struggle that an opponent had appealed openly to either major political party. Hendrick had once asked Republicans to make the Jones bill a partisan contest, but skilled politicians had resisted.

While Hendrick mobilized yet another set of communications to Congress so as to counter the priest's effort, Van de Ven on May 9 widened his attack in a long telegram to Congressman Miles Poindexter. Perhaps his action was a response to a criticism of the Pope that appeared in the Walla Walla *Bulletin*. Penrose maintained that neither he nor any professor had written the editorial against the spiritual leader.[97] But the priest remained unconvinced, stated that he represented 3,000 Catholics in Walla Walla County, and protested "against the proposed graft of transferring under the sham of sale government property" worth $250,000 to Whitman, a school that was "always avowedly sectarian until opportunity to raid the government treasury suggested that it be proclaimed undenominational." Van de Ven charged that the Jones bill would "in a way stamp with Congressional approval the slanders and falsehoods concocted and circulated by Whitman supporters." He attacked Henry Spalding for the Whitman-saved-Oregon myth, for his denunciation of the Reverend Father J.B.A. Brouillet, and for charging Catholics "with having instigated the murder of Whitman." The critic asserted that Penrose "in speech and pamphlet has fathered utterances prejudicial to Catholics and contrary to fact." Van de Ven insisted that "The only claim that Whitman College offers to obtain the bounty of government is the fiction that its namesake [Marcus] Whitman saved Oregon; this is a pretense of his followers never made by him."

The priest also accused Hendrick of deceiving congressmen about the value of the post lands. "Such chicanery while consistent with

Whitman methods," he complained, "are unworthy of any kind of an educational institution and should be investigated." He asked Poindexter to read this telegram into the Congressional Record.

Poindexter refused. Other congressmen, however, received copies and conversed about this sensational charge of vicious attacks on Catholicism. Hendrick telegraphed Penrose about the Walla Walla priest's damaging claim. Penrose responded that local Catholics opposed to their priest had wired a critic of the bill, Congressman Fitzgerald, that the majority of "thinking Knights of Columbus" in Walla Walla supported the legislation. The college asked Bishop Edward J. O'Dea of Seattle to inform congressmen that he disagreed with Van de Ven. Penrose also had Secretary of the Interior Richard Ballinger alert President William Howard Taft about the priest's blow against the college and its leaders.

Penrose, Hendrick, and allies had only a week to counter Father Van de Ven's slashing attack. They failed to convince enough congressmen. Whitman's leaders and Congressman Poindexter eventually concluded that the priest's charge of sectarianism, more than any other factor, led to their defeat.[98] The politician wrote that during the debate little was said on the "religious or sectarian question," but his colleagues stated that it actually prompted their negative votes.[99] Hendrick, who stormed about the "viciousness and unfairness of this attack," urged Protestant denominations across the Pacific Northwest to rally to Whitman's defense. He asserted that Van de Ven's communication was "the most pronounced evidence of Romanism which has ever come before the attention of Congress, and I am told by many members that they would welcome a general attack of the Protestant denominations upon such an effort as is being made by this Catholic priest."[100]

The controversy in their town, the letters in the newspapers, the Van de Ven telegram, and the House's negative vote of May 10, 1910, excited Walla Wallans. Somebody wired the priest that his telegram was a "terrible blunder" and would likely be "disastrous for all Catholic bills."[101] The school's friends denounced the priest and other detractors. One Odessa, Washington, resident sympathized with Hendrick; like many others, he acknowledged the educator's sacrifices for Greater Whitman and then denounced his foes as "a lot of idiots who are too small a calibre to even know what is best for them."[102] He groused: "It is actually strange what a lot of pin heads" Walla Walla had produced.

The writer correctly predicted that Hendrick would continue his fight. As soon as the House's negative vote reached him, the dean began to build an even stronger case and to find additional political allies. It was possible, he thought, that the House might stay in session long enough to reconsider the Jones bill. When it appeared on the floor, Hendrick wanted to be ready to meet the sectarian issue as well as any other criticism. In June Congress adjourned without taking further action on the fort bill.

Thus Hendrick spent much of the summer preparing for the December session. He realized that the college must reach an understanding with regional Catholics and wrote to Bishop O'Dea asking if the Walla Walla priest's "action represents your desire."[103] The dean explained that the college did not seek the land as a reward for the services of Marcus Whitman but as the site to build a great private school. Hendrick stated that heads of some denominations wanted Whitman "to begin a sectarian war because of the priest's attack," but he hoped for some other way to settle the dispute. Wanting no confrontation with Whitman, O'Dea emphasized that he had sent telegrams to congressmen and to Walla Wallans stating that he did not oppose the college's purchasing the military property. The bishop concluded: "I greatly regret the action of the Reverend Father Vander Venn [sic] in relation to the bill, and I did not hesitate to communicate my regrets to him as soon as my attention was called to the telegram."[104] Hendrick persuaded some leading Walla Walla Catholics to write for the Jones bill and against the priest's message to Congressman Poindexter. To show that there was widespread support for the Senate bill and to demonstrate that the college was not sectarian or denominational, the Walla Walla Ministerial Union signed a favorable resolution.

Hendrick mobilized supporters to combat political opponents. He explained to a friend that "The Democrats in Congress seem to have allied themselves in opposition to our measure," and that he hoped to change their minds. To achieve this end Hendrick traveled around the state and convinced Democrats to send William Goodyear of Colfax to Washington, D.C. to assure Democratic congressmen that local party members supported the Jones bill. The dean also guaranteed Poindexter that every Democrat he met in the state supported the college and disliked "the attack of Father Van De Ven."[105]

The board of overseers backed Hendrick's strenuous efforts to acquire the fort property by raising his salary to $2,500 and by passing flattering resolutions; for example, "it could be no pleasant ... task to stand laboring" with politicians who did not consider the aspirations of Whitman College very important compared with national issues or the pressing demands of their own constituents.[106] Politically astute overseers expressed astonishment that Hendrick had even got the bill through the Senate.

In July 1910 Hendrick provided overseers with a sketchy but optimistic report on the Senate bill. He reminded them that the measure provided an opportunity to purchase 611 acres at $150 per acre and that the money must be paid by January 1. The dean explained that the bill failed in the House because of disagreements over the value of the land and because of "sectarian grounds."[107] Hendrick assured the overseers that this opposition had been met: the school would pay a price set for the fort property by government appraisers, and Whitman had assurances from Seattle's Bishop O'Dea that Catholics generally did not denounce the bill. Hendrick explained that church opposition was "entirely local, and probably based upon personal reasons." The lobbyist was not only confident about meeting the two objections to the Senate bill, he also predicted that the college could raise the required land price by the deadline.

To get a favorable House vote Hendrick wrote many letters to both private persons in the Pacific Northwest and to congressmen in the East and South. He asked regional allies to spread the word that "the best men of three states" sided with the college and that the disagreement over the fort property was more important than "a squabble between two city factions."[108] The dean wrote frank letters to Democratic and Republican congressmen informing them that the opposition to the Jones bill was composed of some local Roman Catholics, the city's liquor dealers, and long-time enemy Thompson Elliott. To a congressman who had heard Elliott's testimony before his committee, Hendrick explained that this critic had no local reputation, that he was a "note-shaver and money lender of his wife's money," and that his enmity toward President Penrose was so deep that he would do anything to assure his failure.[109]

But in other letters Hendrick ignored Elliott and placed the struggle in a moral context. The college had long denounced the garrison's influence in the city, especially the fact that Fort Walla Walla enriched the proprietors of saloons and operators of houses of prostitution. Joined by other Walla Wallans who worked to improve society, the school wanted the fort closed. Regional allies, especially the prestigious overseers, applauded the school's efforts to reduce the power of unsavory characters.

Hendrick sought the sympathy of an eastern Republican congressman by emphasizing the moral struggle: "A college located in an old pioneer town that has been used to allowing the town to run open undoubtedly would have made a great many enemies if it did its duty as a Christian institution. We have striven to do this and are willing to take the opposition of the liquor interests and the evilly inclined here because of the principles which we represent. They, of course, have made a great fight upon us, have put up money, and have tried to represent that we are falsifying the value of this property."[110] He continued, "Whitman College is not anxious for any graft ... we are not in the business to steal something."

To Congressman Oscar Underwood of Alabama, Hendrick admitted that about twenty-five years ago a minister—he did not identify Leavitt Hallock—served as a college trustee and had in his "foolish enthusiasm" charged that Roman Catholics had inspired the murder of Marcus Whitman. Such accusations were a thing of the past, the dean assured him, but the liquor men of Walla Walla—most of whom were Catholics—had revived this old sectarian story and had persuaded Father Van de Ven to attack the college.

To another representative Hendrick claimed that Whitman was not a mere local college seeking government favors. It had prestigious overseers and sought "to be serviceable in the educational affairs" of three states.[111] The college also hoped that raising its own standards would prompt other regional schools to do the same; furthermore, Whitman as an educational leader tried to meet "the actual needs and not the fancies and foibles of the populace."[112]

To help win support Hendrick wrote a widely disseminated essay, "Educational Unity in the Pacific Northwest," which appeared in the August 1910 issue of *Outlook*. In it he explained Greater Whitman, emphasized the support given to this proposal by both regional leaders and eastern educators, summarized the results of Whitman's valuable educational congress, and claimed that the financial campaign for Greater Whitman was succeeding.

In November the overseers, the dean, the president, and friends met to complete plans for the passage of the fort bill in the House. Hendrick encouraged overseers to go to Washington and push the bill while he traveled in the Pacific Northwest finishing the $1,000,000 Greater Whitman campaign. He explained: "I have been spread so thin over so many things that I have not been very effective in anything." At this meeting and in the following weeks, Hendrick constantly pleaded with trustees to write their congressmen in behalf of the fort bill. Probably former senator George Turner of Spokane wrote the most effective letters.[113]

The overseers made two significant decisions about the fort proposal. The board had inspected the land and judged that it was not worth more than $150 per acre. The group feared that foes might offer more than the land's value, so they now opposed an amendment to the Senate bill that would provide for appraisal of the land. The school chose to remain as the preferred purchaser, assuming that congressmen would recognize Whitman as a worthy institution that would use the federal land to benefit western society. The board's second move was an unusual attempt to strengthen its case in Congress by obtaining memorials in support of the Jones bill from the Washington, Oregon, and Idaho legislatures.

A month later Hendrick also modified his tactics in response to new political advice. Congressmen had informed him that the only hope of getting the measure passed in the next session was to have Miles Poindexter, the representative from eastern Washington, serve as its sponsor. This placed the college in an awkward position because its leaders had worked to defeat him. Poindexter was a familiar figure to them: in the 1890s he had practiced law in Walla Walla and then had moved on to greater opportunities in Spokane. In 1908 he won election as a Republican to Congress, where he immediately sided with the insurgents—progressive Republicans who challenged such regular Republicans as President Taft, House Speaker Joe Cannon, and others. Although Poindexter's vocal endorsement of progressivism drew the wrath of many national Republicans, his political opinions appealed to the rank and file of both parties. In 1910 he

Judge Thomas Burke was a prominent Seattle attorney who served as a member of the college's board of overseers from 1908 until his death in 1925. President Penrose praised Burke for his educational vision, friendship, and financial generosity.

sought a United States Senate seat, and the progressive tide swept him to victory.

He easily defeated Seattle judge Thomas Burke, who was a resourceful friend of the college and a leading overseer, and who had, of course, the enthusiastic backing of Penrose, Hendrick, and other Whitman figures. Sharing Burke's political and personal views, Penrose had hoped to have his friend serve in Congress. One board member, Levi Ankeny, had been a senator; it would have been even better for the college to have Burke in that office. Devastated by the election returns, Penrose consoled Burke: "The so-called 'insurgency' of the time is synonymous with hysteria, populism, socialism, anarchy, and almost any other term which indicates a mind diseased and a vision beclouded."[114]

Hendrick now tried to mend political fences. He explained to Congressman Poindexter that in the last session of the Congress, Speaker Cannon and other Republican leaders directed him to have the measure introduced in the Senate because the controversial Poindexter lacked influence in the House. The dean admitted to the congressman that this was a mistake: "the college in its desire to pass this [fort] measure allowed expediency to influence against what would be our right course of conduct."[115] Hendrick frankly admitted: "I am conscious of the fact that there is no one who can pass this measure but you, and unless you undertake it and will become the adviser of us concerning it, we might as well consider the measure lost."

Hendrick admitted to friends that it was not easy to seek the politician's help but stated that "we have to humiliate ourselves, confess our sins, and ask for forgiveness and appeal to the larger manhood of Poindexter."[116] To win his assistance, Hendrick asked the congressman's political friends, especially Spokane publisher William H. Cowles, to help convince him that he should forget the school's opposition and sponsor the Jones bill. Poindexter, however, responded that he would only vote for it as he had in April. The fact that Senator Jones had authored the measure probably contributed to Poindexter's lukewarm support. In the 1910 Senate race, Jones had openly worked for the insurgent's defeat. The resourceful Poindexter could have committed himself to bringing the bill to a floor vote, as experienced politicians had predicted to Hendrick. Very likely his aloofness to appeals from the college was fatal to the bill.

While the conservative dean and others sought to convince insurgent Poindexter to become the bill's sponsor, another awkward problem arose. The city's unions raised against the college an unanticipated negative voice that needed a response. In December the Walla Walla Trades and Labor Council passed resolutions that countered the Jones bill. Boasting of a membership of 700, the council praised the fertile soils of Fort Walla Walla and wanted them sold directly to workers, not to a private interest. The council requested Congress to pass an act subdividing the fort property into acre tracts that would be sold in installments to "industrial toilers" who must make improvements.[117] The council insisted that "We have no fight with Whitman, but we believe we are more entitled to the land."[118] The Walla Walla *Union* sympathized with the union scheme and maintained that many, including friends of the college, also favored it. This newspaper, which reported a rumor that artillerymen would be transferred to the fort, would rather have soldiers than either college students or farmers living on the property. The *Union* emphasized that many petitions had been circulated to keep the local garrison not because of its economic significance but because of the fort's "historic surroundings and the picturesque accomplishments and the matters of interest accompanying it." The council then wrote to Senator Jones that it would pay $300 per acre and requested his support for their proposal. The workers also reminded the senator that their plan made sense because it was "a time-honored custom of the government to help and assist the landless and homeless in acquiring property in used lands"; furthermore, those who owned their homes were more anxious to support the government.[119]

Senator Jones sidestepped these resolutions but quietly informed Hendrick that foes seemed "to be throwing rock after rock in the way of our proposition."[120] Hendrick replied that Richard Johnson and his allies had prompted the council to seek the land in another attempt to prevent the passage of the fort bill and that all who had signed for the Trades and Labor Council resolutions were "Catholics . . . identified with the crowd who have been holding us up so far."[121]

Friends of the college owning property near the fort site responded to the Trades and Labor Council's proposal by offering them even better farm property under the same terms that the unions wanted from the government. Hendrick rejoiced over this countermove, for it would "show the fallacy" of the resolution passed by the workers' organization. But Hendrick privately confessed that the "labor unions have exploded on our hands and have passed a resolution which is causing us some embarrassment."[122] He feared that a state labor organization might endorse the local one. This, of course, would have a negative impact upon politicians in both Olympia and Washington, D.C.

The Fort Property Dispute in State Capitals

The next round in the contest over the fort property was fought in state capitals, not in Washington, D.C. Penrose advocated such a public battle with labor unions because "we must fight it out now or be permanently defeated."[123] Friends assisted the college by flooding state legislators with requests to support a memorial transferring ownership of the fort site to Whitman. Walla Walla businessman Oscar Drumheller's appeal to a legislator included the claim that if the property struggle took place anywhere but in Walla Walla "every man in the place would be in favor . . . for the government in giving to Whitman College means a gift to the people of the city for they get all the benefits."[124]

On January 16 Senator Josiah Collins of King County introduced the memorial addressed to the president and the U.S. Congress on behalf of the college. Collins asserted that "the nation will derive the greatest benefit from the property by entrusting it to an institution in every way worthy, and capable of using it in the cause of higher education."[125] Collins added other arguments provided by Hendrick and allies. He asserted that the Oregon Country became part "of our national domain through the instrumentality of patriotic pioneers, of whom Dr. Marcus Whitman was a type and a leader." Penrose had insisted that the controversial Whitman-saved-Oregon story not be included in the memorial; therefore, Collins simply stated that the missionary and others wrested the region from the Hudson's Bay Company and held it until American public opinion forced the government to make a treaty with Great Britain in 1846, "whereby the American title was finally recognized and established." The senator recalled that the federal government had funded statues and paintings to honor illustrious persons. Granting property to the college honoring Whitman would be similarly appropriate because "the people at large" favored it and because the college would advance the arts and sciences. The speaker also proclaimed that Oregon, Washington, and Idaho residents looked upon the school "as an object of their solicitude and pride."

To block the adoption of the memorial, a few state senators introduced two negative telegrams. One signed by some twenty Walla Wallans explained that a petition favoring sale of the land to laborers had been sent to Congress. The group charged that the college paid no state taxes and that it was better to put the acreage into the hands of workers rather than a college because only one child in 200 would attend college. Richard Johnson, a relentless foe, sent the second telegram insisting that he and other Walla Wallans had legitimately offered the government $300 per acre for the fort property; this was twice the amount that the college would pay.

After each side laid out its position, a lively but short exchange ensued. Senator Collins defended his memorial by insisting that only the University of California had the same high standards as Whitman College, that the school did not have an enemy outside of its home city, and that critic Thompson Elliott was an "erratic" individual who had "flooded the country" with literature attacking both the missionary and the college honoring his memory. Collins hailed Marcus Whitman as a martyr, insisted that the college was centrally located so as to serve three states, and praised the group of prominent men who served as college overseers. A senator from eastern Washington talked about local conditions: "the opposition did not come from the great body of laboring men in Walla Walla but from a few of them who had been deceived by a half dozen contractors who were in fact making fools of these labor leaders."[126] Walla Wallans, he said, were prouder of their college than they were of their "beloved penitentiary." The memorial easily passed the Washington Senate by a vote of thirty-three to seven; some of the negative votes came from those who wanted a senate committee to investigate the dispute further.

On the same day, January 16, the college's friends in the Washington House rushed the memorial to a vote. There was a more vigorous opposition to the memorial in this body because a Democrat from Walla Walla, Francis A. Garrecht, delivered a thirty-minute oration against it. Serving as minority floor leader, Garrecht repeated all of the negative arguments heard in Walla Walla or in Congress; for example, he expounded to fellow representatives that the college wanted the memorial to pass so as to vindicate the Whitman-saved-Oregon story. Garrecht also made much of the fact that laborers, not college students, should utilize the fort property. More important, he charged that the school's leaders had joined local real-estate leaders in organizing a land grab. The Democrat accused the realtors of deliberately undervaluing the land; in turn, he said, the institution had agreed to sell some of the fort property to these fellow conspirators at the low price of $150 per acre.

Whitman's many supporters in the Washington House heatedly denied any underhanded deal, and one by one they answered Garrecht's accusations. One Tacoma legislator rebutted the charge that Whitman did not pay state taxes by pointing out that Gonzaga, a Roman Catholic school in Spokane, was wealthier than Whitman and that it had never paid state taxes even though it enjoyed no exemption in its charter.[127] Walker Moren of Yakima pleased all Whitman supporters by asserting that he and other Roman Catholics scattered across the state approved of the memorial and pointed out that only "the narrow minded individuals" in Walla Walla fought it.[128]

The House adopted the memorial by a large margin, eighty-three to twelve. Walla Wallans supporting Garrecht cried that the memorial was railroaded through the state legislature, warned that laboring men would remember the vote against them, and promised that "the real battleground" would be in the United States House of Representatives where they enjoyed support.[129] On the other hand, Hendrick and Whitman's bursar, Dorsey Hill, heard the debate in both houses and celebrated the sweeping victory. Hendrick summarized: "the discussion was rich; the best I ever heard." He thought it significant that Garrecht was the only Roman Catholic to vote no.[130]

Hendrick and Hill thanked those who had championed the memorial. The dean wrote Governor Marion E. Hay that he appreciated the governor's help in the college's "scrap with the 'bad eggs' from this city." In another letter he informed an alumnus that the University of Washington "boys . . . were of great assistance to us, in fact, they won the victory."[131]

Pleased with the state legislature's endorsement, Penrose traveled to Salem, and Hendrick journeyed to Boise. The administrators guided favorable memorials through the Oregon and Idaho state legislatures. The college assumed that these memorials would be crucial in the congressional debate over the Jones bill, for the documents meant that three states had recognized the importance of Marcus Whitman and the accomplishments of the college. Moreover, a newspaper account published a month after the memorial's passage stated that Washington legislators continually expressed enthusiasm for Whitman College.

After gaining the support of three state legislatures, the dean switched his efforts to Congress. Once more he persuaded allies to shower congressmen with letters endorsing the Jones bill. Penrose again enlisted the help of prominent easterners, including his cousin, Senator Boise Penrose. Two prominent Walla Walla businessmen reviewed this contest for the fort property: Frank W. Paine concluded that the college was combatting "speculators, bigots, false friends and fools;" John W. Langdon accused a few persons of wanting the school "smothered" despite the fact that thousands of regional citizens wished it well.[132] In his correspondence with congressmen, Hendrick complained about "vicious attacks" upon the Jones bill by "real estate speculators and prejudiced Roman Catholics who have succeeded in working all kinds of subterfuges to defeat this bill."[133]

The dean insisted that these two old opposition groups persuaded the local unions to join them in their fight against Whitman. He urged immediate passage of the legislation because the school was ready to start construction, but first the site needed to be determined.

Hendrick also feared that the American Federation of Labor might become a powerful foe if it embraced the Walla Walla Trades and Labor Council's position and worked to defeat the college in the House. Thus the dean wrote to AF of L president Samuel Gompers, summarizing the conflict and listing the college's regional contributions, all made without the use of tax money. The educator wanted the labor leader to know that Whitman did not denounce unions and that he could not comprehend why the local unions opposed it. He explained that the "liquor people" and some Walla Walla Roman Catholics had long been hostile.[134] Hendrick insisted that the school had diverse and deep regional support in its effort to gain the fort site: ninety percent of Walla Walla's population, three hundred businessmen, the Walla Walla Ministerial Union, a regional farmer's group, the Presbyterian General Assembly, three state legislatures, three governors, and the Washington Democratic State Executive Committee. To the dean's way of thinking, local laborers should join this list because they stood to benefit if Whitman erected $1,000,000 worth of new buildings.

In his struggle to get a favorable House vote, Hendrick encountered troubling obstacles. Friends in Washington, especially Senator Jones, Edward D. Baldwin (a former Whitman student who served as secretary to Congressman William Ellis of Pendleton), and Thomas Burke, who was energetically lobbying for the college, provided an accurate assessment of political conditions. They urged the dean to get a vote in the current Republican Congress. However, the bill needed to pass this vote. If it failed again it would be considered tainted and would have even less chance of passing in the new Congress scheduled to convene in April 1911.

These knowledgeable advisors also discussed the problems of getting bills onto the floor in the short session when many representatives battled for time to enact pet ones. Furthermore, political observers noted that currently there was on the House floor an unusual amount of political maneuvering and wrangling. Because of the cluttered schedule, the military affairs committee would not get a chance to report the Jones bill, so it would be necessary to introduce it in the session's last six days when the rules would be suspended. It would take an enthusiastic congressman to convince two-thirds of his colleagues to vote for his bill during the suspension. Baldwin and Ellis emphasized that if Poindexter "takes off his coat and pitches in,"[135] then there was a hope that the Jones bill would be considered in the session's chaotic last days. But the congressman refused. He repeatedly informed friends that he did not believe that the two-thirds vote could be mustered in this session because the bill had no more support now than it had when it was badly defeated in 1910. Hendrick again apologized to Poindexter for the "ignorance or clumsiness" in the management of the fort bill, pondered why the college did not have a friend to fight for it on the House floor, and pleaded with him to be the necessary leader for the "good of education and for the cause of Whitman College."[136]

Although Poindexter resisted the wooing of Hendrick and others, the college's allies prevailed upon House Speaker Joseph Cannon to allow the bill to be brought up at the end of the session under the suspension of the rules. This was a notable success, but other House members rejected appeals for help. Hendrick identified Brooklyn Democrat John J. Fitzgerald as the most vehement critic in the 1910 floor fight. The dean concluded that the Democrat still opposed the Jones bill because he was a Roman Catholic and that members of his faith in Walla Walla furnished him with negative stories about the college. Fitzgerald responded to Baldwin's entreaties by insisting that he opposed the government's giving land to private institutions or selling it at less than its market value. He also discredited the three state memorials and growled that he was now even more hostile to the Jones bill than he had been in 1910. Some notable Roman Catholics in the Pacific Northwest asked Fitzgerald to reconsider. Apparently he did not.

Early in 1911 Hendrick understood there was only a slight chance of a favorable House vote, but the college's friends prevailed upon him to return to Washington to lobby for the bill. Thus for about three weeks he visited congressional offices or huddled with allies and plotted strategy. The dean worked as intensely in Washington in 1911 as he had in 1910, but it was, as he feared, to no avail. The measure was not brought to a floor vote during what observers called "wild disorder." Hendrick explained the failure to newspaper reporters: "Owing to the unsettled condition of political affairs in the House, it was impossible to get consideration of the bill."[137] Penrose's history provides a fuller explanation. Speaker Cannon had agreed to a vote but because of the great confusion the member designated to introduce the bill was not recognized; thus, "the last chance for securing the passage of the bill had been lost."[138] Alumnus Baldwin gave a more precise account. He judged that the Jones bill was not the type that congressmen would "go out of their way to make one of the very favored bills to be taken from the mass in the rush . . . at the close."[139]

Some members of Washington's congressional delegation favored the reintroduction of the measure in the new session. The discouraged Hendrick disagreed. He replied that the school must not delay its building program, and accordingly he traveled from Washington, D.C. to New York, pushing a proposal to get a $100,000 library from the Carnegie Foundation and requesting a monetary gift from John D. Rockefeller's General Education Board.

Upon his arrival home in late March, Hendrick became embroiled in a brief but bitter conflict waged in local newspapers and on street corners. According to local newspapers, Hendrick had confided to an Iowa congressman that Walla Wallan Richard Johnson had for many years been "grafting the government on hay and grain contracts" and that the local union council was "dominated by brewers and saloon men."[140] The dean denied accusing Johnson of graft but did not rebut the other charge.

A few days after this public squabble, Hendrick informed overseers that Penrose and trustees agreed to abandon the struggle for the fort property and to build a set of buildings on the existing campus. The dean promised that he would energetically seek to complete the $1,000,000 endowment campaign by year's end. This would require him to raise $200,000 regionally and to find the rest among "the great educational funds of this country."[141]

On March 31 he issued a press statement for the trustees, summarizing the attempt to acquire the federal property. Hendrick reminded them that despite opposition most businessmen endorsed the effort. But, he boasted, "It is with pleasure . . . and with great satisfaction, that Whitman College realized that there was no one of any political faith or religion outside of Walla Walla, who raised his voice against the college project."[142] (Apparently the dean discounted the votes against the memorial delivered in the state legislature and Fitzgerald's opposition in Congress.) Hendrick also took pride in the fact that in the Pacific Northwest "there is an almost unanimous chorus of acknowledgment that we have here a great educational institution." The educator noted that some supporters believed that the proposed campus at the fort site would better serve Greater Whitman than its current site, but he insisted that the school could not delay its plans for two more years while attempting to secure the federal property. "Whitman College," he assured the trustees, "will make no further effort for the acquisition of the abandoned military reservation ... the incident is closed."

But the matter was not ended. In 1911 the federal government proposed selling the fort property; some of Whitman's supporters recommended that the school bid $300 or more an acre. The college refused to do so, but Hendrick admitted "that a great many of our friends say that we have been wrong in giving up the fight." The administrator stated that if the institution wanted to rejoin the contest, he would not personally participate because he had already spent so much "time and money and worry."[143] Although the defeated dean refused to push Whitman's case, he wrote letters attempting to prevent Richard Johnson and other critics from acquiring the contested property. In July the fort issue was important to Hendrick, Penrose, and their Whitman allies as they successfully worked to defeat old foe Thompson Elliott when he ran for mayor.

The fact that Senator Poindexter introduced a bill that would turn part of the fort property into "a national home for disabled and aged ... soldiers" made it much less likely that Whitman could ever obtain the site.[144] Perhaps the frustrating contest officially ended in September 1912, when Penrose announced that the school had no further interest in the government property and joined other Walla Wallans in requesting the government to re-establish the fort.[145]

Another Crisis Confronts the College

Stephen Penrose considered the time from the failure of the Jones bill in 1911 through the spring of 1912 to be one of the most difficult periods of his long presidency. As in the gloomy days of 1894–1895,

Whitman leaders again talked of removing the school to another city. In April 1911 Penrose presented the difficult financial prospects to benefactor D.K. Pearsons. The president acknowledged widespread local support in the dispute over the fort property but complained that contractors, saloonmen, labor unions, and especially local Catholics had defeated the college. School friends in Seattle, Portland, and Spokane, who had heard Penrose's gloomy assessment, advised him that the school should be moved to a city that would wholeheartedly support it. After furnishing this evidence to Pearsons, Penrose then asked if he should accept an offer from Spokane that included an eighty-acre campus site and $500,000 in cash if the school moved there.[146] Pearsons quickly responded that the school should never be moved and bluntly told Penrose "to settle down to business and stop building castles."[147]

While Penrose pondered the Spokane offer, Hendrick, who disliked his hesitation, urged a change of location. In a discouraging report to overseers, the dean revealed that since the failure of the fort bill he had been unable to find a single subscriber for the Greater Whitman campaign because potential donors "have come to believe that the antagonism of . . . Walla Walla to Whitman College does not warrant them in giving their to money to this institution in preference to one in their own community."[148] Hendrick explained to overseer Thomas Burke why he favored a new site. He emphasized that raising money for Greater Whitman had now become futile because potential donors disliked the hostility of some Walla Wallans to the college. Some wealthy men said they would not support the institution unless the town "assured that the . . . continuous opposition to the college shall definitely and positively cease, and that the city shall show in a substantial way their consciousness of the loss which they inflicted upon the institution [by the opposition] which they permitted to arise against the fort bill."[149] Outsiders told Hendrick they were surprised that there had not been a mass meeting of Walla Wallans supporting their school and denouncing its bitter foes. Such a massive demonstration of support would have "resulted in the withdrawal of this opposition." Hendrick agreed and confided that the college was embarrassed by its defeat in Congress and by the failure of Greater Whitman. The dean predicted that the college had no future in Walla Walla because relentless critics denounced any memorial to Marcus

Whitman, including the school. Hendrick admitted, however, that Whitman might regain outside support if Walla Wallans pledged a new college fund equal to the value of the army post. But he doubted that this would happen. Thus the hostility of a few townspeople and the criticism of the city by potential outside donors led the dean to urge overseers to transplant the college to more hospitable ground.

Hendrick also discussed reactions to the idea of removal. He stated that "the old pioneers" objected to it but thought such action appropriate if it were the only way to honor the missionary. The educator stated that Spokane leaders would raise money to attract the college because they realized that their city needed it to improve the city's culture.

Hendrick concluded, "I am pretty well convinced that nothing can be done locally and that if it is decided to leave the institution here, the Greater Whitman Movement must be abandoned and the college must shrink back into its original condition, and worse, of four years ago, which means a reintrenchment of its aims, desertion of its faculty, and practically starting over again with the probable consequence that it will go under sectarian control." Although Penrose was more optimistic than his colleague, he granted some of Hendrick's arguments. There was, for example, no doubt but that the defeat of the fort bill halted regional fund raising. And surely there was still local hostility to both the missionary and the college. Despite his frustration and anger, however, Penrose had not given up on Walla Wallans. He and some board members decided to seek completion of the endowment campaign by January 1, 1912, promising that if this were done the college would remain at its old site. Walla Wallans hailed this decision and some promised to contribute $10,000 for the school's immediate financial requirements. Most of the community clearly wanted the school to remain. An editor argued that moving the college would destroy it, "as the entire spirit of the founder would be lost, and the memories and traditions surrounding the institution would be desecrated."[150]

Hendrick, who had urged "that the educational interests of the Northwest would be best served by the removal of Whitman College to Spokane," disagreed with the decision not to move and resigned from the college in October. Few people who knew him were surprised. Since the failure of the Jones bill in April, rumors of the dean's resignation had swept the campus and town. His friends hoped that the vital leader would not depart because he had fathered the Greater Whitman plan, had raised about $500,000 to attain it, and had brought prominent men to the board of overseers, and because they thought he possessed the energy necessary to attain Greater Whitman early in 1912.[151]

Although many people speculated about Hendrick's motivation, the college and the city press never offered reasons for his resignation. The inability to acquire the fort property and the decision to reject a move to Spokane seemed the basic explanations. But a third factor was Hendrick's desire to pursue a business career. While serving as dean he had been associated with several businesses. In the summer of 1911 he became involved in a much bigger adventure when he joined overseer Wayne Darlington in establishing a manufacturing plant in Portland. It would produce "lionite," an inexpensive explosive. After resigning, Hendrick moved to the Rose City.

In 1914 Penrose explained his version of Hendrick's departure: "He has a mercurial nature derived, I think, from his Scotch Irish ancestry. It seems to me that every now and then his Celtic temperament shows itself.... He is better in a winning game and does not stand discouragement or defeat well. Our failure to secure the Army Post took the heart out of him, and I think that is a good deal of the reason why he seemed soon after to peter out."[152]

Trustees failed to dissuade Archer Hendrick from resigning but convinced him to serve as an overseer. (Those associated with the college knew that Hendrick's nine years of service as teacher and dean were more valuable than had been Eaton's three years as president.) As a professor, dean, and spokesman, Hendrick had made his mark. The trustees acknowledged his many contributions, especially the Greater Whitman proposal. In a resolution the board wrote that "he was persuaded to take in charge a movement for the strengthening and enlarging of the college, and in this work showed remarkable originality, boldness, and resourcefulness."[153] While the board acknowledged his intelligence, character, and energy, some faculty members, who detested his power, probably expressed pleasure over his departure. Even Penrose may have been relieved by his resignation because some overseers preferred Hendrick's leadership to his own. The president appreciated the dean's energy, imagination, enthusiasm, and fund-raising abilities and always credited him with bringing important persons onto the board of overseers. Nevertheless, Penrose complained that Hendrick's Greater Whitman movement had added to the college's debt. A few years later in a letter of recommendation, Penrose acknowledged the former dean's skills when Hendrick successfully applied for the presidency of the University of Nevada.

Hendrick's departure did not immediately kill Greater Whitman, for Penrose asked overseers to allow him to shed his presidential duties and serve as fund raiser. It was absolutely necessary to do this because the Greater Whitman pledges totaling some $600,000 were only payable after the total goal had been achieved. Thus for several weeks Penrose traveled to both coasts seeking wealthy donors. Portlanders who had subscribed to the Greater Whitman campaign assured him that they would continue to befriend the college even if it moved to Spokane. Penrose emphasized to potential contributors that Greater Whitman needed about $400,000 and that the plan had been modified. The focus was now on a liberal arts college with rigorous standards and an emphasis on the pure sciences. The president explained that he would not attempt to realize the dean's "plan for a great school of technology" modeled after MIT.[154] He would not attempt to establish "a great school of technology in place of the original college," nor would he minimize the traditional curriculum.

Penrose was optimistic about his efforts, but a rejection of his proposal to the General Education Board changed everything. The foundation bluntly told him that the school must pay its large debt before it would donate money. By early February 1912 Penrose resolved that the school must abandon the campaign for Greater Whitman in favor of a more modest drive to eliminate the school's $200,000 debt. Chester Maxey later explained, correctly, that this switch meant that the "Greater Whitman project was laid to its final rest."[155] Student body president Paul Garrett observed: "Whitman has declined to become large and popular that she might remain small and great."[156]

The inability of Penrose to raise the endowment apparently convinced some Spokane businessmen to stir up their efforts to attract Whitman. Aubrey L. White, for instance, entered into confidential negotiations with Penrose. A February 1912 newspaper report stated that a group of unnamed Spokanites offered a campus site (probably

Fort George Wright), the payment of moving expenses and all college debts, and the establishment of an endowment fund of $500,000. Even if this rumored offer was not valid, obviously Spokane desired a college. In 1914 it would attract Whitworth College, a Presbyterian school, away from Tacoma. According to Maxey the Spokane men who wanted to secure Whitman were the same who found the funds to move Whitworth.

Just after the public learned that outsiders had made a proposal to attract Whitman, Penrose launched an effort to cover the nagging college debt. He assumed that if the community saw how important the institution was to the city, then its leaders would work to retain it. The president demonstrated leadership by publishing the school's financial standing. In his report he stressed that since 1895 Whitman had spent more than $1,240,000, mostly for salaries, buildings, and equipment; furthermore, students spent an additional $510,000. During these same seventeen years the college had received about $375,000 from residents of the region outside of Walla Walla. Townspeople had given about $86,000, with the Reynolds, Baker, and Ankeny families providing the largest gifts. Whitman's underpaid faculty had donated nearly $12,000. Penrose knew that few readers understood college finance. Thus he explained why there was a debt: the school's expansion meant that it had had to borrow local money to pay for land, buildings, and equipment that would "maintain the college at a high degree of efficiency."[157] Penrose then addressed the debt issue: the school did not make an annual appeal to its friends to pay current expenses because "an institution which is always begging retards its own growth and wears out its friends." The college had elected to build a reputation and then raise money to cover its debt. Finally, the president emphasized that tuition income covered only about one-sixth of the actual education cost. Because the institution did not receive tax money, it had to raise the rest of the funds from private sources.

Penrose rarely publicized the sources from which Whitman borrowed, but he later revealed that the prime lender was Levi Ankeny, who personally held notes worth $33,000. Ankeny's First National Bank held another $35,000. The president considered the banker's role "indispensible in Whitman's long process of development."[158] Penrose hoped that if he presented the college's economic conditions, community leaders would soon propose a plan to pay the $200,000 debt. Their failure to act discouraged him. By March he was pessimistic: "I doubt whether the Walla Walla people will do what we have asked them to do, and in that case I shall favor going to Spokane, where a very real and splendid offer and opening await us."[159] Penrose confidentially explained to close friends the advantages and disadvantages of a move to Spokane. For the school it would mean a large endowment, a suitable campus, the support of millionaires, and the advantage of being in "a town which is alive and enterprising, where the people pull together, and where a spirit of energy is in the air."[160] He also argued that there was a historic reason for moving to Spokane in that the school would be located near the Cushing Eells mission site. But the president worried about moving to a large city, warning that Whitman "might become a city college and unable to hold our present ideals."

In May Penrose's gloom lifted when Walla Wallans launched a new campaign to save their school. That month Congregational minister Raymond C. Brooks spurred Whitman's friends to take action. A popular minister, an active Whitman trustee, and a part-time Whit-

The Whitman Conservatory of Music (now called the Hall of Music) was completed in 1910, the only campus structure built during the Greater Whitman era. Designed by Ellis Lawrence and costing about $50,000 from funds donated by D.K. Pearsons, the handsome building contained studios, offices, a large lobby, McDowell Hall (a small concert hall), and practice rooms. It stands on the site of the original Whitman Seminary building.

man professor, Brooks enjoyed enormous community support. His emotional sermon, "The Crisis in Whitman College," moved his listeners and those who read it in the local newspapers. In this sermon, designed to win immediate financial support for the beleaguered college, Brooks recalled its history, underscoring the sacrifices of Cushing Eells and others who financed it in the troubled early days. Brooks also elaborated on many points made in Penrose's sober financial report; for example, "To every college worthy of the name either a permanent endowment or an annual subsidy is an indispensable necessity, a matter of life or death." He showed that in no collegiate institution could a student's tuition cover all actual costs. Brooks sympathized with the reasons why the college had accumulated a debt and warned that unless the debt was paid by the June commencement, Whitman would not open in September 1912.

The clergyman bluntly stated that the desperate financial situation meant that the college had to make one of three choices: it could declare bankruptcy and close; it could relocate in Spokane; or it could launch a drive to raise $200,000 locally with the school's promise that if this were accomplished it would remain in Walla Walla. Brooks discussed each option, acknowledging that "there has been much short-sighted and deplorable opposition which has helped to bring about the present embarrassing situation." The minister assumed that most citizens favored the third alternative and thus would generously contribute to the vital institution. Brooks argued that "Whitman College is the most important asset Walla Walla possessed or is ever likely to possess" and that its loss would be deplorable. He then appealed to the congregation: "Permit the dauntless heroism of Marcus Whitman, the lofty, simple, heroic devotion of Cushing Eells to stir your hearts today that we may worthily enter into their labors and put as fine devotion and as genuine sacrifice into the present Whitman as went into its beginning." He asked emotionally: "Shall Whitman College live or shall it die?" Brooks then reminded his congregation that other communities had carried out costly enterprises, including the Seattle regrades (the city had moved hills to increase the downtown area). This same we-can-do-it spirit should be manifested by Walla Wallans as they struggled to save their college.

The sermon had the desired effect, for the aroused congregation voted to delay a new church building and turn over to Whitman the

The Reverend Raymond C. Brooks served Whitman as a professor of philosophy, an overseer, and a fund raiser. A good friend of Stephen Penrose, he was an enthusiastic spokesman for the college and for Christian education. Few Walla Wallans before the First World War did more for the school than Brooks.

subscriptions it had raised. Penrose stated that the church's donation of $60,000 was "a splendid act of self-sacrificing generosity which honored pastor and people."[161] The First Methodist Church also elected to set aside its building plans to help erase the school's debt.

Brooks' action launched a more energetic campaign to cover the debt. Shortly after his appeal, overseers issued a statement to the press alerting the public to the crisis. Indebtedness was a major reason for the failure of Greater Whitman; furthermore, the school was unable to pay all of the May faculty salaries. The board summarized the college's situation: Whitman had a fine campus, possessed valuable equipment, "gathered one of the most capable, loyal and enthusiastic faculties that can be found in any college," enrolled the region's most able students, and enjoyed a national reputation. But unless the debt of $225,000 was paid, the school would not open in the fall of 1912. The board acknowledged that a group of Spokane businessmen would propose to move the college if it closed. The board preferred to retain the college in Walla Walla because of "sentiment, tradition, and long association." The statement predicted a solid future for Whitman if it met this crisis because there were opportunities to raise an additional $500,000 by 1914. The board assumed that this money would come from two sources: those who had pledged to Greater Whitman and the General Education Board. This agency would be generous with Whitman after it balanced its books. So the college's future—in the short and long run—depended upon a campaign to cover its debts. The board also warned that if the city allowed "its greatest asset to perish," then potential investors and homeseekers would look elsewhere. Therefore, there should be wide public support for a fund drive. The school's leaders set a deadline of June 1 for making a decision to continue in Walla Walla.

Brook's emotional sermon and the board's sober statement fired immediate action. Businessmen, not Penrose, led the unusual campaign waged to eliminate the college debt. They selected an executive committee under the chairmanship of the Reverend Brooks and also chose ten captains, each of whom in turn assembled a team to work a section of town. Chester Maxey, who as a student participated in many rallies by singing in a college musical quartet, remembered the effort as "a high-pressure, almost hysterical debt-raising campaign."[162] Others disagreed. They thought that the month-long drive was an enjoyable and worthwhile community project. Fund raisers met with potential donors, held public meetings, and reported total contributions. The names of donors were not published until later. Walla Walla's two newspapers gave ample space to the teams, which, in two weeks, accumulated about $135,000, mostly in the form of subscriptions.

The executive committee, trying to raise the whole fund as soon as possible, broadened its effort. On May 28 a hundred members of Walla Walla's Commercial Club went by special train to Waitsburg, Prescott, Dayton, Starbuck, and Pomeroy. Accompanied by musicians (Prescott had a piccolo band), the excursionists marched down village streets, urging crowds to help save Whitman. Everywhere their speeches and personal appeals received a fair hearing. The train travelers enjoyed themselves—a barber chair was erected and victims received a limburger cheese shampoo, and a kangaroo court forced Walla Walla Mayor Andrew J. Gillis to gulp a soda pop in one minute's time. The trip was not only fun, it was also successful because tiny Dixie and other communities subscribed. Probably a Waitsburg attorney furnished the best explanation for this assistance: Whitman belonged to the region, not only to Walla Walla, and it deserved help.

The second action by the executive committee was a call upon Walla Walla women. Apparently the biggest contribution of these female volunteers resulted from a tag day. Many respected women, including Mrs. Penrose and faculty wives, joined chaperoned young women in taking positions in public buildings and streetcars or at busy intersections where they sold promotional tags (equivalent to modern campaign buttons or bumper stickers) for amounts ranging from ten cents to $1. This activity netted more than $1,000. Mrs. Max Baumeister explained why the women's committee worked for Whitman. She stressed that the town owed much to Dr. and Mrs. Penrose and that "The time is coming when college-bred men will rule the world." More specifically she wanted the college to remain in Walla Walla because local children benefitted from it.[163]

At a concluding rally held on June 15, campaigners compiled lists of donors and learned that they had raised about $212,000. It must have surprised Penrose to learn that his old opponent, Thompson Elliott, contributed a generous $3,000. Among the hundreds of donors were groups, including the Whitman faculty, which subscribed $1,300, and the Sharpstein Grade School, which gave about $5. Some supporters had simply switched their subscriptions from the defunct Greater Whitman list to the college debt fund. Chester Maxey wrote that some subscriptions went unpaid but added that "enough came in to stave off imminent disaster and keep the college in Walla Walla."[164] The *Bulletin* hailed the campaign as the "biggest attempt in Walla Walla." Mayor Gillis acknowledged the old city factionalism but emphasized that the campaign had demonstrated a remarkable "spirit of fellowship."[165] Penrose publically thanked the community during the baccalaureate service, explaining that the effort succeeded because of farsighted "farmers, businessmen, professional men, and private citizens." He promised that the college "will ever try through simpleness and faith, to exert an influence worthy of the efforts and the sacrifices."[166]

During the month-long drive the college received publicity as well as subscriptions from new supporters. The campaign also prompted considerable discussion about college financing. Many citizens wondered how the school had acquired such a large debt. Maxey later argued that "a very considerable amount of endowment income, tuition fees, and board and room charges had been diverted to the underwriting of the Greater Whitman Campaign."[167] Others also assumed a connection between the unsuccessful drive to fund a greater college and the accumulation of a crippling indebtedness. But Penrose disagreed. He pointed out that his school operated more economically than similar colleges and reiterated that the debt result- ed from the purchase of property, buildings, equipment, and books. Hendrick had correctly stated in 1911 that Greater Whitman had attracted more students, which rapidly increased the college debt. During the drive for subscriptions Penrose apparently did not criti- cize Hendrick for the financial problems, but in his history he stated that the "heavy debt" resulted from the dean's campaign for Greater Whitman.[168] During the campaign the weary president emphasized that he would not apologize for the debt; in fact, he snapped that regional citizens "should deem it a privilege and an honor to assist the college in its hour of need."[169] Penrose, however, did promise that no new departments—he had learned from the engineering program— would be added until the college possessed appropriate funds.[170]

Many fund raisers applauded Whitman's community influence. Mathematics professor Walter Bratton, for example, published a pa- per demonstrating Whitman's importance to Walla Walla's intellec- tual, social, and financial status. He pointed out that worthy families moved to the city and remained there because of the college, but he highlighted economics. Bratton calculated that students annually put about $200,000 into the local economy and noted that twenty-three faculty and administrative homes were a net addition because they were generally "built with resources brought with them . . . for facul- ty salaries have never been large enough to provide any margin for saving."[171] A colleague, English professor Norman Coleman, spoke on "The Moral Value of the College." He judged that comradeship and ideals "make a manly man"; furthermore, "both are available at Whitman . . . [and] not . . . in a larger university."[172]

The Reverend Brooks also championed small colleges. From his experiences, especially at Yale, he pronounced that students from "Whitman-type" institutions did better in graduate school than grad- uates from the larger universities. Serious students chose smaller col- leges, where they were much less likely to cram. Late in the campaign, the minister responded to a popular question: Why was it necessary to preserve Whitman when young people could enroll in a university, a college, or one of the normal schools operated by the state? Brooks said, "I believe that a college like Whitman, where the teachers are in close touch with the students and can use their influence for good upon them, can turn out more reliable citizens than a state institution where more than fifty per cent of the students are going to school for the fun they can have."[173]

Mayor Gillis revealed that he had moved to Walla Walla after hearing a Penrose lecture. The politician also praised Whitman's faculty: "The work of an educator ... goes on forever. And no faculty has ever given more than that of Whitman College. The character of its instructors has made that of the college."[174]

Alumni and students lauded their alma mater. One graduate stated that he and others owed an "immense obligation" to the college; students also appreciated the institution, partly because it sought to build character. The *Pioneer* rejoiced over the successful drive: "Whitman College will never die! She is destined to go on through the years turning out men and women of real stuff." And the student body president, who struggled with a $1,700 associated student debt, thanked Walla Wallans for "their many gifts, which had meant real sacrifice, and have thus made it possible for Whitman College to remain on the spot made historic by Marcus Whitman."[175] Chester Maxey, then a senior, wrote that the present campaign drew students and townsfolk "closer together," and he wished that the campaign had occurred in his freshman year so he could have become better acquainted with townspeople.[176]

And so the crisis passed. The community would have its college, the students would have instruction, and the relieved president and his family would enjoy summer camp on Puget Sound. From there Penrose wrote to an eastern friend that he was "absolutely lazy" and that "the pen is the last thing I wish to see."[177] In September he returned to campus and discovered that Walla Wallans took a greater interest in the college. "The raising of the debt seemed to have taken away the bitterness engendered by our efforts to secure the army post, and only friendliness has been manifested." He predicted a brighter future for his beloved institution, but events during the next dozen years would again dampen the educator's optimism.

8

The Closing of the Academy
And the Greek Decision

1909 – 1912

Between 1907 and 1912 Greater Whitman consumed more time than any other other educational policy matter, but there were two additional important matters decided in 1912. The less important in the long run was the decision to close Pearsons Academy; the other was to allow the Greek system.

Pearsons Academy had its defenders; it was far superior to most secondary institutions—public and private—in the Pacific Northwest. Its high standards and talented faculty gave the school an enviable reputation, for its graduates compiled excellent records at Whitman and elsewhere. But the academy created problems. College students did not like to mingle with youngsters. Faculty, who tired of disciplining and instructing these teenagers, referred back to Henry Pritchett's report, which had insisted that Whitman must either be a college or an amalgamation of college, secondary school, and conservatory. After the easterner's investigation in 1909, the college dropped the academy and conservatory from its college catalog and administered them independently. The academy was in the wooden College Hall (across from Memorial Hall), separate from the college.

Pearsons Academy ran a deficit, most observers reasoned, because it simply could not compete with the growing number of free high schools. Stephen Penrose tried to meet this competition by employing a competent headmaster, sending out a recruiter, improving class work in the sixth through eighth grades, and hiring a teacher of agriculture. However, these efforts failed because parents preferred to keep their children at home and enroll them in free schools.

In October 1911 Penrose wrote to D.K. Pearsons about the academy's status, recalling that he had always wanted it to be a part of "the educational development of the Northwest ... and that it was doing work which I do not think is surpassed, if it is equalled, by any high school in the Northwest."[1] The president then asked if the school should be run at a deficit. He emphasized that a decision on the academy was much more than educational policy because Pearsons had given money for a proposed academy building, and the school bore his name. The president explained to the philanthropist: "I do not like to win your consent to attaching your name to an institution and then let the institution be snuffed out." Thus the academy would continue operating at a deficit if Pearsons so desired, but the educator would prefer to spend the philanthropist's money on a new science building and name it for him. Pearsons immediately responded: "Do as you like and ask no question. Now you manage the academy just as you like and you will please me."[2]

Meanwhile, in November 1911, Dr. Frederick M. DeForest, the capable headmaster of Pearsons Academy, reported to overseers that the school could be continued despite its declining enrollment, especially of girls. He complained that a recent increase in tuition of boarders from $234 to $400 per year and of day pupils from $40 to $75 per year had resulted in reduced class sizes. DeForest was sure that a cut in tuition, along with additional newspaper advertisements, would increase patronage. He predicted that his academy could compete with regional public high schools because there were parents seeking quality private education. DeForest made a strong case for the academy's advantages. "We are free," he maintained, "to study the individual and to look out for his personal needs. We are not bound by a rigid programme of studies provided by the authorities to which we must adhere.... We have discarded or left untried many of the fads and experiments which have tempted public school teachers and even state boards of education." DeForest insisted that the "secondary pupil is not so much to acquire knowledge as he is to learn to think and to prepare himself for the acquisition of knowledge." Thus Pearsons Academy, which had recently introduced four new courses in agricultural studies, still offered a limited curriculum and not "a smattering of subjects" because "we believe ... that for our purposes it is better to shoot with a rifle than with a shotgun."

Despite his eloquent plea and the fact that the academy had operated for nearly half a century, Whitman boards voted to close it.
Board members feared that the institution would never balance its
books. The college faced multiple financial problems, and the academy was a significant one of these. Dean Archer Hendrick disliked the
decision, arguing that to drop the institution would be "a grievous
mistake" because most of its graduates continued at Whitman.[3] A
trustee agreed, generalizing that Pearsons Academy was nearly as
important as the college itself and deserved to be subsidized. But
Walla Walla High School and other competitors—both private and
public—favored the closure. Surely the Whitman faculty later questioned the decision to close Pearsons Academy after noting a decline
in the quality of students, especially in the foreign language classes.
College Hall, which had served as the home of the academy, soon fell
into disrepair. The *Pioneer* of April 12, 1918, joyfully reported that
this "piece of unsightly rubbish" was torn down but acknowledged
the structure's historical value. The writer added, "We feel that we
are superior to most colleges of the west because we have a history,"
one that gave students "righteous pride."

If, as Penrose announced, Whitman was a regional leader in shed-
ding its academy, it was not one of the first institutions to adopt the
Greek system. In 1912 overseers elected to allow fraternities and sororities to be a part of Whitman, a ruling that came after three years
of debate among the boards, administrators, faculty, students, alumni, and friends. More has been written on the establishment and early
struggles of the Greeks than on any other topic of the school's early
history. One explanation for this is that both Penrose and Chester
Maxey—enthusiastic fraternity men—wrote and spoke about this
story. Neither president, however, fully explained the 1912 decision.

There are several reasons for the emergence of the Greek system in
American colleges. The history of fraternities can be traced back to
the 1820s, but their great growth followed the Civil War. They spread
in large part because they filled an emotional and social need. Fraternities were important communities that, as historian Frederick
Rudolph concluded, "offered an escape from the monotony, dreari-
ness, and unpleasantness of the collegiate regimen."[4] Many institutions, such as the University of California, battled over the introduc-

tion of fraternities, and the Whitman community knew that at some point it, too, would join the contest. Thus friends and foes of the Greek system had a long time to stockpile ammunition.

During the years of Greater Whitman, local fraternities appeared. Some Whitman students had friends in fraternities and sororities at other institutions, including the University of Washington and Washington State College, and these students wanted similar chapters, in part, to provide a better social life through dances and parties. Penrose was a critical player, telling the campus community how important his Williams fraternity had been to him and asserting that when Whitman had a large enough enrollment it should establish the Greek system. With a growing student body in 1909, it seemed to students that the fraternity question should be addressed.

Another critical reason for the establishment of fraternities is that they solved the housing shortage. Whitman, like so many other institutions, lacked money for dormitories. Privately owned fraternity houses resolved the problem. Maxey explained that chaotic conditions in Billings Hall also promoted the Greek system. Because there was no compulsory residence rule, the men moved in and out of the dormitory whenever they chose. Some departed Billings because of tasteless meals, dirty rooms and halls, noise, and lack of furniture. Professor Norman Coleman, who had charge of the dormitory, blamed Toy, the Chinese cook, for some basic problems. The professor charged that the bedbugs and cockroaches that infested the hall came "from the kitchen and Toy's room"; furthermore, the cook depleted the building's limited hot water supply.[5] The college fumigated Billings but complaints persisted, including those from college men who did not find grade school boys to be congenial residents. Thus the older residents moved out of the dormitory and rented rooms in private homes and discussed forming either clubs or fraternities. These groups would create hospitable accommodations superior to the much-maligned dorm.

Meanwhile, on the other side of the campus, college women also denounced their living conditions. Because not all female students could be housed on campus, the school permitted women to move into approved private homes. A faculty report explained that "in some cases women students regard rooming with a private family as practical emancipation from college control with regard to study hours, chaperonage, . . . and more or less strict college regulation."[6] Because so many women left the dormitory for the freedom of private homes, the school lost income. Like the men, women living on and off the campus considered forming secret organizations.

The last factor, as Penrose and Maxey both explain, is that with Penrose and Hendrick so involved in the Greater Whitman plan, the school lacked close management. Enjoying more independence than usual, the women and men directly challenged authority.

A local sorority, Gamma Kappa, initiated action. The early history of this and other Whitman fraternal groups is hard to reclaim, but close research in the *Pioneer* during the period from 1900 to 1905 reveals that students formed several groups using Greek names. In 1906 the faculty investigated the matter and reported that it did not find a sorority.[7] The Gamma Kappas, which sponsored social events, later admitted that they were not honest with the investigators. They had lived up to their motto: "A gentle lie turneth away inquiry, and piety covereth a multitude of sinners."[8] In 1909 the *Pioneer* recognized "the only sorority at Whitman."[9] The faculty responded, finding that Gamma Kappa "has the character of a secret organization"; moreover, "it is the sense of the faculty that we do not approve of the organization of secret societies."[10] The group replied to the faculty that it had no "intention to form a society and that it did not intend to maintain a clique."[11]

In 1909 and 1910 male students confronted professors who worried about the growing rift over the fraternity issue. Grumbling about inadequate dormitories and a drab social life, some men formed the Illahee Club and Delta Phi Delta. Both groups wanted houses that would accommodate a few members and provide space for social activities. Partly to overcome faculty hostility, the charter of the Illahee Club included literary as well as social objectives.

Early in 1910 both of these local fraternities requested charters from the faculty but were refused because of low grades. The faculty, however, consented to revive their request for charters in the fall semester after these petitioners had an opportunity to improve their academic records. The students did just that. Apparently the teachers assumed that they would eventually charter these local fraternities, so they adopted rules for them, including one that required the organization's faculty member "to take an active interest in the club and to keep the faculty informed as to the character and efficiency of the club as an aid to good morals, etc."[12] The faculty actually sanctioned local sororities when it granted a charter to Gamma Kappa in March.

It is not clear why professors changed their minds about fraternal groups. Probably the Gamma Kappa experience made it clear that there was no way to prevent them from operating. Thus it seemed wiser to recognize them and regulate them than to let them operate illegally and uncontrolled. No doubt Penrose helped to bring about a faculty change. Realizing that this group was dubious, if not hostile, he ruled that the governing boards, not the faculty, would decide whether to admit fraternal groups. Thus for the first time social organizations would not be approved solely by the faculty, a decision that Chester Maxey later thought had been appropriate. The overseers chose to make the final decision. Although professors recognized local fraternities, a poll taken in 1912 demonstrated that several of them still disliked the 1910 decision.

President Penrose understood that many faculty members worried that the Whitman community would be shattered by elitist fraternities. He also knew that few overseers had been fraternity men, and that they had grave reservations about the Greeks. In his 1910 report to the overseers, he addressed the issue: "Though no fraternities have existed heretofore, carefully considered rules were adopted by the faculty at the beginning of the year under which these social clubs came into existence." Under these rules no group could pledge members before the end of the first semester, a faculty advisor must be in each group, and the fraternal organizations must maintain good scholarship and character. Penrose evaluated the national fraternity system, frankly acknowledging that at many colleges the fraternities presented "grave dangers." He cited "poor scholarship, idleness, dissipation, and actual immorality." Despite the fact that the record of college fraternities was "a shocking chapter in the history of American education," he explained that this sad account resulted from the "careless attitude of the colleges themselves and their faculties towards the social life of their students." The educator insisted that the colleges must be as concerned with a student's social life as it was with his or her scholarly life.

Having made the case against the Greeks, Penrose then presented their advantages. Using the example of his own fraternal experience, the president assured this audience (as well as others) that members and alumni of a chapter would have a positive impact upon younger men. Penrose added, "I believe that the fraternity affords a marked opportunity for the development of what I might call the educational continuity of an institution in that it serves to maintain continuously the interest of undergraduate and alumnus in the progressive life of the college." Surely this thought came from Penrose's experience as a student, professor, and alumnus of Williams with its influential fraternal life. The president explained that he wanted the alumni interested not only in the school's finances but also "in the social, moral, religious scholarly progress of the undergraduate student body." The Greek system could help attain this goal.

He repeated that the faculty, upperclass students, and alumni must work for higher scholarship and "a worthy culture." Penrose emphasized: "I should not want to allow fraternities to be established ... unless the faculty first of all recognized their responsibility in the matter and were disposed to remember it steadfastly." Thus the faculty should establish rules preventing the use of intoxicating liquors in fraternities and should revoke "the charter of any fraternity where drunkenness or immorality is tolerated."

Penrose stressed the attitude of students. He wrote that their sentiments were "the most powerful factor in the life of an educational institution. If fraternities will develop a sentiment which shall be for scholarship, fine culture, and noble character, they would be welcomed to the college. If not, they should be rigorously excluded."

Then the president made his recommendation: "I believe that the experiment is worth trying, particularly when we are well warned in advance of the dangers to be avoided." The college must not simply tolerate fraternities but must "watch them with unfailing interest and anxious solicitude."

The board of overseers, however, surprised Penrose by rejecting his recommendation to permit the fraternities even on an experimental basis. The board decided that the matter needed further study; thus three of the overseers, joined by two faculty members, formed a committee chaired by the Reverend Raymond Brooks to investigate the Greek system both nationally and locally.

In November 1910 this committee presented its lengthy report in answer to the question, "What should be the attitude of Whitman

College toward fraternities?" Realizing that this was a "difficult question of college administration," the committee provided a historical background, traditional arguments that had been made about fraternities and their impact on other colleges, and recommendations and regulations. This thorough report would be cited for years and borrowed by other schools. It contained a criticism that would prompt heated debate among Whitman groups: "the fraternity seriously threatens the life of the college because it fosters a class spirit which is undemocratic, un-American, and un-Christian."[13] The committee reported other troubling conclusions: in fraternities "men morally weak are confirmed in vicious habits," and independent men compiled better academic records than did the Greeks.

In making a case for fraternities it quoted President William DeWitt Hyde of Bowdoin—a leader who had considerable standing at Whitman and other small schools—as saying that "fraternities exert twenty times as much influence for good as . . . for evil." Hyde and others argued that the fraternities frequently advocated scholarship and morality. The committee also recognized the value of fraternity fellowship and the savings to colleges, which did not have to build expensive dormitories. The committee answered objections to the Greek system; in fact, it seemed to assume that the system was, as President David Starr Jordan of Stanford judged, "a permanent part of American college life," which would inevitably be approved at Whitman. Perhaps for this reason the committee championed national over local fraternities and provided regulations for fraternities if they were permitted. The committee, however, did not favor immediate approval. Instead, it recommended that overseers immediately build cottage-style dormitories—a type that had been adopted by the overseers two years earlier. If the dormitories could not be built, then the committee advised the college to "permit the establishment of chapters of good national fraternities."

Penrose's history mistakenly stated that this report ended the long debate over fraternities. While it aided the pro-fraternity group, the overseers did not immediately adopt its recommendation. The overseers delayed action probably because Archer Hendrick had convinced them to poll various groups about the Greek system. In his 1911 attempt to block the approval of fraternities, the dean (who disagreed with the president) launched his own investigation. Just after the fight in Congress over the fort property, he battled the proponents of the Greek system.

While Hendrick compiled data and opinions as ammunition for his position, the faculty sought ways to regulate the Greeks. In November 1910 the faculty had established new rules based upon the proposals of the Brooks committee. Late in 1910 the faculty chartered the Illahee Club and Beta Sigma, a sorority, and early in 1911 it sanctioned Delta Phi Delta, a fraternity. Now the school had two local sororities, including Gamma Kappa, and two local fraternities; each male group rented a house. In the spring of 1911 campus debate was lively. The faculty had grudgingly approved groups it distrusted; the president supported groups but insisted upon close regulation; the dean worked to influence the overseers against the Greek system; and the members of the four social groups assured everybody that they would live up to the school's highest ideals. Although nobody bothered to poll them, some students voiced strong opinions about the secret organizations. Everybody awaited the overseers' meeting in June. It must have struck some observers as odd that the small campus community could not resolve the fraternity challenge and that minimally informed outsiders, who made only two campus visits a year, would rule in this crucial matter.

In soliciting opinions about the Greek system during the spring of 1911, Hendrick did not conceal his own contempt. The regional press reported that he believed these new groups were "contrary to the principles for which the college stands" and were also "opposed to true democracy."[14] To a friend, Hendrick complained that colleges everywhere generally feared "offending the wishes of the student body."[15] He faulted the nation's faculties for an indifference to campus conditions and for an unwillingness to remedy them. Hendrick further charged that professors, as well as students, would cover up the misdeeds of fraternity men. He had seen this happen at the University of Toronto and, as an alumnus, he had warned its administration against ignoring a "crime" committed by a fraternity. Such lack of action by the administration, he argued, weakened his alma mater.

Hendrick polled the faculty, alumni, and college friends for their opinions on the "Greek letter societies." He asked about advantages and disadvantages and posed a controversial question: if the fraternities came to the campus, would it be more difficult "to teach the ideals of true democracy?" According to the surviving returns, twenty-one favored the Greeks, twenty-eight opposed them, and six were neutral. The faculty opposed by a vote of five to two and friends of the college by twelve to eight, but alumni voted in favor, twelve to eleven. The dean's poll was unscientific, but the campus was just as divided as the results indicated. The faculty response is the most instructive because faculty members had observed the local fraternities and knew something about Greeks on other campuses from information compiled by the Brooks committee. Two popular professors made the case against the Greeks. History professor William Lyman said that "the only advantage from the presence of such societies would be the gratification of a considerable number of students and the bringing of Whitman into the circle of colleges where such societies exist."[16] He continued: "The presence of fraternities would tend ... to the formation of cliques and a spirit of discrimination and rivalries which would impair college spirit and genuine, whole-hearted democracy." English professor Norman Coleman expressed another line. He criticized the adoption of Greek societies because the present student body was too small; also, students already had so many organizations and activities that "many of them have no leisure for continuous thought and study in their chosen lines of work."[17]

Professor James W. Cooper was not an enthusiastic champion of fraternities, but, like Penrose, he believed that if the school regulated them they could be of service. He pointed out that the two existing fraternities had improved the scholarship of members; on the other hand, he warned about "the danger of establishing a permanent caste spirit and petty rivalries."[18] One faculty member wrote that the fraternity houses provided better living conditions than Billings Hall because their members cared for property and developed "habits of cleanliness and orderliness, and a strong spirit of good fellowship." Librarian Arminda Fix met the often-expressed fear that the Greeks would establish cliques. She noted that students had always formed cliques and that the fraternal groups would "have a tendency to break up the very small select cliquish groups."[19] She also assumed that carefully controlled Greek societies would attract to Whitman good students who otherwise would attend schools with fraternities.

Probably mathematics professor Walter Bratton provided the answers that reflected the majority of faculty opinion. He called secret groups "an evil" and believed that the college could more likely reach its goals without fraternities and sororities than with them. He also was sorry that the adoption of the Greeks would mean "the loss to the Northwest of its one important non-fraternity college."[20] But Bratton was realistic: "It is however questionable whether it is possible for a college to keep all forms of such organizations out after it has reached numbers in excess of two or three hundred, and if we must have them it seems to me advisable to arrange for their entrance under the best conditions for effective cooperation and control by the faculty." He also advocated national over local fraternities.

To get more information for the final decision on the Greeks, Archer Hendrick wrote to several colleges and to individuals about their experiences. The few letters and questionnaires he received covered most of the arguments ever advanced in the endless debate over fraternities. Meanwhile, the dean, who saw a choice between dormitories and fraternity houses as relevant to discussing the Greek system, wrote to several schools about their dormitory policy, especially how they kept them filled.

Hendrick did not complete his study of fraternities for the overseers. In June 1911 he simply summarized his findings and restated the problem: "We are having some difficulty making up our minds whether to admit fraternities, and if we determine to admit them upon what terms."[21]

At the June 1911 overseers' meeting, Penrose affirmed that the local fraternities currently promoted scholarship and the Whitman spirit. But some board members still remained unconvinced. Dr. Park Weed Willis was a vocal opponent, insisting that the fraternities "will be like Jim Hill Mustard once they get started, it will be impossible to get rid of them, and our institution will be more democratic, truer to its traditions, and more in correspondence with western ideas of cordiality without fraternities." Professor Louis Anderson disagreed. He favored immediate recognition and warned that some of the best students had informed him that they would transfer if the school banned fraternities. Raymond Brooks, a cautious spokesman for the secret groups, argued that the faculty, which had approved of the four local fraternities, was really in a better position to judge their value than the overseers. However, the board reiterated that it would decide the matter and then probably angered all the Greeks and many

Dr. Park Weed Willis received his undergraduate degree from Whitman in 1891 and his medical degree from the University of Pennsylvania. He was one of the school's most dedicated trustees and a staunch supporter of Stephen Penrose, but in 1911 he opposed the president on the issue of the Greek system.

others by placing the fraternities on probation for a year, restricting their membership to current numbers, and postponing a ruling on their admittance until the following year. Probably the overseers hoped that Greater Whitman would still be funded and that its dormitories, divided into vertical sections, would serve all housing needs. If this happened, the four existing secret groups would be banished.

Following the overseers' meeting the fraternity controversy simmered; in 1912 it flared again when the overseers voted to recognize the groups and revised the rules regulating them, as had been proposed by the Brooks committee in 1910.[22] Two factors influenced the overseers' decision. In June it was obvious that the school would not soon have money for dormitories; furthermore, Hendrick, the archfoe of the fraternity system, had resigned. He might have won another delay before recognition, but surely the Greek system pushed by Penrose eventually would have been adopted.

Everyone realized that the overseers' favorable decision had significant consequences. During the next dozen years the Greeks would come to dominate Whitman's social and political life as they had at dozens of other campuses. This influence had been predicted during the period from 1909 to 1912 as the Whitman community argued the merits of secret groups. And the issues of that debate continue more than eighty years later.

9

The Maturing College

1913 – 1917

In the period from 1913 to 1917 money problems continued to nag Stephen Penrose. The old problem of a small endowment meant deficits, an underpaid faculty, and an inability to expand the curriculum or construct buildings. In 1913, however, it seemed that the college soon would be freed from its financial woes because the Rockefeller Fund of the General Education Board (GEB) finally provided a matching grant. For years Penrose, Archer Hendrick, and others had called upon or written to the GEB headquarters in New York City seeking financial assistance. Whitman's successful debt-campaign drive and a proposal aimed at establishing an endowment finally convinced the GEB of the applicant's strength, and it awarded $125,000 on condition that the college raise $375,000 by June 30, 1914. Penrose rejoiced over this offer, informing the GEB that "it lifted a great load from my heart"[1] and telling overseers that "it is the first gift made to any institution west of the Rocky Mountains."

Penrose had prepared for the financial challenge he now faced. He had often told potential donors about his GEB application and had received hearty assurances of assistance once its match had been offered. Now in 1913 and 1914, fund raiser Raymond Brooks and Penrose called upon everyone who had pledged to Greater Whitman and requested that they switch their old pledges to the new matching campaign for the endowment. Penrose explained their technique: "Without sacrificing their duties as preacher and teacher, the two men together visited all the subscribers to the Hendrick campaign, leaving Walla Walla on Monday night and returning on Friday morning, in order that Mr. Penrose might teach his Friday and Saturday classes in philosophy and Dr. Brooks might prepare for his regular Sunday services."[2] The campaigners accumulated about $69,000 in the East and about $326,000 in the West. Walla Wallans were not solicited because in 1912 they had subscribed $213,000 to the debt campaign. It was a tribute to Penrose and his college that Pacific Northwest businessmen donated to an out-of-town institution. Clearly, many saw Whitman as the region's best small college and one that might become nationally recognized.

During the 1913 campaign a leader from Whitworth College (which was then located in Tacoma) proposed a merger to Penrose, who immediately asked the GEB if Whitworth's assets could be part of the matching campaign. The organization approved: "The union of the Congregationalists and Presbyterians in the support of Whitman College seems to be a very desirable thing. You could then have two strong institutions in the state, Whitman for the eastern end . . . and the State University for the western end."[3] Penrose, too, advocated the union. "I scarcely dare hope, Whitworth College should wisely decide to seek amalgamation with Whitman."[4] Whitworth, however, maintained its independence and soon moved to Spokane.

If Whitman could have immediately received the $513,000 resulting from this matching campaign it would have had a noticeable impact. Such funds would have paid for campus construction, curriculum enrichment, better salaries, and other desirable goals. Penrose rightly argued that a successful fund drive would have brought additional financial contributions. But such was not to be. Whitman did not receive the full fund from the matching grant until 1919 because the GEB insisted upon Whitman's collecting money, not subscriptions, and paying off all of its debt. The college even sold some property in an unsuccessful attempt to pay its bills.

Thus the shortage of money again retarded the college's growth, and the all-too-familiar deficit problem arose again. But restricted growth suited the temperament of the overseers, a group chastened by the Greater Whitman experience. Seeking direction, the overseers in November 1912 heard two papers on the topic "The Proper Scope of Whitman College." Both presenters used Williams as a model. One speaker, overseer Abbot L. Mills, president of the First National

Bank of Portland, was a graduate and overseer of Harvard. He argued that Whitman should seek to be a small distinguished college rather than a large university because it lacked funds for such a transformation; furthermore, he thought that "more big men in proportion to attendance are turned out from the small colleges than from the big universities." At the smaller institutions, and not at Harvard, the student was in closer relationship with distinguished teachers and more subject to their influence. Mills again emphasized that it was "visionary to attempt to make Whitman College into a great University of the Northwest," but he predicted that it could become a "first-class college with the highest standards and ideals" similar to those of superior small eastern colleges. The second speaker, John P. Congdon, a civil engineer from Boise, reminded overseers that Whitman had the tradition, the curriculum, and the location to be the Williams of the West. He stated: "Theodore Roosevelt is reported to have once said that the mountain country of the Northwest would produce the strongest men in our public life, and if it does, it will need the help of some institution of the Williams type."

There was a spirited debate over Whitman's future mission. Although the arguments went unreported, no doubt Whitman's overseers opposed reintroducing a Yale or MIT model. The goal of emulating Williams was challenge enough.

In 1914 President Penrose stated that the college was small and "must grow slowly." But it grew more slowly than he hoped; for example, the music building was the only new campus building erected between 1910 and 1923. The 1914 college catalog no longer mentioned a fund-raising drive for $2,000,000 or the establishment "of superior courses in engineering." The engineering program simply disappeared.

Launched in 1908 with only rudimentary offerings in drawing and allied courses, engineering had been strengthened so that by 1911 it made up a special group in the curriculum. It was equal on paper to the three curriculum groups into which the other academic departments had been divided: Group I, philosophy, history, and political science; Group II, language and literature; and Group III, mathematics and science. Engineering had its own dean, Wayne Darlington, and the 1913 catalog stated that the engineering courses "are designed to prepare a student thoroughly for practical work in civil, mechanical, electrical, or mining engineering." But students enrolled in this program still had to take many liberal arts classes, and the faculty reminded them that they were a part of the college, not in a separate and superior program. During the summer vacations after their sophomore and junior years, engineering students spent time performing field work, including some time in an industrial plant. It is not clear how many students enrolled in such courses as structural engineering, power plants, and civil engineering, or in the allied program offering courses in applied mathematics and drawing. But three men taught this engineering program, and the 1913 catalog listed only one engineering major.

Because of poor enrollments, Penrose in June 1914 reported that the "proposed Engineering department had been dropped and that students could no longer complete an engineering degree." Penrose used the word "proposed" because the complete curriculum had never been taught. He explained his decision to terminate the engineering program: "We may frankly admit that it was a mistake to project upon so large a scale such technical work," and he claimed that there was a national problem because "engineering education is at the present time greatly overdone."[5] He interpreted this decision as an "honest and open course." A professor further clarified the matter: the college could not compete with state university engineering programs which had superior facilities and no tuition fees.

Another type of practical education replaced engineering. For years the school had recognized that many potential students sought degrees in economics and business. In 1913 Portlander Hollon Parker donated $50,000 to fund such a program. Meanwhile Professor Charles G. Haines requested the establishment of an economics department. He reasoned that the school offered English and music majors that appealed to women; it needed a program in economics that would have a similar appeal to men. Whitman men, he suggested, transferred because they demanded more courses in economics. Haines advocated classes in accounting, farm management, and marketing, so as to serve the community. In 1913 Whitman offered only a modest economics program—principles and money and banking—as part of the political science program. Haines, however, predicted that the economics program would attract so many students that it would pay for itself.

With a student demand for the major and with a generous donation, the college in 1914 opened a department of economics and business. Two faculty members taught a wide variety of courses, including economic and industrial history, commercial geography, business
organization and finance, accounting, economics of agriculture,
commercial law, and even principles of sociology. Penrose hoped that
this new department would "be a means of attracting... many young
men who wish to fit themselves in a most thorough way for the higher
walks of business and professional life."[6]

Business proved to be much more attractive than engineering.
This practical curriculum immediately recorded good enrollments; in
1917 it had become the second most popular major behind English,
and those majoring in it included two women.

Another addition to the curriculum was the history of art. Penrose
applauded this addition because a school that enrolled fifty percent
women should pay attention "to the artistic side of life." He urged
overseers to support this new teaching emphasis. "The life of Whitman College, like the life of the pioneers, has been bare of beauty or of
art. It has practically no painting, sculpture, statuary, or other art
forms to quicken the imagination of our students and to lift their
minds above the commonplace."[7]

Realizing that there was no hope of financing a new science building, the college—responding to the pleas from science professors for
space—converted Billings Hall from a dormitory to a hall of science.
The physics department was on the first floor, biology on the second,
and chemistry on the third. Penrose boasted that the departments
now had well-equipped laboratories and rooms, and that this new
facility attracted greater student interest in the sciences. Billings Hall,
however, was a poor substitute for the modern building that Penrose
had long planned. Once again the shortage of money frustrated him.
It was a great disappointment for him and many others to abandon
the modern science buildings in the Greater Whitman proposal and
come to accept a converted dormitory as the center for the important
science curriculum. And Billings Hall was not to be a temporary science building as Penrose predicted. It lasted for about fifty years.

The death of Greater Whitman not only meant the end of engineering and the conversion of Billings Hall, it also forced Penrose to
lower his educational sights in other ways. Under the Greater Whit-

man scheme, especially if relocated on the old fort site, Whitman would have the resources of a major regional college. Its traditional departments and impressive array of technical courses would have attracted students and supporters. In 1913 Penrose had to discard such a grand vision and modify his goals to match a new reality. In that year he advocated programs that would benefit the region. He favored establishing a department of education so as to influence public schools in three states. The educator emphasized that because Whitman "stands apart from the system of education, [and] has no connection politically with them," it could advantageously participate in the resolution of school problems. Whitman could serve by sending out more talented public teachers, and its education director would become "a leader in educational progress." The president saw some urgency in this because "The life of a people is determined in the last analysis by its system of education," and he warned about "the present stage of our semi-barbarous civilization."

But most of Penrose's message to overseers was aimed not at the states but at Walla Walla and the countryside within a fifty-mile radius. The leader saw that in many college towns "the faculty held themselves superior to the people, and the students rendered themselves obnoxious to the townspeople by acts of lawlessness." Whitman, however, provided assistance to Walla Wallans through its reference library, the free use of its athletic fields, "the lending of fair and impartial officials for high school athletic contests," and the distinguished archaeology lectures. Professors of political science and German prepared printed bibliographies for public school teachers. Penrose proposed even more diverse ways that the college could aid the town: scientists could analyze local water, asphalt, lubricating oils, orchard sprays, road surfaces, and fruit pests. The faculty might offer extension courses in literature, chemistry, political science, and other fields. They also could help churches attain their missions.

The president thought the institution also had an obligation to the rural area. To be of service to farm families, it would need to accumulate a rural extension fund. "A college," he judged, "may be likened to a reservoir, whose waters, as through irrigation ditches, may be conducted under wise direction to making desert places fruitful." The educator asserted that an agricultural college should take care of "crops and stock," and Whitman-type colleges had the responsibility "for the care of parents and their children." He set lofty goals: "Whatever Whitman can do to improve life, to modify environment, to ennoble ideals, to lift thought, . . . to develop the sense of brotherhood and fairness and justice, it will render cheerfully and gladly." To attain such aims in farm areas, he said his professors could promote religion and the liberal arts, including history and philosophy, at schools, farmers' unions, or churches. The faculty could also teach practical courses: farm management, bookkeeping, marketing, and chemical testing of fruit sprays. Penrose summarized: "We shall be able to test the purity of food, the germinal power of . . . grain, the chemical constitutes of the soil, the purity of water, and the healthfulness of the environment [for] children."

The president sent a copy of this report to the GEB thinking it might fund his resourceful plan to instruct farmers and townspeople. A GEB official approved his general concept but feared that it was too ambitious for the underfinanced college. In 1914 Penrose responded that he did not expect to implement his program all at once. He insisted that "The all important thing is that Whitman should devote its attention and strength to its internal work," but he thought that the "overseers should hear a proposal [that] would appeal to their imaginations." The leader insisted that by expending only a few hundred dollars the institution could be of "real service to the farmers." The overseers, however, considered his plan to be too idealistic and too expensive.

Penrose demonstrated his practical side in defending extension courses. He understood that some businessmen liked his proposed "community extension work" more than the college's curriculum. "It was such men, partly," he explained, "that I had in view when I wrote the report." He added, "If I can get fifty thousand dollars as an endowment fund for such extension work from men who would not give to the legitimate work of the college itself, I feel that we shall be that much to the good." He maintained that extension courses would augment inadequate faculty salaries.

The college could not fund classes beyond Walla Walla, but, prior to the First World War, it increased the offerings to townspeople. The "extension course" section of the catalog listed a diverse curriculum: English literature (including social problems in contemporary drama), elementary French, history of art, applied mathematics, Pacific

The official 1914 photograph of President Stephen B.L. Penrose. He was Whitman College's most important president and one of the Pacific Northwest's most respected educators.

Northwest history, and tree study. Although the faculty taught in this program as an overload, they welcomed the $35 they received from each class. Any amount helped them pay their creditors.

But Penrose did not design his "external program" to enhance faculty income. He wanted it to serve about the same purposes as modern community colleges, which seek to provide practical and cultural classes. (Penrose's understanding of the need to improve the quality of rural life dated from his earlier years as a Dayton minister.)

Although board members failed to share their leader's concern for farmers, they generally cooperated with him. Apparently the two-board system worked well. The nine members of the board of trustees, most of whom were Walla Wallans, frequently met and carried out prescribed duties, including hiring and paying the faculty and staff, managing the school's property (many donated farms and lots), granting scholarships and loans, purchasing equipment and supplies, approving and auditing budgets, ratifying decisions of the overseers, employing students (who received twenty-five cents an hour to grade physics and German papers), and publicizing the school (regional high schools received the *Pioneer*).

The board of overseers was the more prestigious board with about fifty notable men from the Pacific Northwest serving four-year terms. This board annually debated educational policy (settling the thorny fraternity issue, for example). The overseers also heard the reports of the president, the deans, the faculty, and others. The overseers' minutes provide many more details about the college's history than do those of the trustees.

Although the record of the faculty is less complete, it is obvious that no group suffered more from the collapse of Greater Whitman. The proposal had held out the prospect of a larger teacher corps and of improved salaries. Neither was to be. In 1908 Professor of English Norman Coleman complained that he had lowered his academic standards because he had to teach some of Dean Hendrick's classes as well as his own and that economic necessity forced him to spend an exhausting summer as a Spokane roofer. (Perhaps his severe academic and financial difficulties made him more sympathetic with the faculty when he became president of Reed College in Portland, Oregon.)

Soon after Penrose abandoned Greater Whitman, Coleman's colleagues met and talked about their plight. In late 1912 chemistry professor Robert H. Clark spoke to overseers on behalf of the faculty. He acknowledged the need for a new science building and a heating plant, but he judged that a more important requirement was "a suitable endowment to enable the college to pay just and honest salaries to its faculty." He discussed the professors' poverty, revealing that one colleague who had taught at Whitman for fifteen years had been forced to borrow for all but two of those years. Clark emphasized: "This professor is not at all extravagant, doesn't smoke, waste money on tennis balls—in fact doesn't know what fun is—lives most economically, and yet what is he coming to in his old age?" Clark answered that his colleague would go to the poorhouse or be dependent upon his children and friends. He continued that those who had prepared themselves for teaching had lost earning power, had no funds to attend meetings or travel to major libraries, and could not even purchase books to keep abreast of their teaching fields.

To strengthen his case, the chemist compared the salaries of Walla Walla ministers with those of the Whitman faculty and concluded that the professors were being paid "just about one-half what the moderately successful Christian minister is being paid." He grumbled that he had been told in Worcester that the cost of living in Walla Walla was less, but he discovered that board, laundry, barbering, clothing, and railroad fares were more expensive in his new hometown. The protester acknowledged that he found vegetables to be cheaper, but he said that he was not a vegetarian and added that "it may be that you can find a chemist that is, but I'll guarantee that you will have an old woman." Clark proposed that faculty salaries should be jumped to a living wage of $2,500 and that money for this purpose could be found by a campaign similar to the one that eliminated the college debt. Such action must be pursued, Clark insisted, because "a college ... is made by the men it has on its faculty and not by the buildings it possesses."

The overseers' minutes note a discussion following Clark's presentation but no remedial action. Salaries remained static, and Clark held on for a few more years. Penrose sympathized with the chemist's ideas and added that the faculty was badly overworked. In 1913 he anticipated an immediate boost of the endowment from the General Education Board, but that money, much to his and the faculty's disappointment, did not come. Meanwhile Dean Walter Bratton also urged salary increases because professors could not attend meetings of professional associations, visit other institutions during summer vacations, or purchase scholarly literature. The faculty allied with him when he judged that salary improvement was "the greatest need of the college."[8]

Penrose kept the pay issue before the governing boards; in 1913 he stated that salaries of these "devoted and sadly underpaid servants" should soon be increased to $2,000 and then gradually boosted to $2,500. Two years later he reported to the board of overseers that the GEB money was still in the distance and that the faculty had immediate financial needs:

The important need of the college now, as always, is for increased endowment for the payment of more decent salaries to ... the faculty. The astonishing thing in the history of Whitman College is the way in which able men and women have stood by it through poverty and want, teaching splendidly upon meager salaries, and exerting a personal influence which has made the college what it is. While you must admire this devotion, you must not rest content to let such poverty continue always.

The president pointed out that men who had come to the college twenty years earlier at a salary of $1,000 now only received $1,800. He warned the overseers not to accept this depressing situation. But apparently board members counted upon the faculty to survive, for salaries remained abysmal.

Besides poor compensation the professors suffered from onerous teaching loads. In 1913 faculty members reported to the overseers about teaching conditions, each report emphasizing that the faculty spent long hours in the recitation room and laboratory. Many departments called for additional teachers: Romance languages and German because the school was promoting these modern languages, history because William Lyman was teaching all of the courses in both European and American history, and physics because Benjamin Brown taught the entire curriculum. Some of the faculty pleaded for the creation of departments of economics and education, but only the former was established.

Benjamin H. Brown (left), one of Whitman's most popular and energetic professors, assists students in removing a stump during a campus cleanup day in 1918.

The requests for more teachers went largely unanswered. Student enrollment increased from 232 in 1913 to 312 in 1917, yet the faculty remained small. It is impossible to give the exact student-teacher ratio or faculty loads, but there was no significant increase in the number of professors. Instead, to help meet the increased enrollments, the school employed inexpensive student assistants; in 1917 seven of them—most of whom graded in the sciences—played a vital role. In 1914 alumna Henrietta Baker assisted in mathematics; she would later go on to become an effective professor of that subject at her alma mater.

Surprisingly few faculty members became fed up with conditions and resigned. A few departed for more profitable business careers, and others went on to universities. The two major losses prior to 1917 were Professor Norman Coleman in English and Professor Charles Haines in political science. Chester Maxey, who, as a student, enjoyed both as his professors, thought that they equalled any teacher he encountered in his long professional career. He credited Haines with influencing him to pursue political science. Both Coleman and Haines continued their distinguished careers in other institutions, but perhaps they might have remained had they received liveable salaries and opportunities to research and write. The rest of the Whitman faculty remained with the institution because they lacked suitable alternatives (the situations at small colleges everywhere were similar to Whitman's), believed in the school's mission, appreciated Penrose's dedication and leadership, and simply hoped for better times. Penrose frequently praised the "permanency" of faculty members because "the life of the institution is safeguarded and enriched by their continued devotion."[9]

Stephen Penrose annually rested at his summer camp on Puget Sound and returned refreshed; the faculty found less impressive conditions in cabins and tents in the Blue Mountains. Some professors succumbed to stress, however. Few could afford to escape the pressure by either a leave or a sabbatical. Inadequate recreation and stressful conditions forced two faculty members to seek leaves to reclaim their health. Librarian Arminda Fix received a two-year leave because she had suffered a nervous collapse resulting from eighteen years of demanding work that required, the acting librarian stated, "a large outlay of nervous force"; cares at home and family illnesses also

Helen Louise Burr graduated from Wellesley College in 1893; in 1906 she became dean of women at Whitman. During her fifteen years of service, some students appreciated her "kindly guidance and unselfish effort that inspired the Whitman Family with higher ideals." But others complained about her authority over them and called her "Helen Brimstone."

contributed to her exhaustion.[10] In 1916 Dean of Women Helen Louise Burr, "after ten years of hard and efficient service," received a year's leave so that she might recuperate.[11] (Burr had impressed Henrietta Baker and classmates with her advice that they should not wear red because it excited men.)

The long hours that the faculty gave to administrative matters were somewhat reduced by a new board of deans. Established in late 1910, the board soon won Penrose's approval because it served as his cabinet. Penrose preferred this board of deans rather than a single dean, so he did not replace Archer Hendrick when he resigned. From each of the academic groups—I, II, and III—the overseers selected a dean and paid him $200 extra per year. The deans had "a special responsibility for the general welfare of the student body" and carried out administrative tasks assigned by the president. The deans shaped educational policy in such ways as advising, pushing for the termination of Pearsons Academy, managing the library, and proposing new academic courses. They also shaped student behavior as they sought to curtail vulgar language, decrease smoking, improve sanitary conditions, enforce chapel attendance, suspend or dismiss students, oversee fraternity rush, and inspect student housing. The most unusual function of the board was to work with a secret committee of junior and senior men and women to aid freshmen. Penrose explained the system: when the students and deans "see a student getting into bad ways, they simply suggest to some member of this committee that they look after him, and they quietly take means either to straighten him out from his bad companionship or bad ways, or do what they can for his benefit."[12] It is uncertain how long this system lasted, but Penrose thought it was a more effective way to help freshmen than to rely upon those teachers who took little interest in young students. Once the fraternities and sororities became established, the college increasingly relied upon them to temper the conduct of students, new and old.

Another way the college relied on students to govern themselves was by adopting an honor system in 1917. Under this code (already practiced in many colleges), the faculty would no longer proctor examinations. Professors anticipated the cooperation of upperclass students, who would advocate the system and would operate a special student court trying those who allegedly violated the code.

But more lasting and influential than the honor system was a unique educational practice: the final comprehensive examination. Starting in 1914 Penrose led the faculty into adopting this system, which he thought was an original American undergraduate practice. In a senior's last semester he or she must take an oral examination in the major, which was administered by the head of the department and two other professors. Penrose outlined the system in an essay that appeared in the June 1917 *Educational Review*. Based upon Oxford's testing system, Whitman's version was an attempt to avoid "choppiness"; that is, Penrose complained, students took a course, then dropped it for a new study. Courses simply did not relate to each other. Under the comprehensive system, however, students would be questioned carefully but not unreasonably about the material covered in every course in their major. Penrose hailed the system because it had stimulated "the intellectual activity of the students to a remarkable degree." He maintained that students now saved their notebooks, reviewed each course, became more serious, and wholeheartedly appreciated comprehensives. A Penrose file is filled with letters from educators across the nation who sought to borrow from the Whitman system. Penrose replied to a question about the value of the final comprehensive examination: "No one here would advocate its abandonment, for we have realized the seriousness with which it invests study and the higher ideal which it provides for the complete mastery of one field of knowledge."[13] Students, too, responded— often emotionally—to comprehensives. A senior in 1917 spoke for hundreds of others who have passed exams during the last seventy-five years: "I was pretty well frightened by it beforehand, but my review of the whole subject gave me a comprehension of it I never had had before, and I am really grateful for what I got out of it."[14]

The faculty became more involved in the college administration not only because some of its members served as part-time deans but also because faculty members assumed administrative responsibilities. A professor took charge of a duty such as scholarships, music organizations, alumni, catalogs, or publicity. Penrose hailed this system as being much more effective than the use of faculty committees. The faculty held two meetings each month: one was a business meeting (student petitions, curriculum matters, and other traditional duties) and the other was an educational meeting where members gave papers on such subjects as "Extension Work at the University of Texas," "The Relation of Work in Freshman English to the Work of Other Departments," and "The Grading System."

By 1917 the faculty had written a set of student requirements somewhat similar to current models. Students had to complete 120 hours of college work, take no more than seventeen hours a semester without faculty approval, have a seventy percent (c) average to graduate, complete required courses (including Biblical literature, English, philosophy, and physical training), complete at least eighteen hours in each academic group, and possess a reading knowledge of a modern language. The women also had to pass a two-hour course in household economics that included instruction in clothing, food, the care of children, and the family as a social unit. Students chose a major in their sophomore year and worked towards a B.A. (it required classical languages), B.S., or B.M. Most majors consisted of ten courses and requirements in collateral fields.

The college annually conferred M.A. degrees in a few fields. The applicants for this degree had to complete twenty hours of advanced work at Whitman, write a thesis, and pass a final oral examination.

To support its demanding curriculum, the faculty expended much energy promoting the library. Despite serious impediments, the library substantially improved between 1913 and 1917. Librarians faced several problems—the library did not have a budget (funds came from small book endowments and gifts), librarians lacked professional training (Arminda Fix was an exception), there was a lack of space for bookshelves and reading tables, and the library received too little attention from governing boards (in 1916 trustees denied a modest $50 request for catalog cards). But a few dedicated amateur librarians, a handful of motivated students, some timely gifts, and the leadership of acting librarian Professor Edward Ruby accomplished much. The small staff catalogued hundreds of items, classified government documents, acquired indexes, bound periodicals, created study space, and provided additional reference service because it is "the most important phase of college library work."[15] Professors and students appreciated the library improvements, stating that these changes meant better academic work. Professors as well as history and political science students used the government documents collections "as a vast laboratory"; these users called the primary materials the library's greatest strength. In 1890 the college became a depository of government documents, and the college received many missing documents when Senator Henry L. Dawes willed his valuable library to Whitman. The Library of Congress provided other items to give the college nearly a complete set. In 1913 the librarian could honestly boast that "Scholars who have worked among the documents in some of the country's largest libraries tell us that on the score of availability for work, our documents are as good as any."

In 1917 the well-trained librarian Harriet L. Carstensen arrived; she would serve for fifteen years. At this time the library occupied one-half of the main floor and one-fourth of the first floor of Memorial Hall and housed 26,500 bound volumes and 18,000 pamphlets. As librarians and readers struggled for space, Penrose proposed an end to this congestion by the construction of a new library. That building, however, would have to wait until after the First World War.

IO

The Impact of the First World War
1914 – 1918

Historian David Kennedy has written that in the early years of the First World War "Americans had profoundly disagreed about the conflict and about America's relation to it."[1] This did not seem to be the case at Whitman, where the students and faculty took little interest in the distant war. The college and the community believed that because the fight was not an American concern, the nation should remain neutral. Campus sentiment held that a democracy should stay clear of a war being waged by aristocracies. The college sources clearly indicate that, from the outbreak of hostilities in August 1914 until President Woodrow Wilson broke diplomatic relations with Germany early in 1917, the conflict seemed to have slight impact upon the Whitman campus. But Wilson's drastic action against Germany aroused the college because students might face combat. In April Congress declared a war that, Stephen Penrose wrote, "profoundly affected the college."[2]

In 1914 students heard Whitman history professor William Lyman and University of Washington history professor Oliver Richardson explain the causes of the war and speculate about its consequences. Chapel speakers sometimes lectured about the war's impact upon the present and future national economy. Whitman's debate team researched the question of American military preparedness. In November 1914 the *Pioneer*, complaining that only two students and two townspeople bothered to attend a lecture on the war, urged students to become interested in the terrible event. The editor declared that "Wealth is being wasted by the millions. Lives are being snuffed out by the thousands.... All this without parallel in human experience. And yet the college students give this great struggle less attention than a common athletic contest."[3] The writer judged that the apathy resulted from the fact that students could not see how the war would affect them. As "one of the great powers," the United States might well become involved, he predicted. If so, students turned soldiers would see "the relation of this war to our own welfare." The editor concluded that classmates were too lazy and only interested in compiling college credits.

Prior to American entry into the war there was no significant campus opposition to Germany. In 1915 a Whitman professor gave a thoughtful explanation of the *Lusitania*'s destruction. In late 1916 the college library established a "Great War" shelf, including pamphlets published by the German government. Whitman's German department actually offered more courses than the French department, and the German club, Der Deutsche Verein, flourished. As late as the winter of 1917, the club attracted good audiences to its programs, including a speaker extolling the German public educational system, a program illustrating Germany in peacetime and wartime, and the lectures of German professor Samuel Kroesch on that nation's life and institutions. Kroesch, who had been an exchange professor at Marburg when the war broke out, prepared a list of German plays suitable for presentation in regional schools. The college hailed this aid to teachers. But the best evidence that the college held little animosity towards the Central Powers is the fact that the YMCA successfully appealed to students to donate money to the relief of college students, including Germans, suffering in European prison camps. The son of Whitman professor Thomas Day supported German and Austrian prisoners in Russia. At a meeting held on campus in December 1916, Professor Day read his son's letter requesting books, food, shoes, and other items to alleviate the suffering of these former students. Speakers urged listeners to donate generously to the relief fund on behalf of these imprisoned German and Austrian soldiers; one professor insisted that "the world is becoming a brotherhood in spite of all hatred, and not to ease a world brother's suffering is to be held responsible in part for that suffering." Students generously responded with $238 to the national YMCA fund.

By such action students supported President Wilson's neutrality, and they seemed to endorse his call for military preparedness. In a straw ballot held in November 1916, they voted for him 111 to 80 over his Republican rival.

The campus attitude toward the brutal stalemate on the western front changed dramatically in early February 1917, after Wilson severed diplomatic relations with Germany. American entry into the war seemed imminent, and the school buzzed with excitement; professors expounded on such important topics as the mobilization of labor and food. In late March, Stephen Penrose spoke to Williams alumni about national affairs, angrily denouncing Germany's submarine attacks upon American shipping. He aroused his audience by thundering "God may hasten the day when America will throw off her lethargy and take her stand for right and humanity.... The spectacle of the United States with her ships kept from the high seas, with her honor assailed and her integrity questioned, is the spectacle of a nation lax of duty, bloated with wealth, and slothful of her destiny." He soon addressed the Whitman student body as well. Attempting to keep eager males from enlisting, he urged them to petition trustees to establish a compulsory military training program. The president knew that eastern schools had followed such a course and reasoned that if the nation raised a massive army, then trained college men would naturally serve as its officers. Penrose invited alumni to participate in campus military drills and encouraged Whitman women to do Red Cross work and organize a college first-aid class.

Students followed their president's bidding. Former army captains came to campus and conducted drills on Ankeny Field and taught military subjects at night. The college granted two hours credit to participants. The *Pioneer* hailed patriotic classmates who were training to become officers as a result of humanity's sending "forth a trumpet call."[4] Townspeople came to watch the drills, and, one woman observed, "The sight causes a thrill ... and tightens one's throat."[5]

After the declaration of war, students talked incessantly about their role in it. William O. Douglas, then a Whitman freshman, recalled that "there was much swearing and boasting and bravado. America was going 'to clean up a few alley rats.' ... The general attitude was 'We'll teach them,'" but he also noted moist eyes when the volunteers said farewell.[6] Whitman men, like those at other regional schools, canceled intercollegiate sports and concentrated on military drills. The *Pioneer* considered this a sacrifice because they denied themselves the honor of winning athletic letters.

About a hundred men in various types of military and civilian dress drilled to the beat of a drummer on Ankeny Field, rejoicing when they received wooden guns to replace sticks. Meanwhile, Whitman women formed four companies to support the war effort. Each sent one member a day to the local Red Cross for sewing. The coeds also sold flags and candy to benefit the Red Cross, and all women enrolled in an early-morning college first-aid class conducted by a local physician.

About a dozen Whitman men who had mastered rudimentary military instruction qualified for the officers reserve corps and prepared to leave school in early May for intensive training at the Presidio in San Francisco. To honor them, students and teachers met at Reynolds Hall. Penrose led the singing of Whitman songs while his daughter Maysie played piano accompaniment. Student body president Pat Henderson urged the volunteers to conduct themselves in such a way as to honor their alma mater and ended by reading a poem, "Thomas at Chickamauga," which, he maintained, "typified the Whitman spirit in war." Several faculty members gave patriotic pep talks, and the volunteers made farewell comments. Meanwhile, other classmates enlisted; they had rejected the advice of Penrose as well as that of the Secretary of War who urged college men to remain in school and prepare themselves for military service. A few Whitmanites were called home to work on family farms. Penrose calculated that thirty-six percent of the males left during the spring semester.

During this time students read a variety of items: editorials in the *Pioneer* on patriotism and conscription, copies of the government's *Official Bulletin* published by George Creel's Committee on Public Information, and letters from classmates serving in the military. The *Pioneer* chided those who cut military drills and those who knew little about the war's background. The editor argued that because of inadequate public school history instruction—dry facts, not interpretations had been emphasized—college students had little comprehension of European history. "One is totally unable to understand present-day Germany," the editor insisted, "without a knowledge of her leaders and her policies of fifty years ago."[7]

The college sent a questionnaire to its alumni asking about their fitness and willingness to serve in the military. Everyone hailed their enthusiastic response for the war.

As the semester ended, Washington governor Ernest Lister spoke in chapel, encouraging everyone to play a role in the war against Prussianism and generalizing that the vast majority of German-Americans were loyal. In his baccalaureate sermon Penrose interpreted the war "as a manifestation of the struggle between democracy and aristocracy, and between the individual idea of man and the German idea that man is merely a machine to perform certain labor."[8]

The students and faculty reflected upon the spring semester, declaring it to have been one of the most unusual and exciting in the college's history. After evaluating the school's experiences, Penrose asked overseers at a June meeting to restore intercollegiate athletics and to install a Reserve Officer Training Corps (ROTC) program. This military program was popular at other schools, and Penrose thought it would have a positive impact upon Whitman. In fact, he advocated ROTC and intercollegiate athletics because they would help recruit hard-to-find male students. The educator warned, "One of the dangers which the war is bringing to our colleges, is the danger that young women will go to college and young men will not; if so, the future intellectual life of the nation will be thereby impaired."[9]

At the 1917 commencement, Penrose announced that the college would operate in the fall despite the war; he urged young men under twenty-one to attend. This thirty-fifth commencement had a military tinge. The women delivering orations chose war topics: one praised David Lloyd George, and the other described the "brotherhood of nations and lasting peace for which the United States and her allies were at present fighting."[10] The audience acknowledged two fathers who received diplomas for sons serving at the Presidio.

The war would have an even greater impact upon the college during the 1917–1918 school year and the fall semester of 1918. Enlistments, the draft, and war work slashed enrollments. The *Pioneer* noted in the fall of 1917 that fifty men who had been at college the previous year were now performing military service. In 1917 the catalog listed 312 students; in 1918 only 249.

Male students who did return to campus in mid-September of 1917 came from communities that encouraged enlistments for a great crusade. Penrose, who always possessed an uncanny ability to assess student morale, understood that excited male students thought that while a war for important goals raged in Europe they were caught up in the humdrum life of classes and examinations. The *Pioneer* also caught the negative male attitude: "Many of us are rather surprised to be here at all. We are filled with the general unrest which wartime brings, and we wonder whether it is worthwhile to bother about the regular attendance of classes, the faithful preparation of lessons, the daily routine of college life." The writer then reminded his readers that "We must not let our end slide when the country asks us, as students, only to prepare ourselves well to meet the problems which the next few years will bring. We must live up to the tradition which says that Whitman College is a college of hard-working, serious-minded, purposeful students."[11] Anxious men nevertheless spoke about enlisting; perhaps sophomore William O. Douglas was typical of those who balanced responsibility to family (his mother depended upon him) with an urge to serve the nation. His inability to pass a color test, however, kept him out of the Marines.

Males complained that there was neither an unofficial military program in the fall of 1917 as there had been in the previous spring, nor an ROTC as was available on other campuses. Whitman men badgered Penrose for an ROTC program. The school had applied for one in the spring of 1917, but the War Department's bureaucracy delayed a response. But the grumbling ended in December when the War Department took the unusual step of granting Whitman's request for an ROTC program, one that required all physically fit Whitman men to join. Participants received military training, especially marching and the manual of arms, three periods a week.

Penrose hailed the ROTC program because it would help keep men on campus and improve morale. He boasted that the unit "was the first to be established in any American college after the war began."[12] The program immediately lifted the campus spirit, in large part because students enjoyed the teaching of Captain Theophilus B. Steele, who came out of retirement to become professor of military science and tactics. Penrose had sought Steele out, impressed by his background as well as his social connections in the Pacific Northwest. Steele had served in the army from 1898 to 1915 and had experienced combat in the Phillipines. He spent six years at Goettingen University, became a New York corporation lawyer, then served as judge advocate in Chicago.

Steele proved to be as effective a teacher as Penrose predicted. Despite the fact that for several weeks the men lacked uniforms and rifles, they mastered drills and enjoyed the tactical problems of simulating trench warfare. In February 1918 a Midwest manufacturer delivered uniforms, and khaki-clad men in class or on Ankeny Field became familiar. In April the state provided aging cavalry carbines to replace wooden guns. To increase the size of formations, the college invited some Walla Walla High School students to join them in campus drills. A regular army officer inspected the Whitman ROTC unit and praised Steele and his cadets. In May the college sent ten men— most of whom were seniors—to Camp Lewis for advanced training. Twenty-one younger men were selected for a month-long ROTC camp at the Presidio. Whitman took pride in the fact that so many students received calls to these spring camps.

During the entire war Penrose and other speakers sought to keep the men from enlisting. The *Pioneer* joined this effort by encouraging

In the spring semester of 1918 Whitman soldier-students conduct military drills on Ankeny Field. Reynolds Hall is in the background.

men to "Sit tight. Keep on with your education." It quoted President Wilson and other officials who urged men to remain in college unless drafted. Apparently this advice had only minimal success because in every semester students departed for military service. The ROTC unit kept many men on campus; its termination at the end of spring semester, 1918, reduced male enrollments for the next school year.

While the men marched on Ankeny Field or studied military topics in Memorial Hall, the women also increased their participation in the war effort. The Red Cross took space in the campus YWCA room, set up a sewing machine, and directed coeds as they basted hems into sheets or comfort kits. A more obvious sign of patriotism was the fact that college women at the start of the fall semester formed a unit of the Patriotic League, an organization sponsored by the YWCA. Members pledged to "express my patriotism by doing better than ever before whatever work I have to do; by rendering whatever special service I can at this time to my community and country; by living up to the highest standards of character and honor; and by helping others to do the same."[13] The league adopted the motto "Practice what you preach," selected a captain from each class (including junior Frances Penrose), and took on a variety of activities. The group sought members and donations for the Red Cross, urged the sale of Liberty Bonds, sold Christmas seals to support the campaign against tuberculosis, supported an Armenian baby, knit squares, sewed a Whitman service flag, gathered magazines for distribution to servicemen, and directed patriotic work in public schools. Patriotic League members assisted overworked grade school teachers who directed pupils in various wartime activities such as making towels, joke books, and gunwipers; collected clothing for the Belgian relief; distributed material on food conservation to homes; and helped raise money for the Red Cross. The women in the Patriotic League dressed as nurses and marched in a local military parade; one participant recalled that these women hoped that they could serve as army nurses in France. The organization also passed a resolution dealing with fashion: "that in keeping with the general trend toward military style, all college coeds should wear their hair in bangs."[14]

Students supported the war in still other ways. They maintained a roll of honor that showed where former students served, honored the service flag that was hung in the chapel, and placed Red Cross service flags in the windows of Reynolds Hall. Students read military letters in school publications, including those from Mary Lyman, who served as a surgical nurse in France. Beta Theta Pi established a regular writing schedule to its members in the service. Individuals and groups lent their support to drives advancing such causes as the Red Cross, the YMCA, the YWCA, Belgian refugees, and French orphans.

Besides working for the war effort, students listened to speeches about the war. A variety of patriotic speakers addressed the Whitman community. Professors from Whitman and regional schools, YWCA leaders, combat veterans, and others celebrated the American war effort. The *Pioneer* saluted these patriots, but it chided male students for not attending all the military lectures and women students for not listening to talks on food conservation, which was "the best way by which they can help to win the war."[15] The editor stated that those Whitman men who did not drill three mornings a week merited the unpatriotic title of "slackers."

The war disrupted the school's social life. A shortage of junior and senior men, especially in 1918, had a profound impact upon fraternities, athletics, forensics, journalism (no yearbook was produced in the war years), and dances. There was only one man in the 1918 graduating class, and he was there only because he could not pass a military physical examination. Students in 1917 decided to abandon the use of taxis and corsages and to have a general school dance rather than individual ones sponsored by groups. At some dances women found it necessary to dance with each other.

The faculty also contributed to the war effort. Because of the age of Whitman's professors, only three entered the service—Latin professor Edward Ruby (who became the librarian at Camp Lewis), director of the music conservatory David Campbell, and director of physical education Vincent "Nig" Borleske. These last two men had played vital campus roles and many missed their contribution.

Other professors served in various ways: Walter Bratton was Red Cross field representative for eastern Washington and Idaho; William Davis chaired the home relief department of the local Red Cross; Dean Helen Burr aided local war agencies in conserving food and in operating a canning club and directed the publication of a leaflet entitled *Practical Suggestions for Food Conservation*; Stephen Penrose served as county food administrator; and Benjamin Brown taught physics at Camp Lewis. English professor Milton Simpson worked in and wrote about a Puget Sound sawmill.

Faculty members spoke across the state on a variety of war topics in an attempt, their president explained, "to develop a spirit of fervent loyalty in the hearts of the people."[16] Penrose, who delivered more talks than his faculty did, spoke on the "Meaning of War" and "Making Democracy Safe for the World"; Howard Brode handled the topic "The Place of Propaganda in Education"; William Davis hailed the talents of Lloyd George; and William Lyman speculated on "America's Twentieth Century Message to the World." The president was quick to acknowledge his faculty's contribution and its loyalty, even though some of its members spoke out against the war. Penrose assured his audiences that at his school "There has been no suspicion of disloyalty, not any whisper of unfaithfulness to the cause of the United States and her Allies."[17] The *Pioneer* also lauded professors for donating their time in organizations and as lecturers; Brode, for example, spent nearly every weekend away from campus on behalf of the Red Cross. The editor observed that the teachers "offer the students . . . a splendid example of those who, in spite of the burdens of the daily routine, are willing to assume more responsibility in order to help the country in its need."[18]

Many schools terminated their German departments during the war and suspended clubs devoted to the "study of the life and customs of the German people." But at Whitman the German club showed as much vitality in the 1917–1918 school year as it had in the preceding spring. In October 1917, at its first meeting, the club attracted many students, who sang German songs, elected officers, and set a program. Der Deutsche Verein provided an opportunity to practice German and to have fun at its German plays and around its Christmas tree in Reynolds Hall. It continued meetings, generally sponsored by a German class, well into the spring semester of 1918. The club promoted a prize essay contest sponsored by the Intercollegiate League of German Clubs of America. Perhaps this contest might have caused opposition to the club, which was last mentioned in the *Pioneer* of April 26, 1918. During the remainder of the war, the *Pioneer*'s list of organizations does not include Der Deutsche Verein.

President Penrose did not discuss the disappearance of the German club in his June 1918 annual report, but he stated that everyone knew about "the wide-spread feeling in the United States against the teaching of German in the schools." He explained that this hostility resulted from several factors, including "a species of hysteria which in its hatred of the Hun thinks that it can banish forever from the world life all things German." Penrose reasoned that at the war's end German civilization "must be studied and understood, not only by scholars, but by those who most come into relations with the German people." American policy makers, he insisted, must understand German language and literature. Penrose thought that high schools might cut German classes but that colleges should offer them. He then described the sorry status of German enrollments at Whitman: in 1914, eighty-eight students took classes, but in 1918 only twenty-five enrolled. He might have added that beginning German attracted only four students in the fall of 1917, only six the next spring. The president asked the overseers to meet the problem of small enrollments. The board responded by terminating the German department and by advising "that any teaching of German ... shall be done through the Department of Modern Languages."[19] Whitman released German professor Charles Goodrich and did not offer German classes from the fall of 1918 until the fall of 1920, despite the fact that they remained in the catalog. It seems that anti-German hysteria off campus was the major reason for the decrease in German enrollments; this, in turn, helped lead to the elimination of the language program. Most likely such overseers as Judge Thomas Burke and the Reverend Mark Matthews brought their deep hostility towards Germany to board meetings. In Walla Walla, as in other regional cities, there was a strong sentiment against the enemy. Here, too, the new phrase "one hundred percent American" found expression.

Walla Wallans heatedly debated the question of offering German language courses after the local school board unanimously voted on April 1, 1918, "that the teaching of German be discontinued at the close of the present school year." Apparently this decision resulted in part from the fact that the powerful German spring offensive prompted fear of an Allied defeat. Hysteria was another factor as townspeople repeated propaganda stories, especially about the German military, and warned that if Germany won the war then the United States must suffer from "a King Hun." The Wilson administration had successfully mobilized emotions; in Walla Walla, as elsewhere, German-

Americans came under attack, especially from Congregational minister Dr. Otis H. Holmes. His fiery words led him to win the nickname
"Walla Walla's Fighting Parson." Meanwhile, advertisements for a
third Victory Loan in local newspapers portrayed the barbarity of the
Huns, including an illustration of a bayoneted child. Newspapers
simultaneously carried stories charging that spies, traitors, and paci-
fists undermined the American war effort. In April the city's Patriotic
League appointed a large and secret propaganda committee whose
task was to put an end "to harmful propaganda being circulated in
southeastern Washington."[20] Townspeople accused each other of being disloyal. The *Bulletin* angrily protested: "A man's loyalty and a
woman's chastity are not subjects for mischievous groups of rattle-
brained magpies to discuss."[21]

The *Bulletin* attempted to alert citizens to the dangers of the hysterical tide that engulfed the region, and ridiculed the local school
board's vote on teaching German. Editor John G. Kelly agreed with
Penrose that banning German was "impulsive and hysterical and that
it would be regretted." Kelly argued that "it must not be forgotten
that a general denunciation of German music, German literature, and
German science not only does no good, but it does actual harm. It
cruelly humiliates a large class of honest and patriotic German citizenship of the United States ... it is German militarism that we are
fighting—not the Germans as a people."[22] But reason fell to fear in
the spring of 1918. Penrose and his faculty understood both the importance of the German language and the power of regional hysteria.
To insist on teaching German would bring Whitman into disfavor.
Defending an academic subject against an unreasoning public was
unwise when the school was already sinking into debt because of the
war. Apparently the termination of the German department did not
upset student editors. When school resumed in the fall of 1918, the
Pioneer carried an editorial, "The New Whitman," and listed such
wartime changes as the absence of intercollegiate athletics and the
declining enrollments in Greek and Latin. Shortly thereafter an editor
complained that there was no Bible department, but at no time did a
writer ever question the removal of a German professor and his classes. Apparently the college community also remained silent after the
state superintendent of education forbade the teaching of German.

Other events during the last few months of the war had a greater impact upon the college than the temporary suspension of the German language program. Most of the major changes resulted from the fact that Whitman, like five hundred other schools across the nation, was made a part of the War Department's Student Army Training Corps (SATC). Announced in the summer of 1918, the program transformed the college into an army training school; the *Pioneer* observed that it had been changed from a private liberal arts college into a government-supervised school. The SATC contract required that all physically fit college men over the age of eighteen become army privates on active duty: they had to wear uniforms, live in barracks, eat at a mess, drill, and study military subjects and military regulations. The cadets received $30 a month and room and board. Officers running the SATC program established the school's schedule, conducted drills, and taught such courses as military law, hygiene, map making, and ordinance. The SATC required Whitman to switch from its semester system to a term schedule. At the end of the term soldier-students could be assigned to officer's training or another military program.

Whitman's experience with the SATC was similar to that of the other schools. As one historian generalized, "The colleges . . . were to become a vast network of pre-induction centers where young men could be temporarily held prior to call-up for active military duty."[23] Whitman and most other schools initially did not object to this outside control. For patriotic and financial reasons college presidents willingly signed SATC contracts. Because of a loss of male students since the spring of 1917, these educators wanted a military program that would boost enrollments. The loss of tuition income had created serious problems from one coast to the other. The SATC provided students with tuition, board and room, and spending money. The government also reimbursed schools for their administrative expenses and use of classrooms.

Because of the war, the faculty had voted to delay fall semester until October 1, 1918. On that day, at Whitman and many other colleges, the SATC program began. Captain Chris Jensen, two lieutenants, and a clerk took charge of the Whitman men assembled in front of Memorial Hall. The cadets heard speeches, listened to the reading of President Wilson's message to SATC units, and were inducted. Most soldier-students moved into the Phi Delta Theta and Beta Theta Pi fraternity houses, which were called barracks. All cadets ate in a specially constructed mess hall. They attended military formations from reveille at 6:00 AM until taps at 10:00 PM. Every evening the men studied two hours under supervision in the college library. Thus their days were completely taken up with drills, required SATC classes, and regular liberal arts classes.

Faculty members had their teaching altered. Those lecturing in foreign languages, mathematics, and social science had to include military material. Three professors team-taught a required "War Issues Course." In some colleges this SATC course consisted of "crude historical simplifications, hate propaganda, and reactionary political views."[24] But at Whitman professor of history William Lyman and his colleagues designed a thoughtful, popular class.

The Walla Walla *Bulletin* approved of the SATC, predicting that it would teach Whitman men responsibility and "how to hustle." But a *Pioneer* editor remembered that before the war men chose the school because of its life, traditions, and spirit. Now a different type of person came, seeking "military advantages," and in his short stay would contribute little to the school. The editor asked, "What then is to become of the old Whitman ... can the new Whitman still retain, with all its new aspects, that old element of ... family-like interest?" Students complained about military courses. William O. Douglas, for example, recalled his experience as a sergeant in the SATC: "We had a colonel [he meant Captain Jensen] obsessed with two ideas. First we must become 'leaping jaguars,' ready with bayonet in hand to run any German through. Second, we must be in the right mood for our role and learn to hate the Germans. . . . I had more disgust for the colonel than I had hate for the Germans."[25] Captain Jensen, however, appreciated Douglas's training in the ROTC and at the Presidio and his current leadership in the SATC. Jensen recommended Douglas and a few others for advanced military training.

President Penrose had much to say about the SATC. At his convocation address delivered soon after the program started, he acknowledged its impact upon the curriculum, especially upon science and mathematics. According to the educator these subjects, and geography, economics, and history "are to be emphasized in college work of today and in the future."[26] The *Bulletin* went even further than Penrose to insist that "Latin and Greek are no longer necessary. Practical knowledge is paramount."

Because Whitman had contracted to enroll 250 in the SATC, Captain Jensen appealed to local men to join his program and train to become army lieutenants. Late in the semester a few men responded, and the registrar enrolled them. To fill the ranks, Whitman received authorization from the War Department to accept men who did not have high school diplomas but who had educational qualifications resulting from their work. Both Penrose and Jensen had to approve their admittance, but only a few men applied because the armistice of November 11 came soon after the authorization.

The reduction of admission standards created less campus comment than a War Department communication asking Whitman and other colleges to suspend all fraternity events except business meetings. This move resulted from the government's conclusion that "fraternity activities and military discipline are incompatible"; thus it was in the best interest of the service to restrict fraternities for the duration.[27] The government's request meant that the Beta chapter, which had its house commandeered by the SATC, hosted social events in some downtown rooms. But the immediate defeat of the Germans meant that the War Department request had little impact on the Greeks, if any. Patriotic students did not complain when the government suspended intercollegiate sports, and they were prepared to accept a limitation of social events.

Penrose provided a humorous assessment of the SATC program at Whitman in the *Outlook* magazine of February 1919. He did not identify himself as the author of "The SATC—A Comedy," because he made fun of government bureaucracy from the implementation of the SATC to its demobilization in December 1919. He recalled the brief history of the organization at Whitman where cadets had to wait for uniforms, and they never did receive their rifles. Students dug trenches and bayoneted dummies, but they did not receive rifles because, Penrose joked, "Someone might be injured—perhaps even shot." He complained about professors having to fill out all kinds of government forms, including those reporting student grades. Penrose even saw humor in the required supervised library study: "Every seat filled with a man, and every man deep in a book. I think that this was the real—and only—miracle which the SATC performed." The educator regretted that by ending payments for tuition, room and board, and the dollar-a-day wage, the government created problems for the former SATC members. Men had to leave school because they lacked cash and the institution had no money to lend. The drop in tuition income ruined college budgets, leading Penrose to observe: "The comic Muse has ordered the wreck of institutions and the ruin of hopes in the high name of Patriotism and Education."

The critic hailed the SATC's objectives—"it undertook to supply swiftly a large number of young officers by obtaining the material from the colleges and sending it in a steady stream to central training camps; it sought to extend government aid to education and to help the colleges while helping the army; and it was deeply patriotic."[28] In his annual report of 1919 President Penrose avoided criticism, preferring instead to generalize: "We endured, and in the end profited by the SATC." He praised Captain Jensen for overcoming bureaucratic problems and the SATC for encouraging men to study more intently.

The demobilization of the SATC created confusion on campus, however. First the school learned that the program would continue until June; then came contradictory orders stating that the men should be immediately discharged. But the demise of the SATC was not the end of military training. Penrose applied for an ROTC program that began in January 1919 under Captain Jensen. All physically fit Whitman men now had to take two years of classes in the department of military science and tactics. To those who complained about the college offering required military classes in peacetime, Penrose replied: "It seemed wise in the uncertainty following the Armistice and before the meeting of Congress that we should continue military training." He added that "If universal military training is established, probably the continuance of the ROTC may not be advisable."[29]

Probably most men considered ROTC so much superior to the short-lived SATC program that they did not grumble very much about its required military classes and drills. Fraternity men spoke instead about how happy they were to get their houses back to redecorate after the SATC had turned them into spartan barracks. As one alumnus noted, "The college has become a college again instead of a training camp, and no one is sorry."[30] Surely some members of the Whitman community must have thought it odd that Woodrow Wilson, who had been a professor and then president of Princeton, would have allowed the federal government through the SATC program to militarize colleges and universities.

While the students adjusted their lives to peacetime, Penrose and trustees worried, as always, about financial conditions. The president wrote: "The effect of the war upon the college was financially disastrous. . . . The war worked havoc with its plans and its property. Its student body was depleted and its income from tuitions reduced; its expenses were increased, and a deficit of $10,000 a year was unavoidable. Its faculty stayed at their posts despite the increased cost of living, though their salaries were already small."[31]

Then in the fall of 1918 the Spanish influenza struck. After the epidemic hit the West Coast, the college and the town dreaded its arrival. The first victims fell just after school commenced; Walla Walla's health authorities immediately responded by closing all schools, churches, theaters, and other indoor public gathering places. The college, however, was allowed to offer classes to campus residents; coeds from Walla Walla moved from their homes to temporary quarters in the school's gymnasiums, explaining to Penrose that they did not want to miss classes. Late in October the flu struck in Reynolds Hall; the college then banned all women from classes so as to protect them and the members of the SATC. In November the disease swept through the various barracks; most victims took beds in the barracks that had been the Beta Theta Pi fraternity house. Captain Jensen swore some freshmen, including Don Sherwood, into the army as nurses so that they might care for their sick classmates. Meanwhile, coeds sometimes entertained the recuperating cadets, who were brought to the windows, with vaudeville acts presented on the spacious porch.

Penrose's attempt to reopen the college in late November failed when city officials, responding to a surge of flu cases, closed all schools. Whitmanites returned home until classes resumed on January 2. Professors crammed assignments into the few teaching days left in the term, and students received full credit despite the shortest term on record. The reassembled students talked endlessly about the flu, mourned the death of a classmate who had succumbed to the disease and blood poisoning, considered the disruption of the past semester, and longed for a return to campus tranquility. Indeed, students and teachers alike anticipated that the coming celebration of Penrose's twenty-five years as president would help them recover from the problems and confusion of war and influenza.

II

Problems of Expansion
1919 — 1924

In the spring of 1919 Walla Wallans anticipated two celebrations: in June Stephen Penrose would be honored for completing twenty-five years as Whitman's president; in July the 146th Field Artillery Battalion, led by a former Whitman ROTC instructor and including some former Whitman students in its ranks, would return from the battlefields of France to the tranquil fields of Walla Walla County. While all the school's constituents adjusted to peacetime conditions and anticipated the celebrations, Penrose again thought about the college's future in relation to society's needs. Because he assumed the United States would play a much larger role in international relations in the 1920s, he sought to bolster the school's offerings in the social sciences. Penrose reasoned, "In the era before the war the department of economics was our chief point of contact with the outside world; business and the college influenced each other. In the new era, the development of political science and history will assume an equal if not greater importance."[1] Therefore, he recommended to the governing boards that they strengthen the departments of history, political science, and economics so as to assist "the large community which the college serves." Penrose also wanted to aid returning servicemen by reducing their tuition and by granting them credit for their military experience.

To get high school seniors thinking about both postwar adjustments and the advantages of a Whitman education, the school offered to three high school senior men and three high school senior women $1,000 in cash and tuition scholarships for the best essays on the causes of the Great War. Despite the college's shaky financial situation, the seniors won prizes and veterans paid only half-tuition.

Penrose pointed out to trustees that the General Education Board would make a final payment on the matching grant in July and that the school must immediately launch still another financial campaign. It should seek $500,000 to be split between the endowment and the building fund. The earnings on the endowment would provide for a larger and better-paid faculty. The president stressed again the deplorable financial condition of professors: "Most of them with families are in a tragic position. They have been brought by the war to the edge of disaster. Their long sacrifice seems hopeless. They cannot continue teaching and pay their bills. They cannot bear to see their children go unclothed or unfed. I know one man who has not bought a new overcoat for himself for ten years or a new suit of clothes for himself for four years."[2] As for the building fund, Penrose listed for the trustees the facilities the school needed: a central heating plant, $50,000; a library, $125,000; two dormitories, $200,000; and a president's residence, $25,000. Penrose complained that Reynolds Hall could not house all of the capable women seeking admission and that the school lacked a men's dormitory and depended upon the fraternities to supply space. The library was crowded into Memorial Hall; furthermore, there was a need to convert this limited library space into classrooms and offices. In addition, the planner insisted that an efficient central heating plant would greatly reduce the cost of janitors and coal.

While Penrose listed ways that money could improve the college, he thanked local overseers who directed the fund drive and thereby spared him this burden. Enthusiastic campaign managers responded that they wanted to provide funds for the expanding enrollment and pledged to have a tidy amount collected by the time of Penrose's anniversary celebration. A successful campaign would show how much the community appreciated its respected educator. Although Penrose did not manage this drive, he did provide its strategy. He advised that potential donors from Walla Walla should be asked to donate to buildings because they liked to walk on a beautiful campus and because they understood that dormitories ultimately aided the local economy; potential donors living out of town should be asked

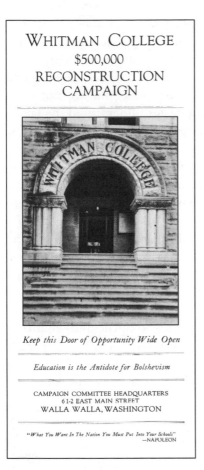

WHITMAN COLLEGE
$500,000
RECONSTRUCTION
CAMPAIGN

Keep this Door of Opportunity Wide Open

Education is the Antidote for Bolshevism

CAMPAIGN COMMITTEE HEADQUARTERS
61-2 EAST MAIN STREET
WALLA WALLA, WASHINGTON

"What You Want In The Nation You Must Put Into Your Schools"
—NAPOLEON

A Whitman fund-raising circular, from around 1920. The slogan, "Education is the Antidote for Bolshevism," reflects the impact upon the college of the national Red Scare of that time.

for endowment gifts because they generally better understood the need. Penrose also pushed an annuity program, thinking it would attract donors.

Chairman John Langdon led the fund drive, which was modeled after the successful Victory Loan drives. He began the intensive April effort with a banquet and notable speakers. Former Secretary of the Interior Richard Ballinger, who had been Penrose's college classmate, addressed an excited crowd, praising his "friend Steve" for making Whitman into a western Williams. Ballinger championed these small institutions: "The difference between a college and a university is that at a college you learn something of everything and at a university you learn everything about something."[3] The speaker applauded Whit-

man-type colleges for graduating solid citizens. Another guest, Episcopal bishop Frederick Keator of Olympia, expanded on this theme.
He was sure Whitman's graduates would not follow such agitators as
had led the recent, menacing Seattle general strike. The Reverend
Otis Holmes spoke about what townspeople could do, not what
Whitman graduates would do. The minister underscored the favorable local financial situation resulting from the fact that wartime
Walla Wallans had accumulated large savings accounts and liberty
bonds and now could be generous with the college.

The intensive drive included daily luncheons, pep talks, competition between female and male fund-raising teams, music, and extensive newspaper publicity. Editor John Kelly of the Walla Walla *Bulletin* championed the campaign because most of the students were
self-supporting and thus deserved assistance. He urged his readers
"to give until your conscience is clear" and recommended that a sign
be placed in the valley: "To rich old men and women: there are no
pockets in shrouds."[4]

Students joined in the effort too. Bringing music and what they
called their famous "Whitman pep," they led a serpentine parade
from campus to city center, delivered one-minute speeches through
megaphones from the upper floor windows of business buildings, and

*This photograph of Walla Walla dates from the early 1920s, when the city had
20,000 residents. It was shot from the same vantage point as the photograph on
page 80.*

placed signs in shop windows. On campus, students assured each other that they faced a brighter educational future if the $500,000 could be raised.

The week-long drive netted close to $81,000, nearly a third of which came from Mrs. William Kirkman's donation of her home and some property. The Oszias P. Jaycox family gave the $5,000 government insurance on the life of their son Arthur, who had died of influenza while serving in the SATC. After a week leaders terminated their work, explaining that poor wheat prices and competition from a new Victory Loan campaign forced this decision. Organizers, however, assured Penrose that a fall drive would flourish because everyone anticipated a good wheat crop and because Seattle businessmen had predicted that half the needed fund could be raised there.

The Walla Walla campaign was but one attempt to meet the college's needs. Penrose carried on a voluminous correspondence with such diverse prospects as the wealthy widow Caroline Gray Kamm and the General Education Board. In 1917 Penrose and Kamm had collaborated in having her father, missionary William Gray, and her mother reburied with the Whitmans at Waiilatpu. Penrose stressed to Kamm that a library honoring Gray would be a fitting tribute. While this was one arrow in his quiver, another was a series of letters to the General Education Board requesting a matching grant similar to the one awarded in 1913.

Despite the president's fervent and frequent efforts to find the money required for an expanding college, he failed to achieve his aims. Still, there were some successes between 1919 and 1923. The General Education Board in 1920 provided another matching gift of $125,000, contingent upon the college's raising $250,000. In 1921 the school received $50,000 from Walla Wallan Miles Moore, $27,000 from the estate of Seattleite Margaret Denny, $10,000 from Portlander Caroline Kamm, and the first payment on a $75,000 gift from the sons and daughters of the late Frederick and Sarah Weyerhaeuser. The timber money created a chair of Biblical literature and prompted great enthusiasm among Whitman's friends, who hoped that other families who had made fortunes in the West would aid the college. During the Greater Whitman campaign Dean Archer Hendrick and others had anticipated such philanthropy. But the Weyerhaeuser gift did not prompt similar donations.

Unfortunately these gifts received in the early 1920s failed to provide any buildings or to increase faculty salaries. Eastern foundations proved less helpful than predicted. The General Education Board gift produced only small yearly amounts, but even more disheartening was the fact that the Carnegie Foundation refused repeated requests to provide $225,000 for a library.

In the early 1920s money problems continually depressed Penrose, who complained that this poor financial situation meant that the school denied admission to impressive applicants, that the crowding in Memorial Hall frustrated everyone, and that the faculty could not pay household bills. The overseers themselves donated a few thousand dollars for salary enrichment, but the fact that the rest of the wealthy community refused to provide much relief must have irritated professors. In a futile effort to improve the situation the president publicly compared their salaries with those of clerks. In 1925 alumnus Chester Maxey returned to campus, discovered the faculty's low morale, and concluded that the school "was sailing without a pilot."[5] He saw that the professors admired Penrose but that they also doubted his ability to remedy their desperate economic situation. Maxey's interpretation of faculty dissatisfaction was probably overstated, but undoubtedly financial problems of the early 1920s hampered the college just as it grew more popular.

While financial matters darkened the president's thoughts in the postwar period, during the summer of 1919 the financial clouds momentarily passed. The college had balanced its annual budget; furthermore, alumni were optimistic about efforts to raise $25,000 for a new president's home. An alumnus said it would be "a beautiful testimony of love and loyalty to President and Mrs. Penrose equally, and especially a tribute to their home life, which has meant so much to Whitman men and women"; furthermore, it would also be important to future presidential families.[6] This drive for the residence succeeded partly because Walter Crosby Eells, grandson of Cushing Eells, controlled the alumni association. As its secretary he began publishing *The Whitman Alumnus* and organizing alumni clubs. These two efforts aroused alumni interest in their alma mater and increased donations, especially for the president's house.

News that there would be a new residence, not the inability to raise $500,000, received emphasis during the celebration of Penrose's twenty-fifth anniversary. For months the college's supporters, led by Walter Eells, had planned a worthy celebration to be held at the 1919 commencement. The alumni's contribution to the affair would include demonstrations of affection, the start of a presidential home, and suitable memorials to the war dead.

The four-day event began with a Saturday night reception honoring Dr. and Mrs. Penrose. Some participants hailed it as the largest ever held in the city. Commencement marshall William O. Douglas joined them in the receiving line. Much of the crowd went to the gymnasium and danced at the junior prom, a joyous event that contrasted with the dull social life of fall semester.

On Sunday Penrose's career was highly praised by Raymond Brooks, who came from the Pacific School of Religion in Berkeley to deliver the baccalaureate sermon. Brooks gave an historical address stressing the contributions of Marcus Whitman, Cushing Eells, and Stephen Penrose, but he also taught that Whitman graduates must "make effective the ideals of America." The minister, who would later be a popular Pomona College professor, explained: "Education is not so much to give instruction as to give vision and purpose. Whitman seeks for its students not knowledge, but power and wisdom."[7] In the afternoon an automobile caravan transported five hundred people to Waiilatpu for the traditional college pilgrimage where regional ministers praised the martyred missionary and the inspirational college president.

Monday was given over to an educational conference. Professor Walter Bratton evaluated Penrose's administration, emphasizing the important educational service that had been rendered and the strong foundation that had been laid for the training of larger numbers of young people. The professor quoted a Penrose writing of 1896: "The college will not undertake more than it can accomplish. It has no university aspirations. It desires to do the work which is set before it earnestly, broadly, and thoroughly. It will tolerate no shams." As Bratton saw it, the aims of 1896 were also those of 1919.[8] University of Oregon president Prince Campbell judged that a presidential term of twenty-five years was unusual. He thought that "college presidencies ought to be classed among the extra hazardous occupations, since the average term of office is something like seven and one-half years."[9] Campbell praised Penrose for guiding his school through "its period of probation," and preparing it to enter "upon its new era of growth, prosperity, and influence." In discussing higher education, he urged educators to look upon students as persons and not as machines. Campbell believed that in the freshman curriculum, students "must acquire self-orientation, and secondly social orientation."[10] The Oregon educator also advocated classical courses. English professor Frederick M. Padelford of the University of Washington commented upon this address, fully agreeing with Campbell's praise of Penrose's educational accomplishments and his support of the classics. Padelford predicted a great emphasis in the study of humanities. "History, geography, and philosophy have all taken on a new life because of the positions of America in the world today." Padelford argued a point Penrose had often made, that those who would handle American affairs overseas must have an understanding "of other peoples which can only be had through a close study of history and languages."[11] The professor repeated an old faculty complaint: college students participated in so many activities that there was "little inclination for serious and thorough study."[12]

Dr. Henry Pritchett, president of the Carnegie Foundation for the Advancement of Teaching, gave a much different speech entitled "Democracy and the American College." He explained that college administrations tended to be autocratic, with the governing body at top, the faculty below, and the students at the bottom. Although the speaker did not call for faculty representation in the governing body or the student's participation in the administration, he did emphasize the importance of providing everyone a chance to voice opinions.

Late in the afternoon, before an audience of a thousand, students presented *The Masque of Marcus Whitman*. Written by students, the play emphasized important aspects of the college, especially the missionary period. In one scene Marcus Whitman pleaded with Daniel Webster (played by William O. Douglas) and President John Tyler not to surrender Oregon to England.

On Monday night, at the nearby Baptist Church, two noted educators praised Penrose and the small college. President Harry Garfield of Williams College, son of murdered president James Garfield, spoke on the subject "The Place of the Small College in American Education." He began by recalling that his college classmate, Stephen Penrose, was a man "of sterling character, of enviable ability, and for whom respect mounted easily to affection." In a tightly argued address, Garfield confessed that "The place of the small college in American education is easier to appreciate than to define." He reasoned that the small college should be maintained only if it served a societal purpose but explained, "I believe not only that the college serves a useful purpose, but that it is indispensable to our system." The educator expounded:

> The safety of the Republic depends upon the quality of its citizens and ... the primary function of a college is to train citizens for citizenship.... It is therefore of first importance that the community sense be educated as the underlying motive of life, guiding the use not only of one's general powers but also of those special powers late developed for one's trade or profession. Man is by nature a gregarious animal, and he is also a greedy animal. A highly trained specialist who keeps out of jail is not necessarily a good citizen. A good citizen is of course law-abiding, but his distinguishing mark is a well-developed community sense based on a comprehensive understanding of the elements necessary to the common welfare.[13]

After making a case for offering a broad liberal arts education, he criticized small colleges. They imitated the universities, provided too many campus activities, and emphasized intercollegiate athletics over the "physical improvement" of all students.

President Henry Suzzalo of the University of Washington then spoke on the subject "Whitman College as a Part of the Educational Life of the Northwest." He recalled that while on a graduate school committee at Columbia University he had found that Whitman alumni were well trained for graduate work. Since coming to the West, Suzzalo had met Penrose, and added that he had "admired him at the first meeting, and loved him ever after." The speaker considered Penrose to "be one of the great educators" and a valued counselor. Suzzalo explained the need for both public and private education and concluded: "I am perfectly frank to say that I believe that I prefer the intellectual small college to the large college of liberal arts or the great university. I believe that if I had a son of my own I would send him to some small college [such] as Whitman or Williams."[14]

Stephen Penrose approved the educational speeches delivered by distinguished guests. They praised the small college, as he consistently did, and pondered higher education's future. His enthusiasm for liberal arts received a needed boost. Undoubtedly the president hoped that this impressive discussion of education would attract more support from townspeople. While it probably had such a result in the long run, it failed to revive the local financial campaign that had faltered in April.

At chapel on Tuesday morning fifty delegates from various schools greeted and congratulated Penrose. Representatives from the University of Idaho and Washington State College gave brief talks. Penrose responded with thanks for the flattering words about his commitment to education.

In the afternoon it was the alumni's turn to honor the Penroses and the Whitman men who had perished in the war. The alumni presented a bronze tablet with the names of the dead, and Captain Russell Miller recalled how his alma mater had contributed to the defeat of "the most barbaric and bitter enemy ever known in history."[15] The alumnus praised Marcus Whitman for "building up our civilization" and the nine former students who "gave all to defend it." Following Miller's speech, a long procession marched to Stanton Street, where a row of nine maple trees had been planted as a memorial, and where ROTC cadets fired three volleys. Then the procession moved to the site of the new president's home for ground-breaking ceremonies. Among the speakers was an alumna who called Mrs. Penrose "the mother-in-love of us your Whitman children." Some alumni predicted that the home designed by alumnus Harold Crawford would soon be erected, but, in fact, high construction costs and some difficulty in obtaining financial pledges would delay completion until late 1921.

In the afternoon several alumni—both men and women—related their wartime experiences to an attentive audience. In Memorial Hall the crowd examined a collection of war trophies brought back by Whitman alumni and charts prepared by Walter Eells showing Whitman's remarkable growth during the Penrose administration. Then the crowd moved on to the commencement ceremonies, where Penrose awarded a degree in Greek to his daughter Frances and honorary doctorates to his old classmate Harry Garfield and to college supporter Henry Pritchett.

The ceremonies ended at the commemoration dinner with Judge Thomas Burke as toastmaster. He, too, lauded Penrose: his efforts "will stand forever in the educational history of the state of Washington."[16] Burke then digressed into an emotional tirade. "We are fighting enemies more deadly and more treacherous than the lurking Indians that Marcus Whitman faced. For years insidious propagandists have poisoned the minds of the children in the public schools." He denounced alien teachers: they were "reptiles ... who had to fly for their lives when the mind of the country was once aroused after the outbreak of war with Germany."[17] Burke was at this stage of his life a superpatriot. According to a biographer, "his judgment of men and events had considerably deteriorated and his course was deplorable."[18] During the war he hounded German-Americans; in 1919 he lashed out at organized labor, Bolsheviks, and "alien enemies." Penrose shared Burke's fear of radicalism, but he did not succumb to his friend's irrationality.

Several guests toasted Penrose, who replied that he did not believe the flattering things that had been said about him and concluded that "if the people have the delusion that they are so, then let's try to make them so."[19] To everybody's delight Garfield revealed that Williams

Built on the southeast corner of the campus, the president's house was a gift of alumni in recognition of Stephen Penrose's twenty-fifth year as president. Early in 1922 the Penrose family moved into the home; Mary Penrose soon made it a social and cultural center.

would bestow an honorary degree of doctor of laws on Penrose.

The Penrose family, faculty, alumni, students, and townspeople enjoyed the exciting anniversary celebration. Editors fully reported the event with pictures and stories, including accounts of the school's history. The Walla Walla *Union* stated that the president had "guided the college through some troubled waters, many, many times. . . . There are still many problems to solve, but they are in Dr. Penrose's capable hands and the . . . celebration—a testimonial of the affection his fellow educators have for him—will strengthen him for the tasks before him."[20] More than 250 alumni had returned for the celebration—half of those who had ever graduated from the institution—and they thanked Stephen and Mary Penrose for having such a positive effect upon them. A distinguished alumnus, Dr. Park Weed Willis, summarized the celebration for Penrose: "It was a great success from beginning to end, and I have no doubt it remains as a pleasant reminder to you and your good wife of the splendid work you have been doing for so many years."[21] In the difficult days of the early 1920s, as the nation shifted from wartime to what President Warren G. Harding called "normalcy," Penrose and his friends could look back and be comforted by a great community celebration.

In 1919 the president had evaluated the college's past; in 1920 he looked to its future. In a report to overseers, he reiterated the school's goal: "the noblest aim for Whitman is to be a small college, with a limited number of students to whom it will give the finest quality of education."[22] For the first time he pushed for limiting the size of the student body to five hundred students taught by fifty faculty members. These professors must have "genuine personalities"; moreover, they must be "warm-hearted, clear-sighted, wise, and generous . . . [and their] thinking and life must greatly inspire their students . . . in the classroom . . . and on the campus."

Penrose proposed an educational program that should be established in the future and the buildings needed to support it. He advocated major changes in the curriculum that he himself taught. The president wanted to establish a separate department of education, which would not only train teachers but also attract men interested in school administration. He also wanted to create a separate philosophy department: "To train adequately businessmen is undoubtedly one function of the college, but it must no less remember its duty to train men of the other sort . . . who like to hold themselves aloof to some extent from the confusion of the marketplace." The educator still favored a department of fine arts because the nation "is still in large degree barbarian, and Whitman College must plead guilty to this impeachment." Penrose wanted to add Italian and geography, grumbling that in America, unlike Europe, geography was improperly relegated to school children. He ruled that "No college man ought to be ignorant of the general geography of the globe, including the strategic values of each national territory" and advocated the immediate termination of the ROTC program, which had declined in popularity since the armistice.

His list of needed buildings emphasized a library because the book collection was "cribbed, cabined, confined, and groaning to expand." Again the leader appealed for two dormitories. Of secondary importance were a new gymnasium for men (to be built off campus at the site of a proposed athletic field), an astronomical observatory, a college church, and a community house, which would have many of the same functions as a contemporary student union. Penrose hoped it could provide "a common social life" to overcome the divisive nature of fraternities.

But in his report to the overseers, the president called for more than bricks and mortar. He never forgot the faculty, who contributed so much to the institution's development, and he pleaded again for salary increases. Penrose did not believe it was necessary to add many more professors until the enrollment increased. Once the school had five hundred students and fifty teachers it would provide, through close contact, a unique and worthy educational experience. The president evaluated a few teachers in this report, including retiring history professor William Lyman, who should write a college history at the school's expense. The institution needed "a full and accurate history of its origin and evolution."

Penrose fully understood that it was much easier to list than to resolve institutional needs. During the early 1920s, as he struggled to attain his goals, he sometimes had to accept substitute measures. For example, since the Carnegie Foundation and another potential donor consistently refused to give money for a library, the school had to take an emergency step. In 1921 Penrose reported to overseers the crisis of overcrowding in the library section of Memorial Hall. "Frequently every seat in the library has been taken and students have had to stand waiting in the halls outside until they could obtain a seat to study."[23] The solution he advanced was the construction of a wooden shack similar to those used in army camps. Measuring forty feet by ninety feet, it would be located at the west end of Memorial Hall. Penrose acknowledged that "It will be unsightly, disfiguring to the campus, and altogether unsuitable except as a temporary solution for a problem which has become acute." The board built the $2,500 structure, but Chester Maxey complained that "it would have been hard to find a barn in Walla Walla County more barnlike than this hideous and dilapidated library annex."[24]

While the leader sought to erect the necessary buildings for a growing student population, he simultaneously dealt with the new problem of selective admissions. He did not believe that increased enrollment was necessarily a benefit. Penrose asserted that "the fad for education is causing people to overlook the psychological fact that not everyone is mentally qualified to go to college." He added: "It is perhaps a departure from our democratic ideas, which would be thought highly dangerous in some quarters, but an unqualified democracy which overlooks natural differences between people is unscientific nonsense."[25]

In 1920 the governing boards voted to restrict the student body to three hundred men and two hundred women. Once this limit had been decided, the president and the faculty intermittently debated the standards of admission. In 1922 Penrose reported their position to the overseers. He assessed the national student population's ability, generalizing that twenty percent were super-normal, sixty percent were normal, and twenty percent were sub-normal. Penrose generalized that up to this time American colleges, including Whitman, had inadvisably treated all students as normal and had assigned the same classwork to each. He criticized such a course: "The result of this rather stupid assumption that all students are practically alike and can best be fed upon the same intellectual pablum . . . has been that many brighter men, young men especially, have lost a considerable part of their interest in their college education . . . [and] many grow mentally lazy [and] careless."

Penrose predicted that American colleges were going to provide better educational opportunities for the top twenty percent. He stated that the Whitman faculty wanted to challenge the top ten percent of students by installing an honors program that would excuse participants from some recitations, provide them with special tutorials and library privileges, and even permit early graduation. The faculty also desired to bestow prizes and graduate scholarships on these talented men and women. The overseers praised the program and then dashed it by saying that it must be delayed until funding was possible.

Professors debated about whether to drop weak students who showed their inability after a semester or whether to deny them admission in the first place. Penrose confided to a friend that he thought that the school could soon scrutinize each application and "be in the enviable position of telling those who are not first-rate in character and ability that we do not want them."[26] Weak students squandered valuable resources. The president explained to board members that selective admissions would save the school time and money since the institution paid two-thirds of the cost of each student. But apparently the board turned a deaf ear to any talk about selective admissions until the student body totaled five hundred.

The board also refused to limit the number of Walla Walla students until the school was full. Penrose had previously tried to shape a policy, stating that there was a need to restrict the number of local men and women because "the college serves the entire Northwest and must hold its doors open to receive students from all portions of the Northwest." He recommended that the number of Walla Wallans be gradually reduced to a total of no more than seventy-five men and fifty women. In 1922 Whitman had twenty-eight percent local students; Penrose wanted no more than twenty-five percent.

Although board members disagreed about the proposed plan of restrictive admissions, they did recognize the need to create room for the growing student body. The construction of the library annex had eased one space problem and so had the conversion of private homes into dormitories. Far more important than these expedient measures was the fact that in 1923 the school erected a heating plant north of Isaacs Avenue and built a large men's dormitory on Stanton Street. The central heating plant meant that coal furnaces could be pulled out of Billings and Memorial halls and replaced with badly needed classrooms; the oil-burning plant also reduced fuel and staffing costs.

But this new heating system, which cost about $40,000, created much less excitement than the addition of new student housing. In the expansion of the early 1920s, everyone agreed that the school required a modern dormitory for each sex. To meet the immediate need of housing women, the college in 1920 added Langdon Hall and Green Cottage. These converted homes, along with Reynolds Hall, meant accommodation for a total of one hundred women. Insisting that women live with relatives or in a dormitory, the school currently had only limited space for additional out-of-town applicants.

President Penrose often stated that the only remedy was the construction of a larger women's dormitory; in fact, he designed one that he called "a new and original solution" to the sorority housing problem.[27] Women had unsuccessfully requested Penrose to allow the sororities to find off-campus housing similar to that of the fraternities. He refused on the grounds that such houses would lead to snobbishness and to an emphasis on sorority rather than school spirit. The educator believed he had an effective compromise with a cottage-plan dormitory that would provide separate sorority sections, each of which would house about twenty-five members. Each section would include a parlor and a chapter room, but it would not have its own dining facility. The leader argued that his plan would spare a sorority

The John W. Langdon house has long been important to Whitman College. In 1907 plans for Greater Whitman were presented in this house; in 1920 the college bought the three-story dwelling and used it as a dormitory for thirty-five women. Since 1927 it has been the home of Beta Theta Pi.

from the problem of buying and managing a house; moreover, by living and dining together the women would become well acquainted. His scheme, he reiterated, could avoid sorority exclusiveness, "which sometimes runs into snobbishness and the loss of true college spirit."[28] Penrose's ideas would prove persuasive and resulted in the design of Prentiss Hall, which opened in 1926.

The men's housing situation was even worse than the women's. The college did not even operate a men's dormitory and had to depend upon the four fraternities for housing. These social groups accommodated a hundred men, and Kirkman House provided space for another twenty-five. Walla Walla lacked suitable boarding houses, so Whitmanites complained about the difficulty of locating accommodations. Aware of the housing difficulties, Penrose reminded overseers that the school should provide "wise supervision and comfortable quarters"; furthermore, it could not grow to the desired five hundred students if it did not erect a men's dormitory.[29] In a rare challenge to board members, Penrose demanded that they solve "two vexing problems, the housing of men and the housing of women." In 1922 the leader again hammered on the need to build dormitories, insisting that the best colleges required freshmen to live in a dormitory so as to become acquainted and "imbued with the spirit and ideals of the college." Penrose regretted that his school "throws the responsibility for its boys upon fraternity houses." Without a men's dormitory, the college lost desirable students who disliked the housing situation. The president lectured: "The reputation of the college for sound scholarship is not powerful enough to overcome their reluctance to submit to the uncertain and unsatisfactory living conditions." He continued: "I urge with all persuasiveness and energy that I can command that the building of a freshman dormitory is the immediate and pressing need."

The overseers favored a library over a men's dormitory, but they responded to Penrose's demands by establishing a special housing committee. Then the full board accepted a unique proposal from the alumni association: a joint-stock corporation that would build a three-story, $100,000 dormitory accommodating a hundred men. This would solve the pressing housing need and also mesh with the financial realities. The school was currently trying to raise money to match that offered by the General Education Board, and it simply could not launch another fund-raising drive. This alumni plan meant that Whitman might immediately provide housing for many freshmen boys.

From the fall of 1922, when the college sought bids for construction, until the dormitory's completion in the fall of 1923, Penrose put tremendous energy into the project. After the O.D. Keen Construction Company of Walla Walla submitted a low bid of less than $100,000, the president tried to convince one wealthy overseer to purchase the construction bonds and have the dormitory named for him. When that attempt failed, the Whitman Building Corporation, established by the alumni association, sold bonds for the dormitory and the heating plant through Carstens and Earles of Seattle. Penrose became very involved with this firm, providing written material for a pamphlet to advertise the bonds and the names of friends and alumni who might purchase them. In fact, he joined the bond-selling effort, convincing Caroline Kamm of Portland to invest $5,000.

Meanwhile, Penrose huddled with Portland architect Ellis Lawrence. Ever since they had worked on plans for the Greater Whitman buildings, the president and the architect had maintained a friendship. Lawrence modified a dormitory plan for men that he had prepared in 1910; he also began work on plans for a women's dormitory that would be started in 1924.

Built in 1923 for freshmen boys, Lyman Hall was divided into vertical sections to avoid long and noisy hallways. Designed by Ellis Lawrence, the building remains one of the most handsome campus structures.

Favorable weather allowed carpenters to lay the foundations for the men's dormitory in January 1923. In September freshmen moved into one of the most beautiful buildings on the campus. The dormitory was named after Professor William Lyman, who had died of a heart attack in 1920. Many of his former students had recommended that the college name the structure after the long-time history teacher. Lyman would be the only professor who would have a building named for him; presidents Stephen Penrose and Chester Maxey have been similarly honored but for their service as presidents, not as teachers. Oddly, the music and science buildings at Whitman still have only generic names.

The reception opening Lyman Hall in 1923 featured a receiving line, a dormitory orchestra, and tours conducted by freshmen who proudly displayed the game room and the electric dishwasher. Penrose explained to visitors that he wished to provide "freshman boys ... [with] a very comfortable home in a beautiful and artistic building, not so elaborate as to fill them with ideas of luxury but comfortable enough to make them feel at home."[30] Visitors and residents assured him that he had succeeded.

In Penrose's thirtieth year at the college, as in his first year, economic conditions forced him to be a fund raiser. In both 1894 and 1924 the school struggled to pay its faculty, to cover a debt, and to

solicit endowment and building funds. In both time periods Walla Walla County farmers also faced economic adversity. Pressured by board members in 1923 to take charge of still another fund-raising drive, Penrose reported to overseers that he did not want to abandon the classroom for a campaign. He favored hiring a financial agent as fund raiser. In one of his bluntest writings to overseers, the president growled that after twenty-nine years of service he would not become "a mere field agent" and argued that he must continue teaching to stay in touch with "the inner life of the college."[31] Chastised by the leader, overseers responded by recommending a campaign to raise $1,500,000 and by instructing the board of trustees and the president to work out its management.

Overseers, however, could not escape involvement. In the fall of 1923, trustees summoned them to a meeting to discuss a new campaign. Penrose had contacted Tamblyn and Brown of New York City, a firm that had conducted a successful fund-raising campaign for Williams. It submitted a proposal to Penrose, who was impressed with its thoroughness, but he warned the firm that the state's "agricultural section" was in a "period of extraordinary stringency."[32] The New Yorkers brushed aside his concerns. In October the college entered into a contract with Tamblyn and Brown, which agreed to run a campaign seeking $1,500,000 at a cost of $32,500. Penrose, who stated that he did not have the skill to conduct such a drive, rejoiced over the contract: "I am happy that we have burned our bridges behind us and launched forth on the open sea."[33] About eight months later he would be less optimistic when the campaign foundered, forcing him back into the exhausting role of fund raiser.

The New York firm elected to run the campaign from January through commencement. The most important representatives of the campaign were director Joseph C. Rivers, a seasoned and energetic person, publicity agent Gerald Bath, and Mildred L. Winship, who took on several tasks, including "the women's end of the campaign."[34] Bath came to the campus and interviewed the president and the faculty as well as overseers, alumni, and students. He then put his findings in five publications. A leaflet contained basic facts about the college; a pamphlet told of the service Whitman alumni had given the nation; and an illustrated pamphlet, *Whitman, the College of the Pioneers*, linked the institution's historical past with its current life

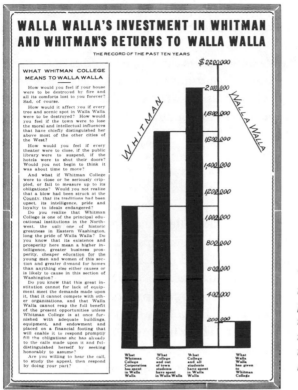

This fund-raising publication from 1924 repeats a frequent message: Whitman has put much more money into the community than the community has put into the college.

and future prospects. A pamphlet entitled *What Whitman College Means to Walla Walla* circulated locally. Alumni received several special appeals.

Besides distributing thousands of these publications, Bath also sent hundreds of news releases to 150 western newspapers. Regional publications received special photographs, and a Seattle audience saw a movie featuring President Penrose and other dignitaries launching the financial campaign. Bath employed a clipping service to measure the publicity's impact. Newspapers published 22,270 column inches of news stories and more than 200 Whitman College pictures. Whitman supporters were pleased by all this attention being paid to the institution.

The campaign waged in Walla Walla was also unique. The drive for the town's college included wide distribution of publications, a forty-foot street banner flying at a busy intersection, and numerous window displays. Everyone on campus became involved by making pledges and by arranging a parade featuring student floats and all of the faculty as marchers.

Seattle, not Walla Walla, served as campaign headquarters. Judge Thomas Burke was national chairman; other college friends took subordinate positions in key locations. The governing boards, which had never possessed the ability to conduct such an intensive drive, applauded both Tamblyn and Brown's resourcefulness and its "admirable college literature."

In June, Bath measured the impact of his publicity and made significant recommendations. He had discovered to his surprise that western newspapers either did not know about the college or did not understand its quality because the college had never informed them about its accomplishments. To overcome this problem, Bath urged it to employ a press agent, who would distribute stories and photographs. He predicted that Whitman releases were more likely to appear in Seattle, Portland, and Tacoma newspapers if accompanied by pictures. Bath recommended that the college list potential donors and begin corresponding with them. These friends could, in addition, recommend potential students.

Penrose anticipated that as college president he would have to play some role in such a major campaign and arranged to leave his administrative post and teaching station. But heavier burdens than he anticipated would fall upon his shoulders and even affect his health. The president absented himself from the campus during the intensive campaign, spending most of his time at the Seattle headquarters with the Tamblyn and Brown staff, ten secretaries, and many alumna volunteers. In April he and Joseph Rivers traveled in western Washington and Oregon, calling upon potential donors. Tamblyn and Brown employees, impressed with his enthusiasm for the college, emphasized to Penrose "that the success of the Northwest campaign" depended upon his efforts.[35] But the failure to harvest significant gifts prompted the president to announce that he would seek them in the East. His wife Mary had already been working the Northeast where she had become the campaign's leading fund raiser. After this strenuous urban effort, the Penroses rushed back home for commencement. He returned "spiritually depleted and mentally as well as physically exhausted."[36] In his report to the overseers Penrose revealed that he had not obtained one great gift in either the Northwest or the Northeast, though he assured them that he had made useful contacts, and that the campaign would succeed if fund raisers did not "sag." Overseers agreed that much had been accomplished but refused to publish the total amount collected in the five-month drive.

Penrose tried to put the best face on the disappointing campaign. In his public report he admitted the temptation to "throw up the sponge . . . allowing the comparatively small results which have thus far been obtained to represent the fruitage of our labors. . . . We are all tired and somewhat discouraged, because we had underestimated the difficulty of the campaign." On the other hand, the president explained that to terminate the exhausting drive would mean that the college would "submit faint-heartedly to . . . [its] poverty and inefficiency." He recommended a renewed effort.

The president's private correspondence reveals that the campaign was even less successful than his public report indicated. Certainly he did not publicize the fact that the school was not collecting enough cash from the campaign to make payments due Tamblyn and Brown, that the miserable financial condition of farmers resulted in a sluggish local campaign, and that tightfisted bankers would not lend. He confided to George Tamblyn that at commencement time Whitman would be "in the most distressing financial condition it has ever known."[37] But he did not express his frustrations publicly, for he did not want to discourage supporters.

Exhausted and frustrated, Penrose, for once, found scant relief at his Puget Sound summer camp. He returned to campus in late summer stating to friends that he was "still nervously depleted," that he suffered from serious eye trouble, and that he dreaded to accept Tamblyn and Brown's advice that he personally seek donors through December. George Tamblyn openly admired Penrose and privately expressed his frustration over his firm's failure to raise the amount predicted. He deducted about $5,000 from the college's bill. After his firm had completed its contract he generously allowed Mildred Winship, whom Penrose wanted as his financial assistant, to continue her work. The decision to allow Winship to remain in the campaign turned out to be critical. In fact, Penrose even predicted that if she left it would die. A graduate of Mount Holyoke, she became enthusiastic about Whitman and surprised Penrose with her extensive knowledge about it. Years before Virginia Dox had played a crucial financial role; now Mildred Winship, another talented young woman, served in a similar capacity. The school appointed her as the president's official financial assistant and, following Gerald Bath's advice, hired a publicity director, English instructor Russell Blankenship.

From the fall of 1924 through the summer of 1925 Winship took the campaign into the homes and businesses of potential west coast donors. Although she did not ask for money, she always glowingly described Whitman, and donations often followed. Tamblyn permitted her to remain at her post into 1925, for he knew that Penrose could not push the effort as he had in 1924; indeed the firm even paid her salary.

In September 1925 Stephen Penrose joyfully announced that the college actually had $250,000 from the campaign on hand (it also had about $400,000 more in pledges). This cash and the General Education Board match of $125,000 would enhance the endowment. The president also proclaimed that at last the school was out of debt. In summary, the campaign for $1,500,000 had fallen short, but the representatives of Tamblyn and Brown—especially Mildred Winship—working harmoniously with Penrose, had raised a significant sum and had won new friends for the college. The great fund drive of 1924 −1925 resolved the financial crisis. Once again an eastern institution —this time a fund-raising firm—had come to the assistance of the western school.

12

After the War:
Recovery, Recognition, and Challenge
1919 — 1924

The faculty emerged from the First World War with an enhanced reputation. Its members had pushed the war effort, and even super-patriots had not questioned its loyalty. An editor boasted, "Whitman stands unique as being one of the few colleges whose faculty and student body were untouched by pacifism or other isms which compelled a house-cleaning during the war. It stood [for] one hundred percent Americanism from start to finish."[1]

Although he knew that the community respected the faculty, Stephen Penrose suspected that townspeople seldom appreciated the multiple demands placed upon it. He explained to many audiences that a small college must have professors willing to labor long hours. He emphasized to overseers the need to implement a ten-to-one student-teacher ratio. This reduced teaching load was necessary because the faculty currently juggled so many responsibilities. Penrose stated: "The supposition of the ordinary businessman that a college professor is like a clerk in a grocery store, who ought to put in eight hours of teaching a day in order to earn his salary, needs only to be stated in order to be laughed at by those who have acquaintance with the ideals and methods of the present good college."[2]

The president knew that the professors worked an exhausting schedule: they taught three or four courses a term (some of which were out of their specialties), conducted comprehensive examinations, served on committees, traveled for the school, chaperoned student social affairs, attended games, debates, and musical performances, and kept long office hours. Department chairmen had the additional burden of academic advising.

The faculty controlled the curriculum and offered a fairly standard set of courses. There were, however, some unusual ones, like Penrose's required freshman class entitled "College Life," covering the "history, ideals, conditions, obligation, and opportunities of the American college, especially Whitman." The economics department offered "The Economics of Agriculture" for the benefit of rural students, and the department of applied mathematics listed a course entitled "Railroad Surveying."

The faculty structure remained unchanged. There were the three academic departmental groups (they were beginning to be called divisions) but some subjects, including music theory, art, and physical education, were not placed in any group.

Three faculty members composed the board of deans, which continued to serve in three capacities—as a board of discipline, as a faculty executive committee, and as the president's cabinet. The deans handled a wide variety of concerns, like the problem of congested automobile parking on Boyer Avenue and "the wisdom of providing parking places on the campus."[3] The deans had the responsibility of placing students on academic probation or expelling them for low scholarship, a task that consumed more and more of their time. In the winter quarter of 1922, five students were on the probation list; two years later, twenty-two. The board must also have wearied itself with investigations into charges that students had violated campus rules, especially those against the consumption of intoxicating beverages. A member of the board of deans probably spoke for the others when he regretted the time spent performing disagreeable and routine tasks. The board, he said, "is a good place for executive training, but it is far more congenial to teach."[4]

During its regular or special meetings, the entire faculty considered familiar academic concerns such as the establishment of a calendar, the effectiveness of the honor system, degree requirements, student petitions (generally seeking relief from physical education), and the awarding of scholarships. The faculty would not award scholarships to "students who have any expensive or unnecessary habits." It did not define these habits, but it may have been that by owning an automobile a student indulged in an "expensive habit."[5] One inter-

esting decision was to allow freshmen to challenge the Biblical literature requirement.

The legacy of the war influenced faculty action, especially the
academic schedule and the restoration of German. In 1918 the SATC
compelled a term system; Penrose and a minority of the faculty unsuccessfully pushed for a return to the semester calendar. In 1920 the
science department led the successful movement to restore the teaching of German, but there was no attempt to re-establish the entire
department.

Various student matters came before faculty meetings, including
the adoption of schedules for athletes, singers, and debaters. The
faculty sanctioned new fraternities and clubs, including a new German club that appeared in 1922. Professors kept a watchful eye on the
fraternities, especially their scholarship and social activities. Dances
were closely regulated: fraternities could not schedule more than two
a year, had to provide proper lighting and a chaperone, and should
keep them inexpensive. In 1922 the fraternities had to include an
authorized chaperone at "informal dinner parties, picnics, sleigh
rides, and other occasions where girls are invited."[6] The faculty occasionally pleaded with seniors not to have a disruptive sneak day,
frequently considered ways to improve chapel attendance, and once
had a member review a proposed student vaudeville show to make
sure it was inoffensive.

Faculty and committee meetings could be long-winded and inde-
cisive. One disgusted young professor wrote that an extended faculty
discussion had been "hampered by intellectual pose and Hamlet-like
indecision."[7] Faculty meetings, however, were made more efficient
by the fact that the three faculty groups dealing with academics, internal life, and external relations had discussed issues prior to introducing them. The external relations group, for example, publicized the
college by arranging faculty lectures and by sending colleagues to
institutes, high schools, and alumni meetings.

The underpaid, overworked faculty was aging. Its low pay was
constantly a campus issue. An editorial in the *Pioneer* reminded readers that poor faculty salaries were a national, not just a local, problem. Plumbers, for instance, averaged an $1,800 yearly income com-
pared to a professor's $1,200. In the early 1920s Whitman salaries
improved but failed to keep pace with inflation and lagged behind

Louis F. Anderson   *Helen A. Pepoon*   *Walter A. Bratton*

In 1924 the six senior Whitman faculty members were honored at a Whitman
commencement and had their photographs taken. Each of them received "a purse

those at the University of Washington. An overseer who owned a
Yakima orchard thought it wrong to pay a Whitman instructor less
than he paid a farmhand, but he added "it is refreshing to know there
are men and women whose real worth to the community is not measured in dollars."[8]

In 1920 Penrose feared that economic want might make his faculty disintegrate. He confided: "already several men are being driven by
the needs of their families to consider the abandonment of teaching
for the sake of a more adequate living wage."[9] The administrator
called attention not only to the salary crisis but also to the fact that
some professors had been in harness longer than twenty-five years.
Pointing out that five members had such longevity, he boasted that no
other western college had such a record of heroic service. Professor
Walter Eells compared the faculty with that of the University of Oregon as to length of service; his findings demonstrated that those at
Whitman had the more remarkable record. Eells joked that Pacific
Northwest professors taught a long period because of the congenial
climate, "where men live longer, serve longer, and wear out more
slowly."[10] At a public reception in 1920, Walla Wallans recognized
five professors who had given their lives to the college—Louis Anderson, twenty-eight years; William Lyman, thirty-two years; Helen
Pepoon, twenty-nine years; and Walter Bratton and Benjamin
Brown, twenty-five years each. In 1924 the senior faculty—the same

Benjamin H. Brown   Howard S. Brode   Edward E. Ruby

of a ten-dollar gold piece for each year of their service at Whitman." This talented group did much to build the college and they were difficult to replace.

group, minus William Lyman and with the addition of Howard Brode and Edward Ruby—was again honored, this time at a Whitman commencement.

Louis Anderson, who refused a salary, was probably the only faculty member who did not worry about retirement. Fortunately, the college entered into an agreement with the Carnegie Foundation for the Advancement of Teaching; it required the faculty to enter into an annuity program funded by both the individual person and the foundation. Lyman at age sixty-five was the first to retire under this program, but Penrose complained that the system would make him only modest payments and that Lyman and his wife would still be in need. However, other faculty hailed the annuity program as a way to escape poverty following long and devoted teaching careers.

Apparently, few professors attempted to supplement their meager salaries by summer work, but some, including Coach Vincent "Nig" Borleske, labored in the wheat harvest. Occasionally a professor taught summer school at another institution; for example, biologist Howard Brode often taught at Friday Harbor, the University of Washington's marine biology station.

With the challenges of a growing student body and a limited budget, Stephen Penrose struggled to retain his talented and respected faculty. Like his predecessor Alexander Anderson, he temporarily employed his own capable children. Frances and Mary had attended

Bryn Mawr after graduation from Whitman and returned to teach briefly in the modern language department.

Chester Maxey, who became a Whitman College political science professor in 1925, wondered whether the 1920s faculty was as effective as the earlier ones. He judged his colleagues to be a weaker group than the faculty that had instructed him as an undergraduate. "After allowing for all prejudices inspired by undergraduate nostalgia, I had to admit to myself that most of the newcomers did not impress me as first-raters."[11] Perhaps his generalization is correct: advancing age, deaths, and resignations had taken a toll. Penrose had appointed some capable additions, but most of them resigned because of unattractive teaching conditions, the good job market, and a desire to research and publish. Rebuilding the faculty in the early 1920s proved frustrating for Penrose, who sought men and women with the patience, dedication, and skill to match those who laid Whitman's foundation between 1894 and 1914. President Henry Suzzalo at the University of Washington, who was also attempting to hire faculty members, told his friend Penrose about problems finding skilled teachers in a time of growing student enrollments and of a shortage of applicants for faculty positions.

Although he allowed the faculty considerable power, Penrose would not share control when hiring professors because "In the small college the selection of the faculty must rest ultimately with the president. . . . He dare not shift the responsibility to other shoulders lest he surrender his chief prerogative." Penrose consulted with the faculty but thought that he alone should select the men and women who would best carry out his educational mission. In the postwar period the president tried to strengthen the faculty by taking into account the needs of society and students. His most significant appointments came in religion, history, and political science. Penrose spent considerable time searching for a scholar to fill the Weyerhaeuser Chair of Biblical Literature because he wanted "a man of virile character, red-blooded, human in his sympathies and companionable with young men particularly, who has the scholarly equipment and the love of teaching which will enable him effectively to interest his students in the literature and life embodied in the Old and New Testaments."[12] The person appointed to the chair would also have to teach in the philosophy department and to offer "a philosophy which is positively

Christian and not negative or atheistic." Dr. Eli T. Allen, who had spent years in Turkey and Persia, seemed suited to handle the diverse responsibilities that Penrose placed upon this valuable professorship.

Trustee Park Weed Willis also lauded the Weyerhaeuser gift and wondered "why more of the wealthy people . . . who had made money out of this northwest country, have not thought of the wisdom of placing some of it in the same district where it would do good."[13] Penrose agreed with these sentiments, which were similar to those voiced in 1907 in support of Greater Whitman.

The president hoped that prominent persons might endow professorships in geography, political science, and especially history, since he believed that students in the 1920s needed more thorough instruction in these fields. His emphasis upon history affected the library and strengthened the history department.

Apparently Penrose alone decided library appropriations. In the depressed 1918–1919 school year he could not provide money for books or binding. Despite these stringent conditions, the collection still grew from private gifts, government documents, and Carnegie publications. In the early 1920s Penrose allotted money for binding, for opening the library in the evening (because the faculty was assigning more reserved reading), and for the history department budget. Responding to the pleas for books by a new historian he had hired and to his own conviction about the importance of historical study, Penrose gave $900 (three-fourths of the book budget) to the history department. By 1923 librarian Harriet Carstensen, who enjoyed the able assistance of alumna Ruth Reynolds, could judge that the history section was a "fair working collection," but she expressed two concerns. Generally, she wanted a larger library allocation because "the library is the very center of the entire college" and, specifically, she wanted larger departmental book budgets because of growing demands. The librarian reminded leaders that economics was a popular field and that the political science professor received only a $20 annual appropriation.

Surely faculty members grumbled about Penrose's division of the book budget and also about the inadequacy of a library totaling only 33,000 books. In fact, professors also disagreed with their leader's emphasis on the study of history and had rejected his request that a modern European history course be a college requirement. The presi-

William D. Lyman taught many courses at Whitman but pre-
ferred American history. A fighter for faculty rights in the
1890s, he became one of the school's most admired teachers.
He published important essays and books on Pacific North-
west history. Lyman is the only faculty member besides Presi-
dent Maxey to have had a building named for him.

dent could, however, make a significant change in the history department. In 1920 William Lyman retired after a distinguished thirty-
two-year career. Called "Daddy Lyman" by admiring students, he
had won regional attention for his Pacific Northwest histories, including those on Indians and eastern Washington. Penrose, who
praised Lyman for his "unparalleled knowledge of Northwest history,"[14] joined those who applauded the professor's long-time advoca-
cy of the Columbia River waterway as a critical trade artery.

Convinced that the college needed an historian trained in foreign
policy, Penrose hired Dr. Samuel Flagg Bemis. With a PH.D. from

Harvard and teaching experience at Colorado College, Bemis became an exceptional faculty member in that he published, delivered scholarly papers at regional meetings, and taught energetically. Bemis had been aboard the *Sussex* when it was torpedoed in 1916, and his exposure in the water had impaired his health. He sought to improve it at Colorado and at Whitman.[15] In 1922 his manuscript on Jay's Treaty won him the Knights of Columbus Award in the form of a $3,000 prize and publication. At the award ceremony in Memorial Hall, an enthusiastic campus audience heard that the manuscript "stood as a beacon light . . . not only as fine history, but as a literary gem."[16] This was the first major book prize ever won by a Whitman faculty member, and it brought considerable publicity to the college, including newsreel coverage. Bemis published other essays (including one on the Mullan Road, which linked Walla Walla with Fort Benton, Montana, on the Missouri River), taught a summer at the University of Washington, and received a leave of absence to do research for the Carnegie Institute. Penrose called him an "invigorating teacher" who had "rehabilitated our run-down history department."[17] But he recognized Bemis as research-oriented and anticipated his 1924 resignation. There was no way that a western college paying small salaries and insisting upon enormous teaching burdens—Bemis had taught all the European and American history classes—could have retained him. He went on to have a distinguished career at Yale.

Penrose, however, hired a remarkable replacement in Clement Eaton. A southerner with plans to complete a PH.D. at Harvard, he was a lively instructor and a popular advisor in Lyman Hall. But he resigned after one year, settled at the University of Kentucky, and became a notable historian of the Old South and of the Confederacy.

The situation in political science was somewhat similar. Dr. Harrison A. Trexler, who had earned his degree at Johns Hopkins University, joined the faculty in 1919 and became the Miles C. Moore Professor of Political Science. Judging that "no more important department at this time can be found than that of political science," Penrose had selected well.[18] But in 1924 Trexler, another capable teacher, resigned. He eventually moved to Southern Methodist University and wrote on American slavery.

While seeking to retain the faculty, the president addressed the problem of the "proper relationship between research and undergraduate teaching." He explained that he was "primarily interested in finding teachers" and was "willing to leave . . . research work to the great universities. If a man on our faculty develops a genius for research work and shows a greater inclination for it than for teaching, I encourage him along his bent but with the definite conviction that sooner or later it may be wise for him to withdraw from teaching at Whitman and give himself up to his first love elsewhere."[19] Penrose argued, however, that teaching at a small college had its compensations in the close personal relationship between faculty members and students. "Our teachers are . . . in contact with individual minds and individual needs instead of dealing only with classes." It was his opinion that the faculty "liked the freedom and the opportunity to teach the active-minded students whom they have found."

Probably most faculty members agreed, and those who did not departed. Professors who remained, however, experienced little improvement in salaries or work loads. They and their families did not participate in the 1920s materialism and feared even more stringent conditions in their retirement. The faculty was in a precarious economic position long before the Great Depression. The solutions to the faculty's professional and personal problems and the restoration of its quality challenged Penrose and the governing boards.

The president did not appoint an all-college dean. Undoubtedly his experience with Dean Archer Hendrick, who had challenged his power, led him to maintain what he called an unusual administrative system. He preferred to give each faculty member an administrative duty—a system he thought was preferable to their serving under "an arrogant dean."[20] While he would not appoint an all-college dean, he retained the position of dean of women and, in 1923, sought to fill the position. "I want a woman of strong Christian character, a genius for friendliness and an unfailing fund of common-sense, with sufficient humor to enter sympathetically into the life of the two hundred girls. . . . I do not know of any place more important." The president anticipated that a "charming woman" would have an impact on the residence hall and the school's social life. He did not believe, however, that the position was too demanding because college women governed themselves, and there was no teaching requirement. "The duties," he summarized, "involve mainly befriending and inspiring the young women, with an oversight of the housekeeping in the dormitories though not the running of the dining room and kitchen." Penrose found Rachel L. Fitch, calling her "a host in herself with reference to looking after our girls."[21]

While Penrose realized that the faculty and deans played a significant role in the life of the institution, he also acknowledged the importance of faculty spouses. Unfortunately, this group provided little information about their lives, but Catherine Brode is an exception. In some ways her long experience as a faculty wife was typical. A graduate of the Illinois State Normal University, she had taught in public schools, married Howard Brode in 1893, and moved to Walla Walla six years later. In 1900 she gave birth to triplet sons, an event that prompted considerable faculty excitement. Besides her duties as wife and mother, she delivered papers at women's reading clubs, was active in the state federation of women's clubs, and worked for the PTA, Camp Fire Girls, the YWCA, a Sunday school, and the garden club. During the war she was active in the Red Cross. She and her husband entertained many students in their home, students who later brought their own children to meet Mrs. Brode, referring to her as one of the "College Mothers." Faculty families, including the Brodes, were close to each other, helping when illness struck, camping together in the Blue Mountains, sharing meals and Christmas parties, and taking a great interest in all their growing children. Penrose boasted about the large size of faculty families, even making this point to President Theodore Roosevelt when he visited in 1903. In summary, faculty wives, like their husbands, were overworked but shared their commitment to the college's ideals. They, too, must have grumbled about a small family income and the difficulty in paying the grocer. The Brodes' tour of Europe was made possible only by a gift from an old friend, and they did not acquire their first automobile until 1929. But Catherine and other faculty wives accepted their husbands' meager earnings about the same way that ministers' wives did. Both groups knew that their families responded to a calling.

Alumni of this era still recall the way that faculty wives played an integral role and that their devotion and compassion added to the quality of campus life. Probably the college community often held these respected women up as models to coeds; these mothers served community, church, and college, and simultaneously reared admirable children, many of whom went on to distinguished careers.

Coach Borleske and the Waning Days of "Big Time" Athletics

Today, the idea of Whitman competing in major sports against institutions such as the universities of Oregon, Washington, or Idaho seems humorous. In the early 1920s, however, Whitman belonged to a conference comprising these and other large institutions, some of which had six to ten times the enrollment of Whitman. In 1926 the college helped form a new conference with smaller schools, such as Willamette and Pacific, and played fewer games with large-school rivals. Although this shift of opponents made great sense, it was not so obvious in the early 1920s because Whitman's competition with larger institutions meant better gate receipts and better sports-page coverage.

In 1908 Whitman invited five institutions to Walla Walla to write rules governing intercollegiate athletics. Thus the University of Oregon, the University of Washington, the University of Idaho, Oregon Agricultural College, Washington State College, and Whitman College formed the Northwest Conference. Referred to as the "Big Six," they drew up rules of eligibility, defined amateur status, and installed an enforcement mechanism. Conference members did not annually schedule each other, which led to endless sports-page disputes over championships. Whitman, however, rarely staked a title claim. From 1900 through 1917 it did not have a total winning record in baseball, basketball, track, or, worst of all, football, where the school compiled a record of thirty-two victories, fifty-three losses, and four ties. Whitman could hold its own with smaller colleges and high schools, but universities generally proved to be too powerful.

Unsuccessful football seasons were not the only difficulty. For a time the game itself was controversial. In a particularly savage game against Washington State College played on Ankeny Field in 1909, five men had to be carried from the field. The Portland *Oregonian* denounced the brutal play, accusing each player of rushing "at the other with hatred almost amounting to murder in his heart." It also reported that hundreds of the estimated three thousand excited spectators cried, "Kill him, Kill him."[22] Walla Wallans protested this account, and a local editor complained that Whitman received bad publicity by charges that its players "are would-be murderers."[23]

Filled with loathing over the brutal spectacle that they had witnessed, the Whitman faculty took action. It voted that "the present game of football was unsuitable for college athletics" and favored a change in the rules that would "eliminate mass plays and other extra hazardous features." The faculty warned that if this reform failed, it would consider abolishing football and replacing it with a safer sport.[24] The resolution appeared in regional newspapers, and some Whitman supporters cautioned that the threat of terminating football would reduce freshman applications.

A few weeks later the school received much worse publicity. A sheriff from North Dakota served a warrant upon football coach J. Merrill Blanchard, charging him with statutory rape. Many people defended the popular coach's character; Penrose assured them that Blanchard had settled the matter and would return. But he did not return, and the scandal embarrassed Whitman. The college also received negative publicity because it was accused of recruiting athletes from other schools and because its players violated playing rules.

Meanwhile, the raging national campaign against football had local ramifications. In 1909 newspapers charged that twenty-nine players had died and that scores of others had suffered permanent knee and shoulder damage. Some writers charged that the duels of German college students were safer than the mayhem of American football. The *Nation* roared that "the whole trend of the play has been towards the old massing of men against one spot in the opponents' line." The editor bluntly charged that "Football is not merely a sport now, it is a contrivance for injuring and maiming."[25] Whitman and its opponents were playing just this type of brutal football.

At Williams Penrose had heard critics denounce football, and he now realized that the attack was broadening to include all intercollegiate athletics. This situation required him, he thought, to analyze intercollegiate athletics in his 1910 presidential report. He began by acknowledging that the public took great interest in sports and then presented the case for intercollegiate athletics. It provided "physical betterment," contributed to college spirit, developed teamwork, attracted boys to college, and advertised the school. The educator elaborated: "Perhaps the cheapest advertising which a college gets is that which comes through the sporting columns of the newspapers." He deplored the national situation: "A boy would value less highly the laurel wreath of Dante or the crown of enduring scholarship than the glory of playing on the Yale or Harvard . . . eleven, and it might truthfully be said that more people today are interested in the Yale-Harvard football game than are interested in the problems of pure scholarship or in poetry." The president also assessed the game's local importance. When the school fielded a weak team, "the men of the community are apt to be indifferent to the college's welfare, but when a strong team is put forth, hearty enthusiasm and generous backing soon develops which is of far-reaching value to the college." Everyone knew that, over the years, successful football and baseball teams had prompted enthusiastic community support.

Penrose then presented a strong case against intercollegiate athletics. He cautioned against "the development of a team of a few individuals and a disproportionate expense and attention focused upon them and their physical development, while the great body of students is disregarded." Because more money was spent for athletics than for any other activity, it distorted college values. The players put too much time into football and too little into scholarship. He judged that "no man can undergo the strenuous life of a football campaign without diminishing his intellectual efficiency or at least limiting his intellectual output." Excessive emphasis on athletics would give the high school student the wrong impression about college life. The president feared that high schools considered colleges to be "a place where a few athletic individuals are developed to compete for the glory of the institution, [and are] applauded by a body of students who feel that their own chance for immortality depends upon the success of the college team."

Penrose denounced the emergence of professionalism. "The professional coach, made necessary by the keenness of athletic rivalry, has introduced a spirit of professionalism into the men of his team. . . . Wherever the spirit of professionalism intrudes, there is a marked lowering of standards. The man who plays football or baseball because he is paid to do so, whether secretly or openly, has no college loyalty . . . no spirit of sacrifice for the general welfare, but is rather apt to become filled with the spirit of the old time gladiator who fought for pay and for his own glory." The leader charged that athletics led the players to drink and to dissipation. He also lamented the fact that intercollegiate rivalries led to institutional jealousy. "I fear that too often we think of ourselves as belonging to hostile tribes rather than as all included in a true Israel of scholarship."

The writer advised that students, alumni, parents, and the public should be polled on the question of intercollegiate athletics. Then the overseers could "decide whether it would be wise to run the risk at Whitman of taking the extraordinary step, unprecedented in any American college, of excluding hereafter intercollegiate athletics." Penrose warned, however, that if the school dropped its program it still must provide physical training.

The trustees and overseers were not about to take such a drastic step as terminating intercollegiate athletics. They knew that sports solidified the campus. All major sports attracted support, but football predominated. During football season there were pep rallies, pre-game parades, organized yelling sections, serpentines at half-time, bonfires, the ringing of the college bell after a victory, and post-game receptions. Many townspeople joined in such activities, rendering Whitman songs and yells. Obviously the game united the town and campus. Many agreed with a *Pioneer* editorial: "If we can't play, we can at least cheer, and cheer to the last down."[26]

In October 1916, in a football game against the University of Idaho, Whitman students (joined by Walla Wallans) participate in a typical halftime rally on Ankeny Field. Whitman won by a score of twenty-six to fourteen.

Supporters of intercollegiate athletics realized that the school needed a coach who would field teams comparable to those of 1906 through 1908. Penrose searched for a man who shared his educational goals, who enjoyed a regional reputation as a player and coach, and who, like many Whitman professors, would not be enticed away by a better salary. In 1915 he decided that Vincent "Nig" Borleske met all the requirements. This was the second time that Penrose went to the Borleske home and asked Vincent to help Whitman.

The most remarkable athlete ever to graduate from Whitman, Borleske was born in 1887 into a blue-collar family that valued hard work and education. In 1906 Penrose recruited him as a student because this young man was exactly the type of person that Penrose wanted to educate. An outstanding athlete, Borleske also was valedictorian of his class at Spokane High School and planned to attend law school. As a freshman Borleske played on one of Whitman's best football teams. After an injury in his sophomore year, he recuperated in the Penrose home and became part of the family. In his last two years, Borleske's play at halfback resulted in his being chosen twice to all-Northwest teams. Some coaches, sportswriters, and fans always argued that he deserved all-American recognition. For years after his graduation in 1910, his skills as a runner, passer, punter, and tackler —especially in games against larger schools—remained the basis for athletic legends. In addition, Borleske was both an outstanding baseball player, especially as a pitcher, and a talented basketball player. His numerous admirers stressed the fact that he was much more than a typical athlete. He worked his way through college, served as a student body officer, was active in the Illahee Club, and taught mathematics at Pearsons Academy. Following graduation he coached at Seattle and Portland high schools; at night he attended the Oregon Law School. Out of a deep sense of loyalty to Penrose and the college, Borleske shelved plans to practice law and returned to his alma mater to be its coach and graduate manager. He and his wife Mignon—she would take charge of women's athletics—came to Walla Walla and scrimped on his $1,250 salary.

Everybody had an opinion about Coach Borleske. His biographer neatly captured the man: "He was at once gruff, stubborn, outspoken, sentimental, opinionated, loyal, and generous." The writer Nard Jones, a loyal alumnus, summarized that Borleske was "A man full of fight and fire and loyalty, and deep love for all humanity. A man worth knowing."[27] Penrose wrote that "Borleske's loyalty to the ideals of his alma mater and his invincible integrity have made him an inspiring influence in the life of the College."[28] But he had his detractors. There were charges that he treated his players unfairly, and some angry athletes departed the squad complaining that he expected too much.

Although observers disagreed over the coach, they could all agree that next to the president Borleske was the college's most famous person. This fame reflected the fact that American society was, as Penrose stated, infatuated with intercollegiate athletics. A colorful coach like Borleske would be at center stage. In 1933 *Oregonian* sports editor L.H. Gregory, who helped place him there, assessed him: "No coach on the Pacific coast is more fertile in football ideas nor more resourceful in their application than Vincent Borleske."[29] Perhaps this was true in the early 1930s, but his career between 1919 and 1924 was controversial.

The First World War interrupted Borleske's attempt to upgrade his teams; his first postwar football season was a long-remembered disaster. The University of Washington team—then called Sundodgers, not Huskies—overwhelmed the Missionaries 120 to 0, and a *Pioneer* writer appropriately described it as the second Whitman massacre. Following a hard-fought tie with the University of Montana, Whitman lost to Gonzaga, 39 to 0. Six players suffered injuries, mostly from clipping, in the bruising contest. For the next game Borleske did not have a squad large enough to compete with the University of Idaho, so he canceled the contest. A student editorial did not ask that football be terminated but requested that the school improve its program: "More athletic support would attract more real athletes to Whitman; more athletes would make possible winning teams. Winning teams would mean more advertising. More advertising would bring more students."[30] Penrose endorsed these sentiments, but there seemed little the hard-pressed college could do for this team other than root.

The football situation improved faster than anticipated, however. Borleske recruited a few solid players, including some from the famous Walla Walla High School team of 1919, which won the state championship. There were other reasons for improvement. For example, Borleske was a resourceful coach; the admission of the University of Montana, Willamette University, and Pacific University weakened the conference; alumni recommended a few outstanding athletes; and Borleske's unusual intramural program supplied still others. Seeking varsity players, the coach developed a required and competitive intramural system. Team competition between housing groups in a variety of sports became very popular. Using the slogan, "Every man an athlete," Borleske had as many as eighty percent of the college men playing football in equipment that he purchased from his athletic budget. He bluntly told entering freshmen that "deep in the heart of every normal college man smolders the desire to earn the college athletic emblem."[31] He advised these new men to achieve this distinction by immediately getting football uniforms and practicing hard. Most freshmen joined these intramural teams, which sometimes played local high schools, and the better players moved up to the varsity team. Borleske often hailed his program, assuring supporters that "the old system of athletics for the best only, is going fast. The new system of athletics for all, properly supervised and financed, is coming."[32] In April 1921 the coach boasted that "It is our intramural system that has brought Whitman to the front in athletics again, and it is in this system that our hope lies in the future." As it turned out, this imaginative but controversial program could not develop enough talented athletes to compete with the superior ones being recruited by the larger conference members.

There is a tremendous amount of information about Whitman athletics in the 1920s—in the Walla Walla newspapers, the *Pioneer*, and the school yearbook, the *Waiilatpu*. Perhaps the best summary is to be found in the monthly *Alumnus*, where Borleske frankly evaluated games and teams and pleaded for alumni support.

In 1921 Whitman claimed its first Northwest Conference football championship by winning three conference games in a league where the Whitman student body was "only a third to a tenth as large" as its opponents.[33] This successful season led Borleske, who sought gate receipts and public attention, to overestimate his prospects and to schedule even more large opponents. (This would not be the last time that a coach at Whitman or at some other regional school would make optimistic predictions and assumptions from an extraordinary season.) The 1921 success opened the way for a disastrous football program that collapsed in the mid-1920s. In the 1922, 1923, and 1924 seasons the Missionaries won only four games while the big schools rolled up large scores against them. In 1922 a spirited Whitman eleven narrowly lost to the University of Oregon in Pendleton. A huge crowd paid a gate greater than any ever received in Walla Walla.[34] Following this contest the Missionary squad made exhausting treks for games against Nevada and Utah; the maize and blue had no chance against either university.

According to one observer, Whitman's squads playing in the early 1920s were "mostly fuzzy-cheeked teen-agers weighing less than 150."[35] Because of its small enrollment, Whitman was the only conference member that was allowed to play freshmen on its team. These young men often played inspired football, but a series of games against more physical squads overwhelmed them. It took courage to be "a fighting Bantam" and face Utah, Washington, and Oregon in only thirteen days!

Injuries, the inability to recruit, and frustration resulting from losses at the hands of powerful teams took their toll. These factors and Borleske's harsh manner meant that many athletes did not play out their eligibility. The campus and town, however, cheered those waging the uneven gridiron battles, noting that the wonderful spirit of the maize and blue teams was more obvious at the start than at the end of the season. A Whitman student correctly analyzed: "The fight and spirit, however, could not stand up against the terrible pounding of heavier opponents when there was no prospect of victory in sight. . . . Whitman had a well coached, fighting lineup but was simply outclassed by the larger schools which had a greater wealth of material."[36] Another student summarized all the losing seasons: "It is trying for any team to have to face big heavy teams, coached by a staff of a dozen men and backed by twenty or thirty good substitutes."[37]

The coach and rooters praised the eleven for holding a big school to a close score; in fact, this became an end in itself. Borleske frankly told alumni that he could not win many games but hailed his dedicated athletes. The outstanding player of this period was Ben Comrada, a rangy lineman who consistently won his coach's accolades. Borleske stated that "such men as Comrada only come to a college once in a generation," and that his play against Washington demonstrated that he was "the best tackle in the west." "He is a power at opening holes, a wonderful defensive tackle, a terrific tackler, a most dependable man advancing the ball, a good [blocker], and an excellent forward passer."[38] The football captain became an excellent student, and one admirer stated that Comrada refuted "the current thesis that stupidity was the first requirement of a good lineman."[39] He was the first Whitman football player to have his name placed on the college's Niles Cup and probably the first Missionary to be honored by Walter Camp as an honorable mention all-American.

Football lore was one thing; lopsided defeats were another. Borleske blamed losses upon inexperienced players, the lack of brawn, and small squads. Poor luck, miserable playing conditions, and unfair officiating were other factors that the coach sometimes added in explaining failure to alumni. In 1923 Borleske correctly assessed the athletic situation: "Fight can hold down scores but it cannot win games consistently in the face of such superior odds." However, instead of scheduling more appropriate schools, he again pleaded with alumni to bolster his program. They should recruit talented players, who, added to the few coming up through his intramural system, would comprise a competitive squad. The coach warned that "If Whitman is going to continue in intercollegiate athletics everyone, including alumni, must realize this and do something to remedy the situation. Otherwise it is folly to even think of remaining in the Conference."[40]

Borleske was wrong about intercollegiate athletics, for they were not imperiled. His failed football program resulted from the folly of playing too many big opponents. The *Pioneer* correctly judged that the 1923 record proved that "light, inexperienced men, no matter how much fight and determination they may have, cannot stand up against the terrific pounding of heavier opponents."[41] This analysis also applied to the disastrous 1924 season. In that fall, the maize and blue played six conference games, losing all but one. More important, Whitman scored only 13 points to 225 rolled up by opponents. Despite Borleske's persistent pep talks and his efforts to build a competitive team, he had failed. The coach and other school leaders should have immediately collaborated with other regional private colleges being swamped by the public school giants and formed a more competitive league. In conference meetings held in 1924 and 1925, the large institutions, who had been in the Pacific Coast Conference since

1915, threatened to pull out of the Northwest Conference because the private colleges provided scant competition. A game with a weak opponent helped the Pacific Coast Conference members improve their record so that they might be invited to the Rose Bowl; however, they preferred to play such foes as California and Stanford because such games brought larger gate receipts. At conference meetings Whitman conferred with other private colleges about establishing a new conference. Borleske, however, opposed secession and vainly labored to maintain the old athletic relationship, which lasted a couple more seasons. But in 1926 the big schools finally pulled out, thus forcing Whitman and other small schools to restructure the conference. From time to time the Missionaries played against a football power, but the days of "big time" athletics had mercifully ended.

Borleske's biographer explained that he had not wanted to leave the old conference because of the blow to his pride.[42] The author should have added that games against the universities on their home fields or at Pendleton brought money that underwrote the intramural program and the other intercollegiate sports. Thus, pride and money influenced Borleske in the same way they tempt some present-day overmatched schools to remain in prestigious conferences.

Borleske, a man of enormous energy, could not concentrate entirely upon football because he also coached basketball and baseball and conducted the physical education program. Whitman could not be competitive in every sport, because the larger schools provided better facilities, hired a separate coach for each team, and drew from larger male populations. Borleske noted that Whitman's higher academic standards made it more difficult to recruit players. Despite these problems, the college came closer to meeting the competition in basketball and baseball than it did in football. In 1920 Whitman's powerful basketball squad won the league championship with an eleven and two record and challenged Stanford, Chicago, and other teams to a three-game series. The 1924 baseball team won regional recognition, but generally Borleske coached losing teams that he evaluated honestly. In 1924, for example, he stated that his inexperienced basketball squad "would look good for a few minutes but just as soon as the other team would spurt, Whitman would go all to pieces."[43] Meanwhile, he praised his baseball team for not falling "to pieces in the pinches, and for a wonderful morale."

Basketball games attracted screaming fans. To demonstrate good sportsmanship, Whitmanites in 1924 adopted the practice that they would not jeer or hoot opposing players. The *Pioneer* described visiting teams as being college guests deserving courtesy.

Tennis matches and track meets drew few fans and fewer athletes. A lack of money meant that these squads did not travel like the popular teams. These minor sports received little coaching, but Bill Martin, who had been a sensational sprinter at Whitman, assisted track competitors.

Of the many Whitman men who enjoyed varsity athletics, one of the most skillful was Sabin Rich, a noted basketball and baseball player. The Sherwood brothers enjoyed the competition too: Cameron was an effective baseball pitcher, and Donald won several varsity tennis matches. The Penrose twins played on several teams, and a photograph of them in basketball uniforms brought Whitman national publicity.

The 1922 varsity basketball team won seven games and lost seven games. The highlights of the season were two victories over the University of Oregon in Eugene. Clem Penrose is at the left in the last row; his twin brother Nat stands second from right, next to Coach Vincent "Nig" Borleske.

Tennis was the only intercollegiate sport open to women. In 1924 Martha McAulay (left), Julia Ferrell (center), and Eunice Marquis composed the squad. The players pose on Ankeny Field; behind them is the gymnasium.

Intercollegiate athletics attracted some minority athletes. A black student from Seattle, Claudius D. Norris, won Borleske's praise as a defensive football player. Two outstanding Japanese baseball players arrived at Whitman, having been recruited by alumnus Jack Stone, secretary to the governor of Hawaii. Walla Walla fans praised Moriso Matsuno and Fred Tsuda, and one wrote: "The boys from Hawaii have been making sensational catches as well as getting their percentage of blows with the willow."[44]

Women's athletics were finally becoming more important. Women competed in intramural basketball; on the other hand, attempts to schedule field hockey failed because men monopolized Ankeny Field. Tennis was their only intercollegiate sport, which began in 1921 with a victory over the University of Idaho. There was considerable campus support for this activity; for example, the *Pioneer* applauded the women's team because it proved "their capability of meeting rival teams."[45] The following year faculty granted the three-woman squad permission to travel to Moscow, Idaho, for a return match. Here were the first small steps on the continuing long march towards athletic equality.

Music, Debate, and Dramatics

Students and townspeople enjoyed and profited from the school's offerings in music, debate, and dramatics. Because Stephen Penrose stressed music, the school enjoyed a highly successful conservatory. This institution operated separately from the college, but its director worked under Penrose. The conservatory attracted three diverse groups: students pursuing a bachelor of music degree (they combined music classes with college courses); adults seeking diplomas in piano, voice, public school music, or other areas; and schoolchildren taking music lessons.

Howard E. Pratt, a voice teacher with training at the University of Michigan, came in 1919 at a difficult time, for his predecessor, Llewelleyn B. Cain, who had been hired in 1918, had been "suddenly and unexpectedly arrested for charges of immorality."[46] The trustees heard testimony and discharged him. Pratt's talent, energy, and administrative ability soon brought order and talented musicians. His catalog stressed the conservatory's advantages: location in a city enjoying "delightful climate . . . near the foot of the Blue Mountains," a competent faculty, and a strong regional reputation. Pratt hired about a dozen capable musicians who, in turn, attracted and retained students. With an enrollment of about four hundred in 1921, the conservatory was as large as the college, and some even claimed it to be the largest conservatory in the Pacific Northwest.

With so many sounds coming out of the busy and cozy music building, one observer likened it to an "insane asylum."[47] Enjoying considerable praise, Pratt pressed for a larger operating budget, more music scholarships, and an enlargement of McDowell Hall—a concert hall in the conservatory—to a seating capacity of six hundred so that he would no longer have to hire the Keylor Grand Theater. Pratt added further to the school's reputation with successful glee club tours. In 1921 he led sixteen male singers and ten jazz musicians on a thousand-mile tour that attracted about eight thousand listeners. A special feature was a radio broadcast beamed at six hundred Seattle receiving sets. Harper Joy, the student tour manager and comedian, won applause for his energetic efforts. In the following year there was another successful tour and a rousing concluding performance in

"The 1921 Men's Glee Club," which presented a program of singing, jazz, and vaudeville acts, "was undoubtedly the best and most successful club Whitman has ever had, successful both dramatically and financially," according to one source. The group included sixteen voices and a ten-piece jazz band. To the far left of the third row is Harper Joy, who was an impersonator and an enthusiastic student leader of the group.

Walla Walla. A shortage of money kept the women's glee club close to home, but it did sing before a penitentiary audience. In 1924 a mixed glee club of twenty-eight and a ten-piece orchestra—properly chaperoned by Mrs. Penrose, who exerted her "motherly influence"—made an extensive two-week tour, publicizing Whitman and earning money for the student body.[48] The college musicians appeared in halls, churches, and high schools. A performance often included classical and popular music, dramatic skits, orchestral music, and the Whitman hymn, composed in 1914 by Stephen Penrose. A Spokane reporter described the performers: "The chorus, a good looking melange of men and girls, the latter in all the pastel shades ... was pleasant to the eye as well as the ear."[49] After most performances alumni arranged for a dance, reception, or chicken dinner.

The director of the Whitman Conservatory of Music, Howard E. Pratt was known for his "sweet and powerful voice of pure tenor quality" and for the enormous energy he put into various musical programs, including a memorable production of Faust.

In March 1923 great crowds came to the Keylor Grand Theater for the opera *Faust*, the most ambitious music production ever presented by the conservatory. For several years afterward, the audience still hailed Pratt's direction and the students' skills. The conservatory became a vital community institution: it furnished musical entertainments for city groups, offered recitals, and presented visiting musicians. Thus the conservatory was one of the institution's most popular components, winning friends for the college. Appreciative of music, Penrose hailed Pratt's efforts, as did students. The *Pioneer* asserted: "The name of Howard E. Pratt has been linked with the word 'Success.' . . . Whitman is indeed fortunate in having on its faculty a member with so much personality, so much enthusiasm, and so much ability—a man who is a natural leader."[50]

While the college's music program rose to its highest level, the intercollegiate debate program declined. The touring glee clubs brought money to the student body; the debate team was, according to Penrose, "a financially unprofitable venture."[51] The English department supervised the team, and the Associated Students of Whitman College managed it. Proponents of debate often remembered the school's impressive history of victories over its large-school competitors. In the 1920s intercollegiate debate required an institution to have both an affirmative and a negative team. Thus in a 1921 men's debate with the University of Washington on the subject "That immigration from Southeastern Europe should be restricted," the Whitman affirmative team won in Walla Walla by using statistics, "straight forward reasoning, and tenacity . . . in rebuttal."[52] In Seattle the college's negative team was also successful. Probably these victories over Washington were the highlight of several debate seasons. Although the team enlisted eager participants—football star Ben Comrada gave up his position on the basketball squad for a place on the debate team—there was less student interest in this activity than there had been a dozen years earlier. Perhaps the competition with other activities, especially athletics and glee clubs, detracted from debate. Male and female teams held their own against the University of Idaho and Washington State College but did not compile victories as they once had.

The reasons for the decline of forensics are not to be found in Penrose's reports or in campus journalism. Student editors provided various explanations for the failure of athletic teams but said little about the reasons for debaters being soundly defeated by Oregon State College or the University of Wyoming. After a mediocre 1924 debate season, the *Waiilatpu* lamely reasoned: "Although Whitman has participated in more defeats, yet she has kept the high standard she has always maintained."[53] The *Pioneer* reported that the debate team had lost "almost consistently" but predicted improvement because underclass students took an interest in forensics.[54] The first-ever freshman intercollegiate debate in 1922 against Pacific University had aroused student interest, but to regain its former standing, the school had to put more effort into this activity, including the addition of a top-flight debate coach. Forensics basically needed a "live-wire" leader like music director Pratt.

While debate lost popularity there was a growing interest in campus drama. Several factors account for this: an active dramatic club, the support of the conservatory, and national interest in the theater. The sophomore class annually staged a popular play, such as *A Tailor Made Man*, at the Keylor Grand Theater to raise money for the following year when the class produced the college yearbook. The dramatic club presented *Secret Service* and several one-acts, which were offered in McDowell Hall. The Spanish, French, and German clubs also staged plays.

Patterns of Student Life

The school retained its stiff academic requirements. Penrose boasted that Whitman offered "a balanced education of high quality"; in 1919 he summarized the requirements for the B.A. degree.[55] Candidates pursuing it had to complete 120 semester hours with grades that averaged a minimum of seventy percent, take a year of Greek or Latin, complete two courses in a foreign language and demonstrate a good reading ability in it, enroll in eighteen hours of courses in each departmental group, and, in the senior year, complete a major program and pass its oral comprehensive examination which lasted from two to four hours. To help students meet these requirements, deans provided academic advice to freshmen; sophomores shifted to a major professor, who served as "guide, philosopher, and friend."

Increased public recognition of Whitman's academic standing pleased the college community, especially in 1919 when the council of Phi Beta Kappa voted unanimously to establish a chapter at Whitman. For years Penrose, Professor Edward Ruby, and other members of the honorary group had asked selected chapters to push the school's bid for membership. These advocates emphasized that a campus honorary group, called "X," had long maintained the same rigid standards as Phi Beta Kappa and would serve as a nucleus for a local chapter. After the installation of Phi Beta Kappa in 1920, Whitman widely publicized the fact that this demonstrated its academic standing because there was only one other Phi Beta Kappa chapter in the Pacific Northwest.

The presence of this prestigious honorary group was the most obvious recognition of the college's scholarship, but there were other indications. Two graduates received Rhodes scholarships—in 1920 Edwin D. Ford, an economics and political science major, and in 1922 Robert Brode, a science major. Several others, including William O. Douglas, won nomination. In 1922 the college received the privilege of appointing a student for a graduate scholarship award in engineering at Columbia. Another honor came in 1924 from another Ivy League school when Walter Bleakney received a $1,000 Harvard scholarship on the basis of achieving the highest score in a national competitive examination in mathematics and physics. Known by his classmates as "Bleaker," the Oregonian was a graduate of tiny Echo High School; at Whitman he was a scholar, athlete, and fraternity man. He was praised for all these achievements and also for working his way through school. He explained the work: "At 4:00 AM I mounted a bicycle ... instead of a horse, and I had four furnaces in town. Everybody heated houses with coal furnaces. They liked to get up in the morning to a warm house, and so they would employ some college boy to fire up the furnace early in the morning before they got up. Sometimes you had to build a whole new fire ... And you had to carry out the ashes, and for this I got the magnificent sum of four dollars a month for each one."[56] On June 6, 1924, the *Pioneer* judged that his award was "without a doubt one of the most significant honors ever conferred upon a Whitman graduate." The school also stressed that another senior, Vladimir Rojansky, stood a close second in the competition and also received Harvard's recognition.

While the college basked in this national attention, it debated its honor and grading systems. Although Penrose and most other faculty members defended the honor system, some teachers and students called it a failure. The 1923 version of the honor code forbade proctoring, required a student to sign on an examination paper that "I pledge my honor that I have neither given nor received aid in this examination," and established an elected student committee to investigate charges of dishonesty and in case of guilt to recommend punishment to the president. The perennial bugaboo—the grading system—prompted disagreement. Teachers awarded percentage grades, but some campus voices advocated the use of numeral grades; for example, "2" would replace "eighty-five percent."

As they debated the student evaluation system, the faculty also considered admission standards. In 1921 it agreed to the general principal of selective admission for a student body that would not exceed five hundred. Penrose spoke to the faculty about admissions. He preferred to admit high school students who had acquired a love of reading. The educator complained: "I am afraid that the majority of students read little outside of school assignments, except perhaps the comic colored Sunday supplement or the *Saturday Evening Post*. We are developing in this country young people who have what I call the 'movie mind' rather than the mind of readers."[57] He sought to measure the ambition of those seeking admission and feared that many young people lacked this trait. "They would like to be great, but they do not have the driving power."

Penrose's concern about college admissions prompted him to write a pamphlet entitled *Choosing a Career and a College*. He discussed the professions, which he identified as law, medicine, the ministry, education, and engineering. He listed several significant occupations, including journalism, business management, and farm management. Between the professions and the occupations, he identified a middle ground composed of banking, diplomacy, and consular service. Perhaps the president's most interesting paragraphs were aimed at young women. He expressed pleasure that all the professions and occupations were now open to both sexes. The president stressed that three occupations—nursing, librarianship, and social service—were "primarily reserved for women." Penrose, however, demonstrated his traditionalism by asserting that "the greatest occupation for the greatest number of women is fortunately the occupation of homemaking." He explained that higher education would "deepen the insight" of women prior to their assuming the critical role of homemaker. Penrose generalized: "Household economics ought to be a part of the education of every girl, and civilization will improve as the makers of homes are educated women." The president was actually re-emphasizing the ideas of Catharine Beecher, who in the mid-nineteenth century had urged women to subject themselves to the larger social welfare through domesticity. The president listed factors that students should consider in selecting a college. If a young person chose to live in the Pacific Northwest, he or she should select a school there. Penrose added that schools should be chosen on the basis of cultivation of "reverence, loyalty, generosity, and helpfulness"; commitment to high academic standards; and small enrollment that would permit the college to take "an interest in you."

Admission requirements were much less an issue to the faculty than was the new pattern of college life—the increased importance of campus activities, including clubs, honoraries, athletics, music, and much more. In the 1920s Americans were joiners, and so it was on the college campus. In 1920 and 1921 many new groups having both a social and educational function appeared; meanwhile, existing ones became more active. Faculty approved four new honorary societies: Mu Phi Epsilon, composed of leading women musicians; Delta Sigma

Rho, a national debating fraternity; a press club advancing campus journalism; and the Order of Waiilatpu, an upperclass group promoting homecoming and the care of Marcus Whitman's grave and monument.

Two new women's groups appeared: the Women's League, which enrolled all college women and tried to develop unity and mutual helpfulness, and the Women's Self-Government League, which was established to devise and enforce dormitory rules. Two existing organizations, college chapters of the YMCA and the YWCA, became much more active. These groups engaged in social service off campus, including visits to old people's and children's homes; on campus they promoted student religious life and hosted social events.

The W Club was made up of lettermen and was a powerful campus force. It drew attention when it allowed female students competing in intercollegiate tennis to purchase the coveted letterman's sweater.

National politics also prompted student activity. In 1920 campus Democrats and Republicans debated the merits of presidential candidates and held a straw ballot in which Warren G. Harding swamped James M. Cox. More important was the International Relations Club operating under the conditions of the Carnegie Endowment for the Preservation of Peace. Advised by Professor Samuel Bemis and open to faculty members and townspeople as well as to students, members listened to lectures about subjects as diverse as Japanese expansion, the future of the League of Nations, and India's independence. In 1922 Thompson Elliott, Penrose's old nemesis, presided over the local club.

In the period following the First World War, Whitmanites involved in the Associated Students of Whitman College were busier than their predecessors. Student body officers served a full year managing school activities and attempting to balance a budget that was continually endangered by intercollegiate athletics.

Meanwhile, the *Pioneer* also demanded an increased amount of the staff's energy. Twice a year the student body selected editors from the English department's approved list. The editors and their small staffs labored long hours to produce and to finance the newspaper. In 1919 the *Pioneer* was increased to eight full-length columns, the size of a city newspaper. The proud creators of this four-page weekly presented a reasonable view of college life. This was not the age of personal journalism; thus the opinion pieces were generally thoughtful discussions of campus conditions. An indication of the administration's respect for the *Pioneer* is the fact that in 1923 five thousand extra copies of an issue were mailed to alumni, regional editors, potential donors, and others.[58]

Students poured considerable time into campus organizations, fraternities, sororities, student government, journalism, debate, dramatics, and athletics. To accommodate student organizations, the faculty permitted them to put on programs for the entire student body during two chapel periods a week. The college community concluded that this major change made students more willing to accept the three other thirty-minute chapel services in the week.

Professors found merit in each new student group they approved, but they soon complained that with students involved in so many of these new or expanded extracurricular activities, there was a decline in the quality of class work. The question was not whether there should be diverse campus groups, the question was how much time students should spend in them. Group leaders competed with professors for the time and energy of able students. And the problem was certainly not unique to Whitman. Social historian Paula Fass wrote that in the 1920s there "was a point of contention between those who believed that [activities] undermined academic interests and channeled too much energy from educational matters and those who believed that they were valuable in the educational process."[59] In the early 1920s the Whitman faculty sought ways to convince students that the curriculum outranked extracurricular activities.

Professors first attempted to resolve the activity problem by advising students that academic commitments came first. Advocating a "middle course," the *Pioneer* responded: "For a student to bury his head in books is just as useless as to run wild over student activities."[60] In the fall of 1920 teachers universally lamented that their advising efforts had failed. Term grades indicated that excessive time given to clubs and societies had resulted in lower scores. The *Pioneer* now sympathized with the faculty's concern about the negative influence of extracurricular activities. It reminded students that "the fact remains that we are in college, first of all for scholarship" and wondered if "we are being clubbed to death."[61]

Convinced that the advising tactic had failed, the faculty took new action to place the classroom over the clubroom. When some delinquents freely admitted that they chose an activity over a lecture, the faculty provided stiffer punishments for those cutting classes. The board of deans ruled in 1922 that any student with three unexcused absences would fail a class; moreover, those who failed forty percent of their classes—not just fifty percent as heretofore—would be placed on probation. The faculty took aim at the Greeks by delaying pledging until second term and by requiring a pledge to have an over-all grade average of seventy percent; previously one could be pledged with sixty percent, the minimum passing mark.[62] To prevent college women and men from participating in too many activities, the faculty enacted a point system. Professors decided that sixteen activity points were the maximum and then weighed all activities on the basis of the estimated time each required; for example, varsity athletes, glee club members, actors, orators, editors, and some club presidents were given ten points; presidents of Greek organizations five points, and a chairman of a dance two points. Anyone who had more than the maximum would have to drop out of an organization so as to be in compliance, although students might petition to carry more than sixteen points. The faculty, after hoping in vain that students would voluntarily accept the new activity point system, enforced its rules in 1923. The point system had friends and foes. Opponents maintained that organizations lost talented leaders; proponents insisted that it enhanced scholarship and gave more men and women an opportunity for leadership.

Meanwhile, the *Pioneer* assisted the faculty by discussing "parasites," which it defined as "students of lazy, shiftless habits [who] copy notebooks and papers." These students would do "anything to obtain a passing grade and to have plenty of time to waste." It also denounced freshmen who participated in numerous activities so as "to glorify themselves in the eyes of the student body." These newcomers frequently lost sight of class work, and the editor feared that "Once the habit is formed it is a difficult thing to break away."[63] The editor, like the teachers, begged freshmen to balance academics with their other activities. At various times students joined with their professors in unsuccessful attempts to identify and terminate superfluous organizations.

Professors could conclude that their effort to regulate extracurricular activities had been successful when Penrose announced in 1923 that more students than ever had made the honor roll. Surely faculty members assured each other that if they had remained indifferent to the challenge of activities, then average grades would have continually slumped. But one senior professor, Louis Anderson, doubted that his colleagues had stemmed the activity tide. In a 1924 report he lamented that ambitious students still tried to do too much: "consequently, health, thoughtful meditation, or lessons have to suffer. Scholarship becomes impaired."[64] He said that some students explained that they had put so much effort into an activity in the mistaken belief that they were actually aiding the college. They assumed that the faculty would indulge their lack of preparation. Anderson did not criticize the students for their lack of intellectual ardor; he blamed "the spirit of the age," a time when there was a "disregard, if not disrespect, for age and for reverence ... for time honored conventions." The professor spoke for other experienced colleagues in advocating for students "the old rule of plain living, hard thinking, wide reading, careful meditation, rigid application to study, with appropriate diet, exercise, and sleep, and just enough of social relaxation to make it the spice and not the subsistence of existence." Alumni also worried about a dilution of the liberal arts with "vocational fads." Werner Rupp, for example, advised the school to remain traditional, for he predicted the nation's inability to develop leadership "if the college and universities continue with their fish-canning courses and all the other vocational pursuits."[65]

The tug between academics and activities, of course, continued. Surely a student editor reflected the majority's viewpoint: "The present day student body is, as a whole, a purposeful and serious minded group of young men and women who look upon all the various sides of collegiate life as having a place in that life and as worthy of consideration."[66]

Another important pattern of student life was the determination to maintain traditions. New students learned about them from older students or from the "freshman bible"; for example, sophomores traditionally produced a school play and juniors published the *Waiilatpu*. Many Whitmanites displayed class numerals at social and athletic functions in an effort to identify their group membership.

One important tradition—the class scrap between freshmen and sophomores—took place as early in the calendar as the faculty could schedule it. This battle was no longer as dangerous to property or to health as it had been early in the century, but it was just as entertaining. The highlight of the day was the male tug-of-war across Lakum Duckum when one or both classes were doused. All the classes wanted to humiliate freshmen; in some years beginning students suffered more indignities than others. Tradition required freshmen boys to wear green dinks (felt skullcaps) and three-inch pompadour haircuts. Sometimes first-year women had to wear green ribbons worn in such an unflattering way as to emphasize their ears. In 1920 the W Club imposed severe rules because the numerals "1924" were dabbed on campus buildings. Determined to teach freshmen that they must "forget high school foolishness," the club issued a new rule, "tieless Friday," a time when freshmen must wear white shirts to emphasize that they lacked ties. They must also doff their headgear to faculty; seniors, and women, must work when ordered; must not smoke; and must use only the lower exits of Memorial Hall.[67]

Every spring the freshmen were permitted to make a huge fire and burn their green dinks. But at some point in the year the lettermen's group established a kangaroo court, where freshmen received punishment for violating traditions and rules. This meant that hapless victims were tossed into Lakum Duckum. There were complaints about the way the club conducted the kangaroo court. A sophomore charged that the court's proceedings were immoral because no faculty members watched them. One of the vulgar remarks the student reported was: "What is a taxidermist?" The answer: "A man who mounts animals."[68] A member of the court asked a freshman if he were a masturbator. Perhaps this letter and other reports of vile comments led the faculty to disapprove of the W Club operating the court and to create a new organization, the Upperclass Association. This group was to devise and enforce freshman rules and to preserve campus traditions. Meanwhile, occupants of Reynolds Hall tried women before its kangaroo court, sentencing them to wash windows and to perform other domestic duties. The *Pioneer* assured freshmen that they suffered less humiliation than those at other institutions, but surely freshmen took little comfort from these words when the tradition known as "frosh get walked on" was practiced. At conference basketball games freshmen had to lie face down in a designated area. The team returning to the floor ran down this path of bodies.[69]

In 1923 the college YMCA published the "freshman bible," containing information on traditions, activities, and organizations. It included Penrose's advice: "Remember that you have come to work. You will have a good time in college, and ought to, but you will get it by not making it your first aim. Faithful study will give a basis to your enjoyment, and will enable you to keep your self-respect." The president, however, maintained that character development ranked higher than academic honors, and that students had a greater respect for classmates who were honest and hard-working than for those who attained high academic records.

Other traditions prompted less controversy than the regulation of freshmen. The school year opened with a student-faculty reception, a stag party for men (there were boxing, stunts, apples, and doughnuts), a kid party scheduled for women (female students came dressed as girls and enjoyed music, stunts, and dancing). Homecoming, class parties, the varsity ball, and other events provided social diversion. In the spring, students journeyed to Waiilatpu, attending a

This two-photograph panorama, taken in 1920, shows tennis courts, the grand-

formal gravesite memorial service, playing baseball against the faculty, and picnicking. A few weeks later students elected a May Queen to reign over Campus Day, an "all-college jollification day." Faculty members and students donned work clothes and beautified the campus. Many commented that on this day the community acted like a family. It was, a student boasted, a time when "Democracy reigns supreme and a closer bond of union is realized between faculty and students."[70] The queen's coronation, a picnic, and a dance concluded Whitman's most popular tradition.

Another long-standing tradition was the teaching of Whitman College's history. A *Pioneer* editor supported this effort by pointing out that a respect for the past inspired present students.[71] There were several ways that the historical tradition was taught—the "freshman bible," Penrose's required class, the Waiilatpu pilgrimage, and Founder's Day. Although some members of the college community embellished the school's history, a student editor explained that just repeating the story of founder Cushing Eells made it possible "to preserve the traditions of the college and to develop historical information concerning the times of the pioneers."[72]

stand, Billings Hall, and the campus pond, Lakum Duckum.

Penrose often praised his students, emphasizing their positive spirit, ambition, loyalty, intelligence, and respect for traditions. He expressed concern, however, about two negative thought patterns. "Since the war" he warned, "we have suffered decidedly from the spirit of cynicism brought back by some of our students from France, and we have also suffered from the general loss of idealism which has so distressingly characterized the period since the war."[73] Penrose assumed that the college curriculum, including his required course in religious philosophy, the YWCA, the YMCA, the faculty, and concerned students would restore the optimistic spirit and religious ideals of prewar Whitman.

Fraternities and Sororities in the Period of Expansion

With a growing student population, Penrose wanted to increase the number of Greek organizations to four sororities and four fraternities. The faculty required the school's locals to seek national charters because, Penrose explained, a local fraternity lacked "the broadening effect of a national outlook." He anticipated that the nationals would supervise and direct their chapters. The faculty investigated a national organization prior to allowing a local chapter to apply for membership; professors favored those fraternal groups that would be most in harmony with their educational and social objectives.

It proved more difficult for Whitman to attract national fraternities than sororities. Western chapters of national fraternities in Seattle, Eugene, and elsewhere seemed indifferent to Whitman's local groups seeking charters. Penrose sighed that eastern chapters had a better understanding of small colleges than did the western chapters. To get support from western schools, Penrose asked the presidents of the University of Oregon and the University of Washington to write about Whitman's merit. Then the college used these presidential statements in letters to western chapters about the history and role of the small college in higher education.

In a bid for a national organization, Penrose described the school's strength, especially the fact that it had a selective admission policy. He stressed that this policy meant that an amount "of good fraternity material is . . . secured, drawn from the four northwestern states and Alaska." Whitman's reputation, the educator asserted, attracted "vigorous and earnest students who prefer to pay tuition rather than go elsewhere to free state institutions."[74]

The president also evaluated the membership of the local groups applying to national organizations; for example, he said of the women seeking a charter from Delta Delta Delta that they were serious about scholarship and that "I like them personally and thoroughly respect their spirit and aim." Penrose stressed that the men seeking a Sigma Chi chapter were some of the college's "most brilliant students" and that "they are earnest and disposed to cooperate for the common welfare of the college."[75]

By 1923 the institution had attracted seven of the eight groups it sought. Two sororities, Phi Mu and Delta Gamma, had been established prior to the war. Kappa Kappa Gamma received a charter in 1917, and Delta Delta Delta received one in 1923. After a tremendous effort on Penrose's part in 1923, Tau Delta Sigma became Sigma Chi. This meant that the college had secured the noted Miami Triad—Phi Delta Theta, Beta Theta Pi, and Sigma Chi. But the other local fraternity, Zeta Phi Epsilon, failed in its effort to receive a charter from Phi Gamma Delta.

Penrose felt that the fraternities helped the college attain its goals. He concluded that "we have found fraternities to be a decided help in the life of the college." The Greeks disciplined their members.

Delta Gamma, probably in 1920.

The educator explained, "In most cases if a boy is going wrong, we find it sufficient to refer him to his fraternity officers who promptly straighten him out."[76] The groups also pressured "the lazy and careless student to study."

Social historian Paula Fass has written about the impact of the Greeks upon campus communities in the 1920s. Although she studied fraternities and sororities at larger campuses, most of her findings can be applied to Whitman. Fraternities held most campus leadership offices, dominated social life, maintained traditions, increased their membership, and provided important residential space. It was obviously everywhere that "fraternities were also encouraged because administrators found them useful in the supervision and control of students" and, because the Greeks "maintained strict internal discipline, they were ready-made administrative units."[77] Penrose practiced such a system: for example, in 1920 there was an act of campus vandalism; the president expressed his dismay; all the Greek organizations expressed regret and sought the perpetrators.

The faculty consistently refined its rules for fraternities and sororities. Although the sororities disliked the decision, pledging was de-

Kappa Kappa Gamma, probably in 1919.

Tau Delta Sigma would become Sigma Chi.

layed until the third term. The faculty possessed the power to remove an "unsatisfactory" student from a fraternity house. It ruled against both gambling and intoxicating liquors, insisted that it control all social activities, and required regular study hours. Rush was deferred to allow freshmen to make wise choices and to make them aspire to good scholarship. The rules governing sorority rush were more complicated than those regulating fraternities. The Pan-Hellenic Association provided a booklet setting forth rules that prescribed a period of silence, that forbade slander of other sororities, that described formal parties as those "where more than three-course meals are served," and that forbade sorority members from studying with rushees. The Inter-Fraternity Council rules for rush were less specific but provided harsh penalties.

The "freshman bible" provided advice for those pondering Greek membership: "the one important thing to remember above all things [is] that it is your individuality that you are seeking to maintain and improve, and regardless of whether you are a member of a Greek letter society or not, that is your most important reason for being here."[78] The Greeks did insist upon conformity brought about by peer pressure; there is no evidence, however, that members surrendered their pins because of oppressive conformity.

Beta Theta Pi. William O. Douglas stands in the back row, sixth from the left.

The president and the faculty kept a wary eye on fraternity scholarship. In 1922 Penrose informed a national Beta Theta Pi officer that their local chapter's low scholarship was owing to the fact that upperclassmen set a poor example for freshmen. He frankly cited the evidence of his twin sons. He admitted that these bright young Betas took "an interest only in athletics, not at all in scholarship." (He did not add that his scholarly daughters had been independents.) Their willingness to be satisfied with only a seventy-five percent average helped lower the chapter's academic standing and gave a negative message to pledges. The president then put this local situation into national context: college men generally were "far more interested in activities than they are in thinking." He challenged the Beta officer: "If you could devise some means by which the men of a fraternity could be made to think and to take a keen interest in world questions . . . you would redeem the colleges from their commonplaceness."[79]

Three years later Penrose expressed a more positive view. Fraternities "stimulate scholarship by bringing fraternity pride to bear upon the lazy and careless students."[80] The educator believed that even those in the Whitman community who damned fraternities as being elitist and undemocratic would not want them abolished because they had been helpful in promoting the school, in working for scholarship, and in regulating behavior. Perhaps some professors disagreed, but surely they all would accept their leader's generalization: "My main contention in respect to fraternities is that they ought not to be allowed to run the college or to become arrogant in their attitude toward college affairs. They need to be held in check and this can be done if the faculty will not throw down the reins of government but will keep firmly in its own hands for wise and kindly use the direction of life on campus."[81]

A few tensions marred the harmonious relationship between professors and Greeks. Sororities, for example, grumbled to teachers that they should have houses like the fraternities, arguing that it was difficult to have chapter meetings in private homes and that they could not build a spirit of sisterhood in a dormitory. Greek groups disliked the faculty's stringent rules for dances and hours for women. There was also complaint about the faculty's insisting upon higher

Phi Delta Theta was the only organization that resided in a house designed for fraternity living.

academic standards for pledging and initiation. All four fraternities reported economic hardship because the college ruled that all first-year males must reside in Lyman Hall. The houses could not balance their books because they now had empty beds; the college replied that it needed dormitory income to pay the Lyman bonds; furthermore, it wanted the freshmen to become well acquainted prior to their living in fraternity houses.

Penrose did not report the percentage of students who were members of fraternities and sororities, but the senior class of 1922 had an eighty percent membership. About sixty-five percent of the student body was Greek. Believing that fraternal life was beneficial, the leader appreciated the fact that nearly all those who wanted to affiliate with a fraternity or sorority had the opportunity. Independents also received his attention—the women formed a loose organization, and so did the men living in Kirkman House.

Whitmanites in the Age of Play

Historians have concluded that "during the 1920s Americans were caught between two value systems. On the one hand, the Puritan tradition of hard work, sobriety, and restraint . . . still prevailed, especially in rural areas. . . . On the other hand, a liberating age of play beckoned."[82] Whitman clearly retained the first value system although its students were aware of movie stars, sports heroes, lawbreakers, flappers, and other alluring types that made up the Jazz Age. Whitman students were not grinds; students of the early 1920s enjoyed more dances, picnics, campouts, dinners, and parties than their predecessors. On the other hand, students often boasted that they were full of the school's traditional spirit, were optimistic, and worked hard. An editor called his classmates "purposeful and serious-minded."[83] One reason for their seriousness was the fact that the agricultural region suffered from economic stagnation. A student explained: "prices are high, jobs are scarce, and money often unavailable."[84] Students as well as faculty members lacked money. Penrose reported that "ninety-five percent of the boys and sixty-five percent of the girls" either worked to pay for all or part of their college costs.[85] Few Whitmanites could afford the outlandish clothing, roadsters, saxophones, ukeleles, movie tickets, beauty products, formal parties, and other items associated with that pleasure-seeking college generation. The faculty preached work over pleasure, but even more important, peer pressure made students reject the new fashions sweeping across the nation's campuses. William O. Douglas recalled that most of his classmates were poor and that "We felt that the fellow with the rich father and the fancy clothes had a dim future."[86]

Whitman students, of course, adopted some fads and fashions. The senior men in 1921 voted against wearing mustaches—some of them confessed their inability to grow one—and adopted canes and monocles. In 1924 some men wore rolled socks and flat derbies, had long hair, and carried bamboo canes. Whitman women adopted the fashion of bobbed hair. In 1922 a student wrote: "A year ago the bobbed-haired co-eds were a real curiosity but today to be really in style and belong to the 'upper crust' one must have the hair clipped and curled."[87]

The flapper—identified as an "independent-minded woman" wearing short skirts—had not made a campus appearance. Sexual fashion had not progressed much beyond bobbed hair. Prohibition seemed to be enforced on the campus. There had always been students who had violated the college's rules about the consumption of intoxicating liquor, but faculty sources indicate that there was no notable increase in the early 1920s. This pleased the *Pioneer*, which reminded readers that the consumption of alcohol broke both national and college strictures. It also denounced bootleggers who were operating at one of the state campuses.

But students did find alcoholic beverages during Prohibition. For years Whitmanites rehashed two famous drinking cases. At 2:00 AM on December 3, 1920, a group of drunks approached Reynolds Hall and sang, shouted, swore, and fired a pistol so as to gain entry into the outdoor cellar. President Penrose and police rushed to the scene. The police easily followed the marauders because they had left an apple trail. Three of the group were Whitman football players, including Ben Comrada, and the faculty voted censure and suspension. In chapel, eager listeners heard the facts of the case and the president's reading of the apology of the guilty men, who were later reinstated by the faculty. William O. Douglas described another case in which his brother Arthur and Harper Joy were traveling in a Pullman car during a glee club tour.[88] Someone furnished whisky, and several stu-

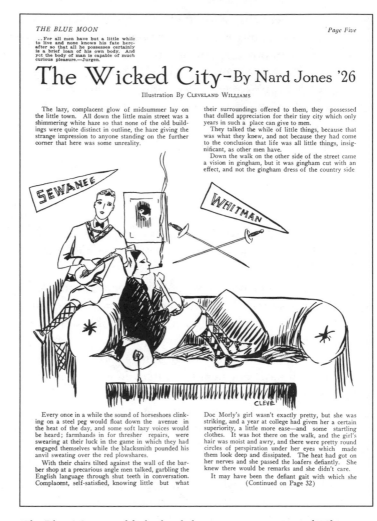

(Continued on Page 32)

The Blue Moon *published a dubious interpretation of Whitman-ites by Nard Jones in May 1924. A 1926 graduate, Jones earned a regional reputation as a writer and biographer.*

dents enjoyed a noisy party. Douglas wrote that Penrose expelled Arthur and Harper but the trustees readmitted them. This party and punishment became a fraternity legend.

Whitmanites adopted a significant national campus custom: they founded a campus literary magazine. In the spring of 1924 students launched the *Blue Moon*, a lively publication featuring art work, poetry, fiction, feature stories, and humor. This was the most striking and sophisticated periodical that students had attempted, and its humor is still appealing; for example: "Even if you do think your school is going to the dogs, you can't save it by howling."

Evaluating the nation's changing campuses of the 1920s, a Princeton dean concluded that "With the general obscuring of the college's original purpose and function, it has unfortunately become a kind of glorified playground. It has become the paradise of the young."[89] Penrose feared the impact of hedonistic students upon American intellectual life: "the quality of our public life is determined sooner or later by the qualities developed in our colleges and universities."[90] He judged that frivolous students doubled the work of professors, demoralized classmates, wasted student time that might be used in learning a trade, and squandered the money of disapproving parents and taxpayers.

In 1924 a *Pioneer* editor wrote that he and classmates resented the fact that the movies and popular fiction had spread the notion that a "collegian" was a carouser and pipe smoker who played a ukelele under a coed's window. The editor defined the word "collegiate." Some students, he said, took it to mean participation in fads and the wearing of outlandish fashions. The editor, however, used a dictionary definition. The word actually meant traditional college practices. The writer expressed pleasure that Whitman students appeared in conventional clothing and that they did not draw looks "filled with mingled amusement and contempt."[91] The writer assumed that student opinion and the kangaroo court would remedy flagrant cases of deviant dress. Probably such writing shaped behavior, for Whitman students remained down-to-earth, rejecting the fashionable and worldly ways of students at distant campuses. There is no evidence that the alumni—a group concerned about the maintenance of traditions and standards—accused the students of overly indulging in the age of play.

In 1921 the institution made its initial study of why students selected Whitman. They responded that parental influence was the major factor in selecting a college and that Whitman's scholarship, not its social life, had influenced their decision to attend. At the same time parents understood that the faculty faithfully practiced *in loco parentis*, guiding and protecting while teaching their children.

The Boards and the Alumni Association

After fifteen years, Whitman's two-board system had changed little. The trustees retained several responsibilities, largely financial. This board managed the school's property, paid salaries, borrowed money, and granted student scholarships and loans. Trustees also approved faculty hirings, leaves, and other personnel matters. Composed of nine men, including Professor Louis Anderson and six other Walla Wallans, the board met monthly or upon call. Occasionally trustees met with overseers, and they always sent their minutes to the larger board to keep it abreast of college affairs.

The overseers remained the more impressive group, annually averaging a membership of fifty-five. Most of them lived in the Pacific Northwest and were influential businessmen, lawyers, ministers, or physicians. A great percentage had college degrees. In 1920 three women, including Anna M. Weyerhaeuser, accepted board membership. Penrose hoped to increase the number of women to six, explaining to one potential board member that her sex could contribute "that sort of insight and sympathy which only women can bring."[92]

At its annual meeting held at commencement the overseers heard reports from the president and others. This body responded to the president's requests, which he often made in his reports. Thus it took action on the library, curriculum, student housing, and many other concerns.

The division of authority between the boards seemed to be free of friction. Both boards tended to follow Penrose's leadership. The president hailed the system and did not propose any major changes. He approved of the fact that members of both boards could remain in office and serve as many four-year terms as they desired. Only about forty-five percent of the overseers generally attended the annual meeting. There is no evidence that Penrose chided them for such poor attendance.

Board members left little information about their service, but some letters indicate that they shared Penrose's enthusiasm for building a liberal arts college. Miles Moore wrote that "it is a great satisfaction to me to have had a part in establishing such an institution,"[93] and Seattleite Thomas Burke, who aided Penrose for thirty years, explained that he supported the interior college because "It stands in precept and example for the plain, homely virtues and the principles of justice and liberty which have endeared every generation of true Americans to the great Republic." Burke also assured Penrose that he favored both strong public and private institutions of higher education. He appreciated the fact that the college prepared youth "to distinguish the true from the false, keeping their heads when so many people are carried about with every wind of doctrine"; furthermore, its alumni did much for the state.[94] These two men and William Cowles, George Turner, Frederic Keator, Dr. Robert Yenney, and Dr. Park Weed Willis were probably Penrose's ablest board members from 1917 until 1924. Penrose praised all his co-workers; for example, he said that Burke "was one of the few men in Seattle who could see across the state . . . and appreciate the honest work and the high though modest standards of Whitman."[95]

From correspondence, especially that kept by overseer Burke and trustee Willis, it is possible to appreciate what influential board members did to assist Penrose. Moral support and personal friendship meant much to the overworked president. Board members also spoke on behalf of the college to influential businesspeople, journalists, and educators; donated money and submitted names of others who might be generous; provided advice on various topics; served on committees; aided Whitman alumni in launching careers; and carried out special tasks Penrose requested.

Between 1919 and 1925 death claimed some valuable board members, including Miles Moore and Thomas Burke. Both had willed large sums to the college, but their friendship and board work were worth far more to Penrose than their financial generosity.

The Whitman Alumni Association, which also lent valuable support, began in the 1890s, but lacked organization. On December 15, 1910, the Walla Walla *Union* embarrassed the college community by revealing a verbal battle between Dean Archer Hendrick and college alumni. The dean wanted the membership of the alumni association to include all men and women who had attended the college and pointed out that eastern schools followed such a practice. Alumni heatedly disagreed. In a bitter argument at an alumni banquet, they accused Hendrick of selling seats on the board of overseers, "of fraud in the building of the Whitman gymnasium, and of undue influence in

Walter Crosby Eells graduated from Whitman in 1908, earned a masters' degree at the University of Chicago, and in 1916 returned to his alma mater as a professor of mathematics. Eells revitalized the Whitman Alumni Association while serving as its secretary.

diverse matters." The angry dean retorted that alumni still owed him money for unredeemed pledges to the gymnasium fund and for operating an inefficient alumni association. This unfortunate disagreement troubled Penrose. In his 1916 report he complained that "the weakest side of the college is the side which it extends to the outer world, and its feeblest effort, the effort which it makes for publicity." He hoped that a stronger alumni association would result in "a closer relationship between the college and the world of business and social life in the Pacific Northwest."

In 1917 Professor Walter Eells, grandson of Cushing Eells and a Whitman graduate, put new life into the organization by getting an alumnus elected as an overseer and by establishing the *Whitman Alumnus*. Penrose applauded these new measures that would bring the alumni "into close and sympathetic relations with the college."[96] The president was convinced "that no college ... has passed beyond the primary state of its development until its alumni have come to participate openly and avowedly in its affairs." Within six years, seventy-five percent of the alumni had joined the association either as graduate members (those who had earned a degree from the college or diploma from the conservatory) or as associate members (those who had attended Whitman but had not graduated). The association greatly assisted the college by recommending it to high school seniors, by raising or donating money, by building campus structures (especially a bridge across the college stream near Billings Hall), and by funding Lyman Hall and the heating plant.

Records of alumni donations are incomplete, but Penrose did not anticipate much help from them because there were too few alumni, and they had not yet attained professional positions that would make substantial gifts possible. One devoted alumna had the "wild idea" of selling her blood for money that would go to her alma mater. Penrose responded that such action "would be an awfully good talking point" but advised against it.[97]

The *Whitman Alumnus* was a vital publication, carrying out tasks similar to those of the modern college quarterly. Published nine times a year, this small journal summarized campus news, reported alumni club activities, carried alumni correspondence and classnotes, provided a class directory, reported on commencement, and included

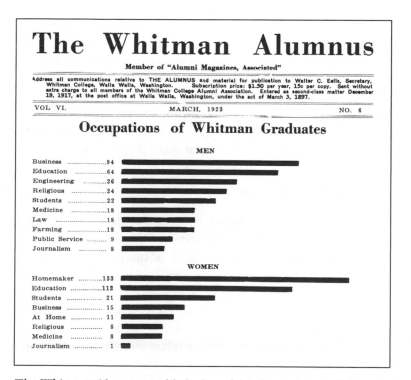

The Whitman Alumnus *published useful information, including details about Whitman graduates.*

Coach Borleske's reports on athletics and a secretary's summary of the conservatory. Its features were informative; for example, in 1921 it published a study on why freshmen chose Whitman; in 1923 it profiled graduates, showing that of the 680 graduates fifty percent were women.

Secretary of the alumni association Eells and allies worked hard to establish local alumni clubs; by 1924 twelve stretched from New York to Willapa Harbor. Nostalgia flowed at alumni meetings, but alumnus Hugh Elmer "Hez" Brown soberly thought back about the sacrifice of teachers. He recalled a look seeming to say: "It is impossible to overestimate the capacity of the human mind for resisting the introduction of knowledge."[98] In Chicago, Los Angeles, San Francisco, and Portland, alumni clubs sponsored parties, picnics, lectures, banquets, and celebrations of Founder's Day, February 16. In fact, the school tried to set up Whitman reunions everywhere on Cushing Eells' birthday and feature a college speaker. In 1923 at a Portland reunion, for example, a professor discussed the current financial campaign with what "seemed to be just one big family seated in a circle."[99] A San Francisco alumnus promised that at a future meeting "empty 'tummies' and full pocket-books will be taken care of."[100]

Undoubtedly the big event for alumni was Homecoming, not Founder's Day. Penrose thoroughly enjoyed these social occasions and joked to alumni: "you are heavier in body, if not in wit, and while your horizon has expanded, so has your waist line."[101]

Stephen Penrose at His Zenith

In many ways Stephen Penrose's best years as president were between his twenty-fifth and thirtieth years of service. Old problems, especially a shortage of money and the allied matter of fund raising, still taxed him. Some new difficulties also beset him, including the death and resignations of professors and board members and the pressures of increased enrollment. But, as has been indicated, the college had evolved into a significant liberal arts college. The school had finally achieved stability—no one even whispered economic collapse or removal to Spokane.

By 1924 Penrose had reached the zenith of his reputation. He was known as an effective educator, a knowledgeable church leader, and an informed spokesman on a variety of political and economic issues. From about 1910 onward Penrose delivered dozens of talks at schools, universities, clubs, societies, churches, and special groups. Following the First World War, he won an even wider reputation resulting from his lectures on numerous topics, including regional history, Marcus Whitman, the need for good roads and improved farm practices, the potential of irrigation, and inspirational themes such as a call for women and men to serve society rather than self.

In the 1920s Penrose received many invitations to speak about the role of education. On one occasion he told journalists that "every problem of society is an educational problem and that the future of the country and of the world depends finally upon education."[102] He stressed the need for intellectual, esthetic, moral, and spiritual education. The educator frequently taught that the "flapper girl" and the "hoodlum boy"—two troubling types in the "so-called decadent generation"—emerged because parents could not be troubled to teach their children good habits. In fact, mothers and fathers wanted children out of the house and did not care whether they attended movies and dances.

Conservative in his politics, Penrose attracted statewide attention in the 1920s as he became involved in state tax issues. He proposed a new equalization plan of taxation for public schools that received considerable attention; in fact, his concern about taxes and government economy led the governor to appoint him to the state tax committee. Many regional leaders applauded his insistence that the state practice economy, enact a better state budget system, and establish a state tax commission. He favored "a stringent budget law ... with penalties against over expenditure."[103]

Penrose also spoke on Asian economics, politics, and religion. The educator anticipated that both China and Japan would become increasingly important to the United States. Therefore he tried to find sponsors for a so-called "Pacific problems endowment" that would provide for Asian classes at Whitman. The president confided to an alumnus that he had always wanted to be a missionary to China because it was "the most interesting place in the world" but that he had not gotten beyond Washington. Penrose commented on American-Japanese difficulties, decrying racial prejudice, especially in California, and advocating "fair-minded justice and honest friendliness" between the two nations as they competed for Asian trade. He wrote the former president of Doshisha University: "Personally I have very friendly feelings towards the Japanese whose development in the last fifty years is one of the most amazing things in history."[104] It was his opinion that most Americans shared his sentiments and hoped that Japanese and American politicians would not destroy the friendship between the two Pacific powers.

Penrose's hostile response to the Ku Klux Klan received far more attention than his friendly pronouncements on Asia. In fact, historian and priest Wilfred P. Schoenberg tells us that Roman Catholics in the 1990s still remember and appreciate his public opposition to the Klan. At a time when many opinion makers chose to remain silent, Penrose attacked the hooded order. Alarmed by the fact that Oregon voters in November 1922 had passed an initiative that would require children to attend public schools and would abolish private and parochial schools, Penrose took action. He lectured on the subject of "True and False Americanism" to the Knights of Columbus in Seattle and to the YMCA in Spokane. He identified "epidemics of false Americanism that have swept over the United States every fifteen to twenty years for the last seventy years."[105] The educator pointed out that the Order of the Star-Spangled Banner of the 1850s, the Ku Klux Klan of 1870, the American Protective Association of 1894, and the Ku Klux Klan of 1920 all boasted that they were totally American. But he maintained that each one was secret and intolerant. Penrose confided that "When a man tells me he is one hundred percent American I wonder what he has up his sleeve." The president defended foreigners, immigrants, Catholics, and Jews, and identified the true American as one who loved the law. "It is a great thing," he concluded, "to be an American in loyalty, tolerance, friendship, and fairplay."

Penrose repeated these points on campus, especially in early April 1923, when the city hosted a regional Ku Klux Klan convention. A visiting Klansman boasted that "Walla Walla, in comparison with population, had the largest and most active klan in the state."[106]

A month later the secretary of Walla Walla Klan Number 3, the Reverend Bert A. Powell, wrote to Penrose that his group had learned that Penrose had called the Klan dangerous and un-American. He added: "Naturally Klansmen and Protestants of the Whitman student body and Klansmen who have children in Whitman College as well as your neighbors who are Klansmen are asking and eager to know what facts you have ... on which you base your judgement of the Klan."[107] Powell, seeking to uncover the "whole facts," invited the president to debate with a Klansman on the question, "Resolved: that the Ku Klux Klan is a dangerous and un-American organization." In accepting the challenge Penrose refused to retract prior statements about "the curious organizations like the Ku Klux Klan which have sprung up, flourished, and died away in each generation of American life." To help regional citizens distinguish "true Americanism from false," Penrose proposed that he and a Klansman debate the question, not in a local theater, but in regional newspapers. The president proposed that he contact regional editors asking for space for the proposed debate. The Klan refused.

In November 1923 the educator's views of the Klan again won attention. To his surprise, the National Vigilance Association in Washington, D.C. announced that it wanted to destroy the Klan and listed him as one of the college presidents who would serve as a national committeeman. Penrose was the only Washington state educator on the list. He refused to be a member of such a group, explaining, "While I am not in sympathy with the methods of the Ku Klux Klan, I do not approve of forming an organization to combat them."[108]

Penrose's opposition to the Klan was part of his educational effort to teach beyond the campus. He was particularly interested in promoting regional history. Patriotic and sentimental, he respected the early settlers and worked to honor them. The leader thought it proper that the first chartered school in the state, the school named after a martyr, should be closely associated with Pacific Northwest history. Penrose wrote in the catalog that the school "has a wider commemorative function than to preserve the name of Doctor Whitman alone. It recognizes the worth of the other pioneers and desires to commemorate them also. It is a monument to the pioneers of Oregon Territory, and it seeks to honor, in its buildings, its professorships, and its various funds for scholarly purposes, the names of the men and women who have played a distinguished part in the making of the Pacific Northwest."[109] A promotional pamphlet published in 1924 bore the title *Whitman, the College of the Pioneers*.

The president brought the aging pioneers to the college for reunions and urged students to meet and honor them. But his major effort to teach Walla Walla Valley history was his pioneer pageant, *How the West was Won*, a drama produced in the springs of 1923 and 1924. It highlighted Lewis and Clark, the Whitmans, Indian Wars, Walla Walla's founders, and the valley's future. In his historical and symbolic account, Penrose identified and portrayed four great types in western history: the explorers, the fur traders, the missionaries, and the pioneers. Each of these groups, he wrote, had played a vital role in the valley's development.

Percy J. Burrell of Boston, an experienced director of pageants, played a pivotal role in the one offered in Walla Walla. For weeks prior to each of the two productions, he carried out many duties, especially the rehearsal of local actors and collaboration with both Mignon Borleske, who had charge of the dancers, and Howard Pratt, who trained the singers. Burrell later wrote about his experiences, stressing the massive scale of the production: 2,500 participated in 1923 and 3,000 in 1924, the enormous outdoor stage was 326 feet wide and 200 feet deep.

Walla Wallans financed, managed, and publicized the show, taking pride in the community effort. More than 250 Whitmanites appeared on stage. There were 600 Walla Walla children in one choir and 800 local adults in another. An estimated 20,000 people attended the 1924 production; many visitors motored from Seattle, Portland, and Spokane, boasting to each other about their worthy vehicles. The audience applauded the beautiful costumes, the natural scenery, the symbolic dancing (including the wheat dance), the massed choirs, the 250 Indians, and the pioneer saga.

Penrose wrote that the pageant was "designed to teach boys and girls the sterling quality of their ancestors as well as the thrilling history of the West."[110] But he had also instructed adults; in fact, in the 1920s Northwest residents probably knew more about the role of the Walla Walla Valley in the pioneer period than they do now.

The success of the production led many Walla Wallans, including the editor of the *Bulletin*, to urge that the pageant should be offered every year like the Pendleton "Round-Up" and the Portland "Rose Show." Those boosting tourism championed Penrose's efforts. Probably the financial deficit was a major reason why the pageant was discontinued. Despite the fact that there were no new productions, citizens, for many years, read the pageant story and recollected the two performances. Townspeople thus came to appreciate not only local history but also the crucial role the college played in promoting such a colorful community celebration.

Penrose wanted a history of Whitman College to be written. He called upon residents to donate material and devised a plan whereby retired Professor William Lyman would write it. Regrettably the skilled local historian died in 1920, so Penrose announced that he and Professor Walter Eells would assume the task. Unfortunately, the press of other responsibilities delayed Penrose's history until 1935. Although the president failed to get a history in the 1920s, he did promote and expand the school's museum. The college took pride in the Myron Eells Indian Collection housed in Memorial Hall and another small collection relating to the Whitman mission. Penrose asked for donations to these and other collections.

Besides supporting the museums and celebrating the missionary in *How the West was Won*, Penrose further sought to perpetuate the story of Marcus Whitman by rebutting scholars who denounced the Whitman myth. In the 1920s he still taught that Whitman rode east primarily to save the region from the English, not to save his Waiilat-pu mission. As proof he stressed that Whitman went first to Washington to see government officials and then to Boston to confer with church officials. Support for his defense of the missionary came from an unlikely quarter. In 1923, President Warren G. Harding, in an address in Meacham, Oregon, advanced the Whitman legend. He stated that upon entering a certain White House room he visualized a dramatic meeting of President John Tyler, Secretary of State Daniel Webster, and Marcus Whitman in which the missionary pleaded for the Oregon Territory. Immediately scholars denounced Harding's sympathetic views of Whitman. Penrose identified these detractors as the staff of the Portland *Oregonian* and "those so-called students of history who follow Professor E.G. Bourne and W.I. Marshall without question."[111] Penrose wrote to the White House asking if the late president had merely read a speech written by others or if he had actually been a proponent of the missionary. He summarized his own position: "I have for thirty years been president of Whitman, endeavoring to honor properly the great missionary and martyr." A secretary replied that Harding had indeed encountered critics after his Meacham address but had consistently defended the missionary because he "was decidedly of the opinion that there are some traditions concerning our national history that ought to be preserved without an undue amount of super-criticism. Among these were numbered the tradition of the Whitman service."[112]

In 1922 Penrose arranged a significant commemoration of the seventy-fifth anniversary of the Whitman massacre. The infirm Nancy Jacobs, identified as the only living survivor of the massacre, was the honored guest, and recalled mission life. The president, of course, used the occasion to honor the martyr and to denounce the "narrow minded critics who would rob Whitman of the credit for saving Oregon from Great Britain."[113] Clifford M. Drury, Marcus Whitman's sympathetic biographer, states that by this time the Whitman-saved-Oregon story "had been discredited and rejected."[114] Penrose, however, remained a believer and expressed confidence that the story would attract adherents. Friendly assessments of the missionary in the 1984 *Colliers Encyclopedia* and the August-September 1986 issue of *American Heritage* would have pleased him.

In summary, during the postwar years the education builder poured his enormous energy into efforts to improve his college and his state and to honor pioneers. Such demands would exhaust anyone, but Penrose shouldered additional tasks. He taught all of the school's philosophy courses, including the philosophy of religion course required of upperclass students, and the college life course, an education class required of freshmen. A gifted teacher, he won the praise of those who studied under him. Chester Maxey considered him to be one of the very best teachers he ever encountered; hundreds of other alumni agreed. Knowledgeable, patient, friendly, and articulate, Penrose impressed those who took his classes. His effective teaching, especially his mastery of the Socratic method, meant that he had become for Whitman students what his old mentor Mark Hopkins had been for students at Williams. Moreover, Penrose tried to become acquainted with each student by advising or visiting, on the campus or in the presidential home. The Penrose family attended campus activities and games. Through all of this contact Whitmanites understood that the Penroses took a keen interest in their education and well-being.

The president squeezed in time to read professional journals and books. He tried to keep abreast of educational issues, especially writings about gifted students. Occasionally he wrote on education, but administration and teaching consumed his hours.

The president's voluminous correspondence demonstrates the variety of his tasks. He personally informed parents about their children who had been punished for violating school rules: for example, he told a father that his son had excessive chapel absences; Penrose had reprimanded the boy by making him read a book and write a thousand-word summary. The leader composed letters of personalized recommendation for some former teachers and for many graduates. In supporting an alumnus for a Harvard Law School scholarship, he emphasized that the applicant was a farmer who had suffered from unfortunate agricultural conditions. He wrote editors in behalf of a faculty member trying to publish a textbook. Penrose helped Bertha L. Compton through the bureaucratic maze of Oregon's department of education so that she might be certified as a public school teacher. He maintained a large personal correspondence with friends and former students; for example, he lent money to alumnus Edwin Ford to help him meet the costs of an Oxford education. Penrose, however, furnished advice as well as money: "Soak yourself in English life and atmosphere without letting yourself be de-Americanized."[115] He wrote recruitment letters, including several on behalf of Nig Borleske's football program. In summary, the president did not spare himself; as Maxey stated, he set high standards and anticipated that faculty and students would do the same.

Much had been accomplished since 1894; and the president's vision, intelligence, and character were the major reasons. He later explained that he "was never satisfied with the college in any respect ... [and] he was secretly its severest critic, planning how improvement might be made within practical bounds."[116] Penrose had a tremendous sense of duty, telling a trustee that "I am willing to do anything for the college."[117]

The president enjoyed his family's devotion. They recognized that they were a part of "a New England college in the process of evolution."[118] The children benefitted from both a loving family relationship and the college community. By living on campus, the sons and daughters became well acquainted with students and faculty members. All the Penrose children attended Whitman and consistently supported their father's career.

Daughter Frances Penrose Owen explained that there was another important person in the Penrose home. Ella Johnson "started as the nurse for the twins ... and eventually became the cook, the housekeeper, guide, philosopher, and friend to the whole family." Mary and Stephen could travel because they completely trusted Ella to run the household. She often dispensed both cookies and advice to students; in fact, she offered opinions to the president too. He once denied that beer bottles found in Lakum Duckum were thrown there by students; she called him naive.

Stephen Penrose acknowledged the importance of his wife to his administration, stating that he relied upon her advice and work. Because of Mary Penrose's "wisdom, patience, humor, tact, sympathy, and unfailing fairness," she became important not only to the college but also to the Congregational church, the YWCA, and the community.[119] The school did not have a professional counselor, so many students turned to her for advice about personal and economic problems. One college woman explained: "All of us have at one time or another fallen in need of help, and have found in her an inspiring adviser. Very early in the college course young men and young women alike have learned to appreciate far more than tongues could tell, the cozy moments spent before her fireplace, when she would make them forget or remember themselves as their moods demanded of a responsive heart like hers."[120] She took a great interest in teaching Whitman women, especially farm girls, about how to act in society; thus she was often found in Reynolds Hall teaching etiquette. Mary assisted students in producing plays and provided advice about musicals, debates, and social functions. She chaperoned on campus and with the traveling glee clubs. She sometimes gave money to needy students and frequently provided advice. Alumnae recall that women looked upon Mary Penrose as a friend and accepted her advice "that Whitman women should not flit about on the tennis courts with their knees showing."[121] As the president's wife she wrote and traveled on behalf of the college, especially as a fund raiser. She persuaded the Shipman family to make financial donations to the college and returned periodically to Hartford to see them because they would not come to Walla Walla.

Mary Penrose was deeply involved with the YWCA, serving as national president from 1913 to 1915 and as a national board member for many years. She also put tremendous effort into the college YWCA, teaching members about womanhood and about the need to render societal service. Students and others often called her "Mother Penrose" and applauded the college for awarding her an honorary M.A. in 1914.

Two years later she and the rest of her family suffered a tragedy when their home burned. Awakened in January 1916 at 4:00 AM to find the house in flames, the family ran out into weather that was fifteen degrees below zero. Word of the fire spread to the fraternities whose members ran to the house and formed a human chain to save books. The family lost clothing, valuable paintings, and other possessions. In early 1922 the family moved into the current president's house, which Mary Penrose made into a new center of social and cultural activity.

While nearly all surviving accounts about President Penrose are positive, there were criticisms of the influential leader. Some people on and off the campus found him to be diffident, strong-willed, self-righteous, or conservative. A few parents resented his authority and removed their children from Whitman. Some liberal women found him to be old-fashioned and patronizing, especially in his opposition to sorority houses and his insistence that women take a course in household management. Undoubtedly several faculty members held him responsible for their continuing financial plight. Another criticism was from the Reverend David W. Ferry, who held several Presbyterian pastorates in eastern Washington. In 1923 Ferry confided to Penrose that several church members had denounced Whitman for not encouraging the students who wanted to render Christian service; in fact, the school "tended to sidetrack young people preparing for definite Christian work."[122] Penrose disagreed, asserting that Presbyterian "zeal for Whitworth" might have obscured the truth about Whitman. He also asserted that many students planned to be ministers and missionaries. Ferry accepted the president's view that "the moral conduct and character of Whitman students will stand comparison to those of any other institution."[123] But the minister later changed his mind and attacked the college for not strengthening its "religious and spiritual influences" upon its students.[124]

The criticism that the college did not emphasize Christianity must have reminded Penrose of the experience of his two predecessors.

Alexander Anderson especially had been denounced by ministers for the school's failure to advance the faith.

Two famous alumni—William O. Douglas and Chester Maxey—wrote critically of Penrose in their autobiographies. Douglas recalled his student days: "Most of us started with a dislike of President Penrose and his pompous manner. He was a good Christian man, with a William McKinley type of political and economic philosophy, who would have fitted snugly into any sector of the Establishment across this broad land. He was a pseudo-intellectual with the instincts of a stuffed shirt."[125]

This negative view surprised many, including the Penrose daughters, who recalled that their parents appreciated Douglas's difficult boyhood and the fact that he, a brother, and a sister worked their way through Whitman and enjoyed successful careers. As a student Douglas was well acquainted with Stephen and Mary Penrose and attended social events with their daughter Frances. In 1919, as a junior, he praised the president and the faculty for cultivating a love of knowledge in their students, for their unselfishness, and for their personal friendships.[126] In his autobiography he recalled that as a senior he loved the college. In 1927 Douglas, then a law professor at Yale, complimented Penrose for being "a man of vision and an educator of incomparable skill" and hoped that Whitman graduates might apply to his school.[127] In 1938 Douglas stated: "Whitman gave us the best teaching I have either experienced or observed anywhere. And I know that it is still strong in that tradition." In his autobiography he admitted: "I have always had a sentimental tie to Whitman that goes very deep."[128] This distinguished alumnus insisted that his son attend his alma mater.

Maxey's criticism was less about Penrose the man than about Penrose the legend. He wrote that after forty years in office the president had left "behind him a vast accumulation of legend which may largely conceal both the real man and the real president." Far better acquainted with Penrose than Douglas was, Maxey in his autobiography provided a critique of the man and his accomplishments. Known for his strong opinions, Maxey criticized Penrose for his financial management of the college during the period from 1914 through 1924. "Starting with a clean slate in 1914, the college closed the year 1924 with depleted resources and a heavy burden of bonded

*In 1920 William O. Douglas—
known by his classmates as Orville
—appears in a natty suit. He thoroughly enjoyed his college years and
would, as a member of the U.S. Supreme Court, become the school's
most famous graduate. A college
dormitory is now named for him.*

indebtedness."[129] However, this assertion fails to take into account
the problems brought on by war, the postwar depression, and
Penrose's many accomplishments in this decade. Maxey stated that in
1925 the buildings and grounds were "decrepit" and that the faculty
was disenchanted. It is difficult to confirm or deny this assessment,
but no other source painted such a dismal picture of the buildings.
The faculty requests of the early 1920s were for the addition of teachers, equipment, and books, and not for the repair of shabby classrooms and leaking roofs. Maxey stated that professors "worried constantly as to whether they would be able to meet next month's bills,
whether they would be able to educate their children, whether they
would be able to lay away saving against the day of retirement."[130]
Undoubtedly Maxey had evidence to support his generalizations; in
fact, the president would have agreed with the political scientist. Maxey stated that the faculty knew that "Whitman was sailing without a
pilot" and wanted a new captain.[131] Stephen Penrose did not write
about such discontent, but Maxey probably had reason to think it
existed. It is unfortunate that other faculty members did not evaluate
the school's leadership.

Epilogue: Penrose's Later Years

Stephen Penrose's herculean labors during his thirty-year presidency had produced impressive results. When asked about his having taken charge first of a church in Dayton and then a college in Walla Walla, Penrose replied, "My job seems to have been reviving corpses."[132] In summarizing his long tenure, Penrose believed that outside experts would consider his administrative accomplishments to be the termination of the academy before any other regional college took such a step, the adoption of comprehensive examinations, the selective admission policy, the requirement that freshmen live in Lyman Hall, and the unusual housing of sorority sections in Prentiss Hall. It was Penrose's opinion that his real achievements, however, were the appointment of a talented faculty, the development of "a first rate college of Liberal Arts and Pure Sciences," and "the creation of an atmosphere of friendliness" that permitted students the chance to develop "their characters and their ideals."[133] All of these achievements, except the construction of Prentiss Hall with its sorority sections, had been accomplished by 1924. In that year Penrose was one of the region's best respected educators. The school had more than five hundred students living on an attractive campus, an effective two-board system that attracted notable members, an alumni association involving seventy-five percent of the alumni, contributions to the financial campaign of 1924 from one hundred percent of students and faculty, and a conservatory of music of the highest quality. In addition, as Chester Maxey emphasized, the faculty enjoyed "an unusual degree of academic freedom." Furthermore, Penrose quoted Henry Pritchett of the Carnegie Foundation as telling a Whitman trustee that "In my judgment Whitman College is the best college in the West." The president responded, "I suppose that I can die happy now in having helped to bring the college to that level."[134]

In 1924 the city was more supportive than ever. The *Bulletin* judged that the college was Walla Walla's "one great and absolutely unique asset."[135] Many townspeople wondered why Penrose did not resign and accept a more prestigious and profitable position. An editor responded that the president "stood by his guns, waving aside temptations to go to the great intellectual centers and gather closer to the flesh-pots, where more liberal portions than he is gathering in here have awaited him. . . . But desertion is not the spirit of Penrose, nor is it the spirit of the really great."[136]

There was still another indication that the college had been successful: by 1924 it had graduated many persons who would make their professional marks and through their donations and board service would strengthen their alma mater. They wanted to make Whitman as important to mid-twentieth century students as it had been to them and their classmates in the early part of that century. Many distinguished themselves in academics: Roland Bainton, Walter Bleakney, Robert Brode, Wallace Brode, John Workman, Vladimir Rojansky, Edith Hinkley Quimby, Walter Brattain, and William O. Douglas. Many became important in American business, including Frances Penrose Owen, Donald Sherwood, Harper Joy, and Ralph Cordiner. Dozens of others would enjoy successful careers in music, law, teaching, medicine, and religion. Walter Eells judged that the school earned its reputation on the basis of its graduates' accomplishments. He might have added that most Whitman alumnae became housewives, as Penrose had predicted and for which career he sought to prepare them, and in this capacity they carried out demanding duties in their homes and took time to participate in churches, clubs, and societies seeking societal improvement. Penrose and the professors delighted in their achievements, for these women rendered meaningful service to society.

Despite all of the evidence that he had succeeded, it was time for Penrose to resign. Frustrated with the exhausting 1924 fund-raising campaign, he considered retirement. Anna Weyerhaeuser disagreed: "Do not for a moment think of resigning. The college needs you today more than ever and the college is doing fine work."[137] Many others echoed these sentiments. But those acquainted with his administration have judged that he remained too long. Some have argued that the school needed new leadership—thirty years was excessive, even for Penrose. Historian Frederick Rudolph has written that many college presidents simply lasted too long. In 1924 Penrose was nearly blind. Some who knew him have argued that owing to this devastating disability he lost energy and enthusiasm for administration, so the school drifted. The president explained that in 1915 he lost the sight of his left eye "by what is called a displacement of the retina," and in the fall of 1924 "the same thing began to happen with my right eye."[138] His daughters remembered that in 1915 when he returned from an eastern fund-raising trip he had eye trouble, and a Spokane physician advised him that his "retina ... was just like a piece of elastic that had been strained too hard, the muscles wouldn't hold."[139] He remained flat on his back for a month, but the treatment failed. According to Frances, the strain of the 1924 campaign damaged the other eye, and the exertion of rowing a boat that summer contributed to the problem. He returned to Spokane and related: "for five weeks I laid flat on my back with my eye tightly bandaged, forbidden to lift my head from the pillow."[140] For a few months he could get himself around in the daytime, but he could neither write nor read. Penrose informed alarmed alumni that he could not recognize people and added that "One ... learns when he cannot read that he must think, a very useful discovery." Meanwhile, the concerned editors of the *Pioneer* hailed the president and reported that students prayed that he might be spared his sight.[141]

Penrose confided that he was again considering retirement, but friends dissuaded him, arguing that nobody could take his place. Trustee Park Weed Willis wrote: "I feel that you are worth very much more to Whitman without any eyes than anyone else ... who could be found with the best of eyesight. I see no reason why the college president needs to use his eyes anyway."[142] But was Penrose's decision wise? His wife, his secretary, the faculty, and others aided him, but the demands of the presidency overwhelmed the blind sixty-year-old. Part of the problem was his attitude. Early in his blindness he explained that he was still effective in the classroom and frankly added: "It is this which interests me most rather than the duties of administration as college president. I think I should suffer the greatest sense of loss if I were unable to continue teaching."[143]

For ten years he attempted to carry on the duties he had shouldered during the previous thirty. But it was impossible. Chester Maxey, who provided the only comprehensive account of Penrose's final decade, ruled that the trustees should not have kept him in office and that Penrose "should have known better than to be so easily persuaded that he could carry on as usual. To me and others who had to watch what followed, the ensuing ten years were both tragic and pathetic."[144] Maxey also related that in his blindness Penrose could not "begin to keep abreast of the memoranda, reports, and other papers which must be read every day if he was to keep up with what was going on." Furthermore, he was uncertain about whom he was talking to, and his travels on behalf of the college ended up as "empty motions." Maxey charged that the leader convinced himself that he was doing well; indeed, Penrose wrote in 1925 that the college was not "a sinking ship or one which is in distress."[145] Maxey disagreed, however, arguing that "from 1924 onward the financial condition of Whitman ... grew worse every day"; even before the crash of 1929 the institution "went down the skids instead of up."

Maxey's assessment seems correct. The boards thought more about what Penrose had done and about their admiration for him in his blindness than about the compelling need to replace him. Surely board members would not have let such sentimentality shape their professional lives. By not acting the boards contributed to the school's enormous difficulties during the Great Depression; Maxey charged them with "callous neglect," but sentimentalism might be a better explanation.[146] In the early 1930s the institution required energetic leadership that Penrose simply could not provide. He continued, of course, to be a challenging and effective teacher and an inspirational figure. It is his positive attributes that the Whitman community remembers and that contributed to what Maxey called the Penrose legend. To shape thousands of lives while building an eastern-type college, however, is more than a legend—it was a great accomplishment. It remained for others to guide the ship through the economic storm and plot a new course. How the Whitman community did this is a fit subject for another historical inquiry.

APPENDIX A

The Career of Dr. Daniel K. Pearsons 1820 – 1912

At the time that Daniel Pearsons—he was better known as "D.K."—offered financial assistance to Whitman College, the philanthropist was a vigorous seventy-one-years old. Pearsons was born in Bradford, Vermont, and was reared on an unprofitable farm.[1] His parents taught him and his brothers to work and to aspire. He attended academies, taught school during the winter season, and prepared for Dartmouth College. But extreme poverty meant that he left the college after only one year. This unhappy experience, he recalled, convinced him that some day he would assist other poor and worthy college students. Pearsons saved enough money to attend Vermont Medical College in the 1840s, where a professor lent him a much-needed $100. This generosity further strengthened his resolve to aid other young students. Soon after graduation he practiced medicine in Chicopee, Massachusetts, and met two women who influenced him. In 1847 he married Marrietta Chapin, who was intelligent, ambitious, and shrewd. The other important woman, Mary Lyon, headed Mount Holyoke College; Pearsons admired her dedication and the fact that many of the women enrolled in her school sacrificed to get an education. He resolved to help this college continue its worthy mission.

Although Pearsons enjoyed a good medical practice, his wife stated: "You are made for something better.... We must get out of here."[2] She wanted her husband to give up eastern medicine for a western business career. Thus in 1851 they left Massachusetts for Illinois. Between that year and 1860, when the couple moved to Chicago, he traveled about the country (especially the South, lecturing on medicine and selling medical books), toured Europe, and practiced medicine and farmed in Illinois. Pearsons visited Beloit College and predicted that one day he would aid this school as well as Mount Holyoke. However, he delayed gifts to these small colleges until the late 1880s; he first concentrated on making himself very wealthy.

In the late 1850s Pearsons began selling eastern-owned Illinois farmland on commission. He was immediately successful, and several other landowners, including the Illinois Central Railroad, asked him to sell land to settlers. He also lent money to farmers for the Aetna Life Insurance Company. Late in the 1860s he wisely purchased Michigan timberland. By investing in banks, railroads, and especially Chicago real estate, he became a millionaire by 1870. Pearsons won election as a Chicago alderman and enhanced his reputation in the business community by protecting the city's credit with New York bankers. Although he was a prominent citizen, he shunned society. From 1875 to 1890 Pearsons donated generously to the Presbyterian church, to the McCormick Theological Seminary and to a variety of Chicago cultural societies. A biographer explained that Pearsons was one of those generous Chicagoans "who labored for ideal ends in a city where materialism is not difficult to adopt as a philosophy of life."[3]

D.K. and Marrietta Pearsons moved to Hinsdale, Illinois; in 1890 he retired from business and the couple worked out a system to give away their fortune of $5,000,000. Pearsons thought it a disgrace to die rich and stated that his philosophy was "to do all the good I can, and to do it while I am alive."[4] He and his wife concluded that the largest part of their money should go to small colleges, especially those located in the West, because the couple believed that such institutions, like the common schools, had been a powerful force in American society. They appreciated the fact that small schools emphasized Christianity and close relationship between professors and students. Pearsons argued that it was unnecessary to establish new colleges. He wanted to assist those that had already achieved academic reputations, that served important areas, and that had a good chance of surviving.

In the late 1880s many denominational schools struggled with debts and lacked endowment, professors, laboratory equipment, books, and buildings. Pearsons wanted to meet these problems at selected schools. He decided that before he gave money to a small college, it must raise financial gifts on a matching basis. His donations generally went for an endowment, whose income would provide for such basic needs as student loans and faculty salaries. In the spring of 1889 Pearsons assisted two Illinois colleges, Lake Forest and Knox; both accepted his offer to match money. At about the same time he fulfilled his pledge to assist Beloit College by offering $100,000 if the school raised a similar amount. News of these unusual and unanticipated gifts to struggling colleges, most of which were Presbyterian or Congregational, swept across the nation's campuses. The ACES in Boston alerted beleaguered college presidents about the Chicago philanthropist. Many institutions reacted eagerly. In 1894 Pacific University, for example, asked Pearsons for money to build Marsh Hall. He responded that he would do more: if the university raised $100,000 he would give $50,000. Whitman joined the long list of young colleges seeking similar matching gifts.

Pearsons explained to reporters, educators, businesspeople, and others why he aided small colleges. He gave to "Beloit, Drury, Berea, Colorado, Whitman, and many others" because he wanted them "to be to their sections what Bowdoin, Williams, Amherst, [and] Oberlin ... have been to New England and Middle States."[5] In the case of Whitman, his hopes were fully realized. The educational aspirations of President Stephen Penrose could not have been realized without the assistance of benefactor D.K. Pearsons.

Whitman Fund Raiser Virginia Dox
1851 – 1941

Undoubtedly Virginia Dox was the most unusual fund raiser ever to work for the college, and her name was long familiar. Although she never visited Walla Walla, many of its citizens knew about her successful work from 1896 to 1901 in finding dollars for the endowment and for buildings. In an exhausting canvass of the Midwest, New York, and New England she raised at least $100,000. Dox collected more in the late nineteenth century than Stephen Penrose did, and the total resulting from her work was second only to the amount given by D.K. Pearsons.

Appreciative of her leading role in the school's formative years, Penrose wanted to honor her. He requested biographical data and a photograph, and suggested that a small statue of the fund raiser be placed in front of Memorial Hall. Dox declined. "You will," she warned, "lose all your pupils, for when they approach it . . . they will be so frightened they will leave town. . . . No! No! You can't even have a picture of me. . . . I wish to be remembered by what I have done."[1]

Dox lived an extraordinary life. Born in the mid-1850s into a devout Presbyterian family, she was reared in and near Lockport, New York. Dox attended several schools, working her way through a nearby academy. She moved to the Midwest, continuing her education in Illinois and at the University of Michigan. Between attendance at schools she became a successful teacher.

As a restless young woman she took some medical training, but in the 1880s she became a missionary serving the New West Education

Commission, a Congregational organization. For six years she labored for its objectives: to counter Mormonism in Utah and Roman Catholicism in New Mexico. Dox also sought to improve the conditions of Indians in New Mexico and Oklahoma. Although the dates and places of her assignments are uncertain, she made a reputation as a devoted teacher in Mormon areas, especially in Oxford, Idaho.[2] The teacher recalled her work among the impoverished inhabitants of New Mexico and boasted that she had been adopted by one Indian chief and made a daughter of two tribes.[3]

Dox became friends with Daniel Pearsons and Oliver Nixon; both of these men supported her energetic missionary labors. When she was about forty, Nixon introduced her to Stephen Penrose. Dox shared Penrose's enthusiasm for Marcus and Narcissa Whitman and the young college honoring them. From 1896 through 1901 the advancement of the school became an obsession: "Whitman College is bound to become," she assured its president, "the greatest Christian institution of our country. No other College has such a history back of it."[4]

She mastered Nixon's biography and other accounts of the Whitmans and then set out to tell ordinary citizens about this remarkable couple. She expected that her listeners would give generously to a college honoring the missionaries. From January 1896 through October 1899 she labored without a rest. With headquarters in Chicago, she concentrated on Michigan, Ohio, and New York. In October 1897 she shifted her activities to Massachusetts and Vermont.

Her fund-raising techniques were fully explained in the numerous letters she wrote to Penrose. Typically she went by rail to small towns and appeared in a Presbyterian or Congregational church, where she emotionally told the Whitman story and made an impassioned plea for the college. What made her an unusual college field agent is that she also went from door to door. In 1898 the canvasser summarized her method: "I go from house to house and from shop to shop; I climb fences over into the fields; take long walks in the country; visit wagon shops, blacksmith shops, stables, even cigar shops, to get the little money I raise."[5] She worked one village so thoroughly that a resident called her "a fine comb."[6] Only about one of every twenty persons gave her money; usually the donation was one dollar or less. Some promised to give fifty cents annually, and for years she attempted to collect these modest pledges. Once a widower took an interest in Dox; she discouraged him and informed Penrose, "I am not afraid of anything on earth, but a bumble-bee and an old widower."[7]

Dox explained why potential donors rejected her: ministers were disinterested, businessmen insisted that the Pacific Northwest, not the East, should fund the college, and other people explained that they gave to other educational institutions. A most unusual competitor in Massachusetts infuriated Dox and Penrose. A traveling lecturer of seedy appearance, calling himself the Honorable John W. Fairbank, delivered talks on Marcus Whitman. Fairbank implied that he was raising money for the college; Dox was furious because some churches had turned her away after donating to him.

In the spring of 1899 she offered her resignation to Penrose, assuming that somebody else would have greater success. She gave a rambling description of what her replacement should be: "a big powerful man, strong in body as well as in brain, one who can get up and tell these ministers what we think of them, for they refuse to sanction our work and so rich people refuse to give—one who can knock the Education Society into smithereens" for not being more supportive. She remained in harness, however, because Penrose flattered her as the best college agent in the nation, because she had promised Pearsons and Nixon that she would not leave without their permission, and because of her "love for Whitman College."[8]

The high point of her campaign was the $5,000 note she received from Julia Billings. A few months later Dox became ill and had to reduce her work. A physician told her that she suffered from "overtaxed nerves." The patient, however, informed Penrose that "I have worn a hole in my stomach from constantly explaining our work as I tramp all day long, day after day, among the homes."[9] A Caribbean vacation failed to improve her health, and a disagreement with D.K. Pearsons led to mental depression. In March 1901 Dox resigned as Whitman's field agent. Penrose desperately tried to get her to take a long vacation and resume her work or to come to Whitman and teach American history and physiology as Pearsons had recommended. She refused. "I am not able to do any hard work. . . . I would rather die than continue in such weary, wearing, discouraging work as that in which I have been engaged for the past few years. I am worn out and am not worth ten cents to anybody."[10] In a last letter she maintained that "I shall always have a deep and loyal affection for Whitman."[11] Penrose, who had often shared his administrative work and dreams for the college with this remarkable woman, explained her resignation. She had overworked herself so that she became very nervous; furthermore, she deluded herself into believing that he, as well as Pearsons and Nixon, had turned against her. These men sadly concluded that Dox "had lost her mental balance."[12]

In his history Penrose fully acknowledged her significant fund-raising efforts. "It is faint praise to say," he concluded, "that but for the labors of this gifted, eccentric, indomitable woman the first financial campaign ... would have ended in a failure or been long delayed."[13] Surely Penrose long remembered and hundreds of other fund raisers would accept Virginia Dox's definition of a fund raiser: "To be a successful College agent, one needs to be as patient as Job; as wise as Solomon; as meek as Moses; and as persistent as Paul."[14]

Notes

Abbreviations

The collections in which cited materials are found are referred to in these notes by the following acronyms:

AHC Archer Hendrick Collection, Whitman College Archives

CEC Cushing Eells Collection, Whitman College Archives

CL Congregational Library, Boston

JEC James Eaton Collection, Whitman College Archives

MEC Myron Eells Collection, Whitman College Archives

PCC Peasly Chamberlain Collection, Whitman College Archives

SPC Stephen Penrose Collection, Whitman College Archives

UWA University of Washington Archives, Seattle

WCA Whitman College Archives, Penrose Memorial Library

Chapter One

1. Cushing Eells to Secretary of the American Board Committee for Foreign Missions, January 6, 1855, CEC.
2. C. Eells to Secretary of the American Board, August 25, 1859, CEC.
3. C. Eells to secretaries of the American Home Mission Society, October 24, 1859, CEC.

4. George H. Atkinson, Peasly B. Chamberlain, and P.H. Hatch to Secretaries of the American Home Mission Society, October 26, 1859, CEC. On September 1, 1859, the Oregon Congregational Association met in Salem and passed resolutions favoring the establishment of Whitman Seminary with Eells as "a home missionary in the Walla Walla Valley." Minutes of the Congregational Association of Oregon, 7.

5. *Whitman College Catalogue*, 1882–1883, 16.

6. "An Act to Establish an Institution of Learning in Walla Walla County." Passed December 20, 1859. Published in Stephen B.L. Penrose, *Whitman: An Unfinished Story*, 243-244.

7. Ibid., 77.

8. C. Eells to American Board, January 5, 1855, CEC. Although Henry Spalding took no interest in honoring Marcus Whitman's life through a school named for him, he hailed his colleague's accomplishments. The year the seminary opened he wrote that Whitman was "emphatically a patriot without guile, a Christian whose faith was measured by his works; who counted not his dear life unto him if he might but do good to his fellow-beings, white or red; whose forethought, whose hazards, labors, and sufferings, self-devised, unsolicited, unrewarded, to reach Washington through the snows of New Mexico, did more for Oregon and this coast than the labors of any other man." *Walla Walla Statesman*, March 16, 1866.

9. Whitman Seminary Trustee Minutes, December 17, 1860, WCA.

10. Myron Eells, *Father Eells*, 180.

11. Penrose, *Whitman*, 67-68.

12. For the naming of Walla Walla see in Frank T. Gilbert, *Historic Sketches of Walla Walla, Whitman, Columbia and Garfield Counties, Washington Territory*, 222; William D. Lyman, *History of Walla Walla County, State of Washington*, 87.

13. M. Eells, *Father Eells*, 182.

14. One historian has summarized the influence of the Oregon Institute: "So completely did the Institute dominate the little city of Salem in its early years that it was commonly spoken of as 'The Institute.'" Robert Moulton Gatke, *Chronicles of Willamette*, 91.

15. Chamberlain, "The Early History of Whitman Seminary," M. Eells Scrapbook, MEC.

16. Ibid.

17. Ibid.

18. *Walla Walla Statesman*, June 8, 1866.

19. Few Whitman Seminary financial records have survived. Trustee Minutes and some newspapers, including the *Walla Walla Statesman*, October 19, 1866, provide some useful facts.

20. Whitman Seminary Trustee Minutes, June 22, 1866, WCA.

21. Whitman Seminary Trustee Minutes, September 5, 1866, WCA.

22. *Walla Walla Statesman*, October 5, 1866.

23. *Walla Walla Statesman*, October 19, 1866.

24. Chamberlain, "Address delivered at the opening of Whitman Seminary," October 13, 1866, PCC.

25. C. Eells Journal, October 13, 1866, CEC.

26. Chamberlain to Henry Spalding, November 30, 1868, PCC.

27. Whitman Seminary Trustee Minutes, March 25, 1867, WCA.

28. M. Eells, *Father Eells*, 192.

29. C. Eells to M. Eells, June 1, 1869, CEC.

30. Myra Eells to M. Eells, October 29, 1862, MEC.

31. C. Eells, "Reminiscences," *The Home Missionary*, March 1893, 533.

32. Lyman, *History of Walla Walla County*, 179.

33. C. Eells to M. Eells, June 1, 1869, CEC.

34. Whitman Seminary Trustee Minutes, September 5, 1868; July 16, 1869; WCA.

35. C. Eells Journal, February 4, 1869, CEC.

36. C. Eells Journal, January 4, 1869, CEC.

37. Penrose, *Whitman*, 68.

38. "From the Address of Cushing Eells," September, 1884, M. Eells Scrapbook, MEC.

39. C. Eells to Charles Eells, March 21, 1877, CEC.

40. Lyman, "The Old Seminary Days," *Whitman College Quarterly*, June 1900, 30.

41. Penrose, *Whitman*, 83.

42. C. Eells Diary, January, 15, 1868, CEC.

43. Chamberlain, "Early History of Whitman Seminary," M. Eells Scrapbook, MEC.

44. Chamberlain to M. Eells, November 6, 1869, PCC.

45. M. Eells to Chamberlain, November 29, 1869, M. Eells Corre-

spondence, MEC.

46. Whitman Seminary Trustee Minutes, December 9, 1872, WCA.

47. George Somerdyke to C. Eells, January 11, 1873, Whitman Seminary Records, WCA.

48. *Walla Walla Statesman*, August 26, 1876.

49. Report of the Bishop, June 13, 1880, St. Paul's School Records, WCA.

50. Alexander Jay Anderson, "The Beginnings of Whitman College," *Whitman College Quarterly*, March 1899, 21.

51. Gilbert, *Historic Sketches*, 325.

52. Chamberlain to C. Eells, July 4, 1873, PCC.

53. *Walla Walla Statesman*, August 30, 1873.

54. C. Eells to John F. Boyer, January 28, 1874, MEC.

55. C. Eells to M. Eells, February 3, 1880, MEC.

56. C. Eells to Edwin Eells, October 2, 1871; C. Eells to M. Eells, May 23, 1872, CEC.

57. C. Eells to John Wood, March 24, 1879, CEC.

58. C. Eells to Dorsey Baker, November 10, 1875, CEC.

59. Baker, Deed to Whitman Seminary, June 1, 1866, Whitman Seminary Records, WCA.

60. C. Eells to M. Eells, October 7, 1879, CEC.

61. Whitman Seminary Trustee Minutes, June 18, 1881, WCA.

62. Penrose, *Whitman*, 88.

63. C. Eells to Mrs. Henshaw, February 10, 1879, C. Eells Letter Book, CEC.

64. *Minutes of the Congregational Association of Oregon and Washington Territory*, 1882, 16.

65. Penrose, *Whitman*, 85.

66. Lyman, "The Old Seminary Days," 34.

67. *Walla Walla Statesman*, September 7, 1878.

68. Whitman Seminary Trustee Minutes, October 7, 1880, WCA.

69. Whitman Seminary Trustee Minutes, June 8, 1881, WCA.

70. Ibid.

71. Lyman, "The Old Seminary Days," 34. By 1886 the Beaches had settled in Lexington, Oregon, where he became a controversial Congregational minister. Lucie won approval for her Sunday school and public school teaching.

72. Ibid., 32.

73. J.D. McConkey, *From New York to Portland, Oregon Via Straits of Magellan*.

74. Lyman, "The Old Seminary Days," 32.

75. *Walla Walla Union*, September 7, 1872.

76. *Walla Walla Union*, August 30, 1873.

77. *Walla Walla Union*, August 28, 1875.

78. Myra Eells to M. Eells, October 29, 1866, M. Eells Correspondence, MEC.

79. Penrose, *Whitman*, 88.

80. Lyman, "The Old Seminary Days," 37.

81. Jo. Keon, "Whitman Seminary Reminiscences," Whitman Seminary Collection, WCA.

82. Baxter Renshaw to William Clark, February 9, 1906, Whitman Seminary Collection, WCA.

83. *Walla Walla Union*, August 16, 1873.

84. Mack F. Gose, "Recollections of Whitman Seminary Days from 1876 to 1880," Whitman Seminary Collection, WCA.

85. William O. Metzger to Clark, February 14, 1906, Whitman Seminary Collection, WCA.

86. Gose, "Recollections," Whitman Seminary Collection, WCA.

Chapter Two

1. Questionnaire for the *National Cyclopaedia of American Biography*, July 8, 1904, Box 71, Accession Number 106-70-12, Edmond S. Meany Papers, UWA.

2. An uncritical biography of Alexander Jay Anderson is Florence Bennett Anderson, *Leaven for the Frontier: The True Story of a Pioneer Educator*, 1953.

3. *Knox College Catalog*, 1856, 23. Two useful accounts of the formation and development of Knox College are Paul John Plath, *The Secularization of Knox College*, M.A. thesis, University of Illinois, 1977, and Hermann R. Meulder, *Fighters for Freedom: The History of Anti-slavery Activities of Men and Women Associated with Knox College*, 23.

4. F. Anderson, *Leaven for the Frontier*, 160.

5. Pacific University Board of Trustees Minutes, May 4, 1869, Pacific University Archives. Useful information on Pacific and oth-

er regional colleges is in James H. Hitchman, *Liberal Arts Colleges in Oregon and Washington, 1842–1980*, Center for Pacific Northwest Studies, Occasional Paper Number 17, Bellingham, Washington, 1981. Clipping, *Schoolmaster*(?), June 1869(?), A. Anderson Scrapbook, WCA.

6. A. Anderson to "Friend Fisher," unidentified clippings, September 14, 1869, February 12, 1870, A. Anderson Scrapbook, WCA.

7. *Pacific University Catalog*, 1869–1870, 6-7, 11; Pacific University Trustee Minutes, June 4, 1872; paper presented by Sidney Harper Marsh to trustees, in Pacific University Trustee Minutes, June 5, 1878, Pacific University Archives.

8. Clipping, A. Anderson Scrapbook; F. Anderson, *Leaven for the Frontier*, 202, explains A. Anderson's responsibilities at Pacific.

9. A. Anderson to George Atkinson, May 25, 1874, George H. Atkinson Correspondence, Pacific University Archives; Pacific University Trustee Minutes, June 2 and June 3, 1874, Pacific University Archives.

10. Victor J. Farrar, "History of the University," *Washington Alumnus*, May 1921, 9. The best summary of the university's history, and of A. Anderson's tenure, is Charles M. Gates, *The First Century at the University of Washington, 1861–1961*.

11. *University of Washington Catalog*, 1874, 13; *Register of the Territorial University*. One editor warned about sending daughters to college: "A young lady of sentiment and vivacity may find a deal of poetry and romance in going away from home to attend boarding school; but experience attests the fact that, where one pure minded girl goes away to remain for a term of years and returns the same modest, loving, and confiding daughter she was when she crossed her father's threshold for a first experience of the world, a hundred girls will come back so inflated with pride and vanity that the quiet of her father's house and the simplicity of her younger brothers and sisters are forever, thereafter, intolerable to her own false refinement"; see *Olympia Washington Standard*, January 18, 1879.

12. A useful summary of the early history of the University of Oregon is Henry D. Sheldon, *History of University of Oregon*, 30-46. Sometimes A. Anderson and others pointed to the University of Oregon's success, which, one editor stated, made it superior to

Pacific and Willamette; see *Seattle Daily Intelligencer*, July 19, 1879.

13. *University of Washington Catalog, 1877; University of Washington Territory Annual Announcement; Report of Regents of the Territorial University*, 8.

14. Farrar, "History of the University," *Washington Alumnus*, January 1922, 10; *University of Washington Catalogs*, 1878–82.

15. *Seattle Weekly Intelligencer*, January 25, 1879; clipping, *Seattle Puget Sound Dispatch*(?), March 22, 1880(?), A. Anderson Scrapbook, WCA.

16. James McNaught quoted in *Walla Walla Union-Bulletin*, January 11, 1953.

17. *Laws of Washington Territory*, 277.

18. *Seattle Weekly Intelligencer*, June 21, 1879; University of Washington president's report to regents, August 15, 1881, A. Anderson Scrapbook (apparently the only extant copy of this document), WCA.

19. A. Anderson, "Territorial University," unidentified clipping, January 1, 1881; unidentified, undated clipping; both in A. Anderson Scrapbook, WCA.

20. University of Washington president's report to regents, August 15, 1881, *A Plea for Aid*, A. Anderson Scrapbook, WCA.

21. William A. Newell, October. 5, 1881, in Charles Gates, *Messages of the Governors of the Territory of Washington*, 224; unidentified clippings, 1881(?), A. Anderson Scrapbook, WCA. Gates, *First Century*, 41-42, discusses the reasons for the negative vote.

22. Henry Villard to A. Anderson, unidentified clipping, *Seattle Post*(?), December 1, 1881(?) and January 9, 1882, A. Anderson Scrapbook, WCA.

23. Regents Minutes, Box 1, Accession Number 81-102, University of Washington Regents Records, UWA. Alexander Anderson wrote to Henry Villard asking for $2,000 per year for salaries, $100 for science and the library, and between $1,200 and $1,500 for desks and repairs of buildings and grounds. Anderson said that the regents hoped that Seattleites would cover this last request but concluded that for the other amounts "our sole reliance is upon you"; see A. Anderson to Villard, February 4, 1882,

Box 1, Accession Number 70-28, Presidents' Papers, UWA. Villard's assistance to the University of Oregon is neatly analyzed in George Belknap, *Henry Villard and the University of Oregon.*

24. A. Anderson to H.G. Struve, April 22, 1882, Box 1, Accession Number 70-28, Presidents Papers, UWA. In this and another letter to the regents, Alexander Anderson failed to explain why he was resigning. The newspapers, however, carried the story that Louisa Anderson's "health has been very delicate for some time, and her physician has prescribed a warmer, less humid climate. In this fact alone is found the reason for President Anderson's acceptance of the invitation given him by the city of Walla Walla"; see *Seattle Daily Chronicle*, May 6, 1882. Anderson himself gave that story to some papers; see *Waitsburg Times*, May 13, 1882.

25. Stephen Penrose, *Whitman: An Unfinished Story*, 92.

26. Atkinson to A. Anderson, January 6 and January 26, 1882, A. Anderson File, WCA.

27. President's Report, December 18, 1882, WCA.

28. It was necessary for Whitman's first president to have the prestige of a doctorate, for this degree had attained national importance. One authority has explained: "The rise of the honorary PH.D. in the 1870s and 1880s was ... striking evidence of the need everywhere for being called 'Doctor.'" Frederick Rudolph, *The American College and University: A History*, 397.

29. Clippings, A. Anderson Scrapbook, WCA.

30. A. Anderson, "Essay read before the Congregational Association, July 12, 1883," A. Anderson Scrapbook WCA; President's Report, December 18, 1882, WCA.

31. *Minutes of the Congregational Association*, 1883, 6-7.

32. A. Anderson "Essay," A. Anderson Scrapbook, WCA.

33. *Walla Walla Daily Journal*, October 31, 1883.

34. *Walla Walla Union*, November 10, 1883.

35. *Walla Walla Union*, November 2, 1883.

36. Whitman College Trustee Minutes, June 4, 1886, WCA.

37. Rudolph, *The American College*, 190.

38. *Seventh Annual Report of the American College and Education Society* (ACES), 1881, 66, CL.

39. *Ninth Annual Report of the* ACES, 1883, 19, CL.

40. *Boston Congregationalist*, October 28, 1883, CL.
41. *Boston Congregationalist*, November 8, 1883, CL.
42. Increase Tarbox to A. Anderson, December 11, 1883, A. Anderson File, WCA.
43. Cushing Eells Scrapbook, CEC.
44. C. Eells to A. Anderson, July 1, 1884, A. Anderson File, WCA.
45. C. Eells Diary, July 21, 1884, CEC.
46. C. Eells to Myron Eells, July 3, 1884, MEC.
47. M. Eells, *Father Eells*, 205.
48. Whitman College Trustee Minutes, December 18, 1884, WCA.
49. Whitman College Trustee Minutes, April 16, 1884, WCA.
50. *Tenth Annual Report of the* ACES, 1884, 35, CL.
51. *Walla Walla Watchman*, August 15, 1884. In this issue the editor praised Elvira Cobleigh's ability to raise money.
52. A. Anderson, Whitman Circular, A. Anderson Scrapbook, WCA.
53. Tarbox to A. Anderson, July 31, 1884, A. Anderson File, WCA.
54. *Whitman College Catalogue*, 1885–1886, 34.
55. Whitman College Trustee Minutes, June 2, 1888, WCA.
56. *Whitman College Catalogue*, 1890–1891, 25-26.
57. *University of Oregon Catalogue*, 1887, 27.
58. *Walla Walla Union*, October 27, 1883.
59. *Whitman College Catalogue*, 1890–1891, 15.
60. *Whitman College Catalogue*, 1887–1888, 22.
61. *Walla Walla Union*, September 26, 1882.
62. Penrose, *Whitman*, 104.
63. Whitman College Faculty Minutes, April 15, 1889, WCA.
64. Ibid.; April 4, 1889; WCA.
65. Rudolph, *The American College*, 194.
66. Ibid.
67. *Whitman College Catalogue*, 1885–1886, 28.
68. *Whitman College Catalogue*, 1886–1887, 26.
69. Whitman College Faculty Minutes, September 9, 1889, WCA.
70. *Whitman College Catalogue*, 1885–1886, 21.
71. *University of Oregon Catalogue*, 1887, 39.
72. Whitman College Faculty Minutes, February 9 and February 10, 1891, WCA.
73. Whitman College Faculty Minutes, October 14, 1891, WCA.
74. *Whitman College Collegian*, January 1893.

75. Journal of Adelphi Meetings, 1888; Journal of Athenaeum Meetings, 1892; and Journal of Whittier Meetings, 1888, WCA.
76. Newspaper clipping, A. Anderson Scrapbook, WCA.
77. Newspaper clipping, A. Anderson Scrapbook, WCA.
78. A. Anderson, "Whitman College," M. Eells Scrapbook, MEC.
79. *Eleventh Annual Report of the* ACES, 1885, 24, CL.
80. *Fifteenth Annual Report of the* ACES, 1889, 24, CL.
81. F. Anderson, *Leaven for the Frontier*, 392.
82. *Seventh Annual Report of the* ACES, 1891, 42, CL.
83. A. Anderson, *Whitman College*, 1889 circular, A. Anderson Scrapbook, WCA.
84. A. Anderson, *Whitman College*, 1890 circular, A. Anderson Scrapbook, WCA.
85. A. Anderson, *Whitman College*, 1889 circular, M. Eells Scrapbook, MEC.
86. A. Anderson, *Whitman College*, 1886 circular, A. Anderson File, WCA.
87. *Walla Walla Statesman*, January 8, 1883.
88. *Whitman College Catalogue*, 1887–1888, 19.
89. Penrose, *Whitman*, 115.
90. Newspaper clipping, A. Anderson Scrapbook, WCA.
91. Newspaper clipping, A. Anderson Scrapbook, WCA.
92. *Walla Walla Watchman*, December 7, 1883.
93. *Walla Walla Union*, February 4, 1891.
94. ACES circular, A. Anderson Scrapbook, WCA.
95. Allen H. Reynolds, "Recollections," A. Anderson File, WCA.
96. Penrose, *Whitman*, 109.
97. A. Reynolds, "Recollections," A. Anderson File, WCA.
98. *Walla Walla Union*, July 4, 1891.
99. A. Anderson to M. Eells, July 7, 1891, Whitman College Trustee Correspondence, WCA.
100. A. Anderson to M. Eells, September 10, 1890, Whitman College Trustee Correspondence, WCA.
101. Eli R. Loomis to A. Reynolds, November 10, 1890, Reynolds Vertical File, WCA.
102. Jonathan Edwards to M. Eells, April 24, 1891, Whitman College Trustee Correspondence, WCA.
103. Penrose, *Whitman*, 118.

104. Chester Maxey, *Five Centennial Papers*, 8.

105. William Lyman to M. Eells, July 13, 1891, Whitman College Trustee Correspondence, wca.

106. A. Anderson to M. Eells, July 7, 1891, M. Eells Correspondence, mec.

107. A. Anderson to M. Eells, April 8, 1892, M. Eells Correspondence, wca.

108. *A Volume of Representative Citizens of the City of Seattle and County of King*, 567.

109. A. Anderson to John Hamilton, aces Correspondence, Box 15, cl.

110. *Whitman College Pioneer*, March 19, 1903.

111. Penrose, *Whitman*, 115.

112. Frederick E. Bolton, "The Alexander Jay Anderson Family: Pioneer Pedagogues of the Pacific Northwest," typescript, 1952(?), 24, Box 15, Bolton Papers, uwa; Nard Jones, "Educator Extraordinary," May, 1960, A. Anderson File, wca.

113. A. Anderson, "My Schools," A. Anderson Scrapbook, wca.

Chapter Three

1. Biographical material about James Eaton is in "Williams College Class Statistics," 1876, and "Obituary Record of the Society of Alumni," Williams College, April, 1922, 154-155.

2. *Annual Report of the School Committee of the Town of North Adams*, 1891, 24-43.

3. *Walla Walla Union-Journal*, September 30, 1891.

4. *Walla Walla Union-Journal*, September 15, 1891.

5. *Walla Walla Union-Journal*, November 19, 1891.

6. Whitman College Trustee Executive Committee Minutes, September 21, 1891, wca.

7. *Walla Walla Union-Journal*, November 26, 1891.

8. The constitution is in Whitman College Trustee Executive Committee Minutes, April 9, 1892, wca.

9. J. Eaton to the class of 1892, in particular, and in general to the pupils of Drury High School, June 13, 1892, jec.

10. *Whitman College Catalogue*, 1892, 7.

11. *Walla Walla Union-Journal*, April 24, 1892.

12. *Walla Walla Statesman*, September 10, 1892.
13. John Boyer to Myron Eells, April 8, 1892; Eells Correspondence; M. Eells Diary, June 4, 1892, MEC.
14. William Lyman to Allen Reynolds, January 19, 1892, Reynolds File, WCA; Louis Anderson to M. Eells, February 13, 1892, M. Eells Letters, MEC.
15. Whitman College Trustee Minutes, December 10, 1891, WCA.
16. Whitman College Trustee Executive Committee Minutes, December 14, 1891, WCA.
17. Whitman College Trustee Executive Committee Minutes, February 2, 1892, WCA.
18. Whitman College Trustee Executive Committee Minutes, March 11, 1892, WCA.
19. Lyman to A. Reynolds, January 19, 1892 and March 18, 1892, Lyman File, WCA.
20. *Walla Walla Union-Journal*, March 14, 1892.
21. Stephen Penrose, *Whitman: An Unfinished Story*, 134.
22. Ibid., 135.
23. M. Eells Diary, June 26, 1894, MEC; *Olympia Olympian*, June 2, 1968.
24. Robert Gatke, *Chronicles of Willamette*, 406-417.
25. J. Eaton to M. Eells, February 26, 1892, Whitman College Trustee Correspondence, WCA.
26. Boyer to M. Eells, April 8, 1892, M. Eells Letters, MEC.
27. *Eighteenth Annual Report of the* ACES, 1892, 30, CL.
28. Eaton to Harry A. Reynolds, December 2, 1892, Whitman College Trustee Correspondence, WCA.
29. Penrose, *Whitman*, 132.
30. *Nineteenth Annual Report of the* ACES, 1893, 3, CL.
31. D.W. Meinig, *The Great Columbia Plain*, 365.
32. M. Eells to Lyman, May 10, 1894; Lyman to M. Eells, June 25 and September 7, 1894, M. Eells Letters, MEC.
33. Eaton to the ACES, November 25, 1893, ACES Correspondence, CL.
34. *Nineteenth Annual Report of the* ACES, 1893, 32, CL.
35. Eaton to Frank L. Ferguson, January 19, 1894, ACES Correspondence, CL.
36. Ferguson to Eaton, March 14, 1894, ACES Correspondence, CL.

37. Ferguson to Eaton, February 20, 1894, ACES Correspondence, CL.
38. Daniel K. Pearsons to Eaton, March 25, 1894, Eaton Correspondence, CL.
39. Eaton to Ferguson, April 4, 1895, ACES Correspondence, CL.
40. *Walla Walla Union-Journal*, July 14, 1894.
41. *Walla Walla Union-Journal*, July 24, 1894.
42. Eaton to William Kirkman, February 27, 1893, Eaton Correspondence, CL.
43. M. Eells Diary, March 18, 1893, MEC.
44. Boyer to Kirkman, February 19, 1893, Whitman College Trustee Correspondence, WCA.
45. James H. Hamilton to J. Eaton, February 24, ACES Correspondence, CL.
46. Florence Anderson, *Leaven for the Frontier: The True Story of a Pioneer Educator*, 413; Louis Anderson to M. Eells, August 7, 1894, M. Eells Letters, MEC.
47. Penrose, *Whitman*, 130.
48. *Whitman Collegian*, January 1892.
49. *Whitman Collegian*, May 1893.
50. L. Anderson to M. Eells, August 7, 1894, MEC.
51. Ida Mabel Anderson to M. Eells, October 5, 1893, Whitman College Trustee Correspondence, WCA.
52. Eaton to Hamilton, July 29, 1893, ACES Correspondence, CL.
53. Unsigned letter to S.B. Bishop, May 16, 1893, Whitman College Trustee Correspondence, WCA.
54. Whitman College Trustee Executive Committee Minutes, February 21, 1894, WCA.
55. Whitman College Trustee Minutes, June 7, 1894, WCA.
56. M. Eells Diary, June 9, 1894, MEC.
57. Penrose, *Whitman*, 124, 138.
58. Harry Painter to William Worthington, March 25, 1931, Whitman College Alumni Correspondence, WCA.
59. Jonathan Edwards to H. Reynolds, September 27, 1894, Whitman College Trustee Correspondence, WCA.
60. Penrose, *Whitman*, 139.
61. M. Eells Diary, September 25, 1894, MEC.
62. Ibid.
63. Lyman, *Old Walla Walla County*, Volume II, 219.

64. Penrose, *Whitman*, 140; H. Reynolds provides his view of the Eaton controversy in his account in Harry Reynolds Correspondence, WCA.; James Eaton provides his side in a letter to M. Eells, August 29, 1894, M. Eells Correspondence, MEC.

65. Whitman College Trustee Executive Committee Minutes, September 10, 1894, WCA.

Chapter Four

1. *Dayton Columbia-Chronicle*, September 13, 1890.

2. Stephen Penrose's career in Dayton is summarized in his own account in *The Washington Farmer*, April 23 and April 30, 1925.

3. *Dayton Columbia-Chronicle*, August 30 and November 15, 1890.

4. Biographical information on the Penrose family is in *History of the Penrose Family of Philadelphia*.

5. Interview with Frances Penrose Owen, Seattle, October 1985, Oral History Collection, WCA.

6. Ibid.

7. An excellent summary of Penrose's Philadelphia is to be found in Russell F. Weigley (editor), *Philadelphia: A 300-Year History*, 417-523.

8. *Twentieth Reunion Class 1885, Williams College*, 45.

9. Scrapbook of Robert W. Gilbert, 1877, Williams College Library.

10. An excellent summary of Williams College in the 1880s is James R. McDonald, "Social Life at Williams College in the Eighties," *Williams Alumni Review*, May 1932, 305-309.

11. A thoughtful and comprehensive study of Stephen Penrose at Williams College is Frederick Rudolph, "One Hundred Years Ago at Williams College: Ecology of the Student Experience," delivered at Whitman College, September 15, 1982, Penrose File, WCA.

12. Ibid., 3.

13. *Twentieth Reunion Class 1885, Williams College*, 46.

14. Ibid., 47.

15. McDonald, "Social Life," 306.

16. *The Williams Anthenaeum*, December 13, 1884, Williams College, 178.

17. Newton F. Gordon, compiler, *Statistics of the Class of '85*.

18. "Senior Editorial," *The Glvielmensian*, December 1884, Williams College.

19. Stephen Penrose, *Whitman: An Unfinished Story*, 142.

20. *Williams College Catalogue*, 1886–1887, 26.

21. Ibid., 34.

22. *Franklin Carter Report*, 1887, 18, 20.

23. Ibid., 4.

24. Interview with Owen, October 1985, WCA.

25. Newton F. Gordon (compiler), *Statistics*, 16.

26. Penrose, *Whitman*, 142-143.

27. Congregational Association of Washington Minutes, 1891, 33.

28. Interview with Owen and Mary Penrose Copeland, Seattle, October, 1985, WCA.

29. "Penrose Quarterly Report," April 12, 1893, American Home Mission Society Papers, microfilm copy at the Washington State Historical Society, Tacoma, reel 236.

30. Penrose, *Whitman*, 141.

31. Interview with Owen, October 1985, WCA.

32. Harry Reynolds to Myron Eells, September 25, 1894, MEC.

33. David Starr Jordan, "Opening Address," *The Palo Alto* October 1891, 29.

34. Penrose, *Whitman*, 144.

Chapter Five

1. John Hamilton to Whitman College Board of Trustees, August 21, 1894, Congregational Education Society Correspondence, CL.

2. Whitman College Trustee Executive Committee Minutes, October 5, 1894, WCA.

3. Stephen Penrose to Myron Eells, Octobr 17, 1894, MEC.

4. Whitman College Faculty Minutes, October 15, 1894, WCA.

5. *Walla Walla Union*, October 7, 1894.

6. D.K. Pearsons to Penrose, October 23, 1894, SPC.

7. Pearsons to Penrose, November 26, 1894, SPC.

8. Frederick Rudolph, *The American College and University: A History*, 352-353.

9. Pearsons to Penrose, November 26, 1894, SPC.

10. *Walla Walla Statesman*, December 8, 1894.
11. Hamilton to Penrose, January 10, 1895, CES Correspondence, CL.
12. Robert L. Whitner, "The Myth that Saved the College," *Two Essays on the History of Whitman College*, 5.
13. Penrose, *The Romance of a College*.
14. Minutes of the Congregational Association of Washington, 1894, 19.
15. *Portland Weekly Oregonian*, August 3, 1888. Jesse Applegate letter, June 20, 1883 in Samuel A. Clarke Scrapbook, Oregon Historical Society.
16. Penrose, *Whitman: An Unfinished Story*, 145.
17. Ibid., 150.
18. Ibid., 147.
19. *Walla Walla Union*, March 15, 1895.
20. *Walla Walla Union*, March 5, 1895.
21. Oliver W. Nixon, *How Marcus Whitman Saved Oregon*, 5.
22. Ibid., 256.
23. *Whitman College Pioneer*, May 17, 1905.
24. Clifford M. Drury, *Marcus and Narcissa Whitman*, Volume II, 384.
25. Hamilton to Penrose, January 15, 1895, CES Correspondence, CL.
26. Hamilton to George Herrick, February 1, 1895, CES Correspondence, CL.
27. Hamilton to Herrick, January 31, 1895, CES Correspondence, CL.
28. Hamilton to Herrick, February 2, 1895, CES Correspondence, CL.
29. Penrose to Harry Reynolds, April 18, 1895, SPC.
30. Hamilton to Penrose, April 17, 1895, CES Correspondence, CL.
31. Penrose, *Whitman*, 148.
32. Penrose to Frank Ferguson, May 22, 1895, CES Correspondence, CL.
33. *Walla Walla Union*, May 26, 1895.
34. *Walla Walla Union*, June 3, 1895.
35. *Walla Walla Union*, June 8, 1895.
36. *Walla Walla Union*, June 12, 1895.
37. President's Report, June 12, 1895, WCA.
38. Ibid., 7.
39. Penrose, *Whitman*, 145.
40. *Spokane Spokesman Review*, July 5, 1895.

41. Herrick to Hamilton, July 7, 1895, CES Correspondence, CL.
42. Pearsons to Ferguson, August 1 and August 22, 1895, CES Correspondence, CL.
43. Herrick to Hamilton, August 5, 1895, CES Correspondence, CL.
44. J.K.M. Lean to Edward F. Williams, June 3, 1896, Edward F. Williams Papers, CL.
45. Pearsons to Penrose, April, 1897, SPC.
46. Penrose, *Whitman*, 148.
47. Penrose Letter File, 1897, SPC.
48. John Maile to Penrose, March 5, 1897, SPC.
49. Ibid.
50. Maile to Penrose, May 31, 1897, SPC.
51. Penrose to Maile, January 17, 1898 and October 14, 1899, SPC.
52. Penrose to Ferguson, ACES September 11, 1897, CES Correspondence, CL.
53. Pearsons to Penrose, September 23, 1897, SPC.
54. Penrose, *Whitman*, 150.
55. Biographical information on the Shipman family is in *The Shipman Family in America*, 1962, SPC; and *Hartford Courant*, June 27, 1906.
56. Information about Mary's schooling is in Mary Shipman Penrose, "School Days" (undated), SPC.
57. Lucius Baird to his mother, September 20, 1888, SPC.
58. A report of the Penrose wedding is in *Hartford Daily Courant*, June 18, 1896.
59. *Walla Walla Union*, September 11, 1896.
60. *Walla Walla Union*, September 19 and 20, 1896.
61. Penrose to The Perfect Mucilage Co., May 10, 1898, SPC.
62. Richard L. Neuberger, *Our Promised Land*, 4.
63. "The Aim of Whitman College," *Whitman College Quarterly*, January 1897, 22.
64. Ibid.
65. "Safety First," *Whitman College Quarterly*, January 1897, 26.
66. "Mining Stock," Ibid., 25.
67. "A Department of Economics and Social Science," Ibid., 23.
68. *Walla Walla Statesman*, December 4, 1897.
69. *Walla Walla Union* (undated), M. Eells Scrapbook, MEC.
70. *Walla Walla Union*, December 1, 1897.

71. *Portland Oregonian*, December 1, 1897.
72. President's Report, 1898, WCA.
73. *Walla Walla Statesman*, December 4, 1897.
74. *Walla Walla Union*, December 7, 1897.
75. George Lundington Weed, "When Dr. Whitman Added Three Stars to Our Flag," *Ladies Home Journal*, November 1897, 9-10.
76. M. Eells Scrapbook, 48-49, MEC.
77. Ibid., 45-48.
78. Penrose to A.P. Mohler, November 18, 1897, SPC.
79. Penrose to the Reverend A.E. Demming, November 5, 1897; Penrose to Ross R. Brattain, 1897; SPC.
80. Penrose to Maile, 1897, CES Correspondence, CL.
81. President's Report, 1896, 3, SPC.
82. Penrose to Virginia Dox, April 1898(?), SPC.
83. Penrose to Dox, November 2, 1898, SPC.
84. *Whitman College Quarterly*, October 1898, 45.
85. Penrose to Dox, March 12, 1898, SPC.
86. *Whitman College Quarterly*, June 1898, 44.
87. Penrose to Dox, February 17, 1898, SPC.
88. Penrose to Dox, May 28, 1898, SPC.
89. Penrose to Dox, March 7, 1898, SPC.
90. Pearsons to Penrose, January 14, 1898, SPC.
91. Nixon to Penrose, April 20, 1898, SPC.
92. Pearsons advised Penrose in many letters between January and June 1898; Penrose to Dox, February 26, 1898, SPC.
93. Penrose to Dox, March 12, 1898, SPC.
94. Pearsons to Penrose, July 14 and July 25, 1898, SPC.
95. Pearsons to Penrose, November 16 and December 2, 1898, SPC.
96. Nixon to Penrose, February 20, 1899 and March, 1899, SPC.
97. Pearsons to Penrose, February 20, 1899, SPC.
98. *Walla Walla Statesman*, March 11, 1899.
99. *Walla Walla Statesman*, March 18, 1899.
100. Penrose to Dox, April 7, 1899, SPC.
101. Penrose, *Whitman*, 155-157; Penrose to Dox April 7, 1899, SPC.
102. *Whitman College Pioneer*, April, 1899.
103. Pearsons to Penrose, 1899(?), SPC.
104. Whitman College Trustee Minutes, May 4 and May 14, 1899, WCA.

105. *Walla Walla Statesman*, March 25, 1899.

106. Ibid.

107. Dox to Penrose, July 11, 1899, SPC.

108. Ibid.

109. Julia Billings to Penrose, August 4, 1899 and *Whitman College Quarterly*, October 1899, 23-25.

110. Penrose to Dox, August 9, 1899; Penrose to the Reverend Amos J. Bailey, September 22, 1899, SPC.

111. *Whitman College Quarterly*, 1900, 46.

112. *Whitman College Pioneer*, January 1900, 12.

113. Nixon, "Dedicatory Oration," *Whitman College Quarterly*, 1900, 3-24.

114. Miles C. Moore, "Response," Ibid., 24.

115. "A Letter from Dr. Pearsons," Ibid., 26-27.

116. Penrose, "A Word Portrait of a Teacher of Physics," Alumni File, WCA.

117. *Whitman College Pioneer*, February 1898.

118. Penrose, "A Word Portrait of a Teacher of Physics," Alumni File, WCA.

119. Penrose to Lucy H. Baird, October 31, 1900, SPC.

120. *Walla Walla Union*, June 12, 1895.

121. Penrose to Dox, January, 1899; Penrose to Bailey, September 22, 1899; SPC.

122. President's Report, 1895, 2, WCA.

123. Penrose to John W. Martin, March 27, 1899, SPC; President's Report, 1898, 2, WCA.

124. *Spokane Spokesman-Review*, February 25, 1900.

125. *Pacific University Catalog*, 1893–1894, 19.

126. *Spokane Spokesman-Review*, February 25, 1900.

127. President's Report, 1895, 18, WCA.

128. *Whitman College Catalogue*, 1898, 45.

129. Penrose to Dox, February 28, 1899, SPC.

130. Penrose to the Reverend William C. Merritt, September 28, 1900, SPC.

131. *Whitman College Catalogue*, 1899, 17.

132. Penrose to E.G. McGilvary, February 15, 1899, SPC.

133. Interview with Mary Penrose Copeland and Frances Penrose Owen, Seattle, October 17, 1985, WCA.

134. Dean of the College to Mrs. Frank Worsley, January 6, 1902, SPC.

135. Penrose to Mrs. John Mustard, October 31, 1898, SPC.

136. Penrose to Miss Henrietta Moritz, October 12, 1898, SPC.

137. Mrs. J.W. Small to Thompson C. Elliott, October 18, 1898, SPC.

138. Penrose to Charles O. Day, October 20, 1899, SPC.

139. Whitman College Faculty Minutes, 1898, 246, WCA.

140. Penrose to Dox, December 28, 1898, SPC.

141. *Whitman College Catalogue*, 1899, 31.

142. Ibid., 34.

143. *Whitman College Catalogue*, 1900, 24.

144. Penrose to Dox, June 23, 1897, SPC.

145. Penrose to Dox, June 28, 1897, SPC.

146. *Whitman College Pioneer*, December 1896.

147. *Whitman College Pioneer*, April 1897.

148. *Whitman College Pioneer*, February 1899.

149. *Whitman College Pioneer*, November 1898.

150. Penrose, *Whitman*, 203.

151. *Whitman College Pioneer*, April 1898.

152. Penrose to Dox, November 9, 1899, SPC.

153. Libethrean Literary Society Minutes (undated), 3, WCA.

154. *Whitman College Pioneer*, November 1898.

155. *Walla Walla Union*, March 25, 1898.

156. *Walla Walla Union*, March 30, 1898.

157. *Whitman College Pioneer*, January 1899.

158. *Walla Walla Union*, April 30, 1898.

159. *Whitman College Pioneer*, January 1897.

160. *Whitman College Pioneer*, March 1897.

161. *Whitman College Pioneer*, March 1899.

162. *Whitman College Pioneer*, February 1900.

163. *Whitman College Pioneer*, November 1897.

164. *Whitman College Pioneer*, December 1897.

165. *Whitman College Pioneer*, January 1898.

166. *Whitman College Pioneer*, January 1899.

167. *Whitman College Pioneer*, November 1899.

168. *Walla Walla Statesman*, September 15, 1900.

169. *Whitman College Pioneer*, December 1899.

170. *Spokane Spokesman-Review*, February 25, 1900.

171. *Whitman College Pioneer*, May 1898.

172. Penrose, *Whitman*, 162.

173. *Whitman College Pioneer*, December 1896.

174. *Whitman College Pioneer*, December 1898.

175. *Whitman College Catalogue*, 1896, 16.

176. Whitman College Trustee Minutes, 1896(?), WCA.

177. Whitman College Faculty Minutes, December 21, 1897, WCA.

178. M. Eells Diary, June 12, 1896 and June 17, 1899, MEC.

179. Nixon to Elliott, July 28, 1899, SPC.

180. Penrose to Dox, 29 September 1900, SPC.

181. Penrose to H. Reynolds, June, 1896, SPC.

182. Penrose, *Whitman*, 163.

183. Nixon to Penrose, July 31, 1900, SPC.

184. Penrose to A.D. Charlton, May 28, 1898, and October 12 and 16, 1899; SPC.

185. Penrose to Dox, August 9, 1899, SPC.

186. Nixon to Penrose, October 24, 1900, SPC.

187. Penrose to Dox, April 3, 1899, SPC.

188. Ibid.

189. *Whitman College Quarterly*, 1900, 44.

Chapter Six

1. Stephen Penrose to C.A. Osborne, September 8, 1906, SPC.

2. Penrose to Howard A. Bridgman, March 19, 1907, SPC.

3. *Report of the President of Bowdoin College*, 1903–1904, 17, 24-26.

4. President's Report, 1904, 8, WCA.

5. *Whitman College Quarterly*, December 1903, 6.

6. President's Report, 1905, 8, WCA.

7. Stephen Penrose to Frank Whitham, December 9, 1902, SPC.

8. Whitham to Penrose, December 8, 1902, SPC.

9. Penrose to Whitham, February 2, 1903, SPC.

10. Whitham to Penrose, February 11, 1903, SPC.

11. Penrose to Whitham, February 19, 1903, SPC.

12. Penrose to Whitham, April 28, 1903, SPC.

13. President's Report, 1904, 8, WCA.

14. D.K. Pearsons to Penrose, September 26, 1903, SPC.

15. Pearsons to Penrose, May 8, 1904, SPC.

16. Pearsons to Penrose, August 4, 1904, SPC.
17. Penrose to Park Weed Willis, May 5, 1904, SPC.
18. Penrose to James Barton, November 24, 1905, SPC.
19. Penrose to E. Benjamin Andrews, February 8, 1907, SPC.
20. Penrose to Pearsons, September 25, 1906, SPC.
21. Pearsons to Penrose, October 1, 1906, SPC.
22. James Bertram to Penrose, January 23, 1906, SPC.
23. Penrose to Bertram, February 8, 1906, SPC.
24. Bertram to Penrose, March 12, 1906, SPC.
25. Pearsons to Penrose, March 12, 1906, SPC.
26. Penrose to Anna Dawes, December 20, 1906, SPC.
27. Penrose to Albert Shaw, February 8, 1907, SPC.
28. Penrose to Starr Murphy, February 27, 1907, SPC.
29. Penrose to Harry Pratt Jordan, February 18, 1907, SPC.
30. Ibid.
31. Penrose to George Twiner, March 27, 1907, SPC.
32. Thomas Burke to Penrose, March 30, 1907, SPC.
33. Penrose to Pearsons, April 20, 1907, SPC.
34. Pearsons to Penrose, April 27, 1907, SPC.
35. Pearsons to Penrose, May 15, 1907, SPC.
36. Penrose to Pearsons, May 4, 1907, SPC.
37. Penrose to Vahram Davond, September 23, 1907, SPC.
38. Whitman College Trustee Executive Committee Records, June 14, 1907, WCA.
39. *Walla Walla Union*, June 1, 1902.
40. Pearsons to Penrose, March 17, 1902, SPC.
41. Pearsons to Penrose, May 1, 1902, SPC.
42. Pearsons to Penrose, April 15, 1901, SPC.
43. Pearsons to Penrose, June 26, 1902, SPC.
44. Pearsons to Penrose, June 24, 1902, SPC.
45. Penrose to William A. Mowry, February 17, 1904, SPC.
46. *Walla Walla Union*, February 24, 1904.
47. Ibid.
48. Penrose to F. Lewis Clark, 1904, SPC.
49. *Whitman College Pioneer*, February 26, 1904.
50. Ibid.
51. *Whitman College Pioneer*, February 1904.
52. *Whitman College Pioneer*, February 26, 1904.

53. *Walla Walla Union*, February 24, 1904.
54. *Whitman College Pioneer*, April 19, 1904.
55. *Walla Walla Union*, February 20, 1904.
56. *Whitman College Pioneer*, October 18, 1904.
57. *Whitman College Pioneer*, April 5, 1905.
58. President's Report, 1902, 3, WCA.
59. *Whitman College Pioneer*, April 23, 1903.
60. *Whitman College Quarterly*, January 1907, 1-12.
61. *Whitman, the Quarterly Magazine of Whitman College*, February 1985, 13.
62. *Whitman College Catalogue*, 1907, 85.
63. *Whitman College Quarterly*, January 1907, 13.
64. Penrose to Louis K. Stark, May 20, 1903, SPC.
65. Penrose to Frank Newhall White, February 2, 1907, SPC.
66. Penrose to Cephas Allin, March 29, 1904, SPC.
67. Penrose to F.J. Smale, January 15, 1904; Penrose to E.H. Storer, January 29, 1904; SPC.
68. W.T. Sedgwick, to Penrose, April 16, 1904, SPC.
69. Ibid.
70. Penrose to Charles Allen, January 19, 1901, SPC.
71. Penrose to Allen, March 25, 1901, SPC.
72. Penrose to The Military Secretary, September 20, 1904, SPC.
73. Penrose to Walter Camp, November 5, 1904, SPC.
74. Penrose to unknown, November 7, 1904, SPC.
75. Penrose to T. H. McMichael, December 10, 1907, SPC.
76. Penrose to Hamilton Wright Mabie, December 19, 1903, SPC.
77. Gertrude H. Wylie to Penrose, January 13, 1904, SPC.
78. Penrose to Samuel Ives Curtiss, January 18, 1904, SPC.
79. Wylie to Penrose, February 20, 1904, SPC.
80. Penrose to Wylie, January 18, 1904, SPC.
81. Penrose to Professor S. Harrison Lovewell, July 24, 1903, SPC.
82. Quoted in Theron F. Schlabach, *Pensions for Professors*, 2.
83. William Worthington to Penrose, May 8, 1907, SPC.
84. Louis Anderson to Penrose, August 15, 1907, SPC.
85. Walter A. Bratton to Penrose, December 21, 1903, SPC.
86. Penrose to Nicholas Murray Butler, February 12, 1902, SPC.
87. Penrose to Frank B. Cooper, May 5, 1904, SPC.
88. Penrose to J.J. Browne, August 26, 1902; Lovewell to Penrose,

July 30, 1903; SPC.

89. G.W. Sandt to Penrose, March 29, 1906, SPC.

90. Penrose to W.F. Chase, February 26, 1906, SPC.

91. Penrose to Valeria Penrose, December 2, 1907, SPC.

92. William Lyman to Penrose, July 25, 1904, SPC.

93. *Whitman College Catalogue*, 1904, 88.

94. Ibid., 88-89.

95. *Whitman College Catalogue*, 1903, 98.

96. President's Report, 1903, 5, WCA.

97. Quoted in G. Thomas Edwards, "The College, the Town, and Teddy Roosevelt: 1903," *Whitman Alumnus*, November 1977, 5.

98. Frederick Rudolph, *Curriculum: A History of the American Undergraduate Course of Study Since 1636*, 191.

99. Rudolph, *The American College and University: A History*, 298.

100. Rudolph, *Curriculum*, 195-196.

101. President's Report, 1904, 1-2, WCA.

102. Penrose to William Worthington, October 3, 1905, SPC.

103. Penrose to William H. Cowles, January 14, 1904, SPC.

104. *Walla Walla Union*, December 27, 1903.

105. *Walla Walla Union*, February 21, 1904.

106. *Whitman College Pioneer*, October 11, 1904.

107. *Whitman College Catalogue*, 1908, 73; *Whitman College Catalogue*, 1907, 63-64.

108. Bratton to Penrose, July 24, 1907, SPC.

109. Penrose to Cowles, January 14, 1904, SPC.

110. Penrose to Fred Baske, May 2, 1903, SPC.

111. Penrose to Charles Gates, May 19, 1905, SPC.

112. Walter Crosby Eells to Bratton, July 23, 1905, SPC.

113. Penrose to N.W. Durham, August 17, 1904, SPC.

114. Penrose to E.L. Dorr, August 26, 1902, SPC.

115. Penrose to George Marquis, September 15, 1900, SPC.

116. Penrose to John Love, August 30, 1902, SPC.

117. Penrose to Frank Swan, June 14, 1904, SPC.

118. Penrose to William Stoddard, August 14, 1902, SPC.

119. Penrose to James McLean, November 10, 1904, SPC.

120. Penrose to J.A. Clock, December 9, 1903, SPC.

121. Penrose to E.H. Talcot, July 15, 1904, SPC.

122. Penrose to J.A. Dursten, January 12, 1904, SPC.

123. Penrose to Charles Loy, September 16, 1902, SPC.

124. Penrose to James F. Camer, January 11, 1907, SPC.

125. Bratton to John Love, September 16, 1902, SPC.

126. Penrose to Bernard Devin, November 17, 1902, SPC.

127. Penrose to Myrtle Sanders, August 28, 1902, SPC.

128. Unknown to J.E. Springer, September 16, 1902, SPC.

129. Archer Hendrick to Lee Samuels and Sam Davidson, 1905(?), SPC.

130. E. Marlatte to Penrose, April 10, 1907, SPC.

131. Penrose to Charles Gates, May 13, 1905, SPC.

132. Penrose to Charles O. Day, February 11, 1901, SPC.

133. Edward Tead to Penrose, November 21, 1901, SPC.

134. Penrose to Day, February 11, 1901, SPC.

135. Penrose to Miriam Lee, May 30, 1901; Tead to Penrose, November 29, 1902; SPC.

136. A.W. Taylor to Penrose, December 1, 1903, SPC.

137. Charles Palmer to Marion A. Kees, May 12, 1905, SPC.

138. Worthington to Penrose, May 22, 1906, SPC.

139. Penrose to George Littlefield, September 28, 1906; Penrose to W.D. Wood, September 28, 1906; SPC.

140. Charles Timblin to Penrose, July 8, 1904, and Penrose to Timblin, July 9, 1904, SPC.

141. Worthington to Penrose, January 5, 1905, SPC.

142. Fred Lasater to Penrose, October 9, 1903, SPC.

143. *Whitman College Quarterly*, 1903, 6.

144. Penrose to G.W. Estes, September 24, 1902, SPC.

145. Penrose to A.E. Barnes, April 12, 1907, SPC.

146. Penrose to Dr. T.C. Willson, July 9, 1906, SPC.

147. Penrose to Ayers, January 25, 1903, SPC.

148. *Whitman College Pioneer*, April 9, 1907.

149. Ross Brattain to Penrose, September 15, 1901, SPC.

150. W.T. Dodd to Hendrick, September 8, 1906, SPC.

151. Penrose to Mrs. E. Derr, November 14, 1902, SPC.

152. Penrose to H.L. Carl, November 16, 1900, SPC.

153. Hendrick to L.W. Robinson, March 22, 1907, SPC.

154. Hendrick to Mrs. R. Walker, October 28, 1907, SPC.

155. Penrose to Thomas Kane, June 1, 1904, SPC.

156. Penrose to unknown, September 20, 1904, SPC.
157. Penrose to Anna Burrin, April 14, 1904, SPC.
158. Penrose to Lucille Marvin, November 8, 1906, SPC.
159. Penrose to Ira B. Cutting, August 11, 1902, SPC.
160. Penrose to Harriett E. Cushman, June 20, 1907, SPC.
161. Penrose to J.G. Bennett, January 7, 1902, SPC.
162. Penrose to Mrs. M.A. McGee, September 6, 1906, SPC.
163. Penrose to E.F. Mitchell, January 20, 1900, SPC.
164. Penrose to Brattain, December 28, 1903, SPC.
165. S.G. Cosgrove to Penrose, November 17, 1903, SPC.
166. Penrose to L. Stillson, January 6, 1903, SPC.
167. George St. Clair to Penrose, June 25, 1904, SPC.
168. Edna Courtney to Penrose, August 26, 1906, SPC.
169. *Walla Walla Union*, January 31, 1904.
170. Whitman College Faculty Minutes, October 3, 1904, WCA.
171. Whitman College Faculty Minutes, November 19, 1906, WCA.
172. Whitman College Faculty Minutes, March 2, 1908, WCA.
173. *Walla Walla Union*, March 30, 1904.
174. *Portland Oregonian*, December 18, 1907.
175. *Whitman College Pioneer*, December, 1905.
176. Arminda Fix Diary, October 12, 1903, WCA.
177. *Walla Walla Statesman*, October 12, 1904.
178. *Walla Walla Union*, February 25, 1905.
179. Arminda Fix Diary, October 31, 1903, WCA.
180. Hendrick to George North, February 5, 1907, SPC.
181. Penrose to B.F. Morris, July 17, 1902, SPC.
182. Penrose to unknown, March 28, 1904, SPC.
183. Penrose to the Reverend Jonathan Edwards, April 1, 1904, SPC.
184. Penrose to S.W. Bowles, December 17, 1902, SPC.
185. Penrose to E. Benjamin Andrews, February 8, 1907, SPC.
186. Penrose to Rose Tweedy, June 25, 1902, SPC.
187. Penrose to Helen McDougall, June 20, 1907, SPC.
188. Penrose to William Proctor, March 2, 1907, SPC.
189. Penrose to Nelson Franklin Cole, December 21, 1907, SPC.
190. Arminda Fix Diary, May 4, 1904, WCA.
191. Annie J. Rue Collection, WCA.
192. Penrose to Linnie M. Marsh, March 20, 1907, SPC.
193. Penrose to Prince Lucien Campbell, September 13, 1907, SPC.

194. Edward T. Mathes to Penrose, May 21, 1907, SPC.
195. Penrose to Hugh Elmer Brown, February 18, 1907, SPC.
196. Lasater to Penrose, October 9, 1903, SPC.
197. "The Progress of Whitman College," *Up-To-The-Times*, December 1906, 45.
198. Penrose to Burke, June 13, 1907, SPC.
199. Willis to Penrose, October 10, 1906, SPC.
200. Penrose to E.C. Kellogg, June 14, 1907, SPC.
201. Penrose to Masry Young & Co., November 7, 1901, SPC.
202. Penrose to E.C. Patterson, June 4, 1907, SPC.
203. Penrose to Frederic W. Keaton, February 12, 1907, SPC.
204. Penrose to Charles Tibling, April 19, 1904, SPC.
205. Penrose to E.B. Conlin, May 15, 1902, SPC.
206. Penrose to Nathaniel Shipman, May 16, 1903, SPC.
207. Edwards, "The College, the Town," *Whitman Alumnus*, 3-9; 22-27.
208. Penrose to Phi Beta Kappa Chapter, Beloit, February 28, 1907, SPC.
209. Penrose to E.G. Schorrock, November 16, 1906, SPC.
210. M.C. Hazard to Penrose, December 16, 1907, SPC.
211. Penrose to Hazard, December 30, 1907, SPC.
212. Penrose to Durham, November 14, 1901, SPC.
213. Kane to Penrose, December 5, 1904, SPC.
214. Kane to Penrose, January 21, 1905, SPC.
215. Penrose to Albert Mead, January 26, 1907, SPC.
216. Penrose to J.F. Ackerman, May 6, 1907, SPC.
217. Penrose to Charles Connor, December 17, 1907, SPC.
218. Miles C. Moore to Penrose, February 6, 1905, SPC.
219. Allen Reynolds to Moore, February 6, 1905, SPC.
220. Penrose to Cornelius H. Patton, September 8, 1906, SPC.
221. Edward L. Smith to Penrose, April 17, 1902, SPC.
222. Penrose to Anna Dawes, February 1, 1907, SPC.
223. Penrose to Brown, March 13, 1907, SPC.
224. Penrose to L. Anderson, March, 1907, SPC.
225. Penrose to John P. Congdon, April 29, 1907, SPC.
226. Whitman College Trustee Minutes, June 10, 1902, WCA.
227. F.M. McCully to Penrose, October 26, 1906, SPC.
228. "Whitman College and What Some People Have Said About

It," *Whitman College Quarterly* (undated).

229. *Walla Walla Union*, June 15, 1905.
230. Penrose to Pearsons, December 5, 1907, SPC.
231. *Walla Walla Union*, September 8, 1907.
232. *Walla Walla Union*, September 17, 1907.
233. *Walla Walla Union*, September 19, 1907.
234. *Walla Walla Union*, September 21, 1907.
235. *Walla Walla Union*, December 3, 1907.
236. *Walla Walla Union*, October 3, 1907.
237. *Walla Walla Union*, October 24, 1907.
238. *Portland Oregonian* quoted in *Walla Walla Union*, October 29, 1907.
239. *Walla Walla Union*, November 8, 1907.
240. *Walla Walla Union*, November 9, 1907.
241. *Walla Walla Union*, November 15, 1907.
242. *Walla Walla Bulletin*, November 14, 1907.

Chapter Seven

1. Archer Hendrick to William A. Giboney, November 27, 1907, AHC.
2. Hendrick to Harry Reynolds, November 30, 1907, AHC.
3. Henrick to Giboney, November 27, 1907, AHC.
4. Hendrick to George Turner, October 13, 1907, AHC.
5. Hendrick to Horace P. James, November 9, 1907, AHC.
6. *Walla Walla Union*, December 15, 1907.
7. Hendrick to George Pope, November 5, 1907, AHC.
8. Hendrick to Turner, October 13, 1907, AHC.
9. Hendrick to Pope, November 5, 1907, AHC.
10. Hendrick to J.P.M. Richards, January 16, 1908, AHC.
11. Hendrick to D.K. Pearsons, November 11, 1907, AHC.
12. Stephen Penrose to E.C. Sage, November 6, 1907, SPC.
13. Hendrick to James, October 10, 1907, AHC.
14. *Walla Walla Union*, December 16, 1907; *Walla Walla Statesman*, December 16, 1907.
15. Penrose to Levi Ankeny, December 17, 1907, SPC.
16. Penrose to A.M. Yoder, December 21, 1907, SPC.
17. Penrose to W.J. Hindley, December 18, 1907, SPC.

18. Hendrick to Penrose, December 16, 1907, AHC.

19. Penrose to Hendrick, December 5, 1907, AHC.

20. Penrose to Pearsons, December 21, 1907, SPC.

21. Hendrick to H.P. James, January 16, 1908, AHC.

22. Hendrick to William Jones, June 16, 1908, AHC.

23. Hendrick to Cornelius H. Hanford, January 16, 1908, AHC.

24. Hendrick to William M. Ladd, June 4, 1908, AHC.

25. Hendrick to Hanford, May 15, 1908, AHC.

26. Hendrick to Ben Holt, July 23, 1908, AHC.

27. Penrose to Ladd, August 4, 1908, SPC.

28. "Summary of Answers to Questions About Higher Education," 1908, AHC.

29. *Whitman College Pioneer*, May 30, 1908.

30. President's Report, 1908, WCA.

31. Penrose, *Whitman: An Unfinished Story*, 191.

32. President's Report, 1908, WCA.

33. Hendrick to Penrose, August 14, 1908, SPC.

34. Hendrick to Anson Phelps Stokes, October 7, 1908, AHC.

35. Hendrick to G. Scott Anderson, November 2, 1908, AHC.

36. Hendrick to Cyrus Northrup, November 4, 1908, AHC.

37. Hendrick to E.T. Allen, November 4, 1908, AHC.

38. Gifford Pinchot to Penrose, October 23, 1908, SPC.

39. *Walla Walla Union*, November 17, 1908.

40. *Walla Walla Union*, November 18, 1908.

41. *Whitman College Pioneer*, November 23, 1908.

42. *Whitman College Pioneer*, November 23, 1908, and *Walla Walla Union*, November 28, 1908 reported Cyrus Northrup's address.

43. Ibid.

44. *Walla Walla Union*, November 18, 1908.

45. *Whitman College Pioneer*, November 23, 1908.

46. *Whitman College Pioneer*, November 23, 1908.

47. All quotations are from the Whitman College Board of Overseers meeting, November 17 and 18, 1908, WCA.

48. *Whitman College Pioneer*, November 30, 1908.

49. *Walla Walla Union*, November 18, 1908.

50. *Whitman College Pioneer*, November 30, 1908.

51. *Portland Oregonian*, October 15, 18, and 19, 1908.

52. Hendrick to Pope, January 12, 1909, AHC.

53. Hendrick to Joseph D. Neilan, January 15, 1909, AHC.

54. J.P. O'Brien to Hendrick, April 12, 1909; Frederick E. Weyerhaeuser to Hendrick, April 9, 1909; AHC.

55. President's Report, 1909, 9, WCA.

56. Ibid., 15.

57. Ibid.

58. Dean's Report, 1909, WCA.

59. Penrose, *Whitman*, 174-177.

60. Chester Maxey, *The World I Lived In*, 127.

61. Hearing on S. 3196, House Committee on Military Affairs, January 19, 1910, 14, AHC.

62. Hendrick to H. Reynolds, March 30, 1909, AHC.

63. John C. Ainsworth et. al. to Senator Jonathan Bourne, April 7, 1909, AHC.

64. Whitman College Board of Overseers Report, June 1909, 72.

65. Hendrick to Jones, November 20, 1909, AHC.

66. D.W. Standrod to Hendrick, December 11, 1909, AHC.

67. Robert C. Rutter to Senator Wesley J. Jones, December 8, 1909, AHC.

68. Oscar Drumheller to Charles S. Sharton, November 27, 1909, AHC.

69. Penrose to Hendrick, November 4, 1909, AHC.

70. Penrose to Hendrick, November 25, 1908, AHC.

71. *Walla Walla Bulletin*, December 8, 1909.

72. William Worthington to Hendrick, December 18, 1909, AHC.

73. *Walla Walla Bulletin*, December 26, 1910.

74. C.N. Suttner to Hendrick, December 10, 1909, AHC.

75. Penrose to Hendrick, December 29, 1909, AHC.

76. Hendrick to Park Weed Willis, January 5, 1910; Hendrick to N.J.E. Ransom, January 11, 1910; AHC.

77. Hendrick to Thomas Burke, January 11, 1910, Burke Papers, UWA.

78. Hearing on S. 3196, House, 11.

79. *Walla Walla Union*, February 10, 1910.

80. Hendrick to Dorsey Hill, February 10, 1910, AHC.

81. Hendrick to H. Reynolds, February 9, 1910, AHC.

82. Hendrick to Willis, February 22, 1910, AHC.

83. Willis to Fredrick W. Parham, February 26, 1910, AHC.

84. Burke to Hendrick, February 26, 1910, AHC.

85. Penrose to Hendrick, January 25, 1910, AHC.

86. Hendrick to Hill, March 3, 1910, AHC.

87. *Congressional Record*, Sixty-First Congress, Second Session, April 7, 1910, 4365.

88. U.S. Congress, House Report 1259. Sixty-First Congress, Second Session, May 3, 1910, 1-6.

89. *Congressional Record*, House of Representatives, Sixty-First Congress, Second Session, May 16, 1910, 6353. All citations from pages 6353-6355; 6369-6373.

90. Penrose to Hendrick, January 11, 1910, AHC.

91. Hendrick to Penrose, January 18, 1910, AHC.

92. Hendrick's clipping file, AHC.

93. Miles C. Moore to Senator Francis Warren, April 16, 1910, AHC.

94. Hendrick to Hill, April 25, 1910, AHC.

95. Hendrick to James L. Slayden, June 17, 1910, AHC.

96. Hendrick to Hill, April 17, 1910, AHC.

97. *Walla Walla Bulletin*, April 9 and April 16, 1910.

98. Telegram from Father Harry J. Van de Ven to Miles Poindexter, May 9, 1910, found in letter from William E. Humphrey and William T. Dovell, May 10, 1910, AHC.

99. Poindexter to Hendrick, May 17, 1910; Hendrick to Standrod, May 25, 1910; AHC.

100. Penrose to Willis, May 23, 1910, SPC.

101. "K" to Van de Ven, May 10, 1910, AHC.

102. John E. Ransom to Hendrick, May 17, 1910, AHC.

103. Hendrick to Edward J. O'Dea, May 25, 1910, AHC.

104. O'Dea to Hendrick, June 1, 1910, AHC.

105. Hendrick to Poindexter, June 9, 1910, AHC.

106. Whitman College Board of Overseers to Hendrick, June 25, 1910, AHC.

107. Hendrick report to Whitman College Board of Overseers, July 1, 1910, WCA.

108. Hendrick to James A. Moore, November 1, 1910, AHC.

109. Hendrick to Slayden, October 15, 1910, AHC.

110. Ibid.; Hendrick to Herbert Parsons, October 22, 1910, AHC.

111. Hendrick to James A. Tawney, October 22, 1910, AHC.

112. Ibid.

113. In his letters George Turner emphasized that the state had given the national government valuable land for military posts in Seattle and Spokane. He believed that the government should be generous with Whitman because it would contribute to the region's educational and economic progress.

114. Quoted in Robert C. Nesbit, *He Built Seattle: A Biography of Judge Thomas Burke*, 417. Other traditional Republicans, including the *Portland Oregonian*, agreed. It complained that Miles Poindexter attracted "populists, socialists, . . . cranks . . . and discontented souls." Quoted in Howard W. Allen, *Poindexter of Washington: A Study in Progressive Politics*, 57.

115. Hendrick to Poindexter, December 16, 1910, AHC.

116. Hendrick to William Cowles, December 16, 1910, AHC.

117. Walla Walla Trades and Labor Council Resolutions, December 3, 1910; *Walla Walla Union*, December 17, 1910.

118. *Walla Walla Union*, December 17 and 18, 1910.

119. Walla Walla Trades and Labor Council to Senator Wesley Jones, December 15, 1910, AHC.

120. Jones to Hendrick, January 6, 1911, AHC.

121. Hendrick to Jones, January 11, 1911, AHC.

122. Hendrick to James M. Ashton, January 11, 1911, AHC.

123. Penrose to Hendrick, January 14, 1911, AHC.

124. Drumheller to J.A. McLean, January 13, 1911, AHC.

125. Senate Joint Memorial Number 2, *Senate Journal* of the State of Washington, 1911, 102.

126. *Walla Walla Union*, January 18, 1911.

127. Hendrick to Miles Poindexter, January 17, 1911, AHC.

128. Hendrick to W.T. Potts, January 17, 1911, AHC.

129. *Walla Walla Union*, January 17, 1911.

130. Hendrick to Jones, January 17, 1911, AHC.

131. Hendrick to Edward D. Baldwin, January 18, 1911, AHC.

132. Frank W. Paine to Hendrick, February 13, 1911; John W. Langdon to Jones, February 16, 1911; AHC.

133. Hendrick to James R. Mann, February 4, 1911, AHC.

134. Hendrick to Samuel Gompers, February 9, 1911, AHC.

135. Hendrick to Burke, March 24, 1911, AHC.

136. Hendrick to Poindexter, January 26, 1911, AHC.

137. *Walla Walla Bulletin*, March 31, 1911.

138. Penrose, *Whitman*, 173.
139. Baldwin to Hendrick, January 25, 1911, AHC.
140. *Walla Walla Union* and *Walla Walla Bulletin*, March 8 and 21, 1911.
141. Hendrick to Burke, March 24, 1911, AHC.
142. *Walla Walla Bulletin*, March 31, 1911.
143. Hendrick to Jones, May 1, 1911, AHC.
144. *Walla Walla Bulletin*, June 29, 1911.
145. Penrose to Jones, September 5, 1912, SPC.
146. Penrose to Pearsons, April 27, 1911, SPC.
147. Pearsons to Penrose, May 4, 1911, SPC.
148. Whitman College Board of Overseers Minutes, 1911, 67, WCA.
149. Hendrick to Burke, September 11, 1911, Burke Papers, UWA.
150. *Walla Walla Union*, September 26 and September 28, 1911; *Walla Walla Bulletin*, September 26, 1911.
151. *Walla Walla Union*, April 8, 1911.
152. Penrose to Ladd, July 18, 1914, SPC.
153. *Walla Walla Bulletin*, October 20, 1911.
154. Penrose to Henry S. Pritchett, January 9, 1912, SPC.
155. Maxey, *The World I Lived In*, 317.
156. *Waiilatpu*, 1913, 9.
157. *Walla Walla Bulletin*, February 8, 1912.
158. Penrose to the General Education Board, June 27, 1917, SPC.
159. Penrose to Lester M. Livengood, March 11, 1912, SPC.
160. Penrose to William Mowry, April 10, 1912, SPC.
161. Penrose, *Whitman*, 178.
162. Maxey, *The World I Lived In*, 317.
163. *Walla Walla Union* and *Walla Walla Bulletin*, June 14, 1912.
164. Maxey, *The World I Lived In*, 319.
165. *Walla Walla Bulletin*, June 16, 1912.
166. *Walla Walla Union*, June 17, 1912.
167. Maxey, *The World I Lived In*, 319.
168. Penrose, *Whitman*, 174.
169. *Walla Walla Bulletin*, June 6, 1912.
170. *Walla Walla Bulletin*, May 30, 1912.
171. *Walla Walla Bulletin*, May 21, 1912.
172. *Walla Walla Bulletin*, June 4, 1912.
173. *Walla Walla Union*, June 14, 1912.

174. *Walla Walla Bulletin*, June 14, 1912.

175. *Whitman College Pioneer*, June 20, 1912.

176. *Walla Walla Bulletin*, June 15, 1912.

177. Penrose to Mowry, September 7, 1912, SPC.

Chapter Eight

1. Stephen Penrose to Archer Hendrick, October 25, 1911, AHC.

2. D.K. Pearsons to Penrose, October 30, 1911, SPC.

3. Whitman College Board of Overseers Minutes, June, 1911, 73, WCA.

4. Frederick Rudolph, *The American College and University: A History*, 146.

5. Norman F. Coleman to Hendrick, June 23 and 28, 1908, AHC.

6. Report on Housing Conditions, Hendrick Fraternity File, 1911, AHC.

7. Whitman College Faculty Minutes, November 19, 1906, WCA.

8. *Waiilatpu*, 1910, 153.

9. *Whitman College Pioneer*, January 1, 1909.

10. Whitman College Faculty Minutes, February 8, 1909, WCA.

11. Whitman College Faculty Minutes, February 15, 1909, WCA.

12. Whitman College Faculty Minutes, February 14, 1910, WCA.

13. Whitman College Board of Overseers Minutes, November 15, 1910, 181, WCA.

14. *Spokane Spokesman-Review*, April 12, 1911.

15. Hendrick to E.F. Blaine, April 27, 1911, AHC.

16. William Lyman to Hendrick, April 10, 1911, AHC.

17. Coleman to Hendrick, April 1911, AHC.

18. James W. Cooper to Hendrick, April 11, 1911, AHC.

19. Arminda Fix to Hendrick, June 12, 1911, AHC.

20. Walter Bratton to Hendrick (undated), AHC.

21. Hendrick to Ellen F. Pendleton, June 5, 1911, AHC.

22. *Walla Walla Bulletin*, June 19, 1912.

Chapter Nine

1. Stephen Penrose to Wallace Buttrick, January 27, 1913, SPC.

2. Penrose, *Whitman: An Unfinished Story*, 179.

3. Buttrick to Penrose, May 8, 1913, SPC.

4. Penrose to Buttrick, June 10, 1913, SPC.

5. President's Report, 1914, 6, WCA.

6. President's Report, 1914, 8, WCA.

7. Whitman College Board of Overseers Minutes, 1917, 4, WCA.

8. Whitman College Board of Overseers Minutes, 1914, 9, WCA.

9. Whitman College Board of Overseer Minutes, 1915, 5, WCA.

10. Whitman College Board of Overseers Minutes, 1915, 13, WCA.

11. Whitman College Board of Overseer Minutes, 1916, 7, WCA.

12. Whitman College Board of Overseer Minutes, 1911, 298, WCA.

13. Penrose to unknown, November 4, 1931, SPC.

14. Penrose, "A New Requirement for College Graduation," *Educational Review*, June 1917, 53.

15. Whitman College Librarian's Report, 1916, 1, WCA.

Chapter Ten

1. David M. Kennedy, *Over Here: The First World War and American Society*, 11.

2. Stephen Penrose, *Whitman: An Unfinished Story*, 185.

3. *Whitman College Pioneer*, November 17, 1914.

4. *Whitman College Pioneer*, March 30, 1917.

5. *Walla Walla Bulletin*, May 6, 1917.

6. William O. Douglas, *Go East, Young Man: The Early Years*, 91.

7. *Whitman College Pioneer*, May 25, 1917.

8. *Whitman College Pioneer*, June 22, 1917.

9. Whitman College Board of Overseers Minutes, June 1917, WCA.

10. *Walla Walla Bulletin*, June 21, 1917.

11. *Whitman College Pioneer*, September 28, 1917.

12. President's Report, 1918, 4, WCA.

13. *Whitman College Pioneer*, September 28, 1917.

14. *Whitman College Pioneer*, March 5, 1918.

15. *Whitman College Pioneer*, March 22, 1918.

16. President's Report, 1918, WCA.

17. Ibid., 8.

18. *Whitman College Pioneer*, February 15, 1918.

19. Whitman College Board of Overseers Minutes, 1918, WCA.

20. *Walla Walla Bulletin*, April 24, 1919.

21. *Walla Walla Bulletin*, April 27, 1918.
22. *Walla Walla Bulletin*, April 2, 1918.
23. Kennedy, *Over Here*, 57.
24. Ibid., 57.
25. Douglas, *Go East, Young Man*, 93.
26. *Walla Walla Bulletin*, October 2, 1918.
27. *Whitman College Pioneer*, November 5, 1918.
28. Penrose, *Whitman*, 189.
29. Whitman College Board of Overseers Minutes, 1919, WCA.
30. *Whitman Alumnus*, January-February 1919, 15.
31. Penrose, *Whitman*, 192.

Chapter Eleven

1. President's Report, 1919, WCA.
2. Stephen Penrose to Wallace Buttrick, December, 1919, SPC.
3. *Walla Walla Bulletin*, April 3, 1919.
4. *Walla Walla Bulletin*, April 5, 1919.
5. Chester Maxey, *The World I Lived In*, 251.
6. *Whitman Alumnus*, January-February 1919, 5.
7. *Walla Walla Union*, June 9, 1919.
8. *Walla Walla Bulletin*, June 9, 1919.
9. Ibid.
10. Ibid.
11. Ibid.
12. *Walla Walla Union*, June 10, 1919.
13. *Walla Walla Bulletin*, June 10, 1919.
14. Ibid.
15. *Whitman Alumnus*, June 1919, 13.
16. Ibid., 19.
17. *Walla Walla Bulletin*, June 11, 1919.
18. Robert C. Nesbit, *He Built Seattle*, 408.
19. Ibid., 10.
20. *Walla Walla Union*, June 8, 1919.
21. Park Weed Willis to Penrose, July 22, 1919, Willis Papers, University of Oregon Archives.
22. President's Report, 1920, 2, WCA.
23. President's Report, 1921, 10, WCA.

24. Maxey, *The World I Lived In*, 250.
25. Penrose to John Marshall Gest, November 1, 1922, SPC.
26. Ibid.
27. Penrose, *Whitman*, 198.
28. President's Report, 1922, 19, WCA.
29. President's Report, 1921, 13, WCA.
30. Penrose to E.A. Stuart, December 5, 1922, SPC.
31. President's Report, 1923, 17, WCA.
32. Penrose to George Tamblyn, September 27, 1923, SPC.
33. Penrose to Tamblyn, October 23, 1923, SPC.
34. Tamblyn to Penrose, December 28, 1923, SPC.
35. Tamblyn to Penrose, May 19, 1924, SPC.
36. Minutes of the Board of Overseers and Annual Reports, *Whitman College Quarterly*, 1924, 16.
37. Penrose to Tamblyn, June 13, 1924, SPC.

Chapter Twelve

1. *Up-To-The-Times*, September 1919, 9292.
2. Minutes of the Board of Overseers, *Whitman College Quarterly*, 1923, 8.
3. Whitman College Board of Deans Minutes, November 5, 1924, WCA.
4. Minutes of the Board of Overseers and Annual Reports, *Whitman College Quarterly*, 1924, 5.
5. Whitman College Faculty Minutes, January 25, 1921, WCA.
6. Whitman College Faculty Minutes, January 9, 1922, WCA.
7. Whitman College Faculty Minutes, October 1, 1923, WCA.
8. Horace P. James to Stephen Penrose, October 12, 1919, SPC.
9. Penrose to D.C. Sage, January 16, 1920, SPC.
10. *Whitman Alumnus*, February, 1924, 8.
11. Chester Maxey, *The World I Lived In*, 250.
12. President's Report, 1921, 18, WCA.
13. Park Weed Willis to Penrose, May 24, 1921, Willis Papers, University of Oregon Archives.
14. Penrose to Henry Pritchett, April 8, 1920, SPC.
15. *Whitman Alumnus*, October, 1922, 3.
16. Ibid.

17. Penrose to Manly Ormes, November 28, 1923, SPC.
18. President's Report, 1919, 18, WCA.
19. Penrose to Howell Cheney, December 18, 1923, SPC.
20. Penrose, *Whitman: An Unfinished Story*, 218.
21. Penrose to S.R. McCarthy, October 3, 1924, SPC.
22. *Portland Oregonian*, November 26, 1909.
23. *Walla Walla Bulletin*, November 27, 1909.
24. Whitman College Faculty Minutes, November 29, 1909, 2, WCA.
25. "The Football Deaths," *The Nation*, November 4, 1909, 425.
26. *Whitman College Pioneer*, November 1908.
27. Jack Hewins, *Borleske: Never Far From Hope*, 5.
28. Penrose, *Whitman*, 205.
29. *Portland Oregonian*, October 3, 1933.
30. *Whitman College Pioneer*, November 21, 1919.
31. *Whitman College Handbook*, 1923–1924, 15.
32. *Whitman Alumnus*, April 1919, 6.
33. *Portland Oregonian*, December 17, 1921.
34. *Whitman Alumnus*, December 1922, 6.
35. Hewins, *Borleske*, 93.
36. *Waiilatpu*, 1925, 78.
37. *Whitman College Pioneer*, November 26, 1925.
38. *Whitman Alumnus*, December 1920, 8; September 1921, 9; December 1921, 5.
39. Hewins, *Borleske*, 100.
40. *Whitman Alumnus*, October 1923, 8.
41. *Whitman College Pioneer*, June 6, 1924.
42. Hewins, *Borleske*, 108.
43. *Whitman Alumnus*, March 1924, 13.
44. *Waiilatpu*, 1924, 94.
45. *Whitman College Pioneer*, May 20, 1921.
46. Penrose to whom it may concern, January 10, 1924, SPC.
47. *Whitman Alumnus*, October 1920, 8.
48. *Waiilatpu*, 1925, 76.
49. *Whitman Alumnus*, April 1924, 4.
50. *Whitman College Pioneer*, November 29, 1923.
51. Penrose to Stephen Duggan, December 23, 1924, SPC.
52. *Waiilatpu*, 1921, 67.
53. *Waiilatpu*, 1924, 65.

54. *Whitman College Pioneer*, June 6, 1924.

55. Penrose to John H. Finley, January 30, 1919, SPC.

56. Walter Bleakney Alumni File, WCA.

57. *Walla Walla Bulletin*, November 29, 1921.

58. *Whitman College Pioneer*, September 28, 1923.

59. Paula Fass, *The Damned and the Beautiful: American Youth in the 1920's*, 132.

60. *Whitman College Pioneer*, October 8, 1920.

61. *Whitman College Pioneer*, January 14 and February 25, 1921.

62. *Whitman College Pioneer*, January 20, 1922.

63. *Whitman College Pioneer*, October 6, 1922.

64. Whitman College Board of Overseers Minutes, 1924, 9, WCA.

65. "Suggestions to Improve Whitman," Walter C. Eells File, WCA.

66. *Whitman College Pioneer*, March 2, 1923.

67. *Whitman College Pioneer*, October 1 and October 8, 1920.

68. John W. Hoyt to Penrose, December 8, 1922, SPC.

69. *Whitman College Handbook*, 1923–1924, 42.

70. *Waiilatpu*, 1921, 30.

71. *Whitman College Pioneer*, February 28, 1924.

72. *Whitman College Pioneer*, February 11, 1921.

73. Penrose to David W. Ferry, May 18, 1923, SPC.

74. Penrose to Alex Clark, August 22, 1923, SPC.

75. Penrose to the Delta Delta Delta National Sorority, May 22, 1922; Penrose to Ernest O. Holland, May 18, 1921; SPC.

76. Penrose to Herbert Gambrell, February 24, 1925, SPC.

77. Fass, *The Damned and the Beautiful*, 144.

78. *Whitman College Handbook*, 1923–1924, 35.

79. Penrose to Francis Shepardson, October 25, 1922, SPC.

80. Penrose to Gambrell, February 24, 1925, SPC.

81. Ibid.

82. Mary Beth Norton et. al., *A People and a Nation*, 719.

83. *Whitman College Pioneer*, March 2, 1923.

84. *Whitman College Pioneer*, February 3, 1922.

85. Penrose to the Reverend David W. Ferry, May 18, 1923, SPC.

86. Douglas, *Go East, Young Man: The Early Years*, 102.

87. *Whitman College Pioneer*, February 10, 1922.

88. Douglas, *Go East, Young Man*, 98-99.

89. Quoted in Fass, *The Damned and the Beautiful*, 46.

90. Lorna Defoe, "Gin, Joy, or Solid Work," *The Washingtonian,*
    November 1, 1928, 17.

91. *Whitman College Pioneer,* February 29 and March 7, 1924.

92. Penrose to Mrs. J.J. Donovan, June 16, 1926, SPC.

93. Miles Moore to my friends, December 1, 1919, SPC.

94. Thomas Burke to unknown, July 20, 1920, SPC.

95. Penrose to Pritchett, October 14, 1926, SPC.

96. Penrose to Eleanor Hinman, January 25, 1923, SPC.

97. Penrose to Martha Luginbuhl, June 29, 1924, SPC.

98. *Waiilatpu,* 1915, 203.

99. *Whitman Alumnus,* March 1924, 4.

100. Ibid., 5.

101. *Whitman College Pioneer,* November 24, 1922.

102. Newspaper clipping, Penrose File, WCA.

103. *Walla Walla Union,* January 18, 1923.

104. Penrose to Tasuku Harada, November 4, 1920, SPC.

105. *Spokane Spokesman-Review,* November 20, 1912.

106. *Spokane Spokesman-Review,* April 3, 1923.

107. *Walla Walla Union,* May 27, 1923, and *Walla Walla Bulletin,*
     May 28, 1923.

108. *Walla Walla Bulletin,* November 16, 1923.

109. *Whitman College Catalogue,* 1920, 18.

110. Penrose, *How the West Was Won,* 4.

111. Penrose to William Ladd, July 31, 1923, SPC.

112. George B. Christian to Penrose, August 27, 1923, SPC.

113. *Walla Walla Union,* November 30, 1922.

114. Clifford Drury, *Marcus and Narcissa Whitman,* Volume II,
     386.

115. Penrose to Edwin D. Ford, August 16, 1923, SPC.

116. Penrose, *Whitman,* 213.

117. Penrose to William Cowles, December 12, 1924, SPC.

118. Penrose to Frank Cheney, May 27, 1919, SPC.

119. Penrose, *Whitman,* 209.

120. *Waiilatpu,* 1915, 93.

121. Melissa Crumley, oral interview with Almira Quinn, 1991, WCA.

122. David Ferry to Penrose, May 14, 1923, SPC.

123. Penrose to Ferry, May 18, 1923, SPC.

124. Ferry to Penrose, December 21, 1917, SPC.

125. Douglas, *Go East, Young Man*, 103.
126. Douglas, "Souls Tempered with Fire, " *Codex*, June 1919, 3.
127. Douglas to Penrose, October 22, 1927, SPC.
128. Douglas, *Go East, Young Man*, 115.
129. Maxey, *The World I Lived In*, 321.
130. Ibid., 251.
131. Ibid.
132. *Seattle, The Town Crier*, March 29, 1924.
133. Penrose, *Whitman*, 223.
134. Penrose to James, July 14, 1924, SPC.
135. *Walla Walla Bulletin*, 1924 clipping, Penrose File, WCA.
136. *Walla Walla Bulletin*, April 3, 1919.
137. Anna M. Weyerhaeuser to Penrose, June 25, 1924, SPC.
138. Penrose to Mrs. Jacob (Caroline) Kamm, December 18, 1924, SPC.
139. Interview with Frances Penrose Owen, October 6, 1990, WCA.
140. Penrose to Kamm, December 10, 1924, SPC.
141. *Whitman Alumnus*, December 1924, 6.
142. Willis to Penrose, November 7, 1924, Willis Papers, University of Oregon Archives.
143. Penrose to Kamm, December 10, 1924, SPC.
144. Maxey, *The World I Lived In*, 321.
145. Penrose to Stanley Eaton, June 23, 1925, SPC.
146. Maxey, *The World I Lived In*, 251.

Appendix A

1. George Perry Morris, "Dr. D.K. Pearsons, the Friend of the American Small College," *Review of Reviews*, November 1901, 581.
2. Edward F. Williams, *The Life of Dr. D.K. Pearsons, Friend of the Small College and of Missions.*
3. Morris, "Dr. D.K. Pearsons," 582.
4. Ibid.
5. Ibid., 584.

Appendix B

1. Virginia Dox to Stephen Penrose, May 14, 1898, SPC.
2. E. Lyman Hood, *The New West Education Commission, 1880–1893*, 50.
3. *Detroit Free Press*, April 2, 1896.
4. Dox to Penrose, May 18, 1896, SPC.
5. Dox to Penrose, July 4, 1898, SPC.
6. Dox to Penrose, March 23, 1898, SPC.
7. Dox to Penrose, March 26, 1898, SPC.
8. Dox to Thompson Elliott, May 1, 1899, SPC.
9. Dox to Penrose, November 4, 1899, SPC.
10. Dox to Penrose, May 4, 1901, SPC.
11. Dox to Penrose, August 26, 1901, SPC.
12. Penrose to Wallace Nutting, September 4, 1907, SPC.
13. Penrose, *Whitman: An Unfinished Story*, 150.
14. Dox to Penrose, April 4, 1896, SPC.

Sources

Manuscript Collections

American College and Education Society Archives, Congregational Library, Boston, Massachusetts: ACES Annual Reports; ACES Correspondence; Congregational Education Society Correspondence; *Boston Congregationalist*; Edward F. Williams Papers.

Oregon Historical Society, Portland, Oregon: Samuel A. Clarke Scrapbook.

Pacific University Archives, Forest Grove, Oregon: Board of Trustees Minutes; George H. Atkinson Correspondence.

University of Oregon Archives, University of Oregon Library, Eugene, Oregon: Park Weed Willis Papers.

University of Washington Archives, University of Washington Library, Seattle, Washington: Bolton Papers; Thomas Burke Papers; Edmond S. Meany Papers; Presidents Papers; Presidents Report to Regents; Regents Records.

Whitman College Archives, Penrose Memorial Library, Walla Walla, Washington: Alumni File; Alexander Jay Anderson Collection; Biographical Files; Board of Deans Minutes; Peasly B. Chamberlain Collection; Arminda Fix Diary; James Eaton Correspondence; Cushing Eells Collection; Archer Hendrick Collection; Libethrean Literary Society Minutes; Librarians' Reports; Myron Eells Collection; Oral History Collection; Stephen Penrose Collection; Presidents' Reports; Annie J. Rue Collection; Whitman

College Alumni Correspondence; Whitman College Board of
Overseers Minutes; Whitman College Faculty Minutes; Journal
of Adelphi Meetings; Journal of Athenaeum Meetings; Journal of
Whittier Meetings; Allen H. Reynolds File and Correspondence;
St. Paul's School Records; Whitman College Trustee Correspon-
dence; Whitman College Minutes; Whitman College Executive
Committee Minutes and Records; Whitman Seminary Trustee
Minutes.
Williams College Archives, Williams College Library, Williamstown,
Massachusetts: Scrapbook of Robert W. Gilbert.

Original Sources, Special Studies, Articles, and Reports

"A Department of Economics and Social Science." *Whitman College
Quarterly*, January 1897.
Anderson, Alexander J. "The Beginnings of Whitman College."
Whitman College Quarterly, March 1899.
*Annual Report of the School Committee of the Town of North Ad-
ams*. North Adams, Massachusetts, 1891.
Belknap, George N. *The Blue Ribbon University*. Eugene: University
of Oregon Press, 1976.
Bolton, Frederick E. *History of Education in Washington*. Washing-
ton D.C.: Government Printing Office, 1935.
Congressional Record. Sixty-first Congress, Second Session. Wash-
ington D.C.: Government Printing Office, 1910.
Defoe, Lorna. "Gin, Joy, or Solid Work." *The Washingtonian*, November 1, 1928.
Douglas, William O. "Souls Tempered With Fire." *Codex*, June
1919.
Edwards, G. Thomas. "The College, the Town, and Teddy Roosevelt: 1903." *Whitman Alumnus*, November 1977.
————. "Pioneer President: Alexander J. Anderson and the Formative Years of the University of Washington and Whitman Col-
lege." *Pacific Northwest Quarterly*, April 1988.
Eells, Cushing. "Reminiscences." *The Home Missionary*, March
1893.
Farrar, Victor J. "History of the University." *Washington Alumnus*,
May 1921.

Franklin Carter Report, 1887. Williamstown, Massachusetts: Williams College, 1887.

Gordon, Newton F., compiler. *Class of Eighty-Five Quinquennial Report.* Chicago, 1890.

———. *Statistics of the Class of '85.* Williamstown, Massachusetts: Williams College, 1885.

House Report 1259. *U.S. House of Representatives Journal.* Sixty-first Congress, Second Session.

Jordan, David S. "Opening Address." *The Palo Alto,* October 1891.

Laws of Washington Territory. Olympia, Washington: C.B. Bagley, 1879.

Lyman, William D. "The Old Seminary Days." *Whitman College Quarterly,* June 1900.

Maxey, Chester C. *Five Centennial Papers.* Walla Walla: Whitman College, 1959.

———. *Marcus Whitman (1802–1847): His Courage, His Deeds, and His College.* New York: The Newcomen Society, 1950.

McDonald, James R. "Social Life at Williams College in the Eighties." *Williams Alumni Review,* May 1932.

"Mining Stock." *Whitman College Quarterly,* January 1897.

Minutes of the Congregational Association of Oregon. Portland: Advocate Press, 1859.

Minutes of the Congregational Association of Oregon and Washington Territory. Salem: E.M. Waite, 1882.

Minutes of the Congregational Association of Washington, 1891. Colfax, Washington: Palouse Gazette Publishing House, 1891.

Minutes of the Congregational Association of Washington, 1894. Colfax, Washington: Palouse Gazette Publishing House, 1894.

Morris, George Perry. "Dr. D.K. Pearsons, the Friend of the American Small College." *Review of Reviews,* November 1901.

Mowry, William. "Whitman College and What Some People Have Said About It." *Whitman College Quarterly,* 1907.

Nixon, Oliver W. "Dedicatory Oration." *Whitman College Quarterly,* 1900.

"Obituary Record of the Society of Alumni." Williamstown, Massachusetts: Williams College, 1891.

Penrose, Stephen B.L. "A New Requirement for College Graduation." *Educational Review,* June 1917.

————. *How the West Was Won.* Walla Walla: Inland Printing, 1923.

————. "Penrose Quarterly Report." American Home Missionary Society Papers, April 12, 1893 (microfilm copy at the Washington State Historical Society, Tacoma, Washington, reel 236).

————. Summary of his career in Dayton, Washington. *The Washington Farmer*, April 23 and April 30, 1925.

————. *The Romance of a College.* Walla Walla: Whitman College. 1894.

Plath, Paul John. "The Secularization of Knox College." Master's Thesis, University of Illinois, 1977.

Report of the President of Bowdoin College, 1903–1904. Brunswick, Maine: Bowdoin College, 1903.

Ritz, Richard E. "A History of the Whitman College Campus and its Buildings." *Whitman, the Quarterly Magazine of Whitman College*, February 1985.

"Safety First." *Whitman College Quarterly*, January 1897.

Senate Joint Memorial Number 2. *Senate Journal of the State of Washington.* Olympia: E.L. Boardman, 1911.

"Senior Editorial." *The Glvielmensian*, December 1884, Williams College.

Skotheim, Robert A. *Toward a History of Whitman College.* Newcomen Society of the United States, New York, 1987.

Taylor, Richard S. "Seeking the Kingdom: A Study in the Career of Jonathan Blanchard, 1811–1892." PH.D. dissertation, Northern Illinois University, 1977.

"The Aim of Whitman College." *Whitman College Quarterly*, January 1897.

"The Football Deaths." *The Nation*, November 4, 1909.

"The Progress of Whitman College." *Up-To-The-Times*, December 1906.

Twentieth Reunion Class 1885 Williams College. Williamstown, Massachusetts: Williams College, 1905.

University of Washington Territory Annual Announcement: Report of Regents of the Territorial University. Olympia, Washington, 1879.

Weed, George Lundington. "When Dr. Whitman Added Three Stars to Our Flag." *Ladies Home Journal*, November 1897.

Whitner, Robert L. *The Myth that Saved the College: Two Essays on*

the History of Whitman College. Walla Walla: Whitman College.
"Williams College Class Statistics." Williamstown, Massachusetts:
  Williams College, 1876.

Newspapers

Dayton Columbia-Chronicle
Detroit Free Press
Hartford Daily Courant
Olympia Washington Standard
Portland Oregonian
Portland Weekly Oregonian
Seattle Daily Chronicle
Seattle Daily Intelligencer
Seattle Post
Seattle, The Town Crier
Seattle Weekly Intelligencer
Spokane Spokesman-Review
Sunday Olympian
Waitsburg Times
Walla Walla Bulletin
Walla Walla Daily Journal
Walla Walla Statesman
Walla Walla Union
Walla Walla Union-Bulletin
Walla Walla Watchman

College and University Publications

Knox College Catalog
Pacific University Catalog
The Williams Anthenaeum
University of Oregon Catalog
University of Washington Catalog
Waiilatpu (Whitman College yearbook)
Whitman Alumnus
Whitman College Catalogue
Whitman College Collegian

Whitman College Handbook
Whitman College Pioneer
Whitman College Quarterly
Whitman Collegian
Whitman, the Quarterly Magazine of Whitman College
Williams College Catalogue

Books

A *Volume of Representative Citizens of the City of Seattle and County of King*. New York: Lewis Publishing Company, 1903.

Aamodt, Terrie Dopp. *Bold Venture: A History of Walla Walla College*. Walla Walla: Walla Walla College, 1992.

Allen, Howard W. *Poindexter of Washington: A Study in Progressive Politics*. Carbondale: Southern Illinois University Press, 1981.

Anderson, Florence Bennet. *Leaven for the Frontier: The True Story of a Pioneer Educator*. Boston: Christopher Publishing House, 1953.

Attebery, Louie W. *The College of Idaho, 1891–1991: A Centennial History*. Caldwell: The College of Idaho, 1991.

Belknap, George N. *Henry Villard and the University of Oregon*. Eugene: University of Oregon Press, 1976.

Bennett, Robert A. *Walla Walla: Portrait of a Western Town*. Pioneer Press, 1990.

Douglas, William O. *Go East, Young Man: The Early Years*. New York: Delta, 1974.

Drury, Clifford M. *Marcus and Narcissa Whitman and the Opening of Old Oregon*. Volumes I & II, Glendale, California: Arthur H. Clark Co., 1973.

Eells, Myron. *Father Eells*. Boston: Congregational Sunday-School and Publishing Society, 1894.

Fass, Paula. *The Damned and the Beautiful: American Youth in the 1920s*. New York: Oxford University Press, 1977.

Frykman, George A. *Creating the People's University: Washington State University, 1890–1990*. Pullman: Washington University Press, 1990.

Gates, Charles M. *The First Century at the University of Washington, 1861–1961*. Seattle: University of Washington Press, 1961.

————. *Messages of the Governors of the Territory of Washington, 1854-1889.* Seattle: University of Washington Press, 1940.

Gatke, Robert Moulton. *Chronicles of Willamette.* Portland: Binford and Mort, 1943.

Gilbert, Frank T. *Historic Sketches of Walla Walla, Whitman, Columbia and Garfield Counties, Washington Territory.* Portland: A.G. Walling, 1882.

Gruber, Carol S. *Mars and Minerva: World War One and the Uses of Higher Learning in America.* Baton Rouge: Louisiana State University Press, 1975.

Hewins, Jack. *Borleske: Never Far from Hope.* Seattle: Superior Publishing Co., 1966.

History of the Penrose Family of Philadelphia. Philadelphia: Drexel Biddle, 1903.

Hitchman, James H., editor. *Henry Davidson Sheldon and the University of Oregon, 1874–1948.* Bellingham, Washington: Western Washington University, Center for Pacific Northwest Studies, Occasional Paper Number 13, 1979.

Hitchman, James H. *Liberal Arts Colleges in Oregon and Washington, 1842–1948.* Bellingham, Washington: Western Washington University, Center for Pacific Northwest Studies, Occasional Paper Number 17, 1981.

Hood, E. Lyman. *The New West Education Commision, 1880–1893.* Jacksonville, Florida: H. & W.B. Drew Co., 1905.

Kennedy, David M. *Over Here: The First World War and American Society.* New York: Oxford University Press, 1980.

Lyman, William D. *Old Walla Walla County.* Chicago: S.J. Clarke Publishing Co., 1918.

————. *History of Walla Walla County, State of Washington.* W.H. Lever, 1901.

Lyon, E. Wilson. *The History of Ponoma College, 1887–1969.* Claremont, California: Pomona College, 1977.

Maxey, Chester C. *The World I Lived In.* Philadelphia: Dorrance & Co., 1966.

McConkey, J.D. *From New York to Portland, Oregon Via Straits of Magellan.* Walla Walla: Statesman Printing, 1879.

Meinig, D.W. *The Great Columbia Plain.* Seattle: University of Washington Press, 1968.

Meulder, Hermann R. *Fighters for Freedom: The History of Anti-Slavery Activities of Men and Women Associated with Knox College.* New York: Columbia University Press, 1959.

Nesbit, Robert C. *He Built Seattle: A Biography of Judge Thomas Burke.* Seattle: University of Washington Press, 1981.

Neuberger, Richard L. *Our Promised Land.* New York: The MacMillan Co., 1938.

Nixon, Oliver W. *How Marcus Whitman Saved Oregon.* Chicago: Star Publishing Company, 1895.

Norton, Mary Beth, et. al. *A People and a Nation.* Boston: Houghton Mifflin, 1990.

Penrose, Stephen B.L. *Whitman: An Unfinished Story.* Walla Walla: Whitman Publishing Company, 1935.

Reid, J. Juan. *Colorado College: The First Century, 1874–1974.* Colorado Springs: The Colorado College, 1979.

Rudolph, Frederick. *The American College and University: A History.* New York: Vintage Books, 1962.

———. *Curriculum: A History of the American Undergraduate Course of Study Since 1636.* San Francisco: Jossey-Bass Publishers, 1977.

Schlabach, Theron F. *Pensions for Professors.* Madison: State Historical Society of Wisconsin, 1963.

Sheldon, Henry D. *History of the University of Oregon.* Portland: Binford & Mort, 1940.

The Shipman Family in America. Shipman Historical Society, 1962.

Tewksbury, Donald G. *The Founding of American Colleges and Universities Before the Civil War.* New York: Arno Press, 1969.

Weigley, Russell F., ed. *Philadelphia: A 300 Year History.* New York: W.W. Norton, 1982.

Williams, Edward F. *The Life of Dr. D.K. Pearsons, Friend of the Small College and of Missions.* Concord, New Hampshire: Rumford Press, 1911.

Index

G. Thomas Edwards

A native of Oregon, G. Thomas Edwards received his B.A. in history at Willamette University and his M.A. and PH.D. in history at the University of Oregon. Since coming to Whitman College in 1964, he has taught a variety of classes in American history, especially the Civil War and the American West, and was appointed William Kirkman Professor of History in 1986. He received a teaching award from the Whitman College senior class of 1968 and was given a Burlington Northern Teaching Award in 1988.

Edwards has served as a trustee of both the Washington Commission for the Humanities and the Washington State Historical Society. He has presented papers at regional and national historical meetings and was an Oregon Council for the Humanities Chautauqua Lecturer. He has published articles on reformers, women, promoters, politicians, soldiers, and educators. He co-edited *Experiences in a Promised Land* (University of Washington, 1986) and authored *Sowing Good Seeds: The Northwest Suffrage Campaigns of Susan B. Anthony* (Oregon Historical Society, 1990).

His wife Nannette teaches in the Walla Walla public schools.

The Triumph of Tradition has been designed and produced by John Laursen at Press-22 in Portland, Oregon. The type is Sabon, composed by Irish Setter. The paper is acid-free Glatfelter B-16. Printing and binding are by Thomson-Shore, Inc., Dexter, Michigan.

One hundred copies of *The Triumph of Tradition* have been bound in leather and numbered and signed by the author.